# EXALTED SITS THE CHIEF

## THE ANCIENT HISTORY OF HAWAI'I ISLAND

ROSS CORDY

Mutual Publishing

Library of Congress Catalog Card
Number: 00-107918

First Printing, October 2000
Second Printing, August 2001
2 3 4 5 6 7 8 9

Cover illustration, *Olopana,* by Herb Kawainui Kāne. In legend, Olopana was the brother of Mo'ikeha with whom he sailed to Tahiti from Waipi'o Valley (depicted in painting). He wears the whale's tooth pendant of the most ancient form, uncarved, before the typical Hawaiian shape evolved.

Design by Mardee Domingo

Softcover
ISBN 1-56647-340-3

Casebound
ISBN 1-56647-341-1

Mutual Publishing
1215 Center Street, Suite 210
Honolulu, Hawaii 96816
Ph: (808) 732-1709
Fax: (808) 734-4094
e-mail: mutual@lava.net
www.mutualpublishing.com

Printed in Korea

HAWAII STATE ARCHIVES

Part of Webber's illustration of a January 1779 procession of three large double canoes at Kealakekua. This lead canoe held the king and his high chiefs ("the chiefs standing up drest in their Cloaks & Caps"). In the center canoe were two high priests, chanting priests, and four images of national gods ("made of basket work, variously covered with red, black, white, & Yellow feathers, the Eyes represent'd by a bit of Pearl Oyster Shell with a black button, & the teeth were those of dogs"). The third canoe held provisions and ceremonial offerings. The procession greatly impressed the Cook expedition – a realization that they were dealing with a nation not too unlike their's, with a king, nobles, priests and pomp and circumstance. (Quotes from Lt. James King in Beaglehole 1967, 3(1): 512).

# Table of Contents

# List of Figures

# List of Tables

# Preface

This book was essentially completed in 1991. I simply procrastinated submitting it to a publisher. I have continued to update it with recent material, however, so it is still very current.

The book reflects my long interest in blending archaeology, oral history, and history to understand the past. I personally have always enjoyed this approach, and have been doing it in my Hawaiian and Pacific research for over 30 years. More advanced students or scholars may focus on one of these fields and more specific topics, but knowledge from archaeology, oral history, and history provides a broad perspective which is vital for appreciating Hawai'i's past.

This book also reflects my years of work on Hawai'i Island. I have probably worked on and seen hundreds of archaeological projects on the island in the course of my career. And I have spent many hours – enjoyable hours – in archives reading old accounts and letters, and oral histories recorded in the 1800s. I began working on the island in 1968 at Lapakahi in Kohala, as a University of Hawaii student right out of high school, and I did my Ph.D. fieldwork in North Kona in 1975. I was my office's Archaeologist for Hawai'i Island from 1985 to 1987, and have continued to review projects and do research as my office's Branch Chief for Archaeology. Over the years, I have seen most of the places described in this book, some places which are near and dear to me — Waipi'o, Kaloko, Kahalu'u, Kahuwai, and several parts of Kohala, to name a few. In 30 years, I have talked with many people about the island's history – archaeologists, historians, kupuna and others – including friends who unfortunately have passed away.

I did not write this book to be an extremely technical analysis of theoretical research questions, with detailed discussions of dates, food remains and tools, or hundreds of sites. I do that often enough in scientific publications. My aim here is to summarize Hawai'i Island's history, to introduce its rulers and chiefs, and to illustrate certain aspects of the island's history, such royal centers and field systems. There are no overview histories of individual islands written by professional scientists for general readers. I believe they are needed, thus this book. I have included footnotes referencing and elaborating on the material presented, so the reader can use the notes or go to the sources for more detailed information. Hawai'i Island has a fascinating history – as do each of the islands in Hawai'i. Hopefully, this book will enable the reader to better appreciate Hawai'i Island's long and illustrious past.

One problem in preparing a manuscript like this for publication is the use of Hawaiian diacritical markings – macrons and glottal stops, or the kahakō and ʻokina – in spelling the names of Hawaiian chiefs and place names. I have taken the approach that others have advised me to over the years, "If you are not sure, do not add the markings, since you can change the meaning of the name". So, I have used Pukui, Elbert, and Mookini's *Place Names of Hawaii* (1974), Sterling's index to Samuel Kamakau's *Ruling Chiefs of Hawaii* (which only used glottal stops), Barrere's index for the *Tales and Traditions of the People of Old* (Kamakau 1991), the Pukui and Elbert *Hawaiian Dictionary* (1971) which has a supplement spelling some of the names of Hawaiian gods, and the index in the pending publication on Kekūhaupiʻo (Desha in press) where McEldowney, with Barrere's review, carefully checked current spellings. These people are far more knowledgeable than I on spelling of names. If they used kahakō and ʻokina, then I used them. Otherwise, I left the names without markings.

Last, I would like to thank Mutual Publishing and its editor, Bennett Hymer, for taking on the publishing of this book. Summary books on Hawaiian history by professionals probably have limited potential for sales. Yet Mutual Publishing willingly has supported the book's publication to provide the public information on Hawaiʻi's past. Waimea Williams did the copy-editing and did a wonderful job, definitely improving my writing. Eric Komori of the State Historic Preservation Division helped prepare a number of the illustrations, for which I am very grateful. And Bishop Museum and State Archives staff kindly helped me find the photographs that I needed for the volume. Finally, I appreciate the people who looked at one or more chapters of this volume and gave me useful comments – among them H. David Tuggle, Gary Somers, and Douglas Oliver.

I hope you, the reader, enjoy the book. I certainly enjoyed writing it.

Ross Cordy, Ph.D.
Branch Chief for Archaeology
Historic Preservation Division
State of Hawaii
January 2000

EXALTED SITS THE CHIEF

# Prologue

*Fallen is the Chief*

(chant by Keaulumoku) [1]

*Where then are these chiefs? They are gone and dead.... What about their lifestyle? Let those who know and have heard speak forth. At what period did they reign? We know the time of Liholiho, and Kamehameha and Kalanikupuapaikalaniumi, but the majority of them, we do not know.... What did they do? Who were the chiefs under the various chiefs? What about their labors? What did they do? What about the lifestyle of the people during their reign? Who were Hawaii's good chiefs?... Who were the rebel chiefs? Who were the chiefs who truly inherited the government from their parents?*

(Kepoʻokulou 1835) [2]

Today, when many talk of traditional Hawai'i, attention focuses on Kalākaua, Kamehameha I, and other rulers of the 1800s. Yet, Hawai'i's history goes back almost 2,000 years, to when the Polynesians first reached the shores of these islands. What of those times? And what of the period of rich oral histories—the A.D. 1300s–1700s? How many people today can name the powerful rulers and chiefs of those times? These chiefs were renowned in Kamehameha's time, yet they are largely forgotten today. In many ways, these chiefs have sadly fallen—as the chant states—not just died, but with the knowledge of their place in Hawai'i Island's history also passing away.

These earlier times and rulers need to be understood to truly appreciate Hawai'i's history. There are many paths to learning about this past. Oral histories were recorded by many Hawaiians and some non-Hawaiians in the 1800s. These histories are rich sources, and anyone claiming to be a scholar of Hawai'i's past must be familiar with them. Archaeology, too, has opened many doors to the past, and this work has not all been listing fishhooks and pieces of shell. Archaeology has unveiled much about behavior, and is almost our only source of information on early Hawai'i. Those who wish to learn of the years long gone must not reject archaeology as a source of knowledge.

The aim of this book is to blend oral history and archaeology to form an overview of the history of Hawai'i Island prior to its unification by Kamehameha in 1792. It is one person's perspective after over 30 years of work. And certainly, with new knowledge, ideas presented here will change. But, it is hoped it will give readers a picture of earlier times and earlier rulers. These earlier times, after all, span nearly all of Hawai'i's history; the monarchy period of the 1800s was but a very small fragment of Hawaiian history.

# BACKGROUND

**CHAPTER 1**

# The Land, The ʻĀina, in 1795

*Darkness slips into light*
*Earth and water are the food of the plant*
*The god enters, man can not enter.*

*(Kumulipo chant)*[1]

To understand man's history on Hawai'i Island, it is necessary to understand the island's natural environment—the geology, the rainfall, the soils, the vegetation, the reefs. Many aspects of the island have changed since the time of Kamehameha, with differences in the vegetation being particularly striking. Today, the windward sides are, or recently were, cloaked in miles and miles of sugarcane fields, yet none of these cane fields were present in the 1790s. These areas were rolling grasslands and small farm plots with scattered groves of trees, and the forest was nearer the shore. On the dry side of the island, kiawe trees now dominate the shoreline, but this tree was not present in the 1790s; then, the dry shores had strikingly few trees. And it must be remembered too that in certain parts of the island, many of the lands present during the early period of Kamehameha's reign have since been covered by lava flows, for example, the Keāhole flow of 1800 and the Kīholo flow of 1859.[2]

But then too, the natural environment of Kamehameha's time was different from earlier times, a point to be discussed in later chapters. Yet, as a start, the setting in the 1790s will serve as a baseline for discussion.

As all of Hawai'i's residents know, Hawai'i Island is the southernmost island in the archipelago. It lies at 19–20° north latitude and is not in the tropics, but in the somewhat cooler semi-tropics. This island is by far the largest Hawaiian island, having ca. 282 miles of coastline[3] and including 4,030 square miles of land, extending roughly 93 miles north–south and 76 miles east–west. All the other islands—Kaua'i, O'ahu, Maui and the others—would fit within its borders.

Not only is this island of Hawai'i the largest, it is the highest—reaching 13,784 feet at the summit of the massive Mauna Kea, the home of the goddess of the snows, Poli'ahu. Indeed, Hawai'i contains two other high mountains—Mauna Loa and Hualālai. Hawai'i also is the island of active volcanoes—the home of Pele, goddess of the volcano, who often battled with Poli'ahu.

Six traditional districts make up the island—Puna, Hilo, Hāmākua, Kohala, Kona, and Ka'ū (Fig. 1-2). The coasts of eastern

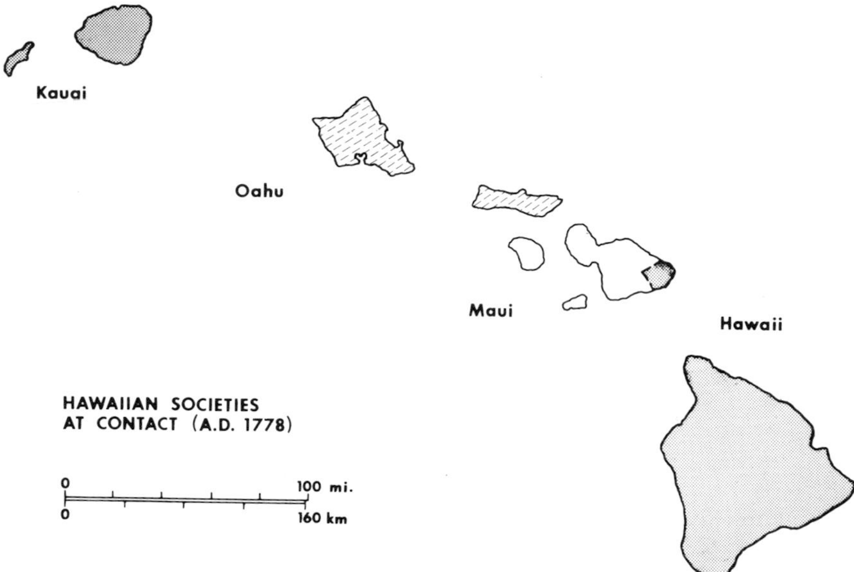


**FIGURE 1-1**
Map of the Hawaiian Islands (Cordy 1981).

Kohala, Hāmākua, Hilo, and eastern Puna are wet and rainy and marked by high cliffs, broken by the gulchlands of Kohala, the large, looming valleys from Pololū to Waipi'o and the low stream lands of Hilo and its bay. The island also has the cool uplands of Waimea, inland from southern Kohala. Yet this land also includes the arid and hot lands of coastal Kawaihae and southern Kohala, of Kona, and of Ka'ū. Hawai'i is extremely varied, and this variation has affected its history.

The lavas from seven volcanoes have formed the island, these volcanoes being Kohala Mountain, Mauna Kea, Hualālai, Mauna Loa, and Kīlauea, and the lesser known Nīnole and Kūlani which have been almost completely covered by Mauna Loa's flows. These mountains are of different ages. Some are heavily eroded, yet lava flows from Mauna Loa and Kīlauea still continue to periodically cover existing land or form new land. Lava even came forth from Hualālai in 1800–1801 during the reign of Kamehameha. Figure 1-3 shows the lands whose surface is covered by the different volcanoes' lava.

**FIGURE 1-2**
Traditional Districts of Hawai'i Island.

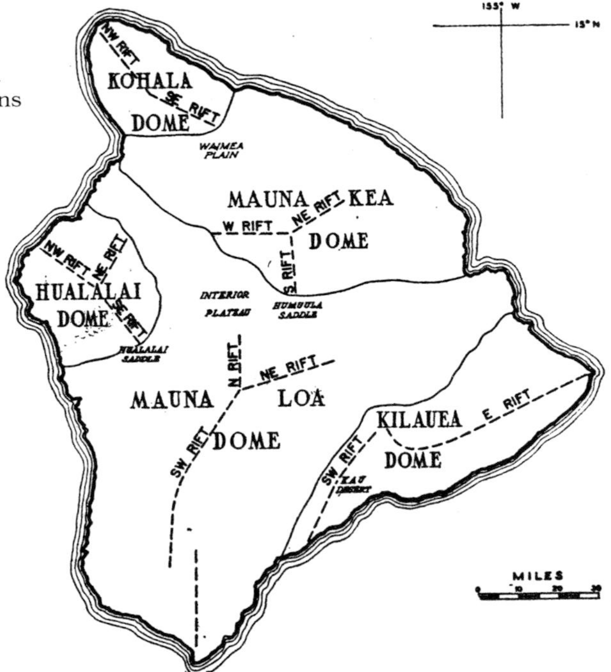


**FIGURE 1-3.**
Land areas currently covered by flows from the different mountains of Hawai'i (Stearns & Macdonald 1946:25).

TABLE 1-1
## The Mountains of Hawai'i Island

| Mountain | Height (feet) | Last Eruption | Traditional District in Which Located |
|---|---|---|---|
| Kohala | 5,505 | Middle Pleistocene | Kohala, Hāmākua |
| Mauna Kea | 13,784 | 15,000–2,000 years B.P. | Hāmākua, Hilo |
| Kīlauea | 4,090 | Currently erupting | Puna, Ka'ū |
| Mauna Loa | 13,680 | A.D. 1986 | Ka'ū, Kona, Hāmākua |
| Nīnole* | — | 100,000 years B.P | Ka'ū |
| Kūlani* | — | 10,000+ years B.P. | Ka'ū |
| Hualālai | 8,251 | A.D. 1801 | Kona |

Information from Stearns & Macdonald (1946); Macdonald & Abbott (1977).

B.P. = before present.
* — almost entirely covered by Mauna Loa flows. The Kūlani cone and a few adjacent exposures are remnants of Kūlani. Remnants of Nīnole are exposed in central Ka'ū.

The age of these volcanoes, their respective locations in relation to the prevailing winds and the most active areas of lava flow are critical factors in understanding Hawai'i's topography, soils, and vegetation, and in turn its history. Kohala Mountain and Mauna Kea are the oldest; they have not erupted since man has been in the islands. As the oldest mountains, they have undergone the most erosion from rain and sea. Kohala is the older of the two. Figure 1-3 shows the current lands of Hawai'i covered by Kohala flows. Kohala erupted in two historical series of flows. The earlier Pololū series was followed by the Hāwī series. Importantly, the Hāwī series did not cover the east and north parts of Kohala Mountain, so these areas have been subject to erosion for longer periods of time and have the only large valleys on the island—the great valleys of Pololū, Waimanu and Waipi'o being the best known.

The areas currently covered by Mauna Kea flows are also shown on Figure 1-3. The Hāmākua volcanic series of Mauna Kea formed the slopes of that mountain and ponded against the Kohala Mountain, forming the Waimea Plains. On Mauna Kea, the Hāmākua series was capped by Pāhala ash, and later by flows of the Laupāhoehoe series.

About the time of the Hāmākua and Hāwī series, Hualālai, Mauna Loa and Kīlauea had early surface flows. But nearly all these early flows have long been repeatedly coated and deeply covered by later flows from these mountains. The land surface covered by these volcanoes' flows is also illustrated in Figure 1-3. Since these three volcanoes are active, it is important to realize that flows often emerge from cracks and cones on their rift zones as well as from the calderas. Mauna Loa's southwest and northeast rifts and Kīlauea's eastern rift are currently frequent sources for flows, with the lava flowing downhill from these areas into southern Kona, western and eastern Ka'ū, and Puna.

What does all this mean in terms of terrain? In the simplest view, the island's topography could be considered gradual lava slopes steepening as summits are approached. Yet reality is obviously much more complex. These lavas were and are generally of two types—smooth pāhoehoe and crumbled, rough 'a'ā. In some cases ash was spewed out, forming thick soil layers on the coastal Hāmākua and Hilo slopes and in Ka'ū. Cinder cones are common along the rift zones of the volcanoes. In a few areas, scarps or cliffs—pali in Hawaiian—formed along fault lines. These are visible today on Mauna Loa and Kīlauea as the 1,250-foot-high Kealakekua pali in South Kona, the 600-foot-high Kaholo pali in South Kona, the 600-foot-high Kahuku pali in Ka'ū, and the 1,500-foot-high and 1,050-foot-high Hilina and Kapukapu pali of eastern Ka'ū and western Puna. These cliffs are nearly sheer drops in terrain—certainly not gradual slopes—and are major features of their districts.

The island's slopes are not barren; many flows have heavily eroded over the millennia and have thick soil—largely from erosion from rain and sea. The age and position of the mountains are the key variables in this process of erosion. Practically everyone in the islands realizes that on the larger islands, there is a dry side and and a wet side, termed leeward and windward today and kona and ko'olau in the traditional Hawaiian reference terms. These windward–leeward patterns are a result of orographic rainfall—mountain–related rainfall. Moisture–laden winds arriving at the islands rise on the mountains, and at the higher elevations the moisture condenses, forming a cloud belt and precipitates as rain, or snow. In the Hawaiian Islands, the prevailing winds, the trades, come from the northeast, so rainfall is by far heavier on the northeast sides of the larger islands—the windward or ko'olau sides—while the west and southwest sides receive little rainfall as the moisture of the winds has been precipitated.

Hawai'i Island largely follows this pattern. East Hawai'i—Kohala east of 'Upolu Point, all Hāmākua, all Hilo and most of Puna—is the wet windward side of the island. Here the trades rise on the northeast flanks of Kohala Mountain, Mauna Kea and Kīlauea, shroud the mountains in clouds and drop high amounts of rain. The cloud belt begins at about the 2,500-foot elevation[4] and "fog drip" also adds to precipitation. Rainfall increases up the mountain slopes with the whole windward side getting over 100 inches per year. As can be seen in Figure 1-4, the high rainfall areas are on the summit of Kohala Mountain, exceeding 200 inches, and between the 2,000–4,000-foot-elevations on Mauna Kea in Hilo, with rainfall up to 250 inches. This rain is fairly evenly spread throughout the year, although it declines slightly when the trades become sporadic in July, August and September.

Because Mauna Kea is so high, at elevations above 4,000 feet, the air flows around the mountain rather than continuing up. The orographic pattern breaks down, and the upper elevations get very little rain. What little precipitation occurs often falls in the form of snow due to extremely cold temperatures on the summit.

West Hawai'i, an area including western Puna, all Ka'ū and Kona, and Kohala west of 'Upolu Point, is the dry side of the island. Marked leeward patterns occur in the rain shadows of Kohala, Mauna Kea and Kīlauea. In these areas, rainfall decreases rapidly down the mountain, with coastal areas getting less than 20 inches of rain per year. It is important to note that on Kohala Mountain the summit rains actually spill over slightly on the leeward sides at upper elevations. Leeward rain—particularly near the shore—is highly seasonal, usually falling in the winter months and often dropping mostly in a few storms when winds arrive from the south and southwest.

Hawai'i with its multiple mountains, however, has two marked twists to this leeward rain pattern. One, Kīlauea is so low that trade winds actually do not drop all their moisture on its slopes. A second orographic rise and high rainfall pattern forms in central Ka'ū at the 300–700 foot elevations on the southeast flanks of Mauna Loa (Fig. 1-4). This area's rainfall rises to 120 inches per year inland, although coastal rainfall is still quite low, less than 4 inches per month from May–September.

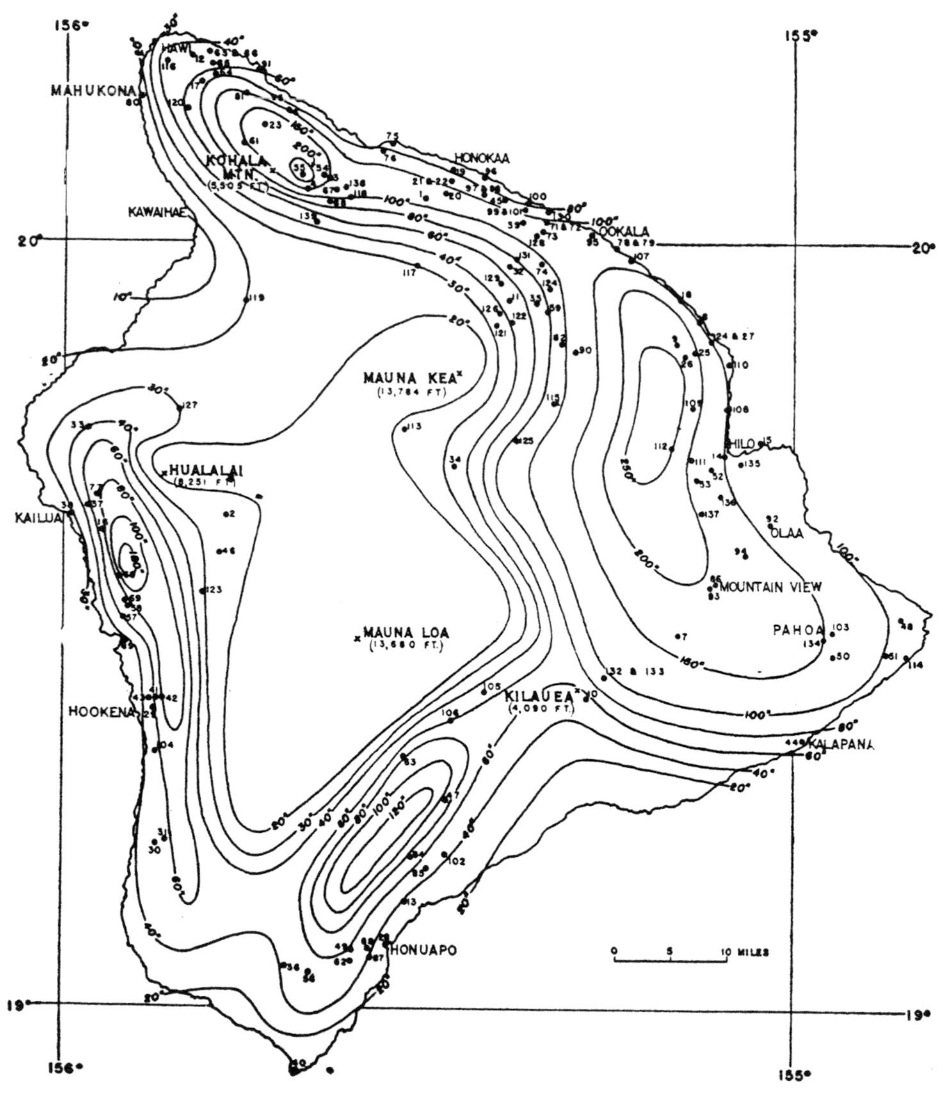


**FIGURE 1-4**
Rainfall patterns on Hawai'i Island (Stearns & Macdonald 1946:212).

The second notable leeward variation is the rainfall pattern of central Kona. Here the trade winds are effectively blocked off by Mauna Loa, Hualālai and Mauna Kea, and local topography and heating effects induce wind and rain patterns. In the mornings as the air is heated, it rises, and this in turn pulls in cool winds from off the sea (onshore sea breezes). Orographic patterns result with clouds forming at the 2,000-foot elevation and rain falling. In the evening, with general cooling of the air, cool air blows out to sea (offshore land breezes). The rainfall highs in Kona exceed 120 inches at about the 2,000-foot elevation, with the highest rains inland of Keauhou. The Kona rains are fairly high from March–October, with lower periods from November–February—just the opposite pattern of the rest of the island. Again, however, the coastal areas of Kona are much drier, 20–40 inches per year, so Kona is still a leeward area.

Interestingly, the high-rainfall areas of Ka'ū and Kona are separated from each other and from the windward districts by extremely low rainfall areas—an important environmental pattern in historical developments.

In Kohala, a high rainfall pattern is found in Waimea, where summit rains spill over the crest of Kohala Mountain. Here rainfall is 40–80 inches. But this is confined to a relatively small area. The rest of leeward Kohala ranges from 30–40 inches, with this rainfall line gradually pulling inland from the shore at 'Upolu Point to ca. 3 miles inland at Kahuā, and in the extremely arid southern Kohala areas 10 miles seaward of Waimea, rainfall is only 10–20 inches per year.

But what does this rainfall mean for topography? On the windward side, on the two older volcanoes of Kohala and Mauna Kea, it means that they have been subjected to high rainfall on their northeast slopes for millennia. The resulting erosion has formed extensive stream systems. On the much older Kohala Mountain, where the early Pololū lava series was not covered, the large and deep valleys of Kohala and Hāmākua have formed—the 1,000–2,500-feet-deep valleys of Pololū and Honokāne in Kohala and Honopue, Waimanu and Waipi'o in Hāmākua. For the younger Kohala and Mauna Kea slopes, shallower gulches reflect younger streams. These gulches are less than

100-feet deep in Kohala and less than 650-feet deep in Hāmākua and Hilo. Outside of these areas, perennial streams are extremely scarce on Hawaiʻi. In windward Puna, the constant lava flows from Kīlauea have inhibited stream formation. Only in the leeward high–rainfall areas of Waimea in Kohala and central Kaʻū are flowing streams present year–round, and today these only flow constantly at upper elevations. During heavy rains, they will flow all the way to the sea, often as small raging torrents which overflow the banks and the highways. Some intermittent streams have developed on the leeward sides of Kohala Mountain and Mauna Kea and in central Kona. These streams flow in upper elevations only during heavy rains.

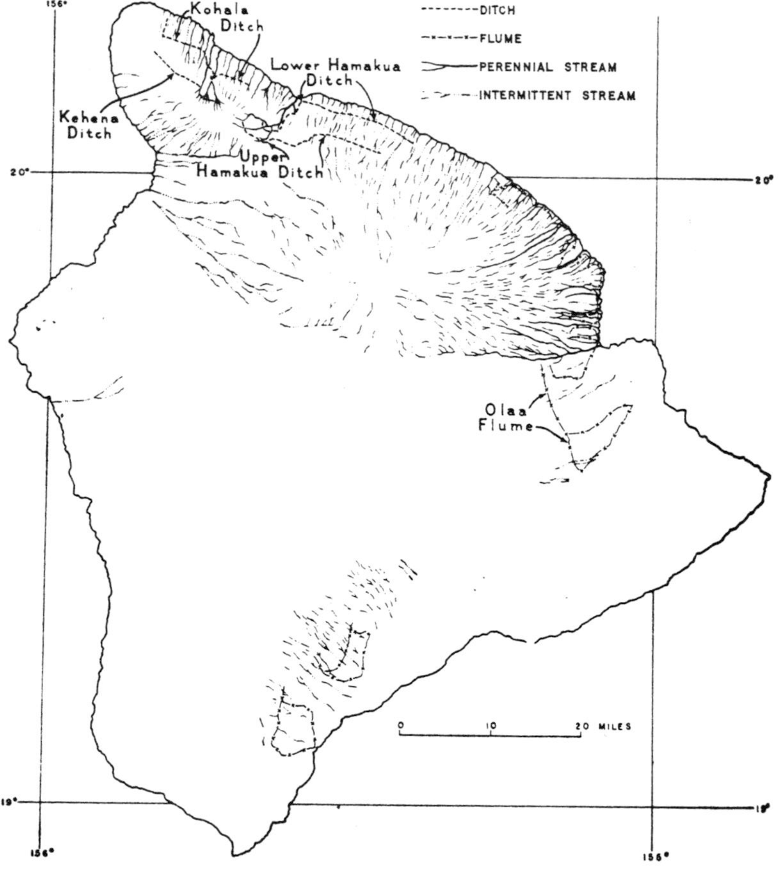


**FIGURE 1-5**
Stream patterns (Stearns & Macdonald 1946:218).

Soils are also linked to rainfall and the age of mountains. Soil development is considerable in the windward areas on the older mountains. A look at a soils map of the island (Fig. 1-6) shows the older Kohala Mountain with near total deep soil development, particularly on the windward side. This includes considerable alluvial deposits on the floors of the large valleys. The windward Hāmākua and Hilo areas of Mauna Kea have deep soil development—although higher mountain elevations above the tree line often have little soil. Deep soils are found in an inland strip in Puna from Volcano to ʻŌlaʻa and Keaʻau. Much of Puna, however, is a patchwork of soils, reflecting the multiple Kīlauea flows of different ages. Deep soils are present on older flows, while shallow soils or bare rock surfaces are present on more recent flows.

Leeward soils generally are shallower. Soils in these areas increase with rainfall up the slopes, with good soil development on the wet upper slopes above the 40-inch rainfall line—although the high mountain elevations, as in windward areas, have little soils. The soils map shows thick soils in central Kaʻū, central Kona, and Waimea. As one descends the slopes below the 40-inch rainfall line, soil depths and coverage dramatically decrease. In the seaward lands of south Kohala, Kona, and parts of Kaʻū there are vast areas of exposed bare rock. This ranges from relatively flat and smooth pāhoehoe, or undulating pāhoehoe with pressure ridges and small domes and low swales, to extremely rugged flows of ʻaʻā with loose stone, making these areas difficult to traverse. Soils have developed in these areas, but with limited extent, filling low swales or drainage fans as a result of wind or sheet-wash from upper elevations. As one proceeds inland, the soil coverage gradually becomes more extensive until one reaches the 40-inch rainfall zone where soils cover much of the landscape.

To this picture of rain and soils, it is important to add two more patterns. One, the high elevations (4,500–7,000 feet) in the Saddle area in the center of the island receive little rain, but cloud cover, fogs and cold are frequent here. Two, the high elevations of Mauna Kea and Mauna Loa are extremely cold and receive snow, particularly during the winter months. Indeed, during the Pleistocene, Mauna Kea had a glacier, Makamaka, which extended down to the 11,000 foot contour. Perhaps an important reminder is that temperatures

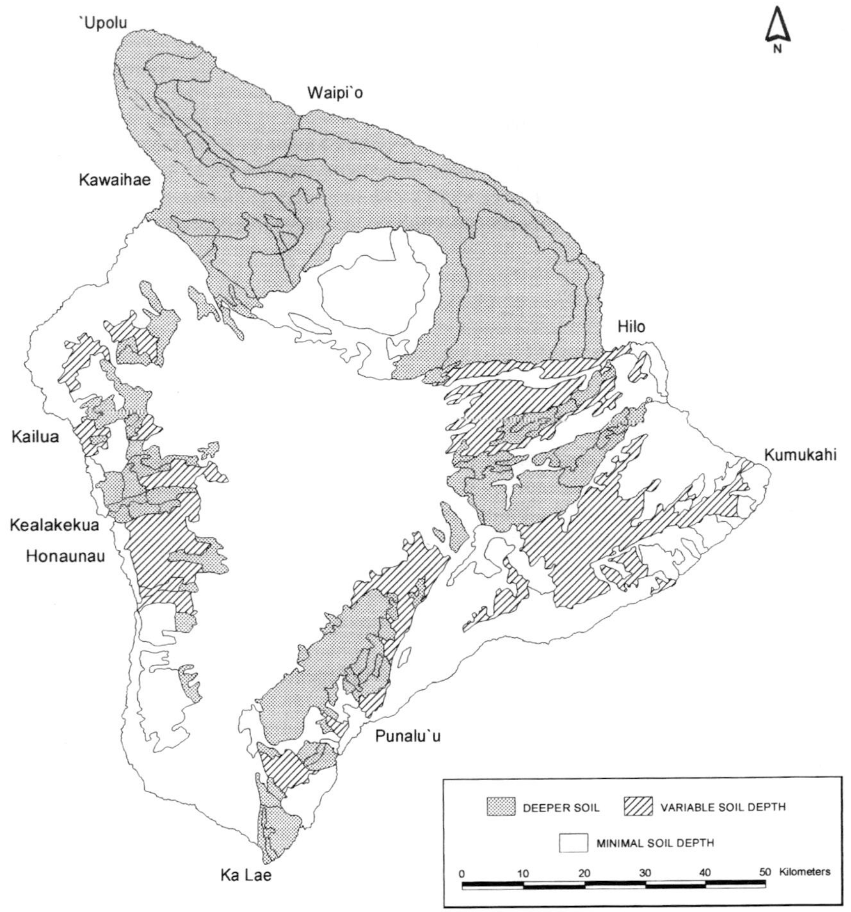


**FIGURE 1-6**
Map showing the major soil patterns of Hawaiʻi Island.

consistently fall as one moves inland. Shore temperatures average 72–75 degrees Fahrenheit. They drop 4 degrees over the first 1,000 feet of elevation to 68–71 degrees, and then 3 degrees for each 1,000 feet thereafter. Thus, at the 5,000-foot elevation temperatures average 56–59 degrees and at 10,000 feet they average 41–44 degrees. For Hawaiʻi, this means it gets quite cold up on the mountains.

Vegetation patterns were linked to these soil, precipitation, lava and temperature gradient patterns. The windward areas of the island had and still have rain forests. In these areas, forests covered all the land from the shore to the summit of Kohala Mountain and

Kīlauea, and to the 6,000-foot elevation of Mauna Kea. These rain forests are usually dominated by 15–50-foot-high ʻōhiʻa trees (*Metrosideros collina*) in an open to closed canopy. From the 2,000–5,000-foot elevations, the forest is labeled montaine, with koa (*Acacia koa*) often a co–dominant with ʻōhiʻa. A subcanopy of 10–30-foot-high trees is present, including kōpiko (*Psychotiia hawaiiensis*), kāwaʻu (*Ilex anomala*), ʻōlapa (*Cheirodendron trigynum*) and alani (*Pelea clusaefolia*). And an even lower subcanopy of 10–15-foot-high tree ferns (hāpuʻu; *Cibotium spp.*) is present. Beneath the canopy various shrubs and vines are present: māmaki (*Pipturus hawaiiensis*), ʻieʻie (*Freycinetia arborea*), olonā (*Touchardia latifolia*). Bogs and assorted wet vegetation and stunted rain forest vegetation are common features, notably on the summit area of Kohala Mountain. And grasses, ferns and herbs line the streambeds and lower stream banks.

From the 2,000-foot elevation to sea level, the forest is labeled submontane. Tree ferns decline at lower elevations, and kōpiko and lama (*Diospyros ferrea*) become more common. But, pandanus (*Pandanus spp.*) becomes a co–dominant with ʻōhiʻa at the lowest elevations, and kukui (*Aleurites moluccana*) is common in gulches and on steep terrain.

In the windward areas of Puna and southernmost Hilo, lava flows of varying ages have disturbed this climax vegetation. Here kīpuka—older lands bypassed by recent flows—may have climax forest, or various developmental stages. It has been estimated that in the high rainfall areas between 1,300–2,200 feet of Kīlauea's east rift zone, it may take about 100 to perhaps 500 years for climax forest to be reached on a new lava flow. Pioneer communities include ferns, lichens and scrubby ʻōhiʻa. Developmental stages include an ʻōhiʻa–uluhe fern (*Dicranopteris spp.*) woodland with widely spaced trees. Nearer the shore, pandanus may be a major element in recolonization.

Above the 6,000-foot elevation on Mauna Kea, this windward rain forest grades into a drier, upper montane forest of māmane (*Sophora chrysophylla*) and naio (*Myoporum sandiwicense*). The 6,000–9,000-foot elevations on Mauna Kea are in māmane-naio forest. Oftentimes the canopy is quite open, forming a parkland setting. The māmane in these areas form clumps to intercept the fog and gain extra moisture. The shrubs in this drier forest include ʻāheahea (*Chenopodium oahuense*) with native grasses such as mountain pili (*Trisetium glosseratom*), and *Dechampsia australis*. Above these māmane-naio forests on Mauna Kea are the alpine deserts, with little visible vegetation—only mosses, lichens, and some grasses and ferns being present.

On the Saddle between Mauna Kea, Hualālai and Mauna Loa at 4,000–7,000 feet, the constant lava flows from Mauna Loa have again led to a mosaic of communities between the pioneer and the climax māmane or climax grasslands: scrub māmane forests and/or scrub naio forests, scrub ʻōhiʻa, and in some cases shrubs such as *Chenopodium*.

Leeward areas with high rainfall also have a similar ʻōhiʻa–koa–hāpuʻu montane forest at the 2,000–5,000-foot elevations—essentially a band from west Kaʻū through Central Kona and around the north edge of Hualālai. And above these forests on Hualālai and Mauna Loa are found the upper montane māmane-naio forest, and then the alpine deserts on Mauna Loa above ca. 9,000 feet.

However, at lower elevations where rainfall drops below 60 inches, the leeward vegetation markedly differs. Between the 40–60-inch rainfall contours, a dry forest was present. Unfortunately, these areas from leeward Kohala through Kona and Kaʻū have long been converted to agriculture, ranches, or housing, so the exact nature of the forests is unclear. Dominant trees seem to vary from location to location. It has been suggested that this upper dry forest was a mixture of koa, māmane, kauila (*Alphitonia ponderosa*), ʻiliahi or sandalwood (*Santalum pyrularium*) and other trees. In the Waimea area, work has indicated that an open māmane forest with koa was present at the 2,000–3,000-foot elevations in an open wooded parkland context in the 1790–1850 period.[5] Sandalwood was also likely present. Relic trees included koai'e (*Acacia koaia*) and kukui in the deep Honokoa Gulch. Today, at the 1,600–2,600-foot elevations in Puʻuwaʻawaʻa ahupuaʻa of North Kona, a remnant native forest is still present—dominated by lama trees, although one area has kauila dominant. Minor trees in this Puʻuwaʻawaʻa forest include māmane, naio, 'ohe makai, wiliwili, and 'iliahi. These patterns tend to suggest local variations in an upper dry forest.

Below the 40-inch rainfall contour, researchers are uncertain what the vegetation pattern was like. From here to sea level, it has been suggested a lower dry forest once was present as an "open parkland."[6] Tree cover is suggested to have been scattered wiliwili (*Erythrina sandwicensis*), naio and lama. In the Kaloko area of northern Kona, 'ohe trees seem to have dominated the open parkland.[7] Various shrubs (hi'aloa, *Waltheria americana*; 'ilima, *Sida spp.*) and grasses (pili, *Heteropogon contortus*) are expected to have been numerous. And, importantly, in the descent down from the 40-inch rainfall line, the tree cover is gradually and substantially reduced, with shrubs and grasses predominating on the lower slopes at European contact. Again, in areas of frequent lava flows—northern and southernmost Kona and eastern Ka'ū—various successions of this dry forest climax would be expected.

On the coastal fringe, common beach plants such as naupaka (*Scaevola taccada*), 'āheahea, and 'ākulikuli were present, and often still are. And around coastal anchialine ponds and marshes in leeward areas, there were various marsh and sedge plants, as well as trees such as hau (*Hibiscus tiliaceus*), wiliwili, 'ohe, naio, lama, etc.

The shoreline of the island also reflects mountain age and prevailing winds. Generally, windward seas are rougher, leeward calmer. The old shorelines of Kohala Mountain and Mauna Kea have been carved back into cliffs by these rough seas over the millennia. The sea has actually cut back about one mile of the Kohala Mountain, resulting in spectacular sea cliffs over 1,000-feet high, broken by valley mouths with sand and cobble beaches (Waipi'o, Pololū). A narrow marine bench also skirts much of this windward shore, with a few wider benches at Laupāhoehoe and 'Āpua in Hāmākua, and at the better known Laupāhoehoe of Hilo district. Easterly swells have also cut fairly steep shores around much of Puna and Ka'ū. Of course, there are rare breaks in this pattern where protected shores, usually bays, are present—for example, Hilo Bay, the now lava-covered Kalapana in Puna, and Punalu'u in Ka'ū. In contrast, the calmer waters off Kona and leeward Kohala have formed fewer sea cliffs, although exceptions exist particularly along central and south Kona.

Since Hawaiʻi Island is fairly young geologically, reef formation is also still relatively limited. Shallow inshore reefs are rare on the windward sides—in small patches in small, semiprotected bays and in a larger concentration in Hilo Bay. In contrast, on the leeward sides shallow inshore reefs fringe most of the coast as a narrow band, ca. 400–800-feet wide being the widest off leeward Kohala. As a result, the leeward side of the island has a much more diverse marine fauna—including inshore reef species of fish and molluscs, as well as the rocky surge species and the offshore benthic/pelagic species.[8] The surge species molluscs include ʻopihi, with uhu (parrot fish) in intermediate depths and with the tunas (ʻahi, aku), scads (ʻōpelu) and the like being the most notable pelagic species. Inshore shallow reef species include cowrie and numerous small varieties of fish.

Also, an associated pattern of the reef and shore terrain is beach patterning. Sand beaches occur only rarely in coves and in protected areas along the windward shores—notably Pololū, Waimanu, Waipiʻo, Hilo and Kalapana. In contrast, Kona has one sandy cove after another along much of its shore, and leeward Kohala and Kaʻū have a fair amount of sandy landings.

Land animals were scarce in the 1790s—ignoring the rat, pig (puaʻa), dog (ʻīlio) and chicken (moa). Primarily, birds were the animals of the lands of Hawaiʻi. These birds' habitats closely follow the vegetation patterns. In the ʻōhiʻa–koa rain forests various types of small honey creepers were present. These honeycreepers often had brightly colored feathers, ranging from red to yellow to green; these feathers were desired status items as will be seen. At high elevations in Kaʻū, Hāmākua and Kona—on the seaward slopes of Mauna Kea, Mauna Loa and Hualālai, and in the Saddle between them—larger birds nested. The most notable of these were the ʻuʻau (dark-rumped petrel) and nēnē (Hawaiian flightless goose). Ducks (koloa) also nested in various areas, such as the higher elevations in Waimea—likely the source of names such as Waikoloa. In the high elevation māmane-naio forests, the small palila were present, feeding primarily on māmane seed pods, but also on naio berries and māmane leaves and flowers. Other relatively small birds were in wetlands along the shore (Hawaiian stilts, flightless rails), and marine birds also nested along the shore. Across all these habitats ranged the predator birds—the owl (pueo) and the hawk (ʻio).

## THE DISTRICTS

A closer look at the island's districts is needed, because the districts and their environments are the key to understanding Hawaiʻi Island's history. Again, there were six districts. Two were entirely windward lands—Hāmākua and Hilo. Two others were solely leeward districts—Kona and Kaʻū. Kohala and Puna straddled both windward and leeward areas.

Hāmākua district is a windward district in the truest sense. It has ca. 29 miles of shoreline,[9] primarily focused on Mauna Kea's eastern slopes with exposed cliffs, rough seas, and narrow reef formations. Above the sea cliffs, the gentle slopes have a thick soil cover and abundant rainfall, and lush vegetation, with the upper slopes from 1,000–6,000 feet in an ʻōhiʻa-koa rain forest. The slopes are cut by deep (up to 300-foot), narrow stream gulches cloaked with kukui and pandanus. Yet Hāmākua is more than these slope and gulch lands. It also incudes the extremely large, deep valleys of Waipiʻo and Waimanu which have been cut over the millennia into the older Kohala Mountain, valleys which, as will be seen, dominated the history of the district and the island. Hāmākua also extended inland, encompassing the high elevation māmane-naio forests of Mauna Kea and the subalpine, oft snow–covered, summit itself. The district continued across the foggy and cold upland plateau or Saddle with its terrain a mixture of bare lava and soils, and with its vegetation a mixture of ʻōhiʻa and māmane-naio forests. This plateau had important nesting grounds of ʻuʻau and nēnē. And, Hāmākua also climbed the interior slopes of Hualālai and Mauna Loa. Few realize Hāmākua virtually spanned the island—reaching to and looking down into the upper edges of Kona.

Hilo district too is a windward district with 32 miles of shoreline. It also is focused on Mauna Kea's eastern slopes with similarly exposed cliffs, rough seas, narrow reefs, rain–shrouded thick–soiled slopes with upper ʻōhiʻa–koa forests and deep gulches. But Hilo also includes the large, fertile flatlands of Hilo Bay formed by Mauna Loa flows. These flatlands with swamps and the wide lower Wailoa River and the calm waters of the bay played a dominant role in the history of Hilo district and the island.

Puna district to the south of Hilo also is largely a windward district. It spans 53 miles of shoreline and has the cliffs, narrow reefs and the heavy seas found in Hilo and Hāmākua. Unlike those two districts, however, it has no large embayments—the sands of Kalapana and Kaimū, (now covered by lava) coming the closest to a bay. Puna's slopes do have heavy rains, but its most striking feature is the fact that it is in an active lava flow zone, a very active zone. The southeast rift zone of Kīlauea runs the length of the district from the caldera of Kīlauea to Kapoho and Cape Kumukahi—with small cinder cones (puʻu) dotting the rift. As a result, most of the lands south and northeast of this rift zone have been overrun by lava at some point over the last 500 years. This created a patchwork of descending land surfaces from barren lava flows to flows with some soil and pioneer ʻōhiʻa and pandanus forests, to deeper soils and thick ʻōhiʻa and pandanus forests. The deeper soils tend to run along the Hilo-Puna border up to ʻŌlaʻa. Another result of the flows is the presence of lava tubes under the ground surface of the flows, some extending long distances from near the rift to near the sea. Puna, in overview, is a wet land, bountiful where soil is present, but definitely within the realm of Pele and frequently visited and inundated by her flows.

To the far north of the island, Kohala forms a striking contrast. Much of Kohala is a land of no volcanic activity and of deep soils. The entire district has 40 miles of shoreline. East of ʻUpolu Point, Kohala is a windward land, once called Kohala iloko.[10] Here, 13 miles of shoreline have steep cliffs, rough seas, and narrower reefs. The older eastern topography is cut by the deep valleys of Honokāne and Pololū; the central slopes are cut by 100-foot-deep gulches with permanent streams. Rainfall is high and soils are deep, and above are the ʻōhiʻa forests. Unlike the other windward districts, however, Kohala has leeward lands—all to the west and south of ʻUpolu Point. Here waters are calm, reefs extend offshore and cliffs are negligible with many coves present. Kawaihae with its long sand shore and wide reef is a notable focal point for this side of Kohala. Interestingly, the land terrain of leeward Kohala falls into three zones. From ʻUpolu Point to Kahuā (Kohala i waho),[11] just north of Kawaihae, the slopes are gradual and dry, with the 30 inch rainfall line and deep soils starting near the shore at the point and gradually pulling inland 2–3 miles. Dryland forest at best would have been present long ago. In the Kawaihae area, slopes are also dry, but the 30-inch rainfall line and deep soils were far inland, over 3 miles. A few deep gulches in Kawaihae serve as conduits for raging stream flow during heavy upland rains. South of Kawaihae are the arid coastal lands of ʻŌuli, Lālāmilo and Waikoloa's Kalāhuipuaʻā and ʻĀnaehoʻomalu. Sizable portions of these lands are barren lava lands; all are arid. The notable features are natural anchialine ponds amidst bare, largely pāhoehoe lava at the shore—with these ponds modified into fishponds. The 30-inch rainfall line for these lands is 7–10 miles inland on the upland edge of the Waimea Plains near today's town of Waimea. Here are deep soils, the higher rainfall, and the perennial streams of Waimea, and at the 2,600-foot elevation, cool temperatures. These Waimea lands are the only leeward Kohala lands with constantly flowing streams. Also, the Waimea area is the origin point for the fierce mumuku winds which blow down off Kohala Mountain and Mauna Kea in the late afternoons.

Beyond Kohala, along 64 miles of the west side of the island was the district of Kona—a completely leeward district focused on the mountains of Hualālai and Mauna Loa, and on the calm western waters of the island. The central portions of Kona had arid shorelines with shallow soil in pockets amidst rocky outcrops and bare lava flows. These central areas had small, protected embayments—Kailua, Hōlualoa, Kahaluʻu, Keauhou, Kealakekua, and Hōnaunau. High rainfall was present ca. 1–2 miles inland, and here soil was thicker, with fewer rocky outcrops. These upper soil areas began at the 700–1,000-foot elevations. Farther above were the ʻōhiʻa forests, and even farther above were the māmane forests and then the cinder lands and high alpine elevations.

North of central Kona, beyond today's Kailua town, the lands are increasingly more arid. The 30–40-inch rainfall line and associated thick soils pull farther up Hualālai through Kaloko, Kohanaiki, the 'O'omas, the Kalaoas, Kau, 'Ōhiki and the other lands; and then these rainier, soil lands are extremely far inland in Pu'uwa'awa'a and Pu'uanahulu. Seaward of the rain areas are grassy slopes with considerable bare lava and eventually the rocky shores with sand coves here and there—at Kīholo, Ka'ūpūlehu, Kūki'o, etc. Anchialine, tidal ponds are present throughout this area. These arid lands of northern Kona were called the Kekaha area.

South of central Kona are the Kipapilua lands, from Manukā at the Ka'ū border north towards Hōnaunau. These lands are subject to frequent lava flows from Mauna Loa. Some of these lands have thick soil above at the 900–1,000-foot elevations; others have recent lava. This pattern of patchy soils and bare lava, and of differing vegetation, continues as these flows of different ages descend to the shore. High cliffs are common along the Kipapilua coast.

Kona, thus, had three marked areas—Kekaha in the north, central Kona, and Kipapilua in the south.

The last of Hawai'i's districts is Ka'ū. Ka'ū is a more isolated land, a land encompassing the homes of Pele—Kīlauea Crater and the crater atop Mauna Loa. Mauna Loa and its slopes make up much of Ka'ū, but as in Puna, it is a land of Pele. Ka'ū was a large district with ca. 64 miles of shoreline. It has four regions. Central Ka'ū from Wai'ōhinu to Wood's Valley has higher rainfall and streams in upland areas ca. 1–3 miles inland. The shore was arid with little soil—albeit with embayments at Punalu'u and Honu'apo. Far inland are the 'ōhi'a–koa forests, but in a patchwork of vegetation communities from pioneer to climax due to lava flows. The South Point area lies between Wai'ōhinu and the high Kahuku pali to the west, and this region is focused on windswept Ka Lae, South Point. Here fertile, deep ash soils were present, but the 40-inch rainfall line was 4.5–5.6 miles inland at the 1,000-foot elevation. To the west of South Point are dry lands, which are often covered by lava from Mauna Loa's southwest rift. These lands formed an environmental buffer of sorts between Ka'ū and Kona. To the east of central Ka'ū is Kīlauea itself, with its vast surrounding lands of lava, cinder and ash, and its southwest rift zone. Included in Ka'ū historically were the lands all the way east to Waha'ula heiau in Pālama ahupua'ā, lands now considered to be in Puna. Also, Ka'ū—like Hāmākua—extended far inland, up to the summit of Mauna Loa and looking down over the lands of southern Kona.

## DISRUPTIONS TO THE LAND

It is important to realize that major environmental disasters periodically struck parts of Hawai'i Island, affecting the vegetation, soils and rainfall and, thus, the lives of the people. Such events were often recalled in oral histories, and often remain as part of the archaeological record.

The most famous of these disasters are lava flows. The people of southern Kona, western and eastern Ka'ū, and Puna were most familiar with these events since Mauna Loa and Kīlauea frequently erupted during prehistory. Truly, the presence of Pele was commonly displayed in these lands. Kīlauea flows tend to be slower flows but high in volume. These flows covered vast tracts of land, fertile land. Sometimes the eruptions lasted for several years at a time. Mauna Loa flows are faster flows, coming down the steep mountain. When they combined with snow or loose ash, mud flows of high velocity could result. In 1868, such a deadly combination occurred

> *[W]e saw...an immense torrent of molten lava, which rushed across the plain below...swallowing everything in its way;—trees, houses, cattle, horses, goats, and men, all overwhelmed in an instant. This devouring current passed over a distance of about three miles in as many minutes...*
>
> [1868 Lyman][12]

Occasionally, a Mauna Loa flow would enter southern Kohala or northern Kona, flowing out of the Saddle area. In rare cases, perhaps once every 200 years, Hualālai would erupt in swift flows. Indeed, a huge eruption of Hualālai occurred in the A.D. 1300s, with archaeological sites showing ash and burned vegetation and soil in the Kailua area.[13]

Although these eruptions led to relatively few deaths, their result was the covering of soils, vegetation, and even bays and reefs in stone. This fact drastically changed the landscape for centuries, until the re-vegetation and marine reef re-formation processes began to establish a new soil–vegetation, reef–marine life community. In the case of Puna, nearly all this district has been covered over in the last 500 years[14]—a pattern of frequent flows that certainly existed back to the times of initial settlement. High rainfall in Puna can begin to convert flows back into soil and promote a rebirth of vegetation within several hundred years.[15] But in arid coastal Kona, the revitalization process is much longer—witness the presence of virtually no vegetation on the 1800–1801 flows.

Perhaps one can best visualize the impact of lava with an example. In 1795, the large black lava flow on which today's Kona Airport is located was not present. Instead, a long narrow fishpond (Paʻaiea) ran for several miles along a sandy shore. Houses were scattered along the shore on the lava of older flows, and fields and more houses were located 2–3 miles inland. The fishpond, the coastal houses, and much of the inland fields were covered in the 1800–1801 lava flow—5 years after the end point of this book. The land remains sealed in stone, with little vegetation growing on the flow to this day, 200 years later.

Unlike lava flows, tsunamis, droughts and floods occurred island–wide and had short-term effects on the land—albeit with greater loss of human life. Tsunamis, or tidal waves, of major scale occur infrequently – ca. 3 times in the twentieth century. Their greatest impact in historic times has been in windward areas on Hawaiʻi Island. The huge waves would flow over low points in the high dunes of Pololū, Waimanu and Waipiʻo valleys and across the low dunes in Hilo Bay, and swirl around in the lower parts of the valleys damaging vegetation, temporarily adding salt water, sand and rock to the taro swamps, and knocking down parts of fishpond walls. The marine benches or low shores could be virtually covered over during a tsunami—as in the case of central Ka'ū in 1868, or Laupāhoehoe in Hilo in the early 1900s when people and houses were literally swept away. On the leeward sides of the island, small embayments were affected by higher wave surges. Impacts were sudden, but relatively temporary, although loss of life was potentially far higher than from most lava flows, and major tsunamis were well remembered.[16]

Large waves from storms could have a somewhat similar, albeit reduced, effect. Twenty-foot waves could, and do, flood low-lying areas and damage fishpond walls.

Similarly, floods from storms dropping large amounts of rain can spill over natural channels. Such floods in Waipi'o, Waimanu and Pololū often breached taro field walls and damaged some fields. In central Kona and central Ka'ū, heavy rain at high elevations can flow rapidly down and over intermittent channels and periodically dump silt and stones in fans at lower elevations—causing localized damage.

Last, droughts, although localized, could also affect the land. Missionaries in the 1800s described a drought which dried up the crops in parts of Kona for several years. Fires occasionally spread during these times, accentuating the drought. Artemas Bishop described such a drought in Kona in 1825, where people stayed "long after the taro & potatoes failed, and subsisted upon the Hapuu...when this was exhausted their only resource was to remove to some distant part of the island until the drought should pass over."[17]

## CONCLUSIONS

This then is a summary of the lands, the 'āina, of Hawai'i Island at the time of Kamehameha in the early 1790s.

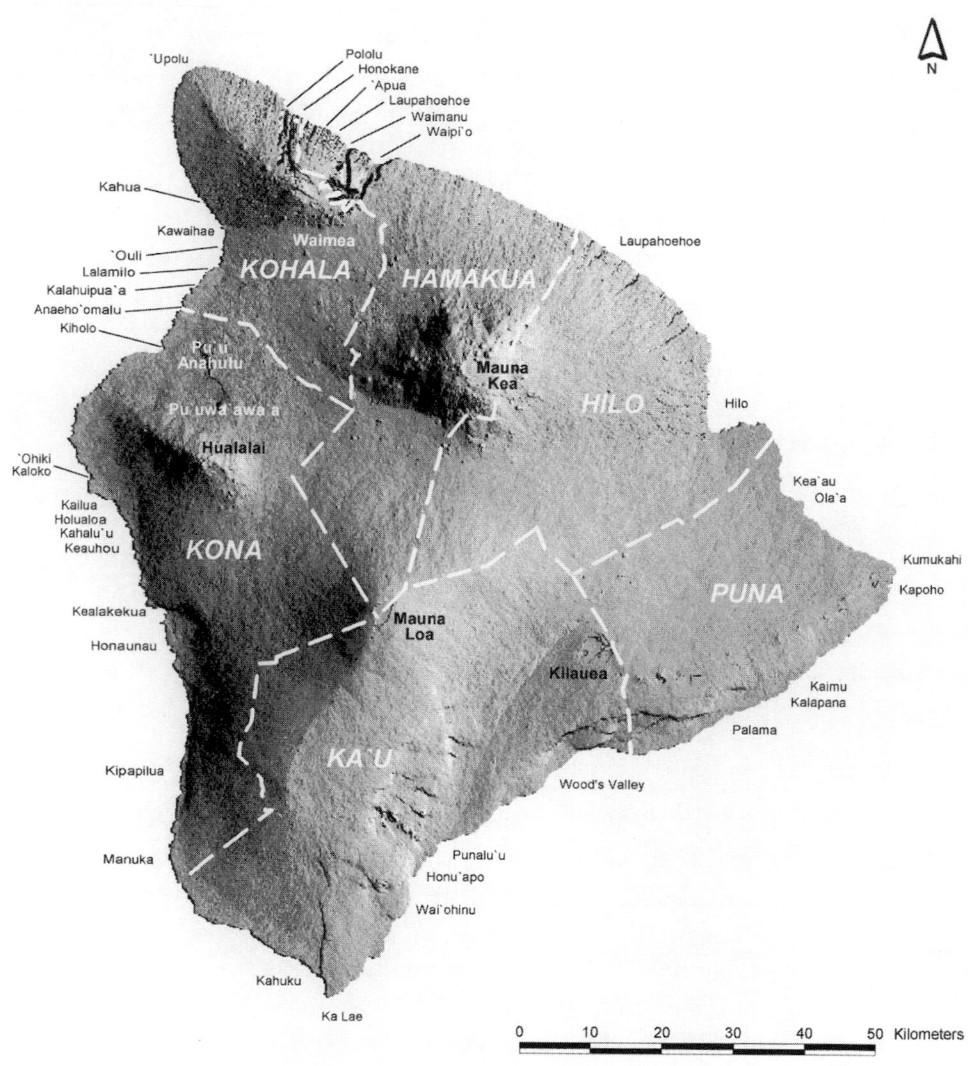


**FIGURE 1-7**
Place names mentioned in Chapter 1.

CHAPTER 2

# Hawaiian Culture Under Kamehameha: The End of the Old Ways

*E one wale no 'oukou i ku'u pono 'a 'ole e pau*

*Endless is the good that I have given you to enjoy*

(1819, Kamehameha's deathbed words to his chiefs)[1]

# INTRODUCTION

The common conception of traditional Hawaiian culture is what existed during the time when the islands were unified under Kamehameha. This is the culture documented by the Hawaiian historians Malo, Kamakau and 'Ī'ī, and by the expeditions, traders and missionaries after 1795. But, this is a view after about 1,500 years of Polynesian settlement in the islands. Generations of Hawaiians had lived and died prior to Kamehameha's reign. Importantly, the culture then was often quite different than it was after 1790. Kamehameha's period marks only the end point of traditional times.

Yet, there must be a starting point for this book, and it is easiest to appreciate the differences in the past if Kamehameha's period is understood first.

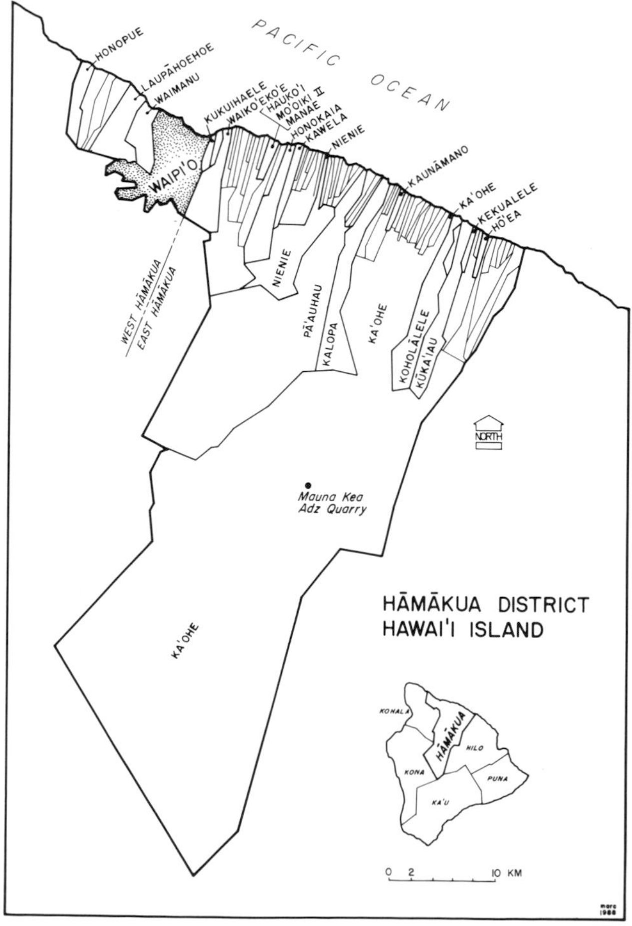


**FIGURE 2-1**
Map of Hāmākua District, Showing its ahupua'a.

# THE LAND

Under Kamehameha's rule, the lands of Hawai'i Island were divided into the six districts, the moku,[2] of Hāmākua, Hilo, Puna, Ka'ū, Kona and Kohala. These covered vast land areas from the ocean depths to the summits of the interior mountains. Hāmākua's shoreline spanned ca. 30 miles, and Kona's extended ca. 64 miles.

Each moku was divided into 70–100 ahupua'a, each of those being the land of an individual community.[3] There were about 600 ahupua'a on the island late in Kamehameha's reign. The ahupua'a has often been presented as a pie-shaped piece of land with its point on the mountain summit and spreading down to the shore. In reality, few ahupua'a fit this concept. Nearly all were roughly rectangular, running lengthwise from near-shore ocean, inland through farmlands, and up into the forest. Commonly, these ahupua'a on Hawai'i Island extended up gradually rising land, what have been called slope ahupua'a. The large valleys of Kohala and Hāmākua were different. Usually, each valley was an ahupua'a with the border being ridgelines. These ahupua'a included nearshore waters, the farmlands on the valley floors and at the base of the valley walls, and the forest above on the ridges. But, these valley ahupua'a were a rarity on Hawai'i Island.

Ahupua'a varied considerably in size; some were quite narrow, some over a mile wide. Some extended far inland, cutting off other ahupua'a and encompassing high forest and subalpine areas on the highest peaks. Others extended farther offshore and included special fisheries.

In Hāmākua district, there were ca. 100 ahupua'a (Fig. 2-1). Most were very narrow, 0.05–0.3 miles wide, and extended only a short distance inland—ca. 1.1–2.5 miles—through the farmlands and up into the 'ōhi'a-koa forests. A few were wider, 0.3–0.8 miles, and spread 3.2–6.5 miles inland, slightly above the 'ōhi'a forests up into the open māmane forest. Three ahupua'a were immense. Ka'ohe and Pā'auhau were not wide in the lower zones where they crossed shore, farmland and montane forests; but above the 'ōhi'a-koa forests, they expanded laterally—"cutting off" all the other ahupua'a in the words of Hawaiian witnesses in the 1870s Boundary Commission hearings—and expanded inland, including the open māmane forests of Mauna Kea's upper slopes. Ka'ohe ran even farther inland, encompassing all the subalpine areas of Mauna Kea above the treeline, including a large adze quarry area, and extending across the inland Saddle plateau, which held important nēnē and petrel nesting areas, and climbing up to the summit of Mauna Loa. Waipi'o was yet another massive ahupua'a in Hāmākua—including the valley and large areas of forested ridges and plateaus to the east (Lālākea) and west (Muliwai).

Not only did the land areas of Hāmākua's ahupua'a vary, but also the extent of the ahupua'a fisheries. Some ahupua'a had access to special resources, cutting off others. For example, Honokaia, Kawela, Kalōpā and Waiko'eko'e had fishing grounds which included the "Uhu Fisheries" (parrot fishes, *Scaridae*).[4] Waiko'eko'e cut off Kukuihaele and Kanahonua to the west and five ahupua'a to the east—it "took all the sea on the Kohala side to Waipio."[5] The point of cut off seems to have been just outside the breakers.[6] Importantly, an ahupua'a with a large land area did not necessarily have a large fishery.

In the moku of Kona, again over 100 ahupua'a were present. In the more fertile central Kona area, many ahupua'a were fairly narrow and included basic fishery, coastal, upland farms, and forest lands. But some extended above to cut off others, and some included huge inland areas. Keauhou was the largest ahupua'a in central Kona, reaching up into and including the vast māmane forests and subalpine areas of Mauna Loa and the Saddle area between Mauna Loa and Hualālai. Keauhou, in fact, shared its border with Hāmākua and its huge ahupua'a of Ka'ohe. In the arid areas beyond Keāhole Point, most ahupua'a had low populations but were fairly broad. Pu'uanahulu, Ka'ūpūlehu, and Pu'uwa'awa'a were 2.0-, 2.6-, and 5.1-miles wide at the shore, and they extended far inland (5–6 miles), also reaching Hāmākua and Ka'ohe ahupua'a.

Another pattern was the inland ahupua'a, usually located 5–6 miles from the shore in the uplands. Such ahupua'a were small, found in clusters in Ka'ū and perhaps in Waimea in southern Kohala, although the nature of the land units in Waimea is not as clear. Usually these inland ahupua'a were in agricultural lands and contained some forest lands. It appears that people living in such communities may have had use rights to portions of the near-shore reef within adjacent ahupua'a.[7]

The size and shape of Hawai'i Island's ahupua'a are cultural features. They reflect a mixture of historical factors keyed to handle special resources (fisheries, meat birds, koa trees, etc.), population, and political factors. Importantly, size does not necessarily reflect population size nor power of a community. Rather, in some cases it simply means that special resources were included within the ahupua'a, with those resources controlled by the resident or absentee landlord—the ruler or a high chief. Or, in arid regions, larger size may have compensated for poorer or more scattered farming soils. Also, it must be remembered that the borders of ahupua'a were not necessarily static.[8] In Kamehameha's time and later, ahupua'a were subdivided and given to different chiefs. Some lands were merged, reducing the number of ahupua'a.

At the time of European contact in 1779, there was another community-level land unit, the 'ili kūpono. This was an area within an ahupua'a which was administered separately under a different chief. For example, in southern Kohala 'Anaeho'omalu and Kalāhuipua'a were established by Kamehameha as 'ili kūpono within Waikoloa ahupua'a, but they were administered separately—half of upland Waikoloa with its grass and farmlands going to Isaac Davis, a foreign advisor and chief of Kamehameha's, and 'Anaeho'omalu and Kalāhuipua'a with their fishponds staying under Kamehameha's direct control.[9] 'Ili kūpono often included only a few resource zones (e.g., shoreline and fisheries).

The last land unit considered here is the 'ili or 'ili 'āina. These were subdivisions within an ahupua'a which were administered by the chief controlling the ahupua'a. On sloping land without valleys—such as Kona, dry Kohala, much of Ka'ū and Hāmākua—'ili have often been described as parallel, shore-to-forest slices. Once again, the picture is more complex. In Hāmākua, blocks of land in the agricultural and housing areas were set aside as ʻili as often as in the long slice pattern;[10] and in Kaʻū blocks seem to be the dominant pattern.[11] In valleys, ʻili became very complicated. Waipiʻo had ʻili which ran across the valley in one piece, from valley wall to valley wall, and others which extended only halfway across from the valley wall to the stream. Still others were in multiple pieces—ʻili lele or jump ʻili.[12] Again, ʻili patterns reflect past historical events related to resource locations, population density, political administration and the like.

## UTILIZED RESOURCES

Land use patterns in Kamehameha's times were linked closely to the major land units. The popular image of traditional Hawaiians as fishermen and users of the sea was true, but Hawaiians were equally dependent, if not more so, on agriculture and raising livestock, and were quite skilled in these arenas.

The basic diet was fish and farm products. Staple crops were taro (kalo), sweet potato (ʻuala) and banana (maiʻa), and to a lesser degree yams (uhi), breadfruit (ʻulu) and sugarcane (kō). Coconuts (niu) were also cultivated. The diet was also supplemented—to an unclear degree—by shellfish (molluscs, crustacea, etc.) and seaweeds. Pigs (puaʻa) and dogs (ʻīlio) were raised, but they served primarily as feast food in association with religious events or as food for the elite. This may also have been true for large wild birds (nēnē, petrel or ʻuaʻu). Chickens (moa) were domesticated, but how they were raised and used has yet to be analyzed in depth by researchers. Additionally, ʻawa (*Piper methysticum*, kava) was grown and prepared as a mildly narcotic drink. Thus, Hawaiians were farmers, stockmen, hunters, gatherers, and fishermen—all in one. Their food varied with the season, rainfall, abundance, and family preferences.

Several aspects of the crops grown need to be understood. Kalo was "king" in the islands. Generally, the kalo root, or corm, matures to sufficient size in 12 months, although different varieties had differing lengths of maturation, some slightly shorter, some slightly longer. Kalo is a plant requiring considerable amounts of water and drainage. It was grown in four major contexts on Hawai'i Island at the time of European contact. The most famous was "wet taro" in irrigated field (pondfield) systems. These fields (lo'i) look much like rice paddies, and many of the kalo pondfields were in fact converted to rice fields in the late 1800s. On flat valley bottoms, pondfield systems often consisted of a number of rectangular fields, usually with earth walls (sometimes reinforced with stone in areas where water flow was rapid) and with carefully prepared muddy floors. Canals—again earth- and stone-lined—led from valley streams, springs and waterfalls to these fields, and water was channeled through at a fairly slow, but constant, pace of flow. In steeper stream areas, such as upper valleys, the pondfields were often stone-walled in descending terraces and canals were sometimes shorter. Classic valley settings for irrigated kalo on Hawai'i Island were restricted to the big valleys of Kohala (Honokāne) and Hāmākua (Waimanu and Waipi'o). Steeper, terraced irrigation kalo fields were present in the upper valleys of these big valleys, in some of the gulches of wet Hāmākua and wet Hilo, and in most of the gulches of wet Kohala.

A second kalo setting occurred in Hilo Bay in the swampy or marshy fringes along the fishponds of the Wailoa and Wailoma rivers. Here mounds of grasses, reeds and marsh soils were formed with intervening ditches, the mounds long, roughly linear, and of different sizes. The kalo was planted on the mounds. This form of cultivation drained water away, as opposed to the lo'i system which supplied water through irrigation.[13]

Hawaiian chroniclers considered farming in these two contexts with flowing water an easy and year-round operation, while cultivation in the dry leeward, or kula, lands of Hawai'i Island was recognized as a much harder task, fraught with problems of heat, drought, and other factors.[14]

> *Kona...frequently suffered from famine in that district. In time of famine the people of Kona performed religious ceremonies with great diligence and carefully recognized the months in which to plant.*
>
> [1838 Malo][15]

In this leeward setting, kalo was cultivated in the well-known "dryland taro" context. Here, kalo was not irrigated for there were no permanently flowing streams, rather it was grown on dry land in areas of relatively high rainfall. In some leeward areas, formal rectangular field systems existed. For example, in Kona ca. 1–2 miles inland, a series of walled field systems existed. Areas had been cleared of stones which were then laid in long, low mounded walls called iwi ʻāina (or kuaīwi in the archaeological literature). These walls ran perpendicular to the sea for long distances with cross-walls forming individual fields. In Puna, a windward district, but one with no streams and often limited soils, dryland taro was grown in some ahupuaʻa in small, walled rectangular fields extending one after another, often for several acres.[16] Besides these walled fields, less formal and scattered kalo fields were present in windward Puna and in drier leeward lands. These usually were small clearings in rocky lands, terraced soil areas, unmodified pockets of soil, etc.

The fourth kalo setting combines the irrigated and dry cultivation methods. The best example is in Waimea in the uplands of southern Kohala. The kalo fields are low-walled plots or unwalled plots in predominantly natural swales or terraced slopes with water supplied by rainfall (10–40 inches per year), and by supplemental irrigation canals which tapped the streams of Waimea.[17] These canals supplied water which spread out and soaked into the fields, rather than flowing through as in the classic pondfield setting. This kind of kalo cultivation also appears in Kaʻū at Waiʻōhinu, fed by springs, and in the uplands of Mohokea and Punaluʻu.[18] It also has been identified recently by archaeologists in a few places in upland Kona, where intermittent streams were tapped.[19]

One important point to realize is that kalo generally does not do well in areas of low rainfall.[20] In contrast, sweet potatoes and yams can thrive in such conditions, with sweet potatoes maturing in 4–6 months.[21] They were grown in windward areas in well-drained soils, often in less formal fields near houses and in mounds of soil and rock which would drain well. In these wet, windward lands, sweet potatoes and yams were dietary supplements. In dry leeward lands, however, sweet potatoes were an important crop, rivaling kalo as the staple and often surpassing kalo in the very dry areas. Apparently, sweet potatoes were grown on an equal basis with kalo in the upland stone-walled fields of Kona in the higher rainfall zones, but they were the dominant crop in the less formal, scattered fields all the way down to the coast. In Ka‘ū, a special variety of dryland kalo was the dominant crop in upper elevations, but sweet potato was the main crop planted at lower elevations, all the way to the shore. In dry Kohala, sweet potatoes seem to have been the major crop in the upland field systems. Here, low stone alignments—perhaps once planted with sugarcane as windbreaks—formed the field borders. Scattered informal fields (the typical clearings, mounds, etc.) were present in rockier areas.

Bananas and the lesser crops—sugarcane, breadfruit and coconuts—were usually scattered among the fields and houses. For example, sugarcane and bananas were often grown on kalo pondfield walls. Bananas were planted in larger numbers in the forest fringe of the island, along with ‘awa.[22] Also, in Kona there was a special breadfruit planting zone, at least in the lands between Kailua and Hōnaunau. This area was just below the stone-walled kalo and sweet potato fields, ca. 0.8–1.2 miles inland, and above the informal sweet potato plots scattered down to the shore. Groves of breadfruit were common as well in windward Kohala, Hāmākua and Hilo, particularly as described in historical accounts along the shores of Hilo Bay. Breadfruit appears not to have been commonly planted in Ka‘ū or leeward Kohala.

In Kamehameha's time, farm plots were claimed and used by individual households within the ahupua‘a. Individual plots within irrigated taro systems were called lo‘i. Dryland plots or sets of fields were called māla and kīhapai among other terms. A household would hold a number of plots in different environmental zones. For example, in valleys, a household's holdings might include lo'i and kīhapai plots. In leeward lands, plots might include low elevation sweet potato fields, upland kalo fields, some breadfruit trees, and a patch of bananas within the forest fringe. Household use-rights were inherited, but they also had to be reaffirmed by the overlord chief's resident agent, the konohiki.[23]

Vegetable food was also collected. In forest areas, mountain apples, arrowroot, Alocasia taro, hapu'u tree ferns and other plants were gathered. Many of these were fallback food sources in the times of famine caused by drought, fire, looting, and the like.[24]

Pigs, dogs and chickens were raised on the island, but exactly how is not very clear. Malo noted that animals, presumably pigs and dogs, were at least partly fed on sweet potatoes, and Ellis in 1823 also stated that dogs were fed vegetables.[25] Dogs were kept in yards, at least in some areas;[26] other references note that pigs and chickens were kept in "small out-houses."[27] On O'ahu in 1809–1810, Campbell said "hogs were kept in pens, and fed on taro leaves, sugarcanes, and garbage."[28] Pigs, dogs and chickens all were used in rituals, as offerings—sometimes in extremely high numbers.[29] The amounts consumed in the normal diets of commoners and chiefs are unknown.

A wide range of marine resources were collected. Along the shore and usually in shallow waters, shellfish were gathered. Cowrie (leho, *Cypraea spp.*) and limpet ('opihi, *Cellana spp.*) were the two with the largest amount of meat, and their shells are often the dominant mollusc remains found in archaeological middens. It does appear, however, that gathering of shellfish was quite varied—a wide range of species being collected, not just a focus on the large meaty species that are used today. Sea urchins also are common archaeological remains, and the historic and oral historic literature note sea cucumbers and other crustacea species being collected. Interestingly, Malo labels shellfish and echinoids as fish which moved at slower speeds.[30]

Fish were also caught in shallow, inshore waters with spears, nets, traps and lines with jabbing and rotating fishhooks of bone and pearl shell. Archaeological evidence (fish remains and small fish-hooks) indicates that inshore fishing was the dominant source of fish. Octopus were caught just off the shallow reef using hand lines with a bone hook point lashed to a stick along with a cowrie (leho) lure and a stone or coral sinker. Line fishing from canoes occurred in deeper waters. Bottom fishing with larger rotating hooks took place to catch jackfish such as ulua and kāhala, using measured lines and exploiting specific fishing grounds (koʻa) identified by sea floor topography, currents and depths.[31] Trolling for larger pelagic fish such as tuna, mahimahi, and the like required long bamboo poles or hand lines with composite fishhooks with a pearl-shell lure and bone hook. Pelagic species that came close to shore—such as scads (ʻōpelu and akule)—were netted.[32] Fishing expeditions of varying size would be mounted for pelagic and benthic fishing.[33]

Importantly, nearshore marine resources were communally accessible to all residents of an ahupuaʻa within that land's fisheries, which extended at least a short distance offshore.[34] These resources were not accessible to residents of other ahupuaʻa without permission. Pelagic and benthic resources which were located well offshore seem to have been open to all members of the Hawaiʻi Kingdom, although some benthic grounds (koʻa) were considered property of a specific ahupuaʻa.[35] The lords of the ahupuaʻa could restrict communal access to the ahupuaʻa fisheries by placing specific fish under kapu for a period of time.[36] Another restriction on communal ahupuaʻa fishery rights were whale bone or large trees which washed ashore. These items were restricted resources for the gods and, thus the king, with the whale bone made into elaborate pendants (lei niho palaoa) and the trees into large hulls for double canoes.[37]

Fish were also raised in fishponds (loko). These were usually mullet and milkfish. Fishponds varied considerably in form, depending on the part of the island. In northern Kona, bays and shallow reef areas were enclosed with large stone walls in the more commonly known form of fishpond. One of these, built by Kamehameha ca. 1805, was at Kīholo Bay in Puʻuwaʻawaʻa ahupuaʻa. It had immense walls running offshore. Another large fishpond was Paʻaiea, extending for several miles just off the coast north of today's Keāhole

Point. Yet another enclosed a bay in Kaloko ahupua'a, the wall extremely thick and high, but fairly short, for the original bay entrance was narrow. Both Kīholo and Pa'aiea fishponds were covered by lava flows, in 1859 and 1801; Kaloko fishpond is still present within the Kaloko-Honokōhau National Historic Park.

Large anchialine or tidal ponds were also modified into fishponds—most notably along the arid south Kohala and north Kona shore. Examples can still be seen today at Kūki'o in Kona and at 'Anaeho'omalu and Kalāhuipua'a in Kohala.

In contrast to these shore ponds, on the windward side of the island inland fishponds were much more common. In the Hilo area, particularly in Waiākea ahupua'a, walled-off sections were built along the Wailoa River behind the sandy beach berm, creating several large fishponds. In Waipi'o, a chain of fishponds were also present behind the berm of high sand dunes, built in the same fashion as taro pondfields, with canals and earth walls. These ponds began fairly small and culminated in the extremely large Muliwai fishpond directly behind Waipi'o's sand dunes.

Fishpond resources seem to have been much more restricted than open ocean resources. A large pond was controlled by the ruler or the high-ranking overlord chief of the ahupua'a and had resident caretakers. The use of lesser fishponds within irrigated taro systems is unclear; possibly lower ranks could use them.[38]

While farming, fishing, livestock-raising and collecting were critical food-gathering activities, another lesser known food source was wild birds. In the interior of the island and on the upper slopes of Mauna Loa, flightless geese (the nēnē) and dark-rumped petrel ('ua'u) nestlings were hunted. Wild ducks (koloa) and plovers (kōlea) were also caught and eaten, as were numerous smaller forest, grassland, and shore birds.[39] Archaeological evidence shows a wide variety of birds were taken, with large meat birds dominating the remains in the Saddle area.[40] Bird-catchers used different techniques ranging from poles and snares, to lime and stoning.[41] Hunting rights to certain birds—particularly the large, meaty nēnē and 'ua'u—were vested to the residents of certain ahupuaʻa, the largest which extended far inland.

Other nonfood resources existed that were critical for daily life. Clothing was made in the form of kapa or bark-cloth. The thin bark from wauke (paper mulberry) and māmaki trees was carefully soaked until pulpy, pounded together on a wood anvil into fine sheets, dried, and then printed or colored with various types of brushes or carved stamps and natural dyes.[42] Paper mulberry was cultivated within the agricultural fields. Māmaki grew wild, with human assistance. It was "owned" in clumps in windward field areas, but usually māmaki was harvested within the ʻōhiʻa-koa forest.

Timber for canoes, houses, firewood, spears, knives, tools and heiau buildings and images was also an important resource. Larger ʻōhiʻa and koa trees were special resources under the control of chiefs, for heiau buildings and images in the case of ʻōhiʻa, and for koa canoes. House posts were made of uhiuhi, naio, māmane, ʻaʻaliʻi and other hard woods.[43] Spears were often made of kauila, as were daggers or clubs—although both the latter could be of uhiuhi or pua.[44] Bowls were made of kou and milo.[45]

Rope and twine were prepared from forest vines (e.g., olonā) and coconut husks to be used as fishnets, fishlines, house lashings, canoe lashings, and slings for warfare. Building thatch was made of pili grass and the leaves of kī, banana, and pandanus from lower forests, grasslands, fallow agricultural fields and cultivated areas. Pandanus (hala) leaves were also collected from lower forest zones in the windward areas and other locations to make mats, sails and the like. The kind of thatch used seems to have varied with the available resource.

Forests were also a source of feathers, a vital and restricted resource for the elaborate feather capes, cloaks and helmets worn by chiefs and their distinguished warriors[46]—striking and well-known elite apparel items. The birds which were the sources for these feathers lived in the forests, often being honeycreepers which relied on ʻōhiʻa blossoms for food sources. Yellow feathers came from the ʻōʻō (*Moho nobilus*) and mamo (*Drepanis pacifica*). Equally valuable red feathers came from the ʻiʻiwi (*Vestaria coccinea*) and the ʻapapane (*Himatine sanguinea*).[47] Feathers were tax items and ahupuaʻa residents had to collect them as tribute.[48]

Forest resources, including meat birds, were communal and restricted to residents of an ahupuaʻa. Residents of other ahupuaʻa could not enter an ahupuaʻa's forest lands without permission of its konohiki and/or residents. There are numerous documented incidents of feathers confiscated from intruders, and a few cases of conflict with intruders.

> *Hamakua natives had the fight when they came onto Kahuku [Kaʻū] after birds.*
>
> [1873 Kamakana][49]

> *in olden times when it was kapu to catch birds on any land but the one you lived on, and if you did so the birds were taken away from you.*
>
> [1873 Kenoi][50]

> *The different lands had different Konohiki, and if we went onto a land we did not belong on, the Konohiki of that land would take our birds away.*
>
> [1873 Kaikuana][51]

Stone for various tools was yet another resource. Basalt was used for stone adzes for woodworking activities, and files and abraders (the old sandpaper) were made from sea urchin spines, small coral pieces and basalt of varying porosity. In many cases, these objects seem to have been prepared from local materials.

High-quality adze basalt, however, was restricted to only a few ahupuaʻa. There were a number of quarries; but at the time of European contact, the fine-grained Hawaiite basalt exposed on Mauna Kea's interior, southwest slopes primarily at the 11,000–12,000-foot elevations seems to have been the major source of adze material on Hawaiʻi Island. The basalt was apparently extracted during summer months by groups working in the open or in rock shelters, breaking down large boulders into smaller, portable adze "blanks" which were then removed to areas, presumably nearer to shoreline houses, for final adze manufacture.[52] This quarry was in Ka'ohe ahupua'a of Hāmākua district, and it is not clear yet if only Ka'ohe people did the quarrying, or if the ruler gave access to quarriers from all over the island. Initial analysis of Mauna Kea adze distributions suggests adzes were traded through small personal exchange systems, not a centralized controlled system.[53]

Another restricted stone was volcanic glass. Tiny, fingernail-sized pieces of this low silica obsidian seem to have been used for generalized cutting. These volcanic glass tools are the most common artifact found in prehistoric archaeological sites. Sources of volcanic glass are found in more locations than adze basalt, and there are even poor-quality chilled glass areas on local flows. Pu'uwa'awa'a, a cinder cone in upland Pu'uwa'awa'a ahupua'a in north Kona, is one known source of high-quality glass. The quarries and quarrying activities are still unknown.

Porous basalt abraders were also quarried from several special spots on the island. So far, archaeological work has identified sizable quarries at the coastal Kohala-Kona border (Waikoloa-Pu'uanahulu ahupua'a), and in Kahuku ahupua'a in Ka'ū.[54] In both areas, cracks in pāhoehoe flows were enlarged to retrieve chunks of porous pāhoehoe, and these were then ground down in abrader basins into "blanks" of approximate tool size. The Waikoloa quarry has small caves and walled surface shelters present amidst the quarry, and interpretations so far suggest brief quarrying by small groups from outside the ahupua'a.[55]

## SETTLEMENT PATTERNS

Generally, permanent housing was predomantly coastal. Nearshore marine resource areas were close to the houses. In windward areas, farms also were nearby and extended a bit farther inland. In leeward areas, primary cultivation areas were predominantly located in the uplands where rainfall was adequate for reliable crop yields, usually at and above the 30-inch rain contour. Farms in drier areas did extend down toward the shore from these higher rainfall areas. And small gardens were even located near houses in leeward areas in pits and mounds. Forest resources were inland of the fields.

There was considerable variation from this general pattern, however.

Hāmākua's large valleys (Waimanu and Waipi'o, and to a lesser degree Honopue) had irrigated taro fields on the valley floors and in the upper valleys, with tree crops (breadfruit, coconuts, bananas) and dryland crops (sweet potatoes, yams) on the drier spots at the base of the valley walls, the valley dunes and in the upper valleys. Houses were scattered along these drier spots, and concentrated heavily in the lower valleys. Major religious structures were at the front in the lower valleys. Large marine benches along the cliffs were used for housing, irrigating taro (tapping waterfalls) and dryland cultivation. Forests above and between valleys were exploited, as were offshore marine resources. The rest of Hāmākua was cliff lands with many small gulches. Housing and associated heiau were just above the cliffs on the gently rolling slopes, extending inland for 0.3–1.3 mile. Dryland taro and other crops were grown in fields around the houses and slightly farther inland. Ahupua'a in these areas exploited the 'ōhi'a-koa forest above, with Ka'ohe and Pā'auhau encompassing the vast inland māmane forest lands and with Ka'ohe including the Mauna Kea adze quarry and the nēnē and petrel nesting ground in the Saddle area beyond. Community rights to marine resources often were restricted to the narrow benches below the cliffs, with some lands having use rights to offshore fisheries.[56]

Most of northern Hilo was similar to the cliff lands of Hāmākua, with some wider gulches such as Mālua perhaps having small valley-type settlement patterns. The ahupua'a of Humu'ula extended far above the 'ōhi'a-koa forest in this part of Hilo, abutting Hāmākua's Ka'ohe ahupua'a on the slopes of Mauna Kea. At Hilo Bay the cliffs ended and the settlement pattern changed. Here houses and heiau were concentrated in clusters near the sandy shore amidst groves of breadfruit, bananas and coconuts,[57] and houses were also scattered inland for 3–6 miles. Dryland fields of kalo and sweet potatoes were around these houses and extended slightly farther inland. Kipikipi wet kalo fields and fishponds were along the Waimoa and Wailoa streams near the coastal houses.[58]

Puna's settlement pattern was a patchy one, affected by the lava flows in the area. Most houses and major heiau appear to have been near the shore, often clustered about small coves, but some inland settlements were found from Kea'au to 'Ōla'a (towards the volcano) and towards Pāhoa. Agriculture was dryland cultivation of kalo and sweet potatoes. In areas where rainfall was high and soil was present, farms were in the form of walled fields. Where rainfall was lower or soil was minimal due to relatively recent lava flows, cultivated areas were informal clearings, mounds, pits and terraces. These fields were located around the houses and extended a bit farther inland, often clustered in kīpuka, remnants of old flows with soil. Forests were exploited as in the other windward lands. Fishery rights extended out to sea, with some fisheries cutting off others.[59]

Ka'ū had four areas with differing settlement patterns.[60] Western Ka'ū and eastern Ka'ū were in active lava flow regions, along the southwest rift zone of Mauna Loa and of Kīlauea, respectively. Here soil was minimal. Houses were on the shore with associated heiau. Informal field areas were far inland, where rainfall was adequate, and a fair amount of houses also appear to have been in these inland areas. Two huge ahupua'a, Kahuku and Kapāpala, extended up to Mauna Loa's summit and encompassed the nēnē and petrel nesting grounds on the upper elevations. Kīlauea Crater and its surrounding vicinity was in eastern Ka'ū. Central Ka'ū had streams which flowed in mid-elevations, and high-rainfall areas approached the shore in some areas. Here houses and major heiau were found about equally on the shore and in the upland fields. Inland ahupua'a were found in clusters in the upland fields. Fields were dryland taro, supplemented by irrigation in a few cases, and sweet potato, with informal fields extending down towards the shore. Fishponds in the form of anchialine ponds and enclosed inlets were present in this area. The last region of Ka'ū, the South Point area, had a settlement pattern somewhat similar to central Ka'ū. Houses and associated heiau were again equally distributed on the shore and in upland fields. Inland ahupua'a were also present. The fields, however, were 6–9 miles inland. No streams were present. Dryland taro and bananas were grown in upper elevation fields, grading into sweet potato cultivation zones at lower elevations and continuing to the shore. The forests of Ka'ū were used as in other moku, and ahupua'a residents had access to fisheries of varying sizes.

Kona's settlement had most of its houses and major heiau along the shore, with perhaps 10% of the houses scattered in the wetter uplands.[61] The main fields were taro and sweet potato parcels in the uplands ca. 2 miles inland, above the 30–40-inch rainfall line, in walled rectangular plots. Breadfruit was planted just below, and then informal sweet potato fields extended down to the shore in soil patches, mounds, clearings, pits and terraces on the drier (kula) slopes. Bananas were grown in the forest fringe above, and the forests were exploited as in the other moku—notably with firewood and fresh water being brought down "on the shoulders of men."[62] Marine resources were gathered on the calm nearshore reefs, on offshore benthic grounds (ko'a), and by chasing pelagic fish in deeper waters. North of Keāhole Point, the upland rainfall became quite low, and inland fields are poorly known—perhaps being only patches in the forest fringe. No walled field systems are known to have been present in the uplands in this area. The seaward lands had vast areas of exposed lava. Coastal fishponds, particularly anchialine ponds, abound in this northern Kona area. Housing and population here were predominantly coastal and low in numbers, and often focused around small sandy coves, with associated coconut groves and some pit cultivation of sweet potatoes in the lava near the houses. Southernmost Kona was subject to frequent lava flows from Mauna Loa, and this area has a typical Kona settlement pattern, occasionally covered, or broken, by flows.

The sixth moku, Kohala, had four basic settlement patterns. In the arid and sometimes lava-covered coastal lands of southern Kohala, there was sparse coastal housing, often clustered around anchialine ponds and fishponds. The bulk of the population was 8–

10 miles inland, scattered among the fields of Waimea, near the present-day town, with supplemental irrigation fed by the streams of Waimea. Larger populations were also present on the coast at Puakō and Kawaihae with major heiau at Kawaihae. Yet Puakō and Kawaihae both seem to have had major inland populations and farmlands. Leeward Kohala north of Kawaihae has the second settlement pattern of Kohala. Here farmlands were only 1–2 miles inland, in the thicker soil above the 30-inch rainfall line, which gradually descended towards the shore heading north. Sweet potatoes were the staple crop of this region. Houses were scattered in the fields, but housing appears to have been predominantly coastal. The third Kohala pattern was found from ʻUpolu Point to the large valleys of Kohala. This is within windward Kohala, and rainfall was high and soil abundant, even on the shore. Irrigated taro was present in the wider stream flats in the gulches and on lower slopes above the gulches 1–2 miles inland, and dryland fields were on the slopes, extending ca. 3–4 miles inland. Houses were scattered about these slope areas, with major heiau near the shore. The large valleys of Kohala (Pololū and Honokāne) had settlement patterns like the similarly large valleys of Hāmākua.[63]

Major trails linked all these moku. A trail ran above the cliffs of Hāmākua and Hilo, passing through the housing and field areas and descending in and out of the numerous gulches. This trail then ran along the sand shore of Hilo Bay. One branch led inland to Keaʻau, ʻŌlaʻa, Kīlauea Crater and descended through the upland fields of Kaʻū. The other branch continued along the shore from Hilo Bay through Puna, and into Kaʻū. (Another upland branch separated near Keaʻau, ran towards Pāhoa and then through the uplands of Puna to Kīlauea.) These two major trails—coastal and in the upland fields—continued through Kaʻū and then through Kona. Near Keāhole Point, the upland trail may have descended to the shore in the Kīholo Bay area. The coastal trail then continued into Kohala, where several branches led up towards Waimea, while the coastal trail continued on through Kohala into Pololū and on up and down the valley region of Kohala into Hāmākua and Waipiʻo, where it rose and joined the trail above the cliffs in Hāmākua. The Waimea branch continued up into Waimea and then over to the trail above the cliffs in Hāmākua, with several branches reaching that Hāmākua trail at different points. These major trails were the main ala loa or ala aupuni of Kamehameha's time—linking all the communities of the nation.

Several other major trails linked the moku across the mountains. For example, a general trail corridor extended from Hilo up across the Saddle and down into Waimea. Puna and Ka'ū had trails linking up with this corridor on the Hilo end, as did Hāmākua and Kohala on the Waimea end. A second corridor ran from Waimea up along the Kona-Hāmākua border to Ahu a 'Umi heiau in the Saddle between Mauna Loa and Hualālai, and then down to the shore in central Kona. Numerous caves which served as rest stops and camps for travelers are still found along this corridor. Another trail led from Ka'ū up along the flanks of Mauna Loa to Ahu a 'Umi heiau, providing access from Ka'ū to Kona, and the corridor beyond to Waimea.

Besides these major trails, numerous mauka-makai (mountain-to-sea) trails ran within ahupua'a, connecting the coast to upland fields and forests. Rest shelters were also commonly found along these trails in the form of caves or small, walled surface structures called o'io'ina.[64]

## THE PEOPLE

For the last two decades, a commonly accepted estimate of population on Hawai'i Island at European contact, before the onset of foreign diseases, was ca. 100,000 people.[65] Early estimates vary wildly, but careful review indicates that 100,000 is a safe figure, and recent work suggests it may even be too low.[66] A polity or nation size of 100,000 was quite large for the Pacific and Americas in the 1700s, approached only perhaps by Tonga in the Pacific and far exceeding the complex chiefdoms of North America (e.g., the Cherokee in A.D. 1700 with ca. 12,000 people),[67] being somewhat equivalent to the pre-Spanish Maya nations, and perhaps only exceeded by the large empires of the Aztec and the Inka.[68]

Population figures for districts in the 1790s are not available. But crude estimates can be gleaned by taking the estimated archipelago total of 300,000, the first archipelago census (1831–1832) total of 130,313 and computing the percentage of decline (57%). Then the 1831–1832 census data for Hawai'i Island can be adjusted up to yield estimates for the 1790s (Table 2-1).

**Table 2-1**

**Population Estimates for Moku, 1778 A.D.**

| | est. A.D. 1778 | Census 1831–1832 |
|---|---|---|
| **Hawai'i Island** | **106,028** | **45,592** |
| Hāmākua | 11,130 | 4,786 |
| Hilo & Puna | 29,070 | 12,500 |
| Ka'ū | 13,488 | 5,800 |
| Kona | 28,837 | 12,400 |
| Kohala | 23,503 | 10,106 |

1831–1832 census information from Schmitt (1977:12). The total, listed as 45,700, actually adds up to 45,592.

One striking pattern here is that Hilo, Kona and Kohala stand out as major population areas. But, the Hilo and Puna populations were combined in 1831–1832, and it appears as if Puna had a sizable population. In the 1790s, Puna may have had 12,000 people and Hilo 17,000; or, perhaps Puna had 15,000 and Hilo 14,000. The census on which these estimates are based occurred 50 years after European contact and well into the trading and whaling eras. Ports for visiting ships were in Hilo (Hilo Bay), Kona (Kealakekua, Kailua-Kona) and Kohala (Kawaihae). No ports were in Ka'ū or Hāmākua. Documents clearly show that sizable amounts of these districts' population were attracted to the port towns for jobs and other reasons—a common Pacific phenomenon.[69] Thus, the figures for Hāmākua and Ka'ū may have been higher, and all the districts' populations may have been more balanced at the time of European contact. We simply do not know.

Within each district, ahupua'a populations varied considerably. Research shows that a common ahupua'a population size was ca. 100–200. Some sparsely occupied ahupua'a may have had 50 residents or less, including many of the inland ahupua'a. Some ahupua'a had up to 300–400 residents. Waipi'o with perhaps 2,600 seems to have had by far the largest ahupua'a population.

Importantly, within each district, the populace was not evenly spread out. For example, in Hāmākua, the bulk of the populace was concentrated in the large valleys, with Waipi'o having perhaps 25% of the district's population. In Kohala, population was concentrated in the windward gulch lands between 'Upolu Point and Pololū, and to a lesser degree in Kawaihae and Waimea. In Kona, the lands north of Kailua were sparsely inhabited, with the central Kona area from Kailua to Hōnaunau evidently having the bulk of that district's population. In part, these distributions clearly reflect abundance of agricultural resources and available agricultural land.[70]

## SOCIAL STRATIFICATION

The populace of Hawai'i was stratified into a number of hierarchically arranged ranks. This has been a subject of attention since the time of Cook and his colleagues.

One separation recognized by all Hawaiians was a sharp division between chiefs and commoners. On the succession of a king, the hale naua ritual identified those who could prove relations to the king within ten generations, and these individuals became the bulk of the kingdom's chiefs. However, highly skilled warriors and other commoners and foreigners of great skill could be elevated to chiefly rank.

## THE COMMON MAN (MAKA'ĀINANA)

The bulk of the population on the island certainly were commoners—perhaps 95% of the population, or 102,000 people.[71] The common man was found in all ahupua'a.

**Table 2-2**
**Idea of Population per Major Social Stratum**

| Administrative Level | Estimated Numbers | Estimated Numbers in Chiefly Family | Total |
|---|---|---|---|
| Ruler | 1 | 10–20 | 20 |
| High Chiefs | 20 | 10 | 200 |
| Konohiki | 600 | 5 | 3,000 |
| Commoners | | | 102,500 |
| Island Population, Table 2-1 | | | 106,000 |

The household was the basic commoner social group. A family household—man, wife, and children and occasionally relatives—typically resided at a pā hale (house lot). Within this lot, they had a thatched sleeping house which was largely used for sleeping and storage. Outdoors nearby were cooking areas (roofed or open) with underground ovens (imu), around which food preparation activities took place. Other work areas would have been present for tool manufacturing, kapa and weaving activities, and the like. Eating was separated by sex (in theory), with the women of the household unable to eat pig, bananas, coconuts, and some other items and being unable to eat in the eating area of men.[72]

The household's agricultural plots were in pieces ('āpana) in the agricultural zones of their ahupua'a. These sections were scattered about, usually within one 'ili. The Māhele records show holdings in several ʻili, but this may reflect post-contact depopulation and activation of land use claims in other ʻili.

Households also had burial areas. Frequently, these were caves or platform areas near the houses. In some areas, burial occurred in family caves in distant cliffs and in platforms and other man-made features on cinder cones.

Households also had religious areas. Recently deceased revered relatives, or associated animals, or auspicious manifestations of gods were considered spirits who could be called on to resolve problems. Male-female separation of worship occurred. Men usually had areas within a men's house (mua) where they made appeals to some of these deities and gave offerings. Several households—often related—shared a men's house. Women were forbidden to enter it.[73] A household's members would also give offerings at other religious places—fishing shrines, agricultural shrines, other occupational shrines, and those associated with deities of a specific place, etc.

Rights to agricultural and house plots were held by the household head or spouse, and could be inherited by designated relatives. The Māhele records show wives or children as frequent heirs.[74] But, superior rights to these land parcels were also held by the overlord chiefs. In theory, the chiefs gave right of use to the commoner household head. Indeed, Māhele claims and testimonies often state that the right to the land was given by the konohiki, and sometimes—albeit rarely—the records in turn clarify that the konohiki's right to allow use of the land came from his overlord chief.

> *It was Umikauikona who gave it [land claimed] to him [claimant's kupuna], and when my kupunakane died, my makuakane inherited the land, and he bequeathed it to me on his death. Kamehameha I was the aliʻi, Heulu was the konohiki, and Umi was the tenant. When Heulu died, Keaweaheulu succeeded him, and when Keaweaheulu died, Naihe succeeded him, and when Naihe died, Aikanaka succeeded him,*

> *and when Aikanaka died, Keohokalole succeeded him. Umi died and was followed by Kua, on Kua's death he was succeeded by Kamalo. [At present] Kamehameha III is the ali'i, Keohokalole is the konohiki, Kamalo is the tenant, and we are the ones who [still] have the mo'o.*
>
> [1848 claim of Kaheananui][75]

Commoner rights could be removed if the household claimants failed to meet the tax, service and behavioral expectations of their chiefs. Before removal chiefly threats often were made, including burning of dwellings.[76] Importantly, rights to land were not held by commoner kin groups ('ohana) at the time of Kamehameha. The household was the commoner unit which held land, and its genealogy was quite shallow, perhaps no more than three generations, in order to substantiate use claims.[77]

This system was feudal. Land ownership was fully separated from kin groups, with duties and obligations held by the commoner household and their overlord chiefs, and with the ultimate rights held by the chiefs.[78] In Polynesia, this system developed only in Hawai'i and Tonga by the time of European contact.

It is important to re-emphasize that there was no larger localized kin group in Hawai'i in the late 1700s, such as the 'ohana which was made famous in Handy and Pukui's ethnography of the 1930s. Research over the last two decades has revealed that there are no references to any such groups in any of the land records of the Māhele of the mid-1800s, or in earlier accounts.[79] There were clusters of households which lived next to each other. These had no name and were often described by referring to a dominant individual, such as Keone ma.[80] Members of these clusters could have been related, brothers, sisters, etc. But they held their property separately as households. These resident groups did share a men's house, the communal gathering spot for the group's men. Here men gossiped, worked, and occasionally ate and slept. Here too they kept images associated with their ancestral spirits and made offerings.

The largest social group in daily life was the community (sometimes given the label ahupua'a, which is actually the name of the community's land). At contact, this was not a corporate kin group. Rather it was the collection of resident commoner households given use rights to residence by the overlord chief, with the konohiki as his representative.[81] A variety of community use and access rights existed: to water in irrigated lands, to reef and forest resources, to trails.

A commoner's daily life was split among the subsistence tasks of fishing, farming, tending livestock, and gathering shellfish; maintenance tasks such as collecting firewood; manufacturing of kapa, mats, fishhooks and tools; religious activities; leisure; and obligations to the chiefs. Full-time specialists may have existed, but they were usually attached to a high chief's or the ruler's court: feather cloak- and helmet-makers, warriors, navigators, priests, fishing specialists, to name but a few. Exceptions may have been sorcerers, medical specialists, and the like.

Obligations to the chiefs were multiple. Every few days, labor was required in the local chief's and overlord chief's fields, the kō'ele plots. Annual ahupua'a taxes were gathered—usually in the form of bundles of bird feathers, kapa cloth, dried taro, other foodstuffs, pigs, and dogs.[82] Nonperiodic demands were also made for labor on heiau, fishponds and paths; for warriors; and for foodstuffs when a high chief or the ruler was in residence nearby, or when he needed food for special ceremonies. Strict respect behavior was owed to the chiefs and to the ceremonies linked to the national religion.

Generally, the lot of the commoner was not unusually harsh, unless beset by drought, lava flows, a demanding chief, or repeated warfare. The land was generally bountiful, and unless gross violations of etiquette to chiefs occurred, life and land rights were safe.

# NA ALIʻI—THE CHIEFS

*[T]he people held the chiefs in great dread and looked upon them as gods.*

[1838 Malo][83]

Although perhaps applying only to the highest chiefs, this comment is a potent one. The renown of traditional Hawaiʻi has been its chiefs. These were the individuals described in detail by the early expeditions. They dominate the oral histories. And they dominated life on ancient Hawaiʻi Island.

The focal point of all the chiefs was the ruler. He was not simply a higher chief; the ruler was in a separate category.[84]

*The king was the real head of the government; the chiefs below the king, the shoulders and chest. The priest of the king's idol was the right hand, the minister of the interior (kanaka kalaimoku) the left hand, of the government.*

[1838 Malo][85]

*Our sources are explicit; the king is the supreme mediator between men and gods...the supreme sacrificer, the man closest to the divine.*

[1985 Valeri][86]

Chiefs primarily held their rank by genealogical affiliation with the ruler, established through the hale naua rites, although some commoners skilled in warfare or other matters might be elevated to chiefly rank.[87] The ruler ultimately controlled all land,[88] redistributing the ahupuaʻa on succession to major chiefs and allocating ahupuaʻa of his own during his reign.[89] The ruler also appointed the highest priests and played the pivotal role in national religious ceremonies; and only the ruler could initiate construction of national sacrificial temples (luakini).[90] Indeed, in concept, the ruler was a living deity (akua)—or the closest possible to a living deity—and he was often called akua in speech.[91]

Accordingly, special respect was given to a ruler. Such behavior included bans on casting shadows on the ruler's back, house or belongings; on using the ruler's clothing or possessions; and on entering the ruler's residential compound without permission. Failure to prostrate or sit when the ruler passed was also punishable.[92] Sitting was even required when the king's food, water, or clothing was brought by.[93] Even high chiefs had to stand and not speak until the king recognized them and asked them to sit.[94] Violations—at least by commoners or low ranking chiefs—could, and did, result in death.[95]

Certain types of elite clothing were restricted to the ruler. For example, feather capes ('ahu'ula) which were made solely of yellow mamo feathers were only worn by him.[96]

The ruler had special burial rites and kapu, with ceremonies usually leading to concealing the bones in a wicker container shaped somewhat like a man (kā'ai), deification as an 'aumakua, and placement in a mortuary heiau or hidden away.[97]

The ruler did not do subsistence work. Kamehameha was known to have sponsored the construction of a large field area in Kona, but it is unlikely he, himself, would have participated in the manual labor to any degree. Food for the ruler came from his ahupua'a, from special small plots in other chiefs' ahupua'a set aside as royal lands (kō'ele) to be worked or to keep pigs on, from demands on the populace near his residence to supply food, and from annual taxes.[98] [In addition, the ruler's food had to be ceremonially clean, with the meat particularly prepared in the major heiau.][99]

The ruler often had multiple wives, and these marriages were frequently intended to consolidate power, sacredness, and alliances. Unions with full sisters (pi'o marriages) and half-sisters (naha marriages) were common, with resulting offspring of extremely high genealogical rank.[100] These children often had special privileges (kapu) such as the kapu moe (prostrating kapu) and the kapu noho (sitting kapu)—formally given in special heiau rites.[101] Marriages with daughters of other kingdom's rulers or with daughters of powerful major chiefs of the Hawai'i Kingdom were also common to strenghten alliances and power. For example, Kamehameha's most sacred wife, Keōpūolani, was from a naha marriage between his slain rival and more senior cousin Kīwala'ō, and Kīwala'ō's half-sister Keku'iapoiwa. But Kamehameha also married the daughters of his major chiefs: Ka'ahumanu and Kaheiheimālie of Ke'eaumoku, and Peleuli of Kamanawa. Children of the senior wife formed the senior line; those of junior wives were the kaikaina (younger brothers and sisters) of the senior children.[102]

The highest chiefs of the island—the ali'i nui—were not numerous and were frequently close relatives, but they also could be aides who were distant relatives or elevated commoners. Power, social rank, was thus acquired through several means, senior genealogical positions, skills, etc. For example, in the early period of Kamehameha's reign, his highest and most powerful chiefs were his younger full brother (Keli'imaika'i), his half-brothers (Kala'imamahū and Kawelo'okalani), his second cousins (Ke'eaumoku, Kame'eiamoku, and Kamanawa), and Keaweaheulu (a distant cousin representing powerful chiefly families), with Ka'iana, Isaac Davis and John Young holding high ranks as skilled generals and advisors.[103] Major chiefs received many ahupua'a from the ruler, although a ruler often only formally renewed the holdings of a powerful high chief to avoid revolt.[104] The major chiefs frequently resided with the ruler at the ruling center, but they did have outlying residences in their own lands. They too received elaborate respect behavior from lower ranking people, had sizable retinues, multiple wives, and often married to build powerful alliances. Some high chiefs were granted kapu moe, noho, or wohi—bestowed upon them by the current or prior rulers.[105] Like the ruler, the highest chiefs did not participate in daily subsistence labor.[106]

One high chief, or several, served as the kālaimoku or secular advisor to the king.[107] On succession of his king, the kālaimoku helped identify people claiming chiefly genealogical ties with the king in the hale naua ceremonies. With his advice, offices and lands were then distributed to these chiefs and to highly skilled unrelated chiefs and commoner favorites.[108]

Beneath these major chiefs were numerous minor chiefs, often called ali'i, kaukauali'i, or ali'i papa.[109] Some junior relatives of the ruler or of the major chiefs were given an ahupua'a or two to control. The same was true for renowned warriors or priests—called ali'i lalo-lalo.[110] Some of these chiefs became the konohiki or haku 'āina of the ahupua'a.[111] For example, in 1792 Vancouver left behind Kualelo, a native of Moloka'i who had been to England, and Kamehameha gave him an ahupua'a, and by marriage with a chief's daughter he gained another.[112] Other junior relatives or skilled commoners became part of the retinue to the ruler or high chiefs. John Papa 'I'i, a distant relation to the Kamehamehas, was assigned to the retinue of Kamehameha's son, Liholiho. The surrounding retinue could be sizable. One evening at Kealakekua in 1794, Vancouver observed 40 guards with pololū spears and daggers surrounding Kamehameha's residence.[113] In 1822, Liholiho had 100 people living in his house.[114]

In the early reign of Kamehameha, he traveled periodically to different royal courts on Hawai'i Island, usually at established centers: Waipi'o in Hāmākua, Hilo Bay in Hilo, Hōnaunau, Kealakekua, Kahalu'u, Hōlualoa, and Kailua in Kona, and Kawaihae and Pu'uepa-Kokoiki in Kohala. In each place, the ruler's residence was the focal point along with the nearby national heiau (luakini) and usually a pu'uhonua (refuge). The houses of major and lesser chiefs were clustered nearby, with commoners' homes farther away.

Life at the court was markedly distinguished from life in the outlying or rural lands, the kua 'āina.[115] Activity in the centers was focused on national religious rites, games, warfare practice, politics, mele composition, and feasts.[116] As an example, late in Kamehameha's reign (1809–1810), an observer noted the popularity of kōnane. "Tamahmaah excels at this game. I have seen him sit for hours playing with his chiefs."[117] Intrigue clearly played an important role, too. To some, the courtly life was considered indolent and lazy, but to others it was a place of fascination and activity.[118] The hangers-on were often called 'ai'alo, "those who eat in the presence," and they were supported in part by the ruler and their immediate lord who supplied food and clothing from tribute, which could periodically run short.[119]

It was to the benefit of the ruler and high chiefs to keep their retinue in plenty.[120] And the ruler was concerned about keeping his highest chiefs pleased, since they were the prime source of possible revolt.[121] If the ruler was charismatic and kept his high chiefs in plenty and satisfied, then they served him faithfully as generals, the honored spitoon and kahili bearers, and close aides. If a high chief was dissatisfied, he could try and gather power by increasing his retinue with promises and goods, and by increasing his alliances through marriage or intrigue, and by attracting a powerful priest to enlist the support of the gods. Often enough—as will be seen—high chiefs attempted to revolt or overthrow a ruler.

## THE GODS (NA AKUA) & THE PRIESTS (NA KAHUNA)

Spirits were a vital part of everyday life in Hawai'i. People worshiped the different gods who were active in the affairs that concerned them.[122] The four major deities—Kū, Lono, Kāne and Kanaloa—manifested themselves in nature in many forms: in places, plants, animals, and phenomena such as thunder and clouds, and in images. For example, Kū had the following manifestations: the dog, the 'ōhi'a lehua and koa trees, coconut, breadfruit, the 'ō'ō bird, the ulua fish, war, sorcery and canoe-building. Lono was associated with the pig, sweet potato, kukui, 'ama'ama and āholehole fish, and the lama tree. Kāne was associated with fishponds, irrigated taro, springs, bananas, cliffs, and so on.[123] Their manifestations were differently labeled in binomial form, such as Kū-nuiakea or Kū-kā'ilimoku.

Other deities were related to sorcery or violent events. Pele and her family were such deities, affiliated with the active volcanoes of Mauna Loa and Kīlauea. The kahu or priests of Pele often were considered possessed by these deities, and their appearance reinforced this fact, for they "were in the habit of dressing their hair in such a way as to make it stand out at great length...having inflamed and reddened their eyes."[124] Fear of Pele and her family was great, for certainly ample proof existed of their ability to devour land, houses and people. Tribute and awe were readily given to avoid Pele's wrath.

Commoners had their own ʻaumākua, recently deceased relatives and special animals, places and phenomena. These were appealed to in men's houses or at special shrines—both being types of heiau. For example, a fishing shrine near the shore in the form of a small stone platform (koʻa) with an upright stone might be used to worship Kūʻulakai and family ʻaumakua to ensure productive fishing.[125] Similarly, an agricultural shrine (unu o Lono) in the fields might have been dedicated to Kūʻulauka or Lono.

Shrines were also present along well-traveled trails, in adze quarry areas, where canoe timber was felled, or feather birds were caught (Kūhuluhulumanu).[126]

The aliʻi had their own differing family deities, with the ruler's being far more important.[127] Appeals were made to them in war, to gain land, for death to enemies, for agricultural prosperity and so on.[128] The war god of the Pili ruling line just before and during Kamehameha's reign was Kūkaʻilimoku. Kūnuiakea was associated with fertility of the land.[129] These gods were appealed to at the major national heiau, the luakini. Only the ruler could build and consecrate a luakini, but he and other chiefs could build several kinds of Lono heiau to appeal for growth of food (hoʻoūluʻūlu).[130] The luakini at the royal center was the focal religious point of the kingdom. These were huge structures—immense stone platforms with a fringing wooden palisade and/or high-walled stone enclosures. Inside, an altar area had images of Kū and a tower (ʻanuʻu) to the gods, and another section had houses to store religious items (drums, feather images of the gods), as well as for priestly prayer and chants, and sacred food preparation.[131]

Attendant priests lived nearby and cared for these heiau and performed the daily rituals, with the high priest, the kahuna nui or kahuna kiʻi, overseeing the administration and major ceremonies and urging on the king to righteous and religious behavior.[132] The priests belonged to formal priestly orders—moʻo Kū from Pāʻao, or moʻo Lono.[133] They inherited their positions or were appointed as junior relatives of chiefs.[134] The high priest was the head of the Kū order.[135] The king's rituals to Kū were again focused in the luakini.[136]

The high priest advised the king on the auspicious timing of war preparations, oversaw luakini services and the general conduct of religious services, directed the daily cooking of the king's sacred food, coordinated the makahiki rituals, distributed offerings and taxes, oversaw sacrifices, and acted as head of the many priests under him.[137] He also apparently appointed the lesser priests.[138]

Ceremonies went through a monthly and yearly cycle. For 8 months of the year, the luakini was dedicated to Kū—with strict kapus. Four periods (kapu pule) each month required strict ceremonies.[139] Violators could have their property seized by priests or their overlord chiefs, or be sentenced to death for serious breaches.[140]

Annually, between the approximate time period of October–January, rituals occurred removing Kū and installing Lono in the luakini—the makahiki season. In theory, this was a period when national heiau were shut down, pig was no longer eaten by those of high rank, and the kingdom was free of warfare and sacrifices.[141] In the second month of the makahiki, tribute was gathered in each ahupua'a and brought to the king, who redistributed it to his gods, priests, and secular retinue.[142] Shortly thereafter, the image of the makahiki god—Lonomakua—was made in the form of a pole with a carved head, a cross-piece with a feather lei, pala fern, and white kapa.[143] Once completed, the image was carried clockwise around the island's coastal trail (ala loa) accompanied by priests and athletes to collect tribute (ho'okupu). This was gathered at each ahupua'a's border, placed between two poles erected next to the shrine of the ahupua'a—a stone platform or mound (ahu) surmounted by a red-ochre-painted kukui board in the image of a pig (pua'a). The tribute included feathers, kapa cloth, hard taro (pa'i 'ai), pigs and chickens.[144] Some of the food was consumed by the retinue of Lonomakua.[145] In 1778–1779, this circuit of the island took 23 days, covering the approximately 600 ahupua'a.[146] If all were passed through, about 26 ahupua'a would be covered in a day—a phenomenal rate. It seems quite likely some areas were bypassed with tribute brought to a gathering place.[147] At certain ahupua'a, the procession halted for boxing matches between local champions and the athletes accompanying the god.

The return of Lonomakua to the ruling center marked the start of a series of ceremonies leading to the resanctification of the temples to Kū. These included the kapu hua rite for the consumption of pork,[148] the ritual removing the kapu on aku,[149] a land purification ceremony (hui kala),[150] the refurbishing of the luakini or building of a new luakini which began with felling an ʻōhiʻa tree for the main image (the haku ʻāina) which marked Kū's return to the luakini,[151] the kauila nui ceremony prior to rebuilding the sacred houses on the luakini, and several concluding rituals.[152] Numerous offerings, including human sacrifices, accompanied these rituals and the return of Kū. Indeed, Valeri cites early references that hogs and dogs were presented when Kūkaʻilimoku's image was brought into Puʻukoholā heiau at Kawaihae, and that dogs were displayed as offerings to Kū at Hikiau heiau in Kealakekua Bay.[153] More striking, human offerings were placed in a prostrating posture on the altars, the same posture as required in the presence of the king and some high chiefs.[154]

Within the luakini, special rituals were conducted for warfare success and to promote agricultural prosperity. Participants were the ruler, chiefs and vital commoner aides, and the priests—often seated in rows. The general commoner populace and women did not participate.[155] Rituals were often quite strict, requiring periods of complete silence and lack of movement. Appeals would be made from the oracle tower by the king and high priest, and could involve appeals to the main images and to the kāʻai of the ruler and high chiefs.[156]

*Favorable are the omens for the service.*
*The voice of the multitude is at rest.*
*Now we must perform the service for the king.*
*An acceptable service, one that reaches its end.*
..................................................................
*The assembly stands before the king.*
*His enemies shall melt away before him.*

[1898 or earlier, prayer told to Emerson][157]

## WARFARE

Warfare played an important role in Kamehameha's and earlier times. In preparing for war, priests would check for favorable signs through prayer and the analysis of slaughtered pigs or chickens.[158] If signs were favorable, messengers were sent to the lords of the ahupuaʻa and an army was gathered, with men of suitable age called up from each ahupuaʻa under the leadership of their chiefs.[159] These warriors would be armed with throwing spears or javelins (ihe, 6-feet long and barbed), jabbing spears (pololū, 16–20 feet long and unbarbed), spear-clubs (lāʻau pālau, 8–9 feet long), clubs (lāʻau, some wooden-headed, some stone-headed), daggers (pāhoa, 1.5–2 feet long of wood and pointed on one or both ends), and slings (of human hair or coconut fiber, with egg-sized stones used as projectiles).[160] Each warrior undoubtedly had favored weapons, so individual armament varied. The most renowned warriors were already in the retinues of the ruler and high chiefs.

The army gathered about the ruler's residence. Small huts and a few larger buildings formed the encampments, which often spanned several ahupuaʻa.[161] Kamehameha is said to have gathered 700 canoes and 20,000 warriors (the latter perhaps overestimated)[162] in his 1791 defeat of Kāʻeo and Kahekili off Waipiʻo, and 10,000–16,000 and then 7,000 men in his two attempted invasions of Kauaʻi in 1796[163] and 1804.[164] Alapaʻi's army in his war with Maui was said to have consisted of 8,500 men.[165] Such an army is quite plausible with 600 ahupuaʻa, each contributing 10–15 warriors. Once the army was gathered about the ruler, human and other sacrifices were offered to the war god—Kūkaʻilimoku—at the luakini heiau.

The army then proceeded to battle by canoe, on foot, or both. Chiefs were usually dressed in feather cloaks or capes and helmets; commoners simply wore malo.[166] In 1823, Ellis was told that there was a regular system for battle array, although there were "various methods for attack and defence, according to the nature of the ground, force of the enemy, &c."[167]

> *When about to engage in an open plain, their army, drawn up for battle, consisted of a centre and wings, the latter considerably in advance, and the line curved in form of a crescent.*
>
> *The slingers, and those who threw the javelin, were in general distributed through the whole line.*
>
> *Every chief led his own men to battle, and took his position according to the orders of the commanding chieftain, whose station was always in the centre.*
>
> *The king generally commanded in person, or that authority was exercised by the highest chief among the warriors; occasionally, however, a chief inferior in rank, but distinguished by courage, or military talents and address, has been raised to the supreme command.*[168]

Prior to engaging, the divining priests continued to check for favorable signs. The principal war god was brought forth and a priest and then the king or general exhorted the army. The armies then engaged, with the king, the priest and gods usually staying in the back ranks surrounded by warriors with the long pololū spears.

> *The national war-god was elevated above the ranks, and carried by the priests near the person of the king, or commander-in-chief. Nor was this the only idol borne to the battle: other chiefs of rank had their war-gods carried near them by their priest; and if the king or chief was killed or taken, the god himself was usually captured also....We have been told, that, in the battle, he [Hewahewa, the kahuna nui of Kamehameha] often distorted his face into every frightful form, and uttered most terrific and appalling yells, which were supposed to proceed from the god he bore or attended.*[169]

Battle often began as skirmishes, or "partial engagements," with insults thrown back and forth. Single combat of champions often took place. Major joinings of warriors eventually would occur. The battle was then continued until a draw, until one side retreated, or until one side was routed.[170]

> *The first slain was the lehua....[The victorious warrior] dispoiled the fallen warrior of his ornaments, and dragged the haena, the slain body, to the king, or the priest, who, in a short address, offered the victim to his god.*
>
> [1823 Ellis][171]

If routed, warriors would flee to waiting canoes or over the mountains. They also might chance an approach to a place of refuge—at the ruler's residential center—or to the ruler, himself.[172] Many were taken prisoner or cut down. If captured, they might be spared or become sacrificial offerings or slaves. Actual numbers slain on a battlefield are difficult to determine. The 'Ālapa division of Kalani'ōpu'u, perhaps numbering several hundred men, was wiped out by Kahekili's forces in one battle. Death figures in the hundreds or less, not the thousands, seems most likely.[173]

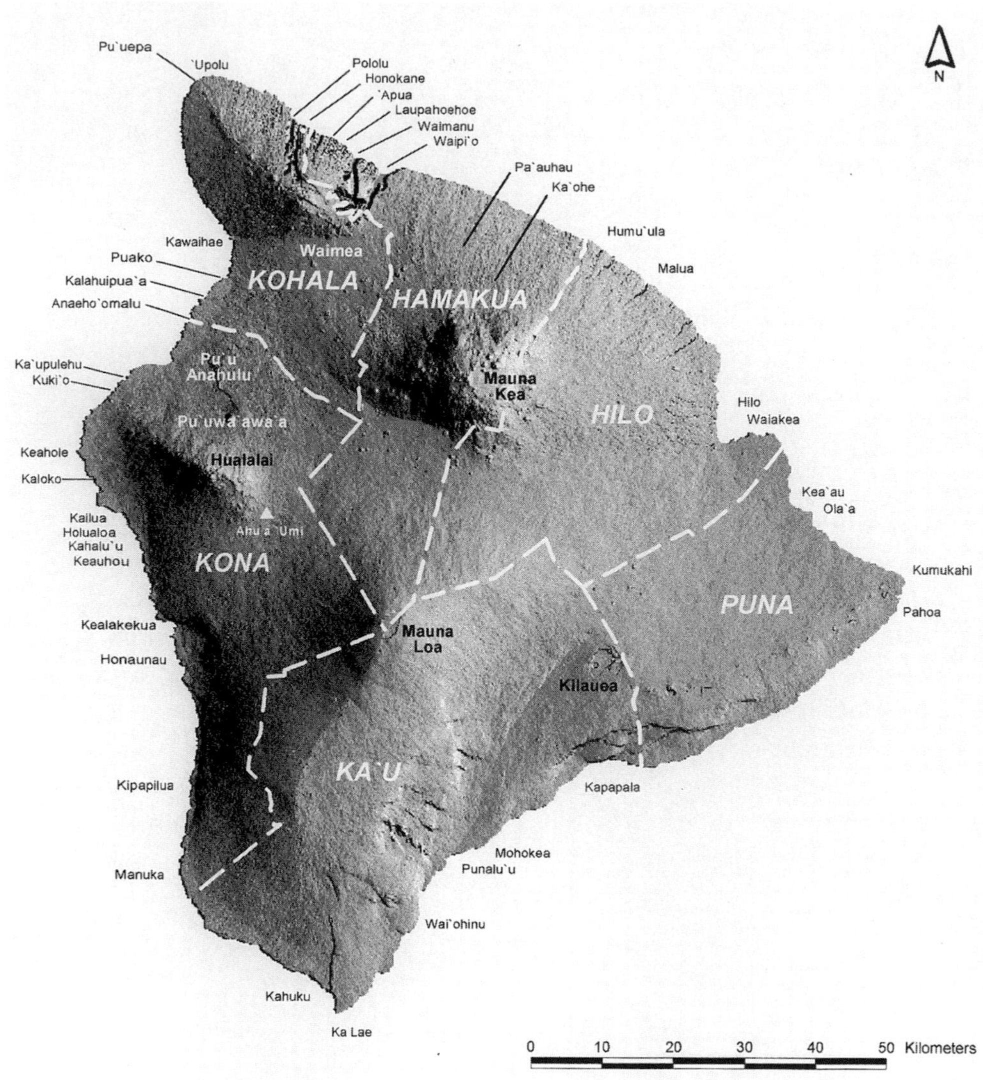


**FIGURE 2-2**
Place names mentioned in Chapter 2.

## CHAPTER 3

# Understanding the Information on History

*The traditions about the Hawaiian Islands handed down from remote antiquity are not entirely definite; there is much obscurity as to facts, and the trends themselves are not clear.*

(1840, Malo)[1]

*This material is extremely uneven in value... and must be used with discernment.*

(1985, Valeri)[2]

*Such a chronology at best can only be an approximation.*

(1933, Stokes)[3]

The scholars of ancient Hawai'i have been many over the years. Today they include academically trained scientists (historians, archaeologists, social anthropologists, linguists, and oral historians), traditionally trained experts, genealogists and interested amateurs. In the nineteenth century, foreigners and Hawaiians recorded knowledge and oral histories, and discussed and analyzed Hawai'i's past. And prior to European contact, unknown kahuna and ali'i were certainly historical experts of their times—knowing the genealogies, chants and stories in great detail. One such acknowledged chief in Kamehameha III's time was Hoapili or Ulumāheihei, a high chief who had been Kamehameha I's main advisor late in his reign, and who was the son of the high chief Kame'eiamoku, one of Kamehameha's main advisors earlier in his reign.

> *Ulu-maheihei was a learned man skilled in debate and in the history of the old chiefs and the way in which they had governed. He belonged to the priesthood of Nahulu and was an expert in priestly knowledge. He had been taught astronomy and the ancient lore. Richards would bring to him any question about the ancient customs or tabus, and he could explain them all. He was proficient in the genealogies of chiefs even where they were obscure; David Malo and others would go to him with puzzling questions, and he was able to explain them.*
>
> [Kamakau][4]

The primary sources of information for the times from initial settlement to Kamehameha's unification of the island in 1792 are direct observations of culture and events, oral histories of events passed down, and archaeology. This chapter gives the reader an initial understanding of these sources and hopefully an appreciation for the problems in using them. Each is valuable in piecing together the past.

# DIRECT OBSERVATIONS OF CULTURE AND EVENTS PRIOR TO 1792

One set of direct observations comes from foreign visitors or residents of the islands. They are dated between 1779, European contact on Hawai'i Island, and 1792—a period only a little over a decade in length. These observations are included primarily in ships' logs, journals, letters and illustrations. The observers range from fur traders to military personnel on exploring expeditions. The Cook expedition is perhaps the richest source—with sizable journals and log entries written by captains Cook and Clerke, lieutenants King, Burney and Rickman, surgeons Samwell and Law, midshipmen Gilbert, Trevenen, Riou, coxswain Zimmerman, artist Ellis, marine corporal Ledyard, and others.[5] Maps were prepared by Bligh and Roberts, and illustrations by Webber and Ellis.[6] This information is fascinating reading, with day-by-day accounts of events and encounters between two cultures previously unknown to each other—with the understanding that one is reading from the English cultural perspectives of the time.

However, caution must be taken when using these sources. The key is to differentiate between observations by the writer versus those by someone else which were passed orally to the writer, to see if the account refers to a specific observation at a specific geographic location or is a general summary of what was seen, to note the time (month and year) of the observation, to recognize facts versus interpretation, and to evaluate the reliability of the observer. For example, many members of the Cook expedition recorded what they observed at Kealakekua Bay. Yet, contradictions among the accounts arise. One problem seems to be that some individuals were far better observers—being more objective and more accurate. An example is house counts at Kealakekua Bay. Surgeon Samwell's and Lt. King's journals are in approximate agreement, 310–320 and 320–350 houses, while Marine Corporal Ledyard's account seems much too high, 1,400.[7] Such problems can be a result of many factors, such as writing and publication of journals years later based on recall, more frequent time spent ashore, or just careful observation. The general conclusion of most researchers has been that Ledyard's and Lt. Rickman's accounts suffer from some inaccuracies, while King's and Samwell's were much more accurate due to careful observations.[8]

On the other hand, King was largely stationed at the astronomical observatory in the coastal settlements, and he did not travel far inland. So his published comments on inland patterns are based on talks with members of the expedition who did travel inland. He mentioned this shortcoming when presenting his information, something few accounts do.

Another caution is to differentiate observations of what took place from interpretations of why, or from what Hawaiians told the early visitors. Many of the visitors had difficulty understanding the Hawaiian language. Misinterpretations resulted. Samwell of Cook's expedition gives a relevant statement.

> *[I]t must be remembered, that there is not much dependence to be placed upon these Constructions that we put upon Signs and Words which we understand but very little of, & at best can only give a probable Guess at their Meaning.*[9]

Another set of direct observations of this time were those of Europeans who resided on the island and gave verbal accounts to others who wrote them down. John Young and Isaac Davis are two of the most notable of these individuals for Hawai‘i Island. Both were captured in 1790, and soon made high-ranking chiefs by Kamehameha. They fought in his wars, playing important roles. Both became fluent in Hawaiian, married ranking women, and had children who became politically important in the 1800s. Many of the fur traders and explorers of the 1790s, and even later visitors wrote down what Young and Davis told them of the events of the years 1790–1792.[10]

Another set of direct observations came from Hawaiians themselves. Most who were old enough to experience pre-1792 events never learned to write.[11] Yet some gave verbal accounts to foreigners and to Hawaiians who wrote them down. Cook's expedition was given brief accounts of the Hawai'i and Maui wars from participants,[12] and information on the genealogies of Hawai'i's rulers.[13] In 1792–1793 Vancouver recorded Kamehameha's rise to power from those closely involved—Ke'eaumoku, Ka'iana, and Kamehameha himself—with differing information from each.[14] In 1823 Rev. William Ellis recorded information from Hewahewa (the high priest of Kamehameha), Kelou Kamakau (a low chief in Kealakekua), and others who had experienced events and culture prior to 1792. For example, Ellis was told of 1780s–1790s battles between Keōua's and Kamehameha's forces, of the 1790 volcanic eruption which killed part of Keōua's army, about the nature of warfare, etc.[15] Rev. Hiram Bingham's accounts of aspects of the 1782 Moku'ōhai battle and of Kamehameha's rise to power were supplied to him by Ka'ahumanu and Kalanimoku, the wife and kālaimoku of Kamehameha I.[16] Many other examples could be given.

Into the mid-1800s, Hawaiians who had lived as adults before 1792 still were alive and providing accounts. Samuel Kamakau, in writing about Kamehameha's first battle with his cousin, Keōua, noted that an informant, Moa, had been at this battle.[17] Remy in 1853 spoke with Kanuha, a man of Ho'ōpūloa in south Kona, who reputedly was 116 years old—although how Remy arrived at such an exact figure is a wonder in itself.[18] Kanuha claimed to have been a runner and a messenger for the rulers Alapa'inui and Kalani'ōpu'u, whose estimated reigns were from 1740–1760 and 1760–1782.[19]

These Hawaiian sources are invaluable. Unfortunately, nearly all the direct observations recorded appear to refer to the period from 1782 on—from the battle between the forces of Kīwala'ō, Kalani'ōpu'u's heir and senior son, and Kamehameha—as the rise of Kamehamcha seems to have been the topic of interest for writers. Events of Kalani'ōpu'u's and Alapa'inui's reigns which had been directly observed do not seem to have been a focus of recording. Most adults from Alapa'i's time probably had passed away by 1800–

1810 (at the age of 60–90), while those who were adults in the time of Kalani'ōpu'u probably were gone by 1830. The intensive recording of times prior to Kamehameha really did not begin until the 1830s, when Rev. Sheldon Dibble and Rev. Lorrin Andrew began teaching at Lahainaluna and encouraged the first post-contact work on Hawaiian history. By then, what was known was primarily indirect observations through oral histories. Nearly all of those who had lived in earlier times had passed on. The Hawaiian scholars of Lahainaluna—D. Malo, S. N. Hale'ole, S. Kamakau, and others—attempted to gather histories of culture and events from those who participated, but pitifully few such elders were still alive. Indeed, many lamented this fact.

> *There are no more people conversant with old history; those who are left try to make out that they are beacon lights on historical subjects, when in fact their knowledge on these subjects is only limited.*
>
> [Kamakau, ca. 1843][20]

It should be noted that the accounts given by Hawaiians who were direct observers sometimes conflicted—just as with foreign accounts. Sometimes the source of conflict reflected political manueverings by rulers and high chiefs. For example, by the 1820s, Ka'ahumanu and others were giving accounts that stated Kalani'ōpu'u had divided the island at his death, with half to Kīwala'ō and half to Kamehameha. This claim gave more legitimacy to Kamehameha's revolt. In fact, from other accounts it seems quite clear that Kamehameha was given no vast lands and was entrusted by Kalani'ōpu'u to serve under Kīwala'ō.[21]

Conflicting accounts were also due to other factors. Sometimes informants may not have been at the event. Ellis' 1823 recording of the volcano disaster affecting Keōua's army differs from other accounts,[22] and some versions may reflect secondhand information. Sometimes, the informants may just have been poor observers. Others may have had poor or confused recollections due to age. The 116-year-old Kanuha may be such a case, for he recalled that 'Umi a Līloa ruled East Hawai'i and Keli'iokāloa ruled West Hawai'i until 'Umi defeated Keli'iokāloa in the battle at Ahua a 'Umi. The other accounts uniformly agree Keli'iokāloa was 'Umi's son and successor, and the battle was between Keli'iokāloa and his brother Keawenui a 'Umi—facts that Kanuha certainly would have known if he was completely lucid.[23] Yet another complication was the competency of the recorder. In 1789, Captain Douglas of the *Iphigenia*, a fur trader, recorded that Keawema'uhili, ruler of the Hilo polity, was the "surviving son" of Kalani'ōpu'u, clearly an inaccuracy, since Keawema'uhili was the half-brother of Kalani'ōpu'u and uncle to both Kamehameha and Keōua.[24] Perhaps Douglas meant Keōua, ruler of the Ka'ū polity, who was indeed a surviving son of Kalani'ōpu'u, but the reference to the weather (windward) side of the island indicates that Douglas probably was referring to Hilo and Keawema'uhili.

Despite these problems, direct observations are fascinating, insightful and extremely useful for understanding Hawaiian culture in the late 1700s. In reading such accounts, one can get a firsthand feel for the events and culture. A researcher simply has to be cautious in using the records.

## INDIRECT OBSERVATIONS OF CULTURE AND EVENTS PRIOR TO 1792

Indirect observations include oral information passed down to generations who did not live in earlier times. These consist of genealogies, stories of kings and battles and revolts, name chants such as the Kumulipo (composed in the early 1700s for Kalaninui'īamamao, son of the ruler Keawe), and other chants and accounts. Information on how fishing and farming was done, on how canoes and kapa were made, on how religious rites were performed, and on how warriors were trained and fought was also passed down.

A father would teach his sons how to fish and farm. An uncle might teach his nephews how to build canoes. A mother would teach her daughters kapa-making. And so on. Some individuals were experts in their skills, and they selected specific individuals to pass their knowledge on to. Rigorous training often was involved. Religious training, chiefly genealogical training, and training of warriors were skills that required a lengthy learning process.

A fact of cultures is that they change over time. In Hawai'i the designs of canoes and kapa changed. Tool styles changed. Low-ranking chiefs rose to power replacing senior lines. The oral recollections of the earlier forms and events of a culture also become altered over time—predominantly unintentionally as a result of the passage of time. In Hawai'i some facts were gradually forgotten. For example, Malo notes the following regarding the reigns of several rulers:

> *Of traditions regarding Lanakawai, Laau, Pili, Koa, Ole, Kukohou, Kaniuhi, I have heard none.*
>
> [1840 Malo][25]

Also stories were embellished, were stylized, and elements were added.[26]

> *A family chant like the Kumulipo, passed down orally from one generation to the next without the stabilizing force of a written text, must have been constantly exposed to political changes within the family to the urge felt by a new song-writer to revitalize the old memorial by giving it a fresh application to the more recent family events. Although as a whole it preserves structural unity, the chant also gives evidence of a piecing-together of genealogies from different branches, together with the myths connected with them, and of changes in mere phrasing to give a different turn to the original design of a passage.*
>
> [Beckwith][27]

Even with rigorous training of genealogists and priests, changes occurred.

Sometimes oral accounts were intentionally changed. For example, when junior lines came to power, often genealogies were changed or story elements were added to help bolster the new line's standing. The version of Kamehameha receiving half of Hawai'i in 1782 from Kalani'ōpu'u seems to be a politically motivated change of the oral histories begun in the late 1700s or early 1800s to better justify Kamehameha's rise to power at the expense of the senior line.

Given any of these factors, two commentaries on events occurring several hundred years earlier may differ, or genealogies may differ. Some accounts may not be very accurate. Older events, aspects of culture, or individuals in genealogies may have been forgotten.

To complicate this picture, on Hawai'i Island, vast disruptions to life occurred immediately after European contact, further affecting the passing on of oral information. Considerable knowledge of ancient history and cultural patterns were certainly lost. Depopulation took a tremendous toll in the early half of the 1800s, with overall population at least halved by the 1830s. Experts died from disease before their time, before their knowledge was passed on. Depopulation and the increasing demands of the chiefs also resulted in the abandonment of rural communities and the end of many community contexts for teaching. Diseases resulted in few or no children per family, affecting who the information could be passed down to.

Changing religious patterns also certainly had an effect. With the abolition of the kapu system in 1820, the need for passing on information related to the national religion ended. Widespread conversion to Christianity later in the century further forced a change in morals and priorities and knowledge, pushing some forms of traditional religious training underground.[28]

Additionally, economic changes had an effect. New tools and status items replaced old ones, leading to a general end in production of old items. Stone adzes quickly were replaced by metal, with the result that stone quarries became abandoned and the skilled craft of adze-making was no longer in demand.[29] By mid-century, bird feathers were no longer royal tax items, and the making of feathered cloaks and helmets diminished.[30] These examples are but a few. New sources of income changed economic patterns, increasing chiefly demands and attracting commoners to port towns for economic gain and to escape the demands of their chiefs.[31]

Political patterns changed too. Kahekili and the Maui polity eliminated the O'ahu kingdom ca. 1782–1785, and the need for lesser O'ahu genealogies to reinforce political positions certainly diminished. Then Kamehameha's conquest similarly reduced the importance of the lesser Maui genealogies. With the new, larger kingdom, more levels of low chiefs were placed over the land, changing the political structure, and eventually altering daily commoner life with increased chiefly demands. And in the late 1840s, the basic ties between the political structure and the land were changed in the Māhele land redivisions.

These changes do not mean that all information on pre-1792 times and culture was lost. Much was retained and passed on. But, certainly the teaching context was disrupted, and probably many areas of information were lost by the end of the 1800s. Many Hawaiians and non-Hawaiians were extremely concerned about this situation in the 1800s.

Unfortunately, few Hawaiians were taught to write until the 1830s, and even fewer elderly Hawaiians. Vital recording of knowledge on ruling histories, genealogies, and basic older ways of culture was needed. Fortunately, Hawaiians who had learned to write did begin to record accounts of past culture and events from older Hawaiians. And some non-Hawaiians also documented recollections.

The major sources that are commonly mentioned are the works of David Malo (1795–1853, born at Keauhou on Hawai'i), Samuel

Kamakau (1815–1876, born in Waialua on O'ahu), John Papa 'I'i (1800–1870, born in 'Ewa on O'ahu), Z. Kahoaalii Kepelino (ca. 1830–1878, born in Kailua on Hawai'i), and Abraham Fornander (1812–1887, married to a Moloka'i chiefess).[32] Other sources also exist: S. N. Hale'ole, Kelou Kamakau, Sheldon Dibble, A. D. Kahaulelio, and Jules Remy, to name a few.[33]

Malo's *Moolelo o Hawaii*, written in 1840, was the first overall summary of Hawaiian culture. His account is based on what elders had told him and what he directly observed in his first 25 years prior to the abolition of the kapu system in 1820. Samuel Kamakau added to this general overview of culture in his newspaper writings of the 1860s–1870s, with much of his information being oral information from elders. Kepelino also wrote a general overview in the 1870s, similarly gathered from elders, for he—like Samuel Kamakau—was raised after the abolition of the kapus. Importantly, others added information on specific aspects of culture in writings and newspaper articles. Kelou Kamakau wrote on religious ritual, Kahaulelio wrote on fishing in 1902. The Hawaiian newspapers of the 1860s–1890s contain many such accounts, most of which are not well-known today.

Besides general accounts of culture, the oral accounts of past events began to be recorded. Malo recorded extensive genealogies, a few brief accounts of rulers' reigns, and a volume on Kamehameha which has been lost. Samuel Kamakau greatly fleshed out stories tied to the reigns of earlier rulers in his newspaper articles. And Abraham Fornander in the 1860s was gathering such stories and published a detailed account of the history of the kingdoms in 1880, *An Account of the Polynesian Race: Its Origins and Migrations and the Ancient History of the Hawaiian People to the Times of Kamehameha I.* Others also wrote on events in the past. 'I'i covered some history of earlier reigns in his newspaper articles between 1866–1870. Other Hawaiian newspaper articles referred to such stories in the late 1800s and early 1900s, often adding to Kamakau and Fornander.[34] A few large unpublished manuscripts from the 1800s exist, including one by Helekunihi in the Bishop Museum.[35] Also, in speaking about events and genealogies related to the rulers, the Kumulipo—a birth chant composed for Kalaninuiʻīamamao in the early 1700s—was published in 1889 by Kalākaua and translated into English by Liliʻuokalani.[36] Indeed, publishing royal and chiefly genealogies became common in the late 1800s, although their accuracy was often questioned by other Hawaiians.[37]

Early foreign expedition accounts included stories of events of earlier times. In 1793, Lt. Puget of the Vancouver expedition was told the story of Pāʻao, the priest from Kahiki—a story set in the A.D. 1300s or early 1400s.[38] Others recorded several generations of rulers' genealogies.

A number of cautions need to be given regarding the oral accounts recorded in the 1800s. Each author must have selected from many stories that were told.

> *Kamakau only gives his choice of the legendary stories current in his day.*
>
> [Kuykendall][39]

And, unfortunately, we have a poor idea of which accounts had differing versions, and who provided these accounts to the authors. This is a topic which would merit considerable study. Malo was evidently attached to Kuakini's household in the 1810s. In 1831 he went to Lahainaluna school at age 38 and began his long association with the missionaries and the church. In the 1830s–1840s, when on Maui, he was closely associated with ʻAuwae, then the appointed chief over Wailuku ahupuaʻa and previously a favorite chief of Kamehameha, evidently having been "Kamehameha's bard, genealogist, and ritual expert."[40] But Malo also went to the high chief Hoapili for information in later years when both lived on Maui. Clearly, Malo must have heard many stories from others, prior to writing his famous moolelo in the late 1830s.[41] Thus, although Malo was highly regarded in his own time as "the great authority and repository of Hawaiian lore," who his informants were and what differing versions of stories he had heard are not known.[42]

This dilemma exists for the other authors of the 1800s. We are not sure who they acquired their stories from. ʻĪʻī, as an attendant of Liholiho from 1810–1820, was trained by relatives and servants at the royal court. His firsthand accounts are invaluable. But, his accounts of Hawaiian history before Kamehameha seem slanted to support Kamehameha's claims, and it is unclear who he learned these accounts from.

Samuel Kamakau was born and raised in Waialua moku on Oʻahu, and much of his information must have come from elders of Waialua. At least two sources were his kahuna grandmother, with whom he lived between about 1814–1825, and his grandfather or granduncle (kupuna kāne) Kuikealaikauaokalani—an Oʻahu or Kauaʻi priest.[43] Kamakau also attended Lahainaluna, from 1832–1836, beginning at age 17. He continued as a teacher there for three more years, and then was a member of the historical society formed by Dibble and his students, which lasted from 1841–1845.[44] Kamakau spent the remainder of his life on Maui and Oʻahu, serving as an educator, a member of the Legislature and as a judge, among other jobs, so many of his accounts may have come from unknown Maui elders, or Hawaiian elders by then living on Maui.[45]

Perhaps this dilemma can best be seen in Fornander's work. Fornander lived in the islands for 34 years, from 1842 until his death in 1887. He was first a newspaperman, then a circuit judge on Maui, then director of education traveling throughout the islands, and then again the circuit judge of Maui. Fornander was fluent in Hawaiian and was married to a chiefess from Molokaʻi, Pinao Alanakapu. He gathered stories from many sources in the 1860s–1870s.

> *Though there is no record of most of their names, Fornander had long made it a point on his journeys to talk to as many old Hawaiians as possible, for he realized that much of what they knew had never been written down.*[46]

In the 1870s, he began more rigorously to collect information.

> *I employed two, sometimes three, intelligent and educated Hawaiians to travel over the entire group and transcribe from the lips of the old natives, all the legends, chants, prayers, &c, bearing upon the ancient history, culture, and customs of the people, that they possibly could get hold of. This continued for nearly three years. Sometimes their journeys were fortunate, sometimes rather barren of results, for the old natives who knew these things were becoming fewer and fewer every year, and even they—as is well known to every one that has had any experience in the matter—maintain the greatest reserve on such subjects, even to their own countrymen.*
>
> [Fornander 1877][47]

Fornander's collectors included S. N. Hale'ole[48] (another of the Lahainaluna students, less well-known today) and evidently Naihe of Kohala—both highly competent individuals.

Supposedly, the collected stories were published by the Bishop Museum in 1914–1920 under the title of the Fornander Collections. But, there are not many stories presented. For example, one would think many versions of different stories would have been collected. Also, only a few of the stories in the published Collections indicate who provided the story. It is my opinion that the vast number of stories collected are not published in the Collections. Rather, the Collections appear to be selected accounts and perhaps even initial meldings of the many stories actually gathered into his published composite story. The original multiple stories would be a treasure-trove of information, if they could ever be found.

Nonetheless, in the late 1870s, Fornander reviewed, matched and evaluated differences among his gathered stories. He consulted with Kepelino and Kamakau, "with whom I have conferred both often and lengthily."[49] And evidently Kamakau's newspaper articles, when relevant, were extensively used to evaluate the accuracy of the stories.[50] After collating the stories, Fornander published *An Account of the Polynesian Race* in three volumes, the second being beyond doubt the most comprehensive account of ancient Hawaiian history from the migratory period to 1795.[51] Still, Fornander clearly realized that his work of selecting out stories was a difficult one.

> *The author has had no easy task in reducing his materials to historical sequence, precision, and certainty. The difficulties he has had to contend with hardly any but Polynesian scholars can fully appreciate, and how far he has succeeded he respectfully leaves to the Hawaiians themselves to decide.*
>
> [1880 Fornander][52]

Because we lack the many individual stories from which the authors wrote their accounts, we actually have relatively few comprehensive recordings of oral histories which were known in the 1800s. There are even fewer, when one realizes that each author emphasized different topics. Malo's emphasis was on general cultural patterns at European contact, and Kamakau in some of his articles tried to expand on Malo, as probably did Kepelino. Fornander's emphasis is on the history of the rulers, expanding on topics that Kamakau partly covered in his newspaper stories. ʻĪʻi provides a glimpse of the details of life at the court, which few others discuss. Thus, these accounts plus shorter newspaper articles and other yet unfound accounts have great value. Each contributes a piece of the picture of Hawaiʻi's past.

One problem—particularly for this volume—is that occasionally the sources conflict, providing different versions of the same historical story. Then one must address the question of determining which version is more accurate. Clearly, this was a problem for Fornander when he compiled his volume from many sources and had to choose. Trying to evaluate is extremely difficult in some cases. When the stories are all early, from the early to mid-1800s, one can carefully check different versions for inconsistencies or contradictions. For example, one story might call a known district chief a king and place the person in the wrong ruler's reign.[53] Another contradiction might be saying district chiefs were replaced, yet in the next chapter referring to their sons having inherited the position from their fathers.[54] Another means of evaluation is to rely on the earlier sources—primarily K. Kamakau and Malo. However, without knowing who gave stories to Fornander or S. Kamakau, it may be unfair to say that their sources were not pre-1795. If sources span many decades, such as the 1850s to the 1930s, then it is often useful to compare stories looking for the amount and scale of changes over time as a measure of reliability.[55]

Interesting and severe conflicts exist between Kamakau's and Fornander's accounts for Hawai'i Island. Fornander consulted with Kamakau, and he largely follows Kamakau's versions for the history of O'ahu and Maui.[56] Why then does he provide differing versions for Hawai'i? Did Hawai'i Island experts give different stories from those recorded by the O'ahu-born and Maui-based Kamakau? One cannot tell, for Fornander does not say why he chose a different story, nor did he give the source of the differing accounts; nor is the source clear in the Fornander Collections. Evaluation is often frustrating at best. I often tend to favor Fornander—given specific inconsistencies in Kamakau and the numerous informants Fornander interviewed. But, as Barrere has suggested to me,[57] in some cases, it may not be possible to determine which account is more accurate, and the different versions can only be given.

One important point to consider with many of the 1800s oral histories is that they were written in Hawaiian. (The stories told Fornander were recorded in Hawaiian.) By the end of the 1880s arrangements were being made for translation of Malo and Fornander's Collection. Malo's Moolelo was translated in 1898 for the Bishop Museum by Nathaniel Emerson (a missionary son, 1839–1915). In more recent years, it has been suggested that the translation "is not always literal or accurate and his voluminous notes [at the end of chapters], while exceedingly helpful and valuable, contain errors."[58]

The manuscript collections of Fornander also began to be translated ca. 1896 under the direction of W. D. Alexander of the Bishop Museum. He had Nathaniel Emerson translating, and in 1907 he was replaced by Emma Metcalf Nakuina and then John Wise—both part Hawaiians.[59] Alexander died in 1913 with the publication almost complete. Thomas Thrum finished the revisions, editing the translations, and added the notes.[60] These collections were published from 1916–1920. Thrum's edited portions are considered to be less accurate than desired.[61] But, the Hawaiian was published along with the English.

The translation of Kamakau's newspaper accounts seem to have fared better. The first set of articles were translated by Mary Kawena Pukui, Thomas Thrum, Lahilahi Webb, Emma Davidson Taylor and John Wise, and published as *Ruling Chiefs of Hawaii* in 1961.[62] Other articles on cultural patterns published in *Ku 'Oko'a* and *Ke Au 'Oko'a* from 1865–1871 also began to be translated by Bishop Museum staff in 1931–1934, and "w[ere] translated piecemeal by a group of Hawaiian scholars and the translations were gone over by Mary Kawena Pukui, the main contributor, and Martha Warren Beckwith, Professor of Folklore, Vassar College."[63] These sections were revised by Dorothy Barrere with the advice of Mary Pukui, and published in 1964 and 1976.[64] And just recently the fourth volume of Kamakau articles has come out, edited by Barrere.[65] These are widely considered to be excellent translations.

The point here is that translations of Hawaiian accounts can have flaws. Today a number of manuscripts are still untranslated or need better translations—a worthwhile series of future projects. For the best accuracy, they should be read in Hawaiian. The symbolism and metaphors need to be understood. Unfortunately, few scholars today have this fluency. English translations are used in this volume.

Importantly, the events described by many different oral stories can be dated. The way that this has been done is to use the genealogies of the ruling lines—the lists of successive rulers. Oral stories often are stated to take place during the reign of a specific ruler. Thus, one can place accounts of events into a relative time sequence. Dates for rulers and events in the 1700s were estimated by Kamakau (often inaccurately).[66] But, in the late 1800s, calendrical dates began to be assigned to each generation of rulers, starting with those individuals ruling at European contact, assigning a fixed number of years per generation, and then calculating back for each generation to key accounts. A generation is the age of a parent when the eldest child is born—when an individual became an adult and might assume the position of ruler. To illustrate this dating approach, Kalaniʻōpuʻu was Hawaiʻi Island's ruler at European contact (1779), and he died in 1782. If one assigns 20 years as an estimate for a generation, Kalaniʻōpuʻu's generation dates 1762–1782. His predecessor's, Alapaʻinui's, reign would date 1742–1762, and so on.

A complication here is that the lists of successive rulers do not correspond to successive generations. In some cases, a brother of the same generation followed as ruler. To calculate by generation, one must carefully determine which generation each ruler belonged to.

It is important to realize that researchers using this dating approach have assigned different spans of time for an average generation. In the 1870s–1880s, Fornander used 30 years per generation. By the end of the 1800s, 25 years per generation became the common standard for the Pacific. Indeed, members of the well-known Polynesian Society seem to have begun to use this figure in 1898, and it has continued to be used.[67] However, Stokes and Cartwright looked carefully at this figure during the early 1930s.[68] Stokes was on the staff of the Bishop Museum and was one of the extremely knowledgeable anthropologists specializing in Hawaiian history of this century.[69] He noted that birth information for Hawaiians from 1919 suggested women had their first child at 18–19 years of age.[70] Discussions with a country doctor in rural Hawaiʻi indicated that women may have been having their first child at 13–14 and men at 15–16.[71] Stokes concluded that an average of 15 years for a royal generation—as suggested by Yzendoorn and Cartwright—might be correct.[72] Yet Stokes noted that these figures might be lengthened in cases where the firstborn does not inherit the reign, or high-ranking marriages occurred later in the ruler's life leading to the heir actually being farther apart in years.[73] Cartwright[74] notes some cases where generations were skipped by rulers marrying very young wives. Correcting for such factors, Stokes concluded that 21–22.5 years per royal generation might be accurate, with a calculation of 20 years per generation being sufficient.[75]

After careful review of the arguments, this 20-years-per-generation figure has been accepted as more reliable by recent scholars doing work with the oral histories.[76] It is used in this volume. But, it must be realized that it is only an estimate. One ruler may have reigned for 40 years, while his two successors, both of the next generation, may have ruled only two and five years. As the quote from Stokes at the start of this chapter notes, such dating at best is an approximation.

For a reference year for the genealogies, Stokes recommends A.D. 1782, which marked the death of Kalani'ōpu'u, the accession and death of his heir Kīwala'ō and the accession of Kamehameha over part of the kingdom. These events occurred between visits by Westerners, so they can be definitely linked to today's calendrical system. For conceptual convenience, this volume uses 1780 as the reference year.[77] Thus, the generation of Kalani'ōpu'u's reign is placed as A.D. 1760–1780; the generation of his predecessor Alapa'inui as A.D. 1740–1760; the generation of his predecessor Keawe as A.D. 1720–1740; and so on. Stokes[78] also pointed out that Kamakau's, and correspondingly many of Fornander's, dates for events in the 1700s were inaccurate. Kamakau evidently had estimated these dates and did not use early historical observations by expeditions. For example, Kamakau, and Fornander following Kamakau, have Peleiōhōlani—ruler of O'ahu—dying in 1770. But Hawaiians told Cook's expedition in 1779 that Peleiōhōlani was quite old, but very much alive, although he did die in 1779 or 1780.[79] Stokes points out a whole list of such errors in Kamakau's dates. Most moved dates a few years; some errors were 20–50 years off. Thus, the reader of Kamakau needs to be aware that some of his dates are incorrect.

Yet one more aspect of the oral traditions as a data base that must be understood is that detailed accounts of kings and of associated battles and other events occur only for the late periods of prehistory—from the A.D. 1500s on. On Hawai'i, these detailed accounts begin with Līloa's reign, ca. A.D. 1580–1600. Often this period of oral histories is called the dynastic period. The dynastic genealogies go back reliably another 100 years or so, but with far fewer associated stories. Prior to the start of these dynastic accounts, the genealogies cannot be considered to be as reliable nor to be as complete.[80] There are a number of reasons for this situation.

> *The traditions about the Hawaiian Islands handed down from remote antiquity are not entirely definite; there is much obscurity as to the facts, and the traditions themselves are not clear. Memory was the only means possessed by our ancestors of preserving historical knowledge; it served them in place of books and chronicles. No doubt this fact explains the vagueness and uncertainty of the more ancient traditions, of which some are handed down correctly, but the great mass incorrectly. It is likely there is greater accuracy and less error in the traditions of a later date.*
>
> [1840 Malo][81]

One period of upheaval—often called the voyaging period—occurred approximately in the A.D. 1200s–1300s, and old ruling lines were replaced by new lines. Virtually nothing was recalled before the late 1300s–early 1400s for many rulers.[82]

> *Hawaiian traditions, on Hawaiian soil, though valuable as national reminiscences more or less obscured by the lapse of time, do not go back with any historical precision much more than twenty-eight generations from the present.*
>
> [1878 Fornander][83]

Fornander specifically discusses this point in relation to the Māweke line's ascendance on O'ahu.[84] While more reliable information—albeit brief—existed for the new ruling lines, the old lines became forgotten in many, if not most, cases. Certainly, this pattern happened often as smaller polities were encompassed into larger ones. Even information on the early founders of the new ruling lines is often confusing. For example, Malo says for four successive rulers after Pili: "Of traditions regarding [these rulers]...I have heard none."[85] Indeed, as will be seen, the different sources fail to agree on the relation of these rulers—whether they were brothers, successive sons, etc. In one account, some were not even considered rulers. Clearly, identification of generations of rulers and dating falls apart in these situations.

As oral traditions extend back beyond the dynastic founders of the 1300s–1400s, the traditions move from real persons to more mythical settings, events and persons.[86] Indeed, these earlier periods have been labelled "mythical" versus "traditional."[87] or cosmogonic (creation) and heroic versus settlement and dynastic.[88] And before the "voyagers" of the 1100s–1300s, the traditions are virtually silent, other than in listing names on the royal genealogies of the Kumulipo, the 'Ulu-Hema and other lines, and other than in the stories of Polynesian culture heroes including Wākea and his children.[89]

Still, despite all these problems, it must be emphasized that the oral histories are extremely vital sources on the past—for many areas of culture and history, they are the best sources on the past. In my mind, the late history of the islands (1200s–1700s) cannot be appreciated or understood without the use of the dynastic accounts. Much still needs to be learned from the oral histories. Better translations are needed for some. Known accounts have yet to be translated.[90] Other oral accounts are waiting to be found and compiled—being hidden away in old journals, letters, and family books. Some accounts have portions yet untranslated, and many articles in Hawaiian newspapers of the 1800s contain untranslated bits of information.

# USING POST-1792 INFORMATION

In reconstructing what Hawaiian culture was like at the time of European contact and quite probably the few centuries before, often researchers have had to use direct observations from the early 1800s. The first detailed population information comes from the 1831–32 missionary censuses. The first detailed descriptions of houses, fields, and life in rural areas such as Kohala, Hāmākua and Ka'ū are not available until the Māhele claims and testimonies of 1848–1849—oral accounts of Hawaiian commoners and low chiefs on what lands they were using. This later information—although direct observations from the 1820s–1850s—is important in attempting to understand the patterns of late prehistoric times.

Life between 1800–1850 had been affected by severe population declines; abolition of the national religion; the move of the rulers and high chiefs to Maui and O'ahu; profilerating middle and lower levels of chiefs; increasing chiefly demands for sandalwood and provisions for ships; and emigration from rural areas to port towns to escape chiefly demands, see the bright lights and/or earn cash. Cultivation increased in some areas with chiefly demands (notably on O'ahu),[91] while in other areas, declines and abandonment seem likely (such as the marginal rural areas of Hawai'i Island).[92] Warfare had essentially ended. Despite these changes many patterns of earlier culture persisted. For example, the basic forms of commoner social organization and land-holding seem to have changed minimally. Sahlins[93] has reconstructed these local patterns from Māhele records. This reconstruction clearly showed—from Hawaiian accounts—that there was no 'ohana kin group owning 'ili lands at European contact. Rather households obtained rights to land use through residency and approval of the overlord chiefs. The 'ohana model presented by Handy and Pukui in the 1930s and widely used in Hawaiian anthropology until the early 1980s has been proven incorrect.[94]

Other patterns of earlier culture changed in scale. An example is land use. The 1848–early 1850s Māhele land records—the claims, testimonies, and awards—show a pattern in most ahupua'a that was similar to pre-1792 times. The major trails (ala nui or ala aupuni) were still in the same locations. Parcels awarded for houses, irrigated taro, fishponds, and dryland fields were probably similarly used prior to 1792. One major change seen in these Māhele records was a reduction in house lots in most areas of Hawai'i Island. For example, many upper-valley houses had been abandoned. By the 1840s–1850s, no houses apparently were in the upper valley of Waipi'o on Hawai'i Island, while in 1823 houses had been found all the way back.[95] Other rural areas in marginal lands away from port towns also lost population. In Kaloko in Kona, archaeological evidence shows only 5 of the 19 coastal houses had historic era artifacts, suggesting dramatic depopulation by 1820.[96] And by the time of the Māhele, no coastal house lots were awarded, supporting this view of depopulation.

It is also likely that many fields had been abandoned. Sahlins has shown that, in Waialua on O'ahu, fields were intensified in upper valleys to supply produce to chiefs in Honolulu to provision ships.[97] However, on other islands, the Māhele and archaeological records so far have been interpreted to indicate abandonment of fields. The upland fields of Kaloko on the northern fringes of Kona seem to show reduction in size, based on limited kuleana claims and lack of post-contact archaeological evidence. This agrees with a reduced coastal population, where no house claims were made and where but a few house sites yielded post-contact archaeological remains. This reduction in field area and outlying house lots indicates that the Māhele land use patterns accurately model pre-1792 land use, but in a reduced fashion.

Other records from the 1800s have proven quite useful in reconstructing likely pre-1792 patterns. Wills (probates) and court testimonies (minute books) record monarchy period accounts of land use. Testimonies also were made before the Boundary Commission in the 1870s when ahupua'a borders were being fixed, often prior to sale. Elderly Hawaiians, born between the 1790s and early 1800s, testified, providing rich information on early 1800s land use in forest lands, and with occasional oral historical accounts of earlier times. For example, Kauhane of Kapāpala in Ka'ū told of ahupua'a lands in

Ka'ū having their borders changed by the high priests of Līloa, which would have been ca. 1580–1600.[98]

There are more modern oral histories. For example, Stokes used old informants in his archaeological studies of heiau in 1906 and 1919. In Kahalu'u in Kona, a primary informant was the grandson of the last priest presiding at Kapuanoni heiau.[99] In the 1930s, Hudson and Reinecke similarly used informants when doing archaeological studies. In Waipi'o, two of Hudson's informants were 70 and 76 years old, and they told him about ancient places.[100] Handy and Pukui used Pukui's elderly relatives in the 1930s. An important caution here again is that the informants came of age in the late 1800s in a setting far different from pre-contact Hawai'i. Stories often blend old patterns, early-1800s patterns, and late-1800s patterns—a complaint of Kepelino's mid-1800s account and one that now appears true for Handy and Pukui's famous Ka'ū family system volume. Great caution is needed in using these accounts.

Use of records of these later times clearly is important. Often they provide the only information on certain areas of Hawai'i Island. Caution and evaluation is needed to try to eliminate post-contact changes.

## ARCHAEOLOGICAL DATA

Archaeological information in Hawai'i is completely different from oral and written histories because archaeology deals with fragmentary material remains, not observations or recollections of behavior. Behavior must be reconstructed. Archaeologists recover artifacts, food remains, debris, plant pollen, and the like within a location called a site. Sites can have remains of surface architecture such as stone platforms or enclosing walls that are ruins of heiau, permanent house sites, and temporary house sites or shelters. Stone and earth walls and canals are left behind in irrigated agricultural areas. Some sites may have no remains of architecture on the surface, such as buried habitation sites in sand dunes, field shelters visible only as a stone hearth, or caves used as temporary shelters or as burial locations. The archaeologist must record the information in a site, often conduct laboratory analyses, and then attempt to reconstruct past behavior.

Archaeology has the advantage of not being confined to a certain time period. Sites from the earliest settlements should still exist even if altered by later settlements and natural events. They can be studied just as easily as more recent sites. Yet archaeology does have weaknesses. The reliability or usefulness of archaeological information varies considerably with the completeness of survey coverage, the accuracy of a site's description, the amount and nature of laboratory analyses, the quality and focus of interpretation, and the basic accuracy problem of archaeological dating.

Survey coverage varies greatly. Many projects failed to adequately cover project areas and find all historic sites.[101] This is particularly true of pre-1970 surveys which tended to be fairly brief surveys of large archaeological ruins (heiau, fishponds, etc.). Many house sites and smaller sites were not identified in these studies. In the 1970s this situation changed with a switch in archaeological focus to settlement patterns—the overall pattern of all sites on the landscape: house sites, campsites, agricultural fields, fishponds, and religious structures.

Still there are surveys in the 1970s and early 1980s which were of poor quality and failed to find most sites. Ways of checking for flaws are to read a report to see if the acreage of land was surveyed in a reasonable amount of time with a reasonable number of workers. One might be dubious of a 300-acre parcel covered by one person in one day, unless much of the land surface had been previously destroyed by bulldozing, sugarcane cultivation, etc. Also, if the project is in a sand area, excavations should have occurred to check for subsurface remains of habitation sites. With survey reports being thoroughly reviewed by the State Historic Preservation Division archaeologists since 1987, and being revised if missing information, survey coverage in most reports today is good.

The completeness of site descriptions is also a problem in using archaeological information. It is vital to have the form of a site be clear (for example, a complex of two rectangular platforms and one C-shaped enclosure), the area of each feature clear (Platform A 4 x 5 meters and 1 meter high), and a description of general types of surface remains such as artifacts and food remains. In a few cases, pieces of this information are incomplete, making the survey report of little use and making interpretations dubious. Most archaeologists do, however, produce quality site descriptions. And again since State Historic Preservation Division review began rigorously in 1987, most reports have these problems corrected before being finalized.

The nature and completeness of laboratory analyses also vary—often as a result of different research interests and funding. For example, one project may analyze stone tool debris in depth; another may not. One may describe and illustrate all artifacts in depth; another may not. The caution here is that reports' interpretive interests are varied. This is not necessarily bad, and the recovered remains are stored and available to other researchers to study differently.

Interpretation is a major problem area of archaeological findings. Archaeologists do not have the benefit of firsthand observations of behavior. They have to interpret or reconstruct behavior from the patterns of debris left behind by a certain event, often altered by later human actions (sweeping out a house, pulling down a wall and rebuilding it, digging a pit through earlier deposits) and by natural events (gradual erosion and rapid flooding or tidal waves). Interpretation involves a complex series of steps to reconstruct general behavior patterns such as population, social ranking, etc. And even lower level interpretations—determining what a house structure was used for—are often complicated.

Some studies carefully present the logic leading to interpretations; others do not. For example, some reports may describe a platform and conclude it was a men's house with little or no justification for this interpretation. Others will note characteristics of men's houses as documented historically—larger size relative

to other house structures, religious altar features, male-specific artifacts, etc.—and then match the archaeological case with these traits and reach an interpretation. It is important for researchers not to blindly accept interpretations. Interpretations are constructs of the archaeologist's logic. They may be poorly thought out and completely inaccurate. Even the good interpretations today may change as analyses improve over time. However, this should not be taken to mean archaeological interpretations are of little value. There are many good, solid studies that advance our knowledge of the past.

Higher-level interpretations such as reconstructing social ranking or population are even more complicated. One method of studying social ranking focuses on permanent house sites—in contrast to shelters found in fields, along the shore, along trails, or camps in forests. Permanent house sites must be carefully identified in an area. Usually, they contain one or more medium-sized house structure (20–60 sq. meters) and are more substantially built (more rectangular, with carefully made stone facings). However, the actual interpretations are more complicated. Once identified, each house site must be test excavated to obtain dates, with several dates processed so the whole span of a site's use is known. This is time consuming and can be expensive. For example, if 30 sites are studied with 3 dates each, 90 dates would be processed. This rarely is done because the cost for dating at $300 each would be $27,000. With good dating, however, the archaeologist can determine which house sites were used at the same time, say A.D. 1500–1600. To identify differences in social ranks among the house sites of this time, labor invested in the site is studied. For example, of 30 sites, 28 may have 1–3 simple platforms or terraces and the labor expenditure on these sites would be similar. One site may have had a large wall built around its five structures, and the last site may have had 10 structures built on an immense leveled area. These last two households reflect greater labor expenditure—and thus two different and higher social ranks. The ranks might be interpreted as a low chief's and high chief's household. Clearly, this study of social ranking is a long and expensive process. So far such studies, which are important for learning about the past, are relatively few in number.[102]

Population reconstructions are equally difficult. Estimates for different places have been reconstructed archaeologically using permanent and/or temporary habitation sites.[103] I personally believe that, at present, only those based on permanent habitations are reliable. These houses need to be identified and dated. Once an idea is obtained of how many such sites were present ca. A.D. 1400–1500, then there are several ways to estimate population. One archaeologist has counted sleeping houses and assigned six people per house, following Lt. King's 1779 estimate from Kealakekua.[104] Some archaeologists have used five people per house, following Rev. Ellis' 1823 estimate for Hawai'i Island.[105] On the mainland, 10% of the area once roofed was long used as a means of estimating population, based on an average of several cultures studied throughout the world.[106] There are other ways of estimating population or studying population trends, some of the more innovative just using radiocarbon dates to give a relative idea of increase or decrease.[107] The whole area of population studies in Hawaiian archaeology is really in its infancy. It takes time and lengthy work.

A benefit of archaeology is that many finds can be dated. Radiocarbon dating of once living animals and plants (charcoal from trees and shrubs, shells from molluscs, fish bone and pig and dog bone, diatoms in fishpond sediments, etc.) is the primary technique for dating pre-Cook sites. These dates are reported as calibrated calendrical ranges, such as A.D. 1410–1664, which means that there is a 95% probability that the true date of the sample lies somewhere within that 254-year range. Such a 200+ -year time span is not terribly useful for reconstructing behavior ca. A.D. 1500–1600, although multiple dates and statistical computations can reduce the span or usefully reveal broad patterns over the years.[108] One caution is that dated samples can sometimes be older than the site they are found in if the charcoal is from driftwood that had died much earlier, or from long-lived trees and the charcoal is from the center of the trunk. Archaeologists hope to correct this problem in the near future by first having the charcoal analyzed by a botanical specialist. But until then, some dates might be too old.

Volcanic glass dating is another technique with great potential. Each site often contains a few to hundreds of volcanic glass flakes (former cutting tools). Each is like a potential penny with a date. When a flake is broken to form a tool, theoretically it begins to alter at a fixed rate based on the chemical makeup of the glass source, and on the temperature within the archaeological site. In theory laboratories can thin-section the glass and measure the width of the alteration rind in microns. The chemical make-up of the glass can also be identified. If the hydration rate over time (number of microns per thousand years) for a certain source is known and how the temperature in the site affected the rate, then the age of the glass could be determined, potentially with smaller error ranges than radiocarbon dates. Lab experiments in the 1980s identified hydration rates for some sources, and dates closely approximated radiocarbon dates in most cases. However recently, the lab-induced rates have been shown to be flawed. Until more lab research occurs to resolve the problems, all volcanic glass dates are suspect, and cannot be reliably used. However, perhaps measurements of rinds can show relative ages of sites—if temperature from where they were recovered is similar. For example, sites with volcanic glass in the same temperature setting and from the same chemical source with rinds of 1.5 microns would be older than those of 1.1 microns. If radiocarbon dates are found with volcanic glass, these relative dates could be tied to those dates.[109]

Dating clearly remains a problem in Hawaiian archaeology. Radiocarbon dates can place sites within broad time periods, and this certainly is useful for interpreting general patterns of change. However, to reconstruct population, social organization and political organization, sites must be shown to be of the same age within a much narrower time span—50 years or less. For example, if 50 house sites are located and dated, and 40 are found to be occupied A.D. 1400–1450 and 44 in A.D. 1450–1500, population changes could be carefully reconstructed. Currently, the 50 sites could be dated only within 200-year or larger ranges, and such refined reconstructions are quite difficult. But, techniques are constantly improving, and dating should greatly improve in the next two decades.

## SUMMARY

These then are the primary information sources used here to analyze the history of Hawai‘i Island. To understand Hawai‘i's past completely, one must know oral histories, archaeology, and history. All have great usefulness. Yet all have weaknesses. Researchers reconstruct the past, knowing the weaknesses and cautiously analyzing the material.

# MYTHIC TIMES

CHAPTER 4

# A.D. 300(?)–800s Earliest Times

*Child in the time when men multiplied*
*Child in the time when men came from afar.*
*Born were men by the hundreds.*

(Kumulipo: Ka Wā ʻEwalu, lines 596–598)[1]

Truly, men must have been born by the hundreds on Hawai'i during this time, which may have spanned 500 or more years. Yet we know very little about this period.

## SETTLEMENT

A number of questions always arise in addressing the settlement of the islands—who, from where, when, how, how many voyages? Over the last 100 years, answers have changed considerably.

## WHO?

Fornander presents one origin story whose "principal facts, and some of the episodes" were repeated to him frequently in the 1860s–1870s.[2] Hawai'i loa,[3] also called Ke Kowa-i-Hawai'i, was a chief, a noted fisherman and a great navigator who lived on the eastern shore of a land known by many names, but most frequently called Kapa-kapa-ua-a-Kāne ("the land where his forefathers dwelt before him") or ka 'Āina-kai-Mele-mele-a-Kāne ("the land of the yellow or handsome sea") or Hawai'i-kua-uli-kai-oo ("Hawai'i with the green back, banks or upland" or "verdant hills and the dotted sea").[4] Hawai'i loa and his navigator Makali'i (Pleiades) made many voyages to fish on a sea to the east (Kai holo o ka i'a, the "sea where fish do run"), and on one voyage the navigator urged him to sail farther in the direction of the stars Iao (Jupiter) and the Pleiades. "They sailed into another sea named Many-colored-ocean-of-Kāne" [Ka Moana kai Maokioki a Kāne] and then "on to the Deep-colored-sea" [Moana kai Pōpolo], where they came to an island.[5] "The discoverer named the island after himself, Hawai'i."[6] Pleased with it, Hawai'i loa returned home, gathered his family and followers, and sailed back and settled the island.

More recent work by Emory has indicated that these Hawai'i loa stories began to be told after the 1840s.[7] They used geographic information obtained through European contact. And none of the earlier sources such as Malo, Ellis and others mention Hawai'i loa at all. Malo suggested Hawaiians had come from an unknown Kahiki, meaning an unspecified foreign land in the Hawaiian language, not specifically Tahiti in the Society Islands.[8] Ellis was told in 1823 that people were either created in the islands as descendants of the gods or had come "from a country which they called Tahiti [Kahiki]."[9] Kamakau stated that people emerged from the gods with different genealogies identifying different people as the first humans[10]—none of which were Hawai'i loa. Kamakau said "it is not clear where the people were born; perhaps they were born in Hawai'i, perhaps somewhere else"[11]—"their homelands and their lands were unknown."[12] Emory bluntly said the Hawai'i loa story "has every appearance of a post-European neo-myth."[13] Thus, current researchers do not consider the Hawai'i loa story to be an older Hawaiian account.[14]

Although this Hawai'i loa story was well-known in the late 1800s, importantly Fornander[15] and Buck,[16] and others pointed out in the late 1800s and early 1900s that this version was but one of several legends potentially identifying different Polynesian discoverers of the Hawaiian Islands. It is virtually impossible to choose the correct discovery story—if such a one exists. This situation is complicated because, as the above scholars have noted, often in excruciating detail, oral histories for this distant period merge references to the Hawaiian Islands with basic references shared by most Polynesian cultures. Traditional figures such as Wākea, his wife Papa, the Maui brothers, Ki'i, Hawai'i loa, and others appear in the origin legends of other Polynesian peoples as do the gods Kāne, Kanaloa, Kū and Lono, and many place names. Scholars have debated long and heatedly as to whether these people, gods and places in Hawaiian oral histories refer to events of discovery and early times in Hawai'i or refer to a pan-Polynesian account for the origin of the gods, land, sea and man. Indeed, great scholarly emphases have been placed on differing interpretations of these names. Buck, a professional Polynesian anthropologist of this century, reached perhaps the wisest solution. He refused to choose and concluded:

> *Certain it is that some Polynesian leader arrived early with his followers.*[17]

## FROM WHERE?

Again, debate has swung widely over the years as to the homeland of Hawai'i's settlers. Cook realized that the Hawaiian language was very similar to the rest of Polynesia, so a Polynesian homeland was obvious. As soon as Hawaiians became aware of other Polynesian lands after European contact, they too realized this point.

> *The Hawaiians are thought to be of one race with the people of Tahiti and the islands adjacent to it. The reason for this belief is that the people closely resemble each other in their physical features, language, genealogies, traditions (and legends), as well as in (the names of) their deities.*
>
> [Malo 1838][18]

Hawaiians used the word Kahiki—often translated Tahiti in English—to refer to an original homeland in central Polynesia.

Fornander in the 1870s used words, place names and comparisons of cultural traits, and seemed to conclude the original homeland may have been in Samoa, and earlier in Indonesian lands farther west.[19] By the 1920s–1930s Handy and Buck of the Bishop Museum had developed the hypothesis that the Society Islands were the homeland of all of eastern Polynesia. They argued that impoverished settlers, called manahune, arrived in the Societies without agriculture and livestock—coming from Micronesia, as the Micronesians were light-skinned like the Polynesians. They concluded these manahune had temples in the form of small rectangular altars in a paved court with stone uprights on the altar. Such temples were found in the inland areas of the Society Islands in the 1920s, where their theories said a much later chiefly wave had forced the manahune.[20] They believed that the manahune people migrated out to Hawai'i and other islands. In Hawai'i, they argued, these were the menehune (the little people of Hawaiian legend) based on the similarity to the word manahune. In the 1920s archaeologists found some temples in Hawai'i with rectangular altars with stone uprights (on Necker Island and at a few places on the main islands—Mauna Loa, Mauna Kea, etc.), and it was argued that these were early temple types brought by the Society Island manahune. Other archaeologists claimed these were not early types of temples and were local developments, but these comments were ignored at that time. (See Chapter 6 for a detailed discussion of problems with these migration theories and why they are no longer followed.) Nonetheless, this idea of a Tahitian homeland for Hawai'i's first settlers continued to be popular.

This view changed in the 1960s when much earlier archaeological sites were found in the Marquesas. And for the last two decades, the southern Marquesas have been considered to be the likely homeland of the initial settlers of Hawai'i.[21] This theory seems reinforced by several lines of evidence.

Linguistic evidence clearly confirms an East Polynesian origin for the Hawaiian language, since on the basis of shared-word lists, the Eastern Polynesian languages share higher percentages among themselves than with Western Polynesia. Certain lexical innovations also developed in Eastern Polynesia prior to dispersal to Hawai'i, Easter Island and New Zealand, so an intact speech community which endured "for several centuries" is indicated as the source—either in one or a few nearby island groups.[22] These innovations formed the basis of Proto–East Polynesian, which became Proto–Central East Polynesian after Easter Island's settlers departed.[23] In other words, the language of the initial settlers in Eastern Polynesia developed differences: "Isolated from the western homeland, they developed distinctive new patterns of speech, technology and other aspects of culture."[24] Unfortunately, most of the Eastern Polynesian languages at European contact virtually shared the same percentage of words in a statistical sense, so comparison of shared words has not proven terribly useful yet for pinpointing a homeland in Eastern Polynesia.[25] Grammar patterns, however, suggest links between the southern Marquesas and Hawai'i.[26] And more recent studies of sound shifts also show Marquesan and Hawaiian ties.[27] This evidence suggests the successful founding population in Hawai'i was from the Marquesas.

Physical anthropological studies of human remains, working with measurements and presence-absence traits (metric and non-metric) identified on skulls, have also shown Eastern Polynesians differ somewhat from Western Polynesians, clearly placing Hawaiians' origins in Eastern Polynesia.[28] Within Eastern Polynesia, Marquesan remains and Hawaiian remains have greater similarities, based on current osteological work,[29] reinforcing the hypothesis that the Marquesas was the likely source of initial settlers arriving in Hawai'i.

Material culture evidence also shows a strong Western versus Eastern Polynesian difference.[30] Within Eastern Polynesia, archaeological dating over the last 30 years shows that the Marquesan Islands were occupied much earlier than the other islands. Archaeological studies from early sites in the Marquesas, Hawai'i, the Society Islands, and New Zealand have led to the identification of certain material culture items shared by the early cultures of the area.[31] Recent analyses indicate that the earliest sites found so far in New Zealand and the Society Islands contain artifacts (war clubs of a certain type, patu; barbed harpoons; whale-tooth ornaments of a certain type), which are found in the Marquesas, but not in the earliest periods of settlement. In Hawai'i and Easter Island, none of these artifact types are found, yet earlier types of artifacts found in the Marquesas are found in Hawai'i and Easter Island. These facts suggest that Hawai'i and Easter Island were settled from the Marquesas prior to the development of these later artifact types, which seem to represent a spread of later patterns within central and southern East Polynesia, after the settlers of Hawai'i and Easter Island had departed.[32] Again, this points to the Marquesas as a likely homeland for Hawai'i.[33]

## WHEN?

Dating the settlement of Hawai'i has been another subject of changing ideas over the years. Fornander, in 1878, reviewed the Hawaiian traditions and concluded that they did not have any historical precision beyond 28 generations.[34] However, he did argue that the Nana'ulu ruling line of Hawaiian chiefs was the oldest, speculatively extending back 43 generations.[35]

Using the then-accepted 30-years-per-generation count, he determined that the first of the Nana'ulu line arrived in the A.D. 400s[36] or A.D. 500s.[37] This hypothesis then became dominant for almost 70 years, with many scholars restating that Hawai'i was settled ca. A.D. 450.[38]

This view gave way in the early 1950s when Kenneth Emory re-evaluated the Nana'ulu genealogy using 25 years per generation and processed the first radiocarbon dates from archeological sites in the islands. His re-evaluation of the Nana'ulu genealogy placed its arrival back 34 generations before 1900, which at the 25 years per generation estimate then used by Pacific anthropologists placed settlement at A.D. 1050.[39] He also obtained the first radiocarbon date for Hawai'i from charcoal just up from the base of the cultural deposits in a cave site in Kuli'ou'ou on O'ahu (called O1). It dated A.D. 1004 ± 180 years,[40] A.D. 760–1320 using today's calibration. About this time, Samuel Elbert, using linguistic approaches, processed a glottochronology date for the settlement of Hawai'i—A.D. 930–1300 based on a multiple cognates list. The single cognate method—more commonly used—placed settlement A.D. 700–1140.[41]

Within a year, Emory had even earlier dates from Pu'u Ali'i Sand Dune (South Point, Ka'ū, Hawai'i Island). Three dates from the oldest layer (III) were rejected as too recent, but the fourth date from a hearth was accepted—a date of A.D. 124 ± 60 (Gron.-2225).[42] Suddenly, scientists were talking about settlement in the A.D. 100s.[43] The fact that this early date was revised by radiocarbon labs to A.D. 290 ± 60 in the early 1960s seems to have drawn little attention;[44] the A.D. 124 date was oft repeated in the public media.

Interestingly, within a year of those findings, Emory and his colleagues had rejected all the early dates from H1. In a 1969 publication, they explained that the early Pu'u Ali'i date was too old and perhaps had been a drift log or from a tree near a volcanic fumerole.[45] Similarly, they rejected three dates from Layer II within the dune, dates between the A.D. 600s–1000s.[46] They then suggested settlement occurred in the A.D. 800s–900s, based on the A.D. 1004 ± 180 date from the base of the Kuli'ou'ou cave on O'ahu, and a A.D. 957 date from near the base of a small cave shelter (H8) near South

Point, and based on a genealogical date of A.D. 900, with 40 generations before 1900, using 25 years per generation.[47]

By the end of the 1960s, Emory and Sinoto had run an extensive series of radiocarbon dates from Pu'u Ali'i Sand Dune and other sites. These remaining dates from Layers II and III were all in the A.D. 1200s–1400s, so they concluded that the Pu'u Ali'i dune dated to ca. A.D. 1250–1350.[48] At the same time, given new earlier dates, they revised their dating for the H8 cave shelter near South Point from A.D. 950 to ca. A.D. 750.[49] Thus, by the end of the 1960s, settlement of Hawai'i was considered to have occurred ca. A.D. 700s–800s, frequently cited as A.D. 750.[50]

This date held for about a decade. In the 1970s, new radiocarbon and volcanic glass dates were recovered from early sites in Hawai'i, which again changed the hypotheses on when Hawai'i was settled. In 1969, the University of Hawai'i excavated Bellows Sand Dune in Waimānalo ahupua'a on O'ahu. Early artifact types were found in the lowest layers. Radiocarbon dates were processed indicating occupation perhaps back to the A.D. 600s.[51] A few years later, work at a sand dune site at the mouth of Hālawa Valley, a windward ahupua'a on Moloka'i, also found early artifact types in the lowest layers and recovered dates which extended occupation back possibly to the A.D. 600s.[52] These dates, the early H8 dates, the early dates at H1, and the 760–1320 O1 date—as well as processing of then-new volcanic glass dates for Bellows and Hālawa—led to the suggestion that early settlement occurred in the A.D. 300s–600s.[53] Additional work at Bellows Sand Dune in 1975 by the University of Hawai'i processed volcanic glass dates which suggested that Bellows could have been occupied beginning A.D. 300–500.[54] By the early 1980s, these dates, plus the fact that a number of dates from the A.D. 800s–1000s were more commonly being recovered throughout the islands, seemed to substantiate the hypothesis being formed by several researchers that the Hawaiian Islands were probably settled between the A.D. 300s–500s.[55] These dates were compatible with Central Polynesian findings. They followed the early deposits in the Marquesas, where settlement began ca. B.C. 200s, and they predate the later changes in central Polyesian culture in which Hawai'i did not share, which seem to date ca. A.D. 900s–1200s.[56]

In the late 1980s and early 1990s, more dates were processed and argued to support the A.D. 300s–500s settlement model. Dates back to the A.D. 500s–800s came from the fertile lowlands of Honouliuli stream entering Pearl Harbor[57] and dates from the A.D. 300s–900s come from the fertile windward lands of O‘ahu—on the sand plain behind Bellows Dune; in Kailua near the entry of Maunawili stream into Kawainui Marsh (site 2022), at a terrace at the back of the marsh (2028), and from two sites in Maunawili Valley; and from the Luluku complex in Kāne‘ohe.[58] Similarly, such early dates began to be recovered on Kaua‘i.[59] And, a number of A.D. 600s–900s dates were processed from charcoal within 20+ sites (mostly short-term habitations in cave shelters) on leeward Hawai‘i Island.[60] This pattern indicated to many researchers that settlers had arrived in the years prior to this increase in sites—in the 300s–500s.

However, in the late 1980s, a number of earlier dates were processcd, and some researchers began considering a A.D. 0–300s date for Hawai‘i's settlement. On the arid ‘Ewa plain on O‘ahu at today's Ko Olina resort, work in 1988 by the Paul H. Rosendahl Inc. archaeological firm revealed that a small stream once flowed into a freshwater marsh flanked by limestone bluffs. This marsh then emptied into a saltwater marsh and through narrow coastal dunes into the sea. Pollen work from the freshwater marsh suggested human manipulation of the flora beginning ca. A.D. 225–565.[61] A deeply buried habitation deposit was found by backhoe excavations on the edge of the marsh, on the slope at the base of the bluffs, and initial human use there has been dated to A.D. 145–600.[62] Initial use of rock shelters right across the marsh also began early—perhaps by A.D. 600s–1000s.[63] And an early date of 410–660 was recovered from buried deposits in the sand dunes.[64] The excavators argued that these occupations were all temporary in nature, used by people who had come there, presumably from permanent settlements elsewhere on O‘ahu, to exploit the rich marine resources.[65] Importantly, the dates potentially alter prior conceptions of when Hawai‘i was settled.

About the same time, two other even earlier dates were processed from windward O‘ahu. A basal habitation layer from a large coastal dune (site 2911 at Kahuku Point) on the north shore of O‘ahu was

B.C 165–A.D. 210.[66] Another early date of B.C. 430–30 was obtained from Kahana Valley on the Ko'olau windward shore. The excavator there argued this date was from charcoal in soils that washed in the coastal marsh from early agricultural clearing on the marsh slopes.[67] However, these dates have been viewed with skepticism by most researchers. Follow-up dating work took place at Kahuku in the deposit which had yielded the early date, and much later dates were processed, making the early date suspect (perhaps dating driftwood of a much earlier age).[68] In the Kahana Valley case (the B.C. 430–30 date), most researchers who have analyzed the information are convinced this date actually is from earlier marine sediments, and that the only solid cultural dates from Kahana are in the A.D. 700s–1200s.[69]

Besides these O'ahu dates, a reanalysis of dates processed from South Point on Hawai'i Island suggested that some of the early dates from that site should not be rejected and that the site may well date ca. A.D. 100s–400s.[70] Indeed, the early date does come from a firepit at the base of the deposit. Later dates could reflect gradual spreading out of the site and building deposits.

The most recent of the advocates of the A.D. 0–300 view identifed all the pre–1000 A.D. dates processed in the islands, assumed they were all correct, and concluded the dates did suggest settlement by the A.D. 0–300s.[71]

More recently, the reliability of many of the pre–700 A.D. dates and conclusions have been considered suspect by some researchers. The Bellows dune radiocarbon dates have been argued to be near worthless due to their wide range (600s–1200s) and inversions (some younger dates are found lower in the deposits), and the volcanic glass dates at Bellows are considered unreliable.[72] Additional dating of previously collected charcoal samples has not been of much use other than showing the dune site was occupied ca. the A.D. 900s. Statistical analysis of the H1 dates from South Point has convinced one researcher that Emory and Sinoto were correct in dropping the early dates.[73] Also, the early dates from Ko Olina have yet to be reported, and some are reserving comment until close analysis can occur. One possible cause for some of these early dates is that old driftwood may have been used in fires. Charcoal from the inner trunks of long-lived trees also might skew dates by several hundred years. To deal with this problem two researchers recently suggested deleting all pre–1000 A.D. dates that did not fit with other dates from a site's deposits and deleting solitary dates that had no supporting dates.[74] This seems likely to be too extreme, however, because dates that could be accurate might be discarded.

However, at this time, three competing hypotheses exist for when settlement of Hawai'i occurred—A.D. 0–300s, 300s–600s, and A.D. 700s. Most seem to still follow the A.D. 300s–600s view. Certainly a large number of sites are now falling into the 600s–900s range, and all of these dates are unlikely to be from "old wood." They suggest population expansion after earlier settlement. But, it should be noted that even a settlement date of Hawai'i between A.D. 0–300 does not conflict with the model of a Marquesan homeland, because the Marquesan early sites seem to at least date to the B.C. 200s and, given the minimal work in that archipelago, perhaps even earlier dates will be found.

## HOW? HOW MANY VOYAGES?

For decades, from the late 1800s into the 1950s, it was assumed that when the Hawaiian Islands were discovered from the Society Islands ca. 1,000 miles away, the discoverer returned for settlers, and one or more colonizing voyages soon followed. Michener[75] popularized the view in his historical novel about Hawai'i in the 1950s. Some researchers in the 1950s and 1960s pointed out that such extremely long-distance voyaging—out to discover, back to the home island, and then back to the discovered island—was unlikely to have been possible.[76] An often bitter debate raged among scholars.[77] On one side were the traditionalists; on the other side were those that argued for one-way discovery and settlement, either through intentional voyages or storm/accidental drift—voyages with no return.[78]

In the 1970s, some researchers perhaps unfairly maligned the one-way settlement theory, claiming it demeaned Polynesian navigational skills and the ability of the canoes themselves by arguing that islands were settled only by drift voyages.[79] A more recent version of this criticism points to 1970s computer simulations which showed drifting was not supported for settlement of Hawai'i.[80] This criticism is not a fair one. The one-way settlement proponents continually emphasized that intentional voyages of discovery were important methods of settlement. Their argument was that localized navigational systems made it improbable to return. These supporters of one-way settlement have lauded the navigators, not critiqued them.[81]

> *The Polynesians...indeed deserve their reputation as outstanding voyagers. In making visits to islands several hundred miles away without instruments, they were heroes of the sea whose like may never be seen again.*
>
> [Sharp][82]

Indeed, those suggesting one-way settlement argued that prior researchers had so idealized and romanticized navigation, that the skilled navigational systems were not properly understood or credited.[83] The 1970s computer simulations did show that one-way settlement voyages to Hawai'i from Central and Eastern Polynesia could be successful.[84] The simulations did not evaluate the probable success of two-way settlement hypotheses.

Recent work on the sailing ability of Polynesian canoes[85] is fascinating, and the Hōkūle'a has shown that the canoes can do even more than expected. However, the one-way settlement advocates never doubted the ability of the canoes to reach the islands. The ability of the canoes does not refute either the one-way or two-way settlement hypotheses.

The key points relevant to analyzing these hypotheses have to do with the nature of Polynesian navigational systems. Were the systems of the type which would enable discoverers to find their way back to their home island, and then return again to Hawai'i? The Austronesian navigational system ancestral to the famous contact systems of Polynesia (the Tongan and the Tuamotuan systems), Micronesia (the central Carolinean and the Marshallese and Gilbertese systems), and of Melanesia (those in the New Hebrides area) has been discussed recently by Irwin, based on the well-known contact systems and logical sailing approaches. Perhaps the best-studied navigational systems in the Pacific that are like the Polynesian systems are those of central Micronesia—the Carolinean system.[86] Indeed, Mau Piailug, a navigator from Satawal in Micronesia, was brought to guide the Hōkūle'a and retrain Hawaiian navigators. The Micronesian navigational system—and the Polynesian ones—are highly localized systems. Journeys began by sailing out from landmarks directed toward a certain course to reach a known island. [In some cases, suitable winds—sometimes seasonal—had to be awaited before starting.] General wave patterns and stars (zenith and rising/setting locations) are used for dead-reckoning navigation.[87] But, local wave patterns which reflect hidden reefs and islands over the horizon serve as a crucial net (or safety factor) in reaching a goal. When a navigator identified such a pattern, he knew where he was and could make corrections if he was off course. [Birds returning to nest at night, reflections of islands off clouds, and other patterns were also used to home in on a goal; or simply to verify that a goal was being passed or approached.] In Micronesia, the two extensive navigational systems were based in areas of numerous scattered small islands—in the western Caroline atolls (within which Satawal lies) from Truk to Palau and up to the Marianas, and in the atolls of the Marshall Islands. These systems covered vast areas, but importantly many islands were present and were never very far apart. In Polynesia, the areas of extensive navigational systems similarly were based in dense, scattered sets of islands—a Tonga-Samoa-Fiji cluster and a Tahiti-Tuamotu cluster. It seems quite likely that these systems increased in area over time, as the new topography of nearby islands was learned. However, the crucial question is, "If sailing far beyond the known net of islands (due to storm or intent, or both), was the navigator able to return to his home island and then able to relocate the island found?"

It needs to be re-emphasized that this question is not one doubting the skill of the Micronesian or Polynesian navigators. Within their net of known islands, their navigational skill is impressive and renowned. The navigator is, and was, a person of great knowledge and a person to respect. The question is what happens when navigators reach islands far outside their known net of islands. Settlement of

Hawai'i is an extreme case. Hawai'i was far from central Eastern Polynesia. New major wind and wave patterns and star-setting patterns which were unknown to the navigator would have been crossed before Hawai'i was found—indeed, several major wave patterns. Could the navigator, sailing north across the equator and far into northern seas searching for land, have learned these wave, wind and star patterns (and seasonal fluctuations) well enough in the course of a 30-day voyage (perhaps with cloud-covered skies on some days) to have returned to his homeland, and then return to Hawai'i again? Most important, without knowledge of the local topographic clues (localized waves arising over undersea reefs and mountains), the safety factor would be reduced, even if the main guiding clues got the navigator near Hawai'i. And an additional problem may have been that pointed out by Finney[88]—to get back to the Marquesas, sailing back against the wind was unlikely. Rather a sail down to the Society Islands–northwest Tuamotus area and then back across would be needed. The following question would arise, "Were those islands known within the navigation net tied to the Marquesas?" Far fewer islands were known or settled then, and the existing archaeological evidence shows no settlement in the Society Islands until well after the settlement of the Hawaiian Islands. This question of whether the discoverers of the Hawaiian Islands could return home and then travel back to Hawai'i again can be, and has been, debated back and forth. As yet, it has not been satisfactorally answered.

In Micronesia, European residents and explorers of the 1600s–1800s did find navigators living on islands far distant from their home islands. These navigators had been sailing within their network and been hit by storms, during which they were flung far outside their net of islands. In each of these cases, they knew generally where their homeland lay. In some cases, they attempted to return home (with unknown success), but in other cases, they did not consider the risk of returning to be sufficient to attempt it.[89] Note that these cases do not even consider the problem of once home, trying to return to the newly discovered island.

Perhaps a test of this question would be to have a Micronesian navigator placed in a situation replicating a successful arrival at

Hawai'i from the Marquesas.[90] A planetarium can re-create star patterns for each night, although perhaps some nights should be eliminated for cloudy situations. But, major wave patterns and localized wave patterns that would be passed over would have to be re-created simultaneously. The knowledge would have to cover a span such as 30 days, with no repetition of a day's or night's information—rather a strict duplication of an actual voyage's situation with constantly changing new wave and star patterns. Then the navigator should be asked to try to return to the Marquesas and then return to Hawai'i. Such an experiment (if carefully controlled) might indicate if the first voyager to Hawai'i—thrust into a vastly new and distant geographic system and having no leisure to study and restudy the new patterns—could have completed a two-way voyage.

Archaeology and ethnobotany, as yet, cannot contribute much to the one-way versus two-way settlement arguments. These sciences have the potential to identify the arrival of new plants or new tools (and thus perhaps new arrivals) several hundred years apart, but not a return to the homeland and a return to Hawai'i within a matter of a few months or a few years. Dating is not sophisticated enough to distinguish events so close together. For example, archaeobotanical work—with soil cores from wetlands and studies of pollen from the cores—can be used to identify when introduced plants appear in Hawai'i.[91] If some plants suddenly appear 300 years after settlement, new settlers could be argued to have brought them. However, for such work to address the nature of initial settlement in Hawai'i, more precise dating will be needed, and widespread and representative pollen samples—all items still lacking. This botanical work has just begun and no definitive results have yet been obtained. Archaeological work could similarly identify new styles of tools or identify off-island stone, but no such items have been found yet, and dating is still not precise enough to distinguish items from voyages occurring over a short period of time.

Given the above concerns and evidence, most researchers today seem to lean toward the view that the initial settlers of Hawai'i arrived on one or a few canoes, and never returned to their homeland.

The numbers of people arriving on the initial voyage is unknown. Predictive studies indicate that 6 people (3 couples) would have had as low as a 33% chance of successfully producing a surviving population, while 14 people (7 couples of child-bearing age) would have had over an 80% chance of founding a colony that would last.[92] Clearly, a double canoe could easily carry 14 people.

A final interesting question on the initial arrival of the settlers is, "Was Hawai'i Island the first one settled in the archipelago, or was it settled later from another island within the chain, such as Kaua'i or O'ahu, both of which have abundant permanent streams and coastal lowlands?" At this point in our understanding of Hawaiian history, this question cannot be answered. Too few early sites have been discovered and studied by archaeologists here.

## THE CULTURE OF THE SETTLING POPULATION

Regardless whether those people settling on Hawai'i Island came from the Marquesas or another of Hawai'i's large islands, their culture would have been similar. This culture—labeled Ancestral Polynesian—has been reconstructed using (1) historical linguistics (reconstructing words of Proto-Polynesian, PPN*) and extrapolating their meanings from post-European contact languages throughout Polynesia, and (2) archaeological evidence.[93] Again, this is the culture that was taken to the Marquesas and began to form differences in that area, and then apparently was taken to Hawai'i.

Archaeological work has found early settlements to be small, coastal, multi-household hamlets or villages.[94] Linguistics indicates that the basic household group was called *kainga, and the larger, blood-related (consanguineal) kin group of multiple households, which held a specific land area, was called *kainanga. One can assume, based on Micronesian and Polynesian ethnology, that several of these larger kin groups were present. [Note: Larger kin groups holding land were not present at European contact in Hawai'i. This aspect of the ancestral culture changed, apparently between the A.D.

1400s–1700s, and maybe kin group control of land ended as late as the 1600s–1700s.]

There was the concept of primogeniture (senior or firstborn), of the firstborn in a family, in a kin group, and among kin groups. The term *'ariki has been reconstructed for this concept, or set of concepts. It is assumed that the presence of this concept meant that a hereditary chieftainship existed, with the senior man of the senior kin group being the chief.[95] Here the reader needs to realize that the polity over which this chief would have been placed would have been a small one on Hawai'i Island. A single small settlement, or several allied settlements, is likely. Logically, any social ranking would be a simple ranking situation, with minimal social distance of the chief from the rest of the population—a lack of elaborate deference, housing, burial, and power. These chiefs were not the rulers, or even high chiefs, over thousands of people which were found in Kamehameha's time. There was no elaborate kapu which distanced them from the bulk of the population, no power in the form of an armed retinue and enforcers, no palisaded chiefly households of 10–12 houses. Even if the settlers had arrived in Hawai'i from a Central Polynesian land with complex social ranking (which no scholars today claim to have existed then), the small size of the settling population is expected to have leveled any marked ranking differences—a phenomenon labeled social leveling in anthropology.[96] And this seems to be the case based on archaeology in early Hawaiian sites. Although there is very limited information on architecture and burials from early sites, there is as yet no archaeological evidence of vastly elaborate housing and burial.[97]

This early culture would have gathered food through farming, animal husbandry, terrestrial exploitation of wild plants and birds, and marine resource exploitation. Historical linguistics show Proto-Polynesian speakers had taro, yams, breadfruit and bananas; and Proto-Eastern Polynesian speakers had the sweet potato.[98] With these plants, undoubtedly the underlying concept of a wet-focused cultivation of taro versus a dry-focused cultivation of taro, yams and sweet potatoes existed, as well as a tree-crop cultivation focus.[99] It is argued also that knowledge of the concepts of drainage and irrigation—as applied in a simple fashion—were also a part of the farming patterns.[100] No evidence of agricultural stone features in early Hawaiian sites has yet been found—although sites on Kaua'i, O'ahu and Moloka'i with soils containing charcoal flecking have been interpreted as early agricultural soils.[101] However, shell scrapers and peelers for preparation of breadfruit and root crops (taro, sweet potatoes, yams) are artifacts found in Ancestral Polynesian sites.[102]

Animal husbandry was present, with pig (*puaka), dog (*kulii) and chicken (*moa) being reconstructed Proto-Polynesian words. Dog and pig bones have also been found in early Hawaiian permanent housing sites—at Bellows in Waimānalo and at Hālawa on Moloka'i—and pig bones have been found at the early temporary habitation sites at Ko Olina on the 'Ewa plains of O'ahu.[103]

Marine resource exploitation was present in a variety of forms based on linguistic and archaeological evidence. Proto-Polynesian words exist for a variety of fishing strategies such as for traps, nets, hooks, and plant poisons.[104] Archaeological remains from Ancestral Polynesian sites in Tonga, Samoa, and the Marquesas include one-piece pearl-shell fishhooks, possible pelagic trolling lures, stone weights for nets, and cowrie-shell lures for octopus fishing gear.[105] In early Hawaiian sites, these items are also found—with the addition of two-piece fishhooks of bone, apparently favored early on in Hawai'i due to the lack of extensive numbers of large pearl shells. Archaeological samples of fish bones from Tonga, Samoa and other Ancestral Polynesian sites are reflective primarily of common nearshore reef fish,[106] which ethnoarchaeological work in Tonga has suggested were probably mostly caught with nets and spears.[107]

Two of the most famous of the early Hawaiian sites with fishhooks are the Pu'u Ali'i Sand Dune in Kamā'oa ahupua'a (which includes South Point) and the H8 Wai'Ahukini cave in Pākini ahupua'a (just west of South Point and below its cliff), both in Ka'ū district on Hawai'i Island. These sites seem to have seen repeated early use as camps by fishermen. They both contained thousands of fishhooks and fishhook-manufacturing tools—coral and sea-urchin files.[108] Large amounts of fish remains also were present.[109]

Besides fish, molluscs and crustacea were also gathered from the sea, again based on historical linguistic and archaeological evidence. Finds from early archaeological sites show a wide variety of species collected.[110]

Terrestrial resources would also have been gathered for food. These include wild birds, which are common components of early layers in sites, though decreasing as time goes on.[111] Wild plants also are expected to have been used.

Bark cloth (*tapa) is also a reconstructed Proto-Polynesian word, indicating that the cultivation of paper mulberry was known.[112]

Mats were woven, given linguistic reconstructions.[113] Food was cooked in earth ovens, *umu, with archaeological evidence of such ovens also found.[114] Cutting tools found in Ancestral Polynesian sites consisted of stone-flaked tools and chisels, and adzes of stone and some shell, with adzes being of various cross-section styles (plano-convex, trapezoidal, reversed triangular, etc.).[115] Basalt hammerstones and abraders of branch coral and urchin spines were general tools for manufacturing other items.[116] Ornaments found include shell armbands, beads, rings, and segment bracelets and pendants of shell, porpoise and whale teeth or bone.[117] Ornamentation through tattooing also existed based on reconstructed words and archaeological finds of tattooing chisels.[118]

Last, weapons of self-defense and war were part of this culture. Archaeological finds include slingstones and spearpoints.[119] Proto-Polynesian words refer to spears, and lances, and the sling.[120]

It is important to note that the settlers arriving in Hawai'i did not bring all their crops and tools with them. Not as many trees and other crops as in the Marquesas and Societies were present in Hawai'i at European contact.[121] The voyagers also most certainly did not bring the full range of the ancestral cultural knowledge. Experts in some areas certainly were not members of the crew on the discovering canoe, or canoes. Experts in other areas may have solely represented a few "schools of thought" as taught by their kin group. So some tool types, designs, rituals, chants, deities, and the like would not have made it to Hawai'i.

If the migration to an isolated place, whether a small island or a large continent, is by a relatively small group of people who are unable to reproduce in full the culture of the population from which they derived, then the culture in the new place will be immediately different from the culture in the homeland.[122] And once the settlers arrived, some crops may have failed, and more culture was lost. These differences helped lead to new forms of culture, which over the years became Hawaiian.

## WHERE DID THE SETTLERS OF HAWAI'I ISLAND FOUND THEIR FIRST COLONIES?

For years it was argued that South Point was the initial settlement location on Hawai'i Island because of the early dates from the site called H1, or the Pu'u Ali'i Sand Dune. This is no longer accepted by archaeologists, although unfortunately it is still printed in newspapers and magazines.

Pu'u Ali'i Sand Dune is located in Ka'ū district. It is ca. 200 meters from Ka Lae, or South Point (Fig. 4-1); but more precisely—and more important culturally for the later periods of the site—it is along Pinao Bay within Kamā'oa ahupua'a. The dune is small and roughly circular, about 12 x 12 meters in diameter and 1.8 meters high (Fig. 4-2). It sits atop a yellow-brown volcanic ash soil, near the edge of a 2-meter bank cut into this soil by the sea. Lava baserock is exposed at the base of the bank along the shore. Out toward the sea this lava area is boulder-strewn and washed by the tides. Pinao cove provides a slightly sheltered inlet. A smaller dune is present farther into the cove (H24) and subsurface deposits (H5) extend 100 meters inland along the south bank of the erosional wash which enters the bay.[123] In brief, there are several small sites along this tiny cove.

This Ka'ū shore is an extremely arid land, with less than 10 inches of rainfall per year, and constantly blowing winds. Vegetation is sparse, yellowed grass. Inland 4.5–5.6 miles at the 600-foot elevation, the 30-inch rainfall line is reached. Here, the vegetation begins

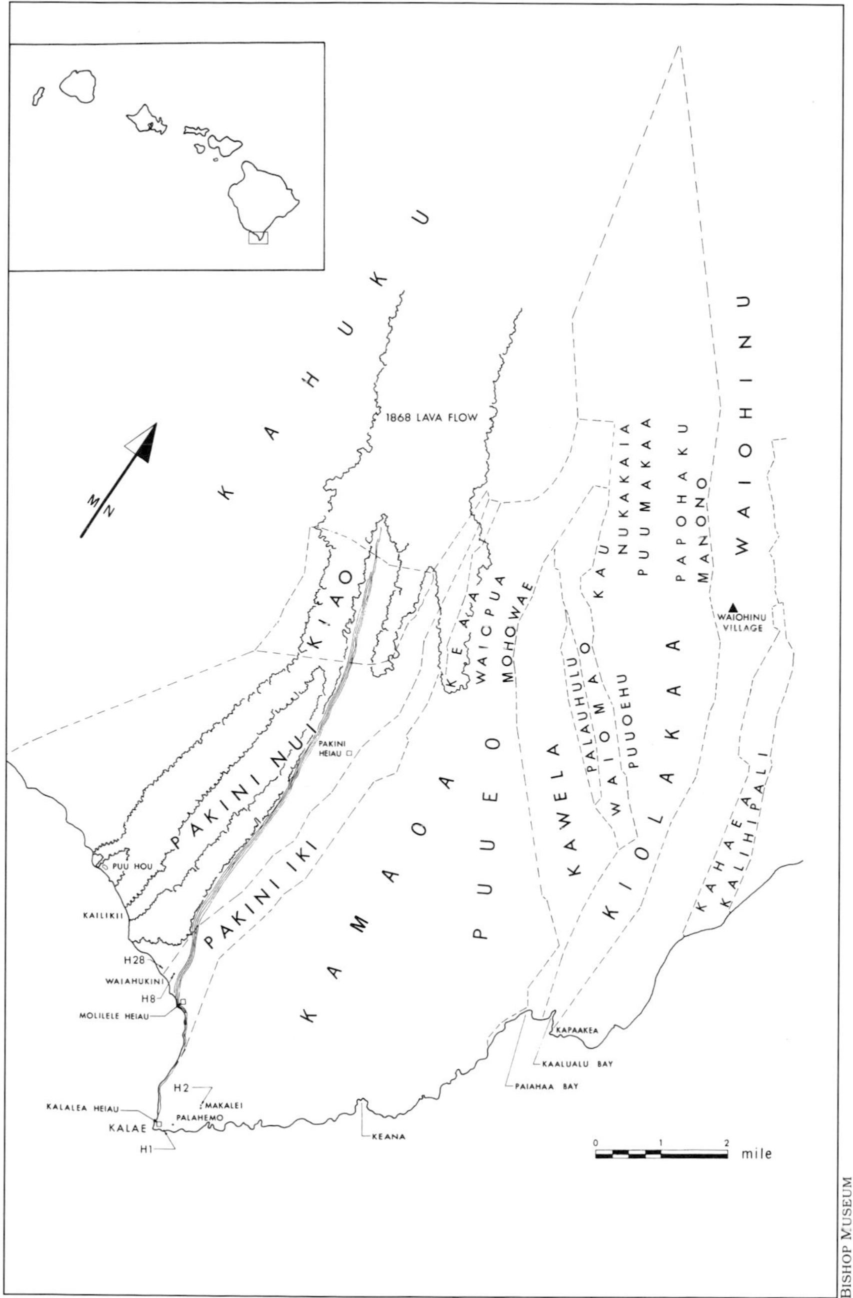


**FIGURE 4-1**

Map of the South Point Area of Ka'ū. H1 is located right near the southernmost point. H8 is located west of the point in Pākini iki. (From Kelly 1969).

**FIGURE 4-2**
Pu'u Ali'i Sand Dune. Note the pāhoehoe baserock in the foreground. Tidal action covers this baserock. (From Underwood 1969.)

**FIGURE 4-3**
The excavations at Pu'u Ali'i sand dune. Much of the interior of the small dune was excavated.

**FIGURE 4-4**
East entrance to H8 cave shelter. The photo shows how small this site was. (From Emory, Bonk & Sinoto 1969.)

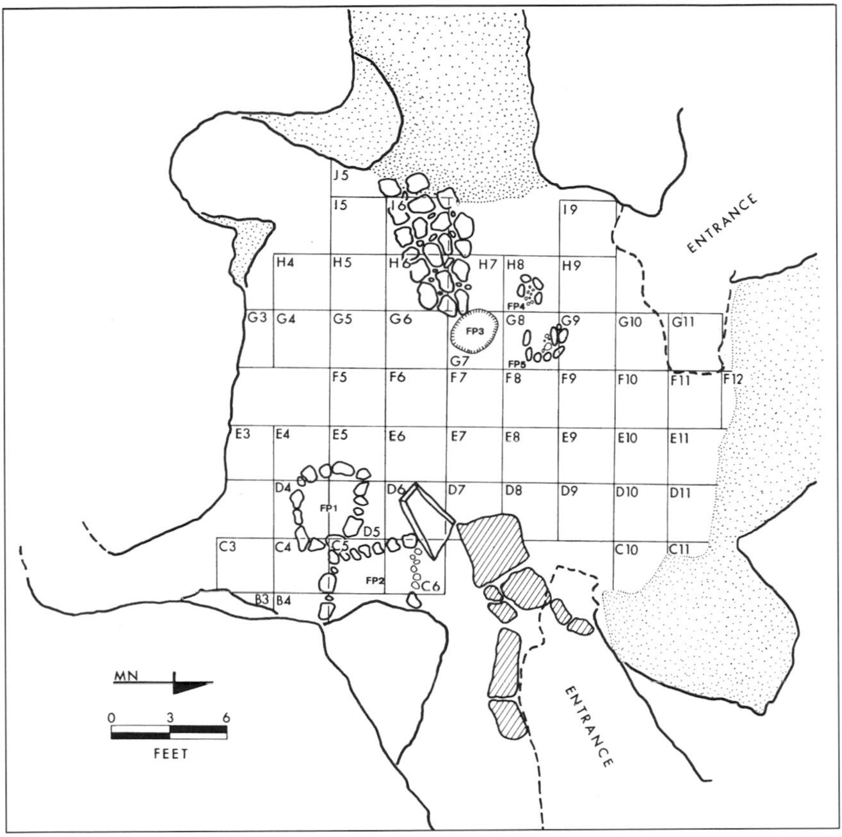

**FIGURE 4-5**

Map of H8 Cave Shelter, showing the test units which were excavated. (From Emory, Bonk & Sinoto 1969).

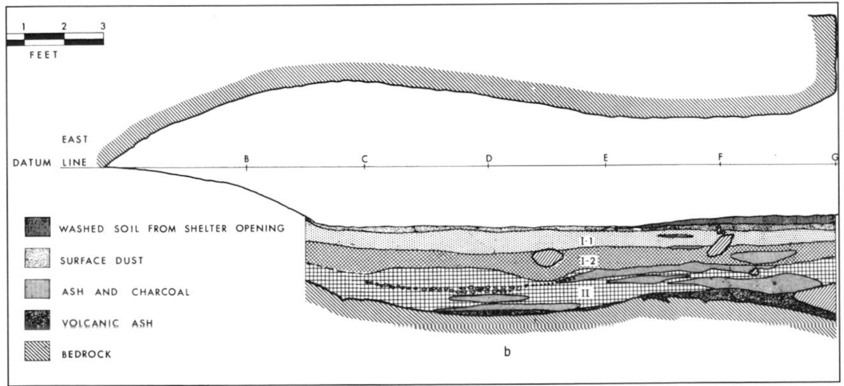


**FIGURE 4-6**

Profile of side wall of the excavations, H8 cave shelter, identifying the main layers, I-1, I2, and II. Many smaller lenses of ash and charcoal are also apparent, indicating frequent reuse over time. (From Emory, Bonk & Sinoto 1969).

to change to the lush green grasslands found above. Not surprisingly, at European contact, this elevation is where the year-round agricultural fields of Kamā'oa began.[124] Seasonal fields were in seaward patches and were subject to drought.

Eroding artifacts were discovered at Pu'u Ali'i in early 1953 by Amy Greenwell, a Bishop Museum volunteer associate.[125] The site was then excavated in 1953–1955 by the Bishop Museum and the University of Hawai'i, in work headed by Kenneth Emory, with William Bonk the overall supervisor, and Yosihiko Sinoto in charge of much of the artifact analyses. Most of the dune was excavated (Fig. 4-3). Four periods of cultural activity were found. The last two belong to recent prehistory—Layer I and the burials above Layer I—and these layers will not be discussed here. Layers II and III, however, contained thousands of artifacts—quite notably over 1,700 fishhooks and over 4,000 coral files and 7,000 sea-urchin-spine files which had been used to make fishhooks.[126] These two layers also incuded numerous post-molds, which indicated multiple house structures.[127] Unfortunately, patterns of house structures have yet to be identified from these post-molds, so the size of these houses cannot be determined—nor can archaeologists tell if several were used at one time. Layer III's artifacts included apparent early types: adzes of a variety of forms (reversed triangular, reversed trapezoidal and quadrangular types), pendants, double-holed trolling hook points, and double-notched line attachments on one-piece fishhooks.[128] Distinctive South Point styles were also discovered, particularly notched lashings on 2-piece fishhooks.[129]

Dates from Layer III were initially considered to contain a reliable hearth date of A.D. 124 ± 60 (Gron.-2225), and Layer II had dates considered reliable which ranged from A.D. 600s–1000s.[130] Indeed, the excavators considered the site to have been abandoned by A.D. 1230.[131] However, today there is considerable disagreement on the age of this site. The reliability of the early Pu'u Ali'i dates was rejected by the excavators in the late 1960s, after processing a large number of new radiocarbon dates.[132] Emory and Sinoto concluded that the early date from Layer III was contaminated (by an old drift log or a tree which had been near volcanic vents), as well as the three earlier dates from Layer II, largely because the bulk of the dates seemed to fall into the A.D. 1200s–1400s.[133] They revised the age of the site to be ca. A.D. 1250–1450.[134] In recent years, several researchers have suggested that the early dates should not be rejected. They argue that a fair number of the dates indicate Layer II was repeatedly used from the A.D. 500s–1300s, making Layer III even older, and the A.D. 290 ± 60 date quite plausible.[135] But, another researcher doing a careful statistical study has concluded that Emory and Sinoto's conclusion on the early dates was probably correct. Thus, the age of H1 is still uncertain.

The H8 site, or Wai'Ahukini cave site, is also often brought into discussions of early settlement in the South Point area. It is located in Pākini ahupua'a immediately below the cliff or pali along the west side of South Point (Fig. 4-1). This land is also extremely arid along the shore. The farmlands of Pākini at European contact were above the pali alongside those of Kamā'oa, above the 30-inch rainfall line, and 4.5–5.6 miles inland. H8, now 50-10-76-10847 in the State numbering system, was 600 feet inland on an old pāhoehoe flow with little soil. This was a small cave shelter (Fig. 4-4). One could enter down through two openings. Floor space was only 6 x 7.5 m (20 x 25 feet).

Almost the entire floor deposit was excavated between 1954–1958 (Fig. 4-5), mostly under William Bonk's direction.[136] Three main layers were identified—I-1, I-2, and II, in descending order (Fig. 4-6). Many lenses of ash and charcoal were present, as well as multiple fireplaces—indicating reuse, time and time again. As in H1, fishing gear and tools to manufacture fishhooks dominated the finds; 1,211 hooks were found and 6,809 files and saws. The interpretation of the excavators was that the cave was a fishermen's shelter, not a permanent habitation.[137] Radiocarbon dates from layers I-1 and I-2 show use in more recent prehistoric times. However, Layer II had multiple early dates—A.D. 755 ± 210, 765 ± 320, 850 ± 140, 985 ± 310.[138] This early layer had 355 fishhooks and large amounts of files and saws.

Regardless of the debate on the dates, several factors strongly argue against the South Point area as a place for early settlement on Hawai'i Island. The first factor is environmental. South Point is an arid land, receiving less than 10 inches per year, and the fertile lands with suitable rainfall for reliable cultivation begin 4.5–5.6 miles inland. Contrary to Handy's claim,[139] there is no evidence that this rainfall pattern was substantially different in the past. Indeed, more recent archaeological work has obtained botanical remains of dry country bushes.[140] An early settler, logically, would opt for the windward side of the island where high rainfall and streams favored the successful planting of crops, without the obvious hazards of drought and crop failure. On these grounds, wet Kohala, Hāmākua, Hilo, and wet Puna all were far more optimal agricultural lands. Probably the large flat lands of Waimanu, Waipi'o and Hilo Bay were the most optimal of these windward lands.

Another major factor arguing against initial settlement at South Point are the archaeological finds themselves in Pu'u Ali'i's and the Wai'Ahukini cave's earliest layers. The finds all point towards the sites being recurrent fishing camps. Indeed, the excavators themselves emphasize this point.[141] Most of the artifacts are fishing oriented—for example, the ca. 2,000 fishhooks and 12,000 abraders for manufacturing fishhooks at Pu'u Ali'i. This is hardly surprising, since the deep waters just off South Point are famous for their pelagic fishing. Also, multiple fires and hearths are found, suggestive of recurrent use. These patterns indicate that permanent settlement was elsewhere on the island. But, they also indicate that the rich fishing grounds of South Point were used frequently and early on—apparently by individuals periodically traveling from their homes in windward Hawai'i.

## THE NATURE OF EARLY SETTLEMENT

When the first permanent settlement was established on windward Hawai'i Island—whether from the Marquesas or one of the other Hawaiian islands—the colonists would have likely faced a wooded 'ōhi'a/pandanus land with coastal dunes and, perhaps in the case of Waipi'o, Waimanu and Hilo, some shallow marshes or lagoonal lands behind the dunes.[142] Larger birds (e.g., nēnē, 'ua'u, and possibly extinct species) perhaps nested closer to the shore. Trees would have to be cleared from small plots to plant crops, and timber and forest products also felled and gathered for houses, tools and firewood. Before the first crop was successfully harvested, the birds and nearshore marine life were undoubtedly the focus of daily food collection along with wild plants, vegetables and fruit.[143] With the crops beginning to bear, diet would have probably switched rapidly back to domesticated vegetables and fruit supplemented by bird and marine protein. As bird colonies moved and/or were depleted, the more common dominance of marine and domesticated animal protein would be expected.

This picture was most likely repeated again and again as windward Hawai'i was settled.[144] Forests would gradually become cleared around growing settlements and newer settlements. The settlers began literally to carve their way in small patches along the shore.

## DEVELOPMENTS

Over the perhaps 500 years after initial settlement of Hawai'i Island, it has been suggested that permanent settlement gradually spread through windward lands.[145] Perhaps this spread was out from Waipi'o and Waimanu into wet Kohala and the cliff lands of eastern Hāmākua, and out from Hilo Bay along the cliff lands of northern Hilo and into the wet areas of Puna.

The nature of this population spread is unknown. It may have been rapid, a pioneer-like situation with so much favorable land available.[146] Settlements may have leap-frogged—first to the most ideal locations for farming and fishing (Waipi'o, Waimanu, and Hilo Bay), then to other favorable locations (perhaps places like Kaimū in Puna and Niuli'i and Hālawa in the gulch lands of wet Kohala), and last into the less favorable, but still wet areas of windward Hawai'i. These ideas as well as others bear checking in future archaeological research.

The nature of polities or countries during this period is also unknown. Several possibilities can be suggested. One would be a large number of small nations—perhaps with 200–500 people each and consisting of a major settlement and several smaller outliers.[147] Social stratification would be expected to be minimal, with a chief of limited power coming from the senior nonunilineal kin group. This is the pattern found in the Marquesas at European contact and in many other areas in the Pacific.

Alternatively, perhaps there were fewer countries which were larger in area. Waipi'o with its vast lands and Hilo with its equally sizable lands may have been able to hold a larger focal population, and as a result more warriors. These larger settlements may have dominated numerous smaller settlements from near the beginning of settlement on the island. For example, perhaps Waipi'o dominated much of today's Hāmākua coast, and perhaps Hilo Bay became the focus of a polity centered on what eventually became Hilo district. Smaller countries might have developed in wet Kohala and wet Puna—either focused about one stable center or cycling among several nearly equal competitors. Such polities may have had a similar social stratification and population picture, or one with a population of ca. 1,000–3,000 and with the ruler from the senior kin group; with multiple chiefs over outlier settlements and from among junior members of the senior kin group in the power center. This latter picture was found in the southern Cooks and perhaps in the Society Islands in Polynesia at European contact, and only in a few islands in Micronesia. It is a situation of complex hierarchical organization. Usually larger public structures begin to appear, and in Hawai'i larger heiau would be expected. To date, we have no evidence for large heiau before the A.D. 1400s, so minimal ranking definitely appears the more probable among the two alternatives discussed here.

Again, these ideas cry out for archaeological testing in multiple research projects along windward Hawai'i—particularly in the near pristine valleys from Waipi'o to Honopue, but also in remnant areas with archaeological sites from wet Kohala through wet Puna. Whichever model of this period finally develops from archaeological research, it is almost certain that Waipi'o and Hilo Bay will prove to be the dominant political and population powers of this period—given their vast optimal lands. This may well account for the wealth of oral histories of a mythical nature linked to these locations.

Throughout this time, the leeward lands of Hawai'i were certainly explored and special resources found. Early on, it must have been discovered that extremely rich pelagic and benthic fishing grounds were present off South Point in Ka'ū, off Kona, and off southern Kohala. Quite definitely, fishermen visited these areas, for we have early dates from campsites—from Pu'u Ali'i (Kamā'oa ahupua'a) and from the Wai'Ahukini H8 cave shelter (Pākini ahupua'a) at South Point in Ka'ū district; from Puapua'a (sites 9962 and 9963) and Kapua (site 3705) in Kona; and from 6 caves at 'Anaeho'omalu (sites E1-24, -28, -67, -68, -133, -148) and Kawaihae (site 14068) in dry south Kohala; and Kapa'anui (site 12444) and Kou (site 12434) in dry north Kohala.[148]

Interestingly, we have early dates from caves along trail corridors linking Waimea and Hāmākua with Kona—running along the border of Hāmākua and Kona and then down through the saddle between Hualālai and Mauna Loa. These dates range ca. A.D. 800s–1000s.[149] Perhaps we are seeing one access route of the Hāmākua people into leeward areas. Maybe the different windward areas had spheres of influence over certain leeward areas.

Besides these leeward places, two obvious natural forces are closely linked with places on Hawai'i Island that would have been observed by the early settlers. These are snow on Mauna Kea and Mauna Loa and lava flows out of Mauna Loa and Kīlauea. Religious ceremonies must have developed to appease the powerful deities identified with these forces and their associated places—particularly at Kīlauea. Oral traditions tell of gods of the volcano before Pele and her family's later arrival, and perhaps these gods were worshiped in these early times.[150]

It appears—based on current limited evidence—that by the end of the A.D. 800s population had built up to a sufficient degree in the windward lands of Hawai'i Island to initiate a spread of pioneer permanent settlements into the dry lands. If settlement had begun ca. A.D. 300, 25 generations would have lived and died on the island before this new settlement shift began. And, they would have lived a culture different in many ways from that of Kamehameha's time.

CHAPTER 5

# A.D. 900s–1100s: To The Dry Side

*Forgotten is the time of this multitude*

(Kumulipo: Ka Wā 'Ewalu, line 662)[1]

This period of Hawaiian history has indeed long been forgotten. The oral traditions are silent for these years, yet archaeological evidence has revealed that one of the great changes in the island's history took place—the founding of numerous permanent communities on the dry, leeward side of the island. For the first time dry Kohala, from ʻUpolu Point to Kawaihae and up to Waimea, began to be settled, as well as all the vast lands of Kona and Kaʻū. In those times, these lands must have been a new frontier for any restless dwellers from windward Hawaiʻi.

The reasons why some of the people of windward Hawaiʻi began to spread into the drier lands are still unknown. Some archaeologists suggest population pressure had built to a sufficient degree, or a socially perceived degree, to initiate the changes.[2] Some of the people that lived on the wet sides may have begun to feel crowded. For those in poorer lands or who felt oppressed by their chief, the new lands may have held promise. Then again, ambitious junior relatives of the chiefs of small polities may have desired to carve out a new country for themselves, and they may have led their followers across the island. Another alternative might have been that these new settlements were official colonies of their home country. Perhaps some place names might reflect this pattern, such as Nāpoʻopoʻo in Kealakekua Bay having ties to Nāpoʻopoʻo of Waipiʻo in Hāmākua.[3] But, the oral histories of immediately following centuries show strongly independent polities present in the leeward lands—for example, a land centered about Kukuipahu in Kohala and perhaps Waimea—which would tend to argue for settlements or sets of settlements which became independent regardless of the nature of their initial origins.

Whatever the reason, current archaeological evidence suggests permanent settlement of the dry side beginning between the A.D. 900s–1100s. In south Kohala, we have a very few sites which have been dated to the A.D. 800s–900s. Dates from the A.D. 800s–1000s have come from ʻAnaehoʻomalu and Kalāhuipuaʻa within Waimea ahupuaʻa—a land which extended from the shore up into the wet Waimea lands far inland and just above Waipiʻo. And a similar early date comes from agricultural soils in Waimea, itself, although this date is being evaluated by additional research. In Kona, early permanent habitation appears to have taken place in central Kona. Early permanent habitation sites have been dated in Kaloko between the A.D. 900s–1200s and other such sites have been suggested for other areas in central Kona.

All of these settlers of dry Hawai'i, as agriculturalists, would have faced new challenges for successful cultivation. With low rainfall in shore areas, taro would have only successfully and consistently thrived at higher elevations where rainfall exceeded 40–80 inches per year. Even at these elevations, land was often rocky with shallow soils and stoney outcrops. The lower coastal and intermediate lands were even harsher, for soil was even shallower and patchier under sparse rainfall, and lava outcrops usually covered more of the landscape. Almost bare lava was present across extensive areas. Given these factors, it seems likely the first families would have farmed lands of higher rainfall—perhaps 40–80 inches—in upland locations Here clearings would have been cut in the existing forests, marking the beginnings of the leeward agricultural systems. And generally, except for south Kohala (Waimea), permanent houses were likely along the coast to better exploit marine resources, with only short walks to the uplands to care for fields.

Not all leeward Hawai'i uplands have rainfall in the 40–80-inch-plus range, so initially the colonists may have moved into the optimal areas of higher rainfall. Cool Waimea with flowing streams, located just over the mountain from Waipi'o and Waimanu, may have been among the first such leeward lands settled—although it lies 8–10 miles from the sea. This expectation could account for the early dates of use along the shore in 'Anaeho'omalu and Kalāhuipua'a—the coastal extensions of the lands which begin in Waimea. If the fields were in Waimea, then occasional exploitation of marine resources and the coastal anchialine ponds certainly must have occurred. The sediment in Keanapou fishpond in Kalāhuipua'a shows it was converted to a fishpond ca. A.D. 1000–1200, if not earlier.[4] Eight caves, as short-term habitation shelters, belong to this period at 'Anaeho'omalu. These caves were located adjacent to the large 'Anaeho'omalu fishpond or in its near vicinity.[5] They may reflect visits to the shore by upland dwellers to gather marine resources. Also, at least one possible permanent dwelling site at Kanikū Point—a set of 4 structures (1 platform and 3 enclosures)—may date to this time.[6] This permanent habitation site may be associated with a few settlers on the shore who had to exchange marine foodstuffs for agricultural products with those living upland. We have but one early date from upland Waimea (along an irrigation canal and still being evaluated).[7] Our archaeological investigations have focused on the drier downslope and central portions of Waimea's agricultural system, which were probably built later. The initial colonists may have settled roughly where Waimea town is today, along the flowing streams at the base of the then forest-covered hills. Archaeological excavation has yet to occur in these areas and hopefully will before large-scale bulldozing of the soils, which probably would destroy any early sites remaining.

No other Kohala leeward area has high upland rainfall patterns. One must travel far south to the uplands of central Kona—from roughly the Kaloko area just north of Kailua-Kona down to Ho'okena, just beyond Kealakekua and Hōnaunau bays. These upland Kona areas are not far from the shore, at approximately the 900–1,000-foot elevations, 2–3 miles inland, only a walk of an hour or two. Because the distance from the sea was short, it appears likely that early colonists in Kona had their houses in easily accessible coves scattered along the shore, and walked the short distances up footpaths to their upland fields. Such coastal houses have been found at Kaloko-Honokōhau National Historical Park. At site D13-3, a smaller and older house platform was found within a larger platform during 1971 excavations. The lower platform yielded radiocarbon dates of A.D. 920–980, 1005–1290.[8] Kaloko and Honokōhau both had sizable protected embayments with large brackish ponds and flowing drainage at their borders, along which D13-3 was located. Farther to the south behind the bay at Kailua-Kona, two small subsurface midden deposits were found a short distance inland in Lanihau ahupua'a. These deposits were uncovered under surface stone platforms during excavations done before the Kuakini Highway was built. The lowest midden dated A.D. 1055–1270, and the excavator considered this midden a temporary shelter probably used by pioneer settlements on the nearby coast.[9] The same could be said for a tube shelter dating to A.D. 1000–1280 found a short distance inland in Kahalu'u.[10]

Besides these habitation dates, early dates from a Kona agricultural site were recently processed, from charcoal found in a walled upland field complex. These fields were in higher rainfall areas in Hōlualoa ahupua'a in central Kona, at the 900–1100-foot elevations.[11] The dates are A.D. 1040–1310, 1360–1380 from prehistoric field soils, and A.D. 1020–1240 from soils within a low, apparently long, earth and stone wall. The excavators believe that these dates indicate walled upland fields began to be built in Kona in the A.D. 1000s–1200s. It is not yet clear if they are dating initial kuaīwi (iwi 'āina) wall construction or earlier agriculture. But these dates do show agriculture in the uplands at this time, as expected.

Settlement of Kona and south Kohala in the A.D. 900s–1100s is also strongly supported by the presence of numerous sites dated to the A.D. 1200s–1300s in these areas. This pattern, on its own, suggests that settlement should have begun a few centuries earlier to account for the larger number of sites found to date just later. Also, the oral histories of north Kohala and other leeward areas show populations of some size in place by the A.D. 1200s–1300s. Again, this evidence suggests initial settlement had to have occurred several centuries earlier.

Ka'ū also holds uplands with rainfall greater than 40–80 inches per year, all in central Ka'ū from Wai'ōhinu east through Honu'apo, Hīlea, Punalu'u and beyond. Wai'ōhinu has springs which formed small rivulets extending out from its cliff for a short distance. The distance from the shore to these inland areas is short in the lands between Honu'apo and Punalu'u, ca. 1–2 miles, and somewhat greater in Wai'ōhinu and the area to the east. Easily accessible coves are few along the Ka'ū shore which has cliffs and strong sea currents caused by easterly trades. Honu'apo and Punalu'u do have shallow coves and perhaps these were early optimal areas of permanent settlement. Unfortunately, we have dates so far only from Punalu'u, and then well in from the shore. Earlier sites could be hard to find in this part of Ka'ū because many shoreline habitation deposits may have been scoured by the great 1868 earthquake and tidal wave. Yet, dates from South Point's sites in Kamā'oa ahupua'a do fall into this period. Here rainfall is only 30–60 inches per year and is 5–6 miles inland. Accessible Mahana Bay has sites dated via volcanic glass hydration to the A.D. 900s–1200s. These may be small early permanent settlements in a slightly less favorable leeward area within Ka'ū, suggesting earlier settlement in central Ka'ū.

The agricultural challenges of leeward Hawai'i were not just those of sufficient rainfall necessitating upland farming. In rocky soils, stones would have been cleared out for taro cultivation, being placed in small terrace facings to hold soil from moving downslope and being placed in clearing mounds. This is the architectural pattern archaeologists have found on the fringes of the final form of the leeward field systems—the systems' greatest extent in the 1700s prior to the early 1800s and depopulation and abandonment. In Kaloko, the upper fields consist of small terraces and clearing mounds, patterns which were interpreted as initial phases of spreading higher into the forest.[12] This pattern is also found at lower elevations throughout Kona, where the people began to farm downslope from high rainfall areas.[13] This type of field has often been labelled an informal field.

Other agricultural changes occurred in leeward Hawai'i. Humidity was lower, with lower rainfall, and evaporation of moisture became a problem. Mulching of crops developed at some point, with fields often covered with cut grass and vines.[14] Seasonal cultivation of lower elevations also may have taken place. When the rainy season set in, planting of crops in lower elevations may have begun.[15]

The most dramatic change in leeward adaptations was the shift to sweet potatoes as a co-dominant crop with taro or as the dominant crop replacing taro. Sweet potatoes could thrive in drier conditions, whereas taro generally could not. In the wet uplands of Kona and Ka'ū and Waimea in Kohala, taro and sweet potatoes seem to have been co-dominants or taro was dominant. As one dropped down to the 30–60 inch rainfall areas, the historical records of the 1778–1850 era clearly show sweet potatoes became the dominant crop. In dry Kohala north of Waimea, rainfall did not exceed 30–60 inches and sweet potato was the dominant crop.

How long it took the new settlers to discover the hardiness of their sweet potato and the limits of their taro, and how long it took them to transfer their cultural focus from taro is unclear. For several generations, people may have continued farming in higher rainfall areas where taro could grow. In Kaʻū, a hardy variety of dryland taro was grown, which may reflect an attempt to push taro into drier areas.

> *The path led us through several fields of mountain taro, (a variety of the arum), a root which appears to be extensively cultivated in many parts of Hawaii. It was growing in a dry sandy soil, into which our feet sank two or three inches every step we took. The roots were of an oblong shape, generally from ten inches to a foot in length, and four or six inches in diameter. Seldom more than two or three leaves were attached to a root, and those of a light green colour, frequently blotched and sickly in their appearance. The inside of the root is of a brown or reddish colour, and much inferior to that of the...lowland taro. It is, however, very palatable, and forms a prime article of food in those parts of the island, where there is a light soil, and but little water.*
>
> [1823 observation of Ellis in the uplands above South Point, Kaʻū District.][16]

By the end of this period, it seems likely that people had settled the drier leeward areas of north Kohala. This region has upland rainfall of less than 80 inches, and sweet potatoes were the staple at Cook's arrival. Archaeological dating of coastal permanent habitation sites is very limited so far in leeward north Kohala. But, Kaoma ahupuaʻa may have begun to be settled in the A.D. 1200s, if not earlier.[17] And adjacent Lapakahi ahupuaʻa saw permanent settlement begin at least by the A.D. 1300s.[18] These are the only well-dated areas in north Kohala, and settlement could have begun earlier in this region—such as in lands farther north (e.g., Kukuipahu) where higher rainfall zones were closer to the shore.[19] Of interest, although not to the time period of this chapter, the most extreme areas of leeward Hawai'i—the Waikā and Kahuā area of Kohala, and the arid, lava lands of north Kona (Kekaha) from the Kohala border to Kaloko, do not seem to have been permanently settled until the A.D. 1300s or 1400s. Both have long distances to upland areas of higher rainfall and, even then, rainfall is low.

Throughout this period, with initial, small permanent settlements occurring in leeward north Kohala, Waimea (south Kohala), central Kona, and South Point and central Ka'ū, it is vital not to forget that the the windward side of the island was where the greater populations were. And the windward populations must have kept growing. And, it is in the windward areas where the polities of greater power and renown probably existed during these centuries. Indeed, oral histories of the 1200s–1300s document the rise of such polities in the windward lands.

# THE TIME OF EPIC VOYAGES

CHAPTER 6

# A.D. 1200s–1300s Centuries of Change Ending With the Arrival of Pili

*The lands of Hīkapoloa were named for the chief to whom all other chiefs of Kohala-waho (outer Kohala) answered.*

(legend of Kamiki)[1]

*The canoes touch the shore, come on board*
*Go and possess Hawai'i, the island.*

(chant of Makuaka'ūmana, priest with Pā'ao) [2]

These centuries mark another period of great cultural change and upheaval on Hawai'i Island. The changes did not focus on agriculture, rather on social institutions—political organization and religion. Archaeology provides some information, while oral histories yield other clues.

Archaeological evidence shows a continuing spread of population through leeward Hawai'i. Much of leeward Kona—from Keāhole Point down to Kapua on the Ka'ū border—was now occupied, although populations in many cases may have been quite low.[3] In original settlements, it appears populations were growing. For example, at Kaloko, new households were established around Kaloko Bay.[4] Forest clearing in optimal rainfall zones for farms undoubtedly increased in leeward upland areas, with these fields probably being in the archaeological form of small mounds, terraces and the like. Indeed, a fair amount of dates from temporary habitations associated with the lower Kona field areas belong to this time.[5] These dated sites suggest fields farther upland in higher rainfall zones were increasing in area along with permanent housing on the coast.

Despite relatively few dated archaeological sites, it also appears that Ka'ū settlements had spread by this time into the drier South Point area, based on dated sites at Mahana Bay, Pinao Bay (Layer II of Pu'u Ali'i), and Kaulana/Kapalaoa bays in Kamā'oa.[6] Some permanent settlement may even have appeared in the more arid land of Kahuku to the west of South Point.[7]

Dry leeward Kohala also has only a few areas with their sites dated. But again new settlements appear. Lapakahi seems to have been settled with habitations on the coast by the A.D. 1300s,[8] and these residents likely cultivated fields in the uplands where adequate rainfall occurred for growing crops. Similarly a permanent habitation has been dated to the A.D. 1200s–1400s in Kaoma, just to the north of Lapakahi.[9] Surrounding areas—north to 'Upolu Point and south towards Kawaihae—may have been settled about this time, but we cannot be sure until more archaeological research occurs. In southernmost Kohala, Waimea's settlement on the coast and in the uplands undoubtedly grew during these centuries and may have spread out towards and into the uplands of Kawaihae.[10]

Some oral traditions belong to this period, although how much they have been altered over the years is uncertain. One such tradition refers to a war between a polity based at Kukuipahu in leeward Kohala and a country focused about Niuli'i in wet Kohala. The warriors of Niuli'i under Hīkapoloa defeated those of Kukuipahu in battle at Kapa'au (at Hinakahua), unifying the northern areas of Kohala.[11] This event can be roughly dated using genealogies. Lu'ukia (Hīkapoloa's granddaughter) married 'Olopana, son of Muli'eleali'i of O'ahu.[12] The O'ahu genealogy extends unbroken back to 'Olopana's time. Using the 20-year estimate, 'Olopana would have ruled ca. A.D. 1340–1360—with Hīkapoloa two generations earlier, A.D. 1300–1320.[13] The Hawai'i Island royal genealogies are less clear this far back, but they suggest Hīkapoloa's reign could date between A.D. 1240–1260 and A.D. 1300–1320.[14] All this is extremely rough estimation, but a date of mid-1200s to early 1300s for Hīkapoloa is suggested. The important point of this oral story, however, is that it clearly indicates that two competing polities were in north Kohala and were combined into one larger unit. Note that Waimea and southern Kohala were apparently separate at this time and are not a part of this account.[15]

This political pattern of polities of greater size forming is paralleled somewhat in Hāmākua. Oral histories from these lands suggest a Hāmākua polity existed and was dominated by Waipi'o at least by the early to mid-A.D. 1300s.[16] A sequence of Waipi'o rulers appears in some of the traditions—'Olopana, Kunaka and Kapawa.[17] 'Olopana was an O'ahu chief, a junior son of Muli'eleali'i who was possibly the nominal ruler of O'ahu.[18] In several accounts 'Olopana became a ruler in Hāmākua, based in Waipi'o, where he married Lu'ukia of Kohala, the ruler Hīkapoloa's granddaughter.[19] 'Olopana's sister also had ties to Waipi'o,[20] as did Mo'ikeha, his younger brother.[21] Eventually, in one set of accounts, 'Olopana left Waipi'o after severe flooding and traveled to Kahiki.[22] The next ruler described was Kunaka—of unclear relation to 'Olopana. Kunaka adopted Kila, a prince of Kaua'i and the castaway son of Mo'ikeha, Mo'ikeha by then being the ruler of Kaua'i through marriage.[23] According to Fornander, the following ruler was Kapawa, also an O'ahu chief.[24] All these rulers controlled Waipi'o, and it seems implied that they controlled a larger polity, quite likely the size of Hāmākua district.

These oral traditions of Kohala and Hāmākua suggest a pattern of competing polities in the A.D. 1200s–1300s, with powerful countries emerging in the 1300s somewhat approximating traditional districts, but not always. For example, Hāmākua with Waipi'o as its ruling center may have been one country, and Hilo speculatively would be another with Waiākea and adjacent areas of Hilo Bay the center. But in Kohala, three polities are suggested for the 1200s—a windward country focused on Niuli'i, a leeward northern Kohala polity with Kukuipahu the center, and another leeward Kohala polity to the south with Waimea and Kawaihae the center. About 1300, the traditions would seem to indicate that northern Kohala was unified by Niuli'i as seen in the Hīkapoloa stories, with one of Hīkapoloa's centers being the Pu'uepa area near 'Upolu Point.[25] In Kona, Ka'ū and Puna the political situation is unknown. Maybe Kona consisted of several nations, or only one. Maybe Ka'ū was also just one and focused at Punalu'u or Wai'ōhinu.[26]

The countries based in windward areas seem to have had a ruler and also lesser chiefs over local areas within each country by the A.D. 1300s—witness Kila as the local chief for Waipi'o under the greater rule of his adopted father, Kunaka. The Ka-Miki stories, published in the early 1900s, state that there were chiefs subordinate to Hīkapoloa in Kohala.[27] This two-tiered chiefly strata (ruler, local chief) is believed to be a new development in political organization. It resulted in countries with three social strata—ruler, local chiefs, commoners. It is often cited as evidence of the initial rise of complex societies, for in such an organization the ruler becomes more isolated from his followers and more powerful.

Also interesting is the presence of Paka'alana heiau in Waipi'o, noted in one version of the Kila chronicle. This heiau is described both as a sacrificial heiau and a pu'uhonua (a refuge).[28] If this account is accurate, it contains the first reference on Hawai'i Island to a major polity-level heiau—not really surprising since major religious structures should be present in such formative complex societies.[29]

One should ask here whether these 3-strata polities were also forming at this time in the leeward lands of Kona, Ka'ū and dry Kohala—particularly since they had only been recently settled and the population was probably lower in these areas. Possibly they remained small countries with a simple 2-strata organization, a chief and the commoners. The Kukuipahu story would tend to argue against this idea for Kohala because Kukuipahu was the center of a leeward polity in this account, and windward Niuli'i polity seems to be considered a similar type of society in the accounts—but the accounts are scanty at best for these centuries.

The Waipi'o stories involving Kila also credit him with establishing the kō'ele tax for his adopted father (Kunaka), with work on the ruler's taro fields required upon certain days.[30] This change—if this account is reliable—also points to increasing power of the elite in the society, another common development in the rise of complex societies.

The above archaeological and oral historical information describes internal, local changes in population, political systems, and religion. Population was growing. Larger polities were forming with more levels of chiefs and with larger sacrificial heiau being built for the rulers. Other oral histories, however, refer to external contact in these centuries—these accounts often being labeled "voyaging traditions," and some researchers claim that it was these people arriving from outside the islands that changed Hawaiian political and religious culture.

Fornander, perhaps, established this voyaging period concept most strongly in the study of Hawaiian history. He gathered stories about voyages to and from Kahiki, Kahiki meaning foreign lands. He considered these voyages to begin in the time of Māweke of O'ahu and Paumakua of Maui, and end with Pā'ao and Pili of Hawai'i and La'a-mai-kahiki of O'ahu. These names appeared on the ruling lines' genealogies at the time of European contact—although at slightly different places in differing versions. So Fornander counted back the number of generations from his time—

the late 1800s—and concluded Māweke's and Paumakua's time was 28 generations before, and Pā'ao, Pili and La'a-mai-kahiki's 21 generations. Assigning the then-standard 30 years per generation, he concluded this voyaging period was in the A.D. 1000s–1200s, 840–630 years earlier.[31] If one uses today's more commonly accepted 20 years per generation, these stories date ca. A.D. 1300s–1400s, 560–420 years back. At 25 years per generation, also used by some scholars today, this dates to the 1150s–1300s.

Today, the popular view of this voyaging period is one of Tahitian fleets of double-hulled canoes bringing new chiefs and gods and culture, and of Hawaiian fleets going to Tahiti.[32] This wave of migration from Tahiti is seen as establishing the culture of powerful rulers, restricted religion and human sacrifice, and island-sized polities. Raiatea and the temple of Taputapuatea are seen by many as the focal center for Hawaiian culture. But these points are not in most cases what the Hawaiian traditions actually document—nor are they supported by archaeology and ethnobotany. There is no doubt that these Hawaiian traditions are important; they are part of the significant period of change in Hawai'i. But careful analysis is needed to attempt to determine how they fit in with the period of change.

First, the Hawaiian oral accounts are not those of fleets of canoes going back and forth over a 140–200-year period. The accounts document relatively few voyages. One researcher counted the voyages in the oral histories and identified only 11 (either one-way and no return, or two-way).[33] I reviewed traditions for this book and came up with a total of 18 for this period (see Table 6-1). These average one voyage every 8–11 years.[34] The accounts, although brief, also indicate only one or at most a few canoes per voyage, which can hardly be called fleets.

How then did the common perception of fleets become established? Largely, I suspect, from anthropological theory of the late 1800s to early 1960s—presented in research publications on the Pacific and which spread to the public. In the late 1800s, anthropology was an emerging science. The appearance of new tools, new forms of political organization, and other new aspects of culture in an area were often explained by migrations. In the late 1800s, this reflected racial and academic biases of the time. For example, certain Polynesian societies well-known to Europeans (Hawai'i, Tahiti, and Tonga) had people much lighter than Melanesians, had consummate sailors, and had nobility. These points often led to the conclusion that Polynesians must have had ancestral ties with Caucasians of Southwest Asia (as European academicians at that time saw Caucasoid culture as one of the dominant cultures of the last several thousand years), or at least with Southeast Asia and Indonesia (where impressive city-states existed). Researchers tended to argue that fleets of migrants left these areas. Fornander was undoubtedly aware of such migration theory through his contacts and reading. For the period of Hawai'i's voyaging traditions—the last phase of the Polynesian migrations—he romantically said "a migratory wave swept the island world of the Pacific," radiating out from somewhere in central Polynesia.[35] He never used the term fleets, however, as far as I can tell from my research. But by the 1920s–1930s, this idea of migratory waves and fleets (at least implied) was the theory of the day—presented by Handy, Buck and Beckwith,[36] all widely read even today. Given these points, it appears that anthropologists have set the concept of fleets in the written record. Hawaiian accounts do not.

Second, the published Hawaiian accounts do not in fact record vast numbers of foreign chiefs arriving. Indeed, most of the voyages described were undertaken by Hawaiian chiefs. Table 6-1 shows 11 of the 18 voyages were by Hawaiian chiefs. Mo'ikeha, 'Olopana, Lu'ukia, Kila, Kaha'i a Ho'okamali'i, Paumakua, Kauma'ili'ula, and Kamapi'ikai were all Hawaiians. La'amaikahiki may have been a foreign chief—although some accounts and many genealogies say he was Hawaiian.[37] Only six voyages were said to have been by foreigners—those of Pā'ao, Pili with Pā'ao, Kaupe'a, 'Olopana 2 and Kahiki'ula, Keānini, and Kamaunu ma. In each case, only a canoeload of people seem to have come—hardly vast numbers of chiefs.

So where did the theory of many foreign chiefs arriving come from? Fornander, in part, seems to have established this idea. From the specific accounts and his awareness of the general development of complex societies in Hawai'i, he apparently assumed more chiefs had arrived from Kahiki. However, he never presented accounts to support this assumption.[38] By the 1920s and 1930s, however, the idea of many foreign chiefs migrating clearly is embedded in the writings of Handy, Buck and Beckwith as if it were fact. Handy spoke of a chiefly (ari'i) culture wave arriving.[39] Buck, too, saw many migrants of "a higher social grade led by chiefs of rank and priests," who sailed to the Society Islands:

> *As population increased and shipbuilding improved, explorers went forth from this center to rediscover islands already occupied by earlier voyagers, and to dominate them by organized forces and a higher development of their own culture.*[40]

Both Handy and Buck believed the voyaging traditions of Hawai'i, as presented by Fornander, documented this wave, although Buck believed it occurred in the 1100s–1300s.[41] "The legends of this period recount many voyages to and from Tahiti."[42] Buck argued that similar waves of chiefs went forth from the Society Islands to New Zealand, Easter Island, the Marquesas and to other islands. Beckwith, an associate of these scholars, repeated this view in her 1940 Hawaiian Mythology volume. As a result of these writings, the idea of many foreign chiefs arriving in the Hawaiian Islands was firmly planted in the literature. Yet, again, the Hawaiian accounts never specifically note any more than a few foreigners arriving, and certainly not canoeloads or fleets of them.

Third, do the Hawaiian voyaging traditions document that voyagers from Tahiti or the Society Islands dramaticaly changed Hawaiian political and social organization—establishing the system of powerful rulers and chiefs (social stratification with kapu), restricting religion and initiating human sacrifice, and founding island-sized complex polities? A look at Table 6-1 shows that only two of the voyagers are said to have brought items that played a role in the development of complex societies. Pā'ao, a foreign priest in the traditions, is said to have introduced religious ceremonies and a new priestly order, involving human sacrifices and new kapu. He brought Pili, a chief, to become a ruler over Kohala on Hawai'i Island. La'amaikahiki, another chief, is said to have introduced the kā'eke drum for hula and the temples. These changes, however, do not document a foreign migration wave which radically changed Hawaiian culture. The traditions do not state that larger temples were introduced from foreign lands, nor larger district-sized and island-sized polities, nor more complex social stratification. I believe past anthropologists incorrectly developed the idea that chiefs from Tahiti established complex societies in Hawai'i.

To understand this situation, one must go back and see how the explanation for a Tahitian establishment of complex societies in Hawai'i came about. We must start again with Fornander. In reviewing Hawai'i's oral histories, he importantly concluded that two periods of culture were apparent, separated by the "voyaging traditions." His work showed that a century or so after the voyages ended, the traditions became fairly factual accounts which described island-sized polities under powerful rulers, strong kapus, restricted worship in heiau to powerful gods, where human sacrifice took place, and social stratification separating chiefs and commoners.[43] These latter accounts have been called the dynastic period of later Hawaiian prehistory. Fornander noted that information was extremely sparse on pre-voyaging traditions, but he concluded a period of simple patriarchical societies with open worship was likely.[44] He called this the Nana'ulu period. Therefore, he felt the complex society period must have been established by the outside immigrants of the voyaging period.

Fornander corresponded with other scholars and followed the migration theory of his time. He was aware of the different items brought in by voyagers (see Table 6-1). Among these items, clearly the placement of Pili as a ruler in Kohala, the new religion, the kapus, and the kapu area markers said to be brought by the "foreign priest" Pā'ao, struck his attention—as well as La'amaikihiki bringing the kā'eke pahu temple drum. These seemed to relate to the strict religion associated with social stratification and island-sized polities in the later dynastic traditions. Also Fornander was aware that Pā'ao was said to have built Waha'ula and Mo'okini heiau. Both were large enclosures in Fornander's time and had been important sacrificial heiau in late prehistory; so it is not surprising that the link between Pā'ao's religion and the religion of the dynastic period was firmed up in his mind. Indeed, he decided that walled enclosures were the new form of heiau introduced by Pā'ao and that unwalled platforms were the older form. From these ties, Fornander concluded the foreign "influx with its new gods, its new tabus, and its greater vigour, and moral and intellectual power" changed Hawaiian culture.[45] He went even further, saying the immigrants took possession of the land and hardened social strata.[46]

> *They moulded, reorganized and arranged everything on their own pattern...[and] left us nearly none of the predecessors.*[47]

While these conclusions might initially seem logical, contradictory evidence was ignored. Fornander had gathered traditions showing increasing polity size under Hawaiian chiefs on O'ahu, Hawai'i, and Kaua'i; and Hawaiian chiefs were considered possible rulers (mō'i) by Fornander. Those on Hawai'i were discussed earlier in this chapter—the Kohala and Waipi'o stories associated with Hīkapoloa and 'Olopana and Kunaka. On O'ahu, the non-voyaging Māweke and his eldest son's line controlled rising polities.[48] And on Kaua'i, ruling chiefs were present; Mo'ikeha married one and became de facto ruler.[49] Other traditions that Fornander collected and presented showed several levels of chiefs had developed before Pā'ao and Pili's time—the formation of social stratification. Also, the 'Aha Ali'i, where genealogies were recited to establish the right to be a chief under a new ruler, and which, at European contact, had feather cloaks and palaoa pendants as insignia,

**TABLE 6-1**
## Voyaging Traditions [50]

| Voyager (Hawaiian or foreign) | 1 way/ 2 way | Items Brought | References |
|---|---|---|---|
| 1. 'Olopana (H) m<br>Mo'ikeha (H) m<br>Lu'ukia (H) f[51] | [1 voyage]<br>1-way<br>and/or<br>2-way | Pā'ū (women's clothing)[63] | 1840 Malo:7<br>1843 Dibble:9<br>1858 Pogue:6<br>1865 K:77<br>1867 K:102,105–106<br>1870s FC 4(1):112–129<br>1870s FC 6(2):323<br>1880 F:9–10,49–54, 62 |
| 2. Kaumaili'ula (H), m[52]<br>Kaupe'a (F), f | [2 voyages]<br>2-way<br>2-way | Pā'ū (women's clothing)[63] | 1867 K:102–103<br>1880 F:57–58, 62 |
| 3. Ho'okamali'i (H), m, Hau-laninui-ai-ākea (H), m<br>Kila (H), m[53] | [1 voyage]<br>2-way | | 1840 Malo:7<br>1843 Dibble:9<br>1858 Pogue:6<br>1865 K:77<br>1867 K:106–108<br>1870s FC 4(1):112–129<br>1880 F:54–56 |
| 4. La'amaikahiki (H or F), m[54] | [1 voyage]<br>1-way or<br>2-way | kā'eke drum (pahu kā'eke) or kā'eke'eke drumming[64]<br>lashing style[65]<br>god Lonoika'ouali'i[66]<br>outrigger[67] | 1840 Malo:7<br>1843 Dibble:9<br>1858 Pogue:6<br>1867 K:108–110<br>1870s FC4(1):112–129<br>1880 F:42–43, 50, 54–56, 60 |
| 5. Kaha'i-a-Ho'okamali'i (H), m[55] | [1 voyage]<br>2-way | Breadfruit, or a "species of breadfruit"[68] | 1865 K:9, 77<br>1867 K:110<br>1880 F:54<br>1898 Emerson in Malo: 250, note 3 |
| 6. Pā'ao (F), m[56] | [2voyages]<br>1-way &<br>2-way | Pili becomes a ruler based in Kohala[69] | 1793 Puget<br>1823 Ellis:283<br>1825 Byron:4<br>1843 Dibble:10 |
| Pili (F), m | 1-way<br>w/Pā'ao | new priesthood[70]<br>Pā'ao = priest of Lono[71]<br>pūlo'ulo'u kapu sign[72]<br>'opelu/aku kapu[73]<br>new images/gods[74]<br>pandanus to Kohala[75]<br>built temples[76] | 1858 Pogue:5-6 47,66–67<br>1862 Hoku Pakipika<br>1865 K:3–5<br>1866 K:97–100<br>1868 Kepelino:20, 58, 197<br>1870s FC 6(2): 252–253, 286<br>1878 F:86, 201<br>1880 F:18–19, 22, 33–38, 53, 62–63<br>1893 Emerson in Malo:248, note 1 |

| Voyager (Hawaiian or foreign) | 1 way/ 2 way | Items Brought | References |
|---|---|---|---|
| 7. Kaulu-a-Kalana (H?), m[57] | [1 voyage] 2-way | edible mud to Kawainui1 on O'ahu[77] some kapu[78] | 1866 K:92–94<br>1878 F:201<br>1880 F:12–15, 45 |
| 8. Paumakua (H), m[58] | [1 voyage] 2-way | brought white men[79] | 1866 K:95–96<br>1878 F:201<br>1880 F:25 |
| 9. 'Olopana 2(F),m Kahiki'ula (F), m[59] | [1 voyage] 1-way | built Kawa'ewa'e temple in Kāne'ohe, O'ahu[80] | 1867 K:111<br>1880 F:43–44 |
| 10. Keānini (F), m<br>Ha'inakolo (H), f[60] | [2 voyages] 2-way<br>2-way | | 1861 Hoku Pakipika in FC 6(2)<br>1867 K:103-104<br>1880 F:56–57 |
| 11. Kamaunu-a-Niho (F), f<br>Humu (F), m<br>Kalana-nu'u-nui-kuamaomao (F), m[61] | [1 voyage] 1-way | | 1867 K:111<br>1880 F:43 |
| 12. Kamapi'ikai (H), m[62] | [4 voyages] 3 2-way & 1 1-way | | 1823 Ellis:284–285 |

1793 Puget = Puget in Sahlins (1981:25–26).
1823 Ellis = Ellis 1963 (originally published in 1825, London).
1825 Byron = Byron 1826.
1840 Malo = Malo 1951 (original 1903 translation from Hawaiian).
1843 Dibble = Dibble 1909 (original 1843 publication).
1858 Pogue = Pogue 1978 (original 1858 publication in Hawaiian).
1861, 1862 = Hoku Pakipika, Hawaiian newspaper articles.
1865, 1866, 1867 K = Kamakau 1991.
1868 Kepelino = Kepelino (1932) (Hawaiian ms, 1868).
1870s FC = Fornander Collection 1916–1917, 4(1); 1919, 6(2).
1878 F = Fornander 1878.
1880 F = Fornander 1880.
1893 Emerson = Emerson 1893.
1898 Emerson = Emerson notes in Malo (1951) (annotated ms, 1898).

**TABLE 6-2**

## Early Versions of the Traditions of Pa'ao-Pili Given in Order of Year in which Recorded

| Year | Source | Information |
|---|---|---|
| 1793 | Puget | "Their religion underwent a total change by the arrival of a Man from Taitah [Kahiki], who was suffered to land. His visit produced the morai [temple] & the present established form of worship, no other account could the Priest give of its origin." [Lt. Peter Puget of Vancouver's expedition, interview with high priest of Hikiau heiau at Kealakekua. Sahlins 1981:25–26.] |
| 1823 | Ellis | Mo'okini heiau, in the ahupua'a of Pu'uepa (Pauepu), was "celebrated in the historical accounts of the Hawaiians, as built by Paao, a foreign priest, who resided in Pauepu, and officiated in this temple." Pā'ao arrives in the reign of Kahoukapu,[1] and Pā'ao was "a white man." Pā'ao's son was Pili (Opiri). [Rev. William Ellis 1963:283. Obtained while passing through Kohala.] |
| 1825 | Byron | "In the reign of Kukanaroa, as one account says; in that of Kahoukapu, according to another, the Islands of Hawaii had been visited. First by a priest, who settled there with his gods, and whose posterity still remains; and secondly, by a vessel with white men, with whom this priest was able to converse." [Byron's source seems to have been Ellis, for Ellis is footnoted.] |
| 1840 | Malo | Pā'ao and Makua-ka'ūmana, with "others" arrive in the reign of Lonokawai, 16th after Kapawa. Pā'ao stays in Kohala; Makua returns to Kahiki. The "kings of Hawaii became degraded and corrupt (hewa); then he sailed [from Kapua in south Kona] away to Tahiti to fetch a king from thence. Pili (Kaaiea) was that king..." (6) Pili was accompanied by two schools of fish, one of 'opelu and the other aku, which led to kapu in "ancient times" (6–7). Genealogy of kings: 28. Kapawa...44. Lanakawai, 45. La'au, 46. Pili (238). [Malo 1951:6–7, 238] |
| 1843 | Dibble | Pā'ao said to be from the Society Islands, a priest to Lono, "the great foreign god" brought by Pā'ao. He went back to bring a chief from afar. [Dibble said the particulars were too detailed for him to give.] [Dibble 1909:10] |
| 1858 | Pogue ed. Mo'olelo Lahainaluna collection of student accounts | One chapter: Pā'ao came to Kohala from Kahiki in the reign of Lonokawai, 16 generations after Kapawa. People were living immorally, so Pā'ao returned to Kahiki and brought back a chief, Pili, to rule. 'Opelu/aku fish accompanied the canoes and calmed storms, so the fish became religiously restricted in parts of the year. [Pogue 1978:5–6. Possibly Malo's contribution, as it is a very close match.] Another chapter: Many beings came to Pā'ao and asked him to worship them. He told them to fly from a cliff and if they returned he would worship them. Makuaka'ūmana successfully did so. Pā'ao and Makua sailed back to Kahiki and returned with a priest who "constructed stone temples for the people to worship in." Before, no idols were in the Hawaiian islands. Pā'ao |

| Year | Source | Information |
|---|---|---|
| | | returned to Kahiki again for another priest to teach people how to worship. Only since Wākea did people engage in idolatory. Other Christian points made. [Pogue 1978:47. Author unknown?] Another chapter: Genealogy shown with Lonokawai the ruler, followed by his son La'au, followed by Pili. [Pogue 1978:66–67. Author unknown?] Another chapter: Pā'ao and his people arrived from Kahiki and lived at Kohala—during the reign of Kahoukapu, or Lonokawai, believed by the learned to be between 1530 and 1600. [Pogue 1978:67–68. Author unknown?] |
| 1862 | *Hoku Pakipika* article | Pā'ao came in the time of Lonokawai. Pili was brought by Pā'ao, accompanied by 'opelu and aku; hence they became kapu fish. [Article in *Hoku Pakipika*, 4/13/1862. In FC 1919, 6(2):320.] |
| 1865 | Kamakau | Lonopele and Pā'ao were brothers. Lonopele accused Pā'ao's son of stealing fruit, and the son was killed. Thus, Pā'ao plans to leave for "another land." Before departing, Pā'ao sacrifices Lonopele's son; Lonopele banishes Pā'ao as an evil man. Pā'ao departs with "Pilika'aiea...the chief, and others" (among them was Makuaka'ūmana, a prophet, who leaped off a cliff onto the canoe). Lonopele sent a storm after Pā'ao and the aku and 'opelu calmed the sea. Fragment of a chant of Makuaka'ūmana included, but not the same as Fornander's and Emerson's. [Kamakau 1991:3–5; originally in *Ka Nupepa Kuokoa*, 6/15/1865.] |
| 1866 | Kamakau | Pā'ao ma lived on "Wawau and Upolu and on islands farther south —" perhaps those called New Zealand by the white people." Same story with Lonopele as in 1865 publication. Pā'ao left with 38 people, including Pili-a-ka'aiea, "the chief." Same account of storms sent by Lonopele, with the aku and 'opelu and the resulting kapu starting here "in the religious services of Pa'ao and his descendants." They reached Puna first, and Pā'ao built a heiau "for his god and named it Aha'ula. It was a luakini." He continued on to Kohala at Pu'uepa where he built a luakini called Mo'okini. [Kamakau 1991:97–100; original in *Ka Nupepa Kuokoa*, 12/29/1866.] |
| 1868 | Kepelino | "According to some authorities it was Paao who turned the Hawaiians to actual image worship." [20] A Tahitian who lived in Kohala, arrived in time of Kahoukapu or perhaps of Lonokawai, both chiefs when 'Umi or Ke'li'iokāloa were king, in 1530 or 1600.[2] [20] [See 1838 Pogue, last entry for a close match.] Lonokawai was the chief and Pā'ao the priest of images when people turned to image worship and "all heiau became heiau for images." "At that time all the kahunas were put to death and the land revolutionalized." [58] Two classes of priests were present in Kamehameha I's time. The class of holoa'e was the class of Pā'ao as handed down. Holoa'e [high priest in the time of Kalani'ōpu'u] was a great kahuna of the Pā'ao line. The other class was of Kūali'i with their god being Lonoika'ouali'i. [p. 197][3] |
| 1853 | Remy | "Paao has always been considered as the first of the Kahuna." (10) [The informant may be referring to one priestly order.—R. Cordy] [From interview with Kanuha, reputedly a 116-year-old Kona resident.] |

| Year | Source | Information |
|---|---|---|
| 1870s | Fornander | Pili was not the son of La'au-a-Lonokawai, rather he was Tahitian (Fornander 1919, 6(2):246). Tahitian meant foreigner from elsewhere in Polynesia (Fornander 1919, 6(2):252–253). Fragment of synopsis of Pā'ao in Fornander's possession. Hawai'i was without chiefs on account of the crimes of Kapawa. [This fragment led to Fornander's conclusion that Kapawa was contemporary with the voyagers and was misplaced in the genealogies as the great-grandfather of Hema, so Fornander places Kapawa as the predecessor to Pili.] [Fornander 1919, 6(2):286] |
| 1878 | Fornander | Pā'ao came with Pili from Tahiti or Kahiki and "was a reformer of the priesthood" [1878:86]. "The legend states...the Nana chiefs of Hawaii were extinct on account of the crimes of Kapawa, the chief of Hawaii at that time." So, Pā'ao sent to Kahiki for Pili [1878:201]. |
| 1880 | Fornander | Pā'ao's homeland: Fornander noted Malo claimed Pā'ao was from Wawao in Tonga, while Kamakau said from Upolu in Samoa and that he owned lands in Wawao and southern lands. Fornander opts for Upolu in Samoa with lands owned in Wawao in Tonga (34).[4] Pā'ao arrived and made his own family "as a hereditary priesthood on Hawaii" and had "more or less to do with the downfall of Kapawa."(22) Pā'ao returned to Kahiki and offered the rule to Lonoka'eho, but he refused and recommended Pili Ka'aiea be sent. [Fornander cites a portion of Makuaka'ūmana's chant here (18–19).] Pili comes and with Pā'ao's aide was established "as the territorial sovereign of that island [Hawai'i], Pā'ao remaining his high priest" (22). When Pā'ao arrived, he landed in Puna and built Waha'ula, but Fornander was unsure what parts of the heiau surviving in the 1800s dated to Pā'ao's time (35); although he concluded that the quadrangular enclosure form was like all those "built under and after the religious regime introduced by Paao" (36). Pā'ao then traveled along the shores of Hilo and Hāmākua, and landed in Kohala at Pu'uepa, and Fornander says "very probably" gave the point there the name Lae 'Upolu. Pā'ao permanently settled there and built Mo'okini (36). Pūlo'ulo'u balls of kapa as signs of kapu in front of heiau dwellings of high chiefs and priests are said to have been introduced by Pā'ao (63). Another story collected by Fornander stated that Pā'ao did not build Mo'okini, rather he added his own gods to those at the altar of the existing heiau (63). |

1. This part of the story would appear inaccurate because Kahoukapu ruled in A.D. 1520–1540, long after Pili.
2. Again, this information seems inaccurate, since Kahoukapu and Lonokawai were rulers who reigned long before the rulers 'Umi (A.D. 1600–1620) and Keali'iokāloa (1620).
3. Lonoika'ouali'i was said to have been brought to Kaua'i and O'ahu by La'amaikahiki [see next part of this table on La'a accounts]. Kepelino may be differentiating between O'ahu priests (Kūali'i was a ruler of O'ahu; Lonoika'ouali'i may have been an O'ahu deity) versus Hawai'i priests (Holoa'e was a high priest of the ruler Kalani'ōpu'u of Hawai'i). Alternatively, he may be looking at Kū vs Lono orders in an unusual phrasing.
4. I could find nothing in Malo which says Pā'ao came from Wawao.

**Table 6-3**

## Early Versions of the La'amaikahiki Stories ('Olopana, Mo'ikeha, Kila, & La'amaikahiki) Given in Order of Year in Which Recorded

| Year | Source | Information |
|---|---|---|
| 1840 | Malo | Mo'ikeha came to the islands from Tahiti in the reign of Kalapana. He went to Kaua'i to live and had a son, Kila. When grown, Kila sailed "on an expedition to Tahiti" from Kealaikahiki off Kaho'olawe. He returned with La'amaikahiki. La'a introduced the kā'eke'eke drum. [Malo 1951:7] |
| 1858 | Pogue | Mo'ikeha came from Kahiki in the reign of Kalapana [of Hawai'i], went to Kaua'i and had a son, Kila. When grown, Kila went to Kahiki, leaving off Kalae Kahiki on Kaho'olawe. He returned with La'amaikahiki. The kā'eke'eke drum and outrigger were introduced by La'amaikahiki. [Pogue 1978:6] (This may be a part that Malo contributed.) |
| 1865 | Kamakau | Mo'ikeha had 3 children—Ho'okamali'i, Haulani-nui-ai-akea, and Kila [Kamakau 1991:36] Nana'ulu genealogy for O'ahu—'Olopana and Mo'ikeha are junior sons of Māweke, with Kumuhonua the senior son. Kumuhonua fought with 'Olopana, and 'Olopana fled by sea, taking La'a and Mo'ikeha, and landed in Kahiki in Moa'ulanuiākea. Mo'ikeha slept with Lu'ukia, 'Olopana's wife, and returned to Kaua'i. The three sons of Mo'ikeha, when they grew to adulthood, then sailed to Kahiki to fetch La'a back. [Kamakau 1991:77; orig. Sept. 1865] |
| 1867 | Kamakau | Lu'ukia went to Kahiki where she married a chief named 'Olopana [Kamakau 1991:102] Another version: Mo'ikeha was Hawaiian. He and his brother, 'Olopana, were taken captive by their older brother Kumuhonua in a sea battle. La'amaikahiki, a Hawaiian (son of Ahukai and Keakamilo), was with Mo'ikeha. [Kamakau 1991:105] Another version: Mo'ikeha was from Kahiki. He was banished due to adultery with the wife (Lu'ukia) of his older brother ('Olopana). Mo'ikeha arrived in Hawai'i and dropped off members of his crew along Hawai'i, Maui, Moloka'i, and O'ahu. Mo'ikeha sailed on to Kaua'i where he married a Kaua'i chiefess and had 3 sons. [Kamakau 1991:105–106]. |
| | | When Kila grew up, Mo'ikeha had him go to Kahiki to fetch La'a; Kila went with his two brothers—sailing to Kahiki-kū and to Kahiki-moe (107). He left Hawai'i from South Point, Kalae. At Kahiki, he found that La'a was the heir to 'Olopana. La'a was to return to Hawai'i after 'Olopana's death. After 'Olopana's death, La'a came from Kahiki with 40+ men and sounded the "pahu drum at sea" off the Hawaiian Islands (the kā'eke or pahu kā'eke). He landed and lived at Kualoa. (Kamakau 1991:105–109). |

| Year | Source | Information |
|---|---|---|
| 1878 | Fornander | 'Olopana and Lu'ukia wed, Mo'ikeha was the grandson of Māweke [Fornander 1878, App. IX, Genealogy of Nana'ulu and Ulu] La'amaikahiki was the son of Ahukai and Keakamilo, both Hawaiians. [Fornander 1878:194]. |
| 1870s | Fornander | Mo'ikeha came from Moa'ulanuiākea, and his son was La'amaikahiki. 'Olopana and Lu'ukia arrived from Hawai'i, and Mo'ikeha took her. 'Olopana "became the prime minister of all the lands of Tahiti." A Tahitian (Mua) created discord between Lu'ukia and Mo'ikeha. Mo'ikeha sailed with Kamahualele (foster-son) and his priest Mo'okini. They arrived off Hilo, Kamahualele's chant was given, then people were dropped off along the islands. Mo'ikeha settled on Kaua'i and married into the Kaua'i ruler's family, and had 5 children. Mo'ikeha recalled La'a (his son) and sent his son Kila with Kamahualele to fetch La'a. Kila sailed to Moa'ulanuiākea and visited Lu'ukia. La'a was at "the mountain of Kapaahu." Kila heard the drum, Hāwea of Mo'ikeha, being sounded on kapu nights at La'a's residence, and realized that human sacrifices must follow. La'a went with Kila, bringing "his priests, his god Lonoikaoualii". As they approached Kaua'i, he had the drum beaten. He took the god to the temple with Mo'ikeha's high prest of Kaua'i—"it is said Laamaikahiki was the first person who brought idols to Hawaii" (128). La'a lived on Kaua'i, at Kahikinui on Maui, on Kaho'olawe, and then returned to Kaua'i. When Mo'ikeha died, and Kila assumed the rule of Kaua'i, La'a returned to Tahiti. The story continues with Kila's brothers abandoning him at Waipi'o, with Waipi'o and environs under the rule of Kunaka (128–152). La'a arrived on his second trip from Moa'ulanuiākea, coming for the bones of Mo'ikeha. He landed at Kā'iliki'i in Ka'ū on Hawai'i Island and sailed up along the Kona coast and on to Kaua'i—introducing hula dancing with drums (154). He returned to Kahiki with Kila and placed Mo'ikeha's bones in the mountain of Kapa'ahu. La'a and Kila remained in Kahiki until their death. ["The History of Moikeha," Fornander 1916–1917, 4(1):112–129]<br><br>Another story (154–159): 'Olopana ruled Hawai'i in Waipi'o (no O'ahu tie mentioned). He was married to Lu'ukia. A flood occurred, carrying them to sea and to Tahiti. Kapukini a chief of Puna was made the ruler on Hawai'i (156). Mo'ikeha and his wife Kapo were the king and queen of Tahiti at this time (156). 'Olopana and Lu'ukia were sent away by Mo'ikeha's uncle, and they returned to Hawai'i (156) and took up residence in Waipi'o. "It is said that Olopana brought the tabu system to these islands" (158).<br><br>Another story (160–173): Mo'ikeha sent Kila to Tahiti to slay old enemies. Makali'i of the net of food was Mo'ikeha's brother. Much fiction is in this story.<br><br>Another story (185), called a "rare version" by Fornander. 'Olopana andMo'ikeha were brothers and were Tahitian. Lu'ukia was also Tahitian. |

| Year | Source | Information |
|---|---|---|
| 1880 | Fornander | Muli'eleali'i's sons are Kumuhonua, 'Olopana and Mo'ikeha. The latter two established themselves on Hawai'i, where 'Olopana ruled in Waipi'o. Here 'Olopana married Lu'ukia, granddaughter of Hīkapoloa, chief of Kohala. Heavy storms in Waipi'o forced 'Olopana and Mo'ikeha to leave, and they sailed to Kahiki where 'Olopana ruled over a district called Moa'ulanuiākea. Mo'ikeha had brought La'amaikahiki (son of Ahukai) as an adopted son. [Fornander's attempt to identify this location: Kapa'ahu was the name of a nearby mountain where La'a was when Kila was sent by Mo'ikeha to bring La'a back to him. Moa tie suggested to Fornander Ava-Moa channel off Opoa on Raiatea—55, but Hawaiian legends make no mention of Opoa, its temple, or Oro, so Fornander concluded they were later in time, 51–52. Fornander could not place Kapa'ahu anywhere.] Mo'ikeha returned when slandered by a Kahiki chief, and the chant of Kamahualele (his astrologer) documents this return (9–10). The legends differ as to his followers, but they agree that places were named after them as they were landed along the islands. On Kaua'i Mo'ikeha married a chiefess and became ruler. He had seven boys.<br><br>One detailed story about Kila was collected (which has "later" embellishments, which Fornander does not identify). Kila went to bring La'a back to Mo'ikeha. In one version La'a returned with Kila, visits, and goes back to Kahiki (55). In another version, La'a came after the death of 'Olopana,with 40+ crew members and resided at Kualoa (55). [Fornander 1880:49–55] La'a introduced the large kā'eke drum when he returned, and it was used at heiau po'okanaka where human sacrifices were offered. [Fornander 1880:63] Lonoika'ouali'i was La'amaikahiki's god, which he brought. The image was taken to the heiau of Mo'ikeha. [Fornander 1880:60, note 8] Nā'ula-a-Maihea accompanied La'a. He was a feared sorceror. Nā'ula built a heiau at Waimalu on O'ahu. [Fornander 1880:42] |

**Table 6-4**

## Locations of the Voyages

| Voyager | From | To | References |
|---|---|---|---|
| 1. 'Olopana<br>Mo'ikeha<br>Lu'ukia | Kahiki (Mo'ikeha not a Hawaiian) | Kaua'i | 1840 Malo:7<br>1858 Pogue:6 |
| | O'ahu ('Olopana & Mo'ikeha) | Moa'ulanuiākea<br>Waihilia = inland | 1865 K:77 |
| | ? (Lu'ukia, a Hawaiian) | Kahiki (married 'Olopana, a Kahiki chief) | 1867 K:102 |
| | Waipi'o (all Hawn)[1]<br>Mo'ikeha returned, | Kahiki, land of Moa'ulanuiākea. | 1880 F:49–52 |

| Voyager | From | To | References |
|---|---|---|---|
| | landing first at Moa'ula in Ka'ū, and then went on eventually to Kaua'i. | Mtn. of Kapa'ahu. Fornander concluded Moa tie to Ava Moa channel at Opoa in Raiatea. | |
| | Kahiki (Mo'ikeha, uncertain if he is a returning Hawaiian, or from Kahiki) | Landed at Puna, dropped off followers along islands, and went to Kaua'i. | 1867 K:105–6<br>1870 FC 1919 6(2):323<br>1880 F:10–11[2] |
| | Hawai'i ('Olopana & Lu'ukia) Mo'ikeha arrived, dropped off followers from Puna on, and went to Kaua'i. | Moaulanuiakea (where Mo'ikeha resided) 'Olopana became ruler of "all the lands of Tahiti." Mtn. of Kapa'ahu | 1870s FC 4(1) 112–129 "The History of Moikeha"<br>1843 Dibble:9 |
| | Waipi'o ('Olopana & Lu'ukia) & returned to Waipi'o | Tahiti (where Mo'ikeha was king of Tahiti) | 1870s FC 4(1) 154–158 |
| 2. Kaumaili'ula Kaupe'a | Kohala & Kailua-Kona | Kuai-he-lani in Kahiki | 1867 K:102–103<br>1880 F:57–58. |
| 3. Ho'okamali'i Haulaninui-ai-akea Kila | All from Kaua'i. | Kahiki "Tahiti" | 1840 Malo:7<br>1858 Pogue:6<br>1843 Dibble:9<br>1866 K:77<br>1867 K:107<br>1880 F:55 |
| | Kaua'i | Moa'ulanuiākea. La'a lived at Mtn. of Kapa'ahu | 1870s FC 4(1) 112–129 "The History of Moikeha" |
| | Kaua'i (Kila) | Kahiki (to slay old enemies of Mo'ikeha). | 1870s FC 4(1) 160–173[4] |
| 4. La'amai-kahiki | Kahiki | [Assume Kaua'i] | 1840 Malo:7<br>1858 Pogue:6<br>1865 K:77 |
| | Kahiki | Passed along islands to Kaua'i, then to Kualoa to live. | 1867 K:107–108<br>1880 F:55 |
| | Kahiki | Kaua'i | 1880 F:55 |

| Voyager | From | To | References |
|---|---|---|---|
| | Kahiki at the Mtn. of Kapa'ahu in Moa'ulanuiākea then back to Kaua'i | Kaua'i, then to Kahikinui, then to Kaho'olawe, | 1870s FC 4(1) 126–128 "The History of Moikeha" |
| | Kahiki Bones of Mo'ikeha placed in mountain of Kapa'ahu | Landed at Ka'ū at Kā'iliki'i, then up along Kona, and to Kaua'i Returns to Kahiki w/ bones of Mo'ikeha. | 1870s F 4(1) 152–154 |
| | Waipi'o (as adopted son of Mo'ikeha) | Moa'ulanuiākea | 1880 F:49–51 |
| 5. Kaha'i-a-Ho'okamali'i | Pu'uloa on O'ahu | Pillars of Kahiki. Kahiki in Ulupaupau "to Kahiki and to the lands to the south—Wawau, Upolu and Savai'i." | 1865 K:77<br>1880 F:54<br>1898 Emerson in Malo:249, note 3. |
| | O'ahu | 'Upolu | 1867 K:110 |
| 6. Pā'ao Pili | Kahiki | unspecified | 1793 Puget<br>1843 Dibble:10<br>1878 F:86, 201 |
| | foreign | Kohala | 1823 Ellis:283 |
| | Kahiki "Tahiti" | Kohala | 1840 Malo:6–7<br>1858 Pogue:5<br>1868 Kepelino:20 |
| | Wawau,Upolu, and islands farther south, perhaps NZ. [Fornander concluded that lived in Upolu and owned land in Wawao and southern islds. Rejected NZ idea.] | Landed in Puna continued on to Kohala | 1866K:97–100<br>1880 F:34–35 |

| Voyager | From | To | References |
|---|---|---|---|
| 7. Kaulu-a-Kalana | O'ahu | Traveled throughout Kahiki, Wawau, Upolu, Pukalia-iki, Pukalia-nui, Alala, Pelua, Palana, Holani, Ku'ina, Ulunui, Uliuli, Melemele, Hi'ikua Hi'ialo, Hakalau'ai, to "the corals of Haluluko'ako'a." | 1866K:92 |
| 8. Paumakua | O'ahu | Ka'apuni Kahiki (around Kahiki), all lands outside Hawai'i. | 1866K:96<br>1880F:25–26 |
| 9. 'Olopana 2 Kahiki'ula | "Kahiki called Keolo'ewa Ha'enakula, 'Ina, & Kauaniani. Where these lands were is unknown; perhaps they were in Ke'e-nui-a-Kāne." | Kāne'ohe, O'ahu | 1867K:111<br>1880F:43 |
| 10. Keānini Ha'inakolo, f | Kuaihelani | Ni'ihau & Waipi'o | 1867K:103–104<br>1880F:56–57 |
| | Waipi'o | Kuaihelani | 1867K:103–104<br>1880F:56–57 |
| 11. Kamaunu-a-Niho Humu Kalana-nu'unui kua-maomao[3] | Kahiki (Humu returned to Kahiki) | Waihe'e, Maui | 1867K:111<br>1880F:43 |
| 12. Kamapi'ikai | Kohala | Haupokane | 1823E:284–285 |

Pogue = Pogue 1978; M = Malo 1951; K = Kamakau 1991; D = Dibble 1909; F = Fornander; FC = Fornander Collection 1916–1920; E = Ellis 1963.

1. La'amaikahiki was the adopted son of Mo'ikeha in this version and was taken to Kahiki.
2. Chant of Kamahualele is given by Fornander (1880:10–11) for this version.
3. Kamaunu and Kalana daughter (Hina) marries 'Olopana 2 of number 9.

was founded by Haho a Hawaiian chief on Maui.[81] Haho is nowhere documented as a voyager. His father, Paumakua of Maui, was considered by Fornander to be of a family of southern element,[82] but no accounts of him or his ancestors coming from Kahiki are presented in Fornander. Indeed, Fornander says the chants were silent on voyages associated with this Paumakua.[83] It seems that once Fornander had come up with the idea of voyagers bringing the elements of complex societies, he overlooked some of the traditions that he had collected.

Again, the Pāʻao and Laʻamakahiki traditions appear to contain the only references to items brought which related to the development of complex political and religious organization. A close look at these traditions shows what they actually state. Table 6-2 shows the Pāʻao-Pili accounts in chronological sequence. The early Hawaiian accounts of Malo, unspecified Lahainaluna students, and Kamakau, emphasize that Pāʻao, a priest, fetched Pili to be ruler. They mention the aku/ʻopelu schools of fish on the voyage which were said to have led to part of the kapu system of contact-era culture—a kapu associated with the strict religious cycle of Kū and Lono. Pāʻao is associated with Kohala and Puʻuepa and Moʻokini heiau. (Moʻokini was a national luakini or sacrificial heiau at contact, located in Puʻuepa ahupuaʻa.) He is also credited by Kamakau with building Wahaʻula heiau in western Puna. (Wahaʻula was also a national-level luakini at contact.) One chapter of the 1858 Lahainaluna moʻolelo ascribes new temple construction and forms of worship to Pāʻao, but this story also has contradictions, at one place saying idol worship began with Pāʻao and in another saying it began with Wākea who was much earlier in time. Kepelino seems to imply that images (new gods?) were instituted by Pāʻao, and he describes a major change in priesthood with old priests slain and Pāʻao establishing the line of priests which led to Hewahewa in Kamehameha's time (priests associated at European contact with Kūnuiākea and the luakini heiau). In 1880, Fornander added the following to Pāʻao's introductions: the walled heiau (Fornander's inference) and the pūloʻuloʻu balls of kapa as kapu markers before heiau and houses of priests and high chiefs. Also, Fornander assumed human sacrifice was introduced or increased in scale—but he did not associate this change with Pāʻao.[84] Indeed, none of the accounts recorded up to 1880 (that I reviewed) say that Pāʻao introduced human sacrifice—contrary to the belief commonly held today. All the above Hawaiian accounts fit reasonably with the two early recordings of Europeans—notably Puget's 1793 account of Pāʻao introducing a new type of heiau and form of worship.

As an aside, after the 1880s, many new elements were inserted into published versions of the Pāʻao/Pili account. Emerson began these changes in 1893 when he retold the story in his own words, with some embellishments, selectively including pieces of many earlier, differing accounts. He added the bringing of the god Kūkāʻilimoku.[85] In the early twentieth century, Westervelt similarly retold the story in his own words, selecting pieces of the old accounts and adding new parts. For example, he has Paʻao installing Pili as a ruler with a feather girdle on their arrival at Hilo Bay.[86] The feather girdle and the arrival of Pili at Hilo are both new elements. Another addition occurred by the 1930s–1940s when human sacrifice was said to have been brought by Pāʻao.[87] I consider most of these post-1890 accounts' new elements not to be reliable as authentic parts of the original story. The older accounts need to be used.

What seems to be documented in all the old stories is the addition of a new form of worship and its associated gods, temples and priesthood in the Kohala area of Hawaiʻi Island. Priests could not build such major heiau without a ruler's permission, so clearly all this was under the approval of a ruler—perhaps Pili? This religion and the ruler Pili's placement occur within a polity which already had complex political organization, probably headed by Hīkapoloa's descendants. Perhaps the prior government was overthrown, which might account for Kepelino's story of the slaying of the earlier priests. Other Hawaiʻi Island polities may not have been directly affected by these changes in Kohala. Importantly, the accounts do not specify how strict the Pāʻao religion was at this time or if human sacrifice occurred, or on what scale. All these accounts clearly realized that by European contact the Pāʻao-introduced form of religion had become strict, and had human sacrifice; but none specifically claim that Pāʻao brought his religion in the form found at European contact.

The La'amaikahiki stories—linked with those of 'Olopana, Mo'ikeha, and Kila, collectively called the stories of 'Olopana ma from here on—have multiple variations (Table 6-3). But in most versions, La'amaikahiki brings a kā'eke drum and a god, adding them to the existing pattern of worship. So, these accounts do not show a dramatic change in religion or political organization.

Thus, the Pā'ao-Pili and 'Olopana ma traditions demonstrate new religious elements added to an existing religious system, and the establishment of a "foreign chief" (Pili) over a single polity, one that was already complex. Yet despite these points and despite the fact that Fornander had other traditions showing that a change to complex societies dominated by Hawaiians had already begun in the islands, the idea of a foreign-caused and completely foreign-dominated change to complex societies was placed in the literature by Fornander. This model of culture change never seems to have been challenged.

Before proceeding, the place of origin of the foreign contacts needs discussion, because this is critical to the foreign-dominated social revolution concept. Table 6-4 notes the places traveled to and from by voyagers. From early European contact times on, it was clear to both Hawaiians and foreigners with a knowledge of the Pacific that Hawaiian culture had developed from some other Polynesian culture—as they shared the same general physical appearance, gods, manners and customs, and substantially the same language.[88] Hawaiians and Euro-american residents of Hawai'i by the early 1800s learned of other Polynesian groups from Polynesians who arrived as crew on foreign ships, from Hawaiians who went abroad, from sailors who had been elsewhere in Polynesia, from Tahitian missionaries who had a large influence in Hawai'i in the 1820s–1830s,[89] and from European exploration and mission accounts. It is important to emphasize that Hawaiian and European knowledge of other Polynesian cultures was hardly as thorough and well-known as it is today—then it was an emerging knowledge, even by the 1890s. This factor plays an important role in evaluating the Hawaiian voyaging traditions.

At European contact, despite having foreign lands named in their traditions and chants, Hawaiians did not know where the place Kahiki was. "Of geography they knew nothing beyond the limits of their own islands."[90] But as a search for the source of the voyaging traditions began, attempts were made to match names and place names in the Hawaiian traditions with known names and place names in other Polynesian islands. The extent of individual researchers' knowledge of the place names of other islands and of their oral history and culture affected the conclusions. For example, one of the first to make such an attempt was the Rev. Dibble of Lahainaluna in 1843. He concluded the following place name matches (place name in Hawaiian accounts first): Kahiki = Society Islands (more properly probably Tahiti), Polapola = Borabora in the Societies, Nuuhiva = the Marquesas (more properly probably Nuku Hiva island), Vavau = the Vavau Islands (in Tonga), 'Upolu = Upolu in the Navigator Islands (Samoa).[91] Dibble also noted that the name Hawaii frequently appeared in the Society Islands' oral histories, that the initial names in the royal genealogies of the Society Islands and in Hawai'i were similar, and that the names of the gods were the same (e.g., Lono = Rono, Kanaloa = Ta'angaloa).[92] Thus, Dibble concluded Pā'ao was from the Society Islands, as were Mo'ikeha and La'amaikahiki—the three voyagers that he mentions.[93]

These two cases—the Pā'ao-Pili and the 'Olopana ma stories—contained place names that Fornander and others also attempted to identify. With Pā'ao and Pili, Table 6-4 shows that the early accounts only said they were from Kahiki. Ca. 1843 Dibble concluded that this Kahiki was the Society Islands. But 20 years later, in 1865, Kamakau concluded Pā'ao and Pili came from Wawau in Tonga, Upolu in Samoa and from islands farther south, perhaps New Zealand. He did not identify other voyagers' origins in his newspaper articles—he simply published the Hawaiian voyaging account. In 1880 Fornander concluded the voyagers came from Samoa, the Marquesas, and the Society Islands.[94] He specifically addressed the Pā'ao/Pili and 'Olopana ma accounts. For the Pā'ao/Pili account Fornander rejected New Zealand as a possibility. He selected Upolu as Pā'ao's residence and agreed with Kamakau that it was Upolu island in Samoa.[95] He argued that Pā'ao had simply owned lands in Wava'u, agreeing with

Kamakau that this was in Tonga. In the case of ʻOlopana ma, Fornander very cautiously suggested that the location Moaʻulanuiākea which ʻOlopana and Moʻikeha traveled to might be tied to the Ava Moa, the harbor entrance at Opoa on Raiatea.[96]

In the 1890s, historians argued further about the migrations and the source of these voyagers. The Hawaiian Historical Society was a center for these discussions—with papers written by members Nathaniel Emerson and W. D. Alexander, and by guest speakers S. Percy Smith of New Zealand and Teiura Henry of Tahiti. Clearly all talked with each other on this subject. Emerson suggested the Marquesas for the ʻOlopana ma, asking if Moaʻulanuiākea might not be Omoa district on Fatuhiva.[97] The papers Teiura Henry presented show that she saw many similarities between Hawaiian and Society Island culture—similarities in dance and amusements.[98] In a 1897 paper she referred to the places Vavau and Upolu in the Kaulu-a-Kalana chant published by Fornander, saying, "It has already been shown that Vavau and Uporu were formerly the names of Porapora and Tahaa" in the Societies.[99] Henry also said that ʻOlopana's Moaʻulanuiākea—as published in Fornander—probably was on the northern shore of the island of Tahiti.[100] Henry matched Moaʻulanuiākea with the ancient name of Tahara'a district on Tahiti, Mou'auranuiatea or Mou'a-ura. And she further noted that nearby Pare district on the north shore was the "cradle and birthplace" of the powerful Oropaa family (Oropaa meaning strong warrior), and implied that this family was descended from the Hawaiian ʻOlopana. Last, she said the mountain Kapaʻahu in Hawaiian legend may be the Tapahi range of hills on the northeast side of Mt. Moua-ura-nui-atea—although the lack of correspondence of Tapahi and Kapaʻahu is not discussed. The prevailing view in both these cases was still that a wave of chiefs from foreign lands changed and dominated Hawaiian culture, leading to the formation of complex societies.

S. Percy Smith seems to play a key role in these findings and in those of slightly later times. From New Zealand, he was interested in Maori origins and the origins of the Polynesians. He used language, oral histories and place names to trace origins and was considered a great authority in his time—1890s–1920s.[101] In an 1897 paper given to the Hawaiian Historical Society, he agreed with Fornander that there were two migrations. He concluded that the first migration to Hawai'i had likely come from the Societies due to people of nearly the same name, Manahune in the Societies versus the first people in Hawai'i "known by the name Menehune."[102] He did not note the source of Hawai'i's second migration other than emphasizing that they came out of Fiji to Samoa and into Central Polynesia ca. A.D. 1100–1350 and were a people "endowed with greater force of character, being more warlike and possessed of greater ability."[103] However, by the 1920s—if not much earlier—Smith had concluded that the Maori had come from the Society Islands and that Samoa was not the key place in Polynesia's second migration. By that time, he was arguing the Havaii, Upolu and Vavau places mentioned in legends of New Zealand were the old names for Raiatea, Tahaa, and Borabora in the Society Islands.[104] He may have even been the source Henry was referring to in 1897 for her conclusion.

The Tahitian location of Moa'ulanuiākea in the Hawaiian 'Olopana ma stories, as argued for by Henry continued to be followed by many researchers into the 1930s–1940s. In 1928 there was an addition, that Pā'ao must have come from Raiatea, also in the Society Islands.[105] In the 1920s Stokes wrote several papers, focusing on three feathered belts or girdles in the Bishop Museum.[106] The result of this work was a revised conclusion on Pā'ao's and Pili's homeland. In one article, Stokes looked at the Pā'ao stories from multiple sources, including twentieth century versions such as Westervelt. He concluded that Pā'ao introduced the pūlo'ulo'u (kapa markers of kapu places), the prostrating kapu, a new walled enclosure temple form, human sacrifice, and Kā'ilimoku as the war god.[107] He decided that these traits were more characteristic of the Society Islands and its more complex societies than any other Polynesian culture. Also, Stokes said the feather belts in the Museum were used in the investiture of Pili-line kings, based on information in Westervelt which said Pili was installed with such a belt, claims by some 1918 informants that one belt was supposedly the ruler Līloa's, and a note written by Kalākaua which said Līloa invested his son 'Umi with such a belt.[108] Since the only other place in Polynesia which used such girdles that Stokes knew of was the Society Islands—with

Raiatea and its Oro cult and kin groups as the center of such practices—Stokes concluded that Pili was "a scion of the sacred royal family of Raiatea."[109] Since one account of Pāʻao placed his home as Savaiʻi (no reference was given by Stokes) and since the ancient name of Raiatea was Hawaiʻi according to Percy Smith, this seemed to clinch the Raiatea tie for Pāʻao in Stokes' view.[110] Stokes ended by stating that Kahiki must have meant the Society Islands to Hawaiians of the voyaging period—although Stokes acknowledged that by European contact Kahiki meant any foreign country to Hawaiians.

In the 1930s–1940s, this theory of the chiefly migration wave was consolidated by Handy, Buck and then Beckwith.[111] Handy's and Buck's theories for the settlement of Polynesia—although slightly different—saw the Society Islands, with its well-known elite, complex societies as the center of East Polynesia society.[112] As seen in Chapter 4, they too argued for an initial wave of settlers into the Society Islands that were low in rank and improverished in culture. They gave this group the name manahune, the Tahitian name for commoners at European contact. Buck felt these people lacked agriculture and livestock. Both argued these manahune had simple temples—a small court with a rectangular altar at one end with uprights. Archaeological surveys in the Society Islands in the 1920s–1930s had determined that this temple type was found solely in the inland areas; large temples were on the shore.[113] Buck and Handy concluded these people spread throughout East Polynesia, and in Hawaiʻi were the menehune (the little people of Hawaiian legends), following Smith's notation of the word's similarity to manahune. Also because a similar type of simple temple with an altar and uprights was found in Hawaiʻi and assumed to be early (found on Necker by Emory and Cartwright—and later near Mauna Kea's summit at an adze quarry and at one site on Mauna Loa on Hawaiʻi and at one location on Maui).[114] To explain the development of complex societies in Tahiti at European contact—with levels of chiefs (ariʻi), large temples and associated human sacrifice, feathered belts as emblems of chiefs, double-hulled canoes (pahi), etc.—Buck and Handy, like Smith and Fornander, had a second migration wave arrive in the Society Islands—a chiefly migration wave. These arrivals with their superior culture swept the manahune into the interior of the islands (thus the small inland temples) and established their own chiefly culture. Since Raiatea and its cult to the gods Ta'aroa and Oro at Opoa was firmly described in Society Island oral accounts as the key sacred place and the original place of kin groups of the highest status, in the hypotheses of Handy and Buck Raiatea was where the chiefly wave first became centered. Handy believed this center on Raiatea began in the late A.D. 500s–600s.[115] Oro had human offerings, and the sacred temple of Taputapuatea in Opoa was an important ritual structure. Buck and Handy then have members of this chiefly wave bear their culture of large temples, human sacrifice, red-feather girdles, and high status kin groups on to Hawai'i, where the migration wave became the Hawaiian ali'i—forcing the menehune out of power.[116] Both, as others before them, felt this chiefly wave was seen in the Hawaiian voyaging traditions, as documented by Fornander. Clearly to them, as to Stokes, Pā'ao came from Opoa on Raiatea (Havai'i) bringing large temples and human sacrifice, and 'Olopana-Mo'ikeha-La'amaikahiki lived on northern Tahiti.[117]

By 1940, Beckwith states this migration as fact in her *Hawaiian Mythology* book, saying the late Hawaiian voyages were definitely migrations from the Society Islands—firmly documented in old Hawaiian chants/legends, linguistic identities (place names), and in corresponding forms of culture (human sacrifice, walled temples, and red-feather girdles) which characterize the Raiatea ritual.[118] She concludes similarly that these migrants from the Societies brought "their superior culture to the simpler islanders on Hawaii."[119]

Notably, these hypotheses again saw similar waves of settlement fanning out from the Society Islands to New Zealand, the southern Cooks, the northern Cooks, the Marquesas, etc. It is important to emphasize again that this migration wave theory for culture change was the theory of the day—established in Polynesia by Fornander, S. Percy Smith and others in the 1890s.

These migration wave theories with Tahiti as the homeland of all Eastern Polynesia held on through the 1940s and 1950s. Linguistic work by Emory and Elbert formed some of the basis of these ideas. In the early 1950s, Elbert's analysis identified an east-west division among Polynesian languages, and he saw the eastern language's proto-speakers living together for several centuries before dispersing. He selected the Society Islands as the likely place they lived together, due to its central location[120]—and perhaps due to its central role in existing theories. He used a date for dispersal to be ca. A.D. 1000, based on Emory's draft manuscript, the "Origin of the Hawaiians," in which Emory used the voyaging traditions (34 generations before 1900, 25 years/generation) and a pending radiocarbon date.

Emory's manuscript was published in 1959, and at that time, he had just received some of the first archaeological dates for Hawai'i from the earliest layers in several Hawaiian sites, with these dates going back to the A.D. 800s–1000s. Since these seemed to be settlement dates and seemed to match the time period of the migration traditions, Emory concluded that there was no earlier settlement prior to these traditions (essentially no Nana'ulu period), and that the menehune were actually commoner crews on these voyages. Very importantly, he also concluded that the Hawai'i loa stories of earlier settlement were post-European stories, as neither Malo nor Ellis had recorded such stories and the stories included elements of clear European influence.[121] Still the Society Islands were seen as the center for the voyages to Hawai'i, as documented in the traditions and given Elbert's shared vocabulary of 76% (versus 71% with New Zealand and 70% with the Marquesas).[122] Not much later, earlier dates were found in Hawai'i, re-establishing the hypothesis of an earlier migration from Tahiti, but the menehune and Hawai'i loa seem not to have arisen again in academic discussions of the earlier period.

By the late 1960s, the Hawaiian migration theory changed due to archaeological evidence. In the 1950s and 1960s, Kenneth Emory and his student Yosihiko Sinoto had been searching for archaeological clues to evaluate the Tahitian migrations. The discovery of rich cave and sand dune sites in Hawai'i—the O1 cave of O'ahu and the H8 cave and H1 dune of Hawai'i—led to the identification of an apparent change in Hawaiian fishhooks, adzes, and ornaments.[123] Early layers seemed to have hooks with notched attachments, untanged adzes of multiple cross-sections, and whale-tooth pendants of simple types. Later layers were dominated by knobbed hooks, tanged adzes of quadrangular cross-section, and whale- and porpoise-tooth pendants of elaborate types (e.g., lei niho palaoa). Dates estimated the change in fishhook style at A.D. 1200s–1500s.

In the early 1960s, work in the Society Islands attempted to locate comparable artifacts. Burials were found at Maupiti Island which dated to the A.D. 700s–900s and contained a knobbed fishhook and simple pendant types.[124] These artifact types were concluded to be evidence of items that were brought to Hawai'i by Tahitian voyagers of the second migration—most notably the knobbed fishhook style. Also, looking at genealogies of Hawai'i again, Emory and Sinoto suggested an A.D. 1100s–1300s date for the migration era.[125] They also reiterated the point made by Stokes in 1928, saying that Hawai'i's elaborate "political organization, temple forms and religious rituals" were "closer to Tahitian culture than either Maori or Marquesan."[126]

In the midst of this search for evidence of the early homeland's culture in Tahiti came the shock of the findings of Robert Suggs's work in the Marquesas.[127] He had uncovered an early settlement with pottery and artifacts—including whale- and porpoise-tooth pendants of simple types—dating back to the B.C. 200s. Quickly, Sinoto began work in the Marquesas and found similar cultural remains—although not quite as early as Suggs's.[128] Despite continued work in the Society Islands, no remains earlier than the A.D. 700s have yet been discovered.[129] Linguistic research has also more recently pointed to the Marquesas as the homeland for Hawai'i.[130] So today, the first half of the old Tahitian migration wave settlement theory for Hawai'i is gone. But into the 1970s, the second wave from Tahiti was still held to be true—marked archaeologically primarily by the knobbed fishhooks.

Here, one must start to unravel the migration theory models. First and most critical, Stokes's, Handy's, Buck's and Beckwith's list of complex society traits—large temples, human sacrifice, red-feather girdles and high status kin groups—can all be thrown out immediately as not being Society Island introductions to Hawai'i in the 1200s–1300s. More recent, careful analyses of Tahitian historical and genealogical information have shown that complex societies in the Society Islands arose much more recently—in the A.D. 1600s–1700s.[131] The rise of the high chiefs of Raiatea and their cult at Opoa with large temples, human sacrifice and feather girdles were all recent.[132] Thus, Tahitian culture in the A.D. 1200s–1300s—the time of the Hawaiian voyaging traditions—lacked the complexity that Stokes, Handy and others thought it had. The set of items Handy and others had Tahitians and Raiateans bringing to Hawai'i did not exist at that time in the Society Islands.[133] There was no Oro cult with human sacrifice, and there were no large temples in the Society Islands at that time. Taputapuatea marae was either not present, or not large.[134] People in the Society Islands could not have brought a "superior culture" with these items, because they had only simple-ranked polities at that time—not district- or island-sized polities and complex social stratification.[135] Indeed, Hawai'i's polities with its Hawaiian-controlled levels of chiefs and district-sized polities were actually more stratified than Society Island polities in those years. Clearly, Fornander's more generalized traits—southern voyagers bringing the concept of island-sized polities under powerful rulers, strong kapus, restricted worship with human sacrifice, and strong social stratification must also be disregarded. So the Tahitian migration model of complex political organization being brought from the Society Islands, which was founded in the 1880s and modified in the 1920s–1930s—with the 1920s–1930s version still popularized today—is based on erroneous information.

Archaeological work in Hawai'i has similarly shown that large temples of Society Island architectural styles did not suddenly appear and dominate temple forms in the Hawaiian Islands in the 1200s–1300s. In fact, after years of research on Hawaiian temples, it is apparent that major national-level Hawaiian temples were not similar to major national-level Society Island temples.[136] Today with the benefit of excavation of more heiau on Hawai'i Island and notably on Maui, no temples in the style of major Society Island types have appeared. The few early Hawaiian temples found are small platforms, pavings or enclosures—dating A.D. 1000s–1300s.[137] We have, as yet, not identified earlier temples. One temple on Maui from ca. 1300 was a larger paving. In the 1400s, national-level temples dramatically increased in size. None have the Society Island style of large coral slab-lined altars or tiered altars with uprights at one end of a court—which again is not surprising, as large temple types did not develop in the Society Islands for another 200 years. The larger Hawaiian temples of the 1400s were platforms, or enclosures, simply larger versions of the Hawaiian forms seen in the 1000s–1300s.

Also, the knobbed fishhook does not suddenly appear in Hawaiian sites during the 1300s–1400s as evidence of the arrival of Tahitians. It appears in the earliest levels of Hawai'i's earliest sites.[138] Indeed, there is no evidence of Society Island influence on fishing gear in general.

> *Other aspects of Hawaiian fishhook technology such as material, barb patterns, use of TPH [two-piece hooks] and so on do not seem to have been influenced by the tradition of the Societies. These traditions are contradictory to the assumption that there was an influence from the Societies.*
>
> (Goto 1986)[139]

Nor have other major aspects of culture shown foreign influxes archaeologically in the 1200s–1300s, or at any time until contact.

As for the three Hawaiian feathered belts being evidence of a Society Islands introduction of royal investiture in the 1200s–1300s, one must again note that such a complex society investiture in the Society Islands did not arise until the late 1600s. The age of the Hawaiian belts is far from established. Other featherwork items (helmets, cloaks and capes) seem rarely to be much older in confirmed age than the 1700s.[140] It would be surprising if the one intact Hawaiian specimen (1910.18.01) is older than the 1700s, if that, given its excellent condition.[141] Some oral historical sources attribute one belt to the time of Līloa and 'Umi—A.D. 1580–1620—but these oral testimonies are recent (1918, based on 1870s recollections), and other contemporary versions are very contradictory, including associations with late 1700s and early 1800s rulers.[142] No informants place the age of these Hawaiian feather belts back to the 1300s. Also, the Hawaiian belts are made with feathers of Hawaiian birds and are different in style from Society Island maro ʻura used at European contact.[143] The Hawaiian cases are not even confirmed to have been used for royal investiture; that is a conclusion solely of Kalākaua in the 1880s and his Board of Genealogy,[144] certainly after he became aware that feather belts were the important royal item in the Societies. Thus, although fascinating objects, the Hawaiian feather belts certainly do not support a hypothesis of Society Island introduction of royal investiture in the 1300s.

Thus, to answer the question, "Do the Hawaiian voyaging traditions document the establishing of a culture of powerful rulers and chiefs (social stratification with kapu), restricted religion with human sacrifce and large temples, and island-sized polities by a chiefly foreign migration wave—particularly from the Society Islands?" They do not. This model of culture change in Hawaiʻi was largely developed in the 1880s–1930s, although it continued until the 1970s. Much of this model assumed complex societies and associated traits were present in the Society Islands in the A.D. 1200s–1300s, but more recent research shows that they did not develop in the Societies until the 1600s–1700s. The Hawaiian traditions do note that Pāʻao, a foreign priest, introduced new religious elements and a new priestly order, and established Pili over a polity in Kohala. But archaeology indicates that larger temples were not introduced from foreign lands. Also, larger district-sized and island-sized polities were not introduced, nor was more complex social stratification. Hawaiian traditions show these developments were already beginning in the Hawaiian Islands in the 1200s and early 1300s, before Pili's arrival. The traditions also describe no massive arrival or replacement by Society Island chiefs. Pili is the only foreign chief who becomes a ruler. Other similar polities were ruled by Hawaiians.

Two or three decades ago, scholars of the Society Islands' culture threw out the idea of migration waves to explain Tahitian cultural development.[145] There is no evidence of an earlier manahune culture being radically displaced by a chiefly culture.[146] Indeed, one of the pre-eminent scholars on Society Islands' culture has stated bluntly that Handy's model of conquest by a superior ari'i culture was "overly simplistic, undocumented, and quite unnecessary."[147] Current theory is that the settling population gradually developed into the complex political culture of European contact[148]—certainly with one or several canoeloads of other nearby Polynesians (Samoans, Cook Islanders, Austral Islanders, Tuamotuans, etc.) occasionally arriving, trading and merging with the populace as amply documented by oral historical, historical and archaeological evidence.

Migration wave theory has actually died away in all areas of Polynesia in favor of models of internal development or complex interactions—except in Hawai'i. In New Zealand, two waves were perceived from the 1890s until the 1960s—and still are by some of the public in New Zealand. But superb and meticulous research with late 1800s Maori tribal records—manuscripts written in Maori—showed that the second wave was actually a series of internal movements of Maori polities within New Zealand, not a wave of new immigrants.[149] Anthropologists in New Zealand (led in part by S. Percy Smith) in the late 1800s misinterpreted the information they had and developed an erroneous two-wave theory. And this published scientific theory was widely read and became accepted as fact by the New Zealand public and by many Maori.

Migration wave theory needs to now give way in the Hawaiian Islands. Clearly, early anthropologists developed erroneous interpretations of the Hawaiian voyaging traditions. These traditions did not describe vast fleets of superior foreigners changing Hawaiian culture and developing the islands' complex societies. I believe we are clinging to the remnants of an overly romanticized and long outdated migration theory—the only place in the Pacific still to do so. In the central islands of east Polynesia, it is now recognized that each island group developed their own patterns of culture and that complex interactions also occurred—exchange, immigration of small groups, stranding of voyagers, etc. For the extreme outlying islands of Polynesia (Hawai'i, Easter Island and New Zealand), two views are now emerging—one claiming these islands developed their forms of culture in isolation, and the other stating that they developed their own culture but that occasional foreign arrivals (from the Cooks, Societies, Marquesas, and other islands) landed throughout prehistory. The former assumes no voyages after initial settlement (due to the extreme distance to the islands and new wave and star patterns precluding successful inclusion of the islands in localized navigational systems—not because canoes were incapable of making the voyages). The latter view assumes voyaging was easier and more frequent. Neither view, however, argues for migration waves which greatly changed culture.

The questions that now must be raised are, "Where were Pāʻao and Pili and the few other foreign voyagers from?" and, "Is there any evidence of foreign arrivals?" Potential information comes from archaeology, ethnobotany, linguistics and place names.

I believe that there is as yet no solid archaeological evidence showing external contact in the Hawaiian Islands after initial settlement. However, a few scholars have suggested evidence of sporadic contact. Knobbed fishhook styles have been suggested to be one foreign introduction in the 1300s from the Societies or Cook Islands, but these fishhook styles were present in early sites and do not show sudden change. Octopus lures with coffee-bean-shaped sinkers have been suggested as evidence of late Marquesan contact,[150] but the time placement for such lures in Hawaiʻi and the Marquesas is far from clear, and the study of this artifact type is still preliminary. Quoits (notched disk gamestones) are said to be evidence of contact with the Society Islands. But this is based on 5 quoits in Raiatea and 15 in the Hawaiian Islands, and no published study of these quoits exists.[151] The vast number of Hawaiian gamestones are unnotched disks (ulumaika). There is no time placement of quoits.[152] Emory argues that their rarity indicates them to be archaic, but they could as easily be independent inventions, or post-contact introductions. Temple syles also have been noted—the small Society Island–style altar platform with uprights seemingly appearing in a few cases in Hawaiʻi. For years, this was considered the initial form of temple brought by the settlers of Hawaiʻi from the Society Islands, but the Societies are no longer considered the initial source of the

Hawaiian settlement population. In fact, these types of temples are not yet dated in Hawai'i (except indirectly at the Mauna Kea adze quarry where they date no earlier than the A.D. 1100s, and more likely after the A.D. 1400s). Their age in the Societies, Tuamotus and other central Polynesian islands is not clear. In Hawai'i, these may simply be versions of a common Polynesian pattern of one or more uprights on an altar that independently developed into many variations—fishing shrines with kū'ula stones, pōhaku o Kāne with one upright stone, and occupation shrines at Mauna Kea with one or several uprights. They may not reflect foreign introductions. Indeed, Emory in 1970 changed his position and suggested the forms may have been introduced at settlement by Marquesans.[153]

One important point to note is that only these few artifact types or styles have been suggested as evidence of contact. If there was contact, one would assume that other more commonly used artifacts of foreign styles would also appear—such as food pounders, ornaments, clothing, headdresses, adzes, weapons, image styles, etc. Yet, they do not. Distinctive Marquesan and Tahitian cultural items of the A.D. 800s–1200s, such as hand clubs (patu) and harpoons, do not appear. Nor do late Tahitian items such as Tahitian food pounders with their distinctive cross-bar.[154] Nor do Marquesan pounders with their distinctive image knobs. Adzes do not show sudden replacement by foreign-favored styles (e.g., the popular reversed triangular adzes of the later period in the Society Islands). Stone used in tool making in Hawai'i that has been sourced by geologists so far is from Hawaiian stone sources.[155] Central Polynesian headgear forms with high frontlets, image forms, and ornament styles do not appear. Thus, no archaeological evidence as yet clearly shows foreign arrivals in this 1300s–1400s period—or in any period until European contact.[156] Such evidence might eventually be found, but the situation is as yet not clear.

Neither does botany yet show any arrivals. If foreigners arrived and brought popular new crops, these arrivals would be expected to proliferate and possibly appear later in the pollen record in Hawaiian sites or swamps.[157] As yet, however, no such evidence of foreign crops arriving has been found.[158] Many varieties of important and popular crops in Central Polynesia were not present in Hawai'i at contact. If Tahitians had come, then as Yen points out[159] why were the red kī plant forms not brought, since they were sacred in Central East Polynesia and surely were known and would have been brought by priests. Only the green kī (ti, *Cordyline fruticosa L.*) was in Hawai'i prior to Cook's arrival. Also, the vast varieties of bananas and breadfruit found in Central Polynesia were not brought to Hawai'i, including the fe'i banana of Tahiti.[160] These patterns run counter to expectation if voyagers had come from or gone to Central Polynesia, since one would expect new food crops and other important plants to have been brought back.

While most researchers have followed the idea that the sweet potato was introduced at initial settlement, it was suggested in the 1970s that rapid settlement expansion to the leeward sides of the islands of Hawai'i and Maui in the A.D. 1200s–1300s must have been due to the foreign introduction of the sweet potato.[161] More recently, it has been suggested that this crop was present in the Cook Islands in the 1000s–1200s and came to Hawai'i from the Cooks.[162] Recent archaeological dates from Hawai'i, however, show that the permanent occupation and farming of dry leeward lands began by the A.D. 900s–1200s on Hawai'i Island, and pollen cores on O'ahu show leeward settlement by the A.D. 1000s, if not earlier.[163] Green has suggested that more fertile leeward areas could have been settled with taro cultivation and that one should look to arid areas where permanent settlement and associated cultivation could have only been based on sweet potato, and to determine when settlement began in these areas. Such areas are very restricted—e.g., dry leeward Kohala on Hawai'i and the 'Ewa Plain on O'ahu, and the islands of Kaho'olawe and Ni'ihau. Limited dates suggest permanent settlement of dry leeward Kohala beginning in the 1200s–1400s, the 'Ewa Plain after the 1400s, and Kaho'olawe in the late 1500s.[164] No clear pattern appears. Thus, it would appear that most massive settlement changes cannot easily be linked to a foreign introduction of sweet potato at this time. Dating of carbonized sweet potato remains may be useful in evaluating this question, but currently few such remains have been dated in Hawai'i or Central Polynesia, so we cannot evaluate how long the plants have been present in either place. Work on dating such remains has just started in Central Polynesia in the Cook Islands, and already its antiquity has been pushed back to the A.D. 900s–1100s.[165] Thus, this question of when the sweet potato was introduced is not clearly resolved. Currently, an equally viable and simpler explanation would be that it was present at initial settlement, and people settling the leeward sides of major islands used taro and sweet potato in various combinations.

Strikingly, I have seen no evidence in published Tahitian oral histories and genealogies which shows knowledge of Hawai'i or the arrival of Hawaiians. Shared names early in royal genealogies of Hawai'i and the Societies probably show nothing more than a sharing of East Polynesian origin accounts of man and chiefs.[166] More thorough study is needed to determine if this sharing is unique to the Societies and Hawai'i. The name Olopa'a appearing in a Tahitian genealogy also is not convincing evidence of contact, for 'Olopana is a name found in many areas of Polynesia. Shared names for deities and general customs—as noted by Dibble—only shows the basic underpinning of East Polynesian culture. All, or nearly all, East Polynesian societies share major deities and many customs. This was evidently information not yet available to Dibble in 1843. Cook asked Tahitians and navigators if there were any known islands to the north or to the northwest, but they said they knew of none.[167] Surely, Hawaiian chiefs would have made an impact in the Societies. Yet, the Society Island traditions are silent on such arrivals. To my knowledge, no one has carefully looked at other East Polynesian oral histories and genealogies for evidence of Hawaiian contact at any point in prehistory.

Linguistics has yet to show whether foreigners arrived. As Green[168] has noted, the common approach of studying ties between languages through percentage of shared words does not work well within the the societies of East Polynesia; their languages are so similar that significant percentages cannot yet be determined. Green's research in the 1960s suggested that Hawaiian grammar was most similar to Marquesan.[169] More recent work apparently has confirmed a strong Marquesan connection based on sound shift forms.[170] These patterns are what would be expected if Marquesans were the initial settlers in Hawai'i and population had grown. Evidence of other contact is debatable. Emory and Green have suggested borrowing from the Society Islands, but linguists have questioned this conclusion.[171] The current status of opinion on borrowing is unclear to me. Green has also suggested that the Cook Island term for the sweet potato shows linkage to Hawai'i with the Hawaiian term deriving from the Cooks.[172] This new conclusion needs presentation and careful evaluation by linguists. Thus, future linguistic work may play a role in addressing this question.

A new line of evidence is just starting to be used to trace distributions over time—DNA analysis of rat bone. In a 1995 presentation, Green[173] cites a yet unpublished study, which he believes shows two separate sources of the origin of rat populations in Hawai'i—one from the Marquesas region and one from the Cook-Societies-Tuamotus region. He indicates that this must have happened early in time in Hawai'i—before the 1200s–1300s.[174] These findings are of interest. When they are published, they too will certainly bear careful consideration.

One line of evidence for outside contact in the 1200s–1300s comes from the Hawaiian oral traditions—place names in those stories which researchers have attempted to link to locations in Central Polynesia.[175] Arguing settlement ties by using place names—without other evidence showing a direct historical settlement tie—is extremely suspect in my view. There are many names shared by most Polynesian cultures—Hawaii (Savaii, Havaii, Hawai'i), Upolu (Uporu, 'Upolu, Upo'u), Moa'ula, etc.[176] Many of these may reflect the original Polynesian homeland in West Polynesia, and have no connection among themselves. For example, Hawai'i in the Hawaiian Islands and Havai'i (if truly the old name of Raiatea) in the Society Islands may both reflect recollections of Savai'i in Samoa—and not reflect Hawaiians coming from Raiatea. This is much like the place name Athens or Sparta across the European/Euro-American world. Historical connections are purely speculative without other evidence showing a direct settlement tie. Thus, in my view, place name evidence by itself is not solid evidence.[177]

The Hawaiian stories, themselves, are seen to be one source of evidence of foreign contact. There are those of the 1200s–1300s (covered here), earlier, more mythical stories (e.g., Wahanui, Hema), and a very few arrivals late in prehistory (e.g., people landing off south Kona).[178] All can be suggestive of limited arrivals throughout prehistory, if the stories are literally correct.[179] Certainly, the possibility exists that the oral histories do in fact refer to foreign contact. However, the striking lack of evidence in the archaeological, botanical and Tahitian oral historical records at this time requires one to consider alternatives. If these oral histories do not refer to actual voyages from lands outside Hawai'i, what could they refer to? One alternative is that these are symbolic, heavily fictionalized versions of internal events and changes. Studies with oral traditions in African complex societies have identified three periods of oral stories: an early mythological era, then an era of migrations with migrants bringing the social institutions of complex societies (basically stories which are largely symbolic in establishing the final era's social institutions), and then that final era which is a history of kings, battles, revolts and the like.[180] Independent of these studies, scholars in Hawai'i have recognized an early mythological period when the gods are present and culture heroes are associated with the gods, then the voyaging period, and last the dynastic period of kings, battles and revolts.[181] Perhaps the Hawaiian voyaging traditions of the 1200s–1300s are in part local events which have been made into symbolic accounts that document the establishing of some social institutions (Pā'ao and La'amaikahiki) and the rise of certain families (Pili on Hawai'i; the hero chiefs of O'ahu and Kaua'i, Māweke's descendants: 'Olopana, Mo'ikeha, Kila, La'amaikahiki; and even some hero chiefs of Hawai'i—Kaumaili'ula of Kohala). To me, the content of most voyaging accounts seem indeed to simply be stories of such hero chiefs. The exception is the Pā'ao account which seems to document social institution changes in Kohala on Hawai'i Island.

A second alternative is that perhaps the foreign lands in the 1200s–1300s stories refer to some of the other many small polities that were present in Hawai'i. For example, Puna polities would be distant foreign lands to small polities on Kaua'i. Perhaps Pā'ao could have developed his new, sterner religion in the lands near Kīlauea to try to cope with the devastation of the volcano. These lands have places with the names Kapa'ahu and Moa'ula. Waha'ula heiau, associated by some with Pā'ao, was built in this area. If he left and searched for another land, he probably would have passed by Hilo and Hāmākua which were powerful polities with established rulers and their own priests, and he could have established himself in Kohala which was likely a polity of lesser power. Yet, one can point out that the voyaging traditions describe too many places in Hawai'i, indicating the voyagers knew the islands and did not consider them foreign lands. But, these could be later embellishments to early traditions.

In either of these alternatives, Kahiki may be a metaphorical word for a distant time or a distant place.[182] Kahiki was a vague place where gods went to/came from.[183] These were "invisible lands beyond the horizon."[184] Great chiefly heroes would certainly travel to such places. Indeed, many of the places visited in the accounts were places associated with the gods—hidden islands where food was abundant.[185] These were associated with clouds—cloud islands which occasionally appeared. Beckwith describes some of these places. Kāne-huna moku ('Āina-Huna-a-Kāne) was one such cloud island,[186] as was Paliuli or Pa-liula.[187] So too were Kahiki-honua-kele, Mole-o-lani, or Hawai'i-nui-kua-uli-kai-o'o in Kahiki-Kū.[188] Kahiki-Kū and Kahiki-moe were two spirit places at two of the four corners of the earth.[189] Kuai-he-lani was another such cloud land, commonly named in voyaging accounts—the land where Keānini and 'Olopana 2 came from.[190] Even the Kealakahiki point on Kaho'olawe—associated with a few voyaging accounts—has earlier associations with gods, with Pahulu the sorcery goddess who came via this "old highway."[191]

Again, the traditions may be speaking of Kahiki as a metaphor for distant times. For example, in "distant times" (Kahiki), Pā'ao established a new religion under Pili in Kohala. Or "in distant times," hero chiefs traveled to places of the gods and brought back marvelous things.

I believe that the oral histories of this period desperately need study by scholars fluent in Hawaiian and trained in the study of oral accounts, individuals who are not biased or feel the need to prove external migrations. Careful comparisons with oral traditions of other Polynesian cultures are also needed. The Hawaiian legends are few, often fragmentary and couched in archaic language and literary fiction. It may be that the accounts have become too muddled over time to provide a clear answer, but more research is needed.

So, were Pāʻao and Pili foreigners? Was there foreign contact in Hawaiʻi in the 1200s–1300s? There is no doubt that the Pāʻao-Pili story documents changes that occurred on Hawaiʻi Island in these years. It seems part of the trend towards complex societies that archaeological work suggests and the other Hawaiian oral histories show had already begun under Hawaiian chiefs. Archaeology has not as yet identified any evidence of foreign contact, nor has botany, nor have traditions in the Society Islands. Place name correspondences are weak evidence at best. This lack of evidence could suggest that there was no foreign contact, that the voyaging traditions are symbolic accounts of internal Hawaiian developments. Pāʻao and Pili may have been Hawaiian chiefs. Yet, foreign contact is a possibility and evidence may be found supporting this idea. So, the question is unresolved. Caution is needed, along with careful objective research. The reader is urged to keep an open mind, as the writer hopes to do.[192]

In these times of celebrating the voyages of the Hōkūleʻa and of forging Hawaiian ties with other islands of East Polynesia—particularly the Society Islands—the findings of this chapter may seem disheartening to some. Possibly contact in the 1200s–1300s never occurred. But, a Hawaiian origin for the foreign voyages mentioned in Hawaiian traditions of the 1200s–1300s should not be viewed as less important than external origins from elsewhere in Polynesia. Hawaiian culture and Society Island culture may have simply developed separately from an ancestral East Polynesian homeland culture into their own unique and impressive forms found at European contact. The important point for today's Hawaiians is that they did share a common homeland; Tahitians and Hawaiians are still related peoples. Maybe the Hōkūleʻa and Hawaiʻiloa are not commemorating voyages of the A.D. 1200s–1300s, and perhaps more caution should be given to such claims to avoid establishing a fictitious history of the Hawaiian people. But, even if so, importantly the Hōkūleʻa and Hawai'iloa are perpetuating a basic Polynesian navigational system—once shared and now being shared again.

To summarize this chapter, archaeology shows growing populations in the A.D. 1200s–1300s on Hawai'i Island, and Hawaiian oral histories suggest the emergence of complex societies under Hawaiian chiefs in the late 1200s–early 1300s—with these polities approaching district size and maybe even island size. The polity of north Kohala under Hīkapoloa and that of Hāmākua based in Waipi'o under 'Olopana, Kunaka, and Kapawa, are examples of these emerging complex societies. Archaeological studies of heiau on Maui also suggest complex societies emerged at this time—with larger heiau developing in the 1300s. However, little of the details of these political changes is yet known. As has occurred throughout the world, these developments of increasing political hierarchies and population were likely accompanied in the Hawaiian Islands by the growing separation of the chiefs through secular and religious kapus, through religious rites in increasingly larger temples, through ornamental insignia, and other forms of respect behavior. Some oral histories for Hawai'i Island note larger sacrificial heiau and the kō'ele work tax. On other islands, other institutions such as Haho's founding of the 'Aha Ali'i are developed. As was shown, the voyaging oral histories of this time do not document the founding of complex societies by foreign chiefs. It may even be that there was no foreign contact. The archaeological record shows no influx of external artifacts or structures, nor external plants. Thus, the oral histories may not be literal accounts of voyages outside Hawai'i. Perhaps they are symbolic accounts of the rise of complex societies—stories of great families and the founding of new institutions. The Hawaiian traditions do show that Pā'ao, a priest, founded a new religion with a new priesthood and gods in a polity in Kohala. The ruler, which he put into power and served, was Pili, whose descendants eventually unified Hawai'i Island.

# DYNASTIC TIMES

CHAPTER 7

# A.D. 1400s–1500s The Ascendency of the Pili Line in Waipiʻo & Līoa and ʻUmi

*This is my command:...He shall be named ʻUmi. I am Līloa, and these are the tokens for the child when he grows up and seeks me in Waipiʻo: the feather cape, ivory pendant, helmet and kauila spear.*

(Kamakau)[1]

*[W]hen ʻUmi-a-Līloa laid the victims on the altar in the heiau—the bodies of the fallen warriors and the chief, Hakau—the tongue of the god came down from heaven, without the body being seen. The tongue quivered downward to the altar, accompanied by thunder and lightning, and took away all the sacrifices.*

(the sacrifice of Hākau by ʻUmi. Kamakau)[2]

With Pili arriving and becoming established as a ruler, so began the Pili line of rulers, leading eventually to Kamehameha. The A.D. 1400s–1500s are the years when the line consolidated power and unified the island under one kingdom. These are also the years when the oral histories begin to move into more factual accounts. This is the start of the epics or chronicles—stories of kings, their rivals and the major battles. Unfortunately, the oral histories speak very little about the early rulers of the Pili line, but by the end of the 1500s, accounts are much more detailed.

The end of the 1500s was the time of the two greatest figures of these centuries—Līloa and his son 'Umi. 'Umi has received the most attention since Europeans arrived, but Līloa deserves equal, if not greater, renown. Both men are the most famous of the early Pili kings who ruled the entire island.

## PILI THROUGH KANIUHI: A.D. 1300s

Following Pili, four rulers' names appear on the genealogy of the Pili line as known at the royal court of Kamehameha I and as written down by Malo: Koa, 'Ole, Kūkohou, and Kaniuhi.[3] Using the 20-year per generation estimates, Pili's reign would begin ca. A.D. 1320 and Kaniuhi's ca. A.D. 1400 (Table 7-1). But, by Kamehameha's time, nothing was recalled of these reigns.

> *Of traditions regarding...Koa, Ole, Kukohou, Kaniuhi, I have heard none.*
>
> [Malo][4]

> *[T]he memory of the names alone were retained. There are no legends serving as commentaries to their genealogy, and the Meles are silent respecting them.*
>
> [Fornander][5]

Indeed, some sources and researchers question whether Koa, ‘Ole and Kūkohou were from succeeding generations.[6] Fornander was aware of at least two other genealogies. One suggested Koa and ‘Ole were brothers of Pili,[7] which would place all their reigns ca. A.D. 1360–1380. The other genealogy stated that Koa, ‘Ole and Kūkohou were sons of Pili,[8] resulting in a time placement of Pili at 1360–1380 and the sons ca. 1380–1400. Other researchers have suggested Koa, ‘Ole and Kūkohou were not rulers, rather contemporaries of Pili who had come with him to Hawai‘i,[9] and this would result in a reign of Pili ca. A.D. 1380–1400.

These alternative views have not been resolved with current information or analyses. As Fornander[10] states, “the order of succession [is] more or less forgotten.”

## THE A.D. 1400s: KANIPAHU THROUGH KALAUNUIOHUA

> *Up to this time [Kanipahu's reign] the Pili family does not appear to have been so firmly seated in the sovereignty of Hawaii, but that occasional disturbances occurred with the ancient chief families of the island.*[11]

This summary statement of Fornander's is extremely important for the history of the island, because it implies that the island was unified before Kanipahu, albeit with control challenged—perhaps from “chief families” which had ruled independent districts. Unfortunately, the specific oral histories leading to this conclusion are not given by Fornander, nor could they be found in his collections,[12] unless he is using the Kama‘i‘ole revolt against Kanipahu as evidence for occasional disturbances. One must assume that he had some specific information with which to make the statement, so his points should not simply be dismissed.

Specific information does refer to Kanipahu's reign within the context of the story of Kama'i'ole's successful revolt against Kanipahu and Kama'i'ole's subsequent assassination by Kanipahu's son, Kalapana. Kanipahu's wives included Alaikauakoko and Hualani, the latter a descendant of the famous chief Māweke of O'ahu.[13] Through the former, he had Kalapana, and through the latter a son, Kalahuimoku, and three other children.[14] Nearly all references describe Kanipahu's kingdom being seized by Kama'i'ole, with Kanipahu placing his sons in hiding in Waimanu and fleeing himself to Moloka'i where he lived as a commoner.[15] Fornander says the histories call Kama'i'ole "a scion of one of those families," the "ancient chief familes of the island."[16] Kama'i'ole, after his revolt, seems to have ruled the entire island since it is noted that he toured the island;[17] indeed, he was killed at 'Anaeho'omalu on his way to Kona.[18] And Kalapana and Kalahuimoku were living at Waimanu in Hāmākua within Kama'i'ole's domain.[19] Eventually, Kama'i'ole began to abuse and oppress the people of Hawai'i, so they approached the high priest of Hawai'i, the head of the Pā'ao family, and he asked Kanipahu to return. Kanipahu refused, embarrassed by his body worn out from years of common labor; instead, he abdicated in favor of his son Kalapana. Kalapana was then found in Waimanu and established in Kohala with the high priest, where they gradually gathered followers and then defeated and slew Kama'i'ole at 'Anaeho'omalu.[20]

The oral histories say nothing further of Kalapana's reign, nor of the reign of his son, Kaha'imoele'a, other than that his royal residence was at Waipi'o.[21] But his grandson, Kalaunuiohua, who ruled ca. A.D. 1480–1500, has several stories. He is said to have "confirmed his sway on Hawai'i."[22] again pointing to an unified island. In a famous story, he had a prophet-priestess (kāula)—Wa'ahia—burned at Ke'ekū heiau at Kahalu'u in Kona.[23] This story points to control of the Kona area and supports the unified island concept. Another story documents his raids from Maui to Kaua'i, known as the war of Kaweleweleiwi, ending with his eventual defeat and capture in a battle at Kōloa on Kaua'i.[24] These battles do not seem to have involved occupation and control of the islands, rather capture of the opposing chief and proceeding on to another area. This warfare pattern is strikingly unlike the wars of the 1700s. Eventually, after Kalaunuiohua's capture, the accounts state that his release was either granted by the ruler of Kaua'i or was negotiated by the chiefs of Hawai'i Island, and he returned home.

## A.D. 1500–1580: KŪĀIWA THROUGH KIHANUILŪLŪMOKU

The information on these rulers is fairly brief.[25] There seems no question in Fornander's account that they were rulers of the entire island. Kūāiwa appointed a junior son, Ehu, as chief over Kona and evidently appointed another junior son, Hukulani, over Kohala[26]—specifically showing that Kūāiwa and probably his successor and eldest son, Kahoukapu, had control over Kona and Kohala. Kūāiwa resided in Waipi'o, so clear control is also documented for Hāmākua.

Little is said of Kahoukapu.[27] His son, Kauholanuimahu, evidently occasionally resided in Honua'ula on Maui, perhaps on his wife's lands. Once while gone, Kauholanuimahu faced a revolt by his wife and her new husband and put down the plotters.[28]

Kihanuilūlūmoku followed his father as ruler. He too seems to have ruled the entire island, with Waipi'o his principal residence.[29] This island control appears confirmed with the appointment of two younger sons to be chiefs of Hilo (Makaoku) and Puna (Ho'olana).[30] Kiha is said to have lived to "a very old age," dying at Waipi'o.[31] His principal wife was Waiolea, sister of his mother, through which his heir—Līloa—was born. Three other sons were borne by Waiolea or another wife—Kaunuamoa, Makaoku and Kepailiula. A later wife, Hinaopio, bore him yet another son, Ho'olana.[32]

> *He is eulogised as a chief of a peaceful disposition, but at the same time always ready to keep peace between the subordinate chieftains by force if necessary. Agriculture and industry received his attention, and the island of Hawaii is represented as prosperous and contented during his reign.*
>
> [Fornander][33]

**Table 7-1**

## Ruling Genealogy of Hawai‘i Island Pili Through Kalaunuiohua

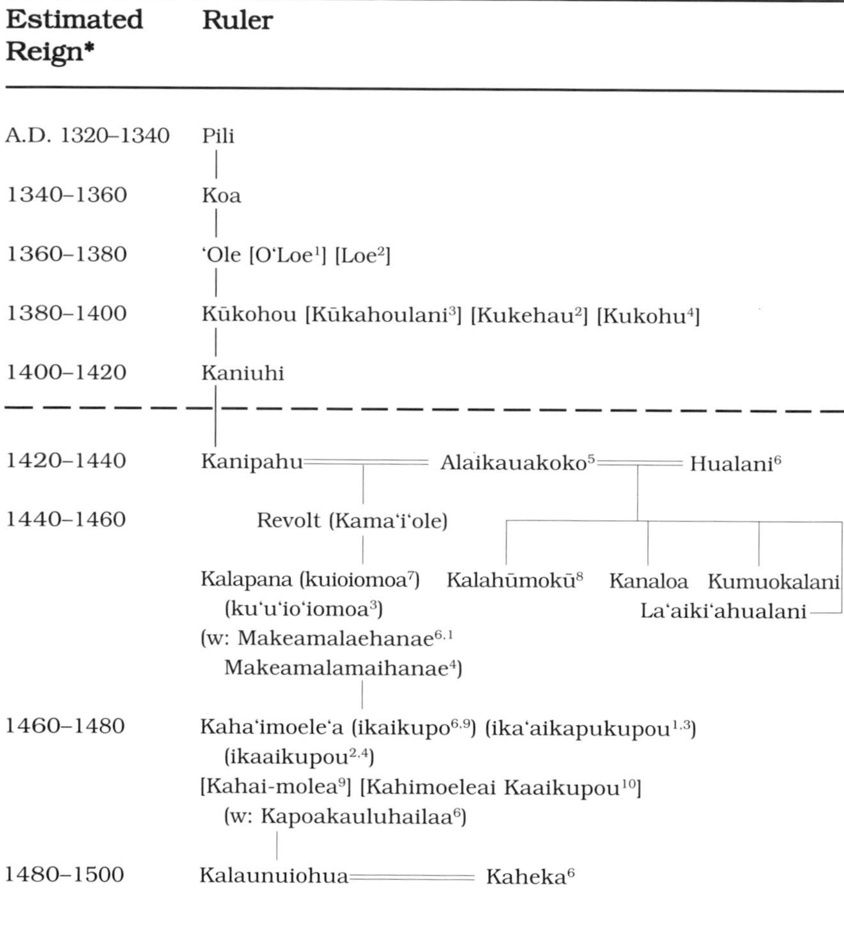

| Estimated Reign* | Ruler |
|---|---|
| A.D. 1320–1340 | Pili |
| 1340–1360 | Koa |
| 1360–1380 | ‘Ole [O‘Loe[1]] [Loe[2]] |
| 1380–1400 | Kūkohou [Kūkahoulani[3]] [Kukehau[2]] [Kukohu[4]] |
| 1400–1420 | Kaniuhi |
| 1420–1440 | Kanipahu ═ Alaikauakoko[5] ═ Hualani[6] |
| 1440–1460 | Revolt (Kama‘i‘ole) (child of Kanipahu and Alaikauakoko); children of Alaikauakoko and Hualani: Kalahūmokū[8], Kanaloa, Kumuokalani, La‘aiki‘ahualani |
| | Kalapana (kuioiomoa[7]) (ku‘u‘io‘iomoa[3]) (w: Makeamalaehanae[6,1] Makeamalamaihanae[4]) |
| 1460–1480 | Kaha‘imoele‘a (ikaikupo[6,9]) (ika‘aikapukupou[1,3]) (ikaaikupou[2,4]) [Kahai-molea[9]] [Kahimoeleai Kaaikupou[10]] (w: Kapoakauluhailaa[6]) |
| 1480–1500 | Kalaunuiohua ═ Kaheka[6] |

* Basis = 20 years per generation. w = wife.

1. Kamakau's 1842 genealogy (McKenzie 1983:xxi-xxv).
2. Kepo'okulou's 1835 genealogy. (McKenzie 1983:xiv-xv).
3. Kamakau 1991[1869]:157–158.
4. 1858 genealogy (McKenzie 1986:2–3)
5. Malo 1951:258; Fornander 1880:70.
6. Malo 1951:258
7. Fornander 1880:40.
8. Kamakau 1991:36.
9. Cartwright 1933.
10. Helekunihi n.d.

**Table 7-2**

## Ruling Genealogy of Hawai'i Island Kalaunuiohua through 'Umi

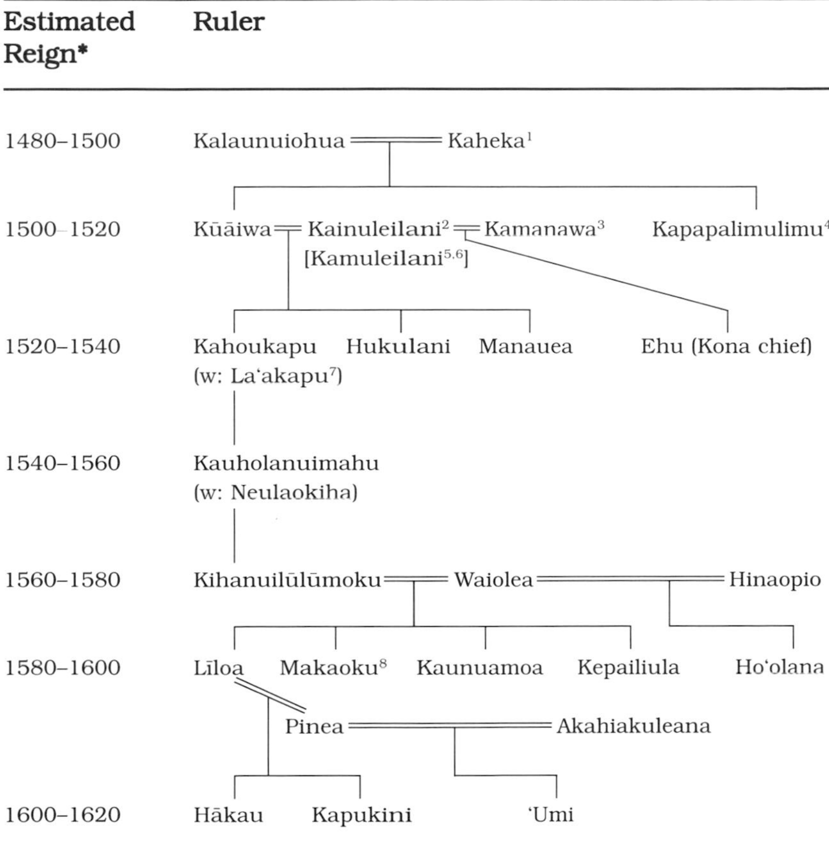


* Basis = 20 years per generation. w = wife.

1. Malo 1951:258.
2. Malo 1951:258.
3. Fornander 1880:70.
4. Fornander 1880:69.
5. Kamakau's 1842 genealogy (McKenzie 1983:xxi–xxv).
6. 1858 genealogy (McKenzie 1986:2–3).
7. Fornander 1880:70.
8. Fornander 1880:69, 72.

One last note relating to Kiha's reign refers to his war trumpet (Kiha pū), "said to have been audible from Waipi'o to Waimea, a distance of ten miles."[34] This was a large Cassis cornuta shell inlaid with the teeth of slain chiefs. It was an heirloom passed down through the Pili rulers to Kamehameha's time,[35] and an artifact reputedly claimed to be this war trumpet is in the Bishop Museum today—a memory of a time and a ruler at the end of the A.D. 1500s.

## LĪLOA
## A.D. 1580–1600

Līloa, as the senior son of Kiha, succeeded his father. While there may be doubts among scholars whether Hawai'i Island was unified by earlier members of the Pili line, nearly all are in agreement that Līloa ruled the entire island.36

> *Liloa...was at that time the king of all Hawaii.*
>
> [Malo][37]

> *Liloa was a tabu chief who was noted for his good deeds. The other chiefs all around Hawaii remained under his rule and placed their sons under his rule. Thus, did the chiefs and sons of chiefs serve Līloa.*
>
> [Kamakau][38]

> *Liloa was the king of the whole of Hawaii.*
>
> [Fornander][39]

In Līloa's time, the following were the high chiefs of the island's districts: Kulukulu'a in Hilo, Hua'a in Puna, Imaikalani in Ka'ū, 'Ehunuikaimalino in Kona.[40] The high chiefs of Kohala and Hāmākua were not mentioned; perhaps Līloa directly controlled these areas. It appears that none of these chiefs were children of Līloa. In Kona, the Ehu line seems to have grown powerful in the three generations that had passed since Ehu, as a younger son of a Pili ruler, had been placed as district chief over Kona. Līloa seems to have adequately kept these chiefs in line, however. He placed their sons at his court in Waipi'o.[41] Also, the Kona district chief's son, Laea (Laeanuikaumanamana) was one of Līloa's closest aides—being perhaps Līloa's high priest or kahu in charge of his spittoon and feathered staff, kahili.[42] Līloa also gave him all of Kekaha (dry northern Kona) in perpetuity.[43] The fact that Līloa granted a district chief's son so much power also indicates that Līloa had considerable personal control over the island.

It appears that Līloa also frequently moved around his kingdom, checking on the status of the chiefs, commoners, farmlands, and heiau.[44] One of these trips within Hāmākua is documented by Kamakau, with Līloa rededicating heiau and overseeing sports of the court (ulumaika, dart throwing, boxing, etc.).[45] It was during this journey that 'Umi, one of his sons, was conceived. Līloa evidently was highly successful in keeping unrest down, for his reign was renowned in the accounts as marked by peace.

One means of keeping peace was use of the religious system as a support base, and Līloa did rededicate many heiau. Examples in Hāmākua include heiau in the ahupua'a of Kukuihaele, Waikoekoe, Kapulena, Kawela and Pā'auhau, and Manini heiau in Koholālele ahupua'a.[46] The main heiau, however, was Paka'alana in Waipi'o, where the court was based. Līloa did not build this heiau, as it was present during Kila's time, over a century earlier. But he may have added to it, and he definitely had the task of annually reconsecrating Paka'alana, sending the chiefs, commoners and priests up into the mountains surrounding Waipi'o to gather 'ōhi'a for new images, fence posts and house posts.[47] This heiau was under the care of the Pā'ao order of priests, with Nunu and Kakohe being named priests who cared for Līloa's major god Kūkā'ilimoku.[48] The use of this heiau also cycled through the annual periods of control for Kū and then use by Lono during the makahiki.[49] Assuming Kamakau has not given his account the religious patterns of his time, the patterns of Līloa's time were highly similar to the situation that Cook's expedition recorded 200 years later regarding the ruler Kalani'ōpu'u, his god and the heiau Hikiau at Kealakekua which Sahlins has carefully documented.[50] The final steps in this cycle saw the resanctifying of the heiau for Kū with the images, fences and houses being replaced, just as in Kamakau's account of Līloa and Paka'alana.[51]

Another means of consolidating his power can be seen in Līloa's marriages.[52] His ranking wife, Pinea, was the younger sister of his mother and was from an O'ahu line of chiefs. With her, he had Hākau, a son and his heir. Another wife, Haua, was a Maui chiefess, and through her, a daughter Kapukini was born. Both these marriages reflected the establishment of ties with high-ranking families outside the kingdom—a common practice in late prehistory of extending a power base.

Although these were Līloa's ranking wives and children, in making a trip to consecrate Manini heiau in Koholālele in Hāmākua, Līloa encountered a commoner woman, Akahiakuleana, and from this affair his famous son, 'Umi, was born. The 'Umi story is well known.[53] The key for discussion here is that after a number of years 'Umi was sent to Līloa with items left by his father for recognition—depending on the account these royal items were the palaoa, a lei-hulu (feather lei) and malo;[54] or palaoa, malo, and lā'au pālau (club-dagger);[55] or palaoa, feather cape, helmet and kauila spear;[56] or palaoa, feather cape, helmet and malo.[57] On his trip to Waipi'o, 'Umi was attended by 'Oma'okamau, Pi'imaiwa'a and, in Kamakau's account only, Ko'i—three youths said to be adopted by 'Umi.[58] Upon arriving at Waipi'o,

> *They descended, walked to Lalakea pond, swam across the Wailoa Stream, and faced Ka-hau-no-ka-ma'ahala, the residence of the chief, Liloa. It was surrounded by a wooden fence. Tabu sticks were placed outside of the enclosure to mark the boundary beyond which commoners were not allowed to go.*
>
> *'Umi went up to lean against the tabu sticks (pahu pulo'ulo'u) at the crossed sticks of the outer entrance. The outermost enclosure had crossed sticks at the*

> *entrance. When these fell, he went on to a fence held together by cords.... 'Umi climbed over the fence, and when the executioners (ilamuku) of the chief saw him [they exclaimed], "The boy has broken the tabu of the chief." He went through the low side door, the tabu door of the chief's residence, and stood looking about him. Liloa sat on an elevated place with his feathered-staff bearers waving their staffs to and fro. 'Umi leaped toward him and sat on his lap. The boy had broken another tabu. The chief looked at the boy sitting on his lap and asked, "Whose child are you?" The boy answered, "Yours! I am 'Umi-a-Liloa." Liloa noticed the tokens he had left for his son and kissed and wept over him. He ordered the kahunas to fetch the pahu and ka'eke drums at once and to take the boy to be circumcized and dedicated, as was the custom for children of chiefs. The chiefly drum, Halalu', and the smaller ka'eke drums were sounded in Paka'alana.*
>
> [Kamakau]5[9]

Līloa, thus proclaimed 'Umi to be his son.

Līloa's heir, Hākau is said to have been extremely angry and jealous of 'Umi, partly through the influence of his mother, Pinea.[60] This intensified as 'Umi and his three adopted "sons" became favorites of Līloa in the ensuing years. All became skilled in courtly manners, including warfare—with Pi'imaiwa'a becoming particularly renowned as a warrior.[61] The accounts speak of beatings and humiliations given to 'Umi by Hākau because of 'Umi's popularity. Līloa continually reassured Hākau that he was the heir, and as Līloa was approaching his death, Hākau was formally declared the heir and all the chiefs were charged to "serve Hakau."[62] But Līloa gave to 'Umi the duties of caring for the god Kūkā'ilimoku, maintaining the heiau, and observing the rituals. This along with Hākau's bitter hatred would eventually cause Hākau's infamous downfall.

Līloa's ruling center was permanently fixed at Waipi'o.[63] It is worth a look at "the glories of Waipio" for as Fornander[64] states:

> *It had been built up and delighted in as a royal residence from the time of Kahaimoelea [6 generations before Līloa, A.D. 1460–1480], the tabus of its great Heiau (temple) [Paka'alana] were the most sacred on Hawaii, and remained so until the destruction of the Heiau and the spoilation of all royal associations in the valley of Waipio by Kaeokulani king of Kauai...in 1791.*

Waipi'o is one of the most striking and impressive places on Hawai'i Island. Approaching from the Honoka'a side today, one drives through cane fields on the gradual slopes of Hāmākua. Suddenly, the valley mouth is visible with extremely steep valley walls dropping 1,000 feet down to the flat valley floor. At the bottom these cliffs block off the valley from outside and result in later sunrises and earlier sunsets in the middle and upper valley reaches. Even today, the quiet and the power of Waipi'o are overwhelming.

But this valley is not just cliffs. It is one of the largest valleys in the islands. At its mouth, lined with a black sand and boulder beach and dunes up to 50-feet high, it is 0.75-mile wide. The main stream, Wailoa, empties out through the beach. Behind the sand, the valley floor remains flat, wide and swampy, extending 2.75 miles inland, with the Wailoa meandering about. Narrow dry slopes are present along each side of the valley at the base of the valley walls. Small streams feed the Wailoa, dropping down from above the valley as waterfalls, cutting through the narrow dry slopes and reaching the valley floor. The larger Hi'ilawe stream forms a small side valley up near the valley mouth, with its waterfall a landmark for those who know Waipi'o in song or legend.

Far inland the Wailoa splits up into four major tributary streams—the Waimā, Kaiawe, Alakahi and Kawainui. The Kawainui wraps around the back of the large Waimanu valley. The valley floor in these upper valleys is quite small, essentially small raised flats along the stream, yet they are spectacular in a different sense from the lower valley. One can walk on the lip above them along the Hāmākua Ditch trail. The cold fog blows around so one can see nothing, and then suddenly it clears, revealing a 3,000-foot drop virtually straight down into the upper valleys.

Traditionally, the ahupua'a of Waipi'o included the valley itself and the adjacent uplands of Muliwai (which extended from Waipi'o to Waimanu across gulches and ridges), and Lālākea (which ran east towards Kukuihaele and inland towards Waimea). These lands made Waipi'o an extremely large ahupua'a.

In Līloa's time, a number of important national places were present in Waipi'o, nearly all at the front of the valley in the sand areas and just behind them. The royal residence, called Kahaunokama'ahala, was located just behind the sand dunes along Wailoa Stream. It included the residential enclosure marked off with kapu sticks, as described in the above quote of 'Umi's initial arrival in Waipi'o. Just inland—probably just across the 'auwai running parallel along the back of the dune—was a taro pondfield (lo'i) called Kahiki-mai-aea with a nīoi wood embankment built by Līloa's great grandfather, Kahoukapu, and this lo'i was also a sacred royal place.[65] Līloa is said to have built a pavement of stones from the bank of this lo'i to the side entrance of his residence, a paving which became known as ka paepae o Līloa or ka paepae kapu o Līloa.[66] Some accounts suggest that this paving led to the heiau Paka'alana, for this heiau was adjacent to the king's residence, probably just on the Kohala side behind the dune.

Paka'alana was a luakini and also a pu'uhonua. It was one of the most sacred religious spots on the island, even retaining its renown into the late 1800s when Charles Bishop specifically called for its protection in the endowment given to the Bishop Museum.[67] Paka'alana was apparently in use as a luakini and pu'uhonua about two centuries earlier as it is specifically mentioned in the Kila-Kunaka stories.[68] More than likely, this heiau was the one being refurbished by Līloa in the Kamakau account mentioned above.

Also associated with the royal residence was a bathing pool called Mōkapu.[69] Possibly this is the Mōkapu pond identified in the 1870s Boundary Commission testimonies, which was located between the dune and Muliwai fishpond on the Kohala side of the dune.[70] This would suggest that the royal residence and Paka'alana heiau spanned about half the back of the dune (Fig. 7-1).

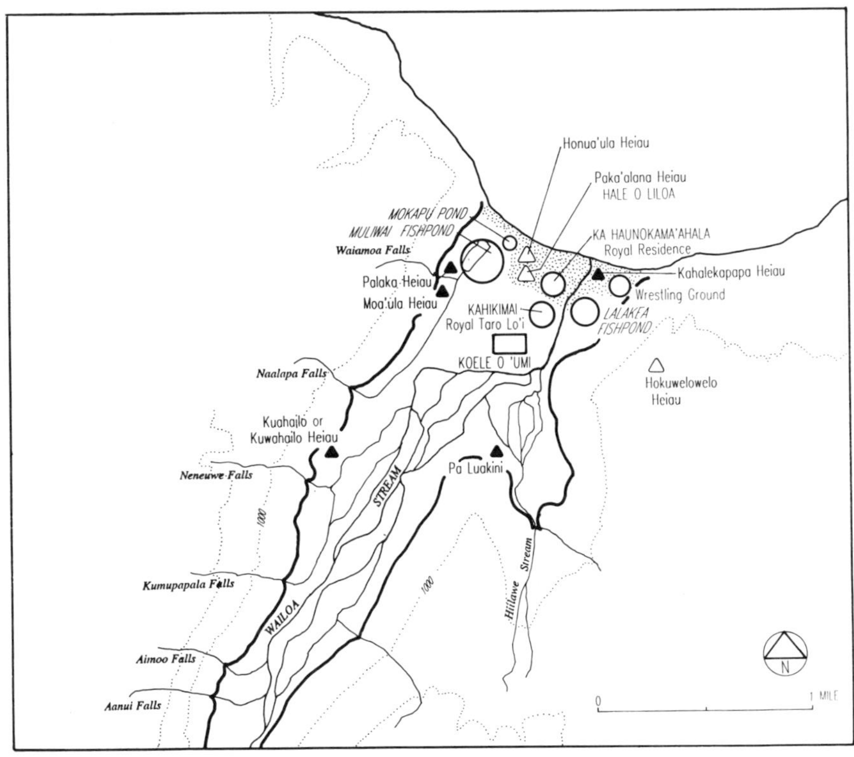


**FIGURE 7-1**

Historic sites in the dune area of Waipi'o Valley. The dunes are the stippled area at the top of the map. (From Cordy 1994).

**FIGURE 7-2**
Sennit burial caskets (Kā'ai), reputedly of the rulers Līloa (left) and Lonoikamakahiki (right). The remains are said to have been removed from the Hale o Līloa in 1830 (Buck 1957:575).

Bishop Museum

Hawaii State Archives, from Ellis' 1825 published account.)

**FIGURE 7-3**
Waipi'o, 1823 view drawn by Rev. William Ellis. The enclosures in the foreground—albeit far from scale—show the royal residential area (abandoned in 1823) and Paka'alana heiau. The royal mausoleum, Hale o Līloa, would apear to be the house under the pandanus tree on the right, since this tree is emphasized in Ellis' journal account. These structures are in the dune area at the mouth of the valley. Inland on the valley floor can be seen taro fields, and at the base of the valley side walls are scattered houses. To the left in the background is Hi'ilawe Valley and its denser cluster of houses.

Other royally related sites were also present near the residence and Paka'alana. Probably on the crest of the dune just seaward was another luakini heiau, Honua'ula.[71] A large fishing shrine may have been present on the dune crest, slightly toward the Kohala side.[72] A wrestling and sporting ground appears to have been in this area, just across Wailoa Stream toward Hilo.[73] And two huge fishponds are located just behind the dune, flanking these royal sites—Lālākea on the Hilo side of Wailoa Stream and Muliwai on the Kohala side of the valley floor.[74]

Probably shortly after Līloa's death, a royal mausoleum was built, likely by Hākau, to house the bones of Līloa. This mausoleum, which came to be known as the Hale o Līloa, was erected within the Paka'alana heiau area. Līloa's bones had been bundled up in a wicker container (kā'ai) and were placed in this house to be revered as deified ancestral remains (Fig. 7-2).[75]

We have no descriptions of this area during Līloa's time, except for the description of Līloa's residence when 'Umi first arrived. The first descriptions of the heiau were written in 1823 by Reverend William Ellis of the London Missionary Society who was touring the island with the American missionaries. It must be emphasized that this was almost 250 years later, and change must have occurred, with heiau being added to and altered. For example, we do know that Kalani'ōpu'u resanctified Moa'ula heiau in 1780,[76] and he may have altered it then. Also, accounts state that Kā'eo, the king of Kaua'i, raided Waipi'o in 1791 during the wars of Kamehameha's time, with his aim specifically to ravage all the signs of royalty.[77] Just what he did is unclear. He may have just burned wooden structures and even then not all, because in 1823 Ellis observed that Paka'alana heiau and the Hale o Līloa (the funerary house for Līloa and his descendants) were intact—although they may have been restored by Kamehameha, who after all was Līloa's descendant. Nonetheless, Ellis does provide a description of Paka'alana and a drawing (Fig. 7-3).

> *Pakalana, the Puhonua, or place of refuge, for all this part of the island. It was a large enclosure, less extensive, however, than that at Honaunau. The walls,*

*tho of great antiquity, were of inferior height and dimensions. In the midst of the enclosure, under a wide-spreading pandanus, was a small house, called Ke Hale o Riroa (The House of Riroa), from the circumstance of its containing the bones of a king of that name.*

*We tried, but could not gain admittance to the pahu tabu, or sacred enclosure. We also endeavoured to obtain a sight of the bones of Riroa, but the man who had charge of the house told us we must offer a hog. [The Hale of Līloa had] a rudely carved stone image, about six feet high standing at one corner of the wall.*[78]

Ellis's drawing shows the stone wall of Paka'alana and the Hale o Līloa with its palisade around it in the center of the picture.

At the same time, Waipi'o must not just be conceived as the ruler's area. At European contact, this valley had perhaps 2,500 people, one of the densest concentrations of people in the entire island chain.[79] In 1823, Rev. William Ellis's party visited Waipi'o. It was estimated that Waipi'o held 265 houses, and Rev. Asa Thurston had specifically gone all the way up the valley to count houses as well as preach,[80] so the house count is probably relatively accurate. These houses were scattered in "small villages" of 20–50 houses, but by this time—almost 45 years after Cook's arrival—the valley's population had vastly declined, so even more houses must have been present at European contact.

These houses were scattered along the dry, narrow colluvial slopes at the base of the valley sides, all the way up the valley, with dense clusters in several spots which were called villages by Ellis (Nāpo'opo'o and 3 unnamed clusters on the opposite side of the valley),[81] and parishes by Rev. Lyons some 20 years later (Nāpo'opo'o, Na'alepa, Kōāuka, Keone).[82] Mahele records indicate many of these house lots were evidently enclosed with stone walls by the late 1840s.[83]

Dryfields were around these houses, and crops noted in the records include taro, sweet potatoes, bananas, breadfruit, coconuts, arrowroot, sugarcane, and 'awa for food and drink; wauke and māmaki for cloth; and kou and hala for raw materials.[84] The specific appearance of these dryfields is not clear.

A vast irrigated taro pondfield system covered the valley floor. This system included at least 14 major canals leading off the streams in the lower valley,[85] but other canals also led off waterfalls. Importantly, Waipi'o also had major fishponds—Lālākea, Muliwai, Mōkapu, and a whole series of smaller fishponds along the Kohala side of the valley, and more in the Hi'ilawe area.[86] Generally Waipi'o had a common windward valley settlement pattern of early historic times, but on a much larger scale.

Waipi'o's land unit patterns also show common valley features, but again reflect this valley's size. The ahupua'a was divided into numerous 'ili, each of which typically contained houses and agricultural lands. In the mid-valley, 'ili contained colluvial slopes with houses and dry fields, and adjacent valley floor sections with taro pondfields. The 'ili stretched half or all the way across the valley. In the front of the valley, all the dune area was Ka'ao, a very large jump 'ili or 'ili lele, which had inland portions. There were also 'ili lele in Hi'ilawe, with dry field lands in this side valley, houses at the front and on one side, and pondfields usually just in front on the main valley floor—e.g., 'ili Waipao, Papalinawao. Also, between the dunes and Hi'ilawe Valley, there were many tiny pieces of 'ili scattered in the pondfields with the main 'ili sections on the west side of the valley—e.g., 'ili Waiamoa, Olowalu, 'Ililīloa, Pahupōhaku, Koloakiu. In all, 49 'ili were counted in one study which covered 50% of Waipi'o's LCAs, a testament to the size of the ahupua'a.[87]

Certainly the valley was different in the 1500s. There may have been fewer houses and taro pondfields. But population was likely to have been dense. Also, we do know the Lālākea Fishpond was present in Līloa's time, for 'Umi passed by it in approaching Līloa's house.[88] A royal pondfield also is noted back to the time of Līloa and his forebears.

The actual documentation of the size and density of population, the general number of houses, and the extent of the taro lo'i and fishponds during Līloa's and 'Umi's time will rest with archaeological research. These specifics are currently unknown. Indeed, archaeological work has been extremely limited in Waipi'o. In the early 1900s, J. F. G. Stokes of the Bishop Museum briefly visited the valley in his island-wide research recording heiau.[89] Thomas Thrum[90] later reported Stokes's results. In 1930–32, Alfred Hudson conducted a survey of major sites along the east coast of Hawai'i Island for the Bishop Museum, and he too briefly visited Waipi'o—again with a focus on the valley mouth and heiau.[91] The valley then remained largely untouched by archaeologists until the 1970s.

The 1970s and 1980s saw the arrival of modern archaeology in the valley with its focus on locating and describing all historic sites from the smallest fields and house remains up to heiau. But only three brief studies were done in Waipi'o during the 1970s and two in the 1980s—each at the reconnaissance level, where sites were located and only very briefly described.[92] Only one of these projects has been in the upper valley. [Just recently, in 1992 and 1993, detailed mapping and excavation of some terraces in Hi'ilawe and taro lo'i on the valley floor and mapping of the dune were done.][93]

These studies have found that the valley is still full of sites. The taro pondfields of Hi'ilawe Valley were found to still be present, along with a large adjacent housing area with numerous walled enclosures with internal mounds, pavings and terraces where houses once would have stood.[94] Abandoned house sites (enclosures, walled areas, plateaus and terraces) and associated dry agricultural fields (terraces and walled areas) abound along the narrow colluvial slopes of the lower valley. And of course, the taro pondfield systems on the valley floor are still present. House sites continue into the upper valley, and irrigated taro terraces on stream benches with long raised canals are present.[95] These sites have only been minimally described. They await detailed mapping and examination to yield the important information on the past which they contain.

# HĀKAU
# A.D. 1600–?

Hākau followed his father ruling the island and is one of the most reviled rulers in the epics, probably—as Fornander notes[96]—to reinforce the claim of 'Umi and his line. Among his reputed evils were that:

> *[h]e dismissed, disrated, and impoverished all the old and faithful counsellors and servants of his father, chiefs, priests or commoners.*
>
> [Fornander][97]

'Umi and his retinue, too, were abused, and 'Umi chose to leave the court and retired into obscurity in Hilo.[98]

Again, the story of 'Umi's exile is frequently told.[99] Ka'oleioku, a priest in Hilo, recognized 'Umi and began supporting him and they raised an army. Two of Hākau's high priests, Nunu and Kakohe, were insulted by Hākau, and they traveled to meet and support 'Umi. A plot resulted to overthrow Hākau. The two priests returned to Waipi'o and advised Hākau to plan to attack 'Umi, and to either send his men to the mountains to get feathers to refurbish his god to initiate war preparation, or to gather 'ōhi'a for the haku 'ōhi'a ceremony rededicating the luakini heiau. While the men were in the mountains, 'Umi's force arrived at Waipi'o.

> *[A] procession of people was seen descending....The people descended on the road from Koa'ekea, and the cliffside was thick with them. One of Hakau's attendants, named Hoe, said to him, "That is not a procession of strangers. It is 'Umi's company....Woe betide you, we are going to perish!" Hakau and all the others were slaughtered—chiefs, personal attendants, and stewards.*
>
> [Kamakau][100]

And, so did ʻUmi become ruler of Hawaiʻi, and Kaʻoleioku his kahuna nui.

## ʻUMI A LĪLOA
## A.D. 1600–1620

One of ʻUmi's first acts as ruler was to offer up the body of Hākau and his attendants to Kū—either at Honuaʻula heiau[101] or at Moaʻula heiau.[102] Here, the stories of old state that the god's tongue came down and consumed the sacrifices amidst thunder and lightning.[103]

There are conflicting accounts on how ʻUmi pulled the kingdom together. Kamakau[104] said the sons of the district chiefs fled home, each district declared independence, and ʻUmi first attacked the chief of Hilo (Kulukuluʻa) after ʻUmi broke the wiliwili pendant of the chief's daughter and insulted this emblem of the Hilo chiefs. The result was a march by ʻUmi and his warriors from Waipiʻo along the mountain trail above on Mauna Kea and down into Hilo. In the battle that followed, Kulukuluʻa was killed. And then, according to Kamakau, ʻUmi subdued Puna, Kaʻū, and Kona—with the chiefs of Puna (Huaʻa) killed at Keaʻau and Kaʻū (Imaikalani) killed by Piʻimaiwaʻa, and with the elderly ʻEhunuikaimalino ceding his lands in Kona. After this time, Kamakau stated that ʻUmi's followers were given certain lands.[105]

However, Fornander's account is quite different.[106] He was told that because Hākau had so greatly abused his power,

> *[T]he great feudatory chiefs in the various districts of the island cordially received and freely acknowledged the sovereignty of Umi as he made his first imperial tour around the island.*[107]

Fornander did state that although some legends referred to problems with Imaikalani, the chief of Kaʻū, his reading of the epics indicated that peace prevailed between 'Umi and his chiefs throughout his reign.[108] He listed the district chiefs during 'Umi's reign:

Hāmākua—Wanua
Puna—Hua'a
Kona—Hoe a pae
Hilo—Kulukulu'a
Ka'ū—Imaikalani
Kohala—Wahilani.[109]

Several of these chiefs obviously were holdovers from Līloa's reign. So, the stories given Fornander indicate these chiefs were not slain by 'Umi in battle, rather that they supported peaceful transition and continuity. [Fornander collected a story which stated that 'Umi's son, Keawe-nui-a-'Umi, slayed the above chiefs' sons, who were district chiefs at the start of his reign. The fact that the above chiefs' sons had been reappointed to their fathers' positions tends to strongly support the version that Līloa's high chiefs backed 'Umi in a peaceful transition.][110]

Resolution of these differing accounts is difficult. It is unclear if 'Umi had to subdue the different district chiefs. It is clear that he did rapidly control the kingdom, and it is also evident that attempts were made to counterbalance the low rank of his mother and thus consolidate his power. He took his ranking half-sister (Kapukini) as one wife. Also, he sent 'Oma'okamau to the Maui royal court, then at Hāna, to ask Pi'ilani, the ruler of Maui, for his daughter (Pi'ikea) as another wife, and she was given to him.[111] She arrived at Waipi'o shortly before her father's death. A third important wife was a woman related to the Kona district chief and the Ehu family, Moku-a-hualei-akea. She had been one of the wives of Pi'ilani.[112]

A marked change occurred during the reign of 'Umi. He discontinued the use of Waipi'o as the sole residence of the ruler. Instead, he moved his court into Kona district, first building the heiau, Ahu a 'Umi, in the plateau between Hualālai and Mauna Loa, in Keauhou ahupua'a. Later, 'Umi seems to have resided in the Kailua area and possibly at Kahalu'u[113] in Kona, for heiau there are said to have been built by him. The reasons for this move are unknown. Some say his chiefs and followers were abusing their power over the commoners of Waipi'o. Others say he wanted to be near the fishing grounds of Kona.[114] Whatever the reason, 'Umi seems to have begun the practice of moving his court about, and having it focused around royal centers in the Kona area—a practice lasting through Kamehameha's time.

The move to Kona seems to have occurred shortly after 'Umi's marriage to Pi'ikea, because the accounts note that her father, Pi'ilani, died soon after. Her eldest brother Lono-a-Pi'ilani became ruler, and after several years a rivalry with his younger brother, Kiha-a-Pi'ilani, arose. This led to attempts to kill Kiha, followed by him hiding in several places. Eventually, Kiha approached his sister at Kailua to ask for aid,[115] giving a glimpse of 'Umi's Kailua residence.

> *[T]hey sailed to Maka'eo in Kailua....According to the number of chiefly wives 'Umi-a-Liloa had, so was the number of their houses. Pi'i-kea and Kapu-kini had the largest houses, and they were near the enclosure of 'Umi's house.*
>
> [Kamakau][116]

Kiha-a-Pi'ilani appealed to 'Umi for warriors to place him on Maui's throne and "[h]aving received favourable auguries from the high-priest, Kaoleioku, 'Umi summoned the chiefs of the various districts to prepare for the invasion of Maui."[117] After a year of preparation, constructing canoes and gathering his men, the force left for Maui. Hāna was attacked, and the high chief of Hāna and Lono-a-Pi'ilani's "great war leader," Ho'olaemakua, held off the Hawai'i forces in a series of engagements and in the defense of the hill fortress on Ka'uiki.[118] Eventually, Pi'imaiwa'a discovered the fortress's entrance was guarded by a huge wooden image at night, and he directed an attack which routed the defenders.[119] Kiha-a-Pi'ilani had Ho'olaemakua hunted down and slain. Lono-a-Pi'ilani, himself, then died.[120] Kiha became ruler of Maui, and 'Umi and his men returned home, ending a rare early foray outside of Hawai'i Island.

The accounts indicate that the remaining years of 'Umi's reign were peaceful ones. He sponsored the building of some large taro pondfields in Waipi'o and farms, notably in Kona.[121] He also erected several heiau or rebuilt existing ones, often with a unique architectural style of hewn stones. A number of these heiau with building or rebuilding ascribed to 'Umi were Kūki'i in Puna, Pohaku Hanalei in Ka'ū, and an unnamed heiau in Kona.[122]

Upon 'Umi's death in Kailua, ca. A.D. 1620 by genealogical approximation, his faithful friend Ko'i, one of the three original "adopted sons," is said to have taken care of the body at 'Umi's request. At night, Ko'i approached the house where it lay, guarded by Pi'imaiwa'a who "knew the body had long been promised to Ko'i."[123] Ko'i substituted another similar corpse and took 'Umi away, burying him in an unknown spot—speculated by many to have been a cave in the cliffs of Waimanu or Waipi'o.[124]

## GENERAL PATTERNS OF THIS TIME AS INDICATED BY ARCHAEOLOGY

### 'UMI'S HEIAU

During his reign, 'Umi built and rebuilt numerous heiau—as did his predecessors and successors. Among the most famous today is Ahua a 'Umi, built on a cold, cinder plain in the saddle between Hualalai and Mauna Loa at an elevation of about 5,200 feet. This heiau, in the ahupua'a of Keauhou of Kona district, is above the forest line and far from the coastal housing areas. The remains were measured by Bingham during an 1830 visit and have been described several times since.[125] Prior to its modification as a goat pen in the late 1800s, the heiau consisted of a stone-walled enclosure (20 x 20 meters) with walls up to 2.5-meters high. This is a rather small area, 440 $m^2$. Four internal areas were walled off within the heiau. Eight very large rectangular cairns—3–4-meters high and 4–7 meters in diameter—were arranged outside the enclosure, a feature unique to this heiau. Recent archaeological work has found a number of other structures scattered nearby, including platforms, enclosures, and fire hearths.[126]

Interpretations vary on the function of this heiau, located so far from populated areas. Bingham in 1830 recorded nothing about its history. In 1841, Wilkes[127] was told the central structure was a "Temple of Kaili," Kūkā'ilimoku, which was "said to have formerly been covered with idols." He was also told that the three front cairns were 'Umi's original districts, that the five other tall cairns were built by "the conquered districts," and that the outside enclosure was the house of Papa, which he called Kā'ili's wife—clearly a reference to a Hale o Papa or women's heiau, often found adjacent to a luakini heiau. Remy in 1853 was told by a very old Kona man, Kanuha, that the heiau was to commemorate 'Umi's conquest over his cousin Keli'iokāloa at that spot,[128] but in 1880 Fornander properly pointed out that Keli'iokāloa was 'Umi's son and successor, and noted "the legends, which I have collected and carefully compared, make no mention of such a civil war [between 'Umi and his son], nor that the Ahua a 'Umi were erected to commemorate this war."[129] Fornander instead says that 'Umi made his residence on this plateau, "choosing to live there on the income or tribute brought him by the chiefs and the landholders of the various districts. This version has six piles of stones reared as peaceful momentoes and rallying points, each one for its particular district, while a seventh pile indicated the court of 'Umi and its crowd of attendants."[130] Alexander[131] repeats this headquarters and cairn explanation. Almost 40 years later, Baker was told that 'Umi had all the people come to the location to conduct a census, with each arriving person placing a stone on an ever-increasing cairn representing their district.[132] More recent interpretations suggest that Ahua a 'Umi was an astronomical heiau with cairns marking certain star patterns.[133]

Clearly, the older Hawaiian-based accounts emphasize three points—the heiau was to commemorate an event, 'Umi and his court were in residence, and the cairns represented the six districts and the court. The commemoration of an event is a common cause for heiau construction or rebuilding, seen from Lonoikamakahiki's celebration of his victories over rebels at a reconsecrated heiau, from Kalani'ōpu'u's rebuilding of Pākini heiau to sacrifice a rebel chief, to

Kamehameha's building of Pu'ukoholā heiau to sacrifice his cousin and unify the island. Perhaps—if Fornander is correct that 'Umi fought no wars to unify his kingdom—this heiau may commemorate the shifting of the royal residence out from Waipi'o and the windward side to Kona and the leeward side, definitely a major departure from traditional Pili line practices and one perhaps requiring religious and political support.

The location of the heiau overlooking Kona and its location next to the junction of two major overland mountain trails—from Hilo-Hāmākua-Kohala-Waimea to Kona and from Ka'ū to Kona—could reinforce this conclusion. A major trail corridor extends up from Kona along the Kohala side of Ahua a 'Umi, goes along the Kona-Hāmākua border, and then swings down into Waimea—where major trails led on to Kohala and Hāmākua. Caves along this trail in Kona quite near Ahua a 'Umi are described as containing water (Waikulukulu), shrines for travelers, and sleeping/rest areas for travelers.[134] Archaeological work in such caves along this trail in the Hāmākua-Kona area have similarly identified sleeping platforms, cooking areas with stone-lined firepits, and rest and working areas—with the caves interpreted as travelers' shelters.[135] Dates have been processed for some of these caves, indicating use back to the A.D. 800s–1000s.[136] Another major trail extends south of Ahua a 'Umi to Ka'ū—branching off immediately to seaward. Descriptions of this trail are limited,[137] and no archaeological work has yet to occur.

Both of these trails had strong links to 'Umi in the 1800s. In the 1870s elderly Hawaiians from this area of Kona and Ka'ū—born in the late 1700s and early 1800s and who had learned of the mountain lands from relatives—called the Ka'ū trail "'Umi's road."[138] Several similarly labeled the trail up towards Hāmākua and Waimea "'Umi's road."[139]

> *Kaohe [ahupua'a in Hāmākua] is mauka side of Umi's road to Waimea and Puanahulu (ahupua'a in Kona] is makai of the road.*
>
> [Keakaokawai's 1873 testimony]

The claim that 'Umi's court was in residence seems quite likely during the heiau's construction, and given the residential features recently found by archaeologists. But the cold at this elevation, the distance from food, and the well-documented use of Kailua by 'Umi, suggests that the court was in residence only briefly.

Last, as to the cairns being linked to particular districts—the earlier accounts all point to some association with the island's districts and the court. Perhaps with the moving of the court, all districts would symbolically participate.

Whatever the exact event and symbolism, the heiau may never have been used frequently for major ceremonies after the initial commemorating event. It is not mentioned in any traditions found after 'Umi, noting ceremonies at, or rebuildings of, heiau. But, the heiau has still survived, with a definite association with 'Umi, and due to its isolation it may well accurately represent a slice of time from almost 400 years ago—'Umi's time.

Several other heiau scattered about the island are also associated with 'Umi, said to have been built when he toured the island after coming to power. Dressed or cut-stone blocks were the hallmark of their construction. One of these heiau was Kūki'i heiau in Kula ahupua'a in Puna. It was built atop a cinder cone, Pu'u Kūki'i. Today it is a moderate-sized enclosure, 37 x 21 meters (777 m2).[140] In 1906, Stokes reported that the interior was paved, with some of the paving being cut-stone, but he noted that the walls were constructed of ordinary stones.

> *Many old natives along the road had described the platform as being constructed of hewn stone and laid so closely "that an ant could not crawl between." I had expected to see a platform built of such stones. In place of that I found retaining walls from 4 to 5 feet high, of ordinary field stones rather loosely laid....It would appear that the hewn stone reference was to the paving blocks of the floor.*[141]

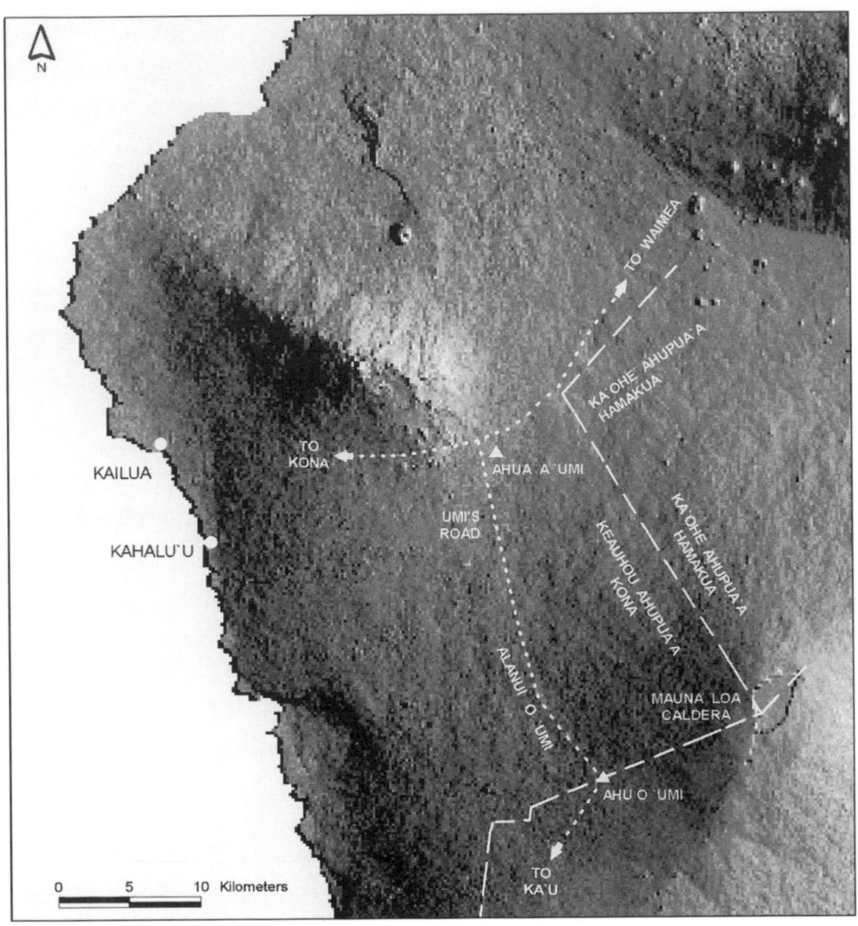


**FIGURE 7-4**
Kona District & place names in 'Umi's Time.

HAWAII STATE ARCHIVES

**FIGURE 7-5**

Ahu a 'Umi, Plan Map done by the Wilkes' Expedition in 1841. Cairns D, E, and F were said to have been built by 'Umi; Cairns K, J, I, H and at edge of G were said to be built by the "conquered districts". G was the Hale o Papa, women's heiau (Wilkes 1844,4:opposite 106).

STATE HISTORIC PRESERVATION DIVISION

**FIGURE 7-6**
One of the Large Cairns at Ahu a 'Umi, Keahou, Kona. Note the size of the cairn in comparison to the car.

BISHOP MUSEUM

**FIGURE 7-7**
Cut-Stone from Kūki'i Heiau, Kula Ahupua'a, Puna. This was one of the heiau associated with 'Umi a Līloa. Note the straight (cut) edges on the bottom and right side of the stone (Bevacqua & Dye 1972:10).

By Stokes's time, the heiau had many of its cut-stones removed—by local residents, and by Kalākaua for some of Iolani Palace's foundations and for Queen Kapi'olani's residence.[142] One of these stones was sent to the Bishop Museum (#4899) by Rufus Lyman.[143] A few still remained on site in the early 1970s with cutting on one or two edges (Fig. 7-7). Like many others, this heiau may have seen additions after the time of 'Umi.

The Kona heiau with cut-stone associated with 'Umi in the oral histories was dismantled early in the 1800s, with many stones said to have been used in the building of Kailua's first church.[144] The Ka'ū heiau associated with 'Umi, Pōhaku Hanalei, appears to have been covered by lava flows in the 1800s.

Another heiau with cut-stone is not listed in the oral accounts as being associated with 'Umi, but possibly its cut-stone construction belongs to the same period. This heiau is found in Kukuipahu ahupua'a in the northern part of leeward Kohala, located inland and still largely intact. It will be open to the public as a state historic park before long. This ruin is a moderate-sized stone enclosure (30 x 45 m, 1,350 $m^2$) with low walls[145] and several internal walls. An internal enclosure—perhaps an older building phase—is faced with cut-stone slabs. Other walls and facings are not of cut-stone, however—suggesting multiple periods of building. This heiau is said to be an old one in local Kohala oral histories, dating earlier than 'Umi. It is not clearly ascribed to his time; however, its cut-stone slabs currently appear to be a rare architectural style which may be linked to him.

Interestingly, of the two existing heiau associated with 'Umi—Ahua a 'Umi and Kūki'i—both were only small to moderate in size—400–800 $m^2$, and some of their area may reflect later additions. These points suggest that the much larger, famous luakini heiau may have had major additions built later—after the early to mid-A.D. 1600s. Nonetheless, these few heiau noted here retain a tie to an earlier era—to the time of 'Umi, last of the windward kings.

## OTHER PATTERNS OF THE 1400S–1500S

During the centuries concluding with 'Umi's acquisition of the rule—the A.D. 1400s–1500s—the archaeoloigcal record indicates that population was rapidly increasing. A great many of our radiocarbon dates fall into these years.[146]

In leeward areas, settlements were growing. In the Kona field system in the uplands, a larger number of field shelters appeared, apparently as if the fields were expanding in many of the ahupua'a.[147] In Waimea, similarly, many new sites and presumably field areas have been found.[148] And on the arid shoreline below Waimea—in Puakō, Kalāhuipua'a and 'Anaeho'omalu—temporary use of caves and other small sites markedly increased, reflective of recurrent use probably by an increasing population in the Waimea area.[149] In leeward, northern Kohala, expansion of the coastal settlement and their inland fields also becomes noticeable in these centuries.[150]

During these centuries many small settlements were founded in arid northern Kona—between Kaloko and Ka'ūpūlehu.[151] This settling of the last marginal lands on the island seems to mark the completion of the major spread of settlement. From this time on, infilling and more dense patterns begin to emerge.

But, these are the leeward areas. The windward areas have received very little archaeological work. As yet, only the Kohala valleys of Pololū, Honokāne nui and Honokāne iki have enough dates to show patterns. In those valleys expanding fields are also apparent in these centuries. In the two Honokānes—both very narrow, steep valleys, subject to avalanche from the cliffs above—the fields are primarily irrigated taro fields, a few fields wide on each bank.[152]

The Hāmākua field systems have few dates. In Waipi'o the irrigated taro fields covered the lower valley floor and smaller taro fields clustered along the upper valley streams, with dryland fields and tree crops mostly along the dry footslopes of the valley sides and in dry spots in the upper valleys. This pattern repeated itself in Waimanu, the other large valley of Hāmākua.[153] Irrigated taro fields were also found on the larger marine benches beyond Waimanu, being fed by waterfalls. These benches include Laupāhoehoe nui and iki and ʻĀpua.[154]

East of Waipiʻo towards Hilo were most of Hāmākua's ahupuaʻa. Here rolling uplands were present above the 100–300-foot sea cliffs, with deep gulches cutting across the uplands and emptying into the sea. At European contact, these uplands—which received up to 180 inches of rain per year—were covered with dryland fields, extending from the sea cliff edge up to the ʻōhiʻa forest.[155]

> *The Country which for a considerable distance has but a gentle ascent, seems fully cultivated & a number of villages interspers'd.*
>
> [King 1779][156]

At contact, scattered groves of trees extended 1–2 miles inland—māmake, breadfruit, coconut, etc. However, what the situation was in the A.D. 1400s–1500s is uncertain. Perhaps, in many ahupuaʻa the forest had only been cleared half a mile or a mile inland, with forest present between settlements along the coast. Perhaps some field areas of newly formed settlements were quite small; other fields could have covered much larger areas.

Importantly, with earlier settlement in Hāmākua and other windward areas, it is vital to realize that windward fields may have had a far greater yield and probably were expanding earlier. Population was also likely to be greater in windward areas at the beginning of these centuries. But, certainly the leeward lands were catching up—if not caught up—by A.D. 1600.

Another subsistence feature that had surely been developed in these centuries, and probably earlier, were larger fishponds. The large Lālākea fishpond at the mouth of Waipiʻo's Valley was noted in the oral histories during Līloa's reign—A.D. 1580–1600.[157] Almost certainly, it was present earlier. The large fishponds at Kaloko and Honokōhau in Kona were mentioned in the oral histories of Lonoikamakahiki's reign,[158] ca. A.D. 1640–1660, and these may also have been present earlier.

As a point of departure, all of these issues indicate a rapidly expanding population and subsistence base, with the leeward areas emerging to rival the older windward lands. With 'Umi's removal of the royal court primarily to Kona locales, Kona emerges as a key power center in Hawai'i Island politics. The Pili line of rulers eventually became known as Kona rulers or Kona chiefs. But, it must not be forgotten that the Pili line rose in the windward lands of Kohala and Hāmākua, and came to dominate the island from the power base of Waipi'o. In truth, unification and power originated in the windward areas—those fertile and long-settled lands of Hawai'i, and the A.D. 1400s–1500s were windward-dominated years.

CHAPTER 8

# THE A.D. 1600s The Reigns of ‘Umi's Descendants in Kona

*O Ku, O Kunuiakea*

*..............................*

*Curse the rebels outside and inside,*
*Who, with bowed head and pointing finger*
*Plot to take the land.*

(sacrificial chant)[1]

*Beware the descendant of ‘Ī, lest the tough roots crawl forth*

(warning given by Palena, a chief of Kohala,
when he saw Kua‘ana a ‘I beaten by a chief of Kona)[2]

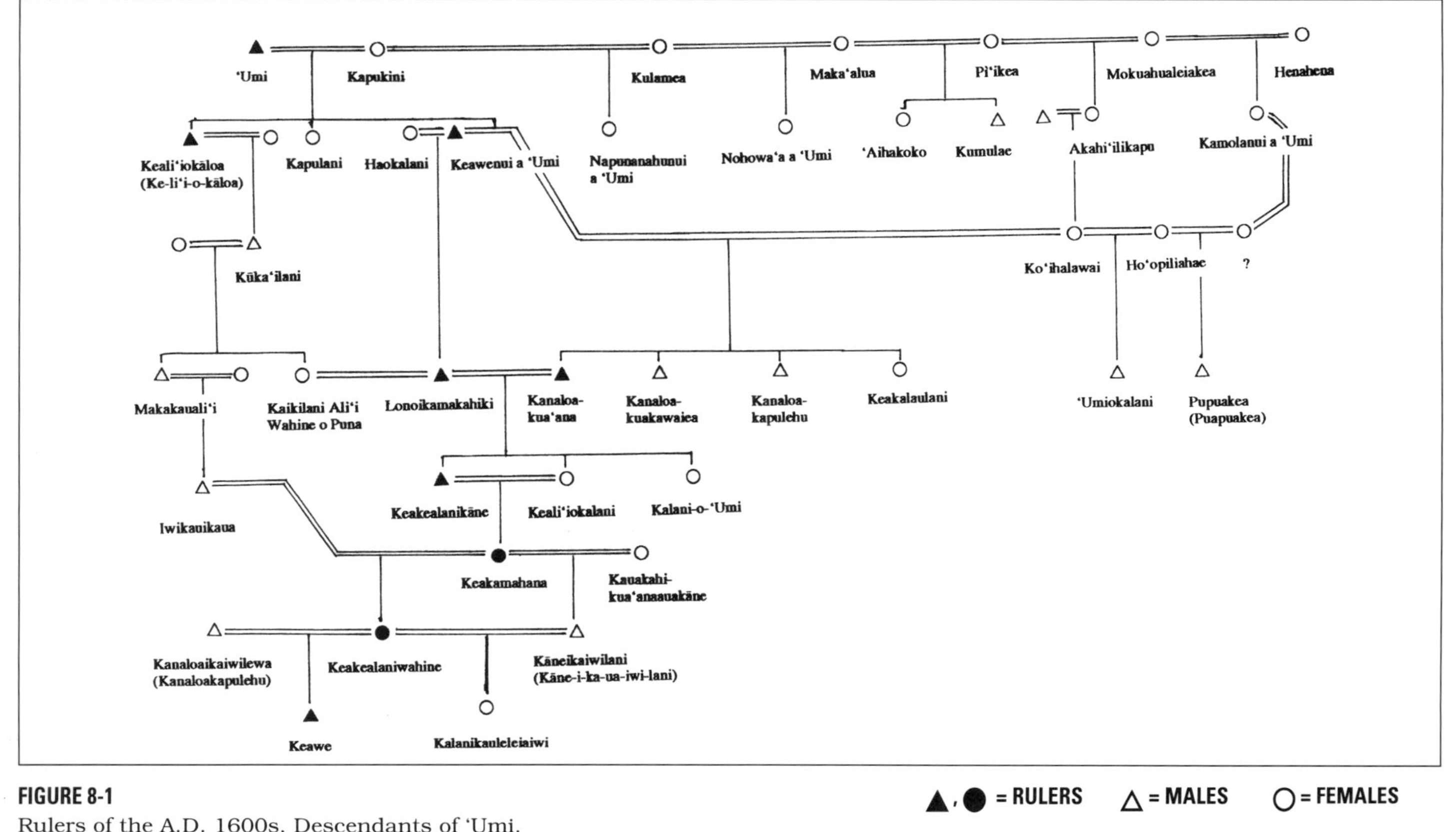


**FIGURE 8-1**
Rulers of the A.D. 1600s, Descendants of 'Umi.

▲, ● = RULERS △ = MALES ○ = FEMALES

# CA. A.D. 1620–1640 KEALI'IOKĀLOA & KEAWENUI A 'UMI— THE SONS OF 'UMI

With the death of 'Umi a Līloa, the rule of the Hawai'i Island Kingdom passed to his eldest son, Keali'iokāloa. 'Umi had at least six wives, and his children are shown in Figure 8-1. Fornander[3] states that little was said of Keali'iokāloa, other than he was unpopular and the cause of his death was uncertain.

Upon Keali'iokāloa's death, warfare broke out within the kingdom. The cause is unclear, but the chiefs seem to have been divided between the two potential heirs—Keali'iokāloa's next oldest brother, Keawenui a 'Umi, and Keali'iokāloa's son, Kūka'ilani who may have still been a child. The district chiefs under Keali'iokāloa supported Kūka'ilani's claim: Palahalaha of Kohala, Pumaia of Hāmākua, Hilo-Hāmākua of Hilo, Lililehua of Puna, Kahalemilo of Ka'ū, and Moihala of Kona.[4] Keawenui a 'Umi defeated these chiefs in battle, with the deciding fight at Pu'umaneo in Kohala.[5] The district chiefs lost their lives either in battle or were executed afterwards, and their bones were bundled and retained by Keawenui and his heirs. The story of Lonoikamakahiki—Keawenui's son and eventual heir—involves the revealing of these bones.[6] They were "plaited with feathers and fastened together by netting." A chant honored each of the high chief's remains. For example, for Palahalaha, "the chief of Kohala, son of Wohilani":

*Level indeed*
*Lies Kohala,*
*Face down.*
*The fragrance is wafted to me*
*Of the flower of Koolau, of Moolau.*
*Low indeed lies Puakea,*
*With Kukuipahu by its side.*[7]

Or, there were the bundled remains of Hilo-Hāmākua, son of Kulukulu'a and district chief of Hilo:

*That is Hilo! That is Hilo!*
*That is Hilo of the incessant rains,*
*The increasing rains,*
*The ceaseless rains of Hilo.*
*That is Hamakua of the steep cliffs.*
*The ti leaf of Kamae is tramped down,*
*Hamakua is indeed withered.*[8]

The remainder of Keawenui a 'Umi's reign passed quietly, with his residence primarily in Hilo, although he did travel about his kingdom and seems to have had a major residence at Nāpo'opo'o at Kealakekua Bay, where his son, Lonoikamakahiki, is said to have been born.[9] Another residence appears to have been at Waipi'o.[10]

Keawenui a 'Umi took steps to consolidate power. In at least one district, he appointed a new line of district chiefs. His half-brother, Kumalae, was made chief of Hilo district, founding the 'Ī family line, which would rival and revolt against the ruling line by the end of the century.[11] He also married five high ranking women (Fig. 8-1):[12] Ko'ihalawai, his niece (daughter of the king of Kaua'i and of Keawenui's half-sister Akahi'ilikapu, a daughter of 'Umi); Haokalani, either of O'ahu's Kalona-iki or of Kona's Ehu family; Ho'opiliahae, perhaps a Maui chief or of the Pae line of Kohala; Kamola-nui-a-'Umi, his half-sister and a daughter of 'Umi; and Hakaukalalapuakea, a cousin and the granddaughter of Hākau. Wisely, he also married off his daughter from Kamola-nui-a-'Umi to Makua, the son of his half-brother Kumalae, the chief of Hilo. This marriage cemented his ties with Hilo, and this daughter became the mother of 'Ī.

His older children through these marriages seem to have been the three sons of Ko'ihalawai—Kanaloakua'ana (the eldest), Kanaloakuakawaiea, and Kanaloakapulehu. Yet, his younger son through Haokalani was apparently the favored or higher ranking son—Lonoikamakahiki.[13] Before Keawenui died

> *he requested Lonoikamakahiki to take the head of the government, but Lonoikamakahiki did not think it proper to do so. What Lonoikamakahiki told his father was, that he did not wish to take charge of the affairs of state at that time, but to defer the time until he was able to master the arts of warfare.*
>
> [Fornander][14]

As another act of consolidation, Keawenui removed the question of usurping his brother's son's (Kūka'ilani's) right to the throne by arranging a marriage between Kūka'ilani's daughter and ranking heir, Kaikilani, first with his son Kanaloakua'ana and then later with his son Lonoikamakahiki. When Lonoikamakahiki initially refused the rule of the land, Keawenui

> *solemnly, and in the presence of his chiefs, conferred the sovereignty, the dignity, and prerogatives of Moi on Kaikilani.*
>
> [Fornander][15]

Kaikilani was the daughter of his brother's son. But, the accounts clearly indicate that Kanaloakua'ana was acting ruler, regent apparently for Lonoikamakahiki.[16]

Kamakau[17] apparently was told a very different account of Keawenui's climb to power. He states 'Umi had commanded that the kingdom be divided in two upon his death. Thus, his eldest son Keli'iokāloa ruled in Kailua over Kona and evidently Kohala and Hāmākua districts, and Keawenui ruled in Hilo over the districts of Hilo, Puna and Ka'ū. Kamakau's version says that while Keli'iokāloa took care of the priests and gods, he became oppressive to chiefs and commoners.

> *He seized the property of the chiefs and that of the konohiki of the chiefs, the food of the commoners, their pigs, dogs, chickens, and other property. The coconut trees that were planted were hewn down, so were the people's koa trees. Their canoes and fish were seized;*

> *and people were compelled to do burdensome tasks such as diving for ‘ina sea urchins, wana sea urchins, and sea weeds at night.*
>
> [1870 Kamakau][18]

Some of his chiefs appealed to Keawenui and offered him the Kona Kingdom. Keawenui then led his army through the Saddle, and two battles were fought, one near Ahua a ‘Umi heiau and the second on the shore near Kailua. Keli‘iokāloa's side lost, and he was caught and killed. And so Keawenui united the kingdom, or so this version goes.

Kamakau's version is clearly different from Fornander's. Which is correct? Or are parts of both correct? This may be impossible to determine without knowing the details and sources of the stories told to Kamakau and Fornander. This is one of the dilemmas scholars face when oral histories of the same time period conflict. I tend to follow Fornander for several reasons.

First, peaceful division of the kingdom among heirs in late prehistory does not seem to have occurred in Hawaiian traditions of the A.D. 1500s–1700s, except in Kamakau's accounts for Hawai‘i in the A.D. 1600s. The senior heir was given the land; sometimes junior sons were given responsibilities for the gods or for certain districts, but always as chiefs under the senior heir. Kamakau's account suggests the reason for the uncertain death of Keli‘iokāloa, but it seems unlikely ‘Umi would split his kingdom with part given to Keawenui.

Second, Kamakau seems not to have had the complete story of Lonoikamakahiki that Fornander obtained. This specified in chant form the unveiling of the bones of all six district chiefs slain by Keawenui,[19] and also discussed Keawenui's melding his junior line with the senior line of Keli‘iokāloa, through marriage of his sons (Kanaloakua‘ana and Lonoikamakahiki) to Kaikilani-Ali‘i-Wahine-o-Puna (Keli‘iokāloa's granddaughter).[20] Kamakau recites pieces of the Lono story in far less detail and with omissions. He did not mention the chants related to the bones of the district chiefs. These chants and their detail argue that Keawenui had to overcome all district chiefs—not just the three of west Hawai'i as in Kamakau's account. Kamakau also does not mention the detailed story or any concerns of Keawenui and others with Kaikilani being a senior line representative. Her clear genealogical position and the fact she was married to Keawenui's sons would seem to support the story of Fornander.

These points make Fornander's version more plausible in my view—although again Kamakau's description of why Keli'iokāloa was oppressive may well be correct and be the basis for his overthrow and death.[21]

## A.D. 1640–1660 KANALOAKUA'ANA & LONOIKAMAKAHIKI: THE GRANDSONS OF 'UMI

Upon Keawenui's death, his eldest son Kanaloakua'ana assumed power as the regent or prime minister for Lonoikamakahiki and Kaikilani-Ali'i-Wahine-o-Puna.[22] Essentially, he was king. His younger brother, Lonoikamakahiki, was placed under his care in a special situation according to which Lonoikamakahiki was to come to power upon passing certain tests, and apparently he did within a year or two.[23] Thus, Lonoikamakahiki came to power, with Kaikilani and Kanaloakua'ana having critical advisory roles.

At some point early in his reign, Lonoikamakahiki and Kaikilani, then his wife, traveled abroad.[24] At Kalaupapa on Moloka'i, while playing kōnane with his wife, he overheard a message from his wife's lover being called down from the cliffs above.

*Say, Kaikilani, Chiefess of Puna,*
*Your lover sends you his love*
*Of the shady cliff that stands,*
*of Uli of Heakekoa.*

[Fornander][25]

In this famous story, Lono then became enraged and struck his wife with the stone kōnane board; and vowing never to live with her again, he departed to O'ahu, where he stayed for several months at the Kailua court of Kākuhihewa, ruler of O'ahu.[26] Word soon reached Hawai'i Island that Kaikilani had almost been killed; all of Lono's brothers and all the district chiefs, save one half-brother—Pupuakea—the chief of Ka'ū, revolted with Kanaloakua'ana "again assuming the regency," and plotted Lono's death should he return.

However, Kaikilani, who had returned to Hawai'i Island, left and sailed to O'ahu to find and warn Lono. There she located him at Kailua staying with Kākuhihewa. After her canoe landed, she approached Kākuhihewa's dwelling and sat outside the walls and chanted Lono's mele inoa (his name chant), breaking down his anger and gaining his forgiveness.[27]

Soon thereafter, Lono and Kaikilani returned to Hawai'i to fight his rebelling brothers. They sailed directly to Kealakekua, bypassing the rebel forces which were arrayed from 'Anaeho'omalu in southern Kohala north along the shore to northern Kohala.[28] Lono made contact with his younger half-brother—Pupuakea, chief of Ka'ū—with the only loyal forces on Hawai'i, and they met at Kealakekua. The Ka'ū warriors then marched north, and rapidly crossed Hualālai's high saddle, and arrived in the uplands of Pu'uanahulu in northernmost Kona, where they were joined by Lono, Pupuakea, and the warriors that Lono had gathered. All this was done before the rebels knew of Lono's return from O'ahu.

> *[A]t Puuanahulu...that was the place where the men were arrayed in battle formation. About this time, however, the rebels who were down at Anaehoomalu observed that the clinkers at Puuanahulu were red with people, which was a matter of surprise to the rebels. Some of them thought there was a battle being fought, while others conjectured they were some of their own men, being under the impression that Lonoikamakahiki was still at Oahu, for no news had*

> *been received that he, Lonoikamakahiki, had arrived at Kealakekua.*
>
> *During the night of the day on which the rebels were surprised, Lonoikamakahiki and his younger brother Pupuakea, together with the men, came down prepared to give battle. On the night the men left Puuanahulu to go down, the rebels realized there was to be war, because there were in the hands of the men torches burning from the van to the rear of the war procession of Lonoikamakahiki. Then it was that the rebels made preparations for battle, sending out messengers to inform the men and the chiefs on their side that had been stationed from Anaehoomalu to distant Kohala.*
>
> [Fornander][29]

The first battle of the day was fought at Wailea with the rebels defeated. Kanaloapulehu, Lono's half-brother and the general of the rebel forces, re-marshalled his men and those of Hilo under his brother Kanaloakuakawaiea at Kauno'oa in 'Ōuli. Later the same day a second engagement resulted, with the rebels again thrown back.[30]

Overnight, Kanaloapulehu regrouped his men and those of Kohala and Hāmākua, who had just arrived, and they encamped near the heiau of Pu'ukoholā and Mailekini at Kawaihae. But Lono, under his priests' directions, outflanked the rebels and attacked the Puna and Hilo forces at night at Puupā on the plains of Waimea. The rebels were drawn out by a small number of men with lighted torches, and then when "the two divisions of Lonoikamakahiki and Pupuakea came together...there was great slaughter of the rebels."[31]

The following night, Lono's men descended to Kawaihae and occupied Pu'ukoholā heiau. The battle called Kawaluna followed, and the rebel general Kanaloapulehu was taken prisoner. The rest of the rebels under Kanaloakuakawaiea were repulsed and fled to Pu'u

'Ainako in Kohala.[32] Kanaloapulehu—despite being Lono's half-brother—"was killed and laid upon the altar."[33]

Lono's and Pupuakea's combined forces followed the fleeing rebels.

> *The conquerors gave chase, meeting them on the beach at Kahua, when Pupuakea slaughtered them on the pili grass as well as at the beach.*
>
> [Fornander][34]

Here Pupuakea was said to have chanted:

> *Routed, are you, indeed you are routed!*
> .......................................................
> *The battle in the shower of sand at Kaunooa*
> *The night battle at Puupa.*
> *In the general war at Kawaluna*
> *The land pirates were easily defeated,*
> *Merely by the wind from the war clubs.*
> *Men are sacrificed indeed, by Lono.*
> *It was a victory.*
> *Lono was victorious.*
> *You treasonable chiefs!*
>
> [Fornander][35]

This battle at Kahuā was called Kai'ōpae, and here Lono's warriors killed Kanaloakuakawaiea, another of Lono's half-brothers and the remaining general of the rebels.

Lono followed up these victories with two final battles at Halelua in Kohala (the battle of Kai'opihi), and at Pu'umaneo above Pololū in Kohala. Again, Lono's half-brothers Kanaloakapulehu and Kanaloakuakawaiea, leaders of the rebel army, had been slain and sacrificed during these battles. Two other half-brothers, the rebel leader and regent Kanaloakua'ana and 'Umiokalani, escaped and later patched up their differences and returned to Lono's service.[36] With this war, Lonoikamakahiki established himself as the sole power on the island. He then returned the land to normal activities, holding several ceremonies at Mulei'ula heiau in 'Āpua, at Pu'ukoholā heiau in Kawaihae, and at Mākole'ā heiau in Kahalu'u in Kona.[37]

Another major event marked Lono's reign. He made a state visit to the court of the king of Maui, the aged Kamalālāwalu,[38] who soon after planned an invasion of Hawai'i.[39] His fleet departed from Hāna and landed at Puakō in Kohala. Kanaloakua'ana (Lono's oldest brother, the former regent) was in residence in Waimea. He met the Maui king with a small holding force at Kauno'oa near Puakō, while Lono was contacted in Kohala. Before Lono arrived with the larger army, his brother's force was overwhelmed, and Kanaloa was taken prisoner. He was unusually tortured, having his eyes gouged out and tattooed; then he was killed. The famous Koauli mele documents Kanaloa's death.

> *Blackened was the face of Kanaloa with fire.*
> *The face of Kanaloa, with burning fire.*
>
> [Fornander][40]

Kamalālāwalu then moved his army up to Waimea atop the hills of Pu'uoaoaka and Hōkū'ula, following false advice given by Lono's agents.[41]

> *During that night and including the following morning the Kona men arrived and were assigned to occupy a position from Puupa to Haleapala. The Kau and Puna warriors were stationed from Holoholoku to Waikoloa. Those of Hilo and Hamakua were located from Mahiki to Puukanikanihia, while those of Kohala guarded from Momoualoa to Waihaka.*
>
> *That morning Kamalalawalu observed that the lowlands were literally covered with almost countless men. Kamalalawalu then took a survey of his own men and realized that his forces were inferior in numbers.*
>
> [Fornander][42]

For three days the armies only skirmished, with Makakuikalani—Kamalālāwalu's nephew and general—dominating the Maui actions. Then the battle was joined with Makakuikalani positioning his warriors at the front below Hōkūʻula and Puʻuoaoaka, and being confronted by Pupuakea and his men. A battle of these two high chiefs alone followed, using war clubs, and Pupuakea emerged the victor with Makakuikalani slain.[43] The Maui forces were then rapidly routed and Kamalālāwalu slain.

> *[T]he slaughter of the Maui-ites continued for three days thereafter and those defeated who ran towards their canoes found no arms and outriggers because they had been broken. The repulsed warriors ran to Puako and noticing the bait boxes floating in the sea mistook them for canoes. They began to waver and were again overtaken by the victors. The destruction of the remaining invaders was then complete.*
>
> [Fornander][44]

Kamalālāwalu's body was taken to Keʻekū heiau in Kahaluʻu in Kona—a large luakini, reputedly in the puʻuhonua of Kahaluʻu when the king was in residence—where his remains were offered up to Kū.[45] Petroglyphs on the pāhoehoe at Keʻekū commemorate this event.[46] So ended the first of the major wars between the nations of Maui and Hawaiʻi.

Not long after, Lonoikamakahiki again left Hawaiʻi to travel to Kauaʻi, to see "the place where the trunkless koa tree was," Kahihikolo. He traveled long in the forests of Kauaʻi and was deserted by all his retinue and joined by a man of Kauaʻi, Kapaʻihiahilina.[47] Upon his return to Hawaiʻi, as a reward Lono made Kapaʻihiahilina his chief advisor (kuhina nui), leading to disgruntlement and plotting by Hawaiʻi chiefs to unseat this foreign advisor.[48] Within a year, when Kapaʻihiahilina was visiting Kauaʻi, he was supplanted. He returned, sailing into Kahaluʻu Bay and approached the fenced compound of Lono, who was then in residence at Kahaluʻu. There, he recited a chant about their wanderings, but Lono failed to respond, so Kapaʻihiahilina departed sailing north.[49] Lono regreted his actions, eventually followed and met his friend at ‘Anaeho‘omalu, where Kapa‘ihiahilina once again was made chief advisor.

To commemorate this reconciliation, Lono built an ahu pōhaku shrine on the main trail at the Kona border of Waikoloa ahupua‘a, which contained ‘Anaeho‘omalu as a seaward ‘ili. This shrine became known as Ke ahu a Lono.[50] An archaeological site called Ke ahu a Lono still exists today on the Kona-Kohala border in the midst of bare, rolling pāhoehoe flows and next to the main prehistoric trail, which cuts inland ca. 0.25 mile from Kīholo Bay in Kona, and passes along the inland border of the ‘ili of ‘Anaeho‘omalu and Kalāhuipua‘a within Waikoloa ahupua‘a in Kohala. This site is a small, flat-topped platform with a stepped tier along the trail. The platform is only ca. 9.8 x 3 meters in area (29 $m^2$) and only 0.75-meter high.[51] Over the years it deteriorated, having been damaged by survey markers and a telephone pole, and generally having its edges collapsing. In 1988, the Waikoloa Beach Resort restored the platform, closely simulating its original appearance.

Evidently Ke ahu a Lono was not just a commemorative marker. Based on archaeological work[52] and recent oral histories,[53] it also seems to have served as the ahupua‘a shrine for this part of Waikoloa. It is on the main trail and on the correct border of the ahupua‘a for such a shrine. If this interpretation is correct, then during the annual makahiki tax collection, tribute may have been laid out here. Some archaeologists have suggested that an adjacent site of numerous, tiny, fragile-walled, rectangular pavings may have been for the storage or display of the taxes[54]—but this has yet to be verified either through oral histories or archaeology. Interestingly, numerous circle petroglyphs, some with dots in the center, are pecked on the pāhoehoe immediately across the trail from Ke ahu a Lono and along the trail to the north. Again, the shrine has been preserved, along with the trail, petroglyphs and part of the adjacent rectangular pavings, and the public can visit this spot.

Other archaeological sites near this commemorative structure of Lono's also date back to the A.D. 1600s. Immediately inland of the trail in Waikoloa and adjacent Pu'uanahulu is a vast acreage of worn basins in the rolling, bare pāhoehoe, each about 1-foot wide and 2-feet long. These basins were used to make hand-sized, light, porous pāhoehoe (scoria) blocks into basalt abraders—the rough saws, files and sandpaper of old. The pāhoehoe blocks were broken loose from cracks in the flow in huge numbers. Indeed, this area is a vast quarry for scoria with numerous workshops where the material was gathered and roughly shaped before being taken away. Small caves, rockshelters, and C- and L-shaped walls are found clustered along the trail and scattered amidst the quarry; these served as temporary shelters for small groups of people collecting the material. Excavations have dated initial use of these shelters and the quarry to between the A.D. 1400s–1800s, with additional volcanic glass dates indicating use beginning in the late 1600s and burgeoning in the 1700s.[55]

Interestingly, just beyond the main abrader quarry, to the north along the prehistoric ala loa trail, is the large 'Anaeho'omalu-Waikoloa petroglyph field. Thousands of figures cover the rolling, almost black pāhoehoe terrain. Recent research suggests that huge concentrations like this were not just the idle work of overnight travelers, but ritual art of an as yet uncertain nature, perhaps tied to the quarrying of the scoria abraders. A striking discovery in recent archaeological work was that many petroglyphs had been cut into abandoned abrader basins.[56] This pattern shows that these specific petroglyphs were made after abrader quarrying began, after A.D. 1400 and probably in the late 1600s, in the time of Lonoikamakahiki and his immediate successors. It may indicate a similar age for the entire petroglyph field.

These sites—Ke ahu a Lono, the prehistoric ala loa or main trail, the quarry and the petroglyphs—appear linked in time, quite likely to Lono and the rulers who followed him. The coastal fishponds at 'Anaeho'omalu were undoubtedly in use then, and were probably where Lono briefly resided while reconciling with Kapa'ihiahilina. But, these fishponds and adjacent shelter caves also were used in much earlier times.

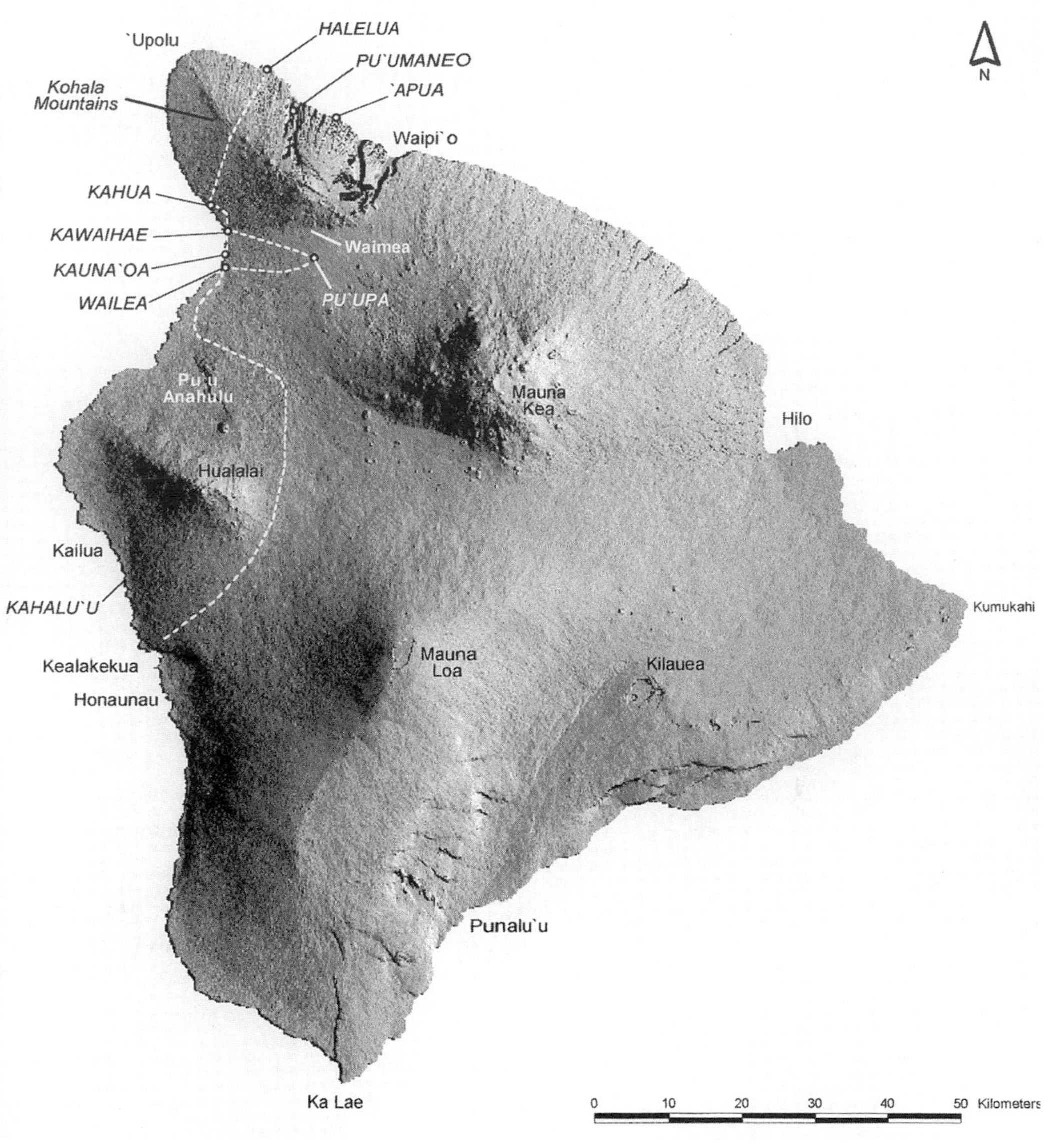


**FIGURE 8-2**
Lonoikamakahiki's campaign against his half-brothers to regain the kingdom. Map shows locations noted in the campaign.

No further major events are noted in Lono's reign. Upon his death his remains are said to have been deified, encased in a kā‘ai container and placed in the Hale o Līloa in Waipi‘o, with the remains of his great grandfather Līloa. One of the two kā‘ai reputedly rescued from the Hale o Līloa during missionary fervor and still preserved today supposedly contains the bones of Lonoikamakahiki.[57] If true, these remains are sacred relics of one of the most famous rulers of the Hawai‘i kingdom, yet one whose reign saw one misadventure after another and periodic losses of power due to his behavior.

Kamakau's account of the life of Lonoikamakahiki contains many of the same events, but not in the same order. And his account omits a number of key stories recorded by Fornander and supported by other sources. Other inconsistencies occur. For these reasons, I am inclined to follow Fornander's account.

Kamakau presents different versions of the succession upon Keawenui's death. In a 1865 article, Kamakau said Lono ruled jointly with his older brother Kanaloakua‘ana, with Kanaloa ruling over Kona, Kohala and Hāmākua and with Lono ruling over Ka‘ū, Puna and Hilo.[58] By 1871, he presented a very different version.[59] In this later version, upon the death of Keawenui, the kingdom was divided into three parts: Kona-Kohala, Ka‘ū-Puna, and Hilo-Hāmākua. Kona and Kohala were said to be ruled by Kanaloakua‘ana (Keawenui's eldest son) and ‘Umi o Kalani (one of Keawenui's junior sons), with ‘Umi o Kalani in control. [One wonders why the very junior son would be given control.] Next, Kanaloakua‘ana was encouraged by his followers to overthrow ‘Umi o Kalani, which he did in a battle at Pu‘uwa‘awa‘a. Ka‘ū and Puna were said to be ruled by Lonoikamakahiki, and Hilo and Hāmākua were said to have been ruled by Kumalaenui a ‘Umi (Keawenui's half-brother) and his son Makua, the founders of the ‘Ī family of Hilo chiefs. Even later in 1871, Kamakau describes Lono as the “chief of the island of Hawai‘i and its people”[60] which implies Lono ruled the entire island. The detailed account of Lono's accession recorded by Fornander makes much more sense than a peaceful splitting of the kingdom into pieces among heirs—which has no precedent other than in Kamakau's versions of A.D. 1600s Hawai‘i. It also conflicts with other oral histories of the 1800s which have Lono residing in Kahalu'u,[61] offering sacrifices at heiau in Kohala and Kona,[62] and dedicating a shrine at the Kohala-Kona border[63]—all acts which imply control over those areas.

Kamakau continues, having Lonoikamakahiki beat his wife (Kaikilani, a chiefess of Puna) to death with a block of wood during a kōnane game at Kealakekua after hearing the story of Heaakekoa being her lover called down the cliff. Then Lono went mad and wandered about, finally reaching Kaua'i, where the story of Kapa'ihiahilina is given.[64] Lono returned to Hawai'i and made Kapa'ihiahilina his aide. Kamakau offers a brief aside about their falling-out and reconciliation with few details. Lono then traveled abroad again, visiting Kamalālāwalu (where the similar Puapuakea story is told). He stopped at Kalaupapa and broke a kōnane board over Kaikilani, "a woman," and then visited Ka'ihikapu-a-Kākuhihewa on O'ahu (where the competitions and Kaua'i chant are noted).

This portion of Kamakau's account is internally consistent, yet it contradicts Fornander's lengthy version.[65] Kaikilani-Ali'i-Wahine-o-Puna is nowhere mentioned as the ranking member of the senior line of 'Umi, nor is the importance of her earlier marriage with Kanaloakua'ana noted. She is killed in Kealakekua, which conflicts with the accounts of Moloka'i elders and with the detailed story of her going to Kākuhihewa's court and returning with Lono. Also, the revolt of Lono's brothers is not mentioned; Lono simply returns from Kaua'i in Kamakau's account. Kamakau ignores the revolt's detailed account and the archaic prayer of Iwikauikaua to escape sacrifice during the revolt, both recorded by Fornander. Kamakau does give a similar version of the Kapa'ihiahilana story, but without the details of his temporary falling-out with Lono. Also, Kamakau has a new Kaikilani hit with a kōnane board at Kalaupapa, and one wonders if this is not the Kaikilani-Ali'i-Wahine-o-Puna story out of sequence. The sojourn at the O'ahu court is now with the son of Kākuhihewa, yet in another story Kamakau says Lono's kahuna left to live with Kākuhihewa[66]—two different versions of which O'ahu ruler was contemporaneous, with the latter agreeing with Fornander's recorded story. Also, Kamakau's stories of the court visit to O'ahu mention some of the competitions, but lack the detail of Fornander's account. To me, this suggests that the overall account and sequence of Kamakau's version may have problems, although some individual events are fairly accurate or at least compatible.

One point is obvious from both accounts. Lono had an up and down career with frequent extended, famous and romanticized departures from Hawai'i. As Kamakau notes, his name was associated with the makahiki god Lono-i-ka'ou-ali'i, and he was thought of as a god of the makahiki—thus his name.[67]

Kamakau's version continues with Kamalālāwalu's invasion of Hawai'i. The spies and Kama's agents are similar to Fornander's story. But, the Maui army lands in northern Kohala in Kamakau's account. Kanaloakua'ana alone is mentioned in the battle of Kohala, with his capture and death given as in the accounts collected by Fornander. Then Kamalālāwalu proceeds to Kawaihae and Waimea. Here the men of Kona, Ka'ū, Puna, Waimea and Kohala—but not Hāmākua and Hilo—advanced upon the Maui army, and the ending is as in the accounts given by Fornander. At this point, Lono is called "ruler of Hawaii," which seems strikingly contradictory to the three kingdoms concept and which actually seems supportive of the Fornander accounts.

One of Lonoikamakahiki's primary residential centers was Kahalu'u ahupua'a in Kona (Figs. 8-3 and 8-4). A small protected, half-moon bay is indented in the shoreline, fringed with sand at its southern end and partly enclosed by a breakwater of large boulders which extends off the southern point of the bay. To the south, a pāhoehoe marine bench is covered by the tides with pockets of sand at the high-tide mark, and with numerous natural pools and succulent growth in low points in the undulating pāhoehoe behind the shore. Upslope behind the bay, the land gradually rises, then steepens to the high-rainfall zone at the 800-foot elevation, ca. 1.2 miles inland. Today, the Keauhou Beach Hotel sits on the south edge of the bay, with the Kona Lagoon Hotel just south on the undulating pāhoehoe. The beach is a county park, and houses line the inland edge of the shore road, Alii Drive. Inland, the land is gradually being developed as the Keauhou Resort.

Surprisingly, within this changing modern context, many important archaeological ruins once associated with the ruling center at Kahalu'u still remain. The luakini heiau of Ke'ekū—where the Maui rulers Kamalālāwalu's body was offered to the gods—is still present on the grounds of the Kona Lagoon Hotel. It is a large, stone-walled enclosure (2,050 $m^2$) extending from the narrow sand shore out onto the narrow pāhoehoe tidal flats.[68] Petroglyphs are exposed at low tide on the pāhoehoe next to Ke'ekū. In 1906, 86-year old Malanui, grandson of the last priest of Kapuanoni heiau, showed Stokes of the Bishop Museum a petroglyph which was said to represent Kamalālāwalu. It is extremely unusual, being cut in low relief.[69] Some oral histories also state that the grounds around and including Ke'ekū were the pu'uhonua of this royal center.[70]

Another large heiau, called Hāpaiali'i, juts out onto the pāhoehoe tidal flats on the grounds of the Keauhou Beach Hotel, less than 50 meters north of Ke'ekū and separated only by a natural, brackish embayment and a tidal pool. These ruins are of a large stone platform, with huge foundation stones. Half of Hāpaiali'i has been severely damaged by waves during storms. Oral histories do not describe Hāpaiali'i as a luakini; it appears to have been another type of heiau associated with this royal center.[71]

Just beyond Hāpaiali'i yet another heiau was built out onto the tidal flats, at the south point of the bay. Kapuanoni consists of several small enclosures and platforms surrounded by a large enclosing wall. The Keauhou Beach Hotel abuts this heiau, which was in part incorrectly restored in the 1960s with rounded corners and cement. Oral traditions identify Kapuanoni as a fishing and agricultural heiau used by the ruler.[72]

Oral histories place the ruler's residence—at least in the time of Alapa'inui and Kamehameha—just inland of Kapuanoni heiau along the sandy south edge of Kahalu'u Bay, near the pond called Po'o Hawai'i. A large structure just south of the Kona Lagoon Hotel on the grounds of the Keauhou Racquet Club has been called Lonoikamakahiki's dwelling. It is a massive stone wall with short side walls. However, such a large structure seems unlikely to have been a dwelling; indeed it has recently been pointed out that this site was called a heiau by local Hawaiians until the 1950s. It seems most likely that Lonoikamakahiki resided close by the large heiau, probably near Po'o Hawai'i.[73]

Mākole'ā heiau, located about 100 meters inland on the grounds of the Kona Lagoon Hotel, is a large stone enclosure. It also was associated with Lonoikamakahiki, having been one of the heiau where he held ceremonies after retaking the kingdom from his brothers. Malanui told Stokes in 1906 that this heiau was for "prayers in general" and not for sacrifice, so it does not seem to have been a luakini.[74] There is also a large surfing heiau on the north side of Kahalu'u Bay, Kū'emanu. It is a large stone platform, currently with the small St. Peter's church built on top of it.[75] Other heiau are scattered inland for ca. 0.5 miles.[76] Importantly, there was another large luakini—'Ōhi'amukumuku heiau—just inland of Po'o Hawai'i. It was largely dismantled in the early 1800s to build the adjacent church, although foundations remain. Oral histories suggest that this heiau became important later in prehistory, with Ke'ekū being the main luakini in Lono's time.[77]

Nearly all these large heiau center around the royal residential area. An archaeological survey from 1929–1930 shows that other residences were clustered around the royal Po'o Hawai'i area[78]—likely the houses of the high chiefs and the lesser chiefs. Few, if any, of these house sites remain today. Other house sites, undoubtedly for commoners, extended inland among the heiau and up into the agricultural fields. These house sites remain today as archaeological ruins, and indicate that Kahalu'u had a very dense population focused on the bay.

Thus, although altered by modern hotels and residences, much remains at Kahalu'u. One need only be at the Keauhou Beach Hotel at dusk and look out toward the sea to the south. The heiau of Hāpaiali'i and Ke'ekū dominate the shoreline, their stone silhouettes gradually darkening. Knowing the history of Kahalu'u, realizing that one is standing on the royal grounds and is looking out on royal, national heiau, one can feel the power of the place. Lonoikamakahiki can be recalled, and the beating of the drums and the chanted prayers at Ke'ekū as Kamalālāwalu's body was offered to Kū in celebration of victory over the Maui invaders.

However, it is important to reaize that not all the heiau and sites visible today were present in the reign of Lono. Some may have been, but they also may have been smaller. Other rulers followed Lono and rebuilt heiau or constructed new heiau. Recent archaeological work mapping Ke'ekū heiau has identified several earlier wall facings. The current walls clearly show an addition of a stone facade, and at least two other different facings have been revealed.[79] Which walls match those of Ke'ekū during Lono's time are still uncertain. As noted, 'Ōhi'amukumuku may not have become a major luakini, or even been built to a larger size, until later in prehistory. The ruins of Kahalu'u represent the era of Lono, as well as earlier and later additions. Indeed, Ke'ekū heiau—in some form—is noted in the reign of Kalaunuiohua, ca. A.D. 1480–1500, long before Līloa.[80]

## A.D. 1660–1680 KEAKEALANIKANE, A.D. 1680–1700 KEAKAMAHANA, & A.D. 1700–1720 KEAKEALANIWAHINE: 'UMI'S GREAT-GRANDCHILDREN & BEYOND

Lonoikamakakahiki had no children from Kaikilani-Ali'i-Wahine-o-Puna and his two sons from Kaikilani-kohepani'o (of the Laea line in Kona's Kekaha area) did not inherit the rule, for reasons unspecified in the traditions.[81] Kaikilani-Ali'i-Wahine-o-Puna's son from Lono's oldest brother, Kanaloakua'ana became ruler. The son was Keakealanikane. Fornander states, "We have no legends of his reign,"[82] which is not quite true because Keakealanikane's son, Keawekuikeka'ai, is said to have built the Great Wall enclosing the pu'uhonua at Hōnaunau.[83] At this time, the power of the great families of 'Ī of Hilo and Mahi of Kohala was increasing. Kamakau goes so far to claim that the 'Ī family ruled independently—with two kingdoms on the island, Kona and Hilo.[84] Fornander says that the 'Ī and Mahi were "enabled to assume an attitude little short of political independence."[85]

Keakamahana, Keakealanikane's daughter through his sister, was the next ruler, as evidently there was no high-ranking male heir.[86] Kamakau stated that she was raised on Kaua'i and had been brought back by the chiefs of Hawai'i as they desired a "sacred ruler."[87] Little is known of her reign.[88] She was married to Iwikauikaua, the son of Makakauali'i (Kaikilani's brother), who was a Kona high chief of the generation before her.[89] One of her main residences was at Hōlualoa in Kona.[90] The Mahi family, with Kanaloauo'o as Kohala's district chief, and the Hilo-based 'Ī family with Kua'ana a 'Ī as the Hilo district chief seem to have been gaining even more power. Kamakau states that Keakamahana ruled all the island except for Hilo and Hāmākua, with these districts supposedly still independent under the 'Ī family.[91] In addition Kamakau says that Keakamahana had her husband's (Iwikauikaua) oldest daughter and his mother killed and their bones mistreated. He then plotted to betray her to the Hilo chiefs, and he left her and went to O'ahu. War followed between the Kona and Hilo chiefs.

Again, no male heir was available, so Keakealaniwahine succeeded her mother as ruler. Her husbands were her paternal half-brother (Kāneikaiwilani, raised on O'ahu and returned to marry her), and Kanaloaikaiwilewa (also known as Kanaloakapulehu), perhaps a Kohala chief.[92] The Mahi family was powerful at this time, and closely allied to the ruler. Mahi'ololī, the district chief of Kohala, was the chief advisor to the ruler.[93]

Civil war with the 'Ī family erupted during Keakealaniwahine's reign.[94] 'I'i[95] provides details for the start of this war. Keakealaniwahine was circuiting the island conducting religious ceremonies at various heiau. 'Ī and his son, Kua'ana a 'Ī, were accompanying her, when 'Ī died. Kua'ana left to prevent defilement of the rituals, and Keakealaniwahine misinterpreted this departure as an act of revolt. Attempts were made to kill Kua'ana. These failed, and Kua'ana and his Hilo followers took Keakealaniwahine and her court hostage in Waipi'o, banished her to Moloka'i for two years, and placed himself and his son, Kuahu'ia, in control of the island. After two years, Keakealaniwahine was reinstated, solely over Ka'ū,

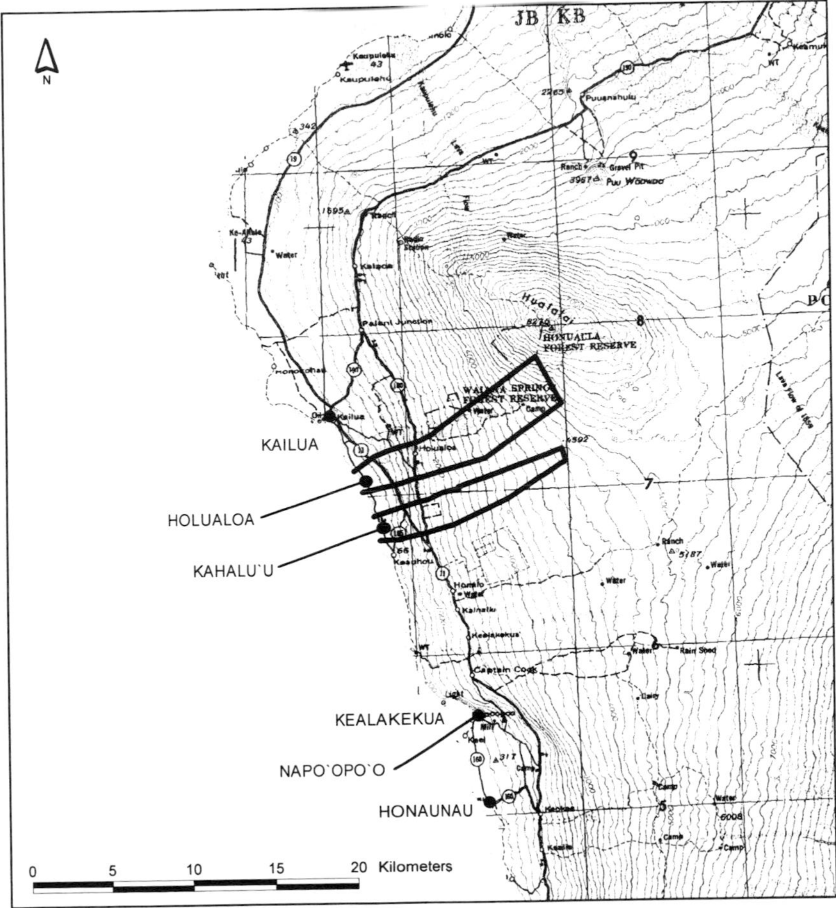


**FIGURE 8-3**

Royal Centers in Use during the A.D. 1600s in Kona.

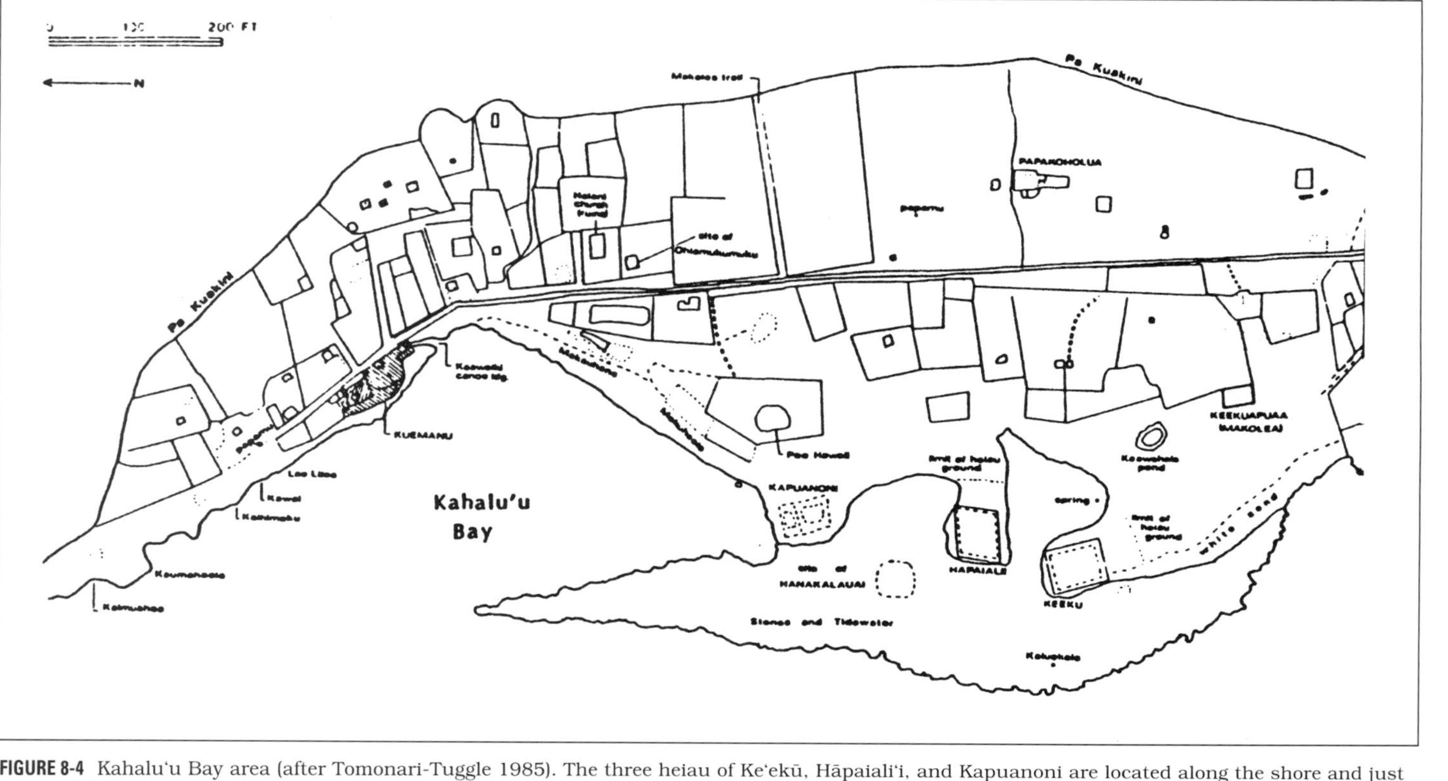


**FIGURE 8-4** Kahalu'u Bay area (after Tomonari-Tuggle 1985). The three heiau of Ke'ekū, Hāpaiali'i, and Kapuanoni are located along the shore and just south of the bay. Po'o Hawai'i, where the ruler resided, is also on the south edge, just inland of the trail (road) behind the center of the bay, and Kū'emanu heiau is on the north edge of the bay. The other enclosures shown on this map are mostly former hoouseyards, bounded by stone walls, which may have corresponded to houseyards or pā hale of chiefs and commoners in the time of Lonoikamakahiki.

Kona and Kohala. Kamakau's presentation is similar. He tells of Kua'ana being taken captive at Kawaihae and almost drowned by the chiefs of Kona. A Kohala chief allowed his escape to his mother's lands in Hāna. Kuahu'ia, Kua'ana's son and Hilo's general, then attacked Kona, and "Kona's chiefs fled to their fortresses." Keakealaniwahine and others were taken captive, sent to Maui and Moloka'i, and later restored over Kona, Kohala and Ka'ū.[96] In contrast, Fornander supplies no details on the war and was told that the war was resolved with the 'Ī family still supplying the district chief of Hilo.[97]

Do these accounts mean the 'Ī family was part of Keakealaniwahine's kingdom, or did they rule over a separate Hilo-Hāmākua-'Ōla'a kingdom? These traditions of the late 1600s and early 1700s can be interpreted to reflect an example of the traditional striving for power and periodic ascendancy of some district chiefs and their families under the king's rule—in this case the 'Ī and the Mahi. Clearly, the 'Ī and Mahi became quitc powerful and perhaps operated virtually independently in their lands, but these families actually seem to have maintained titular loyalty under one kingdom for most of these years, although much of the ruling line's actual control would seem to have been restricted to Kona and their ancestral center of Waipi'o. Only one revolt by the 'Ī family is noted in reference to Kona Pili rulers—that during the time of Keakealaniwahine.[98] The fact that she oversaw national rituals throughout the island before the assault on Kua'ana a 'Ī suggests titular control over the island by the senior Pili line, at least until that time. Much of this control seems likely to have been lost after her capture and banishment.[99] Yet the 'Ī could have in title remained district chiefs of Hilo and in fact have operated independently.

These problems seem finally to have been resolved when Keakealaniwahine's son (Keawe) was married to a granddaughter of 'Ī (Lonoma'aikanaka). The senior son of this marriage was given three chiefly kapu and his name Kalaninui'īamamao or Ka'īamamao (meaning this 'Ī was greater than all other 'Ī), by Keakealaniwahine at his navel cord cutting ceremony at Ke'ekū heiau at Kahalu'u[100]—

apparently late in her reign. Whether the marriage was a forced result of the war, or taken on her initiative to ally with the 'Ī family and strengthen her power, is uncertain. But the marriage and Keawe's heir (Kalaninui'īamamao) brought the Kona and Hilo Pili lines back together.[101]

Under Keakamahana, Hōlualoa ahupua'a became one of the main royal residential centers and remained so through the reign of her daughter, Keakealaniwahine.[102] The heiau of this center seem to have been focused between Kamoa Point on the south side of Hōlualoa Bay and the border with the ahupua'a of Kaumanamana (Figs. 8-5, 8-6). The royal residence and perhaps an associated pu'uhonua (refuge place) were immediately inland.

> *Where the large stone wall is located above Keolonāhihi was Keakealaniwahine's dwelling place, for her parents, Keakamahana and Iwikauikaua resided there.*
>
> ['I'i][103]

High-ranking chiefs' dwellings are believed to have been clustered about nearby, possibly in the form of walled-in house yards.[104]

Deciphering the names and function of the heiau at Hōlualoa has proven extremely difficult, due to the fragmentary, vague and highly contradictory oral and historical records.[105] A large heiau is present on Kamoa Point on the bay (Fig. 8-5). According to the late 1800s Board of Genealogy of Hawaiian Chiefs, this appears to be the likely temple where Keakealaniwahine gave her grandson, Kalanike'eaumoku, the important kapu wohi—in a special ceremony at a heiau called Keolonāhihi.[106] It also seems to be the heiau with a pool described as Kānekaheilani to Ellis in 1823.[107] Other names exist for this heiau; none can be firmly accepted due to inconsistencies in the records, but today Keolonāhihi is being used by the State of Hawaii for the historic park which includes this area. The heiau is surrounded on three sides by a high thick wall; its age has yet to be determined through archaeological work.

The early historic accounts of Ellis also refer to a Hale o Kā'ili ca. 150 feet or so to the south along the same shore.[108] This type of heiau had small structures, but was extremely sacred as it was used to maintain the image of the Pili line's war god, Kūkā'ilimoku.[109] The oral history supplied in 1903 by John Bull, a Hawaiian kama'āina in 1903 to Stokes of the Bishop Museum also refers to two smaller heiau nearby to the south—a hale 'a'ama and hale o kekupa.[110] As seen in Figure 8-5, archaeological remains do exist south of the large heiau, including small platforms within walled areas, and some of these remains may be the ruins of these smaller, ancillary heiau. Again, archaeological excavation has yet to occur, so no dates are available.

In addition to these religious structures, it is possible that a pu'uhonua was just inland. John Bull also told Stokes about this area.[111] And Ellis in 1823 was told about a heiau at the walled enclosure area associated with Keakealaniwahine.[112] The existence of a pu'uhonua in association with the ruler's residence is a typical pattern; the large walled area is similar to the pu'uhonua at Hōnaunau, albeit on a smaller scale.

The area commonly called the residence of Keakealaniwahine, yet clearly also that of her mother,[113] consists of a complex of enclosures, with large platforms and pavings.[114] One large enclosure has walls 9-feet (2.7-m) high and 13-feet (3.9-m) wide.[115] This site has yet to be excavated by archaeologists or even thoroughly mapped. The State of Hawaii hopes to acquire the site or see it preserved as part of the general Hōlualoa royal center historic complex.

Significantly, Hōlualoa seems not to have been used as a royal residential center after Keakealaniwahine's reign. Its temples were still used and refurbished up into Kamehameha's reign,[116] and high chiefs did reside here—for example, Kamehameha's mother and Kamehameha as a youth.[117] It is possible that later rulers briefly stopped and lived at Hōlualoa, but it seems to have fallen back into lesser importance after Keakealaniwahine's reign.

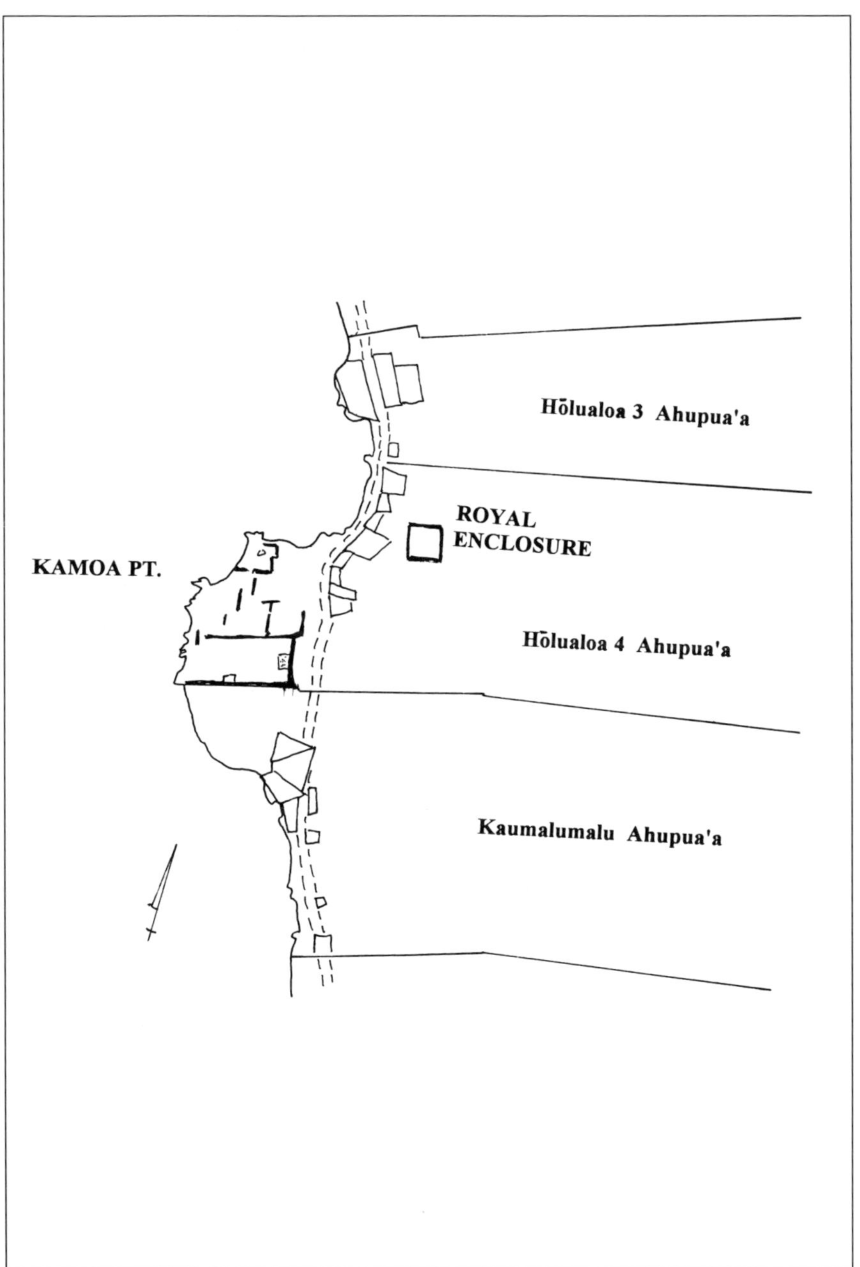


**FIGURE 8-5**

Hōlualoa, coastal portions of the ahupua'a showing royal enclosure, nearby houselots, and the area of heiau near Kamoa Point. (Adapted from McEldowney 1986: Fig. 4).

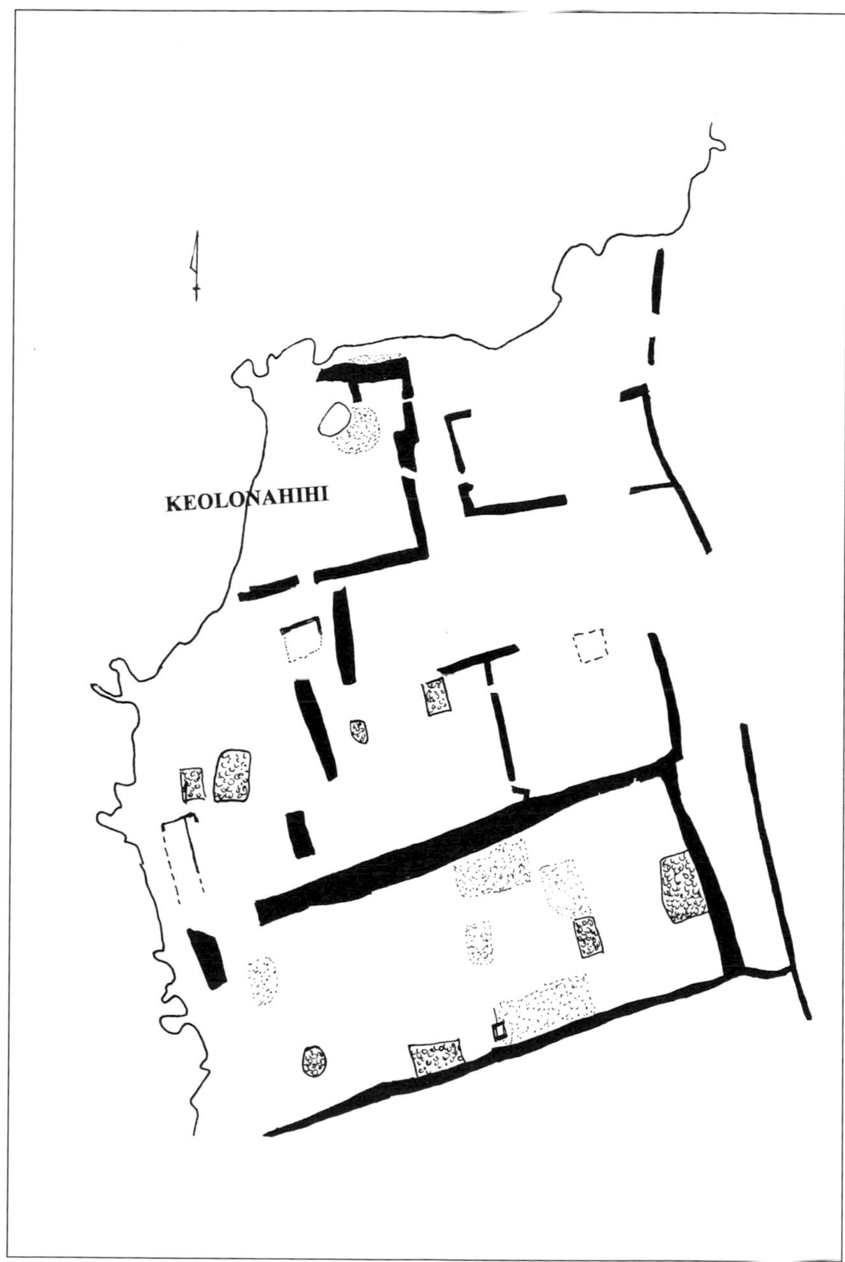


**FIGURE 8-6**

Archaeological features at Kamoa Point, Hōlualoa. The larger heiau is at northwest corner, labelled Keolonāhihi. Smaller heiau, including a Hale o Kā'ili, were located in the southern enclosed area. Nearly the entire area on this map is now Keolonāhihi State Historical Park. (Adapted from McEldowney 1986:73).

# THE KONA FIELD SYSTEM

During the reign of these rulers ending with Keakealaniwahine, the agricultural fields within the district of Kona expanded dramatically—probably partly to support the newly established Kona ruling centers (Kailua, Hōlualoa, Kahalu‘u and Kealakekua),[118] and partly to support a rapidly increasing population. Indeed, based on one experimental simulation, it is possible that in the A.D. 1600s population on Hawai‘i Island increased from ca. 33,000 at the beginning of the century to 61,000—almost doubling.[119] And almost all experimental models of population growth show a marked increase after the A.D. 1400s and 1500s.[120]

In this setting, the field systems of leeward Kohala, Waimea and Ka‘ū undoubtedly also were expanding and approaching the form seen and described at European contact. So too the field systems of windward Hawai‘i—in Puna, Hilo, Hāmākua and wet Kohala—must have expanded.

During the first centuries of permanent settlement in Kona (the A.D. 1000s–1200s), which saw the spread of housing through the district, fields would have been clearings in the forested uplands where annual rainfall was sufficient for reliable crops, probably at ca. the 900–1,000-foot elevation and the 40-inch rainfall line. Over the centuries with population growth, these cleared lands would expand—gradually encroaching into the forest lands farther upslope and spreading downslope onto drier and rockier soils. The originally cleared lands would be more intensively used—well cleared of trees, with rocks removed to increase soil areas, and with many defined plots of land. This latter picture comes close to the Kona fields described by the Cook expedition in 1779, by later expeditions, and by Hawaiians themselves in the 1840 Māhele documents.

The Kealakekua Bay area is perhaps the classic area where the Kona field system has been studied. Commoner farmers cultivated plots of land in four different land zones: kula, kalu‘ulu, ‘āpa‘a, and ‘ama‘u. Above the cliffs in the higher rainfall zones (50–115 inches per year)—at ca. 1,000-2,500-feet elevation and ca. 0.5–2.5–miles inland—was the main farming zone, the ʻāpaʻa. Here taro and sweet potatoes were grown on cleared terraced soil areas and on stone mounds in fields fringed with low mounded stone and earth walls (kuaīwi or iwi ʻāina). These long kuaīwi walls ran toward the sea (mauka-makai). This has been called the formal portion of the field system, or the formal-walled area.

In 1793, Archibald Menzies, the naturalist of Vancouver's British expedition, provided the following oft-cited view of these ʻāpaʻa fields.

> *As we advanced beyond the bread-fruit plantations, the country became more and more fertile, being in a high state of cultivation. For several miles round us there was not a spot that would admit of it but what was with great labor and industry cleared of the loose stones and planted with esculent [kalo] roots or some useful vegetables or other. In clearing the ground, the stones are heaped up in ridges between the little fields and planted on each side, either with a row of sugar cane or the sweet root of these islands [ki, Cordyline terminalis]...where they afterwards continue to grow in a wild state, so that even these stony, uncultivated banks are by this means made useful to the proprietors, as well as ornamental to the fields they intersect.*[121]

Fourteen years earlier, Lt. King and Captain Clerke of Cook's expedition supplied similar descriptions:

> *the regular & very extensive plantations. The Plantain trees... some in the Walls: these walls separate their property & are made of the Stones got on clearing the Ground; but they are hid by the sugar cane being planted on each side, whose leaves or stalk make a beautiful looking edge. The Tarrow or Eddy root & the sweet Potatoe with a few cloth plants are what grow in these cultivated spots.*
>
> [1779 King][122]

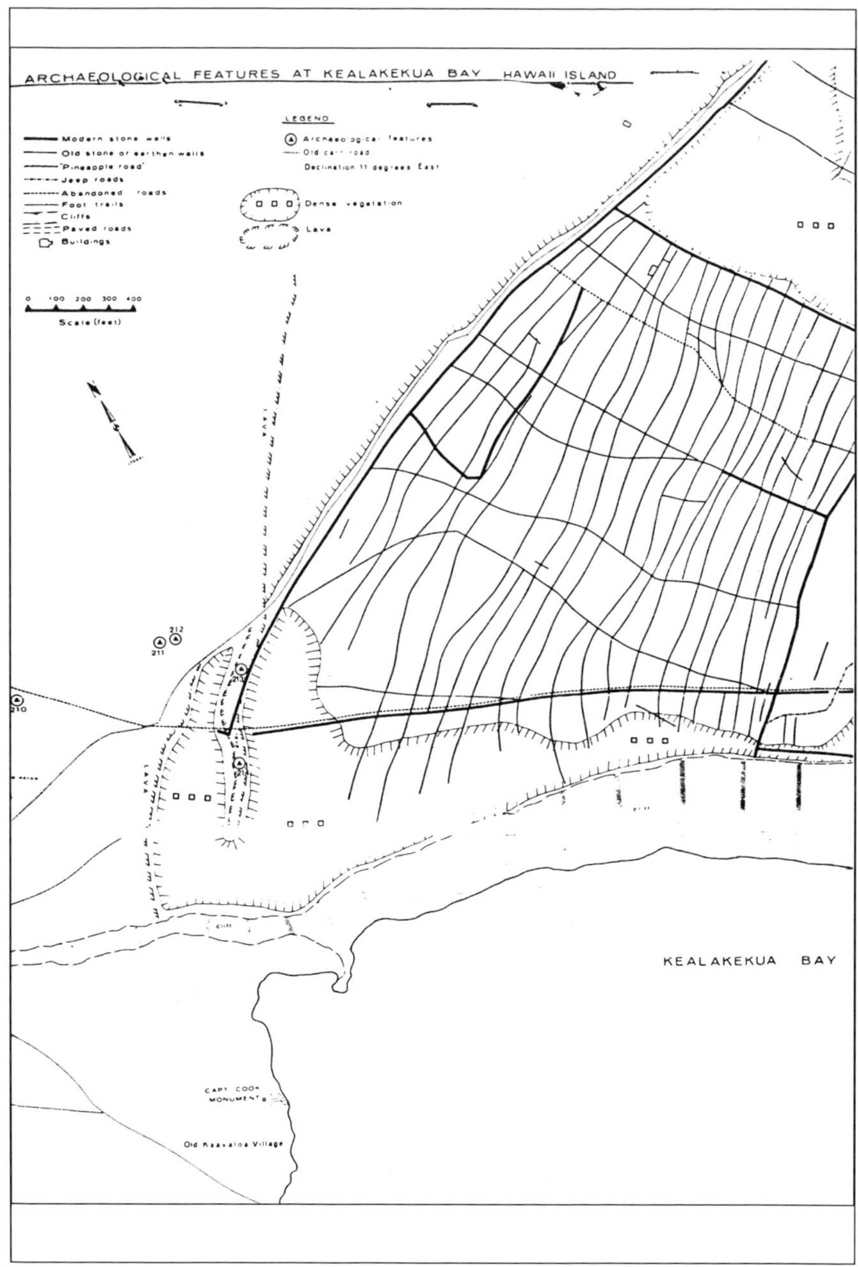


**FIGURE 8-7**

Soehren & Newman's (1968) archaeological map of kuaīwi walls and farm plots above the cliffs of Kealakekua. The shoreline flats of Ka'awaloa ahupua'a are to the lower left, the location of many houses at European contact.

> *At the back of the villages upon the Brow of the Hill are their plantations of Plantains, Potatoes, Tarrow, Sugar Canes &ca, each mans particular property is fenced in with a stone wall; they have a method of making the Sugar Cane grow about the walls so that the stones are not conspicuous at any distance, but the whole has the appearance of fine green fences.*
>
> [1779 Clerke][123]

In the late 1960s, these kuaīwi walls came to archaeologists' attention with the work of Soehren and Newman[124] who used aerial photography to map the walls just above the cliffs of Kealakekua Bay (Fig. 8-7). This zone saw little archaeological work in the 1970s, because development and contract archaeology work was focused nearer the shore. An exception was the founding of the Amy Greenwell Ethnobotanical Park at the 1,500-foot elevation. Archaeological survey of the walled fields and internal terraces and mounds occurred, and test excavations yielded dates suggesting use of the fields in the A.D. 1600s–1700s.[125] Recently, however, development for housing and golf courses has spread into upper Kealakekua, and archaeology has begun anew

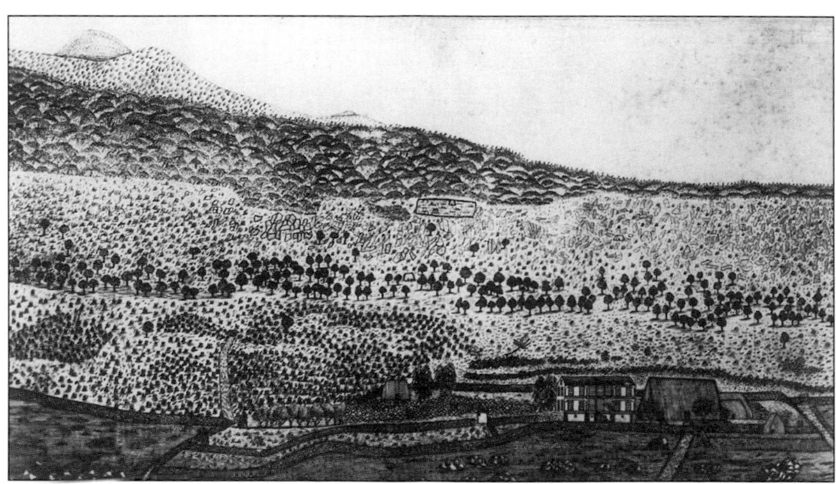

BISHOP MUSEUM

**FIGURE 8-8**

1840 illustration showing the land inland of Kailua's shore. The line of trees is the kalu'ulu (breadfruit) zone. The kula planting zone is below, and the 'āpa'a zone is above the trees and divided into small fields. (Drawing by Persis Thurston, 1840, in Kelly 1983:Fig. 36.)

in the ʻāpaʻa zone. Survey has been done in Kaʻawaloa,[126] Kealakekua,[127] and Kahauloa,[128] and in all cases the walled fields extended down to the 600–700-foot elevations. The few dates from these projects suggest use of the field areas back to the A.D. 1300s–1400s.[129]

Just downslope of the ʻāpaʻa zone, at the edge of the pali above Kealakekua Bay, was the kaluʻulu zone with groves of breadfruit trees. Sweet potatoes and paper mulberry, wauke used for kapa cloth, were planted under these trees.[130]

> *One then comes to breadfruit trees which flourish amazingly. The ground was very uneven & although there was a tolerable Soil about the trees, yet there was constant breaks in the land & large bare, burnt rocks; in the bottoms that these made were planted the Sweet Potatoe roots with earth collected about them.*
>
> [1779 King][131]

Interestingly, this zone cannot yet be distinguished archaeologically from the ʻāpaʻa zone. The walled kuaīwi fields extend right down to the cliff edge at the 600-foot elevation, and their walls go down to 700 feet in Kahauloa south of the pali. It may be that stones were also cleared in these areas to form walls, or the groves were on the steep slopes south of the pali and not above the cliffs, although this seems unlikely.

At ca. 2,000–3,000-feet elevation (2.5–3.0 miles inland) in the forest fringe was the ʻamaʻu or fern zone. Here bananas were planted in small clearings in the forest—an informal part of the field system. Menzies' 1793 account is useful.

> *[W]e... entered the wood by a well trodden path, on both sides of which were luxuriant groves of plantains and bananas reared up with great industry in the neatest order of cultivation. Every step we advanced through these plantations became more and more interesting as we could not help admiring the manner in which the little fields on both sides of us were laid out to the greatest advantage.*[132]

The Cook expedition in 1779 also recorded these banana fields in the woods, marked off by kapa flags.

> *[I]n the woods as far as the horse Plantains extend, they have white flags.*
>
> [1779 King][133]

No archaeological work has been done in this particular zone, although work has just begun in Hokukano and Kealakekua above modern-day Captain Cook.

From the breadfruit zone down to the coastal housing, rainfall was much lower (10–30 inches per year) and the terrain was much rockier. This area was called the kula zone where small patches of crops—mostly sweet potatoes, with some taro—were planted where soil allowed.[134] The Cook expedition described and mapped fields in this kula zone.

> *The Sweet Potatoe grows anywhere, a great part of the ground about the Village yield them.*
>
> [1779 King][135]

> *[F]or the first $2^{1}/_{2}$ miles it is compos'd of burnt loose stones, & yet almost the whole surface beginning a little at the back of the town [the coastal houses on the south side of the bay], is made to yield Sweet potatoes & the Cloth plant.*
>
> [1779 King][136]

A fair amount of archaeological survey has been done in this area, for small house lot or farm lot developments.[137] Agricultural features lack kuaīwi walls, but include clearings, pits, mounds and terraces. In one section near the cliff not far inland from Hikiau heiau, the terrain was considerably terraced in a much more elaborate and intensive fashion.[138] Yet all these features are informal. Unfortunately no dates have been processed from these fields.

Commoners in the ahupua‘a of the bay used small field areas (kīhāpai, māla) in these four zones. In 1779, permanent housing was mostly along the shore as were the large heiau, royal and high chiefs' residences, and court areas. So shore residents had to walk up trails to reach and periodically tend their fields. These trails appear archaeologically as stepping-stone paths or worn areas in 'a'ā flows, or as stone-curbed and straight paths which are modifications of the 1800s. Because of the distance to fields, shelters abound among the fields, their ruins visible as small pavings, platforms and enclosures. Test excavations in these shelters in kula lands have found charcoal, volcanic-glass cutting tools and minimal food remains. Results of testing of shelters in the kulu'ulu and 'āpa'a zones are pending.

Importantly, about 13% of the permanent houses in the Kealakekua area seem to have been in the upland 'āpa'a, based on Lt. James King's count of 50 inland houses, from a total of 400 total houses in the region in 1779.[139]

> *the few Cottages scatterd about...*
>
> [1779 King][140]

> *[W]e came among their Plantations where we saw a few Houses.*
>
> [1779 Samwell][141]

Archaeological work has indeed found a few larger habitation platforms, terraces and enclosures in the 'āpa'a zone above the cliffs.[142] These have yet to be excavated and dated.

This classic Kealakekua pattern has been found elsewhere in Kona. In Kahalu'u and Keauhou, the formal walled fields begin at the 750-foot elevation, ca. 1.0–1.2-miles inland. The kula fields of Keauhou also include several low drainage areas where considerable soil has washed and blown in, and these areas—fairly near the shore—were cultivated. The Māhele records for Keauhou show coastal housing and farm plot claims in these kula soil areas, and also in the upland kuaīwi area.[143] As at Kealakekua, numerous inland-heading foot trails extended up from the coastal housing to these farms in the kula zone and the uplands. Houses were also scattered about, and dates from the house sites in the kula zone range between the A.D. 1200s–1700s[144] and those in the formal field zones have the same time span. [145]

The classic Kealakekua field pattern also seems fairly common between Kahalu'u and Kailua, to the north. Historical documents show a similar kula, breadfruit, kuaīwi taro and sweet potato, and forest banana pattern behind Kailua.[146] Archaeological work has been abundant in the kula zone and has revealed similar kula agricultural sites.[147] This zone—perhaps even drier than at Kealakekua—has field remains in the form of stone planting or clearing mounds, terraces, small soil clearings, and planting pits with stones removed. House remains grade inland from the coastal belt of permanent houses into predominantly temporary habitations: small platforms and terraces, small enclosures (sometimes C- or L-shaped), caves, and modified areas on pāhoehoe outcroppings. Dates—mostly from temporary habitations—suggest use of the kula beginning in the A.D. 1000s–1300s.[148] In some areas, permanent housing has been found to have extended farther inland—to the 150-foot elevation or 0.4 miles inland in Lanihau ahupua'a,[149] and to the 200-foot elevation or 0.6 miles inland in Puapua'a.[150] Dates from these permanent habitations extend back to the A.D. 1400s–1500s. Not long ago, it was suggested that these kula areas began to be used extensively in small and seasonal gardens when the upland fields began to have soil erode downslope into the kula zone, and that this use began ca. A.D. 1400–1550 in central Kona, with drastic increases beginning in the A.D. 1600s–1700s. New findings suggest extensive kula use years earlier, in the A.D. 1000s–1300s, and permanent housing expansion much earlier, in the A.D. 1400s–1600s—this latter pattern perhaps also indicating intensification in the kalu'ulu and 'āpa'a upland fields.

Unfortunately, the kalu'ulu and 'āpa'a zones have received minimal survey between Kailua and Kealakekua. But walled kuaīwi fields have been surveyed in Ke'eke'e, Kanakau and Kalukalu down to the 250-foot elevation ca. 0.25 mile inland,[151] in Kahalu'u and Keauhou down to the 800-foot elevation ca. 1.0–1.2 miles inland,[152] in Kaumalumalu down to the 700–1,100-foot elevation ca. 2 miles inland, [153] and down to the 500-foot elevation in Pua'a ahupua'a,[154] and to the 400-foot elevation in Puapua'a.[155] In Pua'a and Hōlualoa ahupua'a[156] survey at high elevations—2,000 feet and 2,650 feet—found canals leading off intermittent streams to supplement water flow into the fields. A few permanent houses have been found in these zones, in scattered sets of 1–3 structures.[157] Temporary shelters, such as C-shaped walls and small platforms, are more common. Field use has been estimated from charcoal dates in habitation sites and ranges from the A.D. 1200s on.[158] No work has occurred in the forest zone in central Kona.

Outside of central Kona to the north of Kailua, this general field pattern changes. Rainfall decreases with the 40-inch rainfall line much farther inland, ca. 5 miles at Hu‘ehu‘e Ranch. Here archaeological work shows that some ahupua‘a had walled fields—such as Kaloko and Kohanaiki at the 800–900-foot elevation.[159] Other lands had only some kuaīwi walls (e.g., above the 800-foot elevation in Kealakehe),[160] and some ahupua‘a had no kuaīwi, such as Ka‘ū and ahupua‘a farther north.[161] Informal fields abound in this region at higher elevations: mounds, terraces, and the like. In the kula lands, pits and mounds seem to be the common features.[162] Kaloko and Kohanaiki had typical kuaīwi walls aligned perpendicular to the sea from the 900-foot elevation up to ca. 1,600 in Kaloko. However, above 2,000 feet in Kaloko and up to the 2,300-foot elevation, the field walls ran parallel to the ocean, perhaps to check sheetwash and soil erosion in these areas of higher rainfall.[163] What seems apparent in this north Kona work is that with decreasing rainfall, the breadfruit and ‘āpa‘a fields became reduced and sporadic, and even disappeared—making this area the northern end of the vast Kona field system. The work here also points out considerable variation among ahupua‘a due to population, the presence of high chiefs, rainfall, etc. Kaloko appears to have been a higher population area where a high chief dwelled, which probably accounts for the fact that its walled fields extended up the mountain so high and its scattered ‘ama‘u fields even higher, while adjacent ahupua‘a fields were less intensive and did not extend as far inland.

One important finding from archaeological and historical work is that there was considerable variation within the Kona field system, among the ahupua‘a. The fields in some ahupua‘a extended much farther upslope into the forest—a point emphasized by King in 1779.

> *[T]hese Arms [of forest] separated the great Plantations which has been observed to be 4 or 5 miles broad, & which are again divided into Small fields by stone hedges.*[164]

The archaeological survey at Kaloko shows the formal fields up to 2,300 feet, and the informal fields (scattered ʻamaʻu fields) up to 3,500 feet. These fields seem much farther inland than those in the adjacent ahupuaʻa of Kohanaiki, ʻOʻoma and Kalaoa, where the uppermost fields are documented only from historical records at this time.

Variation also occurred in the lower, informal kula fields. The scattered soil patches and field shelters are indeed a common pattern, but in some Kona lands sizable kula soil areas are present, washed down from above, leading to denser clusters of agricultural and housing features in these locations. This pattern has been found in Kapua, Keauhou, Kahaluʻu and Hōlualoa. Some of these soils are remnants of older eroded lava flows. Others are man-induced erosional features, with soils washing down from the cleared fields above. This erosion is visible in archaeological deposits in Keōpū, dating between the A.D. 1200s–1500s.[165]

Another variation is seen in high lava-flow areas—e.g., Kapua in the Mauna Loa flow zone of southern Kona and the Kalaoas in the Hualālai flow zone of northern Kona. In these areas, relatively recent lava flows with virtually no soil are present, resulting in very few agricultural features—a reduced density. Yet another variation occurs in the ahupuaʻa north of Kailua, from Keahuolū to the Kalaoas of Keāhole Point. Here, it is extremely dry and rocky near the shore, and the informal kula fields do not reach the shore, rather they tend to terminate at about the 400–600-foot elevations. Yet another variation has been identified in Kaloko. Just behind the coastal housing are numerous, small narrow-walled oval enclosures which have had soil placed within them. These are man-made fields in lava areas with little soil.[166]

Generally, it appears that the Kona field system gradually formed, with small clearings in the wetter uplands and some use of the kula, beginning in some ahupua‘a ca. A.D. 1000, and in others as late as the A.D. 1400s. Then over time—with growing populations, the chiefly centers, and other factors—the fields gradually expanded and intensified. This appears likely to have taken place at different times in different ahupua‘a. By the end of the A.D. 1700s, the fields of all these lands could be seen by the European visitors as one big complex of near continuous fields. And, as a whole, the field system is truly impressive. It extended from above Keāhole Point south to the border with Ka‘ū district. Its kuaīwi walled areas are striking archaeological ruins. But, the fields also extended down virtually to the shore and well up into the forest—a fact many tend to overlook. Also, these were fields of individual communities with considerable variation and differences in extent. Yet, the archaeological remains of the Kona fields are still present today—from the shore, up into the walled fields and higher still up into the forest. The archaeological sites remaining probably number in the thousands.

CHAPTER 9

# THE A.D. 1700S: Keawe, Alapa'inui, Kalani'ōpu'u & The Rise of Hawai'i as a Power in the Archipelago

*Kane the Earth-shaker,*
*The chief Keawe from the thunder-cloud,*
*The Heavenly-one who joined together the island.*
(chant for Keawe)[1]

*O Ku...*
*Encourage your land to bring forth,*
*Bring forth what? Bring forth men, women,*
*children, pigs, fowl, land.*
(chant recorded by J. Emerson)[2]

*beat the drum and offer the human sacrifice*
(Kalani'ōpu'u to his chiefs)[3]

*Like a dark cloud hovering over the Alapa, rose the destroying*
*host of Ka-hekili....They slew the Alapa on the sandhills....*
*There the dead lay in heaps strewn like kukui branches.*
(the battle lost by Hawai'i under Kalani'ōpu'u on Maui)[4]

## KEAWE ('IKEKAHI-ALI'I-O-KA-MOKU)[5] (A.D. 1720–1740)

With the death of Keakealaniwahine, her son Keawe came to power and rapidly took steps to heal the schism with the windward Hilo family of 'Ī. Evidently, his sister, Kalanikauleleiaiwi, was considered to be equal in rank to her half-brother, indeed even higher through her father's lineage from the ruling line of O'ahu.[6] But, in fact, she was not a co-ruler of Hawai'i's government; Keawe held the reins of power.

Keawe's chief wife, Lonoma'aikanaka, was of the 'Ī family—a daughter of Ahua-a-'Ī, with her mother Pi'ilaniwahine being a daughter of the ruler of Maui.[7] This marriage, which was made in his mother's time must have gone a long way toward patching up the differences with the 'Ī scions, remelding the century-long split between the eastern and western portions of the island. The marriage of his eldest son and heir (Kalaninui'īamamao, an 'Ī himself) to the granddaughter of Kuahu'ia, the leader of the 'Ī family who successfully opposed Keawe's mother, undoubtedly was arranged and intended to reinforce Keawe's situation.[8] Indeed, these actions seem to have diplomatically solidified Keawe's power over the entire island—increasing the strength of the ruler for the first time since Lonoikamakahiki's reign four generations earlier. At the same time, clearly, the 'Ī family lost no great amount of power. The result was a peaceful and unified reign, at least as documented in the oral traditions.

During Keawe's time, estimated as A.D. 1720–1740, it appears as if the island was governed by four district chiefs.[9] Mokulani of the 'Ī family, son of Kuahu'ia and cousin of Keawe's son's wife, administered Hilo, Hāmākua (except Waipi'o) and eastern Puna. The Mahi family still oversaw the affairs of Kohala for the king, with Kauaua-a-Mahi inheriting this office from his father Mahi'ololī. Over Ka'ū and western Puna, Keawe eventually appointed his eldest son, Kalaninui'īamamao. And in Kona, another son (Kalanike'eaumoku), the eldest of his second wife and half-sister, was placed in charge. Interestingly, this patterning still shows the strength of the Mahi in Kohala and the 'Ī in eastern Hawai'i.

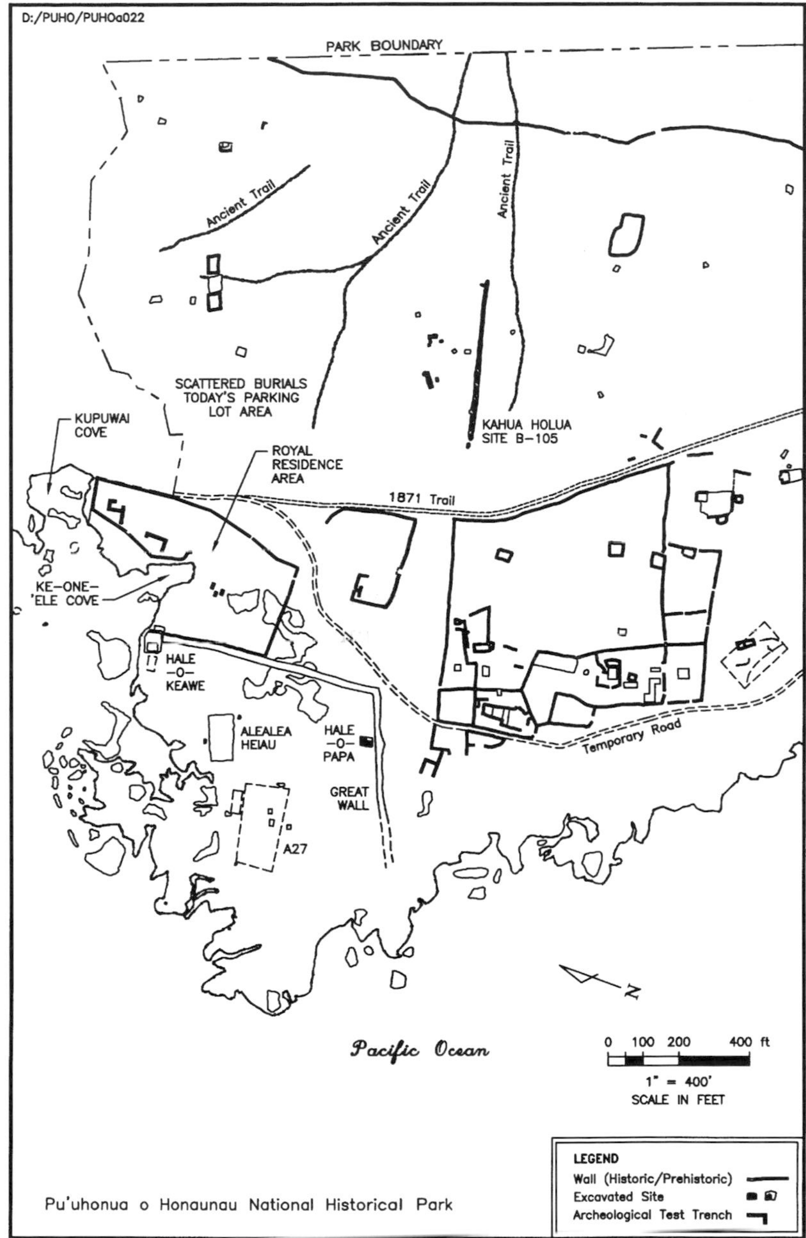


**FIGURE 9-1**

Map of southern portion of Hōnaunau, showing royal residential area and religious sites seaward of the pu'uhonua wall: Hale o Keawe, Āle'ale'a heiau, A27 heiau, and the Hale o Papa. (Adapted from Ladd 1986:2).

Keawe undoubtedly resided at several places during his reign. Evidently one of his favorites was at Hōnaunau in central Kona. There, a small bay was indented among smooth pāhoehoe lands (Fig. 9-1). On the south side of the bay was the royal residence—which may have been called Kauwalonolie—set in a coconut grove among and just inland of several pools of brackish water. This precinct appears to have been marked off by images and/or kapu sticks beginning at Kapuwai Cove to the north. Another cove, Keone'ele, once with a black sand beach, provided access to the royal grounds. Within the precinct in Kamehameha's time (1793), this residence contained a large house and a number of smaller sleeping houses.[10] Also, elderly informants in 1919 told Stokes that a Hale o Lono heiau stood in the area.[11] Ruins of these houses are not visible today, although Stokes identified a large house that was near the cove.

Other chiefly dwelling areas were just inland of the royal compound and to the south, along the main coastal trail which passed just inland of the royal precinct.[12] Commoner dwellings were to the north of Kapuwai Cove and were behind the chiefly residences.[13]

Besides the houses of Hōnaunau, there were major public structures. Hōlua slides were present in the form of long, raised stone ramps, much like a ski jump in appearance—on which one-man wooden sleds were ridden. Three are in Hōnaunau.[14] But, quite definitely, it is the sacred area and heiau of Hōnaunau—support extensions for the ruler—for which the area is renowned today.

Seaward of the royal residence was a large wall 3.7 meters (12 feet) high and 5.2 meters (17 feet) thick (Fig. 9-2), setting off a 5-acre low-lying pāhoehoe parcel which formed the south point of the bay.[15] Within this walled parcel was the pu'uhonua, the refuge, closely associated with the court.[16] Within the pu'uhonua were four heiau. Two were very large—'Āle'ale'a and A27 or the "Old Heiau," whose actual name passed away with earlier generations. 'Āle'ale'a is a 2.4-meter tall platform; 39 x 18 meters, 702 $m^2$ (127 x 60 feet, 7,620 $ft^2$).[17] A27 seems to have been an immense enclosure, 38 x 79 meters, 3,002 $m^2$ (126 x 260 feet, 32,760 $ft^2$).[18] Additionally, there were two smaller heiau; Hale o Keawe, a famed mausoleum; and Hale o Papa, now believed to have been a menstruation house for high chiefesses and not a heiau.

At different times, both of the large heiau must have been the luakini of Hōnaunau.[19] When Menzies stayed overnight at the royal residence in February 1793, he stated,

> *[I]n a large marae [heiau] close to us we now and then heard the hollow sounding drums of the priests who were up in the dead hour of the night performing their religious rites.*[20]

Considerable archaeological work has been done around this royal center of Hōnaunau in conjunction with Puʻuhonua o Hōnaunau National Historic Park, part of the United States National Park system. The "Great Wall" was stabilized with sections removed and rebuilt. Common habitation-related artifacts were found in and around the wall.[21] Unfortunately, no dates have been processed from the wall, but two important facts were discovered. One: the wall was built in part using a rare hollow-construction architectural style, called pao (Fig. 9-3).[22] Excavations in the Hale o Papa,[23] in ʻĀleʻaleʻa,[24] and in a house ruin behind the royal precinct[25] found a similar pao style, possibly suggesting that these sites were built about the same time. Two: the north end of the wall was partly torn down to build the Hale o Keawe, showing that the mausoleum was built after the wall.[26]

Excavations in the ʻĀleʻaleʻa heiau were also made to stabilize the site.[27] There, six different building stages were found, increasing the size of the heiau in increments over time (Table 9-1). Figure 9-4 shows these changes. ʻĀleʻaleʻa I was a much smaller, 352 $m^2$ platform, dated to the A.D. 1000s–1300s from charcoal below its fill. Then in three successive building stages (II, III, IV), this platform was raised to twice its height—first with an elevated platform at one end (II), then another small addition (III), and finally the remainder raised in a substantial re-building. Interestingly, it is the ʻĀleʻaleʻa III and IV stages that have the hollow, pao construction which is similar to the Great Wall. Stages

V and VI saw 6-meter additions placed on the west and east ends of the heiau—greatly increasing the heiau's area and using a considerable amount of stone. A sample from the fill of the eastern addition was radiocarbon dated to the A.D. 1400s–1800s. Last, the heiau's area and fill were increased by a narrow extension added all around the heiau. The end result was the massive platform seen today.

In 1919 and in 1979–80, the large mound of stones known as the "Old Heiau," or site A27, was excavated. The most recent work suggests this was a large stone-walled enclosure with an internal platform. Six volcanic glass samples from this platform all dated in the A.D. 1700s–early 1800s.[28] These dates went against expectations that the "Old Heiau" should be older than the full-sized 'Āle'ale'a, based on A27's name not being recalled in the late 1800s and early 1900s, and its poor condition. Yet, the size of A27 does suggest an A.D. 1500s–1700s age, and many volcanic glass dates tend to be compatible with radiocarbon dates from the same setting. Nonetheless, given the problems with volcanic glass dating, the age of A27 must still be considered uncertain.

The Hale o Papa was excavated in 1963.[29] No dates were processed from the site, but it was built using the pao construction style.

Hale o Keawe, although excavated, also has no archaeological dates. Yet, since it was built as a mausoleum for Keawe, it can be dated by genealogies to ca. A.D. 1720–1740.

Minimal excavations have occurred in the royal residential area, with remains of house platforms found and high densities of artifacts.[30] Unfortunately, these excavations were not expanded, nor do we have any dates from this area. So, archaeologically, it is poorly studied.

Some excavations have occurred in possible high-ranking residential areas to the south of the royal residence. Part of the 20–40 meter wide and 1 meter deep sand deposit was tested, and a cultural deposit 20–60 cm thick with artifacts was found, but again no dates were processed.[31] Othcr tests nearby also found artifacts and habitation features, but also without dating.[32]

Perhaps one of the best studied areas is where today's parking lot and entry road are located, just inland of the royal residential area. Three projects occurred here.[33] Just behind the royal precinct a few possible permanent house sites were found, with an artifact density a bit lower than in the royal residential area. But immediately behind that, numerous burials were found in a belt ca. 50–75 meters wide running parallel to the shore. At least 95 individuals were uncovered here prior to construction.[34] Most of these burials were in crevices or low points in the pāhoehoe, and were covered with a fill of stones, although some platforms were present with burials underneath them. One burial site (Q24/3:site 1), not far behind the royal precinct, held 7 individuals. With one individual was a bracelet of dog tooth plaques and a small bone niho palaoa pendant[35]—the latter artifact often considered to belong to high-ranking individuals. (A coral niho palaoa was also found in one of the house sites—R25/4:site 3.)[36] No dates were processed from this area, but an abundance of earlier notched fishhooks (HT1a, HT1b) suggests some time depth.[37]

The archaeology at Hōnaunau clearly indicates fascinating patterns in this area. Unfortunately, few dates have been processed, and more work is needed. The striking archaeological find, however, has been to show the complexity of heiau building. Obviously, successive rulers added to what was present. Ideas on what structures were present at different times have changed greatly with new archaeological finds.[38] The first heiau appears to have been ʻĀleʻaleʻa I, built in the A.D. 1000s–1300s, well before the royal center was established (Table 9-2). The builder is unknown, perhaps the ruler of the once-independent Kona. The first clear indication we have of a royal center at Hōnaunau is a reference stating Keawe-ku-ʻi-ke-kaʻai built the puʻuhonua during the reign of his father, Keakealanikane, and undoubtedly at the direction of his father—ca. A.D. 1660–1680.[39] This has been interpreted as the time frame for the construction of the Great Wall with its pao construction. This particular style also appears in ʻĀleʻaleʻa III and IV and the Hale o Papa, so these structures were probably built at the same time or soon thereafter. Keawe, the ruler of A.D. 1720–1740—or one of his sons at his death—is credited with the construction of the Hale o Keawe, which is consistent with the tearing down of part of the Great Wall to make room for this mausoleum. Which large luakini heiau was in use at this time—'Āle'ale'a IV, V/VI, or VII or A27—is unclear, or if Keawe added on to 'Āle'ale'a or built the A27 heiau. Given Keawe's use of Hōnaunau as a primary residential base, unlike his successors from Alapa'inui through Kamehameha, he probably built one of the sizable additions or A27. The time sequence of 'Āle'ale'a V/VI, VII or A27 is uncertain. These heiau were undoubtedly used between A.D. 1680 and the 1819 abolition of kapus. A27 with its larger area and more seaward location could be the most recent, but 'Āle'ale'a V/VI and VII could have been built after A27. Regardless, the peak of Hōnaunau's renown must have been with Keawe, who is the only ruler in this last part of prehistory to keep his royal court primarily in Hōnaunau. And, Hōnaunau was still in use during the reign of Kamehameha as a periodic royal residential center and an active mausoleum and religious area.

Keawe had at least 6 wives identified in the oral traditions—Lonoma'aikanaka (of the 'Ī), Kalanikauleleiaiwi (his half-sister), Kāne'alae (daughter of the powerful chief of eastern Moloka'i, who later became a wife of the ruler of Maui—Kekaulike), Kauhiokaka (daughter of his senior wife Lonoma'aikanaka), and two unnamed wives.[40] Twelve resulting children are listed in Table 9-3. Keawe's half-sister was also wed to three other chiefs (Table 9-3). During her mother's reign, she was a consort of the ruler of Maui, Ka'ulaheanuiokamoku, and then was married to Keawe. During his reign or later, she was wedded to Kauaua-a-Mahi, high chief of Kohala and the head of the Mahi family; and eventually she was married to a Kona chief, Lonoikaha'upu.[41] Her children also are listed in Table 9-3. Her marriages suggest unions of political intent, arranged to solidify the power of her mother (Keakealaniwahine) and of Keawe.

Kalanikauleleiaiwi and her offspring, however, proved to be thorns of dissent before, during and after Keawe's rule. Perhaps these actions reflect the scheming of the Kona-Mahi factions versus the Kona-'Ī factions represented by Keawe and his senior wife (Lonoma'aikanaka).

During the reign of Keakealaniwahine, Kalanikauleleiaiwi convinced her mother to bestow the important kapu wohi on her 10-year-old son through Keawe—Kalaninuike'eaumoku—to counter the kapu honors bestowed on Keawe's senior son, Kalaninui'īamamao. The kapu wohi was so given at Keolonāhihi heiau.[42] During Keawe's rule, his eldest son Kalaninui'īamamao—the product of the 'Ī line's joining with Keawe's—was slain, and rumor placed the blame with his half-brother Kalanike'eaumoku, and probably his mother.[43] Apparently, Keawe's 'Ī wife and his sheer force of personality kept the schism with the 'Ī from rending the kingdom apart again. But, upon his death, the kingdom did split.

When Keawe died, Kalanike'eaumoku evidently tried to claim control over the island, but Mokulani of the 'Ī family renounced this claim and declared the independence of eastern Hawai'i, perhaps because of Kalaninuike'eaumoku's reputed major role in the assassination of the 'Ī-related heir of Keawe. The Mahi leader, Alapa'inui (son of Kauaua-a-Mahi and Keawe's half-sister—again a factor from this half-sister) returned from Maui, gathered his warriors of Kohala, and also declared against his half-brother Kalanike'eaumoku. Alapa'inui's forces struck first—defeating Kalanike'eaumoku's army and slaying Kalanike'eaumoku, then swiftly conquering the 'Ī army and killing Mokulani.[44] In this sudden turn of events, Alapa'inui and Kohala's Mahi family and its branch of the royal line ascended to rule the island.

As a last note to Keawe's reign, after his death, one of his junior sons (Kanuha) is said to have built the now famous royal mausoleum at the center at Hōnaunau—the Hale o Keawe.[45] Alternatively, Keawe himself may have had the structure built.[46] Importantly, this structure would have been built just before or soon after Keawe's death, ca. A.D. 1740. If after his death, possibly it was built when Kona was under Kalanike'eaumoku's control.[47] Here Keawe's bones were placed, along with some of his sons and more distant relatives, and revered. This mausoleum also functioned as a heiau (Ka 'iki 'Āle'ale'a)[48] with its remains reinforcing the sacred and royal power over this area, operating in conjunction with the luakini within the pu'uhonua.

The Hale o Keawe was cared for and revered through the reign of Kamehameha. Fortunately, we have descriptions and illustrations of it from 'I'i's and Rev. Ellis's accounts, and from 1825 journals of the members of the HMS *Blonde*. The structure was built at the north end of the Pu'uhonua wall on the edge of Hōnaunau Bay. Nineteen sixty-six archaeological work indicates that ca. 50 feet of the wall was removed to build the site.[49] The structure itself was only 24 feet x 16 feet, and its enclosure but 50 x 50 feet, yet it was striking with its wooden palisade, the carved wooden images of the deities associated with the honored dead and the small, high-gabled mortuary house itself (Fig. 9-5). Within the dark recesses and shadows of the house were the bundled bones of Keawe and his kin.

The exterior was described in 1823 by Ellis, and in 1825 by A. Bloxam.

> *It is a compact building, twenty-four feet by sixteen, constructed with the most durable timber, and thatched with ti leaves, standing on a bed of lava that runs out a considerable distance into the sea.*
>
> *It is surrounded by a strong fence of paling, leaving an area in the front, and at each end about twenty-four feet wide.*
>
> *Several rudely carved male and female images of wood were placed on the outside of the enclosure; some on low pedestals under the shade of an adjacent tree, others on high posts on the jutting rocks that hung over the edge of the water.*
>
> *A number stood on the fence at unequal distances all around; but the principal assemblage of these frightful representatives of their former deities was at the south-east end of the enclosed space, where forming a semicircle, twelve of them stood in grim array.*
>
> [1823 Ellis][50]

*in the interior of the palisade on one side... a kind of stage, about fourteen feet high, of strong poles on which the offerings had been placed. At the bottom lay a considerable number of coconuts.*

[1825 A. Bloxam][51]

Emory pulled together the descriptions of the interior of the house, those by ʻIʻi between 1813–1819, Ellis in 1823, and A. Bloxam, P. Bloxam and Byron of the 1825 HMS *Blonde* (Fig. 9-6).[52]

*Before us were placed two large and curious carved wooden idols, four or five feet high, between which was the altar where the fires were made for consuming the flesh of the victims. On our left were ranged ten or twelve large bundles of tapa each surmounted by a feather or wooden idol, and one with a Chinese mask, these contained the bones of a long succession of kings and chiefs....The floor was strewn with litter, dirt, pieces of tapa, and offerings of every description. In one corner were placed a quantity of human leg and arm bones covered over with tapa. In two other corners were wooden stages, on which were placed quantities of bowls, calabashes, etc. containing shells, fishhooks, and a variety of other articles; leaning against the wall were several spears, fifteen or sixteen feet in length, a small model of a canoe, two native drums and an English drum in good preservation....In the sides of the building were stuck several small idols with calabashes generally attached to them, one of these we opened and found the skeleton of a small fish.*

[1825 A. Bloxam][53]

The bundles of kapa bear more discussion. These were wicker containers (kāʻai) that held a person's bones, and were covered with kapa.[54] These were deified remains which were worshiped as ancestral spirits (ʻaumakua o ke ao).[55]

*On one side were arranged several feathered deities protruding their misshapen heads through numerous folds of decayed tapa. Under these folds were deposited the bones of the mighty kings and potent warriors.*

[1825 P. Bloxam][56]

*a line of deities made of wicker-work, clothed in fine tapa, now nearly destroyed by time, and adorned with feather helmets and masks, made more hideous by rows of shark's teeth, and tufts of human hair; each differing a little from the other.*

[1825 Byron][57]

'I'i stated that Keawe's remains were nearest the door.[58] Evidently the feather deity covering his remains was removed by P. Bloxam in 1825; Emory attempted to trace this image and found it in the American Museum of Natural History (Fig. 9-8).[59]

Rev. Chamberlain in 1829 was given the names of 23 individuals from the Hale o Keawe,[60] and Barrere's analysis indicates that they were all relatives.[61] Ca. 1782, the body of Kalani'ōpu'u, the grandson of Keawe, was also brought by canoe from Ka'ū and laid in a halau in the royal enclosure and then briefly placed in the Hale o Keawe.[62] It was removed after Kīwala'ō was slain, and hidden in a cave in Ka'ū.[63] In 1818, the bones of Ka'ōleiokū, Kamehameha's oldest son, were placed in this house.[64] The bones piled in the corner appear to have been warriors of the family.[65]

The deaths of the kings and high chiefs which once rested in this house would have resulted in outpourings of grief and mourning by tens of thousands of people. Hair would have been torn out, clothes shredded and shed, teeth knocked out; and days of sanctioned chaos occurred. Then after an often lengthy display of the body and proper ceremonies, the remains would be bundled and placed in the mausoleum–adding to the sancity and power of this royal area of Hōnaunau.[66]

BISHOP MUSEUM

**FIGURE 9-2**
Pu'uhonua Wall from south, ca. 1919 (Stokes 1986:166).

BISHOP MUSEUM, STOKES COLLECTION

**FIGURE 9-3**
Cross-section of Great Wall, showing hollow, pao construction. 1919 photo (Stokes 1986;170).

**FIGURE 9-4A**

First Two Phases of 'Āle'ale'a heiau. Phase I is radiocarbon dated to the A.D. 1000s-1300s and is only 352m$^2$. (Ladd 1969a:106).

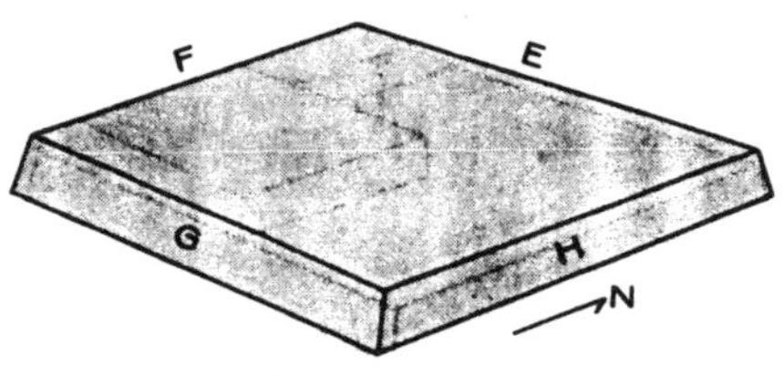


'Alealea I

'Alealea II

**FIGURE 9-4B**

Phases III and IV of 'Āle'ale'a heiau. Both phases used pao construction. Phase III was a quite small addition, while Phase IV completed the doubling of the height and volume of the entire platform. (Ladd 1969a:108).

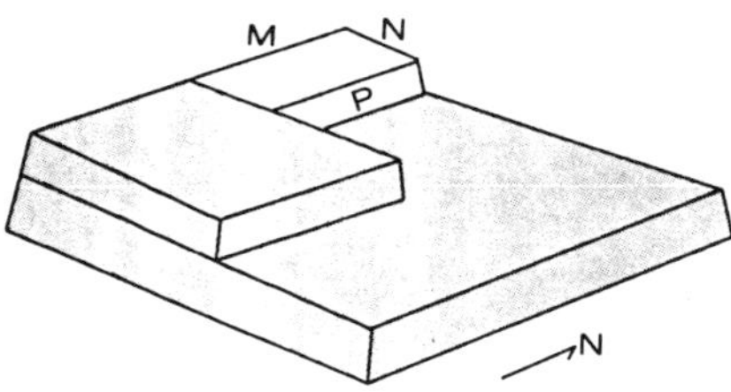


'Alealea III

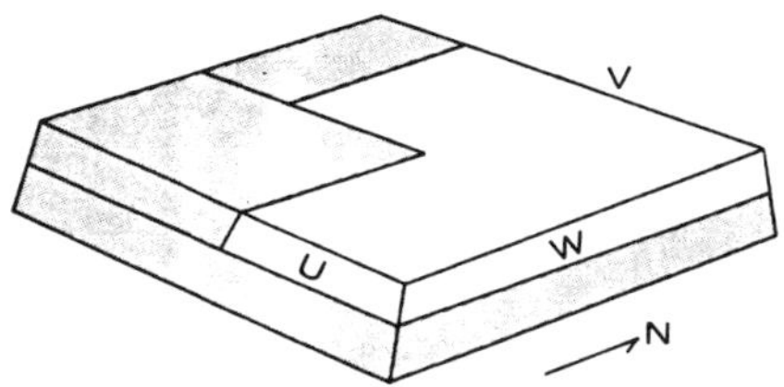


'Alealea IV

**FIGURE 9-4C**
Phases V–VII, ʻĀleʻaleʻa heiau. (Ladd 1969a:112, 114). Phases V and VI saw additions which extended each end of the structure. Phase VII widened and lengthened the heiau platform.

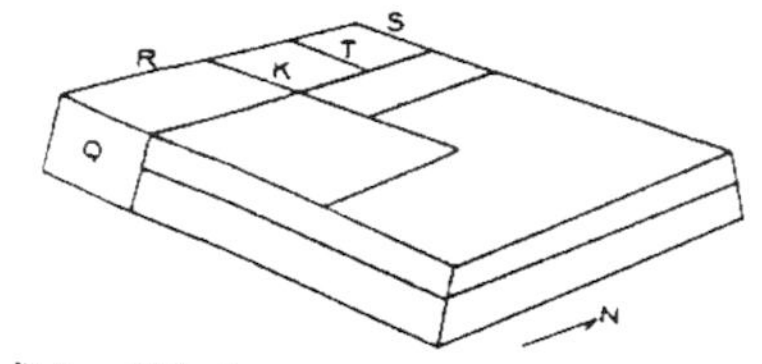


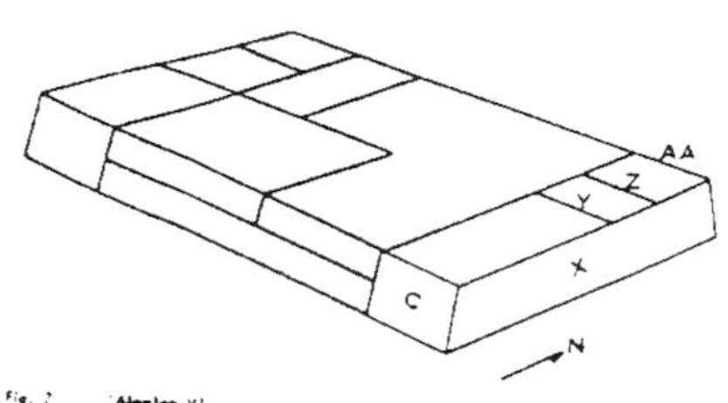


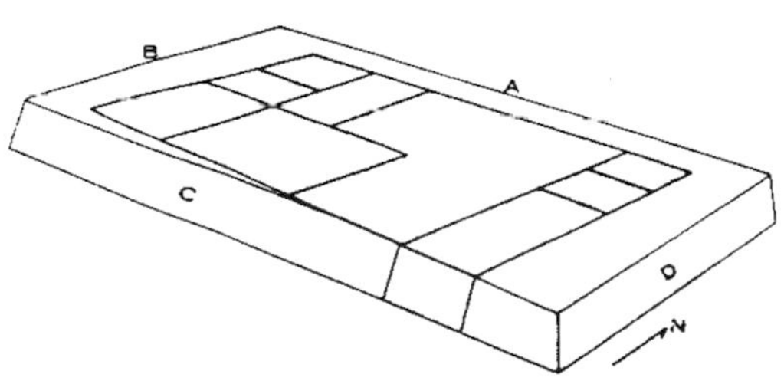


**Table 9–1**

## Excavation Information from ʻĀleʻaleʻa Heiau Hōnaunau Ahupuaʻa

| **Time Stages** | **Construction Units** | **Overall Area m²** | **New Area m** | **Height m** | **Misc. Info.** | **Dates** |
|---|---|---|---|---|---|---|
| I | I | 352 | 22 x 16 | 1.3 | Hakahaka fill ʻiliʻili surface | A.D. 1000s–1300s |
| II | II | 352 | 8 x 12 | 1.1 | Facing of cobble to med-sized stones | — |
| III | III | 352 | 9 x 4 | 1.1 | Pao fill med-large facing stones | — |
| IV | IV | 352 | *see text* | 1.1 | Pao file | — |
| V/VI | V (west)<br>VI (east) | 550 | 6 x 16<br>6 x 17 | 2.4<br>2.4 | Hakahaka fill<br>— | —<br>A.D. 1400s–1800 |
| VII | VII | 702 | *see text* | 2.4 | — | — |

Source of information (Ladd 1969a, 1987).

**Table 9–2**
## Chronology at Hōnaunau

| Site[1] | | Archaeological Dates | Architectural Evidence | Genealogical Dates (20 yrs/genera.) |
|---|---|---|---|---|
| A27 (Old heiau) | 670 m³ | A.D. 1710–1820[2] | | |
| 'Āle'ale'a Heiau | | | | |
| I | 422 m³ | A.D. 1000s–1300s[3] | | |
| II | 537 [115] | | | |
| III | 580 [43] | | Pao | |
| IV | 844 [264] | | Pao | |
| V/VI | 1,319 [475] | A.D. 1400s–1700s[4] | | |
| VII | 1,685 [365] | | | |
| Hale o Keawe | | | Great Wall partly torn down for construction | Keawe—A.D. 1720–1740 Son of Keawe —A.D. 1740[5] |
| Hale o Papa | | | Pao | |
| Great Wall | | | Pao | A.D. 1660–1680 Pu'uhonua (implying wall) in reign of Kekeakealanikane by son.[6] |

1. Arabic numbers in this column are volumes of stone in cubic meters. Each new building stage's volume is in brackets, and the total volume at each building stage is given before the brackets.
2. 6 volcanic glass dates (Ladd 1987:51). Range of means = A.D. 1740–1830.
3. 2 charcoal c-14 dates from base 'Āle'ale'a I. WSU 116 = 790 ± 200 BP; WSU 115 = -800 ± 200 BP. (Dates reported in Ladd 1969a:130; provenience given in Ladd 1987:77.)
4. 1 charcoal c-14 date from fill of 'Āle'ale'a VI (pit 1, ca. 1.2-m level). HH-A26/65 = 320 ± 90 (Ladd 1969a:129). Multiple calibration = A.D. 1410–1670, 1720–1800.
5. Kamakau 1870; Barrere 1957 (1986).
6. Stokes 1930; Emory 1957 (1986); Barrere 1957 (1986).

**Table 9-3**

## The Wives and Children of Keawe & His Half-Sister Kalanikauleleiaiwi

| Keawe | Kalanikauleleiaiwi |
|---|---|
| **Wives/Children** | **Husbands/Children** |
| 1. Lonoma'aikanaka<br>a) Kalaninui-'Ī-a-mamao (m)<br>b) Kekohimoku (m) | 1. Ka'ulaheanuiokamoku, Ruler of Maui<br>a) Keku'iapoiwanui (f) |
| 2. Kalanikauleleiaiwi<br>c) **Kalanikeeaumoku** (m)<br>d) Kekelakekeokalani (f) | 2. Keawe<br>b) **Kalanike'eaumoku**<br>c) Kekelakekokalani (f) |
| 3. Kane'alai<br>e) Ha'o (m)<br>f) 'Awili (m)<br>g) Kumukoa (m)<br>(Kumuhea)(Kamakau)<br>h) Kaliloamoku (f)<br>(Kalilaumoku)(Kamakau) | 3. Kauaua-a-Mahi<br>d) **Alapa'inui** (m)<br>e) Ha'ae (m) |
| 4. Kauhiokaka<br>i) Kekaulike (f) | 4. Lonoikaha'upu<br>f) Keawepoepoe (m) |
| 5. [ ? ]<br>j) Ahaula (m)<br>k) Kaolohaka-a-Keawe (m) | |
| 6. [ ? ]<br>l) Kanuha (m) | |

Underlined = Heir to Keawe
Bold = Became ruler of Hawai'i
m = male
f = female

**Table 9-4**

## Named Individuals Whose Remains Were Within the Hale o Keawe

RULER

Keawe-'i-kekahi-ali'i-o-ka-moku

MEMBERS OF THE GENERATION BEFORE KEAWE

| | |
|---|---|
| Kanaloa-i-ka-iwi-lewa | Husband to Keakealaniwahine, Keawe's father |
| Ku'aiali'i | Uncle to Keawe |
| Lono-a-Moana | Uncle to Keawe |
| Ni'ula | Uncle to Keawe |
| Kawainiulani | Uncle to Keawe |
| Lono-kaua-kini | Chief of Kona & Father-in-law to Keawe's sister-wife |

CHILDREN OF KEAWE

Aha'ula
Kumukoa'a
Keawe-a-Kanuha (Kanuha?)

SAME GENERATION AS KEAWE

| | |
|---|---|
| Lono-ikaha'upu | Son of Lono-kaua-kini, noted above, and last husband to Keawe's sister-wife |
| Ka'aloa | Cousin of Keawe |

LATER GENERATIONS

| | |
|---|---|
| Kala'imamahū | Kamehameha's half-brother |
| Ka'ōleiokū | Kamehameha's son |
| Kaleioku | Chief during Kalani'ōpu'u's or Kamehameha's reign |

UNKNOWN

| | |
|---|---|
| Kekoamano | |
| Keawe Lua'ole | |
| Kala'i-kua-hulu [Okua] | |
| Keawe Kapaulumoku | |
| Hukihe | A Kona chief |
| Keohokuma | |
| 'Umioopa | |
| Lonoakoli'i | |

Information from Barrere 1986.

HAWAII STATE ARCHIVES

**FIGURE 9-5**
1823 drawing of Hale o Keawe, Hōnaunau. (From Ellis' 1826 published account.)

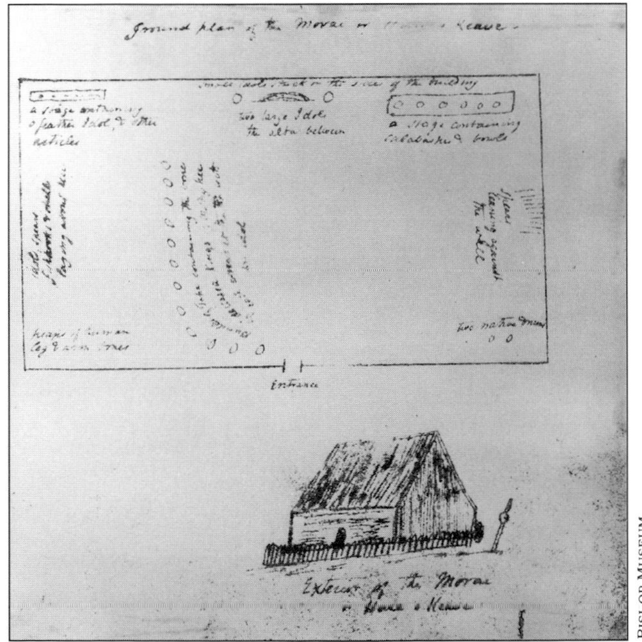


BISHOP MUSEUM

**FIGURE 9-6**
1825 sketch of Hale o Keawe and map of interior of structure, by Andrew Bloxam of *HMS Blonde*. (Emory 1986:95). Inside, next to the entrance was the line of kapa bundles with kāʻai and feathered images.

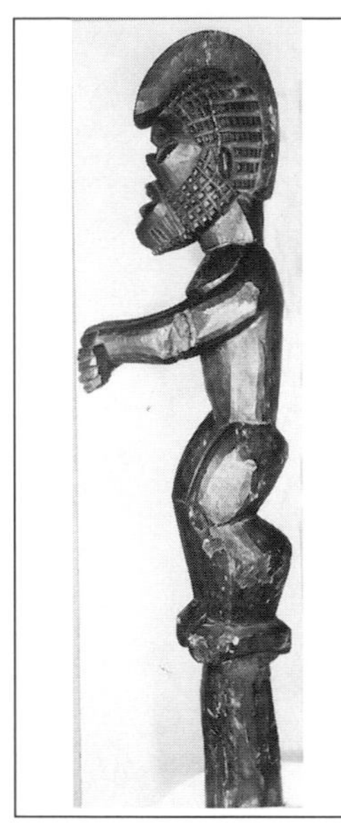

BISHOP MUSEUM

**FIGURE 9-7** Wooden image from the side of the altar within the Hale o Keawe, Hōnaunau. (Emory 1986:101).

**FIGURE 9-8** Feathered image which was with one of the kā'ai in the Hale o Keawe, possibly with Keawe himself. (Emory 1986:102). (Neg. no. 320730, Courtesy of American Museum of Natural History.)

## ALAPA'INUI
## A.D. 1740–1760

Under Alapa'inui, from A.D. 1740–1760, the nation of Hawai'i saw minimal unrest from within until late in his reign. He shifted his ruling center about the island, residing in Kailua in Kona early on, then in Kokoiki near Mo'okini heiau in Kohala, in Waiolama in Hilo, moving up to Waipi'o, then to Waimea, and lastly to Kawaihae where he passed away.[67]

Alapa'inui did have the sizable task of pulling the kingdom together after he seized control. The powerful sons of Keawe were now dead, but the senior half-'Ī son (Kalaninui'īamamao) had two mature sons—Keawema'uhili (through Kekaulike, his half-sister and also a daughter of Keawe and half-'Ī), and Kalani'ōpu'u (through Kamaka'imoku, a daughter of an O'ahu chief and a chiefess of Mahi and 'Ī descent). Kalani'ōpu'u, the eldest son, was the living senior representative of Keawe's senior line—a grandson of Keawe. Additionally, Keawe's next oldest son and his eventual heir (Kalanike'eaumoku)—the ruler slain by Alapa'i in battle and Alapa'i's half-brother—through Kamaka'imoku had a mature son, Kalanikupuapaikalaninui Keōua (or Keōua). [Thus, Kalani'ōpu'u and Keōua were half-brothers.] Also a grandson of Keawe, Keōua was the senior heir of his father who had been ruler for a brief time. In essence, these young men were all nephews of Alapa'i and each of their fathers had once been the heirs of Keawe. They were no longer in the senior line of descent, as that was now Alapa'i's line through his mother (Keawe's more sacred sister), and through the Mahi family. But if these young men gained supporters, they would clearly be high-ranking threats.

Alapa'i's solution to this problem was to keep his nephews at his court, make them his generals, and treat them almost as sons.[68] Also, their mother, Kamaka'imoku, became one of Alapa'i's wives.[69]

Yet another source of threat to Alapa'i's rule was the 'Ī family. Mokulani—slain by Alapa'i—left only an infant daughter (Ululani) as his heir. Alapa'i named her high chief of Hilo-Hāmākua-eastern Puna, which were the 'Ī family lands, undoubtedly placating this powerful family of Hawai'i's wet and fertile side. However, he wed his nephew Keawema'uhili to Ululani, effectively melding the 'Ī family with his own junior lines.[70]

The final cast of players includes Alapa'i's elder half-sister (through his mother) Keku'iapoiwanui, his younger half-brother (through his mother) Keawepoepoe, and his full brother Hā'ae.[71] His half-sister Keku'iapoiwanui was the daughter of Kaulahea, the ruler of Maui. She was married to her half-brother, Kekaulike who was Maui's ruler during Alapa'i's time—giving Alapa'i a direct link to one of Maui's queens. Keawepoepoe and Hā'ae both seemed to play powerful, yet relatively quiet roles during Alapa'i's times. Hā'ae's daughter was wed to Alapa'i's ranking nephew Keōua and was to become Kamehameha's mother.[72] Keawepoepoe's sons, Ke'eaumoku, Kame'eiamoku and Kamanawa, were to play prominent roles after Alapa'i's reign.

**Table 9-5**
## Alapa'inui's Place in Hawai'i's Geneologies

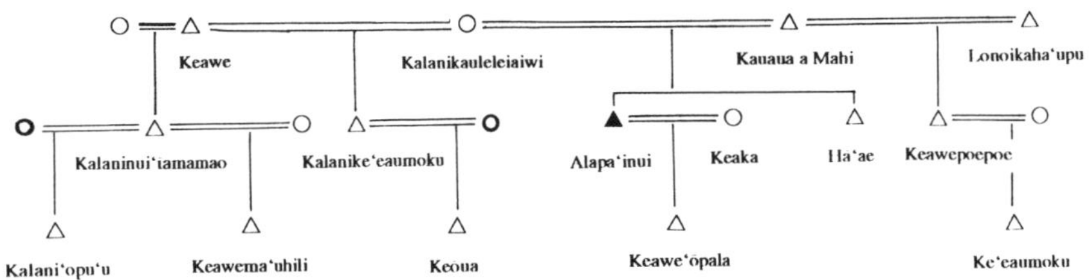


( **O** = Kamaka'iamoku, who also became a wife of Alapa'inui.)

Alapa'i's Wives & Children

| Wives | Children |
|---|---|
| Keaka | Keawe'opala (male) |
| Kamaka'imoku | Manona (female) |
| Kamaua | Kauwa'a (female) |
| | Mahiua (male) |

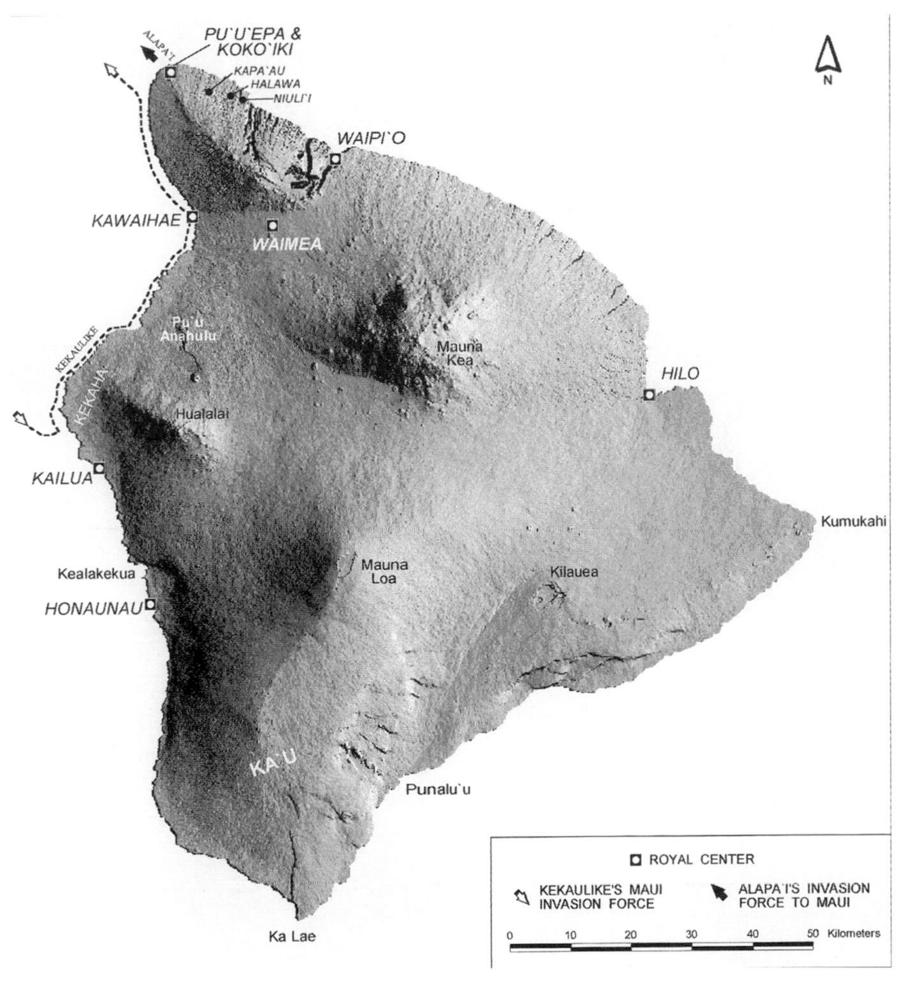


**FIGURE 9-9**

Map, Places of Alapa'inui's reign, ca. A.D. 1740–1760.

State Historic Preservation Division

**FIGURE 9-10**
Aerial Photograph, Mo'okini heiau.

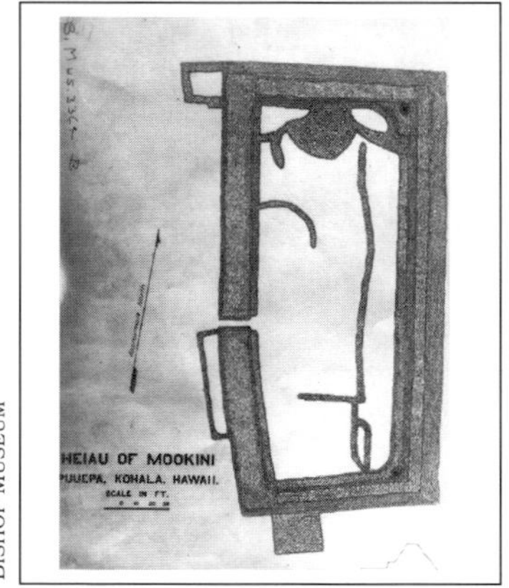


Bishop Museum

**FIGURE 9-11**
Map, Mo'okini heiau (Stokes 1919).

Bishop Museum

**FIGURE 9-12**
Photograph, Mo'okini Heiau, 1931.

Upon Alapa'i's conquest of Hawai'i, he moved his court to Kailua in Kona. And at this early point in his reign, his brother-in-law Kekaulike—ruler of Maui—chose to invade the lands of Hawai'i, evidently assuming weakness after the recent battles among Alapa'i, Mokulani and Kalanike'eaumoku. From Kaupō in eastern Maui, Kekaulike sailed with his fleet of canoes.

> *Kekaulike sailed for the Kona coast of Hawaii where he harried and burned the coast villages. Alapainui was then in Kona, and, assembling a fleet of war canoes, he overtook Kekaulike at sea, fought a naval engagement, beat him, and drove him off. Retreating northwards, Kekaulike landed in several places, destroying villages in Kekaha, cutting down the cocoanut trees at Kawaihae, and plundering and killing along the Kohala coast, and finally returned to Mokulau, Maui [Kaupo], intending to invade Hawaii with a larger force next time.*
>
> [1880 Fornander].[73]

Alapa'i followed north into Kohala where he gathered the chiefs of Hawai'i and their warriors. The army camped in the villages from Koai'e in Lapakahi north to Pu'uepa, with Alapa'i and his court at Kokoiki next to Mo'okini heiau, in Pu'uepa.[74]

Mo'okini heiau and the neighboring ranking residential area in Pu'uepa and Kokoiki were the focal political areas of windward Kohala, while Mailekini and Pu'ukoholā heiau and the Kawaihae residences were the drawing point in southern leeward Kohala. For the Mahi family of Kohala and previous rulers and high chiefs, Mo'okini and Kokoiki were vital areas of sacred and secular power. And Alapa'i—as the first head of the Mahi family to rule—must have placed great importance on this center. It also was used by a later ruler with Kohala ties, Kamehameha.

Mo'okini has a panoramic view of the 'Upolu Point area of Kohala, the shorelines to the south and north, and of Maui. The heiau is a massive structure, set on the gradual slopes back from the sea. It is a large rectangular enclosure (79 x 38 meters, 3,002 sq. meters), with imposing stone walls, 4 meters high and 3 meters thick.[75] Mo'okini is today one of the most impressive heiau ruins on the island. In its day, with its priests and vital ceremonies, it truly must have been awe-inspiring.

Pā'ao, the foreign priest, is said in one story to have built Mo'okini with stones passed by hand from Niuli'i, 9 miles to the east.[76] No archaeological work has been done in recent years here, but the heiau's construction can be expected to have begun in the A.D. 1300s–1400s, and the structure to have been expanded and its walls built higher and/or thicker by successive rulers. Indeed, Alapa'i himself evidently "repaired" Mo'okini during his reign.[77]

But, importantly, one should not forget that Mo'okini was just part of the royal complex at Kokoiki. The residential area and the houses of the high chiefs were undoubtedly immediately nearby. Indeed, Fowke in 1922 conducted a brief archaeological survey in this area and described continuous walled enclosures for a mile south of Mo'okini along the shore, which were probably these residences and those of the surrounding lower ranks.[78] Besides the houses, Hinakahua near Kapa'au was renowned in the oral histories for its boxing and athletic arena,[79] used during the makahiki, with processions leading from Kokoiki, and also used on other occasions. For the makahiki, it appears that a wood god and a feather god were brought up from Mo'okini to Hīkapoloa heiau in Pu'uepa, and that these gods then cycled through different portions of Kohala collecting tribute. Afterwards the two deities returned to Pu'uepa, where they met the "long god" (Lono-makua) coming from Kona, to whom the tribute was then given.[80]

> *At Hikapoloa two gods were set up...a wooden and feather god. The feather god goes mountainward along the cliffs; the wooden god goes on the inside.*
>
> *The day that the gods went out was sacred; no fires were lighted, no cultivating, no fishing, and no other work was done. Merrymaking, pride demonstrations and going to Hinakahua to witness the boxing were the occupations of the day.*

| | |
|---|---|
| *24. Kaloakulua.* | *The god journeys.* |
| *25. Kaloakukolu.* | *The god journeys until it reaches Pololu and stops.* |
| *26. Kane.* | *The god repairs to Mookini.* |
| *27. Lono.* | *Still boxing.* |
| *28. Mauli.* | *The long god comes from Kona.* |
| *29. Muku.* | *The long god arrives at the barren seashore.* |
| *30. Hoaka.* | *The long god reaches Kohala.* |

[Fornander][81]

Unfortunately, Moʻokini heiau is all that remains of this royal center situated in the heart of Kohala. The houses and their foundations are gone, having long since been cleared away during sugarcane cultivation. The stones from these places sit at the base of the nearby sea cliffs and in piles amidst the cane fields. Only Moʻokini remains, standing in the ever-blowing trade winds of Kohala, undoubtedly spared by cane cultivators because of its size and perhaps because of its renown and sacredness.

Here Alapaʻinui gathered his forces to strike back at Kekaulike. His nephews, Kalaniʻōpuʻu and Keōua, were his main generals. At this time, while the army was formed, reputedly during a stormy, thundering night full of omens, Keōua's son, Kamehameha, was born at Kokoiki. Kamehameha was taken by Naeʻole—chief of Hālawa ahupuaʻa in Kohala—and eventually placed with him for his first 5 years, and then raised in Alapaʻi's court with Alapaʻi's senior wife, Keaka, as his guardian.[82]

Shortly thereafter, Hawaiʻi's invasion force sailed for Maui. Landing in Kaupō, Alapaʻi found that Kekaulike had just died and that the son of his half-sister was now ruler, Kamehamehanui. He landed at Kīhei "with all his chiefs and fighting men, commanded by the two leaders, Kalaniʻōpuʻu and Keōua",[83] then met with his sister and nephew at Kīhei, where a peace was agreed to, followed by festivities.

While Alapaʻi was on Maui with his army, Oʻahu's army under its ruler, Kapiʻiohokalani, invaded Molokaʻi. At this time, the Oʻahu nation was approaching its pinnacle of power, flexing its might on

Kaua'i and Moloka'i. It may have been the most powerful polity in the islands in the early 1700s. Alapa'inui brought his forces into the battle—in part since Keawe had sons and grandsons as Moloka'i chiefs through his wife Kāne'alae. A running battle ensued for five days, beginning at Kapualei (Kapulei) and ending at Kawela. O'ahu's forces were eventually trapped between Alapa'i's men under Kalani'ōpu'u and Keōua on the shore, and the forces of Moloka'i in the uplands, "and, after a severe fight from morning till far in the afternoon, he [Kapi'iohokalani] was completely routed with great loss of life, and himself slain."[84] The O'ahu forces, checked by those of Hawai'i, retreated to their island. Alapa'i had raised his nation's station; Hawai'i was now a power in the islands equal to O'ahu. As Fornander notes

> *This famous battlefield may still be seen in the place described, where the bones of the slain are the sports of the winds that sweep over that sandy plain, and cover or uncover them.*[85]

Alapa'i soon carried the war to O'ahu. Blocked from coming ashore from Waikīkī to Hanauma, he landed his forces at Kailua on windward O'ahu and camped in Kāne'ohe ahupua'a.[86] Peleiōhōlani, son of Kūali'i, had meanwhile arrived from Kaua'i with his men to become regent for his dead brother's infant son. Peleiōhōlani—who became one of the most renowned rulers in the islands' oral histories—took command of the O'ahu army. He sent Nā'ili, chief of Wai'anae and full brother of the mother of Kalani'ōpu'u and Keōua,[87] now wife of Alapa'i, to negotiate a truce with Alapa'i. Nā'ili halted the fighting of O'ahu's warriors, found his nephews, who in turn halted their forces and escorted him to Alapa'i. "Na-'ili met Alapai'i, and the two wailed over each other affectionately."[88] Nā'ili was successful, and a meeting between Alapa'i and Peleiōhōlani was arranged.

> *It was agreed that the Hawaii fleet should move to a place called Naonealaa, in Kaneohe, and that Alapainui alone should go ashore unarmed, while Peleioholani on his part would advance from the lines of his army equally alone and unarmed.*
>
> [1880 Fornander][89]

*The two hosts met, splendidly dressed in cloaks of bird feathers and in helmet-shaped head coverings beautifully decorated with feathers of birds. Red feather cloaks were to be seen on all sides. Both chiefs were attired in a way to inspire admiration and awe, and the day was one of rejoicing for the end of a dreadful conflict. The canoes were lined up from Ki'i at Mokapu to Naoneala'a, and there on the shore line they remained, Alapa'i going ashore alone. The chiefs of Oahu and Kauai, the fighting men, and the country people remained inland, the chief Pele-io-holani advancing alone.*

[1866 Kamakau][90]

And peace was made between the rulers.

Alapa'i then withdrew his forces to Moloka'i and then to Lahaina. There he found that Kekaulike's eldest son—Kauhi'aimoku-o-Kama, who had been his father's chief general—had risen against his nephew Kamehamehanui. When mediation failed and Kamehamehanui's forces were routed, Alapa'i withdrew his fleet, took on Kamehamehanui, and returned to Hawai'i to prepare for war against Maui.[91]

The next year, Alapa'i with Kamehamehanui landed his army—8,440 men strong according to Kamakau[92]—in Lahaina district. Kauhi'a had obtained the aid of Peleiōhōlani. Another war began between the powers of O'ahu and Hawai'i. Alapa'i's army arrived first, landing in Lahaina and forcing Kauhi'a to retreat to the uplands.

*It is said that Alapai proceeded with great severity against the adherents of Kauhia in Lahaina, destroying their taro patches and breaking down the watercourses out of the Kauaula, Kanaha, and Mahoma valleys.*

[1880 Fornander][93]

Peleiōhōlani then arrived—with only 640 men according to Kamakau[94]—engaged a section of Hawai'i's army at Honokōwai, and drove them back to the main forces. The following day the entire O'ahu and Hawai'i armies met.

> *The fortune of the battle swayed back and forth from Honokawai to near into Lahaina; and to this day heaps of human bones and skulls, half buried in various places in the sand, attest the bitterness of the strife and the carnage committed. The result was probably a drawn battle, for it is related that, after great losses on both sides, the two kings—Alapainui and Peleioholani—met on the battlefield and, instead of coming to blows, they saluted each other, and, considering their mutual losses on behalf of others, they made a peace between themselves and renewed the treaty of Naonealaa on Oahu.*
>
> [1880 Fornander][95]

Kauhi'a had been captured and killed by Alapa'i's order in this battle, so Kamehamehanui was again installed as ruler of Maui. O'ahu and Hawai'i forces withdrew, departing as equal powers.

Alapa'i is said to have spent his remaining years based in Hilo, but frequently circuiting Hawai'i and checking on his nation's affairs. At Hilo, Keōua died[96] and certain factions claimed Alapa'i was responsible through poisoning or sorcery. Whether this was true or not—and arguments can be made that Alapa'i was innocent or guilty—Kalani'ōpu'u with his kahu Puna and his younger half-brother Keawema'uhili, and other followers, attempted to remove Keōua's son, Kamehameha, from Alapa'i's court. He was opposed by loyal chiefs (Keawe'ōpala; the three sons of Keawepoepoe: Kame'eiamoku, Kamanawa, Ke'eaumoku; and Keaweheulu), and Kalani'ōpu'u openly declared his independence. Battles were fought between Alapa'i's and Kalani'ōpu'u's forces near Hilo, and Kalani'ōpu'u withdrew to his district of Ka'ū–west Puna, along with one of Alapa'i's main kahuna, Holo'ae.[97] There, Alapa'inui left him—"For reasons that have not come down to our day."[98]

After another year at Hilo, Alapa'i moved his court to Waipi'o, then to Waimea, and eventually to Kawaihae where he became ill and died. Prior to his death, at Mailekini heiau, he named his son Keawe'ōpala as his successor.[99] Among his several children from his three wives, Keawe'ōpala was the eldest son.

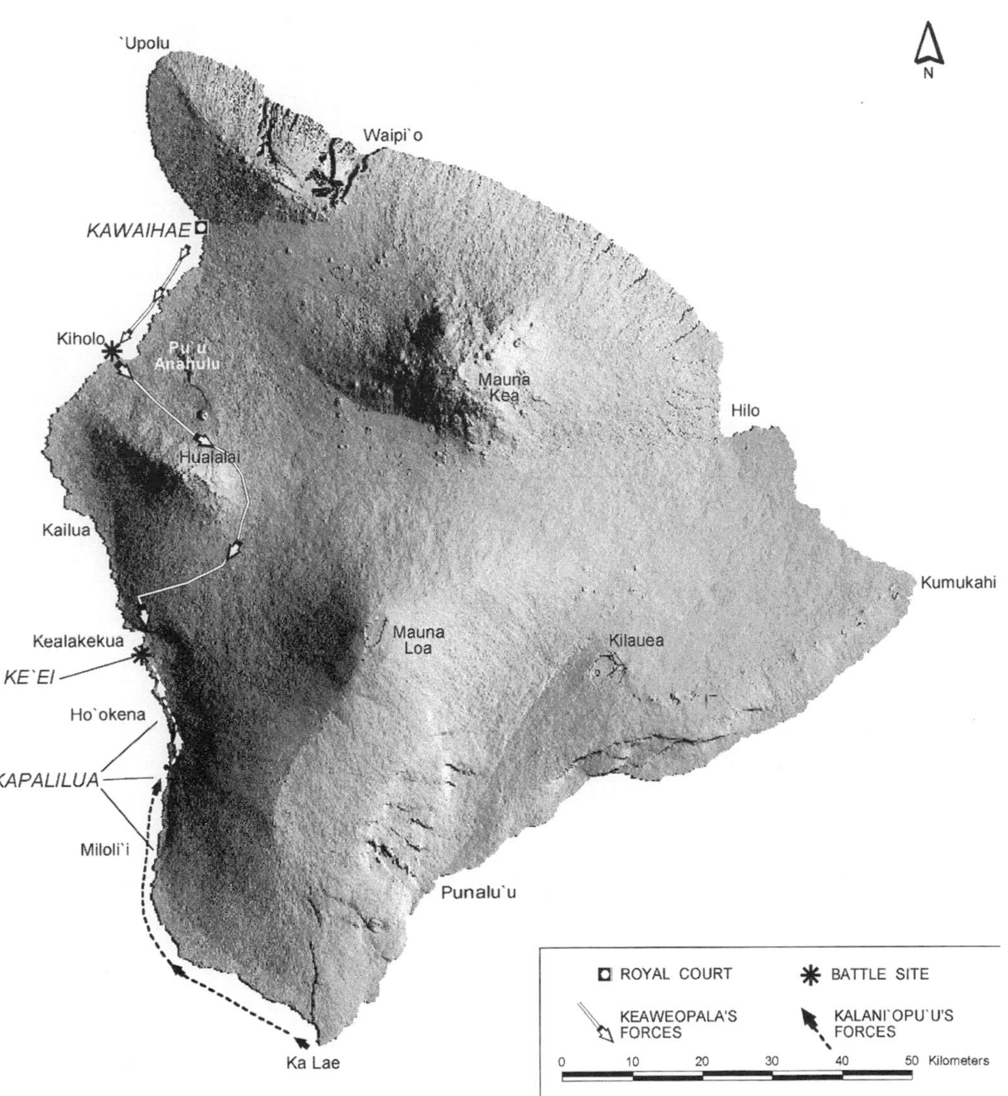


**FIGURE 9-13**
Places mentioned during Keawe'ōpala's brief reign, ca. A.D. 1760.

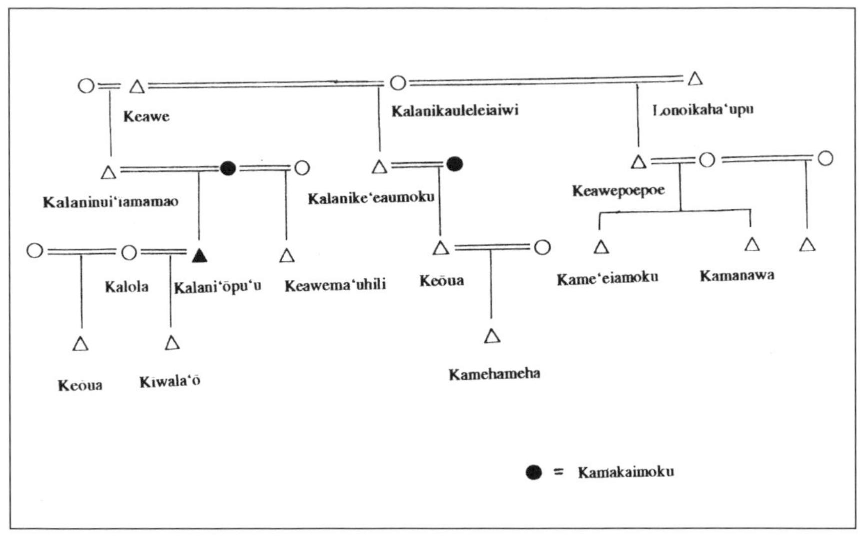


**FIGURE 9-14**
Kalani'ōpu'u's place in
Hawai'i Island's Genealogies

## KEAWE'ŌPALA
## A.D. 1760

Alapa'i's son Keawe'ōpala succeeded him as ruler, with Kalani'ōpu'u still independent in Ka'ū. Keawe'ōpala immediately faced revolt within his country. Redivision of the lands of his kingdom upon his succession failed to satisfy a number of the high chiefs of Kekaha—notably his cousin Ke'eaumoku and his uncle, Keawepoepoe—but Keawe'ōpala defeated their forces in battle.[100] Meanwhile, Kalani'ōpu'u moved his army up into southern Kona (Kapalilua), and Ke'eaumoku joined him with the remnants of his defeated forces. Keawe'ōpala's warriors, under Kamoho'ula, hurried across to meet Kalani'ōpu'u, and they engaged Kalani'ōpu'u's army between Ke'ei and Hōnaunau. The battle lasted for several days and finally turned with the capture and slaying of Keawe'ōpala's [and formerly Alapa'i's] kahuna nui Ka'akau.[101] Keawe'ōpala was slain soon thereafter on the battleground, and the battle and the kingdom had been won by Kalani'ōpu'u.

# KALANI'ŌPU'U
## A.D. 1760–1782

Kalani'ōpu'u, and the senior line of Keawe through Kalaninui'īamamao, thus regained the throne of Hawai'i and reunified the island. He placed his chiefs over the land, and "apparently all were satisfied or none dared to resist."[102]

In the initial years of Kalani'ōpu'u's reign, the court was based in Ka'ū.[103] Here, the military skill of Kekūhaupi'o, one of the most famous warriors in Hawaiian oral histories, came to Kalani'ōpu'u's attention. Kekūhaupi'o was brought to the court and assigned to the service and training of Kamehameha (among other tasks), Kamehameha being treated as a virtual son of Kalani'ōpu'u.[104] In these early years of peace, Kalani'ōpu'u's son, Kīwala'ō, through his wife Kalola, sister of Kamehamehanui and Kahekili (successive kings of Maui), often visited the Maui court.[105]

During the middle of his reign, however, Kalani'ōpu'u spent years warring with the kingdom of Maui. Several years after his rule began, he took the eastern districts of Hāna and Kīpahulu. The ruler of Maui at that time, Kamehamehanui, was unable to dislodge Hawai'i's forces from the fortress hill of Kauwiki in Hana, despite several famous attempts.[106]

Kalani'ōpu'u's next incursion against Maui supposedly occurred almost 15 years later, about 1775. By this time, Kahekili had succeeded his brother as ruler of Maui. Kalani'ōpu'u led a raid into Kaupō district. Kahekili's relief forces routed the Hawai'i warriors, but in a delaying action the great warrior, Kekūhaupi'o, saved Kalani'ōpu'u's men, and in turn his pupil, Kamehameha, eventually saved him. This raid became known as the War of Kalaehohea[107] or Kalaeoka'īlio.[108] And in this raid and the ensuing wars, both Kekuhaupi'o and Kamehameha established their renown as warriors.

> *When Kalaniopuu sailed to Maui to war against Kahekili two persons gained fame, Kamehameha and Kekuhaupio.*
>
> ['Ī'i][109]

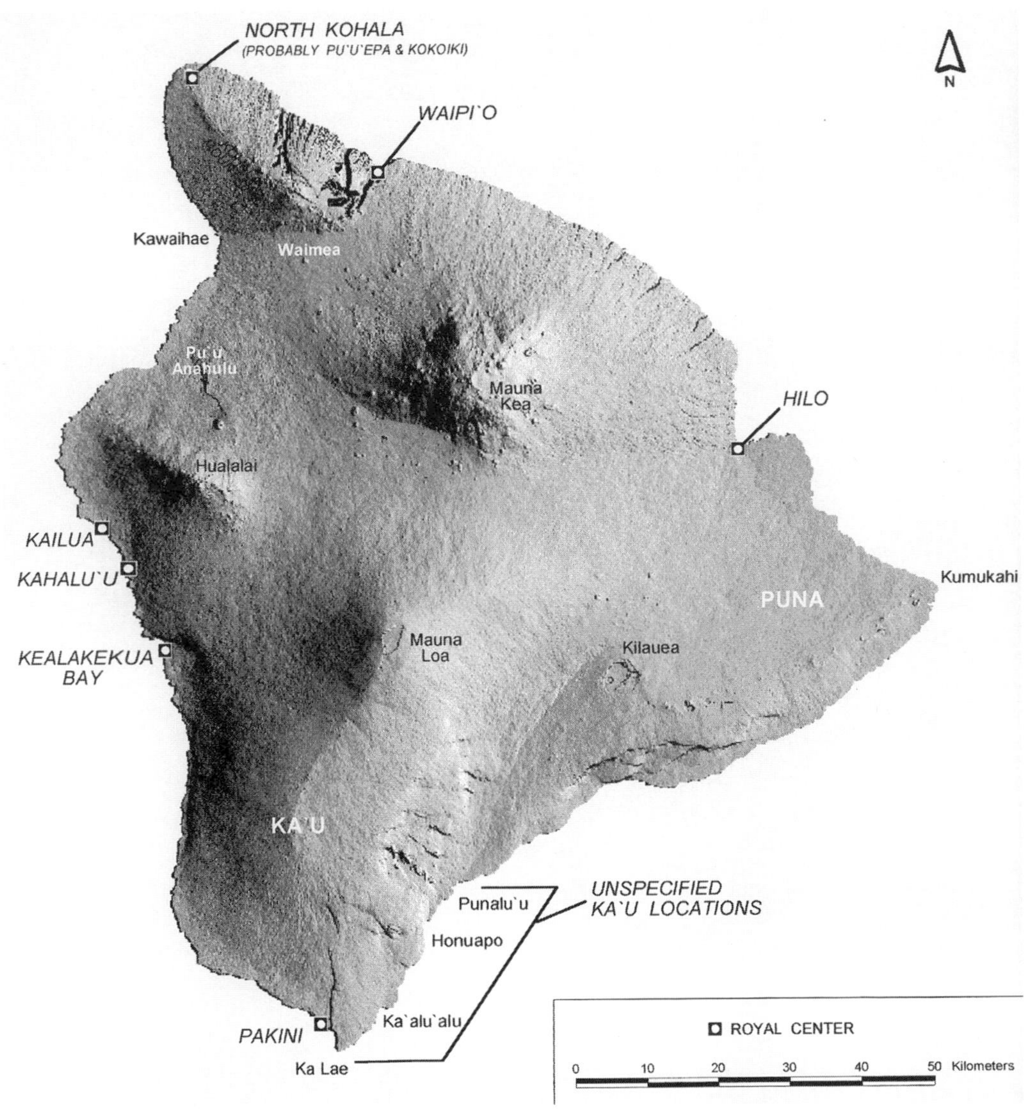


**FIGURE 9-15**
Royal Centers on Hawai'i Island used during Kalani'ōpu'u's Reign.

Kalani'ōpu'u, evidently embittered and sworn to revenge, then regrouped for a year on Hawai'i, recruiting divisions from all six districts and the royal family's guard (Keawe division), and a special elite force called the 'Ālapa or the Pi'ipi'i. He reconsecrated luakini heiau to his war god Kūkā'ilimoku at 'Ōhi'amukumuku (Kahalu'u) and Keikipu'ipu'i (Kailua), this being done under the supervision of his high priest Holo'ae.[110] Then Kalani'ōpu'u invaded Maui once again. His forces landed in Honua'ula district, spread from Mākena to Keone'ō'io, conducted raids, and then moved on to Kula along the Kīhei shore. From there he sent the 800 men of the elite 'Ālapa division across to Wailuku against Kahekili, confident of victory.

> *Across the plains... shone the feather cloaks of the soldiers woven in the ancient pattern and colored like the hues of the rainbow in red, yellow, and green, with helmuts on their heads whose arcs shown like a night in summer when the crescent lies within the moon.*
>
> [1866 Kamakau][111]

And, they were wiped out, all but two warriors who escaped and reported back to Kalani'ōpu'u of the complete defeat. [This battle became known as the Ahulau ka Pi'ipi'i i Kakanilua.][112]

On the ensuing day, Kalani'ōpu'u's full army also suffered a crushing defeat at the hands of Kahekili's army near Wailuku—although Kahekili's army seems to have also suffered great losses. Kekūhaupi'o again delayed disaster with a famous holding action against Kahekili's warriors and the slingstone-thrower 'Oulu.[113] But, it was only by sending his highly sacred son Kīwala'ō, Kahekili's nephew through his sister Kalola, to Kahekili to sue for peace that a total rout was avoided. Kīwala'ō proceeded through the ongoing battle—accompanied only by Kame'eiamoku and Kamanawa, the high chiefs of Kekaha, and said by some to be half-brothers to Kahekili. The sight of them caused the soldiers on both sides to react as expected.

> *As Kiwalao advanced all of the warriors prostrated themselves, putting an end to the fighting.*
>
> ['Ī'i][114]

After an audience between Kīwala'ō and Kahekili, Kahekili granted the truce and peace ensued.[115] [The high chiefs fighting under Kalani'ōpu'u at this time included his brother Keawema'uhili, Kalanimanoiokaho'owaha of the Luahine family of Kohala, Keaweaheulu of the Hilo 'Ī family, 'Īmakakoloa of Puna, Nu'uanupā'ahu of Ka'ū, Nae'ole of Kohala (Kamehameha's kahu), Kānekoa of Waimea (a son of Kalanike'eaumoku and a half-brother of Kamehameha's father Keōua), Nanuekaleiōpū of Hāmākua, Kame'eiamoku and Kamanawa of Kekaha (defacto sons of Keawepoepoe and putative sons of Kekaulike of Maui), and Kekūhaupi'o of Ke'ei and warrior-priest teacher of Kamehameha.][116]

Despite this defeat, within two years Kalani'ōpu'u had regrouped and again invaded the lands of Maui ca. 1778—pillaging Kaupō and Kaho'olawe, landing at Lahaina and engaging some of Kahekili's forces at the fortress of Kāhili, decimating Lāna'i and slaughtering chiefs and warriors at their refuge (the Lāna'i battle known as Kamokuhi), and raiding and engaging Kahekili's forces in Ko'olau and Hāmākualoa.[117] It was during this campaign when Captain Cook arrived off Maui's Hāmākualoa in November 1778. Kalani'ōpu'u went on board briefly, wearing a helmet with yellow and black feathers and a long feathered cloak.[118] Word of Cook's arrival in the islands had spread from Kaua'i, and the Hawai'i island chiefs and priests, according to some accounts,[119] seemed to believe that this was Lono, their ancestor and 'aumakua returned.

Perhaps one of the most stunning events of Kalani'ōpu'u's reign, from the Hawaiian perspective, was this arrival of the British exploring expedition under Cook in the ships *Discovery* and *Resolution*. After Cook's encounter with Kalani'ōpu'u off Maui, the expedition sailed on around windward Hawai'i and Ka'ū, and up to Kealakekua, where they anchored January 17, 1779. Kalani'ōpu'u seems to have rapidly terminated the war with Maui, for on January 22, 1779 he came hurrying back to Hawai'i with Kamehameha and Kekūhaupi'o, other chiefs and several hundred warriors.[120]

> *[S]ome of the chiefs and other warriors who had been at Mauwee came into the bay, and the next day several more hundred made their appearance.*
>
> [1779 Ledyard][121]

Accounts of Cook's visit are numerous—including those by members of his expedition[122] and those from Hawaiian oral historical accounts[123]—and even more numerous studies and analyses have since occurred. Much discussion has focused on the Hawai'i Island priests and chiefs believing that Cook was the deity Lono returned, and Cook's death has also been frequently dwelled upon. Bluntly put, Cook died during an attempt to kidnap Kalani'ōpu'u and hold him as ransom in order to have the *Discovery's* cutter returned—a common approach that Cook and others had used elsewhere in the Pacific. Kīwala'ō was not present, evidently being on Maui, but Kekūhaupi'o, Kamehameha and Kalaimanokaho'owaha were present and certainly would have assisted in aiding their king.[124] Indeed, in Kamakau's account, the slaying of Cook is attributed to Kalaimanokaho'owaha as a reaction to British force.[125] Cook's death and ensuing skirmishes also took the lives of ca. 25-29 Hawaiians, including 4–8 chiefs.[126] This marked the start of a new form of warfare and the vast array of contact with European, American and Asian nations, including the introduction of new status items and new, devastating diseases.

At the time of Cook's visit, Kalani'ōpu'u was described as "an old man and very feeble," ca. 5'8" tall and slender,[127] and the traditional accounts describe him similarly in these his waning years. After the departure of the British expedition, Kalani'ōpu'u spent the remainder of his reign on Hawai'i. His court expended the resources of the Kona royal centers of Kealakekua and Kahalu'u, so he moved the court to northern Kohala.[128] There, two final series of events of his reign began. 'Īmakakoloa, district chief of Puna, revolted, perhaps due to the court's demands for food and tribute; it appears that Nu'uanupā'ahu, a chief of Ka'ū, was also involved in the plot. Both were renowned warrior–high chiefs who had served Kalani'ōpu'u well in his campaigns on Maui. Nu'uanupā'ahu's demise was plotted by Kalani'ōpu'u's kahuna—an attack by a shark while surfing. But, Nu'uanupā'ahu's surfing performance and daring during this attack at Kauhola in northern Kohala—even though he died of his wounds—was so outstanding that it remains fixed in oral history.[129] And, so began the quelling the revolt.

The second series of events began with the installation of Kīwala'ō as the formal heir to the kingdom. The court had moved to Waipi'o, and the ritual occurred at the reconsecrated heiau of Moa'ula on the talus slopes near the front of the valley. Here, Kīwala'ō was given the right to rule the land and dedicate heiau, while Kamehameha—as Kalani'ōpu'u's nephew and virtual hānai son—was given the care of the god Kūkā'ilimoku. With this split of land and god was sown the seed for eventual conflict between Kīwala'ō and Kamehameha.[130]

After Kīwala'ō's consecration, Kalani'ōpu'u and the court traveled to Hilo and then sent warriors into Puna to defeat the rebels and seize 'Īmakakoloa. But 'Īmakakoloa remained at large. From Hilo, Kalani'ōpu'u moved the court into Ka'ū, and while there, 'Īmakakoloa was finally caught in Puna and brought to the heiau of Hālauwilua in Pākini ahupua'a at South Point. Here his body was to be offered up by Kīwala'ō at the end of ceremonies. Instead, while Kīwala'ō was presenting the preceding offering of a pig and bananas, Kamehameha—at the advice of some chiefs—seized 'Īmakakoloa's body and offered it to the god Kū. This act violated protocol, and it appears that many chiefs wanted to slay Kamehameha. But Kalani'ōpu'u ordered his nephew to return to his Kohala lands of Hālawa ahupua'a, and Kamehameha departed with his brother Kala'imamahū and the god Kūkā'ilimoku.[131]

Shortly thereafter, Kalani'ōpu'u became sick and died in Pākini ahupua'a in Ka'ū, in January of 1782. The kingdom passed to Kīwala'ō and soon the conflict between Kīwala'ō and Kamehameha and their subordinate chiefs rose again and split the land apart in revolt. And in these last days of Kalani'ōpu'u, Kahekili recaptured the Hāna and Kīpahulu lands from Hawai'i forces, and reincorporated them within the Maui kingdom.[132]

Kalani'ōpu'u had several wives.[133] His ranking wife was Kalola, sister of Kahekili of Maui. With her, he had Kīwala'ō. A second wife was Kānekapolei, younger sister of Mahi-lele-lima the district chief of Hāna and Kīpahulu under Kalani'ōpu'u. With her, Kalani'ōpu'u had twin sons, Keōua Kū'ahu'ula and Keōua Pe'e'ale, said to be ca.

16-years old at Cook's visit. Another son of Kānekapolei, Ka'ōleiokū, was raised as a son of Kalani'ōpu'u, but all oral histories say that this was a child of an illicit liaison between Kamehameha and Kānekapolei. Four other wives are noted: Kalaiwahineuli (daughter of Heulu of the 'Ī), Kamekolunuiokalani, Mulehu (of a Ka'ū chiefly family), and Kekupuohi.

As a parting comment on Kalani'ōpu'u's reign, although he and his court dwelled in many places—from Kona through Kohala, in Waipi'o and Hilo, in Ka'ū, and even in Puna[134]—perhaps the location most associated with him is Kealakekua Bay. This was but one of many royal residences that he used, and other rulers used it as well. But, it is an appropriate link with Kalani'ōpu'u because of glimpses presented primarily by members of Cook's expedition during their two stays in 1779, from January 17–February 4 and again from February 11–22, a total of about a month. Native oral histories provide additional perspectives, and Māhele period documents and archaeological surveys give more details on structure locations.[135]

The bay of Kealakekua is located in central Kona, south of Kailua and Kahalu'u and just north of Hōnaunau. The bay forms a semicircle open to the west, with Kalaemanō Point to the north in Ka'awaloa ahupua'a, the cliffs Pali Kapu o Keōua on the east, and Palemanō Point in Ke'ei ahupua'a to the south (Fig. 9-16). Seven ahupua'a fringe this bay. Ka'awaloa occupies the northern flats of the bay, with a low pāhoehoe shore and coastal flats, and a rapidly rising slope extending up to the wet uplands where rainfall approaches 100 inches. The ahupua'a of Kealakekua, Kīloa, Waipuna'ula and Kalama all front the low sandy shore and pāhoehoe flats south of the cliffs, then curve around and up the scarp to the high-rainfall uplands above.

In Kalani'ōpu'u's time, the lands around the bay were densely populated. Lieutenant, and later Captain, James King of the Cook expedition counted 350 dwelling houses along the shore and 50 more inland, 13% of the population in the uplands.[136] Surgeon Samwell counted 370–380 houses along the coast,[137] closely agreeing with

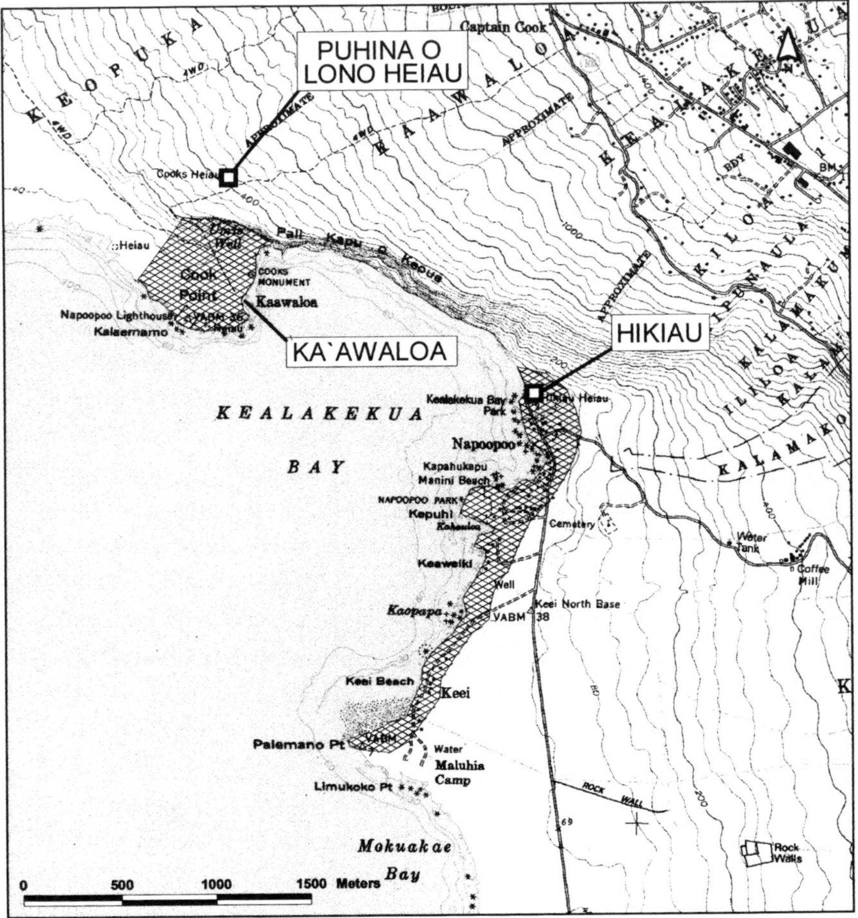


**FIGURE 9-16**

U.S. Geological Survey topographic map of the Kealakekua Bay area, with the Ka'awaloa coastal flats and southern shore shaded. The names of the ahupua'a along the bay are visible; going south from Ka'awaloa, these are Kealakekua, Kīloa, Waipuna'ula, the Kalamas, Kahauloa, and Ke'ei.

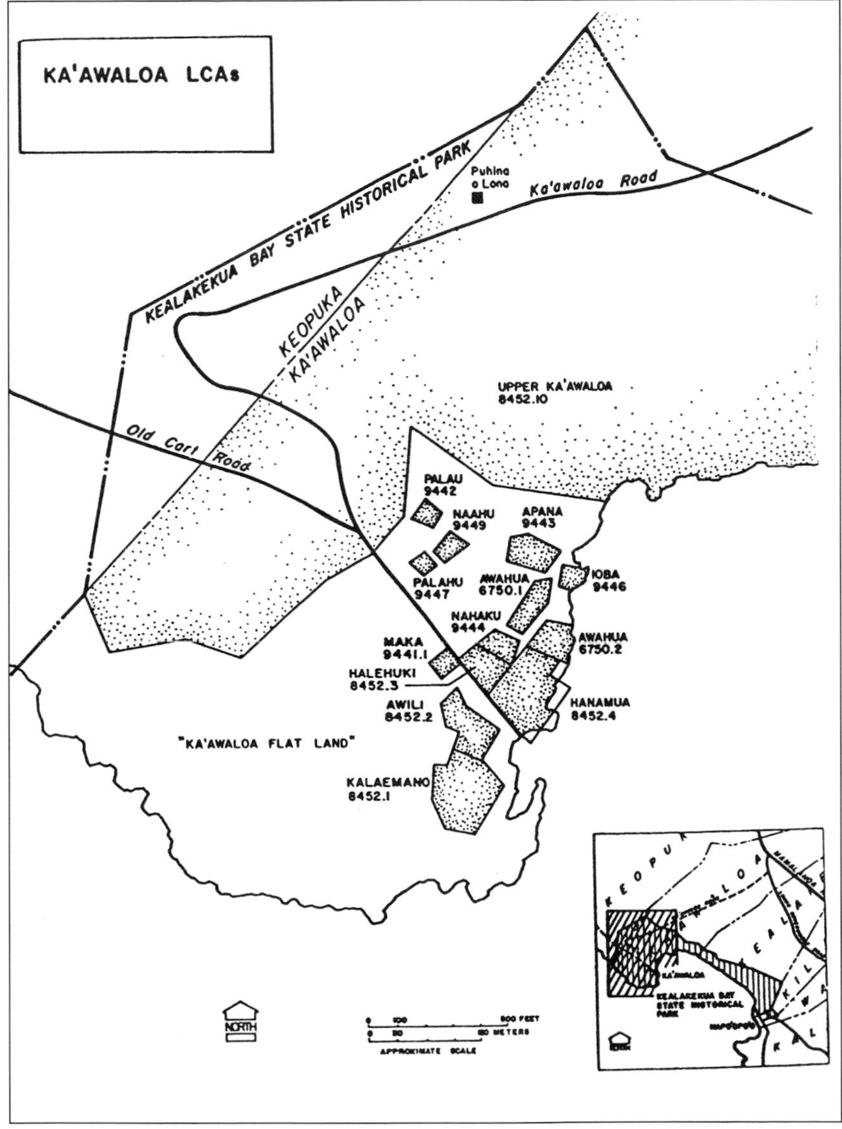


**FIGURE 9-17**
Location of houselots (pā hale) in Ka'awaloa as identified in the Māhele land awards of the 1840s (Alvarez 1989:Fig. 9, p.5.2). In 1779 Kalani'ōpu'u was in residence at 'Āwili; Keaweaheulu at Hanamua.

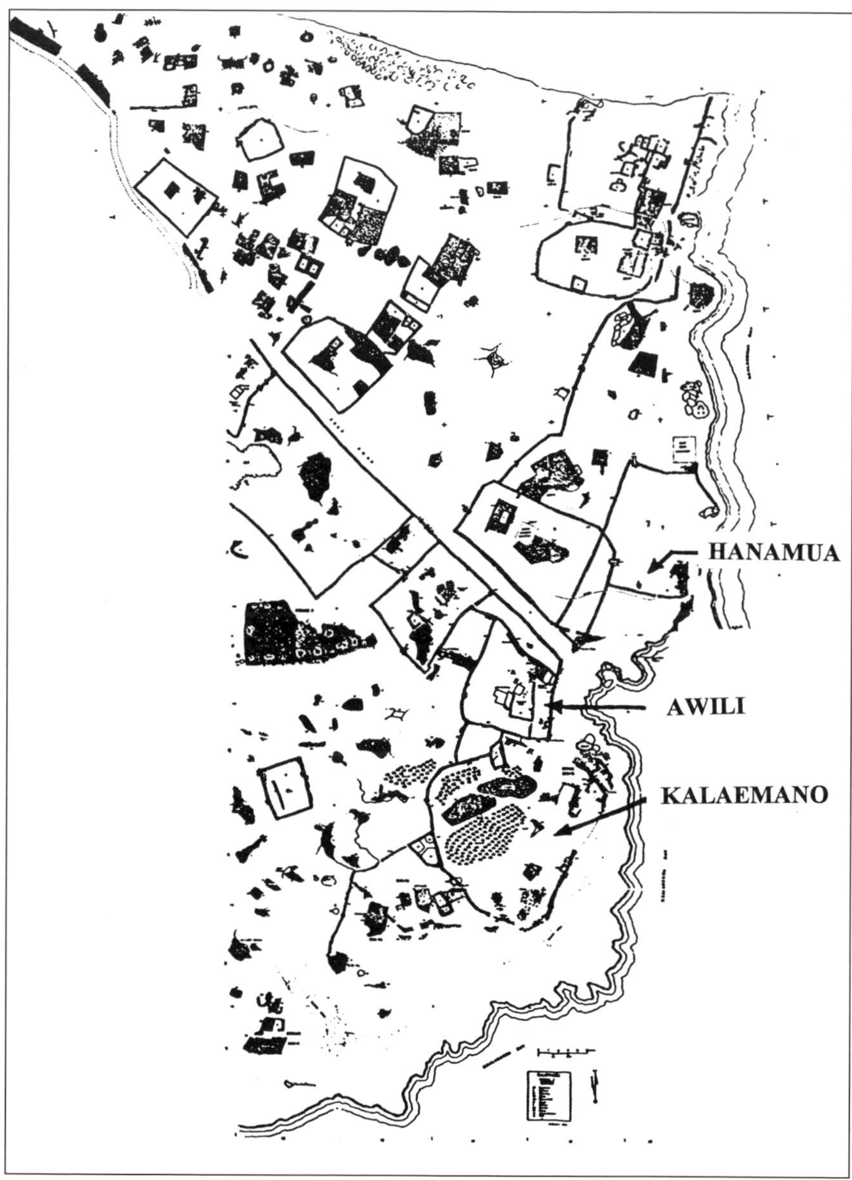


**FIGURE 9-18**

Archaeological map of Ka'awaloa Flats showing major house lots or pā hale. These houselots are often visible as walled enclosures, particularly along the shore, where Hanamua, 'Āwili and Kalemanō are labeled. Numerous stone platforms can also be seen on the map, many of these being house structures. (Composite from Hommon 1969; Hommon & Crozier 1970).

HAWAII STATE ARCHIVES

**FIGURE 9-19**
1779 view of Kealakekua Bay by Webber. Houses to the right are those along the southern shore of the bay. Hikiau heiau is among these houses.

HAWAII STATE ARCHIVES

**FIGURE 9-20**
Close-up of previous figure showing houses on the south side of bay near Pali Kapu o Keōua.

HAWAII STATE ARCHIVES

**FIGURE 9-21**

1779 view of houses at Kealakekua Bay, by Surgeon William Ellis. Presumably these are houses along the southern shore, perhaps near Hikiau heiau.

HAWAII STATE ARCHIVES

**FIGURE 9-22**

The sporting or athletic grounds along the southern shore of Kealakekua Bay in 1779. The wooden image with crossbar is that of Lono-makua, carried about during the makahiki. (Webber illustration.)

King's count. If one uses King's estimated average of 6 people per dwelling house, there would have been an estimated 2,100–2,400 people in this region.

The expedition failed to clearly associate the houses along the south shore with specific ahupua'a—indeed some expedition members appear to have believed the houses belonged to only one village instead of several separately named ahupua'a.[138] This mistake is understandable, since the houses fringed the shore in nearly a continuous pattern. Ledyard, a marine corporal with the expedition, provides a good feel for the housing on the south side of the bay, even though he seems to overestimate the number of houses (also see Figs. 9-19 through 9-21).

> *The Town of Kireekakooa is about a mile and an half in length, but narrow and of an unequal breadth, and as I have before observed contains about 1100 houses, some reckon 1300 including some detached buildings. It is situate along the shore within a few rods of the water, and is in general very compact, and as the houses in those places stand so as to create a breadth there are a number of little streets that intersect each other....There are cocoanut and other trees interspersed artificially among the houses all over the town.*
>
> [1779 Ledyard][139]

> *in different places square elevated yards for bleaching and otherwise manufacturing their cloth.*
>
> [1779 Ledyard][140]

Samwell depicts a similar setting:

> *These Towns, tho' the Houses are close together, are not built regular so as to form anything like streets but have paths running through them in a zig zag manner; most of the Houses have Courts before them*

*railed in, some have large squares walled in near them, covered with small Pebbles on which they dry and stain their Cloth.*

[1779 Samwell][141]

Within this southern area of houses, there was an open arena for boxing, wrestling and other sports—a "level course for running and other exercises... kept very clean."[142] Webber illustrated boxing at this arena in 1779 (Fig. 9-22).

Unfortunately, other than the area around Hikiau heiau, few of these sites along the south side of the bay remain today, due to extensive land disturbance from twentieth-century dwellings. North of Hikiau some enclosures and subsurface cultural deposits are present.[143] South of the heiau, however, remains are spotty, although more may be found in future archaeological surveys.

Across the bay on the pāhoehoe flats of Ka'awaloa were the 80-odd houses of that ahupua'a (see Fig. 9-16). Here lived Kalani'ōpu'u, Keaweaheulu, Palea and other chiefs.[144] Kalani'ōpu'u's housing compound appears to have been at the house lot (pā hale) called 'Āwili right on the shore (see Fig. 9-17), consisting of several houses and a men's house nearby, the latter being where Cook met him to convince him to come on board as a captive.[145] Keaweaheulu's residence was immediately adjacent at Hanamua (see Fig. 9-17).[146] On the other side toward the point was the pā hale called Kalaemanō, which in 1793 was surrounded by a 2-meter- (6-foot-) high wall with a small heiau at the corner nearest 'Āwili.[147] Archaeological survey has identified many remnants of these houses as stone platforms and pavings and house yards with stone enclosing walls.[148] Many of these features are 1800s period modifications. However, kuleana borders and documents, early 1900s maps showing pā hale locations, and archaeological maps show considerable correspondence, and the walls of the pā hale areas of 'Āwili, Hanamua and Kalaemanō are still apparent archaeologically (Fig. 9-18), although the actual walls and many features within may post-date the 1700s. Archaeological work also has shown that many crevices in the pāhoehoe had been filled with stone to level ground around these dwellings,[149] and a number of springs and brackish pools were scattered among the houses, some used for drinking water and others for bathing.[150]

The main coastal trail, the ala loa, connected these coastal houses of Kealakekua, running among the dwellings of Ka'awaloa and up along the top of the cliff and then down to the residences on the south side of the bay.[151] Travel across the bay was by canoe; the Cook expedition frequently saw canoes crossing to Kalani'ōpu'u at Ka'awaloa and returning.

The focal religious structure at this time was the major luakini heiau Hikiau in Kealakekua ahupua'a, on the edge of the shore with a pond adjacent to the north. This area was a religious complex that also embraced priests' houses on the north edge of the pond, and a smaller hale-o-Lono heiau—all bounded on the inland side by a 2.5-meter-high wall.[152]

> *A field of Taboo'd ground separates the Morai from a Village to the south or rather a continued range of straggling houses in that direction.*
>
> [1779 King][153]

> *[W]e discovered in our neighborhood the habitations of a society of priests, whose regular attendance at the morai had excited our curiosity. Their huts stood round a pond of water and were surrounded by a grove of cocoanut trees, which separated them from the beach and the rest of the village and gave the place an air of religious retirement.*
>
> [1784 Cook & King][154]

> *the residence of the priest that conducted the ceremony. It consisted of a circle of large cocoanut and other trees that stood upon the margin of a pond of water in the center of which was a bathing place. Upon the north side of the pond were a row of houses standing among the trees and were most delightfully*

> *situated; These houses extended almost to the morai, nearest which was that of the priest who was the lord of this beautiful recess. Between the houses and the pond were a number of grass plots intersected by several square holes with water in them which were private baths.*
>
> [1779 Ledyard][155]

The foundation of the heiau was an immense stone platform 49 meters (112 feet) long, 34 meters (161 feet) wide, with an area of 1,666 $m^2$, and up to 4 meters (13 feet) high.[156]

> *The top was flat and well paved, and surrounded by a wooden rail, on which were fixed the skulls of the captives sacrificed on the death of their chiefs. In the centre of the area stood a ruinous old building of wood, connected with the rail on each side by a stone wall, which divided the whole space into two parts. On the side next to the country were five poles, upward of twenty feet high, supporting an irregular kind of scaffold [anu'u]; on the opposite side toward the sea, stood two small houses with a covered communication....We were conducted by Koah [a priest] to the top of this pile by an easy ascent leading from the beach....At the entrance we saw two large wooden images, with features violently distorted, and a long piece of carved wood with a conical form inverted, rising from the top of their heads; the rest was without form, and wrapped round with red cloth... they led us to that end of the Morai where the five poles were fixed. At the foot of them were twelve images ranged in a semicircular form, and before the middle image stood a high stand or table...on which lay a putrid hog, and under it pieces of sugar-cane, cocoa-nuts, bread-fruit, plantains, and sweet potatoes.*
>
> [1784 Cook & King][157]

Hikiau heiau's stone foundation remains today, although modified several times in this century.[158]

At least 11 smaller religious structures were also present around the bay, most in the Ka'awaloa area.[159] The hale-o-Lono heiau near Hikiau to the north around the pond, was called Helehelekalani, and Cook participated in a ceremony there (Fig. 9-23). Priests' houses—including apparently that of the high priest—were present around this pond, the whole area being a religious complex.[160] Puhina o Lono heiau in upper Ka'awaloa, overlooking the bay, was where Cook's remains were prepared.[161] This heiau was enclosed by a stone wall ca. 15 feet square. A fishing heiau (kū'ula) (site 70 or C23-9) at Kalaemanō Point, visible in a Webber drawing of Ka'awaloa, has been identified on the shore by archaeologists as a high platform-like structure, ca. 25 x 41 feet (7.6 x 12.5 m, 95 sq. m.) in area.[162] Other heiau are likely to have been affiliated with different high chiefs.

Around all these houses and public structures and just inland below the pali were informal farm plots—patches of sweet potatoes and apparently young taro which were later transplanted to the wet uplands. Archaeological survey on the Ka'awaloa flats has identified agricultural pits dug in the pāhoehoe, often enlarging existing cracks and pits, numerous agricultural mounds, and small soil areas in depressions.[163] On the southern side of the bay, numerous archaeological surveys on the lands between the former houses and the pali have occurred,[164] and a few rare excavations.[165] This work has found remains of the informal fields in the form of small clearings and terraces with stone mounds. Evidence of field shelters has been recovered, appearing as small subsurface soil layers—gray in appearance with occasional stone-lined firepits, a few food remains (shell), abundant small flakes and cores of volcanic glass, and a few artifacts.[166] Beyond these informal fields in the higher rainfall zones on the steep slopes of the pali and the more gradual slopes above were the extensive formal walled fields of the classic Kona field system as described in Chapter 8—taro and sweet potato fields with their long kuaīwi walls running towards the shore.[167]

HAWAII STATE ARCHIVES

**FIGURE 9-23**
Helehelekalani Heiau, a Hale-o-Lono in the ahupua'a of Kealakekua, 1779. This heiau was located on the edge of the pond which had Hikiau heiau on its southern side. (Drawing by Webber.)

## GENERAL PATTERNS OF THE 1700s

Many radiocarbon dates span the period of the A.D. 1600s–1700s, which makes it difficult to securely place sites in time. Volcanic glass dates still have many problems. Yet with these two dating tools—despite their flaws—some ideas on general patterns of life in the A.D. 1700s have been offered by archaeologists.

Some have argued that the limits of agricultural growth had been reached[168]—with cultivation in marginal settings such as washed down soil locations in coastal south Kohala[169] and coastal central Kona.[170] Other information suggests agricultural expansion was still ongoing—evidenced by marginal soil cultivation and expansion farther up into the forests. Survey information from Kaloko in north central Kona shows formal walled field areas up to the 2,300-foot elevation and scattered terraces and mounds up to 3,500 feet. This has been argued as evidence of continued expansion upslope, and interestingly, adjacent ahupua'a fields seem to have been at lower and varying elevations—proof of differential growth of ahupua'a fields.[171] Informal fields had spread downslope in most leeward areas in the form of clearings, terraces, mounds, and pits.

Intensification of fields also seemed to be increasing. In Kaloko, small oval enclosures were built near coastal houses and filled with soil.[172] In central Kona at Puaa[173] and Waiola,[174] and in central Ka'ū at Moa'ula,[175] irrigation canals were extended off streams at upper elevations to provide supplemental water. In the Waimea area of south Kohala, supplemental irrigation reached its extreme in leeward Hawai'i, evidently in the A.D. 1700s.

The Waimea area of Kohala approximates today's growing town of Waimea, extending from the Kamuela Airport and the Parker Ranch Shopping Center at about the 2,700-foot elevation, and dropping downslope along the hills of Kohala Mountain to just below the junction of the Hāwī-Waimea road. Waimea is nestled against the lee of the Kohala Mountain. It is cool (mean = 64°F), often cold, with fine, misty rains. The hills and town are cloaked in green grass, but just outside of town this grass turns yellow-brown.

Although a modern perception of Waimea, the above is not far off the mark for old Waimea. By 1812 it included the large land units of Waikoloa, Lālāmilo [once part of Waikoloa] and 'Ōuli, which extended down to the shore encompassing the arid lands of Puakō, Kalāhuipua'a and 'Anaeho'omalu.[176] Waikoloa originates on the Kohala Mountain, and is associated with the waters of Waikoloa Stream. A green bountiful area, Waikoloa forms the east end of upland Waimea, along with the inland ahupua'a of Pu'ukapu. Lālāmilo is adjacent to Waikoloa, next to Waikoloa Stream, and 'Ōuli is next to Lālāmilo (Fig. 9-24). A number of small inland ahupua'a are above on the green slopes of the mountain.

Two main streams drain off the mountain—Waikoloa and Keanu'i'omanō, which are fed by numerous small streams. These two join and reach the shore as the Wai'ula'ula, which may once have flowed year-round before its waters were partly tapped above, but which today flows only in flash flood conditions. Four major environmental zones bear discussion—first, the hillslopes; second, the flats between the hillslopes and the streams; third, the relatively flat slopes between the airport and town center; and last, the dry swales and rises between Waikoloa Stream and two cinder cones to the south—Pu'u Huluhulu and Pu'u Pā. These four areas were all farmed prehistorically, in what has come to be called the Waimea Field System.

Briefly, the field system consisted of dryland fields fed by low rainfall (15/20–40 inches per year[177]) and supplemented by an irrigation system of wide-basin canals (Fig. 9-25). Irrigation was not into pondfields in most cases, rather it was "a flow-through system" with water seeping into the soil.[178] The hillslopes above had many terraces, in some cases with drainage and/or irrigation into or from streams. The area between the slopes and streams had rectangular fields fed by irrigation canals—the major pondfield area. The area near today's airport had low stone ridges marking off field areas, fed by two major irrigation canals leading off the Waikoloa Stream. The vast swale lands to the south of Waikoloa Stream had rectalinear fields with terrace facings or low-ridged walls, and were fed by six major canals (one an extension out of the airport area) and a vast number of interlinking branches of these canals.[179] The walled fields diminished to the south about halfway to Pu'u Huluhulu and Pu'u Pā, where rainfall and soil quality drop—although the swales were still fed by canals. Canals often branched and ran along both sides of the swales at the base of the ridges. The ridges between the swales had agricultural features also—mounds, small terraces and modifications.[180]

> *[D]own to said hill or mound [Pu'u Huluhulu], was all in cultivation in ancient times, being planted by the natives with bananas, sweet potatoes, sugar cane, and dry land taro.... The land was not all taken up uniformly in planting, but they would plant in available places where the water in the ditch could reach and run.*
>
> [1901 elder Hawaiian's testimony, Carter Case][181]

The density of fields begins to dramatically reduce downslope at the 2,000-foot elevation, and the irrigation system evidently terminates here also. The fields then fade away to virtually none by the 1,800-foot elevation.[182]

House sites were scattered about the fields on knolls and ridges, but many were temporary field shelters—archaeologically appearing as small C- and L-shaped stone enclosures and small terraces and platforms.[183] 1907 testimony by an elderly Hawaiian stated, "People would not live on their farms, but would live in small villages which were scattered throughout this territory, going thence to work their various farms."[184] Historical documents identify three such small clusters of permanent dwellings on the flats between the hillslopes and streams,[185] and archaeological survey has discovered that other clusters of permanent dwellings were in the swale land south of the streams. Some isolated dwellings were on the hillslopes, in the swale land, and on the slopes near today's airport.

One permanent dwelling on the flats between the joining of Lanikepu and Keanuʻiʻomanō streams, site 11,107, was a larger, rectangular stone enclosure, 72 $m^2$. Its low-walled ruins stood amidst the ridged fields of the flat. Extensive excavations found a wide variety of food remains in the rubbish deposits of this site, including chicken, dog, juvenile pig, nēnē goose, flightless rail, and marine shellfish.[186]

Archaeological work in this field system has also shown that activities on the ridges between the swales were more complicated than simply a house site and its associated activities such as cooking, sleeping, tool repair, and manufacturing. The ridges often had a number of features scattered along their sides and peaks. For example,[187] a small C-shaped enclosure with shallow deposits and very small amounts of marine shell food remains may have served as an overnight shelter and would be just below the ridgeline protected from the wind. A thick scattering of volcanic glass flakes and cores may have been 10 meters away atop the ridge, where tiny, sharp volcanic glass cutting tools were made in idle hours. Another 30 meters away, behind a low wall on the ridge top, there may have been a scattering of chipped, fine-grained basalt—where adzes were repaired. Just below, on the side of the ridge, there might have been a stone-lined, rectangular fireplace (hearth) with a scattering of shell and bone nearby—remnants of another shelter and cooking, eating and refuse activities. On the opposite side of the swale, on the side of the ridge, two large platforms may have been present, the foundations of former permanent dwellings. Not all these features would have been used at the same time. They would be the ruins associated with several hundred years of farming in the swale.

Major trails extended up into Waimea from Kawaihae and Puakō, connecting laterally from Puakō into the southernmost Kohala lands of 'Anaeho'omalu and Kalāhuipua'a, and up from Waipi'o and adjacent slopes of Hāmākua, and down from the Saddle area, where major trails led southwest along the Hāmākua/Kona border to Ahu a 'Umi and southeast towards Hilo, Puna and Ka'ū. Multiple internal trails must certainly have branched off to the many dwellings and fields within Waimea.

The questions arise, "How old was this field system?" and "How did it expand over time?" Archaeological excavations are still fairly limited—to the downslope and southern edge of the swale areas,[188] to a few sites within the swale lands,[189] to a small area between the streams,[190] to a few hillslope areas,[191] and to the gradual slopes near the airport[192] (cf. Fig. 9-24). Dates for informal fields (mounds and terraces) and associated habitations in higher rainfall areas near the airport and between Lanikepu and Keanu'i'omanō streams on the flats in 'Ōuli have gone back to the A.D. 1100s–1200s,[193] suggesting incipient farming by this time in Waimea. The southernmost swales have dates for agriculture and housing going back to the A.D. 1300s–1400s.[194] But the bulk of the dates throughout Waimea indicate the walled, irrigated fields and permanent habitations approached their maximum extent in the A.D. 1600s–1700s, and early 1800s.[195] It may be that the hillslopes and upper reaches were among the last cultivated, with a denser forest and steeper terrain.[196] Patches of forest appear to have remained among the fields until the 1800s, based on archaeological finds of tree-adapted land snails,[197] and indeed phytolith studies suggest "[A] number of episodes of forest clearing, both partial and fairly complete."[198]

Much needs to be learned about the chronology of the Waimea Field System; our dates are still extremely limited, but most researchers argue that the A.D. 1700s saw a marked increase in the extent of the fields, likely associated with Alapa'inui's and Kalani'ōpu'u's presence in the Kawaihae and Waimea areas, and with Kamehameha's building of Pu'ukoholā heiau—all requiring greater food production.[199]

Similarly, our dates for other agricultural systems on the island—particularly Kona's—fall abundantly into the A.D. 1400s–1800s range, and particularly the A.D. 1600s–1700s. Expansion and intensification of these systems in the A.D. 1700s seems quite logical, particularly if chiefly demands increased.

Some population models for Hawai'i Island suggest overall population stabilized or declined slightly in the A.D. 1700s.[200] These models are based on volcanic glass dates of sites using the Morgenstein hydration rate. Temporary habitation sites at Kalāhuipua'a (seaward Waikoloa) do show a slight decline,[201] and an analysis of temporary habitation sites and new dates from such sites at adjacent 'Anaeho'omalu show a similar slight decline.[202] But, a recomputation of the Kalāhuipua'a dates using the mean Puakō air temperature, rather than Keāhole's air temperature, show an increase and not a decrease in temporary habitations right up to European contact.[203] Dates from permanent habitation sites at 'Anaeho'omalu also show an increase,[204] and dates from several ahupua'a just to the south in northern Kona show increases in permanent habitations, some slight decreases, and some stability.[205] Based on radiocarbon dates and volcanic glass dates, population growth in upland Waimea is suggested to have continued through the A.D. 1700s.[206] And recent work in the kuaīwi fields of Keauhou in Kona also has processed radiocarbon dates showing population still increasing in the 1600s–1700s.[207]

All of the models on population growth, stabilization, or decline at this time can be called into question. Volcanic glass dates are no longer reliable to such accuracy.[208] Also, sampling of windward regions and optimal leeward regions is quite poor—areas vital to building accurate population models. The value of using temporary housing for population modeling is also suspect, as one family might

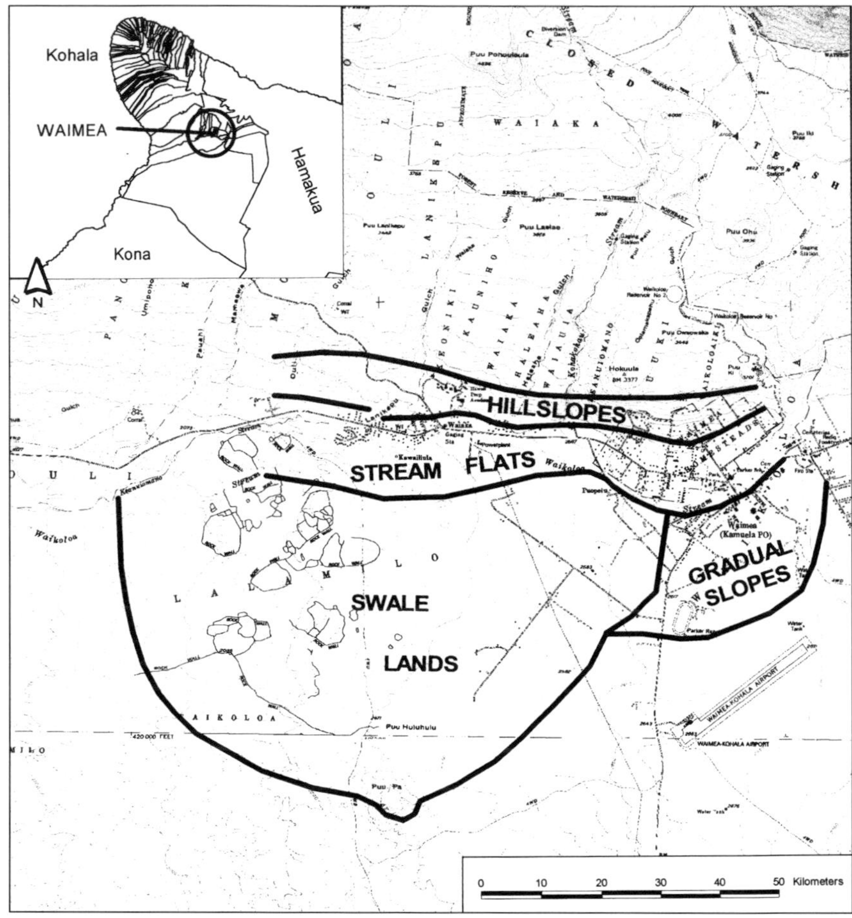


**FIGURE 9-24**

Map of the Waimea Field System & its Zones. Waimea town is to the mid-right edge of the map. The swale lands were planted out on the plain to Puʻupā and down to the 1800 foot elevation.

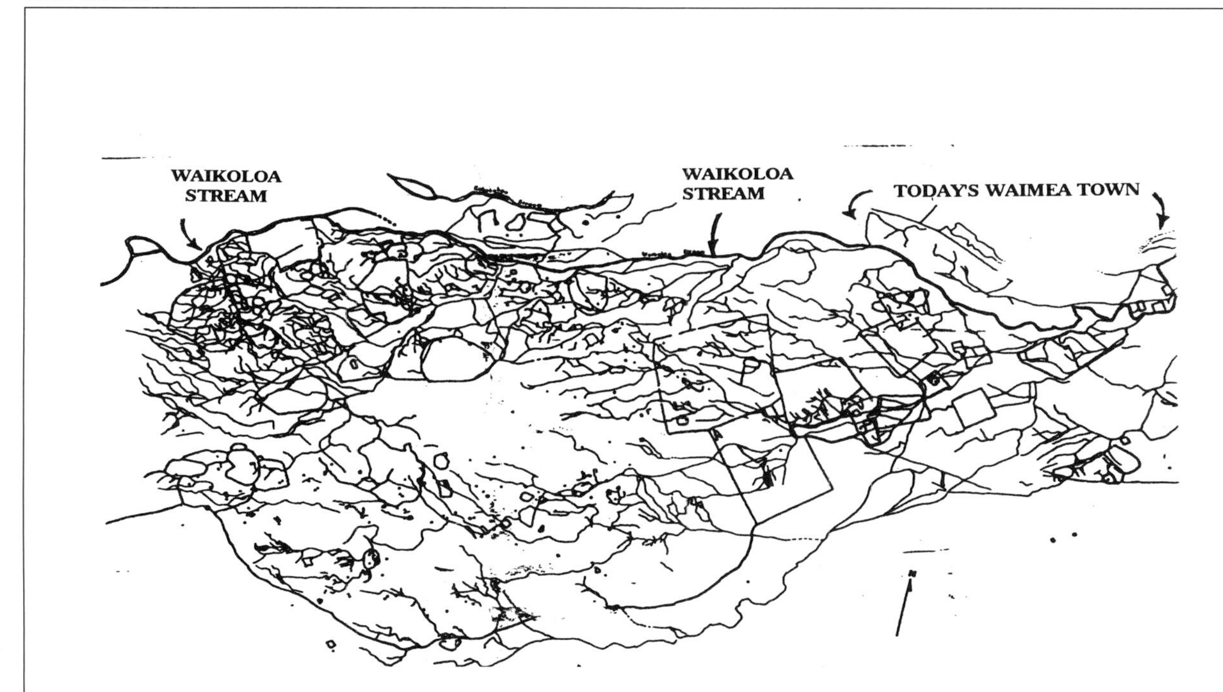


**FIGURE 9-25** Map of the irrigation canals and rectangular houselots and animal pens in the portion of the Waimea field system which extended south from Waikaloa stream to Pu'u Pā. Waikoloa Stream runs right to left (left being downhill) across the top of the map. Pu'u Pā is not shown on this map, but is located at the extreme base of the map. This map was prepared ca. 1915 for the Carter Case, a water case (from Clark 1981). Today's Waimea town is located along and below the Waikoloa Stream at the northeast (upper right) end of the map, and today's Waimea-Kawaihae highway runs just above the Waikoloa Stream, descending down towards Kawaihae which is well off the map to the left.

use five temporary houses, another but one, and both might share the same traveler's shelter. Thus, the question whether population continued to grow in the 1700s or not is still unresolved and is an important subject for future work.[209]

Marine exploitation probably was similar to that of the A.D. 1600s. Residents of the ahupua'a had varied exploitation patterns. Generally, on leeward Hawai'i, the cowrie and urchins remained the dominant marine invertebrates gathered, but a wide variety of species were collected. Nearshore fishing remained dominant, focusing on many species with parrotfish among the more common fishes caught, usually netted. Pelagic fish and benthic fish were caught but did not supply the bulk of the fish which were eaten. Strategies undoubtedly varied between ahupua'a and commoner groups. For example, at Kaloko, a household along the fishpond took greater numbers of eels.[210]

New fishponds may have been built, as periodic public projects. The large Pa'aiea fishpond from Keāhole Point north, which was covered by the 1801 lava flow, was not mentioned in the spy account given to Kamalālāwalu of Maui prior to his invasion of Hawai'i ca. A.D. 1640–1660 in the reign of Lonoikamakahiki. It may have been built later.

Forest exploitation by commoners undoubtedly continued as before, and it may have intensified with the chiefs' demands for feathers as tribute. The Boundary Commission Books document cases of clashes between Hāmākua and Ka'ū commoners who were feather collectors, and these cases likely date to the 1700s.[211] Petrel ('u'au) hunting by common folk may have intensified. Canoe-tree felling and building may have increased—particularly with the kings' numerous armed expeditions which required transport to reach Maui and O'ahu.

Periodic public works projects on heiau certainly were required in this century, with many heiau approaching their final size. Alapa'i was said to have renovated Mo'okini heiau,[212] and Kalani'ōpu'u similarly had men working on heiau throughout the island—renovating and quite likely adding on to the existing architecture. As seen, at Hōnaunau, 'Āle'ale'a heiau may have doubled in size in this century, as well as a new larger heiau possibly being built and used.[213]

Pele and her family also sallied forth in these years in Puna. In Kaimū in Puna, "the lands were overflowed in the days of Arapai [Alapa'inui]."[214] This flow formed the once famous black sand beach at Kaimū, just to the west from where the flow entered the sea.[215] The flow and eruption undoubtedly caused drastic impacts to this area of Puna and probably sent residents off to live in other areas. Yet flows were a common enough event in prehistory in Puna, much of Ka'ū and southernmost Kona—"eruptions from it [Kīlauea] had taken place during every king's reign, whose name was preserved in tradition."[216] Despite their dramatic impact, eruptions were relatively localized.

An even greater disruption and perhaps the striking new pattern of the A.D. 1700s was the extended warfare with the Maui Kingdom, and to a lesser extent with the O'ahu Kingdom. This warfare seems to have been a change in scale and in frequency. It must have disrupted life on Hawai'i for periods of time during the century. Sizable armies with men from throughout the kingdom were off-island for up to several months—some never to return, being casualties of war. Massive pre-invasion preparations involved encampments of the gathering army, which may have taxed the food support base. Whatever the effects, this warfare—planned by the king and his secular and religious advisors, and executed by his armies of faithful commoners and nobles—brought the Hawai'i kingdom to a position as a major power in the islands, rivaling first O'ahu and then Maui. This newly elevated role continued on to Hawai'i's eventual conquest of the archipelago's opposing kingdoms.

Increasing warfare in the 1700s may also partly account for the sudden increase in dog, pig and human sacrifices at luakini heiau on Maui in the late 1600s–1700s as found in recent archaeological work.[217] We do not yet know if such offerings also were increasing at Hawai'i Island luakini, but it would not be surprising. The nature and scale of religious offerings may well have changed as major warfare escalated between island kingdoms.

CHAPTER 10

# Kīwala'ō, Kamehameha, Keawema'uhili, & Keōua

# A.D. 1782–1791 The Decade of Strife & Tears

*The stake was the island;*
*There the property was staked,*
*The game was played to utter loss.*

(Keauhumoku's chant "Haui ka lani" about Kīwala'ō's losing to Kamehameha)[1]

*It is a day of misfortune, with defeat for both sides.*

(1782, Holo'ae, high priest, to Kamehameha prior to his battle with Kīwala'ō)[2]

*The rain drives down from the cliffs above*
*The tears for my chief*
*Drop down on the heads of the people.*

(lament for Keōua, ruler of the Ka'ū Kingdom)[3]

## KĪWALA'O (A.D. 1782)

Kalani'ōpu'u evidently expressed the wish to have his bones placed in the Hale o Keawe at Hōnaunau, so soon after his death Kīwala'ō initiated plans for the transport of his father's body from Ka'ū.[4] The chiefs of Kona became worried over this move and the possible loss of their lands in the traditional reallocation of ahupua'a by Kīwala'ō. Kekūhaupi'o, the renowned warrior and chief over Ke'ei in central Kona, paddled north to Kohala to bring Kamehameha south to the ceremonies.[5] His concerns and statement to Kamehameha foreshadow what was to come:

> *If your brother [Kīwala'ō] does well by us, then all will be well; but if he treats us meanly then the land must go to the stronger.*
>
> [Kekūhaupi'o to Kamehameha, 1782—Kamakau][6]

Kamehameha agreed to go south, and they proceeded south to Ka'ūpūlehu in northern Kona, where they met the powerful chiefs of Kona—Kame'eiamoku and his twin brother Kamanawa, then living at Ka'ūpūlehu, and Kīholo in Pu'uwa'awa'a.

While Kamehameha was traveling south, Kīwala'ō was moving north "in his double canoe accompanied by a double canoe bearing the corpse and by other canoes for the chiefs and commoners."[7] Off Honokua ahupua'a in southern Kona, Ke'eaumoku—the younger half-brother of Kamanawa and Kame'eiamoku—approached and wailed over Kalani'ōpu'u's body, and a critical exchange occurred. Ke'eaumoku asked, "Where will the body be laid?" A guard named Ka-ihe-ki'oi answered rudely, "It will be laid at Kailua."[8] This comment—perhaps just a boast by a man of Hilo or Ka'ū to irritate a chief of Kona—conflicted with Kalani'ōpu'u's wishes and the stated claims of Kīwala'ō, so when the procession reached Hōnaunau and the corpse was placed in the Hale o Keawe with due ceremony, Ke'eaumoku continued north to Ka'ūpūlehu to advise Kamehameha

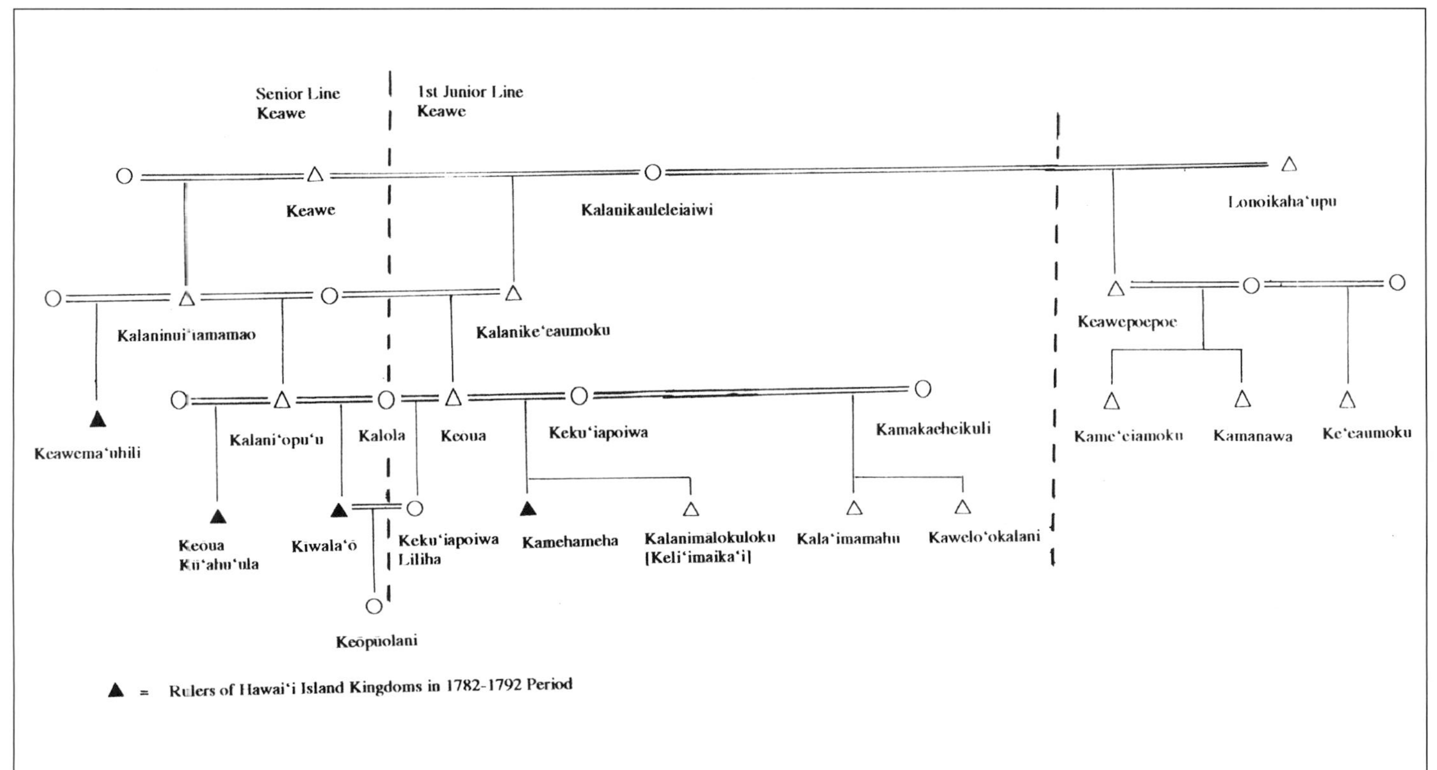


**FIGURE 10-1**
Rulers of Hawai'i Island Kingdoms, 1782–1791.

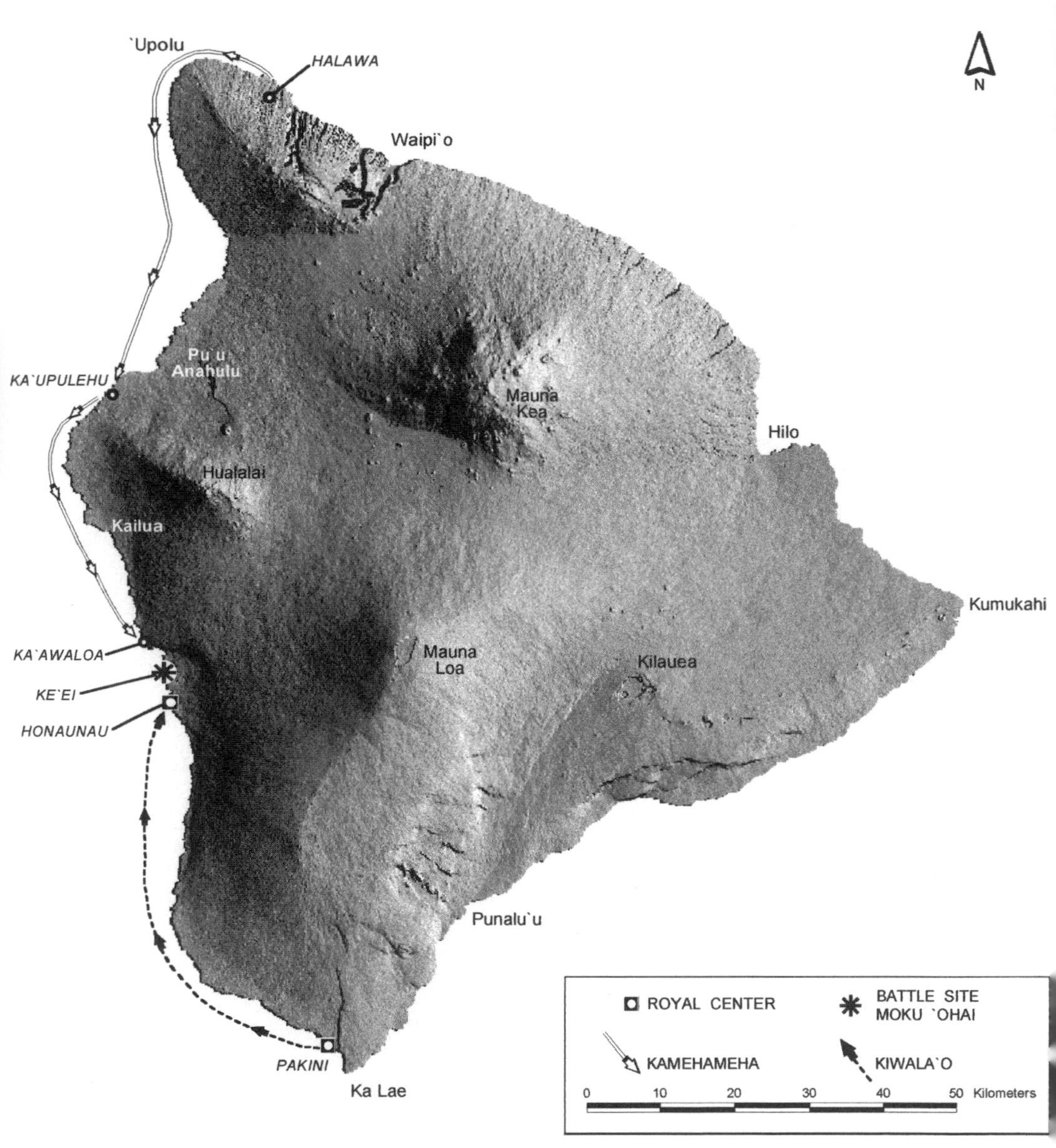


**FIGURE 10-2**
Places mentioned in Kīwala'ō's brief reign, A.D. 1782.

of a possible deception. The Kona and Kohala chiefs decided to sail immediately and disembark from Ka'awaloa to Ke'ei, and, in the worst situation, to prepare for battle at Ke'ei and Hōnaunau.[9]

When Kamehameha arrived at Ka'awaloa, Kīwala'ō came to meet him, and "they wailed and raised loud lamentation for the dead."[10] Here, Kīwala'ō too pointed out the growing tension, stating that Keawema'uhili, his powerful uncle, was advising war, "Here is our father pushing us to fight,"[11] just as Kamehameha's chiefs were advising him.

The next day, Kamehameha and his chiefs traveled to Hōnaunau, to pay respects to Kalani'ōpu'u at the Hale o Keawe.

There, Kīwala'ō proclaimed again Kalani'ōpu'u's command that Kamehameha care for the god and Kīwala'ō the land. Since Kīwala'ō's advisors were Ka'ū and Hilo chiefs, the Kona and Kohala chiefs were dismayed and secretly prepared for war.[12] However, Kamehameha and Kīwala'ō, according to Kamakau and Fornander, still planned to follow Kalani'ōpu'u's wishes.[13]

The following day, Keawema'uhili is said to have urged Kīwala'ō to divide the lands, and Kīwala'ō in agreeing,

> *told him [Keawema'uhili] to divide it, and said, "In dividing it, do not forget to give my brother Kamehameha some of the land." Keawe-ma'u-hili refused, saying, "This is not according to your father's command. He has the god and his old lands as was commanded. You are chief over the island, I am under you, and the chiefs under us. So was your father's command." So in dividing the land he reserved the largest portions for himself, and the rest he divided among the chiefs, warriors, lesser chiefs, favorites, and fighting men.*
>
> [Kamakau][14]

Apparently, none of the Kona-Kohala chiefs or even the Ka'ū chiefs were present.[15]

Keōua, Kīwala'ō's half-brother through Kalani'ōpu'u and Kānekapolei, heard of the divisions. He came to Kīwala'ō and asked which fertile lands in Puna, Hilo, Hāmākua, Kohala and Kona had been awarded to him and Kīwala'ō. Kīwala'ō told him that no new lands had been given; "Our uncle has taken it."[16] Extremely angry, Keōua returned to his camp, and armed his men. He then proceeded to Keomo in Ke'ei ahupua'a, felled coconut trees and killed some of Kamehameha's men. Their bodies were taken to Kīwala'ō to offer up at one of the luakini heiau of Hōnaunau, and Kīwala'ō did so—beginning the war between Kīwala'ō and his Hilo and Ka'ū chiefs against Kamehameha and his Kohala and Kona chiefs.[17]

The oral histories say that the greater number of chiefs remained loyal to Kīwala'ō, even some of Kamehameha's initial supporters—notably two brothers Kānekoa and Kaha'i, the first being a chief of Waimea and a half-brother of Kamehameha's father and thus Kamehameha's uncle.[18] The core of Kamehameha's chiefs were the twin Kekaha (Kona) chiefs, Kame'eiamoku and Kamanawa; the warrior chief of Ke'ei (Kona) Kekūhaupi'o; the half-brother of the twins and the chief of southernmost Kona, Ke'eaumoku; and the chief of the Kealakekua Bay area and the leading "male representative of the proud and powerful 'Ī family," Keaweaheulu—as well as Kamehameha's younger full brother Kalanimālokuloku (Keali'imaika'i), and his fraternal half-brothers Kala'imamahū and Kawelo'okalani.[19]

After two to four days of skirmishing, the major battle of Moku'ōhai began with Kamehameha's side losing in the morning, and Kīwala'ō offering up sacrifices with his force's successes.[20] But as prophets for Kīwala'ō and Kamehameha both foretold, the trend of the fighting would switch in the afternoon.[21] The following famous encounter turned the battle:

> *Ke'e-au-moku was fighting in the rear of the battle and fell entangled by his pololu spear. Kaha'i and Nuhi ran and stuck him through with their daggers (pahoa). Kini came to retrieve his pololu spear and stood at his back and shouted in his harsh voice, "My weapon has caught a yellow-backed crab!" Kini was a person with*

> *a rasping voice (leo'a-'a). Almost dead though he was, Ke'e-au-moku heard the voice of Kiwala'o say, "Guard the ivory whale tooth (niho palaoa)! guard the ivory whale tooth! do not let it become covered with blood!" and he knew that he must die since the chief had no care for his own blood relative (hulu makua). Ka-manawa, meanwhile, seeing his plight, rushed through the thick of the fight to reach his side. As Kiwala'o gazed eagerly at the famous ornament to see that it should not get smeared with blood, Ke-akua-wahine silently aimed (poko) a slingstone (pohaku 'ala') which struck Kiwala'o unaware, and he fell down. The men who were stabbing Ke'e-au-moku fled, and, seeing Kiwala'o lying prostrate, Ke'e-au-moku crawled to him with his shark's-tooth weapon (lei o mano) in his hand and cut his throat with it so that he died.*
>
> *Kamehameha meanwhile had entered the fight and had made an end of Ke-ahia. This was his first victim that day. He tossed him up, and when he fell his bones were broken to pieces. Kamehameha had an affection for Ke-ahia, but Holo-'ae had instructed him to seize a man for the god. Then the chiefs and fighting men of Kiwala'o fled.*
>
> [Kamakau][22]

As prophesied by Holo'ae, the kahuna nui of Kamehameha, it was indeed "a day of misfortune, with defeat for both sides."[23]

Keōua and some of his men reached their canoes and returned to Ka'ū, where he declared independence for his lands of Ka'ū and western Puna.[24] Other warriors of Hilo and Ka'ū escaped over Mauna Loa and returned through the interior plateau to their homes in Hilo and Ka'ū.[25] More chiefs and warriors apparently fled to the pu'uhonua at Hōnaunau for safety. Kalanimoku, the chief counsellor for Kamehameha late in his reign, was one of these, having been a follower of Kīwala'ō. In the 1820s, he showed Rev. Ellis on a drawing which entrance he passed through to reach the pu'uhonua.[26] Still others were slain or captured, including Keawema'uhili, Kīwala'ō's uncle and ill-fated chief advisor, who was held for execution and offering to the gods. However, some chiefs, respecting his extremely high rank, allowed Keawema'uhili to escape, and he returned to Hilo and declared independence for his Hilo lands of eastern Hāmākua, Hilo, and eastern Puna.[27] Kamehameha remained supreme over Kona, Kohala, and the western Hāmākua lands, including Waipi'o.[28] And so the kingdom was split into three warring parts, with near constant warfare to follow for a decade.

Today the battleground of Moku'ōhai remains a historic place and archaeological site, although little visited. In 1823, Ellis traveled to it.

> *The scene of this sanguinary engagement was a large tract of rugged lava...we had seen several heaps of stones raised over the bones of the slain, but they now became much more numerous.*
>
> *As we passed along, our guide pointed out the place where Tairi [Kūkā'ilimoku], Tamehameha's war-god, stood, surrounded by the priests, and, a little further on, he shewed us the place where Tamehameha himself, his sisters, and friends, fought during the early part of the...day.*
>
> *A few minutes after we had left it, we reached a large heap of stones overgrown with moss, which marks the spot where Kauikeouli [Kīwala'ō] was slain.*
>
> *The numerous piles of stones which we saw in every direction, convinced us that the number of those who fell on both sides must have been considerable.*[29]

Archaeological study of this battlefield has been negligible. In 1929–1930 Reinecke found "some puoa [burial platforms], but not so many as one would expect from the old accounts,"[30] and he describes them no further. I made a brief trip to this battleground in the early 1990s, inspecting coastal areas of Ke'ei. Back from the shore, many small clusters of low platforms—apparently burials—are present. In the ensuing 170 years since Ellis saw the battleground, it has slowly become overgrown, with some of the stone platforms worn by time and cattle. But in general, the place remains intact.

Kīwala'ō left behind a daughter, Keōpūolani, through Keku'iapoiwa Liliha, who was Kīwala'ō's maternal half-sister (her mother also being Kalola, the daughter of Kekaulike, former ruler of Maui) and who was Kamehameha's fraternal half-sister (her father being Keōuakalanikupua).[31] Keōpūolani was just an infant at the time, born on Maui ca. 1780, and raised there.[32] Of extremely high rank—tied to the Maui and Hawai'i royal lines through both parents[33]—Keōpūolani was to become a highly desirable marital partner for Kamehameha in the late 1790s.

## KAMEHAMEHA VS. KEŌUA VS. KEAWEMA'UHILI (A.D. 1782–1791)

The decade following Kīwala'ō's death was marked by battles, both on the field and politically. Kahekili, ruler of Maui, hearing of Kīwala'ō's death, sent messengers to Kamehameha requesting double canoes for a war against the O'ahu kingdom. Kamehameha refused, saying he had no canoes as he did not control Hilo or Ka'ū. Keawema'uhili, learning of this exchange, sent double canoes and feather capes and 'ō'ō feathers to Kahekili. In return, Kahekili sent Maui warriors led by Kahāhāwai.[34]

At some point thereafter (perhaps ca. 1783–1784[35]), Kānekoa, Kamehameha's uncle who had joined Kīwala'ō's cause just before the battle of Moku'ōhai, failed in revolts, first against Keawema'uhili and then Keoua. Keōua's men killed Kānekoa, and his younger brother Kaha'i fled to Kamehameha. Kānekoa was still beloved to Kamehameha from memories of his youth, so these events set the stage for retaliation, and Kamehameha sent warriors off to attack Hilo and Ka'ū—a campaign known as Kama'ino due to bad weather.[36] His men faced the allied forces of the Hilo and Ka'ū kingdoms. Kamehameha led a contingent of warriors over the mountains, down between Mauna Loa and Mauna Kea, into Kapāpala ahupua'a in Ka'ū, and then down toward Hilo, where he planned to join with forces brought around Kohala and down the windward side by canoe under Ke'eaumoku. But, Kamehameha's men met the highly trained Maui warriors at Pua'aloa near Hilo and were defeated, fleeing only by getting to Ke'eaumoku and the canoes.[37] Kamakau provides the account of Moa, an eyewitness:

> *The pololu spears and the ihe spears rained down like bath water; blood flowed like water and soaked into the dry earth of that hill. The spears were entangled (hihia ana) like a rainbow arched on both sides.*[38]

Kamehameha's army withdrew to Laupāhoehoe, raided Hilo for a while, and then pulled back to Kohala.[39]

Another failed invasion of Hilo followed ca. 1785. Accounts are largely silent about this campaign, but eventually Kamehameha's forces again withdrew to reside in Kohala. This was called the war of Hāpu'u.[40]

During the ensuing lull in the battles on Hawai'i, ca. 1786,[41] Kamehemeha sent his brother Kalanimālokuloku-i-Kepo'o-okalani to reestablish control over Kīpahulu and Hāna on Maui. Kalanimālokuloku gained the respect and affection of the commoners in his brief governing over these lands, thereby acquiring the name Keali'imaika'i (the good chief) which he retained the rest of his life. However, Maui warriors were eventually sent against him, and defeated his forces, with Keali'imaika'i barely escaping death. Evidently, this event led to Kamehameha's decision to attack the Maui kingdom with a greater army.[42]

The next event of importance noted in the accounts occurred in late 1788 and early 1789. In December of 1788, the trading ship *Iphigenia* under Captain Douglas, in the employee of Captain Meares, arrived off Hawai'i and anchored at Kealakekua. A high chief of Kaua'i, Ka'iana or Keawe-Ka'iana-a-'Ahu'ula, was aboard.

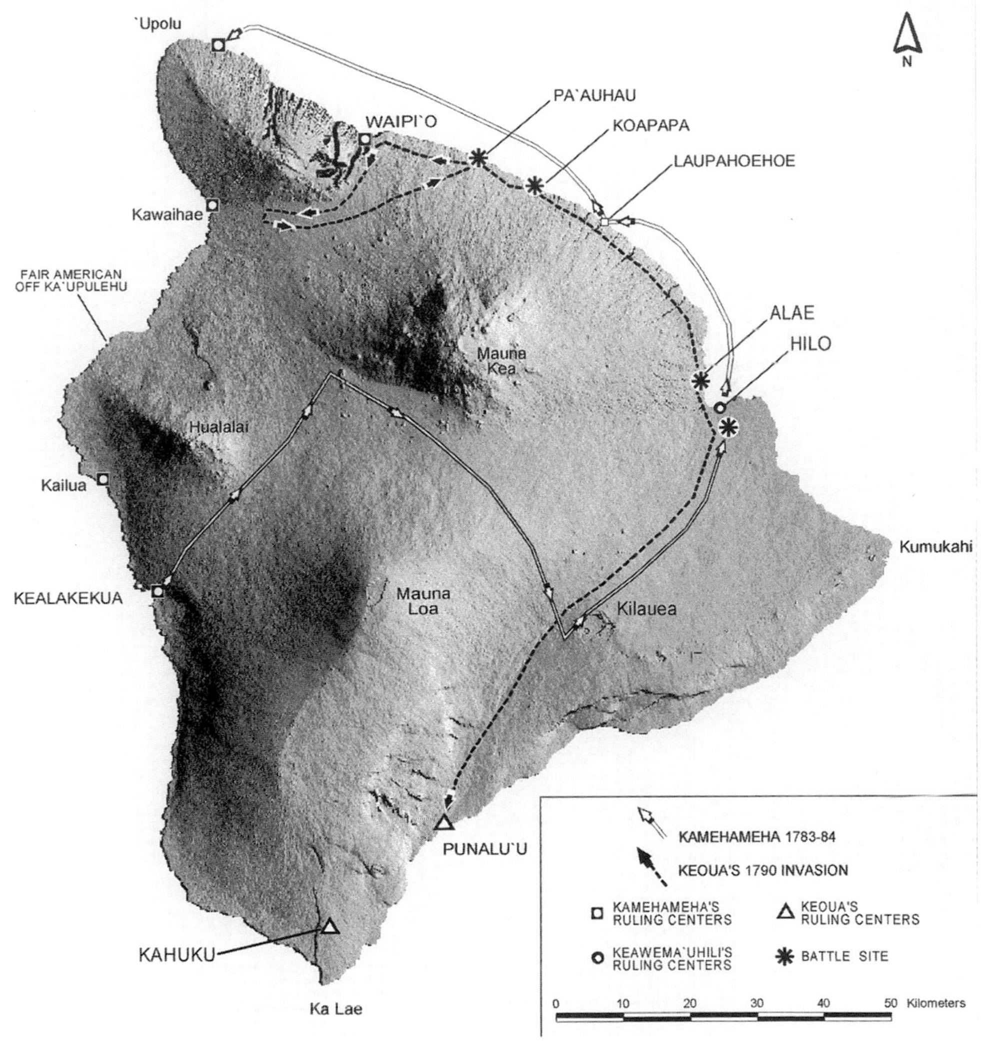


**FIGURE 10-3**
Places & campaigns mentioned during the reigns of Keōua, Keawema'uhili and Kamehameha, A.D. 1782–1790.

Ka'iana had left Kaua'i in 1787 aboard Meares' ship *Nootka*, and traveled to India and the Far East. He was returning with European weapons, ammunition, and other goods, as well as knowledge of foreign ways. Ka'iana was actually Maui-reared and of Hawai'i Island lineage, being a grandson of the ruler Keawe through one of his junior sons, 'Ahu'ula. No longer in favor on Kaua'i and under the urging of Kamehameha, Ka'iana chose to ally himself, his weapons and his knowledge with Kamehameha. He seems to have effectively been made a member of Kamehameha's highest council, virtually equal to the four main advisors.[43]

Several months later (March 1789), Kamehameha told Douglas that Kahekili of Maui and his half-brother Kā'eo, now ruler of Kaua'i, had "entered into a compact with Terreemoweeree, the surviving son of Terreeoboo [Kalani'ōpu'u], who lived on the weather-side of the island."[44] It seems that Douglas had gotten this message somewhat confused, for Terreemoweeree seems to be Keawema'uhili who lived on the windward side, but was not Kalani'ōpu'u's son; rather, he was his surviving brother. Still, Kamehameha seemed to have gotten wind of some alliance between either Keōua or Keawema'uhili and the Maui-Kaua'i kingdoms. He asked for guns and men, and Douglas had a carpenter go ashore and mount a swivel gun on a double canoe and leave firearms.[45] Each side in the wars, thus, were entering a new era in supplementing their forces with Western weapons.

In March of 1790, Kamehameha's forces received added strength. The ship *Eleanor* arrived at Kealakekua after massacring people on Maui, and its companion ship, the *Fair American*, arrived on the northern Kona coast. Kame'eiamoku, the high chief of this area, went aboard and was beaten. In retaliation for this abuse, he took the *Fair American*, a cannon, muskets, swords, and the like, and slew all aboard, except for the master Isaac Davis. These weapons and Davis were passed to Kamehameha, who quickly captured a member of the *Eleanor*'s crew who was wandering ashore, John Young. These two men became valuable high chiefs, soldiers and advisors to Kamehameha, and the weapons amply supplemented his armory.[46]

Evidently, in 1789 and early 1790, Kamehameha had been preparing an invasion of Maui. At some point, he asked Keawema'uhili of Hilo to supply him with canoes, men and feather capes for this invasion. Keawema'uhili consented, sending canoes and warriors under three of his sons—a stunning change in the Hawai'i Island alliances, with a shift of the Hilo kingdom from Keōua and the Ka'ū kingdom to Kamehameha and the Kohala-Kona kingdom.[47]

Finally, in 1790, with his weapons, army and new allies gathered, Kamehameha's first peleleu fleet, with some canoes armed with cannon and swivel guns, sailed to Hāna and then on along the Hāmākua coast of Maui toward Wailuku. At Pu'ukoa'e in Hoalua in Hāmākualoa, they encountered a Maui force under Kapakahili and defeated it. Kamehameha camped ashore nearby, and the next day he reengaged with Kapakahili, and Hawai'i "reinforcements came up, Kamehameha put the enemy to flight, and pursued them along the main road....At the assent of 'Opaepilau, Kapa-kahili was exhausted and was overtaken."[48] One account says that Kamehameha engaged Kapakahili in single combat and killed him.[49]

The Hawai'i forces proceeded on to Wailuku, where a battle was begun and fought for two days—"one of the hardest contested on Hawaiian record."[50] The tide turned finally against Maui, from the havoc caused by Kamehameha's cannon under Young's and Davis's direction, and from the superior guns of the Hawai'i forces. Under duress, the Maui forces retreated into 'Īao valley, an upper valley of the Wailuku River. Here the Maui women, children and elderly watched from the ridges as the Maui forces were routed and slaughtered. Fornander later spoke with Maui folk who had been present:

> *They speak of the carnage as frightful, the din and uproar, the shouts of defiance among the fighters, the wailing of the women on the crests of the valley, as something to curdle the blood or madden the brain of the beholder.*[51]

Many of the Maui high chiefs escaped over the valley, but many warriors were killed. Indeed, "it is said that the corpses of the slain were so many as to choke up the waters of the stream," leading to this battle's name being forever known as Kapaniwai, the damming of the waters.[52]

While the defeated Maui forces retreated to O'ahu to join their ruler Kahekili and his men at Waikīkī, Kamehameha traveled to Kaunakakai on Moloka'i to consolidate his power by taking control of several extremely high-ranking women. These were Kalola (the daughter of Maui ruler Kekaulike, former wife of Kalani'ōpu'u, and mother of Kīwala'ō, and also half-sister of Kamanawa and Kame'eiamoku), and her daughters Keku'iapoiwa Liliha (Kamehameha's half-sister through his father, and former wife of Kīwala'ō) and Kalaniakua, and her 8- or 9-year-old granddaughter Keāpūolani (the daughter of Kīwala'ō and Keku'iapoiwa Liliha). They had stayed on Moloka'i, at Kalama'ula, for Kalola was dying of an illness. There, indeed, Kalola died, first granting Kamehameha permission to take her daughters and granddaughter under his care.[53] The rank of Kalola can be seen in that the Hawai'i chiefs

> *wailed and chanted dirges...and the chiefs tattooed themselves and knocked out their teeth. Kamehameha was also tattooed and had his eyeteeth knocked out.*
>
> [Kamakau][54]

But, importantly, he had gained control of a potential high-ranking wife to consolidate his power and the rank of his future children.

While still on Moloka'i, Kamehameha sent a messenger to Kahekili, to determine if a truce would be arranged or if an invasion of O'ahu would follow. Kahekili opted for the truce.

> *Go back and tell Kamehameha to return to Hawaii and watch, and when the black tapa covers Ka-hekili and the black pig rests at his nose, then is the time to cast stones. Then, when light is snuffed out at Kahiki, that is the time to come and take the land.*
>
> [Kamakau][55]

Another messenger was sent to fetch a woman of great beauty. But finding her and fearing she would rend Kamehameha's kingdom apart, the messenger (an aunt of Kamehameha) approached a prophet of Kaua'i living at Waikīkī—Kapoukahi—and asked how Kamehameha might unify the island. The famous answer followed: to build a great house (heiau) for the god at Pu'ukoholā in Kawaihae.[56]

During this time, Keōua of Ka'ū invaded the Hilo kingdom, slaying his uncle and former ally Keawema'uhili at a battle at 'Alae. The kingdom of Ka'ū in the course of this one, quick battle, expanded its territory on Hawai'i—now including Ka'ū, Puna, Hilo and much of Hāmākua.[57]

Keōua carried his battle on into Kamehameha's undefended lands—ravaging Waipi'o, Waimea and Kohala. Kamehameha heard of these events, and duly embarassed for failing to protect his people, he returned immediately to Hawai'i, abandoning his newly gained Maui lands.[58] His forces met Keōua's—then retiring toward Hilo—at Pā'auhau in Hāmākua. Kamehameha's warriors had cannon and more modern weaponry, but these advantages were neutralized by Keōua's generals Uhai and Ka'ie'iea. The battle ended in a draw. The armies reengaged at Koapāpa'a in eastern Hāmākua, and after heavy fighting, both sides withdrew from the field—Keōua returning to Hilo and Kamehameha to Waipi'o.[59]

In Hilo, late in the year 1790, Keōua redistributed the lands of the former Hilo kingdom among his followers. Some of his army then returned to Ka'ū along the Hilo-Kīlauea-Ka'ū trail. Several varying, but similar, accounts exist of what followed.

> *His (Keoua's) path led by the great volcano of Kilauea. There they encamped. In the night a terrific eruption took place, throwing out flame, cinders, and even heavy stones to a great distance, and accompanied from above with intense lightning and heavy thunder. In the morning Keoua and his company were afraid to proceed, and spent the day in trying to appease the goddess of the volcano, whom they supposed they had offended the*

*day before, by rolling stones into the crater. But on the second night and on the third night also there were similar eruptions. On the third day they ventured to proceed on their way, but had not advanced far before a more terrible and destructive eruption than any before took place; an account of which, taken from the lips of those who were part of the company and present in the scene, may not be an unwelcome digression.*
*The army of Keoua set out on their way in three different companies. The company in advance had not proceeded far before the ground began to shake and rock beneath their feet and it became quite impossible to stand. Soon a dense cloud of darkness was seen to rise out of the crater, and almost at the same instant the electrical effect upon the air was so great that the thunder began to roar in the heavens and the lightning to flash. It continued to ascend and spread abroad till the whole region was enveloped, and the light of day was entirely excluded. The darkness was the more terrific, being made visible by an awful glare from streams of red and blue light variously combined that issued from the pit below, and being lit up at intervals by the intense flashes of lightning from above. Soon followed an immense volume of sand and cinders, which were thrown in high heaven and came down in a destructive shower for many miles around. Some few persons of the forward company were burned to death by the sand and cinders, and others were seriously injured. All experienced a suffocating sensation upon the lungs, and hastened on with all possible speed.*

*The rear body, which was nearest the volcano at the time of the eruption, seemed to suffer the least injury, and after the earthquake and shower of sand had passed over, hastened forward to escape the dangers which threatened them, and rejoicing in mutual congratulations that they had been preserved in the midst of such imminent peril. But what was their surprise and consternation when, on coming up with their comrades of the centre party, they discovered them all to have*

> *become corpses. Some were lying down and others were sitting upright, clasping with dying grasp their wives and children, and joining noses (...) as in the act of taking a final leave.... The whole party, including women and children, not one of them survived to relate the catastrophe that had befallen their comrades.*
>
> [Dibble][60]

Geologists now know that this was a rare explosive (phreatic) eruption of Kīlauea, induced by water mixed with the magma, and it appears as if gases, not ashes, killed the central portion of Keōua's army.[61] Keōua, himself, passed safely into Ka'ū, where he established residence at Punalu'u[62]—surely thoroughly shaken by the event. Exactly, how many people were lost varies with the accounts. The figure of 400 warriors is often given,[63] but some accounts are as low as 80 warriors.[64]

Skirmishes continued between the kingdoms, and genealogists and bards disparaged the rank of the opposition's rulers.[65] Before the end of 1790, Kamehameha sent an army under Ke'eaumoku with Young and Davis against Hilo, and sent another army under Ka'iana into Ka'ū itself.[66] Fornander says "No reminiscences of the operations against Hilo have survived."[67] The Ka'ū campaign was remembered vividly, albeit sometimes in differing versions.

The Ka'ū expedition began with a great battle fought on the lands of Kamā'oa ahupua'a at South Point (Fornander's "South Cape" or Lae a Kalaeloa). "Once Ka'i-ana was forced to retreat to the fleet, once Keoua was forced back by the guns."[68] Keōua retreated into Puna, and Ka'iana followed. Another battle was fought at Pu'uakoki. There, Keōua's generals, Ka'ie'iea and Uhai, captured the cannon, and Ka'iana was forced to withdraw his men, eventually retiring from Ka'ū into Kona.[69]

> *The power of the gods alone remained to defeat Keoua Kuahu-'ula. Kamehameha abandoned war and adopted the advice of Ka-pou-kahi and his aunt Ha'alo'u, to build a house for the god.*
>
> [Kamakau][70]

And so began the construction of the great heiau of Pu'ukoholā at Kawaiahe in Kohala.

Pu'ukoholā heiau's foundations and walls constitute an immense stone structure, built on the seaward brow of a 130-foot-high hill—Pu'ukoholā, the hill of the whale. The heiau is about 200 yards or so from the sea, and its location overlooks Kawaihae Bay and the beach below extending to the north. A second large heiau, Mailekini, lies just below Pu'ukoholā on the side of the hill, also overlooking the water. Oral accounts given by Hawaiians who worked on this project do exist—although research so far has documented only a minimal sketch of what the building project was like. Kamehameha evidently called in people from all parts of his kingdom to work in shifts.

> *The author [Fornander] a few years ago conversed with a centenarian Hawaiian at Kawaihaeuka who had assisted in carrying stones towards building this Heiau. His description of the thousands of people encamped on the neighbouring hillsides, and taking their turns at the work, of their organisation and feeding, their time of work and relaxation, the number of chiefs that attended, and who, as the old man said, caused the ground to tremble beneath their feet; and the number of human victims that were required and duly offered for this or that portion of the building—this description was extremely interesting and impressive.*[71]

Truly, this was a public works project on a massive scale. All the high chiefs and Kamehameha, himself, worked on this task, with the exception of his younger brother Keali'imaika'i, who remained sacred to observe the kapu.[72]

Archaeological work has identified numerous temporary habitation sites on the lower slopes of Kawaihae just to the north and around the heiau. These sites are small pavings, semi-enclosing walls, and platforms with small amounts of food remains and artifacts.[73] They appear most abundant on the slopes above the beach of

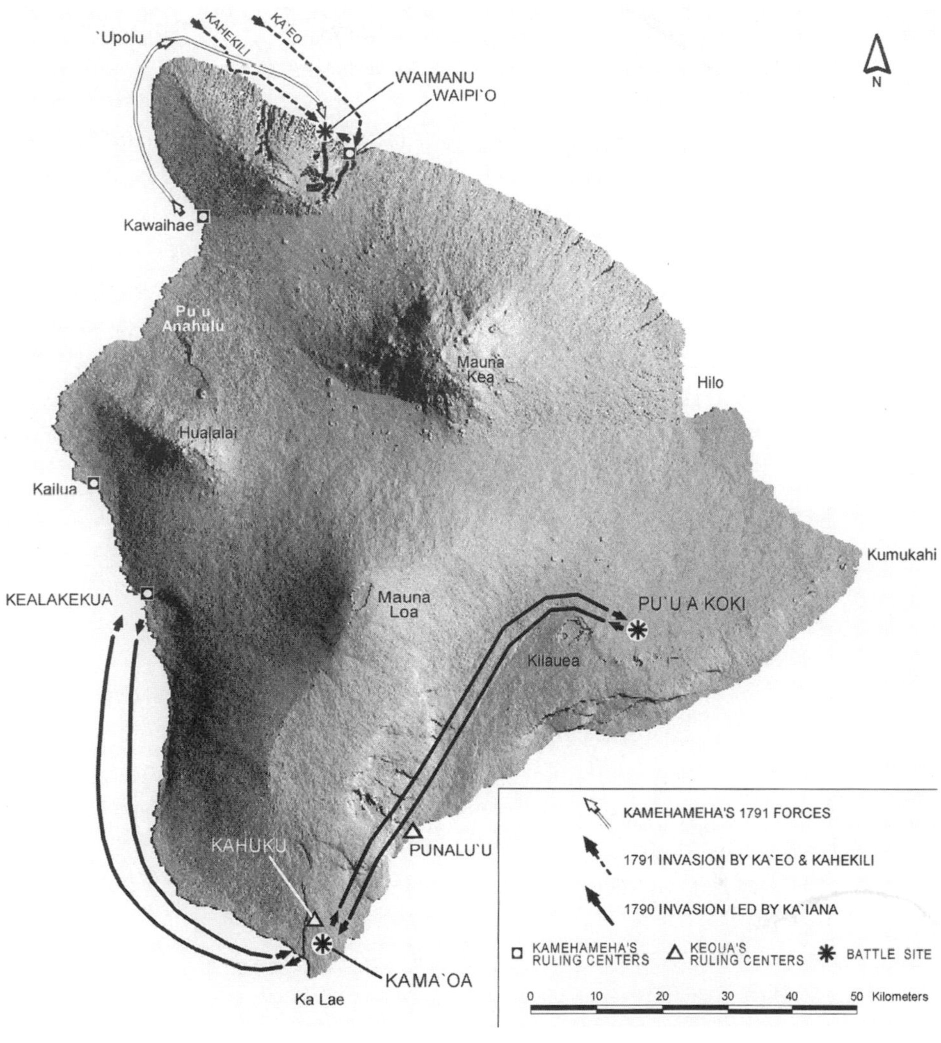


**FIGURE 10-4**
Places & Campaigns mentioned during the reigns of Keōua and Kamehameha, A.D. 1790–1791.

Kawaihae. These temporary habitation sites may have been the encampments of the people working on the heiau. Kamehameha lived immediately below the heiau on the north end of the sand beach, at a spot today called Pelekane, then called Kikiako'i.[74]

The heiau seems to have been finished by summer of 1791,[75] resulting in a huge structure—basically an immense stone platform, with walls on three sides and two terraces descending down the hill. The heiau was 224 by 100 feet,[76] 22,400 square feet, or the size of several large modern house lots (68.3 x 30.5 m, 2,083 sq. m.) The platform was surrounded on the inland side and two ends by 20-foot-high, 20-foot-thick walls which tapered up to a flat top 6 feet wide.[77] The heiau was open towards the sea. The entrance was a narrow walkway along one of the high walls. The platform, or upper terrace, held the heiau structures, and two narrow lower terraces descended down the hill. The upper terrace, as seen in 1823 by Ellis, was "spacious, and much better finished than the lower ones. It was paved with various flat smooth stones."[78] At the north end of this terrace were "the houses of the priests" and in the center was "the king's sacred house...in which he resided during the season of strict tabu."[79] At the southern end of the terrace was an inner court with the offering altar (lele) on pillars at the north end, the 'anu'u tower in the center, and the main and minor images of the gods at the south end.[80] Ellis noted that at the altar, "the pavement around was strewed with bones of men and animals."[81] Wooden images of "varied size and shape" were placed in holes atop the high walls and on the lower terraces.[82]

One of the few rare glimpses of this heiau prior to the abolition of the kapu system is provided by members of a French expedition under Freycinet, who arrived in Kawaihae just months before the kapu system was abandoned. Duperrey of this expedition, later to become an exploring captain himself, drew the heiau from the king's residence. This illustration shows the images clustered at the south end of the upper platform, and the roof of one of the houses at the north end of the heiau can also be seen.[83] Unfortunately, members of the expedition did not go into the heiau.[84]

Archaeological work has confirmed these descriptions. Careful measurements show the maximum outside dimensions of the heiau are 262 feet on the western, open side and 112 feet on the north end (80 x 34 meters), with walls 10–16 feet high, 26 feet wide at the base and 6.5–10 feet wide on top.[85] Two to three house pavings are present on a raised platform at the north end and center of the heiau, and this platform steps down to a slightly lower paving of large, waterworn stones (the inner court) with a raised, rough platform at one end with pits (the image area)(Fig. 10-5).[86] Two pits for offering refuse are noted in oral histories—one near the main altar and one near a sacred house,[87] and archaeologists have found one such pit near one of the houses.[88] Also, archaeological evidence of earlier building phases of earlier heiau has been found,[89] matching oral history accounts of earlier heiau.

The final steps of building this heiau would have been steeped in ritual—the ceremonies when ʻōhiʻa were gathered for images and the palisade of the inner court, accompanied by rigorous prayers, and offerings of fruit, pigs, dogs and human sacrifices to Kūkāʻilimoku. Final consecration may have awaited the attempt to offer up Keōua in line with Kapoukahi's prophecy,[90] but it is also possible that the heiau was fully consecrated and ready to receive Keōua as a special offering, perhaps as a first sacrifice of battle. Indeed, both Fornander and Kamakau do not mention Keōua's sacrifice as the final consecrating step.[91]

Today, the ruins of Puʻukoholā heiau are part of a national historic park. The walls and terraces were stabilized and restored in 1978,[92] resulting in the appearance of nicely faced architecture. A 1928 walkway and steps leading up to the heiau from the sea have been closed. The wooden images atop the walls, the sacred houses, and the ʻanuʻu cloaked in kapa, and the images and altar within the inner court are gone. The priests attending the heiau when it was first built are of course also gone. But, one can stand at the spot and visualize the thousands of workers under the direction of the chiefs, bringing and laying stones, and then as the heiau neared completion, the growing sacredness within its precincts, the chanting of the priests, the beating of the temple pahu drums, and the offering up of pigs, dogs and humans to the god Kūkāʻilimoku. The structure had truly become in 1791, and is still today, a house for the gods of Kamehameha.

Construction was interrupted on the heiau ca. March–May of 1791 when two fleets of invaders arrived—one led by Kā'eo, ruler of Kaua'i and half-brother of Kahekili, and the other led by Kahekili himself.[93] Kā'eo landed his forces in Waipi'o, where he desecrated the royal structures, the paving of Līloa and perhaps the sacred grounds of Paka'alana heiau.[94] Kahekili landed his forces at Hālawa in Kohala and raided east along the Kohala and Hāmākua coastline until he joined Kā'eo in Waipi'o. Kamehameha immediately brought his warriors into action, sailing them around in double canoes with mounted swivel guns and small cannon, with Young and Davis directing the artillery fire. Off the cliffs of Waimanu, the rival fleets met in a battle called Kepūwaha'ula'ula, and Kamehameha's armament prevailed. Kahekili and Kā'eo retreated to Maui.[95] Interestingly, Hawai'i warriors seem to have pursued the Maui and Kaua'i forces, or at least were skirmishing on Maui, because the American trader *Ingraham* was told in May 1791 that while Kamehameha and Ka'iana were at Kawaihae, Hawai'i's warriors were fighting on Maui.[96]

Nonetheless, with Maui and Kaua'i effectively beaten back, Kamehameha had Pu'ukoholā heiau finished in the summer of 1791. He then sent two of his highest chiefs—Keaweaheulu and Kamanawa—to bring Keōua for a discussion of a truce and joint rulership. Keōua was living in Kahuku ahupua'a in Ka'ū, far inland above the Kahuku pali on the fertile ash lands.[97]

> *Close to the extreme edge of the tabu enclosure of Keoua's place the two got down and rolled in the dirt [prostrated themselves according to etiquette] and began to weave their nets of speech.*
>
> [Kamakau][98]

Keōua's advisors—chief counsellor Ka'ie'iea, Uhai and others—urged that Keaweaheulu and Kamanawa be slain. Keōua refused, as they were uncles, younger generational brothers of his father Kalani'ōpu'u. Thus, his "uncles" crawled forward, embraced Keōua's feet, wailed and presented the offer that Keōua come to Kawaihae, meet Kamehameha, and become joint ruler.[99] Keōua agreed.

Many have debated whether Keōua agreed, truly thinking a truce had been offered with joint ruling to follow, or whether he knew he was going to his death.[100] The accounts, however, clearly indicate Keōua knew he was going to die. In the procession north through Kona, his advisors repeatedly urged him to slay Kamanawa and Keaweaheulu. The common people too saw this procession as Keōua's last. At Honomalino, Hōnaunau, Ka'awaloa, Keauhou and Kailua—and at Hōnaunau in particular,

> *the people...crowded around him....Many of them wept...from a foreboding fear of the result of his surrender to Tamehameha.*
>
> [1823 Ellis][101]

As the expedition approached Kohala, Keōua stopped at the pool called Luahinewai at an isolated cove in Pu'uwa'awa'a, and here "he cut off the end of his penis...an act which believers in sorcery call 'the death of Uli,' and which was a certain sign that he knew he was about to die."[102]

One wonders why Keōua gave up. Perhaps, it was for a variety of reasons. His forces may have been diminished and exhausted by the battles, which though never lost, were renowned as encounters with great losses. Also, the fact that Pele had wiped out a part of his army—even though a relatively small force—may have been viewed as a disastrous sign from the gods, particularly from a god so crucial to Ka'ū and Puna as Pele.[103] Perhaps, Kamehameha's successful acquisition of powerful new weapons—the cannons and muskets—were also seen as signs of the gods' displeasure. Or possibly the complete defeat of the seemingly powerful armies of Kaua'i and Maui by Kamehameha was viewed as a sign that he was now the most powerful. Regardless, Keōua clearly went to his death fully realizing it.

At Luahinewai, Keōua

> *ranged his chiefs about him in his own double canoe, those with high rank and those who had lived with him and upon whose love he could count and who would die with him.*
>
> [Kamakau][104]

State Historic Preservation Division

**FIGURE 10-5**

Pu'ukoholā Heiau. The raised platform on the north end (left) of the upper terrace can clearly be seen, and this is where the houses of the heiau stood. Another smaller raised platform on this upper terrace is visible to the right and a lower, lighter-colored area between the two platforms. This smaller platform and lower area are where the images and altar area of the heiau were located.

**FIGURE 10-6**

Aerial photograph of the Pu'ukoholā area. Pu'ukoholā heiau is the large rectangular structure on the hill. Mailekini heiau is immediately downslope, a long and thin rectangular structure. The sandy area is the shore at Pelekane.

Twenty-seven were in this canoe, selected as moepuʻu (death companions), including Uhai who carried the kāhili.[105] Keōua was on the platform of the canoe with Uhai and a ipu bearer next to him. Passing Puakō, they came in sight of Kawaihae with the new huge heiau of "Puʻu-kohola standing majestic," and they approached with the double canoes in crescent formation.[106] On landing, Keʻeaumoku and his followers approached and surrounded Keōua's canoe.

> *Keoua arose and called to Kamehameha, "Here I am!" Kamehameha called back, "Stand up and come forward that we may greet each other." Keoua rose again, intending to spring ashore, when Keʻe-au-moku thrust a spear at him which Keoua dodged, snatched, and thrust back at Keʻe-au-moku, who snatched it away. Kua-kahela, who was an eyewitness, says that if there had been weapons aboard Keoua's canoes some [of Kamehameha's warriors] would have been killed. Muskets were then fired from the shore, and a great commotion took place among the people, during which Kua-kahela, Keoua's kahuna, jumped overboard and, disappearing under the eyes of thousands, hid in the tabu house of Ke-kuʻi-apo-iwa where he lay concealed in a roll of mats. Men said, "You were saved by your family god." This man and one other were the only ones saved of those who came in the canoe with Keoua. Laʻanui jumped overboard secretly while off Puakoʻ. Keoua and all those who were with him on the canoe were killed.*
>
> [Kamakau][107]

The rest of Keōua's people were spared by Kamehameha, so proclaimed to all by Kalaʻimamahū.[108] Keōua's body was "born on men's shoulders" to the altar on Puʻukoholā and offered up to Kū, along with his companions.[109] And Kapoukahi's prophecy came to be:

> *War shall cease on Hawaii when one shall come and shall be laid above on the altar (lele) of Puʻu-kohola.*
>
> [Kamakau] [110]

Peace came to Hawai'i. The Kingdom of Ka'ū ceased to exist, and the entire island was unified. The senior line of Keawe—through Kalaninui'īamamao, his son Kalani'ōpu'u, and his sons Kīwala'ō and Keōua—again lost its power with Keōua's death. The second line of Keawe—through Kalanike'eaumoku, his son Keōua, and his son Kamehameha—which had once ruled the land briefly under Kalanike'eaumoku, regained power.

*He is the chief who staked the island. ...*
*The divine Kamehameha the Great is this.*[111]

## THE WIVES & CHILDREN OF THE WARRING RULERS

Kamehameha's wives of these years of ascending power are less well known than some of his later wives. They reflect ties to his allies in his rise and consolidation of power. During Kalani'ōpu'u's reign, his wife was the daughter of one of Keawe's junior sons, Kaloloa a Kumuko'a. But during his rule of Kona-Kohala–west Hāmākua, Kamehameha had married Pele-uli, the daughter of Kamanawa, one of his closest advisors and one of the most powerful of the Kona chiefs. In 1785, he also married Ka'ahumanu, the daughter of Ke'eaumoku, another close advisor and high chief, the younger half-brother of Kamanawa and Kame'eiamoku, and one of the most agressive Kona high chiefs. Clearly, these marriages cemented ties with his powerful high chiefs. And, most important for eventual political purposes, after his victory at 'Īao on Maui, he followed up and took custody of the much more sacred Keōpūolani—Kīwala'ō's daughter—undoubtedly with the intention of future marriage and consolidation of power through children which would effectively reunify the senior and junior lines of Keawe. Table 10-1 lists Kamehameha's wives and children of these years.

Keawema'uhili's wives and sons are now largely forgotten, even though he had been ruler of the Hilo Kingdom. Of the generation before Kamehameha and Keōua, Keawema'uhili had consolidated his power during his brother Kalani'ōpu'u's reign. As a junior brother of the ruler, he married Ululani, the oldest member of the senior 'Ī line and thus the hereditary chief over Hilo district.[112] Through this marriage, Keawema'uhili effectively gained control of Hilo district under Kalani'ōpu'u. When the kingdom unexpectedly collapsed with Kīwala'ō's death, his Hilo lands automatically became the base for Keawema'uhili's kingdom.[113] Whether he married other women to increase or consolidate his power is unknown. Three of his sons—Keaweokahikona, 'Ele'ele, and Koakanu—led the Hilo forces which accompanied Kamehameha, as allies, in his first invasion of Maui.[114]

Even less information about Keōua's wives and children is published, although evidently one wife's name was Hi'iaka and another Kaiolani.[115] This is a striking example of how rapidly a defeated ruler's history often fades into oblivion.

**Table 10-1**
### The Wives & Children of Kamehameha, Pre-1792

| Wives | Children |
|---|---|
| Kānekapolei, wife of Kalani'ōpu'u[1] | Pauli Ka'ōleiokū, male[2] |
| Kalola a Kumuko'a—early 1780s marriage, daughter of Kumuko'a, one of Keawe's junior sons[3] | No children |
| Peleuli, daughter of Kamanawa[4] | Kaho'anaoku Kina'u, male[5]<br>Kapulikoliko, female[6]<br>Kaikookalani, male[4]<br>Kiliwehi, female[4] |
| Ka'ahumanu—1785 marriage daugher of Ke'eaumoku[7] | No children |

1. Illicit liaison (Kamakau 1961:127, 208, 311; Fornander 1880; 'I'i 1959:7). She was also the mother of Keōua through Kalani'ōpu'u.
2. Half-brother of Keōua and raised as a Ka'ū chief in the court of Kalani'ōpu'u and then in the court of Keōua (Kamakau 1961:156–157, 208; Fornander 1880; 'I'i 1959:7).
3. Kalola was Kamehameha's wife when he left the court of Kalani'ōpu'u and returned to north Kohala. Later, she married the younger brother of Kahekili (Kamakau 1961:311; Fornander 1880:203, note 1).
4. Kamakau 1961:127, 208, 311; Fornander 1880:320.
5. Kina'u boarded Vancouver's ships in 1793 and was ca. 9-years old (Fornander 1880:336, note 1).
6. Kapulikoliko may have been the ca. 9-year-old daughter that Vancouver said was a ward of Kame'eiamoku in 1794 (Vancouver 1798[1967], III:48).
7. Ca. 17 years of age in 1785 (Kamakau 1961:127, 311; Fornander 1880:320). (Her sister, Kaheiheimalie, was the wife of Kala'imamahū ca. 1794, and later became a wife of Kamehameha—Fornander 1880:338).

## THE ROYAL PLACES OF THIS DECADE

Kīwala'ō and the rulers of the three and then the two Hawai'i kingdoms frequently moved their royal residences—following a common pattern of late prehistory. During his brief reign, Kīwala'ō dwelled primarily in two places—at Wai-'Ahukini in Pākini ahupua'a in Ka'ū, where his father had died, and at Hōnaunau, where he took his father to the Hale o Keawe.

Kamehameha rotated his residence among several places over the course of the decade. He was frequently at Kealakekua[116] and Kawaihae[117] during the latter part of the decade to take advantage of trade with Western ships and acquire weapons and ammunition, and to oversee the construction of Pu'ukoholā heiau. He also appears to have resided in the Kailua-Kona area,[118] and earlier in the decade he was in Kohala several times and in Waipi'o in Hāmākua.[119] Quite likely, he spent time at the other established royal centers of Hōnaunau, Kahalu'u and Hōlualoa in Kona.

Kawaihae ahupua'a extends from the shore below Waimea, at the joining of today's north and south Kohala, and runs inland up into the forests of Kohala Mountain adjacent to Waimea (Fig. 10-7). In the 1800s, Kawaihae was divided into two pieces; at the end of prehistory it seems to have been one ahupua'a. This land had a sand beach which stretched north from Pelekane below Pu'ukoholā and Mailekini heiau to Pāhonu Point. Beyond this point, the shoreline is rocky lava. The beach and immediately adjacent land was relatively flat, and then rose in a heavily undulating slope up the mountain. Several large gulches cut through this slope to the shore—Makeāhua, Pohaukole, Makahuna, and Pohi'iohua near Pelekane; Keauhuhu behind the north end of the beach; and Honokoa and Kalopae gulches to the north. The streams in these gulches flow only during and immediately after heavy rainfall in the uplands, and at those times they can become raging torrents. All run down from Kawaihae uka, except Makeāhua, which is the channel for the Waikoloa and tributary streams from Waimea itself. [120]

The coastal lands of Kawaihae are, and were, extremely dry with the slopes behind quite barren with only grass cover until well inland.[121] Even the coastal kiawe trees were not there prehistorically, only sporadic coconuts and native trees. The famous, strong mumuku winds which blew down from Waimea further dried out the coast. Because it was so arid, from the limited records it appears that much of the produce and pigs were raised in the uplands and brought down to the shore.[122] A large population still lived along the shoreline amidst the coconut groves, particularly when the ruler was in residence.

At Kawaihae, the king stayed at Pelekane, below the major heiau of Mailekini and Pu'ukoholā. In 1819 in the first year of Kamehameha II's reign, the royal residence consisted of multiple houses—the king's (10–12 feet long by 8–10 feet wide), his adjoining eating house, a house for his father's widows, and a larger open building for meetings, among other structures.[123] Today, archaeological remains exist in the Pelekane area—pavings, walled enclosures and platforms[124]—but these ruins have yet to be studied to any extent. Oral histories place Lonoikamakahiki and Alapa'inui and his son Keawe'ōpala at Kawaihae using Mailekini heiau,[125] the main luakini here before Kamehameha's rebuilding of Pu'ukoholā. Thus, royal use of Kawaihae goes back at least to A.D. 1640–1660, and quite likely Pelekane was the residential area of the ruler then.

The remainder of the houses of Kawaihae extended north along the beach and farther along the rocky shoreline, with the main trail (ala nui) just seaward of the houses.[126] Among these houses were those for "the purposes of shading, building, and repairing their canoes."[127] In 1819, the high chiefs' houses were scattered up the beach, undoubtedly surrounded by the houses of their retinue. Kalanimoku, then the kālaimoku, had his houses at the north end of the beach; John Young had his on the slope just behind the center of the beach (Fig. 10-9). Whether the high chiefs' houses were as scattered when Kamehameha or earlier rulers were in residence is uncertain.

In 1823, 100 houses were still to be found in Kawaihae.[128] With an estimate of five persons per house, perhaps 500 people lived in the village. Probably more were in residence when the ruler was present.

When Kamehameha lived there during the years of the building of Pu'ukoholā heiau, European and American traders encountered the major high chiefs—each arriving offshore in large double-hulled canoes. One canoe carried 40–50 men.[129]

Sizable parts of Kawaihae's royal center are now gone. The bulk of the houses along the sandy shore have been inadvertently destroyed in this century by the few houses and stores of the twentieth century village, and by the immense deep draft harbor. The sandy shore of old Kawaihae actually has been covered by the dredged coral fill of the modern harbor. Yet, despite these changes, the heiau of Pu'ukoholā and Mailekini and the royal residential area of Pelekane still survive. Some house sites (platforms and enclosures of stone) can still be found scattered along the rocky coast north of the former beach. Other remnants of old Kawaihae exist just inland of today's highway and adjacent houses and stores—including a few platforms and exposed, eroding deposits. These can still yield considerable information on the history of Kawaihae as a ruling center and an earlier village. Archaeological research has begun recently in the form of surveys for the Department of the Hawaiian Home Lands,[130] the National Park Service,[131] and Mauna Kea Resort.[132]

Kawaihae was widely recorded as one of Kamehameha's ruling locales; in contrast, the ruling centers of his rivals, Keōua and Keawema'uhili, are little known and rarely described. In Keōua's case, we know that he used upland Kahuku and coastal Punalu'u as capitols of his Ka'ū kingdom. Virtually nothing is known of the Kahuku center, other than the oral historical references covering the arrival of Kamehameha's emissaries and some 1840s and 1850s Māhele land records. The oral histories note only that Keōua lived within the typical enclosure marked off by kapa-covered kapu stakes.[133] Māhele records provide clues as to general settlement patterns for upland Kahuku. The inland ala nui, main trail, rose up through the Kahuku escarpment from the western lava lands of Kahuku ahupua'a, then descended gradually seaward through the rich, high-rainfall, ash lands above the pali, passing amidst house lots and farms.[134] When the cinder hill of Pu'u Po'o Pueo was reached, the road turned east and headed across the upper fields of Pākini and Kamā'oa, the large

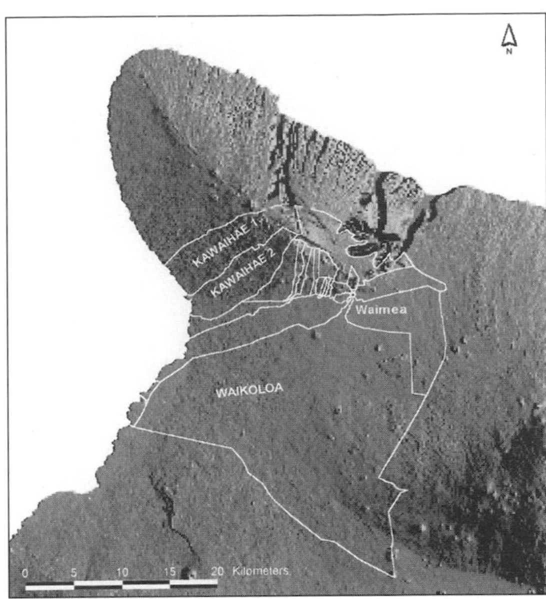


**FIGURE 10-7**
Location of Kawaihae Ahupua'a.

**FIGURE 10-8**
Kawaihae in 1889. Note Pu'ukoholā heiau on the hill to the right and houses scattered along the beach. Note also the marked lack of trees. Although houses in this photograph include wooden frame structures, the general pattern of settlement is quite similar to that of the late 1700s. The heiau clearly dominates the landscape. (After Kelly 1974:20).

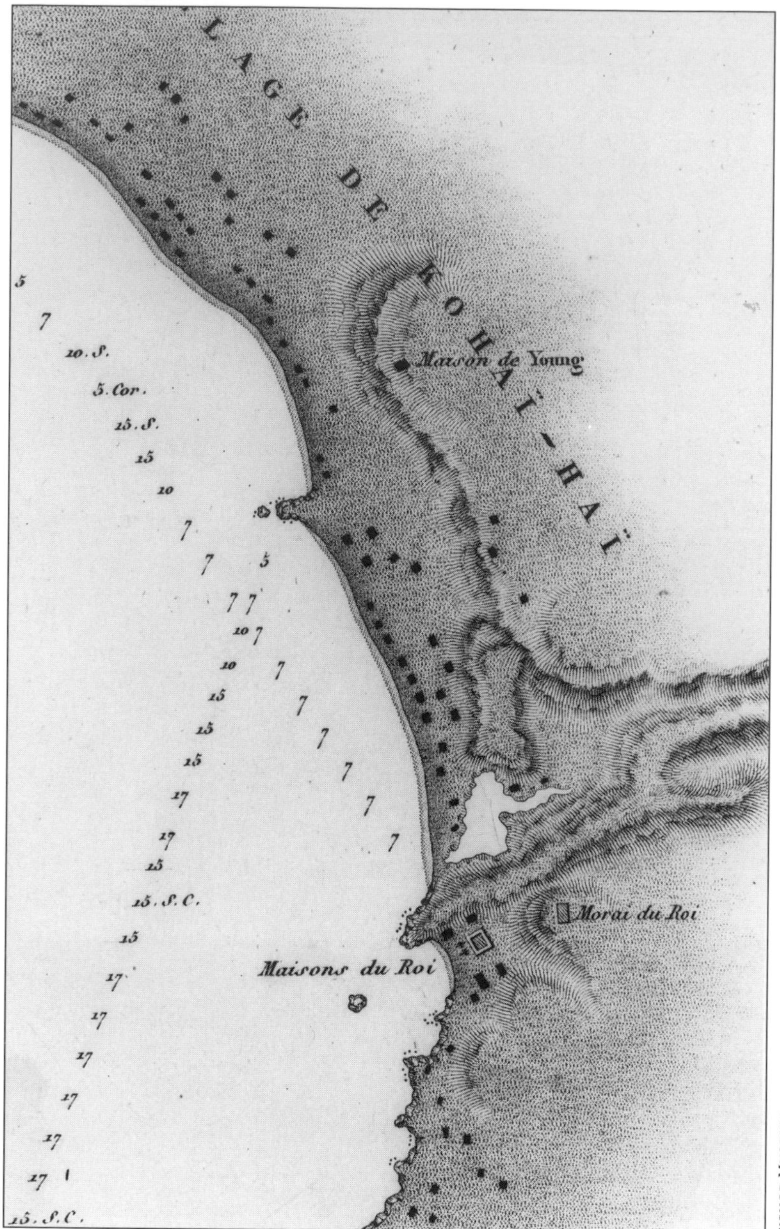


BISHOP MUSEUM

**FIGURE 10-9**

1819 map of the Kawaihae Village area. Pu'ukoholā (Morai du Roi) is to the south with Mailekini (large enclosure) and Pelekane (Maisons du Roi) just seaward. The bulk of the royal center's houses spread north along the sandy shoreline. In 1819, two high chiefs' houses were noted: John Young's (Maison de Young) near the center of the village and Kalanimoku's to the north (just off the map). Map by Duperrey of Freycinet's Expedition, titled "Plan de la Baie de Kohai-Hai."

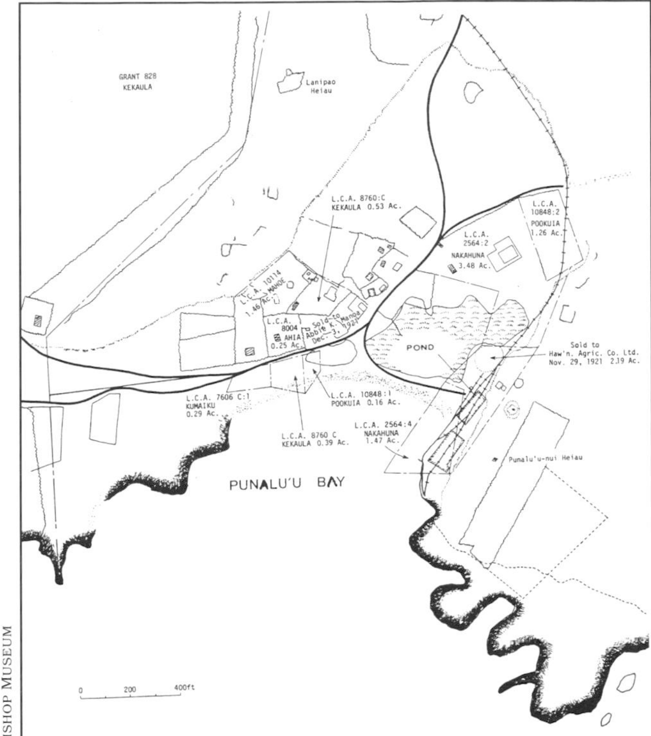


BISHOP MUSEUM

**FIGURE 10-10**
The coastal area of Punalu'u ahupua'a, Ka'ū. Punalu'unui heiau is visible on the lower right, Lanipao heiau in the upper center, and the Māhele period housing awards (L.C.A.s) around the pond between the two heiau. (Kelly 1980:Fig. 28 on p. 66).

**FIGURE 10-11**
Aerial view of Punalu'unui heiau – the major luakini heiau of Punalu'u during Keōua's reign. View is to the east. (Kelly 1980:Fig. 36 on p. 78).

BISHOP MUSEUM, GLEN KAYE, 1974)

ahupua'a reaching down to South Point, towards Wai'ōhinu and the eastern lands of Ka'ū. I have found little other information on upland Kahuku; no archaeological survey has taken place here, so we do not know if any sites remain.

In the case of Punalu'u—the other known royal center of Ka'ū during Keōua's time—archaeological survey has been done.[135] Māhele period historical records are also available. These show a dense cluster of land awards around Punalu'u Bay, just west of the huge luakini heiau of Punalu'unui and along the edge of a pond (Figure 10-10).[136] Most of these awards seem to be house lots. A second cluster ca. 2 miles inland at the foot of Pu'u 'Enuhe hill seem to be farm lots. The major inland trail through Ka'ū passes by these inland parcels, while the major coastal trail passes through the coastal awards and then heads diagonally inland, where it eventually joins the inland trail east of Punalu'u and continues to the crater of Kīlauea.

Archaeological surveys in the 1970s amplified this 1840s picture of Punalu'u. Although the 1868 tidal wave scoured much of coastal Punalu'u and scattered archaeological remnants, the surveys found many of the 1840s house lots around the bay and pond, and additional ruins of house sites behind the pond.[137] The sites are mostly platforms, walled areas, and some stone terraces on the low bluff edge overlooking the shore. Older archaeological work done in 1906 documented the luakini heiau of Punalu'unui.[138] This heiau is a very large rectangular enclosure, 648 x 230 feet (197.5 x 70.1 m, 13,845 sq. m.), with a wall up to 9 feet thick and almost 9 feet high. It was paved with beach pebbles, and no internal features were visible in 1906; but an aerial photograph seems to show some features (Fig. 10-11). This luakini was definitely used by Keōua;[139] his residence would likely have been immediately adjacent.

A second heiau was mapped by archaeologists in 1906 and again in 1972.[140] Lanipao heiau, a smaller temple, just behind the Punalu'u Bay houses was also enclosed by a large stone wall, 6 feet high and up to 7.5 feet thick. It was much smaller in area, however, 70 x 45 feet (21 x 14 m, 294 $m^2$). This heiau seems to have been dedicated to agriculture.

Therefore Keōua's royal center at Punalu'u clearly contains the vital ingredients of large luakini heiau, lesser heiau, and numerous house sites around a major cove—all within an ahupua'a with bountiful farm lands. Some of Punalu'u's agricultural lands at European contact included lo'i (irrigated taro fields),[141] attesting to the productive nature the area.

But what of Keawema'uhili's royal centers? He ruled out of Hilo Bay, through his role as chief of Hilo district and his marriage to Ululani of the 'Ī family, dating back to the reign of his brother, Kalani'ōpu'u. It is quite likely that he had one fixed center—at Waiākea ahupua'a in Hilo Bay. This would have probably been the same one used by prior rulers and by Kamehameha after unification of the island in 1791—with the obvious changes of housing locations and heiau sizes made over the years.

Hilo Bay's sand beach fronted the low land from Wailuku Stream in the west to Wailoa Stream in the east, and the adjacent low rocky shore extending up to Coconut Island bounds the inner bay to the east (Fig. 10-12). The eastern half of this shore was in the large ahupua'a of Waiākea with the narrower ahupua'a of Kūkūau, Pōnahawai, Punahoa and Pi'ihonua along the west half of the bay.

Behind the beach were low swampy lands around the edges of several fishponds. These were walled-off, spring-fed ponds, drained by the Wailoa and Wailoma rivers. The Wailoa fishponds—Hoakimau, Waiākea, Mohouli, Waihole and Kalepolepo—were the larger. Farther back from the ponds and swampy edges were the dry lowlands.

Houses were concentrated in clusters near the beach on the dry lowland, set among groves of breadfruit, coconuts and kou trees. Dryland farms were nearby, stretching far inland along with scattered houses. Wet taro was grown in the marshlands on raised beds, using the kipi ditch-bed method.[142]

> *Round the bottom of this bay was a track of low land that extended a considerable distance to the eastward and adorned with beautiful groves of cocoa nut palms*

> *and bread fruit trees, amongst which were scattered the habitations of the natives.*
>
> [1794 Whidby][143]

> *[Houses are amidst the groves]...not in a village, but scattered everywhere among the plantations.*
>
> [1825 Stewart][144]

The fisheries of the ahupua'a were in nearshore areas, up to a man's neck, with Waiākea's fisheries including the deeper areas of the bay.[145] Forty-five years after Cook and after considerable island-wide depopulation, Ellis counted 400 houses along the bay in 1823, estimating 2,000 residents.[146]

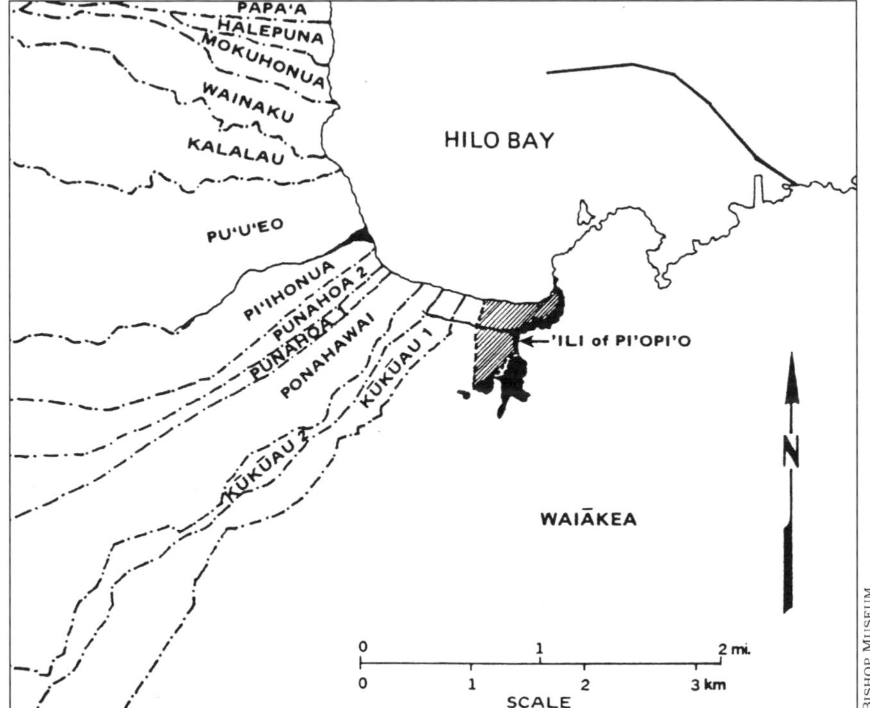


**FIGURE 10-12**

Map of Hilo Bay. The royal center was focused in Waiākea ahupua'a probably within Pi'opi'o 'ili. The ahupua'a of Kūkūau, Pōnahawai, Punahola and Pi'ihonua also fronted the sand beach of the bay and included housing areas of this center. (Kelly, Nakamura & Barrere 1981: Fig.1).

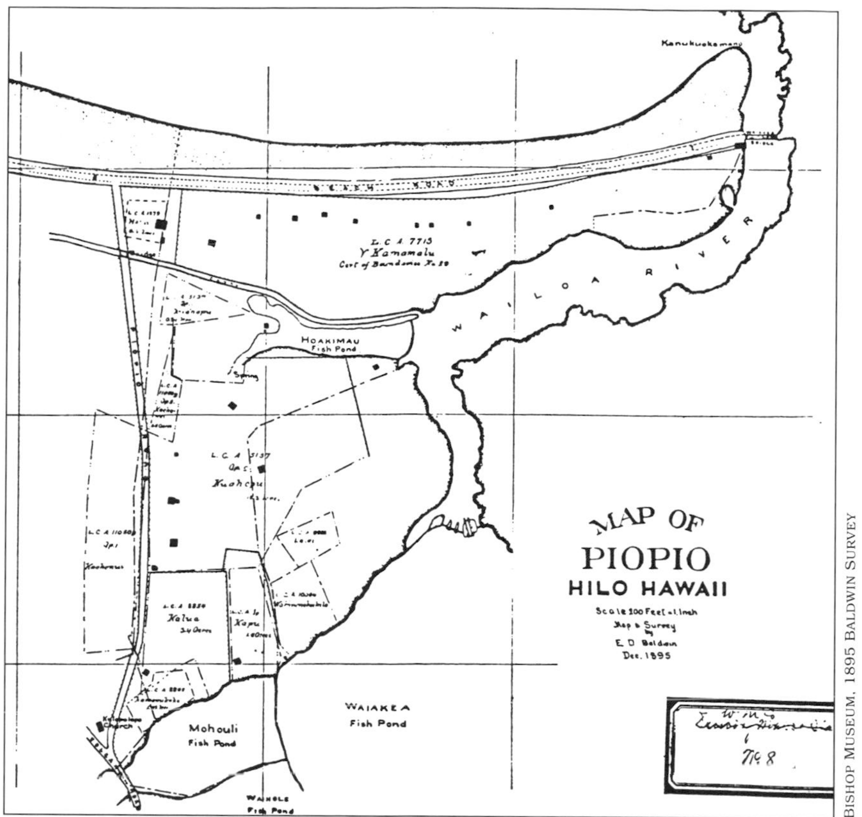


BISHOP MUSEUM, 1895 BALDWIN SURVEY

**FIGURE 10-13**

Close-up of Pi'opi'o 'ili within Waiākea Ahupua'a, showing Wailoa River and its fishponds – Hoakimu, Waiākea, Waihole and Mohouli (clockwise from top). The beach is at the top. (Kelly, Nakamura & Barrere 1981:Fig. 2).

The royal center at Hilo Bay seems to have been focused in Waiākea around the Wailoa fishponds and just to the west—primarily the 'ili of Pi'opi'o. During Alapa'inui's reign, Kamehameha's father died here at Pi'opi'o, when the court was in residence at Hilo.[147] And in Kalani'ōpu'u's reign, the story of Kekūhaupi'o mentions that during a visit by Kekūhaupi'o to Hilo, Keawema'uhili's wife, Ululani, was living at Pi'opi'o. Keawema'uhili was off at Kalani'ōpu'u's court at that time.[148] After 1791, Kamehameha also resided in Waiākea,[149] and the 'ili Pi'opi'o was clearly his property, being given to Ka'ahumanu as an 'ili kupono.[150] The adjacent fishponds of the Wailoa River were known as "the royal fishponds" and were kapu to commoners.[151]

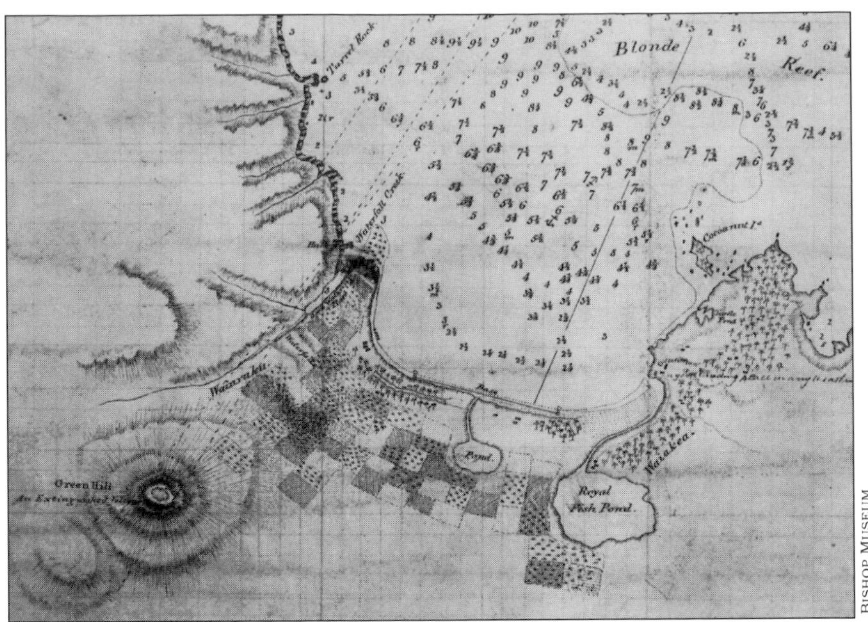


BISHOP MUSEUM

**FIGURE 10-14**
1825 Chart of Hilo Bay by Malden of H.M.S. *Blonde*. The bay spans from Coconut Island (middle right) to Wailuku River (Wainruku, Waterfall Creek) (middle center), east to west. The Wailoa River and its fishponds are marked "Royal Fish Pond" (lower right) and the Wailoma River and its fishponds are labelled "Pond". The Wailoa is in the Waiākea ahupua'a; the Wailoma in Kūkūau. The royal residence is likely to have been between the Wailoa and Wailoma rivers. (Kelly, Nakamura & Barere 1981:fig. 5.)

**FIGURE 10-15**
1824 view of Hilo Bay, view from near the shore looking inland. The drawing shows open fields, scattered houses and groves of breadfruit, kou, and coconuts. (From Byron 1826.)

HAWAII STATE ARCHIVES

Exactly where the ruler resided is unclear; the location may have varied from ruler to ruler. But, ʻili Piʻopiʻo is a likely possibility for the rulers in the 1700s. High chiefs probably resided along the beach in the various ahupuaʻa of the bay.[152] Indeed, in Kamakau's story of ʻUmi, the chiefs gathered along the beach for hula, chanting and games.[153]

Major heiau were present. The luakini heiau of Kānoa was mentioned in Kamakau's ʻUmi account, and it was located in Puʻueo just to the west of the bay.[154] The rebel Nāmakehā was offered up at Kaipalaoa heiau in Piʻihonua in 1796 by Kamehameha.[155] And Ohele heiau in Waiākea is said to have been a luakini heiau.[156] These heiau are all long destroyed.

Indeed, very little is left of the royal center at Hilo. Some of the fishponds are present, in greatly altered condition. All the other remains have been destroyed or dismantled, succumbing to the urban sprawl of Hilo—although some deposits containing important information on the old royal center may be buried under the modern city.

## GENERAL TRENDS OF THE DECADE BASED ON ARCHAEOLOGY AND HISTORY

Archaeology, other than at Kawaihae and Puʻukoholā, has so far told us little about this period. Radiocarbon dates usually span several hundred years, and it is impossible to say that a site belongs to the 1790s when a radiocarbon reading of A.D. 1660–1810 only indicates that the true date lies, with high probability, somewhere within that range. If volcanic glass dating techniques improve, or if dating historic period artifacts (bottles, ceramics) becomes refined, then perhaps sites can be definitely placed to this period.

Historical information does suggest some likely archaeological site patterns, however. Generally, with warfare not leading to great numbers of deaths, with no epidemics yet noted (the great and lesser chiefs did not die off in epidemics until ca. 1803–1804), and with venereal diseases not yet causing marked declines in child births or infant survival, it seems reasonable that the massive population declines of early historical times had not quite set in. Periodic disruption of life certainly must have taken place—through battles and raids and demands of standing armies, the traditional movement of royal centers within the three kingdoms, and periodic planting and heiau building undertakings.

Disruption from battles and raids would suggest that many refuge caves may have been re-used or many new fortified caves were built—particularly in the Hilo, Puna and Ka'ū areas which were often attacked and raided by Kamehameha's forces, and probably in Kamehameha's lands also. Indeed, since this decade appears to have been one of the few times in late prehistory–early history when battles and raids abounded on the island, perhaps many of the refuge caves actually date to this period. These fortifications served as easily defendable temporary hiding places for the common people. The caves vary greatly in size and internal features, but a basic element of all is a walled-off entrance with a narrow, defensible opening. Large refuge caves are fairly common from northern Kona down through Kona, Ka'ū and around through Puna. A few examples bear description.

Site 900 in Pu'uwa'awa'a ahupua'a in northern Kona, in Kamehameha's former realm, is located about a half mile from the shore. Here a large pāhoehoe sink, formed by a collapsed lava tube, has two tube caves leading off its sides. One of these caves was fortified. "The openings at this side of the sink...have been completely blocked off, except for two long passageways which taper off to narrow entranceways."[157] Both passages curve slightly. Outside in the sink, the walls were disguised with a covering of loose stones, and large cap-stones were used to cover the entrance. The interior walls were vertical, sturdy, and well-faced (Fig. 10-16). Within the cave were stone platforms believed to be for sleeping, as well as circular hearths and work areas.

A fortified cave in Keonepoko ahupua'a in Puna, in the former lands of Keawema'uhili, located 6 miles inland, has some similar features. This long tube runs several miles farther inland and extends down toward the sea. It is large, perhaps 10–12 feet high and

20–30 feet wide, with a fairly even floor. Periodic collapses have created a series of entrances to the cave along its inland side. One entrance, ca. 7 miles from the shore, is walled completely around—easily 7 feet high and equally thick. Two entrances pass through this wall into the seaward and inland continuations of the cave, and it is necessary to crawl through both. These walls are extremely well made, being vertical with nicely fitted stone-work. The entrances have stone lintels above them. A narrow walkway extends behind the entire wall, providing a circular corridor without having to go outside the fortification. A few small platforms are just within the entrances of the wall, and quite likely these are for sleeping.

An even larger fortified cave is Lua Nunu in Wai'ōhinu ahupua'a in Ka'ū, within Keōua's Ka'ū kingdom, located about one mile from the sea. Here a deep sinkhole formed by the collapse of a lava tube, and two caves lead off it towards the sea and inland. The latter cave is 42 feet high and 55 feet wide. About 193 feet from the entrance is a large stone wall built atop a natural raised outcrop of stone, with a combined height above the floor of 12–18 feet. One entrance passes through this wall. Farther back within the cave are 102 platforms, most small, averaging 2.4 x 1.2 meters in area (ca. 3 $m^2$). In 1953, "decayed remains of grass and matting were found on many of them," leading to sleeping-platform interpretations.[158] Hearths and scattered ash and charcoal were present. Archaeologists recovered 159 artifacts from this cave, including common tools (a basalt adze, abraders and files, scrapers, awls, fishhooks) and a rare wooden niho palaoa pendant. It was estimated on fishhook typologies that the cave was used between A.D. 1500–1800, which certainly places it within the late prehistoric period.

A fourth notable refuge cave is in Kapua, in Kamehameha's southern Kona lands just beyond the border with Ka'ū.[159] Site T-126 is large—200 meters long, 8.25 meters wide and up to 7 meters high. It is located in an area of undulating pāhoehoe, with its main opening 1.2 miles inland, off a large sinkhole. This entrance has been artificially narrowed with a well-faced wall, allowing access by only one person at a time. The floor of the cave had shell, cobbles, ash and charcoal, and an interior stone terrace with ash

**FIGURE 10-16**

Drawing of fortified entry into site 900, Pu'uwa'awa'a ahupua'a, Kona (Ching 1971:portion of Figure 4). The view is from the inside of the cave looking out. A well-faced ceiling to floor wall is visible on the left. In the center the narrow entryway descends into the cave.

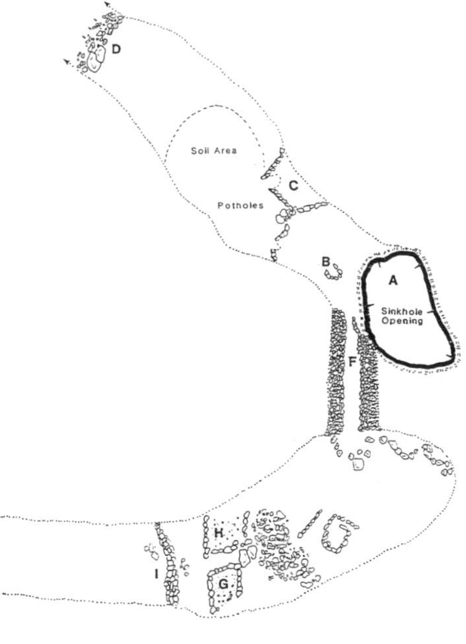


**FIGURE 10-17**

Plan map of a refuge cave's entry area and adjacent habitation platforms, site 5751, Kalaoa, Kona (Walker & Rosendahl 1989:A7). The cave's opening ("sinkhole opening") has a narrow walled corridor, marked "F", which opens into a tube with the habitation platforms, labelled H and G. Refuge cave entries vary from narrowed entryways, to low crawl spaces, to small openings dropping down on to a cave floor. All were easily defended.

which was radiocarbon-dated to A.D. 1420–1650 (B-25310). Twenty meters into the cave is another wall with a small window, beyond that a crawl space with ash and a tiny exit. The ash here was submitted for radiocarbon analysis, yielding a date of A.D. 1453–1651 (B-25311). This refuge, thus, may predate the decade of strife and belong to an earlier era, the time before or just after Līloa and 'Umi.

These dates show that the problem of dating refuge caves, studying their spatial distribution in each time period, linking them to the political events and improving an understanding of warfare and raiding awaits a future researcher. Were most of these fortified caves used between 1782–1791, during the intense battles and raids between Kamehameha's, Keōua's and Keawema'uhili's realms? Or were most of these refuges from an earlier age, perhaps during the A.D. 1600s, when the Hilo chiefs were said to periodically clash with the Kona-based rulers? Perhaps these caves were even used before the A.D. 1400s, when Kona, Kohala and the other districts may have each been independent and fighting with each other.

Despite the disruption from warfare and raiding, during these years an increase in cultivated lands (spatial increases and intensification of existing farm lands) probably also occurred at royal centers—at least Waiākea in Hilo, Punalu'u and Kahuku in Ka'ū, and Kealakekua, Kawaihae, Kauhola, and Waipi'o in Kona and Kohala. Periodic influxes of laborers on building projects undoubtedly also occurred. Pu'ukoholā's construction was such a project—on a huge scale. Certainly Keōua and Keawema'uhili must have been refurbishing heiau to acquire the aid of their gods. Indeed, Keawema'uhili is said to have built Kālepa heiau in Puna. This means that some heiau in all three kingdoms probably saw alterations dating to this decade. The temporary houses of laborers are likely to be found among the archaeological ruins near these heiau.

In many cases, archaeologists should be able to discover remains of the battlefields and temporary encampments of the armies. Despite rumors of eroding skeletons and battlefield graves and battle camps, this topic has yet to receive scientific study.

Historically, a major economic change of this decade must be emphasized. Within several years after the departure of Cook's expedition, commercial traders began to arrive to obtain food supplies, water, and wood before or after proceeding to the Northwest Coast of America to get furs, or before or after traveling to China, or before returning to America or Europe. The ships of Portlock and Dixon (*King George* and *Queen Charlotte*) in 1786–1787, of Meares (*Nootka*) in 1787, of Colnette (*Prince of Wales*) in 1788 are but a few examples. These traders, which were relatively few in number in this decade, initiated several major changes. New status goods were recognized. The demand for weapons—knives, muskets, cannon and ships—began, and these weapons changed warfare. A desire for new materials for practical tools—iron for fishhooks, adzes, etc.—and for new tools started. The need for foreign warriors, craftsmen, and translators arose. The common use of leeward ports, Kealakekua and Kawaihae, certainly began to affect decisions on the locations of the residences of the ruler, chiefs and commoners. It definitely was an advantage to Kamehameha when Ka'iana was brought into the Kealakekua port by Douglas, and when the *Fair American* and *Eleanor* coasted along and anchored in the leeward Kona ports. One might wonder what would have occurred if Hilo had been the port. Perhaps, Keawema'uhili or Keōua would have acquired the services of Ka'iana, Young and Davis, and abundant weapons—swaying the fight for dominance of the island in their favor. But, these are only thoughts, for Kamehameha did predominate—leading to the eventual unification of all the islands under the Hawai'i Kingdom.

CHAPTER 11

# The Search for Greater Understanding

*Fallen is the Chief*

.............................

*Exalted Sits the Chief*

(chant by Keaulumoku)[1]

The ruler, the chiefs, and the priests of old are now gone from Hawai'i Island. The Kingdom of Hawai'i was overthrown just 100 years ago. Yet new changes are emerging. Large double-hulled canoes are sailing again, with true Pacific navigators. Remains of deceased Hawaiians which were removed, often without permission, in the 1800s and early 1900s are being returned and placed to rest. Ruins abandoned for two centuries—houses, heiau, trails, and fishponds—are now being studied before development and are being preserved. The true culture of old is beginning to be seen by residents and visitors alike. Indeed, the issue of sovereignty is now being seriously discussed, and we may yet see the rise again of a Hawaiian nation.

In all these new stirrings, the history of Hawai'i Island before Kamehameha must not be forgotten. That Hawaii'i changed greatly—from the first few early settlers; to a time of spreading windward population and the rise of multiple polities; to the later settlement of leeward lands; to the emerging of complex political systems centered on the districts or parts of the districts; to the unification of the island by the Pili kings ruling out of Waipi'o; to the Pili line's move to the Kona side and their alliance with the emerging Mahi of Kohala and their conflicts with the 'Ī of Hilo; to Alapa'inui and his elevation of the Hawai'i Kingdom to a prominence in the islands; to Kalani'ōpu'u and his clashes with Kahekili of Maui. We still know little of these times, and this must be realized.

Truly, in many ways, the kings and chiefs and the people of old are still with us. They have left remnants of their oral stories, and remnants of their houses and farms and heiau. One needs only to hear the words of a chant and an image of the past comes to mind. Similarly, if one walks among the stone ruins of houses, one can feel those who once dwelt there. Just as knowledgeable navigators must be trained, so too must skilled historians be trained to search out and study oral histories (notably manuscripts written by Hawaiians in Hawaiian in the 1800s), historical documents (old journals, letters and illustrations by Hawaiians and non-Hawaiians), and archaeological ruins. These sources—oral history, history, and archaeology—are the paths to a better knowledge of the past.[2] Together, they should help those living today, and our children and their children, understand those who went before and, in turn, provide a link and a balance for moving into the future. The multitude should not be forgotten, and the chief should remain exalted.

# Glossary

**Ahupua'a:** The land of a community, which commonly extended from the shore inland to the forest. Ahupua'a included nearshore reef, housing and farm lands, and forest. Hawai'i Island had about 600 Ahupua'a at European contact.

**'Āina:** Land.

**Aku:** A fish, the bonito or skipjack (*Katsuwonus pelamys*).

**Akua:** A deity, a god.

**Ala loa:** Literally, long trail. These were the main trails that linked communities together.

**Ali'i:** Chief.

**'Ama'u:** A cultivation zone in Kona, the fern zone on the forest edge where patches of bananas were planted.

**'Āpa'a:** A cultivation zone in Kona, the main farming zone with formal walled fields. The field walls were the kuaīwi or iwi 'āina.

**'Aumakua:** Family or personal gods.

**'Auwai:** A canal feeding water to irrigated kalo fields.

**'Awa:** A plant, kava (*Piper methysticum*).

**Hala:** A plant, pandanus (*Pandanus odoratissimus*).

**Hāpu'u:** A plant, tree fern (*Cibotium spp.*). Common in wet inland areas.

**Heiau:** A religious place. This can range from a single rock, to a small, man-made shrine, to a very large temple. In this book, heiau discussed are usually larger temples.

**'Ili:** A subdivision of the Ahupua'a land unit. 'Ili 'āina were simple subdivisions. 'Ili kūpono were administered separately from the Ahupua'a by another chief.

**Kā'ai:** Sennit caskets holding the bones of a ruler or high chief. Often shaped somewhat like a seated person.

**Kāhili:** Symbol of high rank. Feathers atop a long wooden handle.

**Kahu:** Caretaker, attendant.

**Kahuna:** Priest.

**Kahuna nui:** High priest.

**Kālaimoku:** Chief secular advisor to the ruler. Sometimes called 'prime minister' in the literature.

**Kalo:** Taro (*Colocasia esculenta*).

**Kalu'ulu:** A cultivation zone in Kona, the breadfruit farming zone with which sweet potatoes and wauke (paper mulberry) were also planted.

**Kapa:** Bark cloth, made most commonly from wauke (paper mulberry) or māmaki (*Pipturus spp.*) trees.

**Kapu:** Prohibition or ban, special privilege or sacredness (notably in named kapu given high chiefs and the king), collectively the kapu system could be considered the national religious system.

**Kapu wohi:** A special kapu given certain high chiefs, with special privileges.

**Kipikipi:** A type of wet taro cultivation occurring in marshlands, with raised mounds of mud and vegetation and drainage channels between.

**Koa:** A tree (*Acasia koa*), often co-dominant with 'ōhi'a in wet, inland areas.

**Kōnane:** A game played with stone pebbles on a stone or wooden board. Often said to resemble Chinese checkers, although not actually the case.

**Kou:** A common tree (*Cordia subcordata*), its wood often used for bowls and platters.

**Kuaīwi:** Term applied to the long, low, mounded walls of the upland field system in Kona. These walls ran perpendicular to the sea, and with smaller cross-terrace walls bounded the formal fields within the 'āpa'a cultivation zone. These fields were planted in both dryland kalo and sweet potatoes.

**Kula:** Term of multiple meanings. A cultivation zone in Kona, the dry zone near the shore which had informal fields (mounds, clearings, etc.) planted in sweet potatoes. Also, a general term for dryland areas which were often in shrub and grass, a term for dryland farming areas.

**Kuleana:** In this book, the term refers to commoner land awards awarded during the Māhele in the 1840s. The awards were usually small house plots or farm parcels.

**Kū'ula:** A stone (carved or natural) considered to be the representation of a deity associated with fishing, or a fishing shrine.

**Lo'i:** An irrigated kalo field.

**Luakini:** A national sacrificial temple (heiau). These were often very large stone structures, and humans were occasionally sacrificed to the gods at this type of heiau.

**Māhele:** The division of the lands of the Hawaiian Kingdom in the 1840s, in which commoners, low chiefs, high chiefs and the king obtained private title to lands. In this book, the term is often used in reference to Māhele documents—the claims, testimonies and actual awards of these lands.

**Makahiki:** The period from approximately October to January of every year when rituals removed the god Kū, closed down the luakini heiau, and installed the god Lono. In theory the kingdom was free of war and sacrifices. Taxes (tribute) were collected during this period of time. In the later months of the makahiki, a series of rituals began which re-installed Kū and activated the luakini. Sometimes called the new year festival, but actually the makahiki 'season' was far more complex.

**Malo:** Men's loincloth, made of kapa (bark cloth).

**Māmane:** A tree (*Sophora chrysophylla*). One of the dominant trees above 6,000 feet, and a common dryland tree on the leeward sides of the island.

**Mamo:** A bird, a yellow-feathered honeycreeper (*Drepanis pacifica*). Its feathers were collected to make helmets, capes, and cloaks.

**Marae:** A pre-European temple in the Society Islands and nearby areas in Central Polynesia.

**Moku:** Used in this book primarily to refer to one of the major districts of an island. On Hawai'i, such districts were Hāmākua, Hilo, Puna, Ka'ū, Kona, and Kohala, and each contained 70–100 ahupua'a land units.

**Naio:** A tree (*Myoporum sandiwicense*). Common in dry areas above 6,000 feet or on the dry, leeward sides of islands.

**Nēnē:** The Hawaiian flightless goose.

**'Ōhi'a:** A tree (*Metrosideros collina*). A dominant tree once present from the shore to the uplands on the windward side of Hawai'i Island, and still a dominant tree in the wet upland areas on both the windward and leeward sides of the island.

**'Ō'ō:** A bird, a yellow-feathered honeycreeper (*Moho nobilus*). Its feathers were collected to make helmets, capes, and cloaks.

**'Ōpelu:** A fish, the mackerel scad (*Decapterus pinnulatus)*.

**Pā hale:** A house lot or house yard.

**Pāhoehoe:** Smoother lava. Often flat or gently rolling, with billowy or rope-like features.

**Palaoa, Niho palaoa, Lei niho palaoa:** Stylized, large, single-tooth pendants, of whale bone in pre-European times. Often with a human hair necklace. Symbol of high rank.

**Pali:** Cliff, or steep drop in terrain.

**Pōhaku o Kāne:** Often a small shrine with a single, upright stone (natural or carved), with the stone representing a form of Kāne. Frequently found in the forest or agricultural fields.

**Pololū:** A wooden jabbing spear, 16–20 feet long and unbarbed.

**Pu'u:** A small cinder cone or hill.

**Pu'uhonua:** A place of refuge. Usually refers to a place where criminals or those defeated in battle could flee to for safe protection.

**'U'au:** A bird, the dark-rumped petrel (*Pterodroma phaeopygia sandwichensis*). This petrel was a seabird which nested at higher elevations at European contact.

**Ulumaika:** A game stone, a stone disk which was rolled on edge between distant stakes in the game of maika.

# Chapter Notes

### NOTES FOR PROLOGUE

1. From a chant titled, "A Prophecy of the Overthrow of the Kingdom by Kamehameha" in Fornander (1920, 6(3):363).

2. McKenzie 1983:xvii.

### NOTES FOR CHAPTER 1

1. Beckwith 1972:59, lines 37–39.

2. Primary geological information for this chapter comes from Stearns & Macdonald (1946) and Macdonald and Abott (1970), including rainfall and stream data. General soil and vegetation patterns come in part from Sato, Ikeda, Paeth, Smythe & Tekehiro (1973). The vast amount of environmental information—botanical and other—comes from Environmental Impact Statements and Environmental Assessments for specific development projects (e.g., Belt, Collins & Associates 1981, 1985; Char 1986; Char & Kjargaard 1986; Dollar 1986; DOT 1975; DOT & FHWA 1980; Group 70 1979, 1985; Helber, Hastert, Van Horn & Kimura Planners 1986; O1 Consultants, Inc. 1986; Puna Geothermal 1985; The Traverse Group 1985; U.S. Army Corps of Engineers 1971, 1979, 1980, 1985; U.S. Dept. of Commerce 1976; Wilson, Okamoto & Associates 1981), and from archaeological and ethnohistorical sources (e.g., Goto 1986; Hommon & Ahlo 1982; McEldowney 1979, 1983; Newman 1970; Renger 1970; Schilt 1984).

3. Two hundred eighty-two miles of coastline is a crude estimate which the author computed off the U.S. Geological Survey quadrangles.

4. Sato, Ikeda, Paeth, Smythe, & Tekehiro 1973:110.

5. McEldowney 1983.

6. Kirch 1985.

7. See 1848 Māhele references from Kaloko in Cordy, Tainter, Renger & Hitchcock 1991:412.

8. One example of variation is that *Zebrasoma flavescens* (lau'i pala) is abundant in leeward waters and is rare in windward waters (Goto 1986:100).

9. Shoreline estimates were compiled from U.S. Geological Survey quadrangles and are not exact measurements.

10. Fornander 1880:288.

11. Fornander 1880:288.

12. F. Lyman 1868:109.

13. S. Clark 1986.

14. According to Somers (1991:136), 70% of Kīlauea's surface (primarily in Puna) is younger than 500 years, and 90% is younger than 1100 years. Also, not widely realized is that about 40% of Mauna Loa's surface is less than 1,000 years old (mostly in south Kona and along the upper north and northeast rift zones), and 25% of Hualālai is less than 1,000 years old (cf. Somers 1991:136).

15. Atkinson 1970; Gagne & Cuddihy 1990.

16. In the 1870s Boundary Commission testimonies, Haahea, a man who was born at Waikoloa in Hāmākua district, linked his birth in testimony to the time of "the first Tidal wave at Hilo" (the tidal wave of 1832) (BCB n.d., A:12–13).

17. Bishop 1825 in Kelly (1983:16).

### NOTES CHAPTER 2

1. Kamakau 1961:211.

2. Malo (1951:16) termed these moku-o-loko ("interior districts" in the published translation), as opposed to the island being called moku-puni (surrounded moku). Administratively, Waimea in today's South Kohala was handled almost as a seventh moku. It had a special land status as an 'okana (Barrere 1983), and it appears to have had a separate historical development from the rest of Kohala (see Chapter 6, note 15).

3. There were named land units larger than ahupua'a and smaller than moku—such as 'okana and kalana (Malo 1951:16). However, the nature of these units is not clear.

4. BCB n.d., A(1):95, 100, 110–111.

5. BCB n.d., A(1):99–100, B:79–80, 110–111.

6. BCB n.d., B:97.

7. For example, in the Māhele, a resident in the inland ahupua'a of Waiopua and Mohowae above South Point claimed fishing rights in coastal waters (Native Register n.d., 8:666).

8. Boundary Commission testimony in Ka'ū stated that in Līloa's reign—ca. A.D. 1580–1600—some ahupua'a borders were changed by two of his agents (major priests) (BCB n.d., A:439). Sahlins described some examples of this process in post-Kamehameha times for Waialua district on O'ahu. He noted that pieces of Kamananui ahupua'a were moved into Kawailoa ahupua'a—a result of high and low chiefs] granting of rights (Sahlins 1992:20).

9. Barrere 1983.

10. Cordy 1994.

11. Cordy 1986a, 1987b.

12. Cordy 1987a, 1994.

13. Kelly, Nakamura & Barrere 1981:20. Handy (1940:10–11) and Handy & Handy (1972:90–91) say the general form of planting on mounds in spring-fed marshlands on O'ahu was called pu'epu'e and that Hilo's kipi kalo or kipikipi seems to have been a variant of this general type.

14. Malo 1951:204.

15. Malo 1951:206.

16. Cordy 1988b, 1989a.

17. The best documentation of the Waimea field system is in J. Clark (1981, 1983b, 1987).

18. Cordy (1986a, 1987b) summarized these Ka'ū cases, identified from the Native Registers and Native Testimonies of the Māhele records and from the Boundary Commission testimonies of the 1870s.

19. M. S. Allen (1984) documented a case in Hōlualoa ahupua'a and Kawachi (1989) identified a case in Pua'a ahupua'a—both in the high-rainfall uplands above Kailua.

20. As usual, there are exceptions. In dry Ka'ū, a hardy variety of dryland taro was grown in the uplands in rainfall as low as 30–40 inches per year (Ellis 1963). At Kealakekua, Māhele documents (Native Registers and Native Testimonies) described kalo being grown on the flats below the cliff in the Kalama ahupua'a (Cordy 1985a). Kelly (1983) discussed kalo being planted in the dry lowlands, and then being transplanted into the uplands.

21. Malo 1951:42, 205.

22. Wao generically referred to the forest. Wao kanaka or ma'u referred to the lowest forest zone where 'ama'u ferns grew and men cultivated crops, mostly bananas (Malo 1951:17).

23. This reaffirmation or validation of commoner household use-rights can be seen in the Māhele's Native Testimonies which stated who the rights were obtained from. Some testimonies and claims actually documented the history of use rights. For example, a grandfather received use from a konohiki, the father from another konohiki, and the son from another. Sahlins provided an excellent analysis of inheritance and acquisition of use-rights by commoners (1992:192–208).

24. Malo 1951:43.

25. Malo 1951:42; Ellis 1963:249, 347.

26. Ellis 1963:347.

27. Dixon 1789:274.

28. Campbell 1967:118.

29. Kuakini gave a feast for Ka'ahumanu ca. 1823, with 400 dogs prepared (Ellis 1963:247).

30. Malo 1951:45.

31. See Hommon (1975:124–129); Goto (1986:92–99); and Malo (1951:211) for jackfish techniques.

32. Goto 1986:161.

33. Kahaulelio 1902; Goto 1986.

34. Campbell (1967:142) described the limits of the ahupua'a fisheries to be "as far as the tallest man in the island can wade at low water."

35. Hommon 1975. Such a case was described in Honokōhau ahupua'a in the Boundary Commission Books (BCB n.d., B:452).

36. The monarchy's fisheries law of 1839, as revised in 1845, required the landlords of each ahupua'a to notify the Minister of the Interior annually which fish they were placing under prohibition for the year (Barrere 1970:7). Paki, the chief controlling Mākaha on O'ahu, placed a kapu on he'e (octopus) in 1852 and 'ōpelu in 1854 (Barrere 1970:7).

37. Malo 1951:47, 189; Buck 1957:5.

38. Commoners did have access to some of the larger ponds. In the royal pond of ʻUkoʻa in Waialua district on Oʻahu, commoners could gather seaweed, shrimp and gobies and fish for mullet and āholehole when the winds blew heavily from certain directions (Sahlins 1992:187). But the king had to give permission, and in 1815 no fish had been taken from ʻUkoʻa "for several years" (Whitman in Sahlins 1992:95).

39. Malo 1951:37–40.

40. Cf. Haun 1986; Athens & Kaschko 1988; Reinman & Schilz 1992.

41. Malo 1951:37–40.

42. Malo 1951:48. Kapa was also made from olonā, hibiscus and young breadfruit shoots (Malo 1951:48;50, note 1; see also Kaeppler 1975). The cloth could also be scented by mixing in fragrant plant and wood fragments prior to pounding (Malo 1951:50, note 4).

43. Buck 1957:83. See Malo (1951:21–22) for timber uses.

44. Buck 1957:425, 418, 442.

45. Buck 1957:38; Malo 1951:122.

46. Malo 1951:77.

47. Malo 1951:38–39.

48. Malo 1951:76–77; Kamakau 1961:177; 1808–1809 observation in John Young's journal (Sahlins 1992:51); 1820 observation by Rev. Samuel Ruggles on Kauaʻi (Sahlins 1992:88)

49. BCB n.d., A:142. Kamakana was from Kahuku in Kaʻū.

50. BCB n.d., A:436–438. Kenoi was from Kapāpala in Kaʻū.

51. BCB n.d., A:95. Kaikuana was from Honokaia in Hāmākua.

52. Cleghorn 1986; McCoy 1977, 1986.

53. Withrow 1989.

54. Jensen 1988:134–141; 1991b; Haun & Walker 1987:18.

55. Jensen 1991b:7, 11; Walker & Rosendahl 1986.

56. See Cordy, 1994, for a detailed summary of Hāmākua settlement.

57. In 1825 Bloxam said that Hilo's groves were the "best we have seen of breadfruit and coconuts" (A. Bloxam 1925:51).

58. See McEldowney (1979) for a summary of Hilo settlement.

59. See BCB n.d., B:403, testimony of Kahula on Kahuwai's larger fisheries. See Cordy (1989a) on walled fields in Kahuwai; Cordy (1987c) on Keauohana settlement; Dunn, Franklin & Goodfellow (1995) on Ahalanui settlement; Ladefoged, Somers and Lane-Hamasaki (1987) for settlement in the Hawaiʻi Volcanoes area. See also McEldowney (1979) for a general summary of parts of Puna. See Ellis (1963) for a walk-through account.

60. See Cordy (1987b) for a summary of Kaʻū settlement patterns and Cordy (1986a) for a detailed view of South Point region settlement. See also Kelly (1980) for an general introduction.

61. This 10% figure is based on Lt. King's 1779 observation of 50 of 400 houses being in the uplands at Kealakekua Bay (Cook & King 1784, III:128) and on the archaeological information to date for Kona. See Newman (1974b), Kelly (1983), and Cordy (1995) for summaries of Kona field patterns.

62. Thurston 1824, in Kelly 1983:16.

63. Cf. Tomonari-Tuggle's summary of North Kohala settlement patterns (1988).

64. Malo 1951:17. There are numerous references to oʻioʻina in the Boundary Commission testimonies for Puna.

65. Schmitt 1971, 1977.

66. Stannard 1989.

67. Ehle 1988:7.

68. Mayan city-states may have been similar in population size to Hawaiian polities, with their average polities having 30,000–50,000 people (Schele & Friedel 1990:57). The largest kingdom, Tikal, may have had 500,000 people, but Tikal seems to have been an unusual case. In contrast, estimates have the Aztec empire's capital, Tenochtitlan, alone between 60,000–150,000 (Sanders & Price 1968:151), and some recent estimates indicate it could have had 200,000–300,000 people. The Aztec empire, which included many other cities and towns, would have had a population far beyond that of the Hawaiian polities. Similarly, the Inca empire had a much larger population, some population

estimates suggesting 3,000,000–6,000,000 people (Bennett & Bird 1960:161).

69. Thurston & Bishop 1833, in Kelly (1983:17) on emigration with Kuakini to O'ahu in 1831–1833.

70. This uneven distribution of population, even in windward lands, affects population estimates. For example, Stannard (1989:17–23, 30) constructed his higher population estimates in part on the assumption that windward population densities and populations were constant and higher than optimal leeward areas (such as Kealakekua in Central Kona) (at a 3:2 ratio, in his view). My research on Hāmākua, however, found that many areas of that district had low populations (Cordy 1994), much less than Central Kona, so a constantly higher windward estimate cannot be applied. Also, some Central Kona areas rivaled Waipi'o numbers and density, so a higher windward density may not hold; rather perhaps similarly high-density areas in each district occurred. Differential distributions of population within districts need to be considered in a complex manner in estimating island populations.

71. Charles Stewart noted commoners made up "at least one hundred and forty-nine thousand of the hundred and fifty thousand" total archipelago population—99% (Stewart 1970 [1830]:141).

72. Malo 1951:29.

73. Malo 1951:29; Campbell 1967:92–93, 131; 'I'i 1959:111.

74. Sahlins' Waialua study showed the details of inheritance (1992:204–205). One child often inherited the household's primary land, and junior children had to affiliate with the heir, acquire other land in the ahupua'a, or go elsewhere.

75. NR 1848, 8:330–331. In this quote, konohiki refers to the high chief (the konohiki to the king), and tenant refers to the local chief, who was the tenant under the high chief above him. This quote shows that konohiki was a more general, relative term than usually implied in the anthropological literature. It referred to a hierarchical land relationship between chiefs or between chiefs and ruler. It did not just refer to a low chief placed in control over an ahupua'a by a high chief.

76. Sahlins 1992:71, 87; I'i 1959:29. Regarding burning of houses, in 1825 Chamberlain stated: "This we understood had been a custom formerly when persons refused or neglected to turn out in obedience to orders." (Chamberlain 9/22/1825 in Sahlins 1992:71). In the same year Mathison wrote that if the chief's will was still not followed, "The next process was to seize his [the commoner's] possessions, and turn his wife and family off the estate" (Mathison 1825:451 in Sahlins 1992:87).

77. Cf. Sahlins 1992:33, 193–206.

78. Kelly (1983:70) noted that in 1839 and 1840 the relation of farmer to chief was codified by the monarchy in poll taxes, land taxes, and labor taxes owed to the king and landlords. In 1841, after living in Hawai'i since 1823 and serving the ruler, William Richards emphatically stated that the system was of a "feudal character" (Sahlins & Barrere 1973:21–24). Sahlins (1992) called these overlapping chiefly rights "infeudation". His volume is the most detailed available on the various duties, obligations and maneuverings of all participants.

79. Sahlins 1973:13, 1992:33, 193–200.

80. Sahlins (1992:208–211) identified the dominant individuals as commoner "big men" in a fascinating discussion. They expanded their lands and often intermarried into local chiefs' families in trying to maintain or raise their place in the commoner stratum of their ahupua'a.

81. Commoners could choose to move from an ahupua'a. Most likely they would activate rights in nearby ahupua'a through kin ties—either blood ties or affinal (in-law) ties.

82. Sahlins' work has revealed that taxes may have been gathered twice a year—once during the winter Makahiki festival and "the second annual land tribute may have corresponded to the 'ōpelu (mackerel) tabu of midsummer" (1992:51, note 17; see also 87–88).

83. Malo 1951:61.

84. Valeri 1985:141.

85. Malo 1951:187.

86. Valeri 1985:140.

87. Malo 1951:191–192.

88. Valeri 1985:154.

89. Ellis 1963:302.

90. Malo 1951:160.

91. Valeri 1985:143–144.

92. Many of the bans and respect behavior were documented by Malo (1951:56–57) and Ellis (1963:301).

93. Campbell (1967:94); ʻIʻi (1959:28). "When his [Kamehameha's] food was carrying from the cooking-house, every person within hearing of the call Noho, or, sit down, given by the bearers, was obliged to uncover himself, and squat down on his hams" (Campbell 1967:94—1809 observation). "In the middle of this crowd a man passed us with a piece of cloth in his hand to which all the people cowered down as he went along. This, Kualelo told us, was a malo for the king" (Menzies 1920:91—1793 observation).

94. Ellis 1963:30.

95. Malo 1951:56. ʻIʻi (1959:23) gave an example of a low chief who was under suspicion for wearing Kamehameha's malo. ʻIʻi, in an 1841 talk, described the cases of three men sacrificed in 1818 at Hikiau heiau. One had put on a chief's malo, one had eaten sacred food, and another had exited a kapu house and entered a house that was not kapu (ʻIʻi 1889).

96. Malo 1951:77. See Kaeppler, 1985, who proposed that the long capes were worn only by a few high-ranking chiefs. All yellow capes were rare, Kamehameha's being perhaps the only known case. Kīwalaʻō's also was almost entirely yellow. The triangle motif seems to have been a trait of rulers of Hawaiʻi versus Maui's circles.

97. Malo 1951:104–106.

98. Malo 1951:195.

99. Malo 1951:189.

100. Malo 1951:54–55.

101. Malo 1951:54–55. Rights to these kapu privileges were in some cases bestowed during childhood by the reigning ruler (Keakealaniwahine examples in McEldowney 1986:9, 30). In effect, kapu was conferred and enforced by the ruler's power.

102. Malo 1951:55.

103. Sahlins (1981:62) pointed out (citing 1793 evidence from Puget) that Kamehameha intentionally gave few lands to his full brother. Later falling-outs occurred between Kamehameha and several of these chiefs (e.g., Kaʻiana, Kalaʻimamahū, Kīnaʻu, and Isaac Davis). See Kamakau (1961:172), Fornander (1880:344–348), and Vancouver (1798, II:128–129, 143–145) regarding Kaʻiana; ʻIʻi (1959:49–50) regarding Kīnaʻu and Kalaʻimamahū, and Kuykendall (1957:50–51) and ʻIʻi (1959:79, 83) regarding Davis.

104. Ellis 1963:306.

105. An example of a high chief holding such kapu was Keawemaʻuhili, junior brother of the ruler Kalaniʻōpuʻu, and later chief advisor to Kīwalaʻō (Kalaniʻōpuʻu's son and heir) (Fornander 1880:311). Also, in the reign of Keakealaniwahine, she gave her senior grandson (Kalaninuiʻīamamao) the kapu moe and a junior grandson (Kalanikeʻeaumoku) the kapu wohi (McEldowney 1986). Clerke, in summing up the islands, stated that the people fell on their faces to "the King and two or three of their principal chiefs" (Clerke in Beaglehole 1967; 3:596), so these kapu seem to have been restricted to only a few high chiefs.

106. Malo 1951:152, 192.

107. Malo 1951:188. This position is often called the prime minister in the literature.

108. Malo 1951:191.

109. Valeri 1985:135; Malo 1951:55–56; Kamakau 1991:40.

110. Malo 1951:56.

111. Ellis 1963:301.

112. Kualelo had been brought back from England (Menzies 1920:66, 91; Vancouver 1798, I:156, III:66). Another example is Kalehua ["Tarehooa"] who spoke English and had been abroad with Ingraham; he became an aide to Keʻeaumoku (Vancouver 1798, I:157). Yet another example is Kahikona (a Tahitian preacher) who received Onouli ahupuaʻa in Kona from Kuakini, the Governor of Hawaiʻi Island (Barrere 1989:75).

113. Vancouver 1798, III:46.

114. Barrere & Sahlins 1979:30.

115. Malo 1951:58–59, 63–64.

116. Malo 1951:65–67.

117. Campbell 1967:147.

118. Malo 1951:58, 65.

119. Malo 1951:59, 65. The initial tribute gathered from each ahupua'a's konohiki during the makahiki season supplied feathers, kapa, dogs, and food (hard taro) to the immediate landlord and the king. The king redistributed his share to the high chiefs and to his own retinue (Malo 1951:142).

120. Malo 1951:194.

121. Malo (1951:195) and others referred to commoners overthrowing rulers, but the examples actually documented were high chiefs being deposed by commoners or rulers being ousted by close relatives (high chiefs). Thus, there is no definitive evidence of commoners overthrowing rulers; rather rulers' competition came from closely related high chiefs. To address Malo's list: Kama'i'ole was the ruler through a coup, but he was slain by a high chief, Kalapana, the rightful heir. Hākau was a ruler, but he too was slain by a high chief, 'Umi, his half-brother. Koihala, Koha-i-ka-lani and Halaea in Ka'ū (Malo 1951:195; Kelly 1980:1–5) are not recorded in the genealogies as rulers, rather they appear to have been high chiefs in Ka'ū (cf. Kamakau 1991:76). 'Ehunuikaimalino was not a ruler (Malo 1951:195), rather the high chief of Kona, and he was removed by 'Umi, the ruler. 'Umiokalani was not a ruler, rather a high chief of Kona under Lonoikamakahiki, his half-brother. Last, Lono was a ruler, but was not overthrown by commoners; his half-brothers rose against him, and ruled in his place for a while.

122. Malo 1951:81; J. S. Emerson 1892.

123. Malo 1951:82–84; Valeri 1985:15, 45, 178.

124. Malo 1951:116. Rev. W. Richards described the arrival of a priestess of Pele in Lahaina in 1824—"This woman who is called Ke Akua Pele" (Richards 1824–1825, Aug. 13, 1824 letter to Evarts).

125. Valeri 1985:122.

126. Malo 1951:82.

127. Malo 1951:81; Valeri 1985:13–14. Malo noted (1951:81) that the chiefs and ruler worshiped on the same nights, but to different gods with different kapu.

128. Malo 1951:142.

129. Valeri 1985:184.

130. Malo 1951:159–160.

131. Valeri 1985:237–243.

132. Malo 1951:188–190.

133. Valeri 1985:135–136. Mo'o Kū was also called the order of Kanalu and mo'o Lono called the order of Palikū (Malo 1951:159–160).

134. Valeri 1985:136.

135. Valeri 1985:136.

136. Malo 1951:159–160.

137. Malo 1951:188.

138. Malo 1951:190.

139. Based on a lunar calendar, the kapu periods were Kū (nights 1–3 of the new moon), Hua (nights 12 and 13 before the full moon), Kāloa (nights 23 and 24), and Kāne (nights 27 and 28) (Malo 1951:32, 35). This meant ca. 72 kapu days per year (Emerson in Malo 1951:36, note 7).

140. Bell 1929–30, Pt. 3:77).

141. Malo 1951:142, 143; Valeri 1985:200–213. In December 1788, Douglas of the *Iphigenia* was on Hawai'i and said chickens were also prohibited—"at this season of the year even the chiefs are forbidden to eat hogs and fowls, from the King down" (Meares 1790:339).

142. Malo 1951:143; Valeri 1985:204. Among the tribute "dogs were contributed until the pens were full of them" (Malo 1951:143).

143. Malo 1951:143–144.

144. In 1841, William Richards gave an example of an annual tax owed by an 'ili within an ahupua'a: 1 pig, 1 dog, 1 fishnet, 1 cluster of feathers, 20 kapas (Sahlins & Barrere 1973:24). Richards also noted that "Vast amounts however were secretly retained in the hands of the various grades of chiefs" before taken to the king (Sahlins & Barrere 1973:24). In 1779, Cook described the tax of an ahupua'a ("district") in Kealakekua Bay given the king: "we found the ground covered with parcels of cloth, a vast quantity of red and yellow feathers fastened to the fibers of cocoa-nut husks, and a great number of hatchets and other pieces of ironware that had been got in barter from us. At a little distance from these lay an immense quantity of vegetables of every kind, and near them was a very large herd of hogs" (Cook 1944:400).

145. Malo 1951:145; Valeri 1985:209–210.

146. Sahlins 1981:19, 21.

147. Fornander 1919–1920, 6(1):204–205. In the Fornander collections it seems to be suggested that Kohala tribute was collected and taken to Hīkapoloa or Mo'okini heiau where the Lonomakua procession arrived coming from Kona. "The deity is out on the public highway. The god journeys until it reaches Pololu and stops. The god repairs to Mo'okini. ... The Long god comes from Kona. The long god reaches Kohala."

148. Malo 1951:152; Valeri 1985:228.

149. Valeri 1985: 231–233; Malo 1951:152. Vancouver was in Kealakekua Bay on February 1, 1794, when this strict 10-day kapu began (1798, III:18–19).

150. Valeri 1985:257–261.

151. Valeri 1985:264–275; Malo 1951:145.

152. Valeri 1985:279–282, 334. Vancouver (1798, III:22–23) was in Kealakekua with Kamehameha on February 12, 1794, and observed some of these final rites including a sunset ceremony at Hikiau heiau with strict silence the following dawn.

153. Valeri 1985:353.

154. Sahlins 1981:34.

155. Cf. Sahlins 1981:52–53.

156. Malo 1951:160–167.

157. Prayer told N. Emerson (Malo 1951:185, note 39).

158. Ellis 1963:97.

159. Ellis 1963:99.

160. Ellis 1963:101–102.

161. Ellis 1963:100.

162. Hommon's caution (1975:154). Estimates come from Ingraham (1918:23; Kuykendall 1968:24, 37, note 39.)

163. Broughton 1804:34; information given by John Young in 1796 to Bishop (Roe 1967:136; Joesting 1984:59).

164. Told in 1804 to Capt. Lisianskii (Barratt 1987:5, for 1812 Russian publication's translation; Lisiansky 1814:133) and V. Berkh (Barratt 1987:105) of the Russian ship *Neva* by John Young.

165. Kamakau 1961:74.

166. Ellis 1963:102.

167. Ellis 1963:103; see also Malo 1951:197.

168. Ellis 1963:101.

169. Ellis 1963:103–104.

170. Ellis 1963:104–105.

171. Ellis 1963:105.

172. Ellis 1963:105.

173. One battle on Kaua'i, ca. Feb. 28, 1779, was fought between the Kaua'i-O'ahu faction of Kāneoneo and the Kaua'i-Maui faction of Kā'eo and Kamakalei. Kāneoneo's side withdrew with 26 dead (3 chiefs) and Kā'eo's side lost 1 man—or so Clerke was told (Beaglehole 1967, 3(1):577). But this battle appears to have been quite small in the scale of the major wars of the 1700s between Hawai'i and Maui. In the 1795 battle of Nu'uanu, Ka'iana and supposedly 300 of his followers died (Broughton 1804:41), and another source suggested 500 or more Maui Kingdom warriors were slain (Bishop 1967:143).

## NOTES FOR CHAPTER 3

1. Malo 1951:1.

2. Valeri 1985:xvii.

3. Stokes 1933:24.

4. Kamakau 1961:354.

5. Some Cook expedition references: Cook & King 1784 (official published account); Burney 1776–1780 ms. Rickman 1781; Clerke in Beaglehole 1967, 3(1); King in Beaglehole 1967, 3(1); Samwell 1786 (also in Beaglehole 1967, 3(2)); Law 1779; Gilbert 1982; Trevenen 1959; Riou 1778–1779 ms. Zimmerman 1781; Ellis 1784; Ledyard 1783 (1963).

6. Illustrative material of the Cook expedition has recently been discussed in a publication by Joppien & Smith (1988).

7. Samwell in Beaglehole 1967, 3(2):1175–1176; King in Cook & King 1784, III:128; Ledyard 1963:128.

8. Cf. Valeri 1985:xix; Beaglehole 1967; Stannard 1989:15. Ellis (1784, II:113) noted that King was held "in great esteem with all the principal people of the island."

9. Samwell in Beaglehole 1967, 3(2):1223. Cf. Valeri 1985:xvii–xix.

10. For examples of stories collected from Young and Davis, see Vancouver (1798, II:136–145), Bell's 1792–1794 log on the *Chatham* (1929:67–69), accounts from Lisianskii's 1804 trip (Lisianskii 1812 Russian text translation, in Barrett 1987:51; Lisianskii's English publication 1814:129–132; Berkh in Barrett 1987:105), and Campbell 1967 [1822]:96–98. Young actually kept a log for some years, but it is in a private collection.

11. A major exception is Kelou Kamakau who was ca. 19 in 1792 and who wrote on ritual (Fornander 1919, 6:2–45) (cf. Valeri 1985:xxvi).

12. Cf. Ellis 1784:186; Law 1779:Jan. 18.

13. King in Beaglehole 1967, 3(1):614-615; Ellis 1784:184–187.

14. E.g., Vancouver recovered differing information on Kamehameha's rise to power from Ke'eaumoku (1798, I:157–158) and Ka'iana (1798, I:155).

15. Ellis on 1780s–1790s battles (1963:93–107; 143–144), on the eruption (1963:174–175), on the nature of war (1963:95–107), etc.

16. Bingham on Moku'ōhai (1847:36–37) and Kamehameha's rise to power from Ka'ahumanu and Kalanimoku (1847:38–42).

17. Kamakau 1961:125 [Mar. 1867, *Ka Nupepa Kuokoa*].

18. Remy 1979. Beckwith (1932:4) stated that Kepelino's father, Namiki, was this Kanuha, or "vieux savage." Her reason for this conclusion is not given. It seems unlikely though, because Kepelino was born in 1830 and Kanuha would have been 93 then—if his age in 1853 was anywhere near 116. Kepelino's father would more realistically seem to have been in his 20s–40s in 1830. This does not seem to match Remy's informant.

19. If Kanuha was 116 in 1853, he would have been born in 1737 and been 23 by the end of Alapa'inui's reign—a probable age for a runner-messenger during Alapa'i's and Kalani'ōpu'u's times. Other examples of extremely old people surviving in the mid-1800s existed. Fr. Marechal at Ka'ū in 1844 knew an old woman who had seen Alapa'inui (Remy 1979:4). She probably was well over 90 years in age. In general though, few people who had lived as adults in Alapa'i's or Kalani'ōpu'u's reigns would still have been living in 1850. To be an adult (20 years of age) during Alapa'i's rule (1740–1760), one would have to have been born between 1720–1740 (or earlier). By 1850, such people would be 110–130 years old. Adults in Kalani'ōpu'u's period (1760–1782) would have been born between 1740–1760 (or earlier)—making them 90–110 by 1850.

20. Kamakau in Thrum (1918:43) (see Chun 1988:14).

21. Ka'ahumanu (Bingham 1847:36) and 'I'i (1959:13) versus Kamakau (1961:107,109, 118–119) and Fornander (1880:201, 299–302, with pages 299–302 being a critique of the opposing view).

22. Differing versions of the volcano's impact on Keōua's forces exist (cf. Ellis 1963: 174; Kamakau 1961:152; Fornander 1880:324–325; Dibble 1909:41).

23. Remy 1979:18–19. Alternatively, Remy might have recorded the story incorrectly.

24. Douglas in Meares 1967:354.

25. Malo 1951:247.

26. See Elbert (1951) on exaggerating, embellishing, symbolism, word play, etc. In the 1860s Kepelino also noted that tellers altered stories, "rearranging them from time to time and casting out all that was unsuitable in the tales" (Kepelino 1932:6).

27. Beckwith 1972:153.

28. One should note that in the early 1820s in Lahaina and other mission stations, even though the national religion had ended, many lower levels of religious activities still remained, including praying individuals to death (cf. early ABCFM letters of Richards from the Lahaina station).

29. In 1809–1810 on O'ahu Campbell stated that adzes were "now universally made of iron" (1967:143). Brigham (1902:5, footnote) seemed to imply that stone adzes were rare by the mid-1800s.

30. Sahlins (1992:113) noted bird feathers still were a tax item as late as 1842, but evidently not much longer.

31. Sahlins (1992) has vividly shown in detail for Waialua district on O'ahu the shift of commoners out of rural areas to avoid the increasing demands of the chiefs.

32. Malo contributed to a 1838 *Ka Moolelo Hawaii*—a Lahainaluna school student compilation, written in 1835–1836 and published in Hawaiian in 1838 (Dibble ed. 1838; 2nd rev. edition published in 1858, Pogue ed. 1858). Malo's contribution can be seen when comparing the English translation (Pogue 1978) with the English translation of Malo's own mo'olelo (Malo 1951). Malo's own *Moolelo o Hawaii* was written in 1840 (Malo 1840) and translated to English in 1903 (Malo 1951). Malo also compiled a genealogy of chiefs (Malo n.d.). Kamakau published a 1842 genealogy in a Hawaiian newspaper (McKenzie 1983: xxi–xxv). Over 20 years later Kamakau published numerous newspaper articles from 1865–1871. Several were run in serial chapters—e.g., "Ka Moolelo o Hawaii Nei" in *Ka Nupepa Kuokoa*, "Ka Moolelo o Kamehameha I" in *Kuokoa*, and "Ka Moolelo Hawaii" in *Ke Au Okoa*. These articles were translated into English and published in recent years (Kamakau 1961, 1964, 1976, 1991). 'I'i also wrote newspaper articles between 1866–1870 in *Kuokoa*; and these were translated into English and finally published in 1959 ('I'i 1959). Fornander gathered accounts from Hawaiian informants in the 1860s–1870s; some are in Hawaiian and English in the Fornander Collection (1916–1920). He published a synthesis from this material (1878, 1880). Kepelino wrote his *Mooolelo Hawaii* ca 1868 (1868 ms), and it was translated into English and published in 1932 (Beckwith 1932).

33. S. N. Haleole (1862 ms. in Fornander 1916–1920, 6:56-159), K. Kamakau (ms. in Fornander 1916–1920, 6:2–45), S. Dibble (1843), A. D. Kahaulelio (1902), Remy (1979).

34. For example, Nakuina (1992) and Desha (in press). Cf. Kawaharada (1992:viii) on Nakuina's use of Kamakau's and others' stories and Frazier (in press:Foreward) on Desha's use of earlier sources.

35. Helekunihi ca. 1873 (cf. Helekunihi n.d., 1893).

36. The Kumulipo was published in Hawaiian in 1889 by Kalākaua, translated partly into German by Bastian (1881) from Kalākaua's manuscript, and translated into English in 1894–1895 by Lili'uokalani (1897). A recent, well accepted English translation is that of Beckwith (1972), which also includes the Hawaiian.

37. Cf. McKenzie 1986:129, 140–141. William Brigham, the first President of the Bishop Museum, emphasized the abuse of the genealogies of those years, saying I "care little for ... the genealogies for I have seen them falsified to satisfy ambition" (1902:iv).

38. Puget's Pā'ao story came from an interview with a priest at Hikiau heiau at Kealakekua (Sahlins 1981:25–26).

39. Kuykendall 1957:37–38. One should note that Kamakau's versions often changed and were embellished in later publications.

40. Quote from Valeri 1985:xxiv. Information supported by N. Emerson (1951:viii).

41. Malo's mo'olelo was completed in 1840 (W. D. Alexander 1951:xviii).

42. N. Emerson 1951:viii. For details on Malo in these years, see N. Emerson (1951), W.D. Alexander (1951), Lieb (1949).

43. Barrere 1976:146, note 13; Chun 1988:12.

44. For details on Kamakau's life, see Spoehr (1961), Loeb (1949), Thrum (1918), and Chun (1988).

45. Kamakau did apparently learn genealogies from two Hawai'i Island chiefesses, Hoapili-wahine and Kekauluohi, who had themselves been taught by Kalaikuahulu at Kamehameha's court (Kamehameha having assigned Kalaikuahulu to teach them) (Kamakau 1991:79).

46. Davis 1979:199.

47. Fornander 1878:v.

48. Fornander 1880:279, note 1.

49. Fornander 1878:vi.

50. Barrere 1969:2; Hommon 1975:12.

51. Fornander's volumes 1 and 3 analyze Hawaiian and Polynesian origins, in a typical fashion of his time period. These interpretations reflect long outdated anthropological theory. Today's reader, a century later, thus finds "the first volume of Fornander's history...an inextricable mixture of facts and absurd interpretation" (Valeri 1985:xxviii). The second volume, however, remains an excellent presentation and analysis of Hawaiian history based on oral historical accounts.

52. Fornander 1880:v.

53. See Fornander's Collections for examples of stories which called a known district chief a king (e.g., Fornander 1918, 5(1):150) or which placed a known district chief in the wrong ruler's reign (e.g., Fornander 1918, 5(1):80).

54. Kamakau (1961:chap. 1) had the district chiefs slain by 'Umi's followers, but later in the reign of 'Umi's son, Keawenui a 'Umi, the Hilo district chief (Kulukulu'a) was clearly alive and still the district chief (1961:17).

55. McEldowney's (1983) analysis of stories related to the Kamoa Point area of Hōlualoa (north Kona) shows just how much some of the accounts changed from the 1800s–1900s.

56. Barrere, 1987 personal communication.

57. Barrere, 1987 personal communication.

58. Emory 1971:xix. See also Valeri 1985:xxiv. Interestingly, Lieb (1949:12) said that others criticized that Emerson was too literal and missed the figurative language.

59. Davis 1979:276.

60. Davis 1979:276.

61. Davis 1979:277; Lieb 1949:18–20.

62. Kent 1961:ix.

63. Barrere 1964:vii.

64. Barrere 1964:vii, 1976:v–vi.

65. Kamakau 1991.

66. Stokes 1933:23.

67. Emory 1977; Barrere 1986 (1957).

68. Cartwright 1930; Stokes 1933.

69. For the beginning reader's information, Stokes was extremely knowledgeable on Hawaiian oral history, history and archaeology (cf. Dye 1991). This can be seen in the following comment by the Museum director, Brigham: "Mr. Stokes has accumulated in his more than twenty years in the Bishop Museum, a knowledge of Hawaiian matters greater than any man I know" (Brigham 1921 ms. in Kelly, 1980:69). Even today, Stokes' insights are quite impressive. Cartwright, too, was extremely knowledgeable about Hawaiian genealogies.

70. Stokes 1933:53–55.

71. Stokes 1933:56.

72. Yzendoorn 1927:7; Cartwright 1930:47.

73. Stokes 1933:58–59.

74. Cartwright 1930.

75. Stokes 1933:62.

76. Hommon 1975, 1976; Cordy 1974d, 1981, 1987a, 1994, 1996.

77. Following Hommon 1976. See also Cordy 1987a, 1994.

78. Stokes 1933.

79. Stokes 1933:26, 47; Kuykendall 1957:30. On February 27, 1779, Hawaiian women aboard the ships noted that fires seen on Moloka'i were signals of war between Peleiōhōlani and Kahekili of Maui (King in Beaglehole 1967, 3:584).

80. Malo 1951:1; Hommon 1975.

81. Malo 1951:1.

82. Cf. Fornander 1878:165, 1880:5; Malo 1951:238–247. This was to the time of Māweke, Paumakua, and Hīkapoloa (Fornander 1878:165).

83. Fornander (1878:165). This would be back to A.D. 1320, using 20 years per generation.

84. Fornander 1878:197.

85. Malo 1951:247.

86. Stokes 1932:48; Barrere 1961:63; Sahlins 1981:15–16.

87. Stokes 1932:48.

88. Barrere 1961:63; Emory 1977.

89. Fornander 1880:5.

90. Helekunihi's *Moolelo Hawaii* manuscript was written ca. 1873, but it was never translated or published. Helekunihi (1838/1839–1896) lived with 'Ī'i in 1868, and 'Ī'i said Helekunihi was very accurate (Helekunihi 1893). Other manuscripts have yet to be published (cf. Kaneinei n.d.).

91. 'Ī'i 1959:68–69; Sahlins 1992.

92. Cf. Cordy (1994) for Waipi'o in Hāmākua and Lyons (1842, 1847) for other Hāmākua areas; Cordy, Tainter, Renger & Hitchcock (1991) for Kaloko in Kona; Ka'ū Station Reports (1846:5; 1852:3) and Cheever (1851:269) for Ka'ū; Kohala Station Reports (1845:2; 1848, 1849) for north Kohala.

93. Sahlins 1971, 1973, 1992.

94. Handy and Pukui are not totally wrong. Rather their work is a blend of precontact to early 1800s patterns, mid-1800s patterns, and late 1800s/early 1900s patterns. The 'ohana was a bilateral kindred (cf. Sahlins 1992:193–200) focused about an individual, with the kindred's membership different at each event. However, the 'ohana was not an enduring kin group. Nor was it a group which held an 'ili land at European contact.

95. Ellis 1823 observation (1963:260–261), Māhele records of 1840s–1850s. See Cordy (1987a, 1994) for summary of Māhele patterns.

96. Cordy, Tainter, Renger & Hitchcock 1991:569.

97. Sahlins 1992:41, 51–52.

98. BCB n.d., A:439.

99. Stokes 1991:71.

100. Hudson (1932:145), who worked in 1930–1932.

101. Even the excellent surveys may miss one or two small sites due to thick vegetation and other factors.

102. Cf. such work at Kaloko ahupua'a (Cordy, Tainter, Renger & Hitchcock 1992; Tainter & Cordy 1977; Cordy 1978, 1981) and in other communities in north Kona (Cordy 1978, 1981).

103. Cf. Cordy 1978, 1981, 1984; Cordy, Tainter, Renger & Hitchcock 1992; Hommon 1980; Kirch 1979, 1984:104–111; Jensen 1990b:8–10, 17, 110–112; Welch 1988.

104. Cordy 1978, 1981.

105. Barrere 1971b:18, counting the heads of household from the taxpayers roll, and multiplying by 5 people per household (following Ellis's 1823 estimate).

106. Naroll 1962. See also Brown 1983, 1985.

107. Dye & Komori 1992a, b; Dye 1994.

108. Dye 1992, 1994, 1995; Dye & Komori 1992a, b.

109. New and promising research on obsidian hydration dating is occurring in New Zealand (Sutton & Sheppard n.d.; Stevenson, Ambrose, Sheppard & Sutton in press).

## NOTES CHAPTER 4

1. Beckwith 1972:87.

2. Fornander 1878:24. See also Kepelino (1932:76–79) regarding Hawai'i nui.

3. Fornander 1878:22–24, 132–134; Buck 1938:248–249.

4. Fornander 1878:23, 133.

5. Fornander 1878:24.

6. Buck 1938:249.

7. Emory 1959; Barrere 1967, 1969.

8. Malo 1951:6.

9. Ellis 1963:54, 311–312.

10. Kamakau 1991:129.

11. Kamakau 1991:129 (1869).

12. Kamakau 1991:91 (1866).

13. Emory 1959:32.

14. Nor do they consider Fornander's placement of Hawai'i loa on the genealogies to be accurate of contact era genealogies. The placement is seen as a late 1800s insertion.

15. Fornander 1878:22.

16. Buck 1938:248–249.

17. Buck 1938:249.

18. Malo 1951:7.

19. Fornander 1878:cf. 24, 133, 167–168.

20. Handy 1930; Buck 1938.

21. Kirch (1984:76; 1989:25) cautioned that since earlier sites in the Society Islands have only been found by accident and are submerged, perhaps early sites exist in those islands and have yet to be found. So far, however, dates from the earliest sites in the Society Islands are ca. A.D. 700s–900s, after settlement of Hawai'i and Easter Island.

22. Kirch 1984:77; Green 1966; Pawley 1966; R. Clark 1979:258; Elbert 1953: 165–166.

23. Kirch 1985:62.

24. Kirch 1985:58.

25. Green 1974. As an interesting note, Elbert's (1953:161) early study, which concluded Hawaiian was closer to Tahitian than Marquesan based on a multiple-

cognates approach, also presented findings of the more common single-cognate approach: Hawaiian-Marquesan 64% shared cognates vs. Hawaiian-Tahitian 51%.

26. Green 1966; R. Clark 1975; Elbert 1982.

27. Green 1995, describing the work of Elbert and Biggs.

28. Pietrusewsky 1970, 1971.

29. Pietrusewsky 1971:30.

30. Burrows 1938.

31. Cf. Sinoto 1967, 1970, 1979; Emory 1968 and Green 1968 on adzes.

32. Kirch 1989:24; 1986, 1985, 1984.

33. There is an alternative view recently developed by some researchers that early culture across Central East Polynesia was very similar and any of these islands—the Cooks, the Societies or the Marquesas— could have been the source for Hawaiian culture. A few researchers have even raised the idea that contact was maintained for a while with Central Eastern Polynesia and that there could have been multiple sources for Hawai'i's early population (cf. Cachola-Abad 1993; Green 1995). Cachola-Abad (1993) points out that the early archaeological samples from the Marquesas and other Central East Polynesian islands are minimal. While this may be true, no pre-700s–1200s culture has yet been found in Central East Polynesia, except in the Marquesas (cf. Spriggs & Anderson 1993; Kirch 1986). And this early Marquesan culture lacked the harpoon and hand club (patu), which were found later in the Marquesas and in the early periods of occupation in the Societies and New Zealand. Again, Hawai'i lacked these items, suggesting settlers of Hawai'i had already left East Polynesia. So far, the Marquesas are the only candidate for a population source for this earlier time, based on current archaeological dates. This alternative view also needs to address the linguistic and osteological evidence pointing to origins in the Marquesas. The linguistic evidence seems particularly telling—at present— for arguing that the successful settling population was from the Marquesas.

34. Fornander 1878:165.

35. Fornander 1880:3.

36. Fornander 1878:168.

37. Fornander 1880:3.

38. For example, Buck 1938:249. One must point out—with the benefit of hindsight— that these dates would change radically using the 25 years/generation count of the 1950s–1970s, with 43 generations yielding a settlement date of A.D. 805. If 20 years/ generation is used—the count in vogue by a number of researchers—a date of A.D. 1020 results.

39. Cf. Elbert 1953:168; Emory 1959.

40. Libby 1951; Elbert 1953:168; Emory 1959.

41. Elbert 1953:167–168.

42. Emory, Bonk & Sinoto 1959:viii.

43. Emory, Bonk & Sinoto 1959:vii.

44. Emory & Sinoto 1969:10.

45. Emory & Sinoto 1969:10.

46. Emory & Sinoto 1969:12–14.

47. Emory & Sinoto 1969:10–14.

48. Emory 1959.

49. Emory & Sinoto 1969:10.

50. Cf. Emory, Bonk & Sinoto 1969.

51. Pearson, Kirch & Pietrusewsky 1969.

52. Kirch & Kelly 1975.

53. Cordy (1974a, b) and particularly Kirch (1973, 1974). Hommon (1976) suggested A.D. 400s–600s.

54. Cordy & Tuggle 1976; Tuggle, Cordy & Child 1977.

55. Cordy 1984; Kirch 1984.

56. Sinoto (1970, 1979) has long not accepted Sugg's early dates, and he argues that the Marquesas were settled ca. A.D. 300s, and therefore Hawai'i ca. A.D. 500s or 650–800s. But as, Kirch pointed out (1984:73–78, 1986), problems with the radiocarbon lab's dating of Sinoto's material may have existed and other Polynesian island dispersal dating is consistent with Suggs's dates. Also, Sinoto's early Hane site does not have its earliest layer, Layer VII, dated (Sinoto 1966, 1970), so Hane may date before the A.D. 300s.

57. Site 3321 in Honouliuli (Dicks, Haun & Rosendahl 1987:45). Recent work suggests that site 3321's early date may come from soil layers dating before human occupation

and that the site may have been first used in the 900s–1000s (Wolforth, Wulzen & Goodfellow 1997:4–2 to 4–3).

58. Bellows (Streck & Watanabe 1988; see also Tuggle 1997); site 2022 (J. Clark 1980; Erkelens 1993), site 2023 (J. Clark 1980; J. Allen 1981), and Maunawili sites (J. Allen 1993, 1989, and personal communication); Luluku sites (J. Allen 1987; Williams 1992). See Cordy (1996) for a summary of these sites.

59. Temporary habitations have been dated at Pāʻā ahupuaʻa on the shore, in the Kōloa district—A.D. 220–690 in Keoneloa Dune (site 4001) and A.D. 660–1270 in site 475 nearby (Firor and Rosendahl 1990:8, 35–36). A date in the A.D. 500s–900s from Hanalei (site D10-12) (Schilt 1980:57, 60) dates lithics which may have been associated with an agricultural site. A date possibly associated with an agricultural site, and thus perhaps permanent settlement, also came from an unclear context in Lumahaʻi, A.D. 200s–1000s (calibration in Hunt & Holsen 1991).

60. Cf. Hunt & Holsen (1991) for a list of dates. Contract archaeology projects continue to recover early dates in small numbers.

61. Davis, Haun & Rosendahl 1986:22; Chavet-Pond & Davis 1991:163–167.

62. Chavet-Pond & Davis 1991:169.

63. Chavet-Pond & Davis 1991:179; Davis, Haun & Rosendahl 1986:20.

64. Davis, Haun & Rosendahl 1986:20; Chavet-Pond & Davis 1991:61.

65. Dunn, Haun & Goodfellow 1991:9; Davis, Haun & Rosendahl 1986:19, 25.

66. Bath, M. Rosendahl & P. Rosendahl 1984:53.

67. Beggerly 1990:309–313.

68. Walker, Haun & Rosendahl 1988:113.

69. Cf. Spriggs & Anderson 1993; Cordy 1996. Also, Dye 1993, personal communication.

70. Kirch 1985: 84-85.

71. Hunt & Holsen 1991.

72. Tuggle 1997.

73. Dye 1992.

74. Spriggs & Anderson 1993.

75. Michner 1959.

76. Cf. Sharp 1956, 1963.

77. Cf. Golson (ed.) 1962.

78. Interestingly, many of the knowledgeable explorers and missionaries of the late 1700s and early 1800s observed actual cases of one-way settlement within Central Polynesia (see examples in Sharp 1963). This is not to say two-way settlement did not occur in Central Polynesia. It did (cf. Irwin 1992, for the theoretical basis).

79. Finney 1977:1277, 1283–1284; 1991.

80. Finney 1977:1283–1284; 1991.

81. Sharp 1963:16, 34.

82. Sharp 1963:32.

83. Sharp 1963:35.

84. Levison, Ward & Webb 1973.

85. Finney 1967, 1977, 1979; Lewis 1972.

86. Gladwin 1970; Lewis 1972.

87. Tongans and Tahitians told Cook that sun, stars and direct wind and surface seas (run of the seas) were key variables (Sharp 1963:34–35).

88. Finney 1979:348.

89. In the late 1600s and early 1700s, a number of Central Carolinean canoes had been blown off course and landed on islands in the Philippines 1,200 miles directly west, as documented by Spanish mission enquiries (cf. Hezel 1983:36–43). In two observed cases in the 1690s, the castaways married into the Samar Island population and stayed (cf. Hezel 1983:436–439). The same was true for most cases (Hezel 1983:40–41). But, apparently at least one canoe returned home successfully with tales of the new islands (Hezel 1983:41), although it is not clear if any navigator attempted a voyage back to the Philippines. In the early 1800s, two Woleai islanders from the Central Carolines were found in the Marshall Islands, 2,000 miles to the east (Kotzebue 1821, 1830). They were survivors from a canoe that had been lost in a storm and sailed on. They were so far out of their navigational net that they did not attempt to return. Another example comes from Kosrae. Kosrean clan origin myths document several canoes arriving at different times from the Marshalls to the

northeast and from the Gilberts to the southeast—one-way voyages with no return (Sarfert 1920). However, by the early 1800s, the Marshallese were expanding their navigational net and raiding to quite near Kosrae, and had become aware of the island's location.

90. But recall Micronesians would be more familiar with northern hemisphere stars and major wave patterns than would have Central Polynesians. So, this test is somewhat biased towards success.

91. Cf. Beggerly 1990; Wickler, Athens & Ward 1991; Athens & Ward 1991.

92. McArthur, Saunders & Tweedie 1976:313. Their predictive modeling is more complex.

93. Cf. Kirch 1984, 1989. See Pawley and K. Green (1971), Biggs, Walsh & Waga (1970), Pawley & R. Green (1984) for language reconstructions.

94. Kirch 1984:62–63.

95. Kirch 1984; 1989:21, 23.

96. Harner 1970; Cordy 1974b.

97. Kirch 1974:63; Cordy 1974a, b.

98. Kirch 1984:57. See Yen (1971, 1974) on sweet potato dispersal out of central East Polynesia.

99. Yen 1973; Kirch 1984:55.

100. Yen 1973; Earle 1978; Kirch 1984:57; Spriggs 1982.

101. Schilt 1980 for Hanalei; Kailua's site 2002 on O'ahu (J. Clark 1980; J. Allen 1981; Erkelens 1993); Riley (1975) for Hālawa. J. Allen (1987:249) argues that an early truncated layer (VIII) exposed in G5-85 in Luluku, Kāne'ohe, O'ahu, included pondfield soils once associated with terraced fields.

102. Kirch 1984:56.

103. Pearson, Kirch & Pietrusewsky 1967; Kirch & Kelly 1975; Davis Haun & Rosendahl 1986. Bellows may well not have been a permanent habitation site (cf. Tuggle 1997; Cordy & Tuggle 1976). Also, pig and dog often are not yet clearly established in the earliest layers of these sites (e.g., at Bellows).

104. Kirch 1984:59.

105. Kirch 1984:53; Sinoto 1979.

106. Kirch 1984:59.

107. Kirch & Dye 1979.

108. Emory, Bonk & Sinoto 1968; 1969:10–11.

109. Goto 1986; Emory, Bonk & Sinoto 1969:9.

110. Kirch 1984.

111. Dye & Steadman 1990; Emory & Sinoto 1961:17.

112. Kirch 1984:57.

113. Kirch 1984:57.

114. Kirch 1984:53.

115. Kirch 1984; 1989:21.

116. Kirch 1984:53.

117. Kirch 1984:53.

118. Kirch 1984:53.

119. The "patu" hand clubs once considered part of Archaic East Polynesian Culture appear now to have been developments after the voyagers left for Hawai'i, since they were not found in Hawai'i nor in the earliest layers in the Marquesas (Kirch 1984:78; 1989).

120. Walsh & Biggs 1966; Biggs, Walsh & Waga 1970.

121. Kirch 1984:88.

122. Vayda & Rappaport 1963:134–135; see also Kirch's (1985:285–286) excellent emphasis of this point, using this quote.

123. Emory & Sinoto 1969:Fig. 1; Cordy 1986b.

124. Cordy 1986a.

125. Kelly 1969.

126. Emory, Bonk & Sinoto 1969:19.

127. Emory & Sinoto 1969:13.

128. Kirch 1985:285; Emory, Bonk & Sinoto 1969:27.

129. Kirch 1985:286.

130. Emory, Bonk & Sinoto 1959; 1969:vii, 37, 43.

131. Emory, Bonk & Sinoto 1959, 1969.

132. Emory & Sinoto 1969:10.

133. Emory & Sinoto 1969:12–14.

134. Emory & Sinoto 1969:12–14. Green (1971) in a reevaluation of the fishhook seriation agreed with this revision.

135. Kirch 1985:83–85.

136. Emory, Bonk & Sinoto 1969.

137. Emory, Bonk & Sinoto 1969:10.

138. Emory & Sinoto 1969:5.

139. Elizabeth Handy 1972 (1958): 210–212.

140. Beggerly 1987.

141. Emory, Bonk & Sinoto 1959 (1968):6; 1969:10.

142. Muliwai fishpond just behind the dune in Waipi'o might have been reclaimed lagoonal lands. Muliwai refers to an area where a stream mingles with seawater (Malo 1951:18).

143. Newman 1968.

144. Outlier settlements would not have needed to forgo eating agricultural produce, as they could have obtained these from the original settlement until their crops were sufficient.

145. Cordy 1974a.

146. Cf. Birdsell 1957; Kirch 1984:96.

147. Cordy 1974a, 1974b, 1978. See also Tuggle, 1979:190.

148. Pu'u Ali'i and Wai'Ahukini (Emory & Sinoto 1969); Puapua'a (site 9962, C-shape and 9963, a cave; Landrum, Haun, Rosendahl & Delimont 1990), Kapua (site 3705, tube cave: Haun & Walker 1988:34, D-19), Kapa'anui (site 12444, L-shaped enclosure; Dunn & Rosendahl 1989), Kou (site 12434, terrace; Dunn & Rosendahl 1989), Kawaihae (site 14068, midden deposit; Carlson & Rosendahl 1990a), and 'Anaeho'omalu (pre-A.D. 900 volcanic glass dates at E1-24, -67, -68, -133 and a radocarbon date of A.D. 890–1210 from E1-28—Jensen 1989b; 2 radiocarbon dates at E1-148 of A.D. 640–1040 and 890–1300, 1364–1375—Jensen 1990a).

149. Cf. Cordy 1994.

150. Fornander 1880:44, 60–61. Westervelt (1987:35–36) and Beckwith (1940:178) identify 'Ai-lā'au as the earlier god to whom Kīlauea belonged.

## NOTES FOR CHAPTER 5

1. Beckwith 1972:105.

2. Cordy 1974b; Burtchard 1996. Kirch (1985:303–304) also emphasizes population growth fueled this expansion.

3. I believe that place name studies usually have very weak arguments for historical connections with distant Polynesian islands. However, a study of place names on each island in the Hawaiian Islands, which looks at distribution of names that are not generic names, might possibly suggest historical links. Thus, I have noted this Nāpo'opo'o name tie as a lure for future work.

4. Welch 1988.

5. Three caves (E1-148/State site 12,387, E1-103A, and E1-297) were located adjacent to the fishpond. Another (E1-54/ 12,362) was behind on an inland-heading trail. Four other caves (E1-24, E1-28, E1-67d, E1-68a) were not far to the north of the pond. E1-148 has radiocarbon dates of A.D. 640–1040 and A.D. 890–1300, 1364–1375 (Jensen 1990a:45) and 4 volcanic glass dates in the A.D. 1000s–1100s (Barrera 1971:101). E1-103 has a radiocarbon date of A.D. 1040–1400 (Barrera 1971:103—750 BP) and 8 volcanic glass dates in the A.D. 1000s–1100s (Barrera 1971:101). E1-297 has 4 volcanic glass dates in the A.D. 900s–1000s (Barrera 1971:103). E1-54 has a radiocarbon date of A.D. 980–1420 (Jensen 1990a:46). E1-24 has 10 volcanic glass dates between the A.D. 600s–1100s and two radiocarbon dates in the A.D. 1100s–1300s (Jensen 1989b:63-64, 69). E1-28 has one radiocarbon date of A.D. 890–1210 (Jensen 1989:69). E1-67d has 4 volcanic glass dates in the A.D. 600s–1000s and one radiocarbon date of A.D. 1030–1290 (Jensen 1989:67, 70). E1-68a has 4 volcanic glass dates in the A.D. 700s–1000s (Jensen 1989:67–68). Abundant fishing tools and fish remains were found in many of these caves (cf. Barrera 1971; Jensen 1989b, 1990a).

6. E1-277 is the structure which has the early date. See Barrera, 1971; see Cordy (1975, 1981) for permanent habitation site interpretations. A second permanent habitation site at 'Anaeho'omalu pond (E1-126 and -127—two enclosed platforms) might also date to this time period—if the firepit (dating A.D. 1030–1410—745 + 115

BP) from the outside midden is contemporaneous with the platforms. However, no radiocarbon dates are available from the structures, and volcanic glass dates go back only to the A.D. 1500s, so contemporaneity of the platforms with the early date in the midden is still questionable. (See Barrera, 1971, for data.)

7. Thompson & Rosendahl (1992:7), A.D. 770–1020 from darkly stained soil in an irrigation canal.

8. Cordy, Tainter, Renger & Hitchcock 1991:465.

9. Schilt 1984:276.

10. Walker & Rosendahl 1994. A.D. 1000–1280 in site 4659 (lava tube).

11. Hammatt, Borthwick, Chiogioji, Robins, Collins & Novak 1995.

12. Cordy, Tainter, Renger & Hitchcock 1991:560.

13. The reader who wishes details is encouraged to browse through the State Historic Preservation Division's library of contract archaeology reports for Kona district. These contain numerous references to small irregular terraces, mounds, modified outcrops, and pits—all features associated with lower elevation and low-rainfall cultivation in Kona, associated with the informal fields of Kona.

14. Handy & Handy 1972:164–5; Kepelino 1932:152–156; Wilkes, 1845, 4:105 (central Kona).

15. This issue of seasonal planting is a complex one. Staple crops (taro, sweet potato) required 6–9 months to mature at a minimum. The rainy season in leeward areas is at best only 7 months long—and more realistically 5–6 months—and even then rain mostly comes in a few storms. A question arises, "Is this really enough rainfall to argue for seasonal cultivation?" Also, no one has yet gone through the historic literature and documented in what months crops were planted, cultivated, or harvested in these areas. We do know that some farm lots were awarded in these zones (e.g., in Keauhou and Kealakekua). It may be that year-round cultivation occurred—with occasional loss of crops to drought. More work is needed on the questions of seasonality in Hawai'i and how cultivation in lower elevations on slope lands on leeward sides was done.

16. Ellis 1963:131.

17. Burgett & Rosendahl 1993:36.

18. Tuggle & Griffin 1973.

19. In Waikā and Kahuā at the border with south Kohala, dating has occurred, but only informal fields have been found in the uplands, and findings suggest cultivation and permanent settlement began quite late.

## NOTES FOR CHAPTER 6

1. Maly translation in Graves & Goodfellow 1993:B-13.

2. Fornander 1880:18.

3. Some dates for permanent housing from Keāhole to Kapua in the 1200s–1300s follow. This is far from a complete list; these are only examples from the archaeological reports.

**Kohanaiki ahupua'a**: site 14630, complex of 4 rectangular platforms on shore A.D. 1020–1400, 1040–1420, 1150–1520; site 14627, complex of 1 enclosure and 2 terraces on shore A.D. 1327–1334, 1390–1660; site 14583, complex of paving, enclosure and smaller structures on shore A.D. 1327–1334, 1390–1660 (O'Hare & Goodfellow 1992:102, 114).

**Kaloko ahupua'a**: see note 2.

**Pāhoehoe ahupua'a**: site 19668, buried habitation deposit of some size on shore, which may well reflect permanent habitation. It has two dates ranging back to the late A.D. 1200s and early 1300s (A.D. 1289–1670, 1784–1794; A.D. 1301–1523, 1562–1630) (Head, Pua-Kaipo, Goodfellow 1994).

**Kapua ahupua'a**: Three temporary habitations in the informal agricultural areas behind the shore (note 5 below) suggest some permanent habitations on the shore were in use at this time—although no shore sites have as yet been excavated or dated.

**Keōpū ahupua'a**: A large cemetery was here at European contact. Burials began in the A.D. 1250–1400 period (Han et al. 1986), suggesting associated permanent habitations in Keōpū.

4. Cordy, Tainter, Renger & Hitchcock 1991.

5. Dated temporary habitations in the lower Kona field zone (the kula zone), which indicate upland fields were increasing in area and coastal population was increasing. This is also not an exhaustive listing.

**Kohanaiki ahupua'a**: site 14611, paving A.D. 1260–1670 (3 dates); 14574, lava tube A.D. 1180–1400s (O'Hare & Goodfellow 1992:102, 114).

**Honokōhau ahupua'a**: 13019, lava tube A.D. 980–1650 (Donham 1990a); other sites late 1300s on (Jensen & Goodfellow 1993).

**Lanihau ahupua'a**: D8-20, midden A.D. 1305–1420 (Schilt 1984:276).

**Keōpū ahupua'a**: D8-33 (cave) A.D. 1300s-1600s (Schilt 1984:276).

**Puapua'a ahupua'a**: 14074, C-shaped enclosure A.D. 1030–1470 (Carlson & Rosendahl 1990b); 14081, cave A.D. 1160–1480 and 1280–1640 (Carlson & Rosendahl 1990b).

**Hōlualoa ahupua'a**: 18046, subsurface deposit AD 1159–1415 at 400–500-foot elevation among formal walled fields (Fager & Graves 1993:17); 7976, terrace A.D. 1335–1640 at 140–255-foot elevation below informal fields (Hammatt, Borthwick & Shideler 1986).

**Keauhou ahupua'a**: 15,192, platform A.D. 1240–1450 in formal agricultural field zone (Burtchard 1996).

**Kapua ahupua'a**: 9906, C-shaped enclosure within complex in lower kula zone near informal agricultural features, A.D. 1238–1386; 11727, L-shaped enclosure in upper kula near informal agricultural features, A.D. 1384–1464 and 1389–1513 (two dates); 11749, C-shaped enclosure with branch coral, possibly shrine, associated with informal agricultural features in the lower kula zone, A.D. 1303–1467—all volcanic glass dates (Haun & Walker 1988). Two other temporary habitations in non-agricultural areas fall into the 1300s–1400s period, based on volcanic glass dates (Haun & Walker 1988). As noted in earlier chapters, while volcanic glass dating is currently in disrepute, work has shown close correspondence with paired radiocarbon dates (cf. most recently Komori 1993). Thus, these dates might not be far off true dates. Future radiocarbon dating should clarify the findings.

6. Mahana volcanic glass dates of A.D. 935 (site MB-1) and 980 (MB-4) (Hunt 1976); radiocarbon dates for Pinao Bay (Layer II Pu'u Ali'i), and Kapalaoa/Kaulana bays—A.D. 1240–1385 for a fire hearth in an extensive subsurface burn layer associated possibly with agriculture (Cleghorn 1984:16). An increase in the number of dated fishing shelters in the Wai'Ahukini area of Pākini ahupua'a (Sinoto & Kelly 1975) might indicate an increasing permanent population—although the sample is quite small and still could reflect visiting fishermen from other ahupua'a.

7. Nine sites at Kahuku have had volcanic glass dates in the A.D. 1200s–1300s (Haun & Walker 1987:28–30). At least one is from a permanent habitation site; the others are from temporary habitations.

8. Tuggle & Griffin 1973:56–66.

9. Burgett & Rosendahl 1993:36—site 13639, rectangular terrace.

10. Cf. Hammatt & Shideler (1989:26); S. Clark & Kirch (1983); and Welch (1983:175) for Waimea upland sites dating to these years. The shore areas of Kawaihae have at least two temporary habitation sites of similar ages—site 14068 (midden) with an A.D. 1160–1400 date (and an earlier date) and site 14063 (tube cave) with an A.D. 1220–1430 date (Carlson & Rosendahl 1990a:23–24).

11. Fornander 1916:215–220. Kamakau (1991) noted Hīkapoloa married a Kona woman and lived inland at Pu'uepa. Another story involving Hīkapoloa (the "Legend of Kaulanapoikii") placed him as chief of Pu'uepa (the location of Mo'okini heiau) and had his house on Pu'uiki above Kukuipahu (Fornander 1917(4):560–568). These stories might reflect post-unification times after the conquest of Kukuipahu. Pu'uepa is a central location in northern Kohala and may have become more important with unification.

12. Fornander 1880:49.

13. Cf. Cordy 1996.

14. The Hawai'i genealogies place Pili ca. A.D. 1320–1340, 1360–1380 or 1380–1400, depending on how one interprets the successive four names after Pili—as sons, contemporaries, etc. (see chap. 7). Fornander's account has Pili replacing Kapawa in Waipi'o, possibly two generations after 'Olopana, with Kunaka representing the intervening generation. Thus, the Hawai'i genealogies suggest 'Olopana could have ruled as early as A.D. 1280–1300 or as late as A.D. 1340–1360. Hīkapoloa would be two generations earlier—1240–1260 or 1300–1320.

15. Interestingly, in dry Kohala two different settlement and political zones seem to have developed prior to the 1200s and to have lasted until late in prehistory—one focused on Waimea and Kawaihae in the south, and the other in north Kohala up to 'Upolu Point. The uplands of Waikā and Kahuā at today's border between North and South Kohala may mark an environmental border between these zones. Archaeological survey suggests that Waikā and Kahuā evidently never had formal terraced fields, in contrast to the low terraced fields in the rest of leeward north Kohala and in contrast to the fields with supplemental irrigation found in the southern Kohala uplands of Kawaihae and Waimea. The informal fields and associated temporary habitation shelters dated so far in Waikā and Kahuā are post–A.D. 1400 in age (two temporary habitations in upland Waikā—Hammatt & Borthwick 1986:65), as are permanent and temporary habitations on the shore (two permanent habitations and one temporary habitation in coastal Kahuā—Graves & Franklin 1994:44), so perhaps this environmental border area was not fully used until after this time.

It is suggested here that these two zones of leeward Kohala—Waimea and the south versus the lands to the north—had different settlement origins and histories, perhaps with Waimea and south Kohala settled out of nearby Waipi'o and Hāmākua and with the northern leeward Kohala areas colonized from wet Kohala settlements. A separate historical development may be the reason why Waimea was a special large land unit, an 'okana, within Kohala until ca. 1865 (Barrere 1983:25–26). This hypothesis has yet to be tested with archaeological evidence. One could equally argue that all of leeward Kohala and Waimea were settled from wet Kohala or that all settlers of dry Kohala came from Waimea, or varying combinations. But the nearness of Waimea to Waipi'o and much earlier dates for permanent habitations and agricultural sites in Waimea and from permanent habitations on the coast seaward of Waimea (in the lands of 'Anaeho'omalu and Kalāhuipua'a) are intriguing clues perhaps pointing to a different homeland for the Waimea and Kawaihae areas than that for leeward Kohala settlements.

16. Using the O'ahu ruling-line genealogy, 'Olopana's and his brother's (Mo'ikeha's) generation is estimated at A.D. 1340–1360. Kila, Mo'ikeha's son, and Kunaka would be at A.D. 1360–1380, and Kapawa would then be at 1380–1400, with Pili supplanting Kapawa.

17. Fornander 1880:49 ('Olopana), 21–22 (Kapawa); 1917, 4(1):128–152 (Kunaka).

18. Fornander stated that Muli'eleali'i's senior son, Kumuhonua, "seems to have remained in possession...possibly of the nominal sovereignty of the island" of O'ahu (1880:49).

19. Fornander 1880:49; 1919, 6(2):246. Lu'ukia's brother was Kaumaili'ula, a noted Nana'ulu chief of Kohala (Fornander 1880:57).

20. Fornander 1880:56–57.

21. Fornander 1880:49.

22. Fornander 1880:50.

23. Fornander 1880:53–54 on Mo'ikeha being ruler on Kaua'i. Kunaka's rule in Waipi'o is described in part of "The History of Moikeha" recorded in Fornander's Collections (Fornander 1917, 4(1):128–152).

24. Fornander has Kapawa born at Kūkaniloko, the son of Nanakaoko, a chief of O'ahu (Fornander 1880:21; see also Malo 1951:5 noting Kapawa was an O'ahu chief). Fornander then has him become ruler on Hawai'i (Fornander 1880:22). No other accounts, however, associate Kapawa with Hawai'i or Waipi'o; rather they have Lanakawai (or Lonokawai) and his son, La'au, as the last Hawai'i Island chiefs before Pili, and they identify Kapawa as a ruler in that line 16 generations earlier (1840 Malo 1951:6, 238; 1858 Pogue 1978:5–6, 66–67; 1868 Kepelino in Beckwith 1932:20, 58; 1862 *Hoku Pakipika* article—Fornander Collection 1919, 6(2):320). Fornander collected a fragmentary account of Pā'ao which specifically stated that Hawai'i was without chiefs due to the crimes of Kapawa, so he concluded that Kapawa was misplaced in the genealogies and should actually have been the last ruler prior to Pili (Fornander 1919, 6(2):286). Post-1880 researchers have been split in their acceptance of Fornander's conclusions. For example, Cartwright (1933) and Kalākaua (1990 [1888]:97) followed Fornander; Stokes (1930b) agreed with Malo and the others.

25. Fornander 1917, 4:560–568, see note 10.

26. No archaeological evidence has yet been used to successfully identify polity sizes of this period. Several years ago it was suggested that there were unoccupied buffers between Kona and Kohala (Cordy 1981) and Kohala and Hāmākua (Tuggle & Tomonari-Tuggle 1980). More recent information in the proposed buffer in the Kona area suggests that permanent settlement had begun somewhat earlier. Thus, the buffer concept needs reconsideration given new information. Rather than lack of population, perhaps low population density in buffer zones is the key variable to focus on. No early heiau have been identified or dated, so styles of heiau reflective of different polities cannot yet be identified. No early high chiefs houses have been found either, so evaluation of political hierarchies cannot yet occur.

27. Ka-Miki story, Maly translation, in Graves & Goodfellow (1993:B-13).

28. Fornander 1917, 4(1):134, 142—The History of Moikeha. This assumes the Kila story had not been altered later in prehistory, and reflected the late prehistoric situation with its luakini and pu'uhonua.

29. If Paka'alana heiau was a human sacrificial heiau in Kila and Kunaka's times, it predated the arrival of Pā'ao, who is today given credit by many for the first building of sacrificial heiau.

30. Fornander 1917, 4(1):136–137.

31. Fornander 1878:165–169.

32. Cf. Reeve 1994:163.

33. Hommon 1989:8.

34. In the Carolinean navigation system in Micronesia, where active voyaging takes place, each navigator would undertake several voyages per year; some to nearby islands, others to islands farther away (Gladwin 1970). This might account for 4 long voyages per year for a small island with but four navigators, 560–800 such voyages over 140–200 years. If active voyaging was truly occurring in Hawai'i, surely more long voyages would be expected.

35. Fornander 1880:7.

36. Handy 1930; Buck 1938; Beckwith 1940.

37. Fornander 1880:3, 5.

38. Fornander's assumption is seen in this quote: "Doubtless many other southern chiefs visited the Hawaiian group and established themselves there, but time has blotted their names from the traditional record" (1880:46).

39. Handy 1930.

40. Buck 1938:63.

41. Buck 1938:95. Buck listed a number of chiefs as voyagers arriving from Kahiki (1938:252); yet nowhere in the 1800s accounts that I have seen are there traditions for these chiefs being voyagers.

42. Buck 1938:255.

43. Fornander 1880:7, 59.

44. Fornander 1919, 6(2):251–252.

45. Fornander 1919, 6(2):252.

46. Fornander 1919, 6(2):253.

47. Fornander 1919, 6(2):253. Here his conclusion was based in part on the fact that the traditions of the "pre-voyaging" period were no longer recollected. He assumed this was because of the dominating replacement by the chiefly voyagers.

48. Fornander 1880:48–49.

49. Fornander 1880:53–55.

50. All voyages in table 6-1 date to the late 1200s–early 1300s A.D., except for Kamapi'ikai whose period is not stated in the one account found for his voyages. Also, the Kamaunu-a-Niho & Humu story is only referenced to the migration period in general (Fornander 1880:43). Other voyagers are mentioned in the accounts, but they belong to the earlier, mythological periods and they are not covered in this chapter or table: Wahanui of O'ahu, Hema of Hāna, Kaha'i-a-Hema of Hawai'i, Pupu-hulu-ana of Hawai'i or Kaua'i, the Pele family, Lonoka'ehu, and the brothers Aukele-nui-aiku and Kāne-apua. Kaulu-a-Kalana, Pupu-hulu-ana, and Aukele and Kaneapua stories are trickster stories (cf. Beckwith 1940). Also, the Hema and Kaha'i stories, along with those of 'Aikanaka, are similar to those found throughout Polynesia, also pointing to an early shared mythology (Beckwith 1940:240–258).

51. 'Olopana and Lu'ukia were husband and wife. Mo'ikeha was 'Olopana's brother. They were sons of Muli'eleali'i of O'ahu. Lu'ukia was the granddaughter of Hīkapoloa of Kohala. Different versions of the story exist, see table 6-3.

52. Kaumaili'ula was a brother of Lu'ukia. Kaupe'a was a daughter of 'Olopana. Kaumaili'ula and Kaupe'a were temporarily married, which is the core of the story.

53. All were sons of Mo'ikeha.

54. La'a was a son of an O'ahu chief (Ahukai). He was adopted by Mo'ikeha in one account. See table 6-3.

55. Son of Ho'okamali'i, noted in Voyage #3 of table 6-1.

56. See table 6-2 for variant stories.

57. A chief of O'ahu. This is a trickster story (cf. Beckwith 1940).

58. A chief of O'ahu.

59. Brothers. Both had children by the daughter of Kamaunu and Kalana, who were voyagers noted in Voyage #11 of table 6-1.

60. Ha'inakolo was a sister of the 'Olopana in Voyage #1 of table 6-1. The core of this story is her failed marriage with Keānini.

61. Kamaunu and Kalana were husband and wife.

62. A Kohala priest.

63. Lu'ukia's invented the pā'ū, and it was said to have been brought back by her daughter Kaupe'a (Fornander 1880:62).

64. Pogue 1978:6; Malo 1951:7; Kamakau 1991:109; Fornander Collection 1916–1917:128; Fornander 1880:62. These drums' association with La'amaikahiki are mentioned in a Pukui proverb, "Na pahu kapu a La'amaikahiki, 'Ōpuku lāua o Hāwea" (Pukui 1983:249, Item 2283). See Barrere's discussion of this drum form (Kamakau 1991:122, note 15).

65. Malo 1951:7.

66. Fornander 1916–1917, 4(1):128; Fornander 1880:60, note 8.

67. Pogue 1978:6.

68. Kaha'i is said to have brought breadfruit and planted it at Pu'uloa on O'ahu (Kamakau 1991:9, 77, 110). Fornander (1880:54) said this was but one "species" [variety probably] of breadfruit. Other accounts existed for the origin of breadfruit (Beckwith 1940:98).

69. Pogue 1978:5–6; Malo 1951:6; Kamakau 1991:100; Fornander 1878:201; Fornander 1880:22, 36, 63; Emerson 1893.

70. Dibble 1909:10.

71. Kepelino (Beckwith 1932:58, 197); Kamakau 1991:97–100; Fornander 1878:86; Fornander 1880:22, 38.

72. Fornander 1880:63.

73. Pogue 1978:5–6; Malo 1951:6–7; *Hoku Pakipika* Feb. 13, 1862 article in Fornander 1919, 6(2):320; Kamakau 1991:3–5, 100.

74. Ellis 1963:283; Pogue 1978:47; Kepelino 1932:20, 58; Kamakau 1991:100; Fornander 1880:37.

75. Beckwith 1940:370 [no source].

76. Puget in Sahlins (1981:25–26); Pogue 1978:47; Fornander 1880:36.

77. Kamakau 1991:92.

78. Fornander 1878:201, 1880:45. "Some legends attribute to Luhaukapawa [Kaulu's astrologer-priest-navigator], in a general way, the introduction of the tabus; but it is most probable that he only enforced their stricter observance, and perhaps added some new regulations..." (Fornander 1880:45).

79. Kamakau 1991:96; Fornander 1880:25.

80. Kamakau 1991:111; Fornander 1880: 43–44.

81. Fornander 1880:28–29.

82. Fornander 1880:23.

83. Fornander 1880:28. Based on Fornander's presentation, Hommon (1989:4) also noted that Haho and the 'Aha Ali'i were foreign.

84. Fornander 1880:61. Seven years later, in the introduction to Kalākaua's volume of legends (Kalākaua 1990 [1888]:20–21, 39, 47–48), Daggett followed Kamakau's and Fornander's Samoa origin for Pā'ao and Pili, and he said Pā'ao "somewhat disturbed the religious practices of the people by the introduction of new rites and two or three new gods," "strengthened and enlarged the scope of the tabu," and changed the form of the heiau "with the masses mingled less freely in the ceremonies of sacrifice." He did not associate human sacrifice with Pā'ao, and one assumes that he consulted with Kalākaua in the preparation of the volume. So, this may have been the prevailing view of that time. Kalākaua, himself, in his Kanipahu story, said Pili came from Samoa (1990:97).

85. N. Emerson 1893:5–12.

86. Westervelt 1913:57. This is a long, interesting story, with many new elements

87. Stokes 1928:41; Handy 1930:87; Buck 1938:255; Beckwith 1940:370.

88. Cf. Malo 1951:7; Dibble 1909 [1843]:4–5.

89. It is worth noting that Tahitian missionaries were present in the 1830s and had a considerable influence in the courts of Ka'ahumanu in Honolulu and Kuakini on Hawai'i (cf. Barrere & Sahlins 1979; Barrere 1989). They definitely transferred information. One Tahitian, Apo, in the time of Kamehameha I was noted for his ability to chant genealogies (Kamakau 1991:79).

90. Dibble 1909:89.

91. Dibble 1909:8.

92. Dibble 1909:8–9.

93. Dibble 1909:9–10.

94. Fornander 1878:168–169; 1880:45–46. Fornander's claim for a Marquesan link—not noted in this chapter's text—was that the Puna family of Kaua'i was likely to have been from Hiva Oa, because Fornander saw a Marquesan genealogy that had several Punas at about that time (1880:46).

95. Fornander 1880:34.

96. Fornander 1880:51–52. Huahine Island in the Society Islands also has such an Ava Moa, as may other islands.

97. Emerson 1893:15, his footnote 28.

98. Henry 1896:9–13.

99. Henry 1897:18.

100. Henry 1897:19; 1928:567. One might note here that mou'a is Tahitian for mountain and that the similar Hawaiian word is mauna. The Hawaiian traditions do not refer to Maunaulanuiakea. Although not a linguist, I wonder if an error exists here in Henry's argument.

101. Later, however, some of Smith's conclusions and methods were questioned. See Buck (1938:112) doubting the traditions of Rarotonga as completely factual, particularly in tracing distant origins. See Simmons (1976:38–42, 58, 71–73, 108) on Smith's unreliable dating of traditional stories and genealogies; (1976:8, 17) on problems with Smith's methods and translations ("Smith, on occasion, allowed his preconceived theories of migration sequences into New Zealand to affect his reliability as a translator and editor and his ability to draw objective conclusions from traditional evidence," p. 8); and on Smith's inaccurate interpretations of oral traditions as evidence for migration waves (cf. 1976:315–321).

102. Smith 1897:12.

103. Smith 1897:14.

104. Smith 1920, 1910. Interestingly, in the early 1920s, some scholars in Hawai'i still held to the Samoa source for Pā'ao (Thrum 1924:17).

105. Stokes 1928; Buck 1938:255.

106. Stokes 1921, 1925. See also Brigham (1899, 1903) and Rose (1978) on these belts.

107. Stokes 1928:41; 1921:32–33.

108. Stokes 1921; 1925:26; 1928:42; Rose 1978:33–38, 45.

109. Stokes 1928:42.

110. Stokes 1928:42–45.

111. Handy 1930; Buck 1938; Beckwith 1940. Handy noted that periods of culture were apparent in Polynesian linguistics (he referenced Churchill), myths (Dixon) and other areas. Handy again explained the origin of these periods via migration.

112. It is quite likely that Cook and Banks may have popularized Tahiti and the Society Island's centrality in anthropological theory. Although Tonga was far more complex in hierarchical political organization than the Society Islands, Cook and Banks heavily emphasized the chiefs and political organization of the Society Islands.

113. Emory 1933.

114. Emory 1928; Walker 1931:294; Emory 1943:11 (respectively). Other archaeologists working in Hawai'i disagreed that such temple types were early. McAllister, who surveyed O'ahu and Kaho'olawe for the Bishop Museum, found no such heiau on those islands. He argued that if there were earlier forms they should have been present. So, he concluded that these were local developments and that there was no temple evidence for two migrations (1933:60). Bennett, who surveyed Kaua'i for the Bishop Museum, found no such early temple forms either and no temple evidence for two migrations, although he cautioned that the old forms might have been destroyed (1931:53).

115. Handy 1930:6.

116. Cf. Buck 1938:255. and Handy 1930:87. It is important to emphasize that Handy closely interacted with Kenneth Emory. Indeed, Handy (1930:87) noted that Emory had pointed out to him that the feather girdle, human sacrifice and ahu of marae were features brought to Hawai'i by Pā'ao and Pili.

117. Buck (1938:255) supported the Pā'ao-Raiatea tie, but he saw complications with the 'Olopana ma tie to northern Tahiti because he knew 'Olopana and Ru'utia were also in New Zealand lore (Buck 1938:49). His argument for Raiatea as Pā'ao's home was that the things Pā'ao brought were clearly from Central Polynesia, thus Savaii in Samoa could not be Pā'ao's origin place. He concluded Havai'i (Raiatea) in the Societies was the correct origin place (1938:255–256). One wonders how Buck transformed Kamakau's and Fornander's 'Upolu to Savai'i. Buck did note that Pā'ao had landholdings in Vava'u (corresponding with Kamakau and Fornander), but he claimed this was Borabora in the Societies, whose old name was Vava'u (1938:255). This conclusion probably was based on Stokes's (1928) analysis that 'Upolu and Vavau were the old names for Taha'a and Borabora in the Society Islands. Beckwith (1940:440) linked the old names for Taha'a and Borabora to a translation of Ka'ulu's chant by Emory. The original source for this linkage again may well have been Percy Smith.

118. Beckwith 1940:370. As an aside, Beckwith (1940:38) did note that Oro worship may have been later than the migrations to Hawai'i—apparently because Oro did not appear in Hawai'i. But, Handy's entire list of Society Island traits was based on Raiatean and Society Island culture during Oro's time. They cannot be separated.

119. Beckwith 1972:141.

120. Elbert 1953:165–166.

121. Emory 1959:32. The stories included knowledge of geography gained through European contact. Emory (1959:32) said the story "has every appearance of a post-European neo-myth, of which there are many composed in answer to questions and suggestions made by foreigners." See also Barrere (1969).

122. Emory 1959:32.

123. Emory, Bonk & Sinoto 1959; Sinoto 1962.

124. Emory & Sinoto 1964.

125. Emory & Sinoto 1964:159.

126. Emory & Sinoto 1964:159.

127. Suggs 1961.

128. Sinoto 1966, 1970, 1979.

129. Spriggs & Anderson 1993; Kirch 1986; Emory 1979; Sinoto & McCoy 1975.

130. Green 1966.

131. Cf. Oliver 1974:1105.

132. Archaeological dates for large temples on Mo'orea (Green 1967:155, 157, 160–162), at Taputapuatea on Raiatea (Emory & Sinoto 1965), and on Tahiti (Garanger 1967) have placed them only in the A.D. 1600s–1700s.

133. One item that Handy credited to later chiefly times in the Society Islands has been found archaeologically, but in earliest times in the Society Islands. A large double-hulled sailing canoe was found in waterlogged deposits on Huahine by Sinoto dating quite early—the A.D. 800s–1200s (Sinoto 1979). Thus. Handy was also wrong in attributing simple canoes to early settlers and "complex" large double-hulled canoes to later settlers.

134. Taputapuatea's original name apparently had been Feoro (Oliver 1974:892)—perhaps an association with Oro and late Tahitian culture?

135. As an aside, it should be noted that the Hawaiian traditions as recorded in the early and mid-1800s did not list large temples, red-feather girdles, human sacrifice, or high status kin groups as items brought by the voyagers. These were all interpretations and later assertions by anthropologists and historians. Fornander assumed temples of large sizes were brought. Red-feather girdles do not appear as a voyaging item until Westervelt's 1913 story of Pā'ao and Stokes' articles of the 1920s. Human sacrifice links to Pā'ao do not appear in the literature until well after Fornander—and Fornander did not associate it with Pā'ao; he only assumed it was introduced or was present and increased. The arrival of high status kin groups is strictly a 1920s–1930s migration invention—the arrival of the chiefly wave. The Hawaiian traditions clearly did not label the voyagers as any higher ranking than existing Hawaiian chiefs.

136. In Stokes's 1928 article "Whence Paao?," he said that temple forms in Hawai'i

were more characteristic of the Society Islands than of any other Polynesian island (1928:41). This might seem to contrast with his earlier heiau work where he said he could not find any introduced style (cf. Dye 1989:5). But, in 1928 he seemed to have been referring to the presence of large, national-type temples in both island groups. The forms were not similar; their sizes were.

137. Kolb (1991:151, 167, 178, 184) has recently dated several small (200–400 $m^2$) platform and enclosure heiau on Maui to this period. Also, the earliest phase of ʻAleʻaleʻa heiau at Honaunau, a luakini at European contact, was a small (352 $m^2$) platform with a date in the A.D. 1000s–1300s (Ladd 1969a). The small temples with an altar and upright stones found on Necker, Mauna Kea and elsewhere were not major national heiau, nor were they like such major temples in the Societies which were said to be brought by voyagers. They were small occupational heiau as on Mauna Kea, or were probably small family heiau as on Necker. The Mauna Kea shrines probably date no earlier than the A.D. 1100s and most probably to the 1400s–1700s, based on dates from the associated adze quarry. The Necker shrines are undated.

138. Cf. Goto 1986:281; Cordy 1974. These sites include H1 and H8. Although some doubt H1's early age (cf. Green 1971, 1995; Dye 1992), H8's early age does not seem to be in question.

139. Goto 1986:281.

140. Cf. Kaeppler 1985. Also, this is true in the Societies. There, surviving belts date to the 1700s (Rose 1978:1–17).

141. Stokes (1921) argued the technique used to make the belts was more primitive than that used to make feather cloaks, so he concluded that it must be older (cf. Rose 1978:24). However, a cruder technique could just as easily be more recent. The anthropological literature is full of errors of assuming simpler forms to be earlier.

142. Cf. Rose 1978:24, 27, 29–38.

143. Cf. Stokes, 1921:76–77, on the Hawaiian examples being completed objects versus the Society Islands' specimens being intentionally incomplete so new rulers could have new sections added on. Rose (1978:1–16) showed the Society Islands' cases having lappets (lobes) extending off the belts, which are quite different from the Hawaiian examples.

144. Rose 1978:45.

145. Cf. Oliver 1974:1126.

146. The inland type of Tahitian marae has been found along the shore in the last 60 years of archaeological work. These marae are simply smaller temples of lower ranking kin groups within a polity (cf. Oliver 1974); while the larger temples were those of the polity chiefs.

147. Oliver 1974:1126.

148. Oliver 1974:1126; Piddington in Williamson 1939:225; Goldman 1970; Sahlins 1958.

149. Simmons 1976. Also, see Emory and Sinoto (1964:159) for archaeological evidence of but one migration.

150. Emory 1979; Pfeiffer 1995.

151. Emory 1979:217.

152. One quoit from site G6-40 in Kailua town on Oʻahu has been noted by at least one author to be dated to the A.D. 1200s–1400s. However, the excavation report indicates that much of the site has been highly disturbed (Athens 1983). Intact portions do have three dated features (a hearth, firepit, and charcoal lens) from the base of the site which all date in the A.D. 1200s–1400s. However, the quoit (with a minimal notch) comes from a disturbed landfill layer. Thus, the quoit is not accurately dated; it could date to any time after the A.D. 1200s–1400s, including the 1700s or 1800s.

153. Emory 1970:90. Emory came to this conclusion because Necker Island also had stone images and octopus lures which he thought showed similarities to the Marquesas, as well as the temples. The simple types of temples with a courtyard, an altar at one end, and backrest/upright slabs in the court were noted by Emory as a common type in the Marquesas and Tuamotus, as well as in the Societies (1943:20). The reader might be aware of hewn stones used in heiau said to be associated with ʻUmi, whose reign was A.D. 1600–1620. While long after voyaging traditions, the reader might wonder if these heiau's stones were similar to hewn coral marae of the leeward Society Islands. Kūkiʻi

heiau in Puna has only a paving of such stones—a non–Society Island usage. Kukuipahu's heiau in Kohala—not specifically associated with 'Umi—has a low-walled enclosure faced with cut stones. Again, this is not a Society Island style—it is not a walled, narrow, rectangular platform at the end of an open yard. The only possible association with these Hawaiian heiau might be the hewing of stones, but this easily could have been independently developed, or it could have come from other islands where stones were hewn (e.g., the Marquesas, etc.).

154. Brigham (1902:43) stated that Hawaiian food pounders were similar to Marquesan pounders (without the image knobs) and that Tahitian pounders with the bar handle were held quite differently.

155. Unlike in west Central Polynesia where recent work has shown Samoan stone was widely circulated in late prehistory (cf. Best, Sheppard, Green & Parker 1992).

156. Other contact has been suggested in the past, such as Spanish contact late in prehistory (based on iron and possibly a sword being present at European contact and/or based on Spanish maps showing islands in the general area of Hawai'i) (cf. Fornander 1880:109–110, 158–159, 359–364; Fitzpatrick 1986:128–130). Spanish contact has not yet been substantiated. Dye (1989:17) noted that archaeologists should pay some attention to possible Hawaiian artifacts appearing in Central Polynesia. He noted that perhaps the Maupiti knobbed fishhook might even be evidence of Hawaiian contact in the Societies. A better sample than just one artifact is needed to evaluate this point. Currently, I know of no evidence for such contact, but, the possibility of Hawaiian contact in islands to the south should be kept in mind by future researchers.

157. Cf. Athens & Ward 1991:27.

158. A recent study analyzed a portion of a soil core which contained coconut pollen. It dated later in time, and it was suggested that coconut might be a later foreign introduction in Hawai'i. However, very little pollen of food crops has been identified in any soil cores, and there are not enough dated samples to confidently claim when specific crops made their initial appearance in Hawai'i, using this approach. Additionally, identification of crop pollen, or other signs of crops, in soil cores is still not terribly successful. For example, taro pollen often does not show in layers associated with archaeological ruins of known taro fields. Thus, more work is needed in this area before solid conclusions on outside contact can be made.

Yen 1987:10–11.

160. MacDaniels 1947:3–4, 12, 51; Milleaux 1990, personal communication.

161. Hommon 1976:258–269, 1989:12; Kaschko & Allen n.d.

162. Green 1995.

163. Cf. Cordy 1996; Wickler, Athens & Ward 1991; Denham, Brennan, Ward & Avery 1993.

164. Cf. Burgett & Rosendahl (1993:36) and Tuggle & Griffin (1973) for leeward north Kohala dates; Tuggle & Tomonari-Tuggle (1994:122) for 'Ewa Plain dates; Rosendahl, Haun, Halbig, Kaschko & Allen (1987) for Kaho'olawe.

165. Hather & Kirch 1991.

166. Fornander said that in the time of Kamehameha, it became known that the rulers up to Nana'ulu on the Hawaiian genealogies were shared by the Society Islands and the Marquesas (Fornander 1919, 6(2):233).

167. Cook in Beaglehole 1967, 3(1):256. See also Daws (1968:1).

168. Green 1974.

169. Green 1966.

170. Green 1995, describing the work of Elbert and Biggs.

171. R. Clark (1979:265). He stated "There is no intrinsic evidence that the forms in question are borrowed, however; and their distribution can easily be explained in other ways."

172. Green 1995.

173. Green 1995.

174. Green, 1995, personal communication.

175. One of the most recent of these place name studies argued that Moa'ulanuiakea was on the eastern peninsula of Tahiti island, in Tai'arapu district (Johnson 1979).

176. Cf. Handy on the Marquesas. In his research, he found a Vavau on Hiva Oa Island in the Marquesas. By 1920 this place name apparently had changed to Atu Ona (Handy 1923:11).

177. The same is true with certain names of gods (Kanaloa, Lono, Kane) and hero chiefs (Olopana, Maui). They appear all over Polynesia. Interestingly, Buck critiqued S. Percy Smith's turn-of-the-century New Zealand studies in which he used isolated word comparisons and loosely interpreted legends (Howard 1968:75). Place name sourcing still has much of this same problem.

178. Fornander 1880:107; Kamakau 1991:114–115.

179. Cachola-Abad 1993.

180. Cf. Vansina 1960.

181. Emory 1977; Barrere 1961; Hommon 1976.

182. Cf. Sahlins 1981:16; 1985:74. See also Alexander, 1893, quoted in Finney (1991:388).

183. Beckwith 1940:29.

184. Sahlins 1981:10.

185. Beckwith 1940:75.

186. Beckwith 1940:46, 68; Kaleo 1930 in Beckwith 1932:189.

187. Beckwith 1940:72.

188. Beckwith 1940:73. Hawai'i kua uli was also used as a name for Hāna (Beckwith 1940:245). Indeed, kua o ka moku was a term for the windward side of an island in Hawai'i (Malo 1951:8). These points show the complexity of place name analysis.

189. Beckwith 1940:54.

190. Beckwith 1940:78–79.

191. Beckwith 1940:108.

192. I am aware of another source of information on possible contact. Some families on Hawai'i Island claim that they have genealogies which show ancestors from the Society Islands, and from other Polynesian islands. However, I have not seen these genealogies, so I cannot evaluate if they reflect recent arrivals (post-1778), rely on the Fornander genealogies, or are an entirely different source of information.

## NOTES FOR CHAPTER 7

1. Kamakau 1961:3.

2. Kamakau 1961:14.

3. Malo 1951:238. A 1835 genealogy of Kepo'okulou published in *Kumu Hawaii* (McKenzie 1983:xiv–xvii), a 1842 genealogy of Kamakau (McKenzie 1983:xxi–xxv), and a manuscript in the Bishop Museum's Poepoe Collection (Beckwith 1932:192) show a similar succession. The same genealogy was in Pogue's 1858 edition of the Lahainaluna students' mo'olelo (Pogue 1978:66–67).

4. Malo 1951:238.

5. Fornander 1880:39.

6. Helekunihi n.d.:115–116; Stokes 1930b; Cartwright 1933:10.

7. Fornander 1880:39.

8. Fornander 1880:39.

9. Cartwright 1933:10.

10. Fornander 1880:39. However, in a 1869 article Kamakau did present a detailed list of rulers, giving the names of their 'aha kapu (sacred cords of coconut fiber strung outside their houses) and describing how their bones were bundled (Kamakau 1991:157). This list has Koa as the son of Pili, 'Ole as the son of Koa, and apparently Kūkohou and Kaniuhi as successive rulers. These are details, beyond a simple list of names, which support the Malo genealogy.

11. Fornander 1880:40.

12. Fornander 1916–1920.

13. Fornander 1880:39.

14. Malo 1951:247; Fornander 1880:40; 1917, 4(2):180–181. A 1842 Kamakau genealogy had Kalapana being the grandson of Kanipahu, through Kanipahu's and Hualani's son Kanaloa (McKenzie 1983:xxi). This is the only such account I have seen, and it is not followed here. Three other children of Hualani were named in this genealogy.

15. Malo 1951:247; Fornander 1880:40. Kalākaua (1990 [1888]:95–113) provided a more detailed story about Kanipahu, Kama'i'ole, and Kalapana although this seems considerably reworked and embellished.

16. Fornander 1880:40.

17. Malo 1951:248.

18. Fornander 1919, 6(2):319.

19. Fornander 1919, 6(2):319.

20. Malo 1951:247–248, 251; Fornander 1880:40–41.

21. Fornander 1880:73. Kamakau in 1869 did record the names of the 'aha for Kalapana and Kaha'i-moe and how their bones were prepared in kā'ai (1991:157–158).

22. Fornander 1880:67.

23. Malo 1951:251–252; Fornander 1880:69. Fornander said that he received this legend from Samuel Kamakau.

24. Malo 1951:251–254; Fornander 1880: 67; Beckwith 1940:382. Kalākaua (1990 [1888]:208–225) combined and altered these two accounts into an amplified story of his own.

25. Again, see Kamakau's 1869 names of their 'aha cords (1991:158).

26. Fornander 1880:notes on pp. 70, 76. This Ehu's descendants formed a powerful chiefly line within Kona.

27. Malo 1951:255.

28. Malo 1951:255–256; Fornander 1880:71. See also Kalākaua 1990 [1888]:213–215.

29. Fornander 1880:71. Kamakau (1991:21) noted that, at one point, Kiha was in residence at Kawaihae building a heiau.

30. Fornander 1880:71.

31. Fornander 1880:72.

32. Fornander 1880:72–73.

33. Fornander 1880:72.

34. Fornander 1880:72. See Kamakau (1991:19–22) for more on the Kiha-pū. Also, see Kalākaua (1990 [1888]:249–265) for a lengthy and apparently embellished version of this story.

35. Fornander 1880:72; Cleghorn & Rogers-Jourdane 1983.

36. Barrere 1959:15–16; 1970:7; 1971a, 1971b; Cordy 1987a; Hommon 1976. Others have noted that island was unified by Līloa's son 'Umi, but, as seen, the traditions unanimously show Līloa controlled the island.

37. Malo 1951:258.

38. Kamakau 1961:1.

39. Fornander 1917, 4(2):178.

40. Kamakau 1961:19.

41. Kamakau 1961:1. Also, Līloa's high priests, Nunu and Kakohe changed land borders between Kapāpala and Ka'ala'ala ahupua'a in Ka'ū; showing Līloa's direct power within a distant district (BCB n.d., A 1873:439, testimony by J. Kauhane).

42. Fornander 1880:76; Kamakau 1961:2, 5.

43. Fornander 1880:76.

44. Fornander 1880:73. Thrum (1924:20) was aware of an account which noted that Keikipu'ipu'i heiau in Kailua was built or refurbished by Līloa, although he did not cite the story.

45. Kamakau 1961:2–3.

46. Kamakau 1961:2. In Kalākaua's story of 'Umi, Manini heiau was said to be in use during the reign of Kalaunuiohua; Līloa rebuilt it. "Its outer walls had been enlarged, raised and repaired" (1990 [1888]:302).

47. Kamakau 1961:1–2.

48. Kamakau 1961:1, 14.

49. Kamakau 1961, Fornander 1880 and others noted the use of Paka'alana for Kū; Thrum (1908) referred to its use for Lono.

50. Sahlins 1981. See also Valeri (1985) for annual ritual sequences in general.

51. Sahlins 1981; Kamakau 1961:1–2.

52. Malo 1951:257; Fornander 1880:74; Kamakau 1961:1.

53. Malo 1951:257–265 (written ca. 1840); Pogue, 1978 [1858]:148–150, revised the 1838 Lahainaluna student mo'olelo, and his 'Umi story followed Malo's version almost identically (apparently an inclusion of Malo by Pogue?); Remy (1859; translated by Alexander 1887); Kamakau 1961:3–15 (1870 articles); Fornander 1880:74–78; 1917, 4(2):178–209 (story collected probably in 1860s–1870s); Kalākaua 1990 [1888]:265–315. For a modern analysis, see Valeri (1985).

54. Fornander 1880:74.

55. Malo 1951:259; Fornander 1880:74, note 2; 1917, 4(2):180–181; Pogue 1978 [1858]:148–149.

56. Kamakau 1961:3.

57. Kamakau 1961:5.

58. Malo (1951:261) said ʻOmaʻo was ʻUmi's mother's brother. (See also Pogue, 1978 [1858]:150.) According to Malo (1951:263) and Fornander (1880:76; 1917, 4(2):186-187), Koʻi was adopted as ʻUmi fled Waipiʻo during Hākau's reign. Kamakau (1961:3), however, had Koʻi adopted on ʻUmi's initial trip to Līloa.

59. Kamakau 1961:7.

60. Malo 1951: 262; Fornander 1880:75; Kamakau 1961:8–9.

61. Malo 1951:256; Fornander 1880:75; Kamakau 1961:9.

62. Malo 1951:256; Kamakau 1961:9; Fornander 1880:76.

63. Fornander 1880:73; Malo 1951:256; Kamakau 1961:1–3.

64. Fornander 1880:73.

65. Kamakau 1961:2. See also Kamakau (1991:154, written in 1869).

66. Kamakau 1961:2; 1991:43, 154; Fornander 1880:73; Emerson's note 2 in Malo 1951:257.

67. Charles Bishop, Feb. 22, 1897 letter to Trustee Henry Holmes. See also P. Smith (1898) for a contemporary description.

68. Fornander 1916, 4:128–158; 1916, 6:313; Beckwith 1940:357–358.

69. Kamakau 1961:1–2.

70. Boundary Commission Books (BCB n.d.,B:83-84).

71. Stokes 1919; Hudson 1932; Loo & Bonk 1970.

72. Hudson 1932; Loo & Bonk 1970.

73. Hudson 1932:170. Hudson's information came from elderly informants in 1930.

74. Lālākea is mentioned in Kamakau (1961:7). Muliwai is documented in the 1870s Boundary Commission Books (BCB n.d., B:83–84).

75. Ellis 1963:260–261; Stokes 1930; Buck 1957:574; Barrere 1975.

76. Kamakau 1961:107–108; Thrum 1908:41; Fornander 1880:201.

77. Fornander 1880:73.

78. Ellis 1963:260–261.

79. Cordy 1994:18. Figures of 40,000 etc. that are occasionally seen in publications are totally fictitious.

80. Ellis 1963:260.

81. Ellis 1963:256.

82. L. Lyons 1842.

83. Native Testimony n.d., 4:172, 174, 176, 183, 188, 192–193, 196, 199, 204–205, 208, 211–212, 218–220, 298, 311–313; J. S. Emerson 1880,I.

84. Bingham 1847:379; Native Register n.d., 8:108, 342–344, 346–348, 350, 364, 377, 491–492; Native Testimony n.d., 4:176.

85. Cleghorn & Rodgers-Jourdane 1983.

86. BCB n.d., B:83–84, 116.

87. Cordy 1987a, 1994.

88. Kamakau 1961:7.

89. Stokes 1919.

90. Thrum 1908.

91. Hudson 1932.

92. Loo & Bonk (1970) from the University of Hawaiʻi at Hilo; Martin (1971) of the State of Hawaii's Historic Preservation Office; Barrera (1977); Cleghorn & Rogers-Jourdane (1983) from the Bishop Museum; Cordy (1988a) from the State of Hawaii's Historic Preservation Office.

93. The State Historic Preservation Division, under the author's direction, conducted this work, with the first radiocarbon dates for the valley being processed. One date was in the A.D. 1400s–1500s, for the earliest cultivation layer in a set of kalo fields in the middle of the lower valley. Thus, by that time, much of the lower valley floor may have been in irrigated kalo.

94. Barrera 1976.

95. Cordy 1988a.

96. Fornander 1880:76.

97. Fornander 1880:76.

98. Fornander 1880:76; Malo 1951:263.

99. Fornander 1880:76–78; Kamakau 1961:11–14; Malo 1951:264–265.

100. Kamakau 1961:14; Fornander 1880:76.

101. Kamakau 1961:14; Fornander 1880:76–78.

102. Kamakau 1961:14.

103. Kamakau 1961:14.

104. Kamakau 1961:14–18.

105. Kamakau 1961:15,32.

106. Fornander 1880:96–101.

107. Fornander 1880:96.

108. Fornander 1880:99; 1917, 4(2):214.

109. Fornander 1880:100–101. Fornander (1880:78, note 2) said Hoe-a-Pae was the daughter of Pae, Līloa's priest and a high chief.

110. Fornander 1917, 4(2):314–321. In a story published by Kamakau in 1870, Kulukulu'a (chief of Hilo) was still alive during 'Umi's son's reign (Keawenui a 'Umi) (Kamakau 1961:43). This seems to contradict Kamakau's earlier 1870 articles on 'Umi's rise to power.

111. Fornander 1880:97; 1917, 4(2): 214–219.

112. Fornander 1880:87.

113. Tuggle (1990:App. II) pointed out that 'Umi is associated with Kahalu'u only by place names—Pā o 'Umi and Kapukini heiau. Note Kapukini was also the name of one of 'Umi's wives.

114. Fornander 1880:100–101.

115. Fornander 1880:98; Kamakau 1961:22.

116. Kamakau 1961:27.

117. Fornander 1880:98.

118. Kamakau 1961:29–30.

119. Kamakau 1961:31.

120. Kamakau 1961:31–32; Fornander 1880:198–199. Fornander said that Kamakau's account which had Lono-a-Pi'ilani at Waihe'e or Wailuku was a Maui account. He gathered a Hawai'i Island account which said that Lono-a-Pi'ilani was at Hāna and was slain.

121. Kamakau 1961:19.

122. Fornander 1880:101.

123. Kamakau 1961:32–33.

124. Fornander 1880:105; Kamakau 1961:32–33; Remy 1979 [1859].

125. Bingham 1847; Wilkes 1845, 4:106; Fornander 1880; Baker 1916; Newman 1974a; Watanabe 1986).

126. Watanabe 1986:5.8–5.14. "Low level aerial flyovers...confirmed the presence of additional surface features and structures in sight of Ahu-a-'Umi heiau which appear to be unrecorded at present in the archaeological record." These features included enclosures and platforms.

127. Wilkes 1845, 4:106.

128. Remy 1979:18.

129. Fornander 1880:99–100.

130. Fornander 1880:101. In 1870 Kamakau simply noted that at this spot "stood the mound (ahu), the road, the house, and heiau of 'Umi" (1961:35). While also implying a residence of unspecified duration, he offered no explanation why these structures had been built so far inland.

131. Alexander in Fornander 1917, 4(2):232, note 2.

132. Baker 1916. With perhaps 50,000 residents on the island at this time (Schmitt & Zane 1977:97, in an experimental study had 53,000 people ca. A.D. 1500)—or even less—and certainly not that many stones in the cairns, this interpretation can be discarded as a recent elaboration.

133. Cf. DaSilva & Johnson 1982. A more extreme interpretation is Thrum's editorial note that this was the tomb of 'Umi (Fornander 1917, 4(2):232, note 2).

134. Menzies 1920:163–164; Baker 1916.

135. Haun 1986; Streck 1986b; Watanabe 1986; Cordy 1994.

136. Watanabe 1986:5.5–5.6; Streck 1986; Haun 1986; Cordy 1994. Dates from Waikulukulu cave range back to the A.D. 1500s, and those from a nearby cave to the A.D. 1300s–1600s (Watanabe 1986).

137. Cf. BCB n.d., Hawai'i, A:136–148, 256, 258, 268; B:312.

138. Anonymous 1874. Journal of Trip to the Summit of Hualalai Mountain taken June 10th and 11th 1874. Party C. Wall, S. R. Folsom, the Commissioner (R. A. Lyman), kamaaina Keakaikawai and Kanakainai (BCB n.d.,B:257). Also, Keakaokawai's and Waiau's 1873

testimony on the borders of Keauhou 2 ahupua'a (BCB n.d., A:256,258, 268). Keakaokawai was born in Kealakekua in the 1810s a few years before the death of Kamehameha I (BCB n.d., A:256). Waiau was born in Kanauwae in 1812 (BCB n.d., A:268).

139. Keakaokawai's 1873 testimony on the borders of Keauhou 2 ahupua'a (BCB n.d., A:260; see also 258). Interestingly, the Hawaiians testifying before the Boundary Commission in 1873 and 1874 on the borders of Keauhou (Kona) and Kahuku (Ka'ū) noted that there was another Ahua 'Umi and also a Hale o 'Umi.

There are a good many places on the mountain called Ahu a Umi, and Hale o Umi and Alanui o Umi between Kahuku and Kona.

(1873 testimony of Kaiwi, born in Kahuku—BCB n.d., A:146–147)

Have seen several Kauhale o Umi in the mountains and a heiau o Umi...on my way home I saw a road which the kamaainas told me was Umi's road and led to Ahuami in Kona...have not seen the famous Ahuaumi.

(1873 testimony of Paahao, born and lived in Pakini—BCB n.d., A:148)

The accounts when compared seem to indicate that when one went up the Alanui o 'Umi from Ka'ū (with the lower road often "paved with flat rocks"—R. A. Lyman 1874, BCB n.d., B:312), some "stone houses" ("Na Hale o Umi") and a small heiau were encountered well up the mountain near Ka'aoaehu on the pāhoehoe above the woods (Konaka 1874 testiimony on Kahuku, born in Kukuiopae in Kona one year before Naihe died, BCB n.d., B:318; Kumauna 1873 testimony on Kahuku, born before Kamehameha I invaded Maui, BCB n.d., A:127, 141). The heiau was variously called "heiau Wakaiokaaha (he heiau no Umi)" (Kumauna—BCB n.d., A:141) and "Kakaiokaaha heiau o Umi" (Kumauna—BCB n.d., A:142).

this place Kakaiokaaha heiau o Umi on the road to Kona Kaala o Ehu a small heiau there are many stone houses there...

[Kumauna 1873, BCB n.d., A:142]

The stone houses were called hale o 'Umi or kauhale o 'Umi (Kumauna BCB n.d., A:142). This Hale o 'Umi may have been covered by a 1845 lava flow (Hall BCB n.d., B:255). From this place, Kahuku joined Keauhou at a cave called "Keanahua" and then the border went up a ridge between the two lands to Maunalei where "Ahu a Umi" was located and then to Pōhakuhanalei where Hāmākua, Kona, and Ka'ū joined (Kenoi 1873 testimony, born Kapapala ca. 1804, BCB n.d., A:436; Kumauna BCB n.d., A:127, 142; R. Naike BCB n.d., A:136; J. Kaulia 1873 testimony, born in 1823 and had been konohiki and was told the information by Halulu). This "Ahu a Umi" was on the 'Umi road from Ka'ū to Kona "way above the woods" and it was different from "the famous one in Kona" (R. Naike BCB n.d., A:136). It was described as "four or five piles of stone in a mawae or crack" (C. Hall 1873, BCB n.d., B:255).

140. Bevacqua & Dye 1972:8.

141. Stokes 1919:588. There is a 1871 description of this heiau which talked of a platform, terraces and stairway of hewn stone (LaPaz 1871).

142. Bevacqua & Dye 1972:8; Thrum 1907:55.

143. Stokes 1919:588.

144. Fornander 1880:101.

145. DLNR Site Inventory File 10-02-4135.

146. Dye & Komori 1992a.

147. In the area north of Kailua to Keāhole Point, field shelters among the kula fields date frequently in the 1400s–1500s (Jensen & Donham 1991; Jensen & Goodfellow 1993; Donham 1990a, b, c). Dates from the Kailua to Keauhou area are similar (e.g., Hōlualoa, Puapua'a, Kahalu'u, Keauhou ahupua'a)—from both informal field areas and from lower elevations where formal walled fields (kuaīwi) were present (Tomonari-Tuggle 1985; Schilt 1984; Burtchard 1996; Liston & Burtchard 1993:9–10; Hammatt, Folk & Shideler 1992; Fager & Graves 1993; Hammatt, Borthwick & Shideler 1986; Hammatt & Clark 1980).

148. J. Clark 1983b; Reeve 1983:212–215; Hammatt & Shideler 1989; S. Clark, E. D. Davidson & Cleghorn 1990; Head, Goodfellow & Wolforth 1995.

149. Kirch 1979; Jensen 1988, 1989a, b, 1990a, b, 1991a.

150. Newman 1970; Rosendahl 1972; Cordy & Kaschko 1980.

151. Cordy 1978, 1981; Cordy & Kaschko 1980.

152. Tuggle 1976; Tuggle & Tomonari-Tuggle 1980.

153. Cordy 1991, 1994; Shun & Schilz 1991.

154. Cordy 1994.

155. Cordy 1994.

156. King in Beaglehole 1967, 3(1):605.

157. Kamakau 1961:7.

158. Kamakau 1961:56.

## NOTES CHAPTER 8

1. Kamakau 1976:143,

2. Pukui 1983:31, Proverb 253.

3. Fornander 1880:106.

4. Fornander 1880:111; Fornander 1917, 4(2):314–320. These were all sons of the high chiefs who held these lands under Līloa, so stated in the famed chant given when Lonoikamakahiki displayed their bones to Kākuhihewa, the O'ahu ruler (Fornander 1917, 4(2):314 320). This strongly points to a peaceful transition to power of 'Umi and retention of his father's chiefs as claimed by Fornander. If 'Umi had conquered and slayed the district chiefs, as claimed by Kamakau, the district chiefs' sons would likely not have inherited their fathers' lands, and not been in those positions in the time of Keali'iokāloa. [These chiefs' fathers were recorded by Nakuina as being the sons of Keawenui, appointed as his district chiefs (1990:27). This clearly does not match the earlier traditions or the genealogies of Keawenui's children.] These chiefs of Līloa were recalled in other stories, but they were often given more authority or were placed in the wrong generation. For example, in some accounts recorded in Fornander's collections, Kulukulu'a and Hua'a were erroneously called the king of Hilo and the king of Puna and were sometimes placed in the generation of a ruler other than Līloa. These stories were recognized as flawed by Fornander, and he did not use them in his published 1880 summary.

5. Fornander 1880:111.

6. Fornander 1917, 4(2):314–321.

7. Fornander 1917, 4(2):314–315.

8. Fornander 1917, 4(2):316–317.

9. Fornander 1917, 4(2):256–257, 266–267; 1880:112.

10. The Kū-a-Nu'uanu and Paka'a stories also describe Keawenui residing at Waipi'o (Nakuina 1990:1, 20).

11. Fornander 1880:128.

12. Fornander 1880:113–114, 281. Fornander (1880:113, note 1) had but one genealogy for Ho'opiliahae which tied her to Maui, while Kamakau said she was of the Pae line from Kohala (1961:45; Barrere 1983:26).

13. The story of Lonoikamakahiki given in Fornander's collection said his mother was Kaihalawai (Fornander 1917, 4(2):256–257), yet interestingly Fornander did not follow this version in his published book (Fornander 1880:113). Also, a 1896 newspaper article stated, "The writer has been told Hoopiliahae is his [Lono's] mother as well as Umiokalani['s] (McKenzie 1983:7), which varied from earlier genealogies.

14. Fornander 1917, 4(2):266–267.

15. Fornander 1880:114.

16. Fornander 1917, 4(2):266–267; 1880:114.

17. Kamakau 1961:34–36.

18. Kamakau 1961:35.

19. Fornander 1917, 4(2):314–321.

20. Fornander 1917, 4(2):266–267.

21. To add to the confusion, in 1853 Remy gathered an account from Kanuha, a very elderly man in South Kona, in which he said 'Umi ruled over east Hawai'i and his cousin Keli'iokāloa ruled over west Hawai'i at Kailua. He said a battle was fought at Ahua a 'Umi, and 'Umi won (Remy 1979:18–19). This story is somewhat similar to Kamakau's, with 'Umi inserted rather than Keawenui—clearly a confusion of generations. Kanuha knew about Keawenui; indeed he argued he was the only Keawe of Hawai'i. Definitely, some muddling of facts occurs in Kanuha's account, whether because of his age, unreliability or other reasons.

22. Fornander 1880:115.

23. Fornander 1917, 4(2):268–271.

24. Fornander 1880:116; 1917, 4(2):270–275.

25. Fornander 1917, 4(2):272.

26. Fornander 1917, 4(2):274–321.

Fornander visited Kalaupapa and found that "the old inhabitants...pointed out the very broad stone on which Lono and Kaikilani were said to have been sitting and playing when the game was so fatally interrupted" (1880:116, note 1).

27. Fornander 1917, 4(2):302–307.

28. Fornander 1917, 4(2):320–323.

29. Fornander 1917, 4(2):322.

30. Fornander 1917, 4(2):322–323. About this time, the young high chief Iwikauikaua, a nephew of Kaikilani and supporter of Lono, was captured and almost sacrificed. Fornander collected an oral account of his prayer which saved his life—full of archaic expressions (1880:126).

31. Fornander 1917, 4(2):324–327.

32. Fornander 1917, 4(2):326–327. A 1867 map of "Waikoloa, Waimea, Hawaii" by J. L. Kaelemakule (Hawaiian Government Survey, Reg. Map 574) showed a Pu'u 'Ainako near the shore, back of Puakō Bay.

33. Fornander 1917, 4(2):326–327.

34. Fornander 1917, 4(2):328–329.

35. Fornander 1917, 4(2):328–329. This last battle may have been fought at or near a fortification on the ridge between Honokāne nui and Honokāne iki valleys—a fortification which still survives today (Tuggle 1976). This site had a ditch cut across the ridge to prevent entry, and several piles of waterworn stones (slingstones) (Tuggle 1976:111–113).

36. Kanaloakua'ana evidently became the chief over Waimea, based on the Kamalālāwalu invasion accounts (Fornander 1917, 4(2):342–343. 'Umiokalani is sometimes claimed to have been a ruler who was so cruel, he was deposed (Malo 1951:195). But clearly, at best, he was a high chief, perhaps a district chief, under his brothers Lono and Kanaloakua'ana.

37. Fornander 1917, 4(2):330–331.

38. This court visit was described in a story involving Pupuakea, Lono's half-brother. There is a very detailed account in the Fornander Collection (1917, 4(2):330–335). Kamakau presented a similar, but somewhat shorter version (1961:53–54).

39. Fornander 1917, 4(2):330–341. Lono had counterspies among Kamalālāwalu's advisors, and these spies planted misinformation regarding the conditions of potential battlegrounds.

40. Fornander 1917, 4(2):342–343.

41. Fornander 1917, 4(2):342–343.

42. Fornander 1917, 4(2):344–345.

43. Fornander 1917, 4(2):346–349.

44. Fornander 1917, 4(2):348–349.

45. 1906 informant Malanui, grandson of last priest of nearby Kapuanoni heiau, told Stokes (1919:12–21; 1991:77); 1929 informant Kahulumu told Reinecke (1930:4, 6); Kekahuna (1952).

46. Stokes & Dye 1991; Stokes 1909; Kekahuna 1952.

47. Fornander 1917, 4(2):350–355. In his published work, Fornander (1880:124–125) discussed the possibility that aspects of this Kaua'i story had been romanticized over the years. Pukui (1983:154, Proverb 1419) cited a proverb about this tree, "To say one has found the trunk of Kahilikolo is to say that he has found nothing," and suggested a search for the tree had little point. Thus, Lonoikamakahiki's story involving this tree may indeed be more symbolic.

48. Interestingly, the whereabouts of Pupuakea was not mentioned in this story. Presumably, if the story is truly from Lono's reign, then Pupuakea had either died or had returned to Ka'ū.

49. Fornander 1917, 4(2):356–359.

50. Fornander 1917, 4(2):360–363.

51. Cordy 1987d:7.

52. Barrera 1971; Walker & Rosendahl 1986; Cordy 1987d; Jensen 1990a.

53. At the blessing prior to beginning the restoration work, which the author attended, several members of the Waimea Hawaiian Civic Club recalled stories of this site. Robert Keakealani had passed this way with his elders in the early twentieth century, and they always stopped, placing offerings and giving prayers at the site. It was his understanding that this was indeed an ahupua'a shrine. Mr. Keakealani has since passed away—a graphic reminder of how the oral histories are disappearing.

54. E.g., Barrera 1971.

55. Jensen (1988, 1989b) has conducted nearly all the recent archaeological work in this quarry area, with preliminary surveys by Walker & Rosendahl (1986) and Donham (1987).

56. This pattern has since been found at smaller petroglyph clusters found along trails which connect the main ala loa to the shore areas of 'Anaeho'omalu (Jensen 1989a, b, 1990a).

57. The kā'ai are illustrated in Buck (1957). See Barrere (1975) for a discussion of the differing accounts from the 1800s about whose remains actually are in the kā'ai. Also, see Rose's more recent study (1992). It appears that these kā'ai cannot be as firmly claimed to be those of Līloa and Lono as long thought, due to considerable mixing of the kā'ai from Hale o Keawe and Hale o Līloa. These two could very well be later Kona chiefs.

58. Kamakau 1991:175.

59. Kamakau 1961:45–46.

60. Kamakau 1961:54.

61. Fornander 1917, 4(2):356–359.

62. Fornander 1917, 4(2):330–331; 1906 Stokes work quoted in Reinecke (1930:4).

63. Fornander 1917, 4(2):360–363.

64. Lord Byron, who commanded the HMS *Blonde* when it was in Hawai'i in 1825, published a slightly different version, a "Song of Lono" ("O Lono Akua"), which had been translated by the American missionaries for him (Byron 1826:20–21). This had Lono living with his wife at Kealakekua, where he killed her after her lover saluted her. He then traveled through Hawai'i in "a state of frenzy," boxing with every man that he met—starting games to commemorate her death. He then sailed off to a foreign land, promising to return. This story seems to be a stylized account linking Lono, the makahiki, and his departure and promised return. [Lono was definitely linked with the makahiki after his death. His canoe evidently had feathered skins as banners and a large kahili (Kamakau 1961:52–53), both of which have parallels to the Lono image in the makahiki.]

65. It should be noted that the "Ka Moolelo o Lonoikamakahiki" in Fornander's Collections is sixteen chapters in length (Fornander 1917, 4(2):256–363).

66. Kamakau, 1961:70, identified the kahuna as Lanahu'imi.

67. Pogue [1858] (1978:32) even went so far as to say that "Lono originated the Makahiki"—particularly the festivities similar to those that Lono participated in during his wanderings.

68. Archaeological studies of Ke'ekū include Stokes (1919), Reinecke (1930), Kekahuna (1952), McCoy, Emory & Barrere (1971), and Tuggle (1990). These studies include oral historical analyses.

69. Information on these petroglyphs was well discussed by Tuggle (1990).

70. Oral historical information on the pu'uhonua is covered in Stokes (1919).

71. Archaeological studies of Hapaiali'i include Stokes (1919), Reinecke (1929), Kekahuna (1952), Cordy (1986c), and Tuggle (1990). These studies include oral historical information.

72. Archaeological studies of Kapuanoni include Stokes (1919), Reinecke (1930), Kekahuna (1952), Cordy (1986d), and Tuggle (1990). These studies include oral historical information.

73. Sources on the residence of the ruler include Barrere (McCoy, Emory & Barrere 1971), Cordy (1986c), and Tuggle (1990). Tuggle (1990:61) pointed out that what today is called "the Lonoikamakahiki dwelling" was known by Hawaiians earlier in the century as a heiau with a quite different name.

74. Stokes 1919.

75. Kū'emanu was described by Stokes (1919).

76. The scattered inland heiau were described by Stokes (1919), Hammatt & Folk (1980), and Tomonari-Tuggle (1985).

77. 'Ōhi'amukumuku heiau was discussed in Kamakau (1961), Emory, McCoy & Barrere (1971), Cordy (1986a), Tuggle (1990), and Anderson (1998).

78. Reinecke 1930.

79. Tuggle 1990.

80. Malo 1951:251.

81. Lono's two sons were Keawehanauikawalu and Ka'ihikapumahana through Kaikilani-kohepani'o (Kamakau 1961:61). Possibly these sons did not inherit due to their

lower rank, in comparison to Kaikilani-Ali'i-Wahine-o-Puna's higher rank and that of her children. Keawe married a Kaua'i princess, Akahikame'enoa (a granddaughter of 'Umi). Ka'ihi, born during the O'ahu visit, was named after the ruler of O'ahu's (Kākuhihewa's) son Ka'ihikapu (Fornander 1880:125). Kamakau (1961:47, 54–55) said that Ka'ihi was raised on O'ahu, and Fornander noted that he later married into the Kaua'i royal family (1880:125). An 1896 Hawaiian newspaper writer said he was told these two children were Kaikilani Ali'i Wahine o Puna's through Lono (McKenzie 1983:7), but this clearly disagrees with the earlier accounts.

82. Fornander 1880:127.

83. Stokes 1930a; Emory 1986; Barrere 1986; Kamakau 1961.

84. Kamakau 1961:61–63.

85. Fornander 1880:127.

86. An 1896 Hawaiian genealogy noted Keakealani had a son Moana through Kaleiheana (McKenzie 1983:44), and another 1896 genealogy noted a son Keawekuikaai through Kaleimakali'i (McKenzie 1983:52–54). This latter son reputedly built the Great Wall at Hōnaunau (see Chap. 9).

87. Kamakau 1961:62.

88. Fornander 1880:127–128.

89. Kamakau 1961:60.

90. 'I'i 1959:6.

91. Kamakau 1961:61–63.

92. Fornander 1880:129; Kamakau 1961:74.

93. Fornander 1880:128–129. Mahi'ololī was given Ka'awaloa ahupua'a at this time, which eventually descended to Keaweaheulu in the time of Kalani'ōpu'u and Kamehameha (Fornander 1919, 6(2):320).

94. Fornander 1880:128–129.

95. 'I'i 1869; McEldowney 1986:24–26.

96. Kamakau 1961:63. Four battles were noted—at the "sheer cliffs," at Kahina'i, at Hu'ehu'e in north Kona where "the secret places and burial caves in Kona were broken open," and at Mahiki between Waimea and Hāmākua.

97. Fornander 1880:128–129.

98. Kamakau said that war broke out during Keakamahana's reign and "lasted through several centuries" (1961:62). The true situation is difficult to discern, but perhaps Kamakau was referring to tension and periodic small raids, as well as outright battles. Based on genealogies the severe "tension" with the 'Ī actually lasted from 1680–1700 (Keakamahana's reign) to the start of Keawe's reign (c. 1720), with its last flare-up in 1740—clearly not a period of several centuries. Cases of full-scale war were rare. Only two are apparent—Kua'ana and Kuahu'ia versus Keakealaniwahine and Mokulani versus Kalanike'eaumoku ca. 1740. Possibly some of the battles between the 'Ī and Keakealaniwahine may have occurred after she was reinstated—attempts by her and the Mahi to regain control of the island. For example, in the Mahiki battle between Waimea and Hāmākua (in which Kauaua-a-Mahi, Keakekalaniwahine's daughter's husband, was slain), Mokulani was a general of Hilo's forces (Kamakau 1961:63). Since Mokulani was of Keawe's generation, he could only have led Hilo's forces late in Keakealaniwahine's reign. Again, Mokulani was a contemporary of Keawe (1720–1740), and the traditions have him living peacefully under Keawe's rule. Mokulani did revolt when Keawe's Kona son, Kalanike'eaumoku, came to power—the last rise of the 'Ī. Kamakau said that in these battles, the Hilo chiefs were victorious more often. This was certainly true against Keakealaniwahine. But Alapa'i crushed Mokulani's forces, making the Hilo forces victorious in only one of two wars.

99. The Kumulipo, Kalaninui'īamamao's name chant (Keakealaniwahine's senior grandson through an 'Ī woman) goes, "to 'I is the chiefship, the right to offer human sacrifice, The ruler over the land section of Pakini, With the right to cut down 'ohi'a wood for images, the protector of the island of Hawaii" (Beckwith 1972:139). This is an acknowledgement of 'Ī power, likely as a result of the war. Alternatively, it could indicate the extent of the 'Ī family's independence in Hilo.

100. Lili'uokalani 1897; McEldowney 1986:31; Beckwith 1972:8. His birth name was Lonoikamakahiki, resulting in his confusion with the earlier Lono (Beckwith 1972:8).

101. Kūali'i, ruler of O'ahu, also raided the Hilo coast early in his reign, and probably quite late in Keakealaniwahine's (Fornander 1880:281). Given this timing, one wonders if this might have been in support of Kona. He had to withdraw to put down an uprising on O'ahu.

102. 'I'i 1959:6; McEldowney 1986. She is also said to have resided at Waipi'o and in Kohala (McEldowney 1986:27; 'I'i 1869: Apr. 24, May 8; Kamakau 1961:63).

103. 'I'i 1959:6.

104. McEldowney 1986:60. Kamehameha had lived here for a while in his youth on the flats near the heiau (McEldowney 1986:160).

105. McEldowney (1986) has compiled an excellent summary of these records. This study carefully reviewed early records and showed the changes in oral accounts told by Hawaiians over almost two centuries. Her study is a superb cautionary case on the problems of modern oral histories. It also illustrates that the public often does not realize that older oral histories (told by resident Hawaiians) exist and probably are more accurate versions of the stories.

106. McEldowney 1986:9; Board of Genealogy of Hawaiian Chiefs n.d.:8–11.

107. Ellis 1963:121.

108. Ellis 1963:121; Stokes 1919 (Stokes & Dye 1991:61–63); McEldowney 1986.

109. McEldowney 1986:46.

110. Stokes 1919 (Stokes & Dye 1991:62–63).

111. Stokes 1919; McEldowney 1986.

112. Ellis 1963:74–75; McEldowney 1986.

113. 'I'i 1959:6.

114. Hammatt 1994; Kekahuna 1950; Stokes 1991 [1919].

115. Stokes 1991:58–60.

116. Ellis 1963; McEldowney 1986.

117. McEldowney 1986:40–41, 159.

118. This pattern could hardly have been new. Ruling centers of earlier times, even when polities were district-sized or less, undoubtedly created a demand for greater food production, which would have led to expansion of fields.

119. Schmitt & Zane (1977:97) taking one-third of their totals as Hawai'i Island, with 300,000 being the total used for 1778 for the archipelago.

120. Kirch 1979; Hommon 1976.

121. Menzies 1920:75–76.

122. King in Beaglehole 1967, 3(1):521.

123. Clerke in Beaglehole 1967, 3(1):592.

124. Soehren & Newman 1968.

125. Kirch 1985:230; 1984:187; Yen 1978.

126. Barrera 1990a; Walker, Kalima & Goodfellow 1991.

127. Kaschko & Rosendahl 1987; Walker, Kalima & Goodfellow 1991; Burgett & Rosendahl 1994.

128. Barrera 1990b.

129. Walker, Kalima & Goodfellow 1991; Burgett & Rosendahl 1994.

130. Menzies 1920:75–76; Kelly 1983:57.

131. King in Beaglehole 1967, 3(1):521.

132. Menzies 1920:80–81; Kelly 1973:63.

133. King in Beaglehole 1967, 3(1):617.

134. Māhele records indicated taro was planted quite abundantly in the kula zone of Kealakekua (Kelly 1983; Cordy 1985a).

135. King in Beaglehole 1967, 3(1):602.

136. King in Beaglehole 1967, 3(1):521.

137. Cf. Cordy 1985a.

138. Cordy 1990 notes in fieldbook, on file, State Historic Preservation Division.

139. Cook & King 1784, III:128.

140. King in Beaglehole 1967, 3(1):521.

141. Samwell in Beaglehole 1967, 3(2):1167.

142. Kaschko & Rosendahl 1987.

143. Cordy 1989c; Burtchard 1996.

144. In Kahalu'u and Keauhou habitations in kula zone mostly date from the A.D. 1400s on (cf. Burtchard 1996; O'Hare & Rosendahl 1993; Walker & Rosendahl 1994; Liston & Burtchard 1994; Walker & Rosendahl 1989). One mound with an associated subsurface paving and habitation deposits (site 10941, Feat. D) had a date of A.D. 1260–1440 (Walker & Rosendahl 1989) and one habitation cave (site 4659) at the 140-foot elevation in Kahalu'u had a date of A.D. 1000–1280 (Walker & Rosendahl 1994). [Note: the above is based solely on radiocarbon dates.]

145. Burtchard 1996. Site 15192 is a cave used for habitation, and it has one date of A.D. 1240–1450. Other dates in the formal field zones of Kahalu'u and Keauhou are later, although dating is still limited in this zone. In Onouli between Keauhou and Kealakekua, two dates associated with the walled fields may go back to the 1300s (A.D. 1295–1420 and 1295–1645), and other dates go back to the 1400s (Wolforth 1998:26, 30, 41).

146. Menzies 1920:154–155; Ellis 1963: 31–32; Kelly 1983:52–58.

147. Those interested in detailed accounts should consult the Kona section of the State Historic Preservation Division's library. Among the numerous reports documenting kula zone archaeological work are the following: Schilt 1984; Hammatt 1992; Landrum, Haun, Rosendahl, & Delimont 1990; Carlson & Rosendahl 1990b; Kennedy, Maigret & Moore 1993.

148. Schilt's work (1984:276) dated a midden in site D8-20 in Lanihau to A.D. 1055–1270 (lower deposit) and 1305–1420 (upper deposit) and a cave (site D8-33) in adjacent Keōpū to the A.D. 1300s–1400s.

149. Hammatt, Shideler, Chiogioji & Borthwick 1993.

150. Landrum, Haun, Rosendahl & Delimont 1990.

151. Hammatt, Borthwick, Colin, Masterson & Robins 1994:109–110.

152. Crozier 1971; Tomonari-Tuggle 1985; Burtchard 1996.

153. Barrera 1990c.

154. Walker & Rosendahl 1988.

155. Graves & Goodfellow 1993:figure 3.

156. Kawachi 1989; M. S. Allen 1984:21.

157. Cf. Kaschko & Rosendahl 1987; Barrera 1989; Kawachi 1989; Henry & Rosendahl 1993; Burtchard 1996; Graves & Goodfellow 1993.

158. In Keauhou a date from a cave with temporary habitation deposits (15192) at the 800–900-foot elevation was A.D. 1240–1450, and one from a permanent habitation (15213) at ca. 800 feet was A.D. 1670–contact (Burtchard 1996). Using volcanic glass dating, Crozier (1971) dated habitations in this formal field zone in Kahalu'u back to the A.D. 1100s, although most of his dates are in the A.D. 1600s. In Puapua'a, based on dates from 9 features, initial occupation of the upper field zone was suggested to have begun as early as the 1000s–1100s (Graves & Goodfellow 1993). Other dates exist, and studies in this zone are increasing. The interested reader should consult archaeological reports in the Kona section of the State Historic Preservation Division's library.

159. Cordy, Tainter, Renger & Hitchcock (1991) for Kaloko; Barrera (1988, 1990d) for Kohanaiki.

160. Hammatt, Shideler & Borthwick 1987.

161. Schilz, Shun, Williams & Nees (1994) for Kau.

162. Donham (1990b) for Kealakehe, (1990c) for Keahuolū.

163. Tainter in Cordy, Tainter, Renger & Hitchcock (1991:Chap. 9A).

164. King in Beaglehole 1967, 3(1):608.

165. S. Clark 1986:49–52.

166. Cordy, Tainter, Renger & Hitchcock 1991.

## NOTES TO CHAPTER 9

1. Beckwith 1972:26.

2. Beckwith 1940:13–14.

3. 'I'i 1959:6.

4. Kamakau 1961:85–86.

5. Kamakau's account of Keawe's rule (1961:64–65) contains some major inconsistencies with other sources. He had Keawe ruling only over Kohala, Kona and Ka'ū; evidently with the 'Ī family independent in windward Hawai'i. It is clear that the 'Ī line remained a powerful feudatory family, but Keawe's marriages with the 'Ī family line and the general account of events in his reign point to a united island under Keawe. Kamakau also had his son Kalaninui'īamamao alive at Keawe's death and the kingdom split between this son who received Ka'ū and his other powerful son, Kalanike'eaumoku, who obtained Kona and Kohala. This is not consistent with Fornander's account where Kalaninui'īamamao died before Keawe, and Kalanike'eaumoku inherited. Also, having Keawe split the kingdom does not conform

with Kalaninui'īamamao having been the designated heir. And, giving Kohala to Kalanike'eaumoku as a district chiefship would be inconsistent with the Mahi control of that district; it would have been a direct slap in the face of that family line. Kamakau's account (1961:65-66) continues to differ from Fornander's into the initial year of Alapa'i's reign. On one page (65), Kamakau had Alapa'i defeating Kalanike'eaumoku's Kona-Kohala polity before the attack of Maui, but not defeating Hilo. On another page (66), he had Alapa'i defeating both Kalanike'eaumoku and Mokulani before the Maui attack—this version matching Fornander's account. [Kalaninui'īamamao was not mentioned in either of these versions of Kamakau, suggesting he was not alive—contrary to Kamakau's earlier claim.] Once Alapa'i conquered Hawai'i, then Kamakau's and Fornander's accounts are in agreement through the remainder of Alapa'i's reign and through Kalani'ōpu'u's reign.

6. Fornander 1880:130.

7. In a 1869 article Kamakau presented an account of Lonoma'aikanaka felling the sacred 'aha of Mokulani (her junior cousin) and Hilo chiefs, and visiting the royal places of Waipi'o (Kamakau 1991:155–156).

8. Fornander 1880:129. As seen in the prior chapter, the 'Ī may also have pushed these marriages upon the Kona family of Keawe, due to the indiscretions of his mother (Keakealaniwahine).

9. Fornander 1880:132.

10. Menzies (1920:86–87) visited Hōnaunau Feb. 28, 1793.

11. Stokes 1986:223.

12. Soehren & Tuohy 1987.

13. Emory 1986.

14. Ladd 1986:4–5.

15. Ladd 1969a:9. Stokes informants in 1919 told him the wall was said to have been built by men impressed from 9 adjacent ahupua'a (Emory 1957:147–149).

16. Cf. Kelly (1986:38–39) on pu'uhonua.

17. Ladd 1969a.

18. Ladd 1987.

19. Hale o Keawe also was associated with human sacrifices, but not in the same manner as the large luakini heiau (cf. Barrere 1986:123–128).

20. Menzies 1920:86–87.

21. Ladd 1969b.

22. Stokes 1986; Ladd 1969b.

23. Tuohy 1965.

24. Ladd 1969a.

25. P23/3:site 5, a rectangular platform (Soehren & Tuohy 1987:102, 130).

26. Emory 1986; Ladd 1985.

27. Ladd 1969a; 1987:77, is the source of information for this paragraph.

28. Ladd 1987:51.

29. Tuohy 1965:129–130.

30. Tuohy 1965. His S27 and T26 excavation areas correspond to areas within the royal residential area.

31. Soehren 1962.

32. Ladd 1986:58–72.

33. Soehren 1962; Ladd in 1963 and Tuohy in 1963 (Tuohy 1965).

34. Tuohy 1965.

35. Tuohy 1965:114, 198.

36. Tuohy 1965:125, 144.

37. Tuohy 1965:220, 181. Fishhook head type counts were 5 of type HT1a, 5 of HT1b, and 16 of HT4.

38. Emory 1986; Barrere 1986; Ladd 1969a; Somers 1986; Ladd 1987.

39. Kamakau 1870 in Barrere 1986.

40. Fornander 1880:130–131. 'Umiula-a-Ka'ahumanu, Mokulani's mother, was named in a 1896 genealogy as another wife, with a son resulting, Kauhiololi (McKenzie 1983:82).

41. Fornander evidently confused this man with Lono-i-kai-hopu of Kaua'i (Barrere 1986:134). But see Fornander (1880:131–132) for information on husbands and children. Also, Kamakau (1961:63) said Kauaua-a-Mahi died at Mahiki in a battle with the 'Ī apparently during the reign of Keakealaniwahine, so his marriage to Kalanikauleleiaiwi would appear to have been prior to Keawe's reign.

42. Board of Genealogy of Hawaiian Chiefs n.d.:8–11; McEldowney 1986:9, 30.

43. Fornander 1880:132.

44. Fornander 1880:132–133.

45. Fornander 1880:131; Stokes 1930:66.

46. Cf. Barrere 1986:122–123.

47. Cf. Stokes 1930a.

48. Stokes 1930a; Barrere 1986:118.

49. Ladd 1985:60.

50. Ellis 1963:110.

51. A. Bloxam 1925:74.

52. Emory 1986.

53. A. Bloxam 1925:75.

54. Barrere 1986:122.

55. Barrere 1986:132. These kā'ai seem to have been occasionally moved, for Cook's men visited the Hale o Keawe in 1779 and learned that the deified bones were at Hikiau heiau at Kealakekua Bay, although without their feather images (Cook in Barrere, 1986:129, note 2). Indeed, Valeri (1985:281–282) notes that during the annual building of sacred houses on the heiau (kauila nui rite), "the keepers (kahu) of the ka'ai gods belonging to the king and nobles enter. Each keeper sits in front of his god."

56. R. Bloxam 1924:29–80.

57. Byron 1826:199.

58. 'I'i 1959:139.

59. Emory 1986:100, 102.

60. Chamberlain ms.

61. Barrere 1986:132–135; see also Stokes 1930a:66–68.

62. Barrere 1986:124–125.

63. Barrere 1986:127.

64. Emory 1986:93.

65. Barrere 1986:135.

66. With the abolition of the kapu system and the conversion to Christianity, Hale o Keawe and its remains received less respect. Kamehameha III and his regents, Ka'ahumanu and Kalanimoku, who were strongly influenced by the church, allowed images—including the feathered images—to be removed by members of the HMS *Blonde* in 1825. In 1829, Ka'ahumanu in her religious zeal had the house and palisade demolished and had the remains placed in two large coffins and then hidden in the cliffs of Kealakekua Bay, along with those of the Hale o Līloa from Waipi'o. Thirty years later in 1858, Kamehameha IV brought them to Honolulu. Today, they either rest in Mauna 'ala in Nu'uanu, the Pohukaina mausoleum on the 'Iolani Palace grounds, or are still in the Ka'awaloa cliffs. Just which remains are where is still uncertain (Barrere 1986:136; Stokes 1930a:71; Rose 1992).

67. Kamakau 1961:75–176; Fornander 1880:133–144; 'I'i 1959:3.

68. Fornander 1880:134, 138–140, 142–143.

69. Fornander 1880:135.

70. Keawe-a-heulu, one of the most senior 'Ī chiefs with some Mahi blood (nephew to Kalaninui'īamamao, Kalanike'eaumoku and Alapa'inui's wife and first cousin to Kalani'ōpu'u and Keōua), had been married to Ululani—evidently in her infancy—but he was replaced by Keawema'uhili (Fornander 1878:189; 1880:134–135, 309, note 1). Kalani'ōpu'u was district chief of Ka'ū, allowed to retain his father's right (Fornander 1880:133). Perhaps Alapa'i retained control over Kohala as the senior Mahi male, or his brother, Hā'ae. Possibly Keōua served as Kona high chief, as his father Kalanike'eaumoku appears to have had control over this district (Barrere 1986:122).

71. Fornander 1880:131, 132, 136.

72. Hā'ae also married Keawe's daughter, Kekelaokulani, the defeated Kalanike'eaumoku's sister (Anonymous 1896 in McKenzie 1983:67).

73. Fornander 1880:133.

74. Fornander 1880:134.

75. State Historic Preservation Division's Site File 10-01-2328.

76. Fornander 1880:36–37; Ellis 1963; Stokes 1919. Some said that these stones came from Pololū Valley (Varigny 1981; Remy 1979; Bond 1885). Fornander (1880:53) also mentioned another oral tradition stating the heiau was named after a priest of the Hawaiian voyager Mo'ikeha,

called Mo'okini who was dropped off from Mo'ikeha's canoe on his return from Kahiki.

77. Fornander 1880:38. In the late 1700s, in the reign of Kalani'ōpu'u or Kamehameha, additional building at this heiau may have occurred, because a dedication was held there with 10 human sacrifices offered to the gods (Bond 1885, based on information which he gathered in the 1840s from eyewitnesses).

78. Fowke 1922. Bill Sproat, a long-time Kohala resident (born in 1903), also said that numerous stone walls were once in this area, "Where they [the people in the past—RC] had their houses and what-nots..." (1981 interview in Napoka n.d.:28).

79. Fornander 1919–1920, 6(1):202–204.

80. Fornander 1919–1920, 6(1):202–204.

81. Fornander 1919–1920,6(1):204.

82. Kamakau 1961:68–69; 'I'i 1959:3. Here, one must mention that some place Kamehameha's birth 18 years later in 1758. Kuykendall (1957:430) suggested 1758 based on the mention of a bright star being present and interpreted this star to be Halley's comet. As Stokes (1933:47) has noted, this 1758 birth date—which also marked the invasion of Maui and the death of Kekaulike—would place these events later than given in Kamakau's and Fornander's accounts. If one uses 1740–1760 as Alapa'inui's reign, then these events would have occurred later in his reign, if one assumes 1758 was the date of Kamehameha's birth.

83. Kamakau 1961:70.

84. Kamakau 1961:70.

85. Fornander 1880:138.

86. Kamakau 1961:71.

87. Fornander 1880:139.

88. Kamakau 1961:72.

89. Fornander 1880:139.

90. Kamakau 1961:72.

91. Kamakau 1961:73.

92. Kamakau 1961:74.

93. Fornander 1880:141.

94. Kamakau 1961:74.

95. Fornander 1880:141. Peleiōhōlani is mentioned no further in the accounts related to Hawai'i Island, but he lived to an old age, until ca. 1779–1780, outliving Alapa'inui by 25 years. The Cook expedition, on February 27, 1779, passed off Moloka'i and saw large fires burning ashore. Hawaiian women on board said it was a signal that Peleiōhōlani was at war against Kahekili and Maui (King in Beaglehole 1967, 3:584).

96. 'I'i (1959:3) provided one version of this death. Also, Keōua, "the high chief of Kona" had his bones buried in a cave in the Ka'awaloa cliff, Ka Pali Kapu o Keōua (Barrere 1986:122).

97. Kamakau 1961:75–78.

98. Fornander 1880:144.

99. Kamakau 1961:77.

100. Fornander 1880:145.

101. Kamakau 1961:78; Fornander 1880:145. 'I'i (1959:4–6) gave a slightly different account of this battle.

102. Fornander 1880:146.

103. 'I'i 1959:6.

104. 'I'i 1959:9–10. Kekūhaupi'o eventually married the daughter of Kalani'ōpu'u's high priest, Holo'ae (Fornander 1880:192, note 1).

105. 'I'i 1959:9.

106. Kamakau 1961:79–81; Fornander 1880:146–148.

107. Kamakau 1961:84; Fornander 1880:150–151.

108. 'I'i 1959:10.

109. 'I'i 1959:10. See Kamakau (1961:84) for a similar statement.

110. Fornander 1880:151–156.

111. Kamakau 1961:85.

112. Fornander 1880:153.

113. Fornander 1919, 5(2):452–457. See Kamakau (1961:87–88) for a short version. See also Desha (in press:1921, Apr. 28). This delaying action was said to be at Waikapu at Pu'uhele among ilima thickets ('I'i 1959:10).

114. 'I'i 1959:11.

115. 'I'i 1959:11; Kamakau 1961:85–87; Fornander 1880:154.

116. Kamakau 1961:86; Fornander 1880:154. Keaweohano, a chief of Hilo who also held Lanihau ahupua'a in Kona, was slain with the 'Ālapa as a well-known part of this story (Kamakau 1961:86, 130–132). Stokes (1930a:27–28) argued that this battle occurred after 1779 because iron daggers were said to have been used by the Hawai'i side and because Kahahana could not have been supplying aid as the O'ahu ruler, since Peleiōhōlani was still alive and was the ruler of O'ahu. While Peleiōhōlani was alive, one wonders whether Kahahana, then living on Maui, could not simply have led the O'ahu force. In his "A Tale of Kekuhaupio," Desha said Kahahana was sent by Peleiōhōlani (Desha in press: 1921, Mar. 10). Also, the source on the daggers is not clear. I wonder if this conclusion of Stokes might bear more analysis.

117. Fornander 1880:156–157; Kamakau 1961:89–91.

118. King in Beaglehole 1967, 3(1):499.

119. Kamakau 1961:96–99.

120. Ledyard 1963:111.

121. Ledyard 1963:111.

122. Cook & King 1784; Samwell 1786; Ellis 1784; Ledyard 1963; the accounts of Cook, Clerke, King, Samwell, and others in Beaglehole 1967, 3.

123. Kamakau 1961; 'I'i 1959; Fornander 1880.

124. Fornander 1880:192–197.

125. Kamakau 1961:86. Samwell said Kalaimanokaho'owaha (Kalima-nou-ka'aha) struck Cook first with a club and then Nu'a killed Cook (Beaglehole 1967, 3(2):1202).

126. Kalimu was one of these chiefs (Fornander 1880:194, note 2). See also Clerke (Beaglehole 1967, 3(1):545, 547) and Samwell (Beaglehole 1967, 3(2): 1203, 1207).

127. Ledyard 1963:112. See also Samwell (Beaglehole 1967, 3(2):1168); King (Beaglehole 1967, 3(1):499); and Law (1779:Jan. 26). King described Kalani'ōpu'u as an "old immaciated infirm man" (Beaglehole 1967, 3(1):512). Burney said he was "a tall thin old Man...though in walking he still carries himself upright and erect" (Beaglehole 1967, 3(1):512, note 4). Daws (1968:29) summed these descriptions—"Kalaniopu, shrunken with age and palsied by a lifetime of awa drinking." However, one should add the caution made by Stokes (1933) that people were regarded as old at a much younger age by observers in the 1700s. Old was being in one's 40s, unlike today. And 'awa drinking increased the appearance of age. Stokes (1930a:36) suggested Kalani'ōpu'u was 53 at his death, instead of the 79 or 80 that Kamakau and Fornander indicated.

128. Fornander 1880:200.

129. Fornander 1880:200–201; Kamakau 1961:106–107. Desha, however, wrote that Nu'uanu was seized by Keaweaheulu at Kalani'ōpu'u's command, and the corpse was offered up at Mo'okini (in press:1921, July 7). But Samwell of Cook's expedition stated that a woman from Hawai'i Island, who was on board the ship, told of the death of "a Chief called Nanoo-ano" [Nu'uanu] from a shark (Samwell in Beaglehole 1967, 3(2):1220).

130. Fornander 1880:201. King's account in Beaglehole (1967, 3(1):616) identified Kamehameha as second in succession to Kīwala'ō. The splitting of the god and land has parallels with Līloa's similar division between 'Umi and Hākau. In Līloa's case, 'Umi seems to have perhaps been a favored son. In Kalani'ōpu'u's case, Kamehameha certainly served him well in war and peace; perhaps this was an attempt to reward him.

131. Fornander 1880:201–203; Kamakau 1961:109.

132. Fornander 1880:204.

133. Fornander 1880:204; Kamakau 1961:81, 119–120; 'I'i 1959:7.

134. Cf. Kailua (Fornander 1880:152; Kamakau 1961:85); Kahalu'u (Fornander 1880; Kamakau 1961:85, 105); north Kohala (Fornander 1880:200; Kamakau 1961:106–107); Waipi'o (Fornander 1880:201; Kamakau 1961:107–108); Hilo (Fornander 1880:201; Kamakau 1961:108); Puna (Clerke in Beaglehole 1967, 3(1):606); and places in Ka'ū (Fornander 1880:201–204; Kamakau 1961:108–110; Desha in press).

135. Archaeological work done in Kealakekua Bay's coastal area: 1909 study of Hikiau area (Stokes 1919), 1929 brief survey (Reinecke 1929–30), 1968 brief survey (Soehren 1968), 1969–70 mapping of much of Ka'awaloa (Hommon 1969; 1970), 1977 two test pits in Hikiau area (by Hommon, reported in Yent 1985:61–62), 1981 reconnaissance (Yent & Ota 1981), and 1984–85 mapping of the Hikiau area (Yent 1985).

136. Cook & King 1784, III:128.

137. Samwell in Beaglehole (1967, 3(2):1175–1176). Marine Corporal Ledyard (1963:103) suggested 1,400 houses were present, but his figures seem greatly exaggerated; and in fact, Ledyard's account often suffers from flaws in details, while Samwell and King both seem to have been quite reliable recorders (cf. Valeri 1985:xix; Beaglehole 1967).

138. Ledyard (1963:128) misinterpreted these south shore houses to be one "town," which he called Kireekakooa. Cook & King (1785, III:2) called it Kakooa. In contrast, Samwell realized the houses were in the different lands of Kealakekua, Waipunaula, Kalama, Kahauloa and Ke'ei (Beaglehole 1967, 3(2):1175–1176). Probably the confusion arose because the expedition's members spent much of their time in the Hikiau heiau vicinity in Kealakekua ahupua'a, and they mistakenly assumed that name applied to the entire sourth shore area. Kamakau (1961) and the Fornander Collection stories show that Nāpo'opo'o was the broader term for this settlement along the south shore, as it is today.

139. Ledyard 1963:128. Note Ledyard's house count is much too high, yet the quote portrays the appearance of the dwelling areas well.

140. Ledyard 1963:129.

141. Samwell in Beaglehole (1967, 3(2):1176).

142. Ledyard 1963:114–115, 129. These areas also seem likely to have been used for the game of pahe'e (2–5-foot darts) and 'ulu maika (Ellis 1963:134, describing an arena in Ka'ū).

143. Yent 1985.

144. Samwell counted 70–80 houses and mentioned Palea's and Kalani'ōpu'u's house (Beaglehole 1967, 3(2):1165–1166, 1175–1176,1195–1196), Fornander (1880:185, note 2) and Kamakau (1961:101) referred to Kalani'ōpu'u and Keaweaheulu's dwellings.

145. Kamakau 1961:102; Fornander 1880:185. Kamakau (1961:102) described the presence of the men's house.

146. Kamakau 1961:102.

147. Manby 1959:29–30; Fuller 5/30/1853 (Letter to A. Thurston); Alvarez 1989:5.6.

148. Reinecke 1929–30; Hommon 1970. There are also modern alterations of the Ka'awaloa sites, and many of the enclosures and platforms may be more recent.

149. Reinecke 1929–30:1; Hommon 1970:12.

150. Reinecke 1929–30:1; Soehren 1968:7.

151. This trail is discussed in Bloxam's 1825 account, referenced in Soehren & Newman (1968:15–16).

152. Yent 1985:4–9, 37; Stokes 1919. The wall has been called the "Great Wall" by some archaeologists.

153. King in Beaglehole (1967, 3(1):607).

154. Cook & King 1784:394–395.

155. Ledyard 1963:110.

156. Yent 1985:Table 1. See Samwell (Beaglehole 1967, 3(2):1177).

157. Cook & King 1784, III:6. See also Fornander (1880:174–175), Samwell (Beaglehole 1967, 3(2):1177–1178), King (Beaglehole 1967, 3(1):505) and Ellis (1784, I:180–182) for descriptions. King stated that the skulls were from Maui men (Beaglehole 1967, 3(1):505. On departing, Cook was given permission to remove the railing for fuel, and the sailors also took all the temple images, except perhaps the central image (Fornander 1880:186, note 2; Cook & King 1784, III:25; Ledyard 1963:136–137). The central image was Kūnuiākea (King in Beaglehole 1967, 3(1):621).

158. Thrum 1924:23; Soehren 1968:6; Yent 1985:20. A 1917 restoration

evidently changed the internal features somewhat (Thrum 1924). Modification in the 1950s saw a new ramp and stairs added, walls slanted, and small pebbles ('ili'ili) placed on the surface (Yent 1985:20).

159. Lisiansky 1814:105.

160. King in Cook & King (1784:394–395); Samwell in Beaglehole (1967, 3(2):1169).

161. Ellis 1963:36.

162. Reinecke 1929–30:9–10; Hommon 1970:15.

163. Reinecke 1929–30; Hommon & Crozier 1970:12.

164. The State Historic Preservation Division's library should be consulted. Among these surveys are: Rosendahl (1984a, 1984b), Connolly 1974, Soehren (1977, 1980), Walker & Rosendahl (1985), Yent (1984), Komori (1984), Cordy (1985a).

165. Cordy 1985a.

166. Cordy 1985a.

167. Soehren & Newman 1968:12–13.

168. Kirch 1984, 1985.

169. Rosendahl 1973.

170. Schilt 1984.

171. Cordy, Tainter, Renger & Hitchcock 1991.

172. Cordy, Tainter, Renger & Hitchcock 1991; Renger 1973.

173. Kawachi 1989.

174. M. S. Allen 1984.

175. Cordy 1987b; BCB n.d., A:419 re: Moa'ula. Lo'i were evidently also present near the pond behind Punalu'u Bay (NR n.d., 8:144, 656).

176. Barrere (1983:26–29) showed that many of these Waimea lands were created as independent lands by Kamehameha between 1795–1812, by splitting lands to award to his chiefs. For example, the subdivided pieces of Waimea ahupua'a became Waikoloa (farmlands and kula grasslands held by Isaac Davis's descendants), Lalamilo (the drier farmlands and kula belonging to the king), Waikoloa iki (the king's stream-watered property in the Waimea hills) and the coastal 'ili kūpono of 'Anaeho'omalu and Kalāhuipua'a (kept by the king).

177. At 2,750 feet in Waimea, rainfall is 40 inches per year, but in most of the swale area at 2,280–2,480 feet, rainfall is only 15–20 inches per year (J. Clark 1981:4).

178. J. Clark 1981:24.

179. Ten fields were measured and averaged 122 x 27 meters, 3,110 $m^2$ (J. Clark 1981:24).

180. J. Clark 1981, 1983b, 1987. These divisions (hillslope, flats, airport area, and swales) correlate roughly with ClarKūs (1983b) Field Complexes 1, 2, 4 and 3.

181. Carter Case 1915:1295–1303; in Reeve 1983:235.

182. J. Clark 1983:295–296, 308.

183. J. Clark 1983:295; Reeve 1983:193, 210, 234.

184. Carter Case 1915:1295–1303; Reeve 1983:235.

185. Where the Lanikepu, Waikoloa and Lanimaumau streams were present were three named clusters of houses—Keali'i, Waikoloa, and Pu'ukapu (Ellis 1963:289; Mission Committee Report of 1830:Map of Waimea; Barrere 1983:30–31).

186. Hammatt, Borthwick & Shideler 1988; Hammatt & Shideler 1989. Fifty-one percent of the shellfish was cowrie, a common pattern.

187. This example is similar to sites 2776, 2779 and 5947 in the southern edge of the swale area, except no permanent dwellings were present at those sites (Reeve 1983:191–202, 221–231). It is also similar to the features found around the stream flat swale studied by Cultural Surveys Hawaii (Hammatt, Borthwick & Shideler 1988:30; Hammatt & Shideler 1989).

188. J. Clark 1983b; Reeve 1983.

189. J. Clark 1981, 1983.

190. Hammatt, Borthwick & Shideler 1988; Hammatt & Shideler 1989.

191. Franklin, Maly & Rosendahl 1994; Barrera 1994.

192. J. Clark 1983; S. Clark, E. D. Davidson & Cleghorn 1990; Thompson &

Rosendahl 1992; Head, Goodfellow & Wolforth 1995; Erkelens 1995.

193. Head, Goodfellow & Wolforth 1995; S. Clark & Cleghorn 1990; Hammatt & Shideler 1989; J. Clark 1983b. Clark (1983b) had an earlier date of A.D. 800–1325 in the airport area, but he considered this date too early and suspect. PHRI recently also obtained a very early date associated with a canal on the airport area's slopes (A.D. 770–1020, Thompson & Rosendahl 1992), but this may be from stream layers predating settlement (Wolforth 1999:17).

194. Reeve 1983:212–215 on site 5945.

195. Reeve 1983; Hammatt & Shideler 1989; Barrera 1994.

196. Hammatt & Shideler 1989:47; Barrera 1994.

197. Christensen 1983.

198. Pearsall & Trimble 1983:495.

199. J. Clark 1987; Barrere 1983:27.

200. Hommon 1986, 1976; Kirch 1979, 1984, 1985.

201. Kirch 1979.

202. Jensen 1990b.

203. Welch 1988.

204. Cordy 1975, 1978; Jensen 1990b:9–10, 111.

205. Cordy 1978, 1981.

206. J. Clark 1987.

207. Burtchard 1996.

208. This is a point archaeologists in Hawai'i have known since the early 1980s. Some now totally ignore volcanic glass dates. However, when paired radiocarbon and volcanic glass dates are available, they often seem relatively compatible (cf. Komori 1993). More work is clearly needed on the volcanic glass dating issue.

209. New work solely using radiocarbon dates suggests a stabilizing of population after the 1600s (Dye & Komori 1992a). This work is fascinating, using hundreds of dates from habitation sites. But, the finding of a late stabilization of population may be a result of archaeological sampling problems. Archeologists typically submit radiocarbon dates from basal layers of their sites. If more dates were submitted from upper layers, the number of dates in the prehistoric times of the 1600s and 1700s may well dramatically rise.

Certainly, by the end of the 1700s population did crash due to foreign diseases. Epidemics seem to have begun clearly ca. 1803–1804, with the 'ōku'u, when high and lesser chiefs are first noted in the histories to die from outside disease. Family size decline probably became apparent in the late 1790s due to sterility and increased infant deaths caused by venereal diseases (Pirie 1972; Schmitt 1979). The result was likely a new generation of drastically reduced size. This would have been the start of Stannard's "the horror" (1989).

210. Leach et al. 1988; Cordy, Tainter, Renger & Hitchcock 1991.

211. BCB n.d., A:142 under Kahuku ahupua'a.

212. Kamakau 1961.

213. See Kolb (1991) for a discussion on changes in heiau construction, based on Maui findings. On Maui, heiau continued to be dramatically increased in size up until European contact.

214. Ellis 1963:194.

215. Wright, Takahasi & Griggs 1992:fig. 25, p. 23).

216. Ellis 1963:194.

217. Kolb 1991.

## NOTES TO CHAPTER 10

1. Kamakau 1961:123.

2. Kamakau 1961:121.

3. Kamakau 1961:158.

4. Kamakau 1961:117; Fornander 1880:302.

5. Kamakau 1961:117. According to Fornander (1880:303), Ke'eaumoku, Kamanawa, Kame'eiamoku, Keaweaheulu, and Kekūhaupi'o had already identified Kamehameha as a potential leader for their claims, and he believed that these chiefs were truly

partners in the conquest that followed (Fornander 1880:315).

6. Kamakau 1961:117. This statement and the rest of Kamakau's account agrees with Fornander's and Ellis's (1963), in contrast to 'I'i (1959:13), Dibble (1909 [1843]:42), Jarves, and Bingham (1847:36) who said Kamehameha was given Kona, Kohala and Hāmākua and Kīwala'ō given Ka'ū, Puna, and Hilo. The former is much more in line with common patterns of succeeding rulers; the latter appear likely to be justifications or "fabrications by partisans of Kamehameha" (Kuykendall 1957:32, note 7; Fornander 1880:299–302).

7. Kamakau 1961:118; Fornander 1880:304; Desha in press:1921, Aug. 18.

8. Kamakau 1961:118; Dibble 1909 [1843]:42.

9. Kamakau 1961:118; Fornander 1880:304; Bingham 1847:36. 'I'i (1959:13) claimed that Kekūhaupi'o had heard the chiefs of Ka'ū planning to bring the remains to Pa o 'Umi in Kailua in order to gain more Kona lands, so he went north to warn Kamehameha. 'I'i's accounts of times before his own, however, are often fraught with error, and it is likely that this account may not be accurate in its specifics. Another version stated Ke'eaumoku met the funeral procession at Hōnaunau and not off southernmost Kona, but otherwise this followed the story given in the text (Fornander 1919, 5(2):466).

10. Kamakau 1961:118. 'I'i (1959:13) had Kamehameha in residence at Ke'ei before Kīwala'ō arrived at Hōnaunau, disagreeing with all other accounts—which makes 'I'i's specifics unreliable.

11. Kamakau 1961:118; Fornander 1880:305; Bingham 1847:36.

12. Kamakau 1961:119; Fornander 1880:305–306.

13. Kamakau 1961:119; Fornander 1880:306.

14. Kamakau 1961:119.

15. Kamakau 1961:119; Fornander 1880:307.

16. Kamakau 1961:120; Fornander 1880:308.

17. Kamakau 1961:120; Fornander 1880:308; Bingham 1847:37. N. Emerson (1903:18–19) pointed out that it was rather strange that Keōua did not align himself with Kamehameha's forces as an aggrieved party, rather than attack Kamehameha; and he suggested it may have been a plan by Kīwala'ō, Keōua and Keawema'uhili to provoke Kamehameha's forces, defeat them, and acquire their lands. Kuykendall (1957) commented that Emerson's argument may be a logical explanation.

18. Kamakau 1961:120; Fornander 1880:309.

19. Kamakau 1961:120, 123; Fornander 1880:315.

20. Kamakau 1961:121; Fornander 1880:310.

21. Kamakau 1961:121. Kala'imamahū, Kamehameha's half-brother, was said to have been the war leader at Moku'ōhai for Kamehameha's forces ('I'i 1959:49). Warriors slain or captured by Kamehameha's forces during the battle were evidently ritually offered up at Hikiau heiau, the luakini. Notable among these warriors were Ahia, a high chief of Puna, and Kīwala'ō himself (Desha in press:1921, Sept. 22 & 29, Oct. 6, 13, 20 and 27).

22. Kamakau 1961:121. See also Fornander (1880:309–310; 1919, 5(2):466–468); Ellis (1963:94); Dibble (1909 [1843]:43).

23. Kamakau 1961:121.

24. Kamakau 1961:122; Fornander 1880:310. Ellis (1963:94) was told that Keōua had been wounded in the thigh by a spear about the same time that Kīwala'ō was killed.

25. Fornander 1880:310.

26. Ellis 1963:94. Ka'ahumanu, daughter of Ke'eaumoku, then 8 years of age, had been taken to the pu'uhonua prior to or during the battle, and "after the battle, thence removed by her wounded father" (Bingham 1847:37).

27. Kamakau 1961:122; Fornander 1880:310–311.

28. Fornander 1880:301. During this time of multiple kingdoms, Kamehameha

was called the "kona Haku Alii, Kamehameha" (HEN II:56). Keawema'uhili, thus, might have been labeled "Hilo Haku Ali'i" and Keōua the "Ka'ū Haku Ali'i." In an article written in 1865, all three rulers are called "ke Ali'i"—Keōua, "ke Alii o Kau a me Puna," Keawema'uhili, "ke alii o Hilo"; Kamehameha, "Moi ... no Kona, Kohala a me Hāmākua" (Ke Au Okoa, May 22, 1865).

29. Ellis 1963:95.

30. Reinecke 1930b:151.

31. Fornander 1880:212.

32. Kamakau 1961:259.

33. It is usually noted that Keōpūolani was tied to the Hawai'i royal line through her father and to the Maui line through her mother, and indeed her mother (Keku'iapoiwa Liliha) evidently considered herself a Maui woman and apparently despised the royal Keawe line of Hawai'i (Kamakau 1961:260). Nonetheless, Keku'iapoiwa was related to the Keawe line through her father Keōua, the son of a Hawai'i ruler (albeit a ruler with a brief reign), and her great-grandfather was Keawe himself. Also, Kīwala'ō was related to the Maui royal line through his mother, Kalola, and was a grandson of a Maui ruler.

34. Kamakau 1961:124; Fornander 1880:220–221.

35. Kuykendall 1957:33–34. A 1865 *Ke Au Okoa* list of dates places Kānekoa's death in December of 1782 (May 22, 1865), as did F. S. Lyman's list of dates compiled in 1857 (Lyman 1857).

36. Kamakau 1961:124; Fornander 1880:316–317. This war was also called the Kaua Awa, bitter war (N. Emerson 1903:20).

37. Kamakau 1961:125; Fornander 1880:317; Dibble 1909 [1843]:46.

38. Kamakau 1961:125.

39. Kamakau 1961:126; Fornander 1880:318–319; Dibble 1909 [1843]:46; Desha in press:1922, March 16. One of these raids at Kea'au in Puna was where Kamehameha almost lost his life. While attacking a group of fishermen, his foot was caught in a crevice and he was struck over the head. However, the fishermen or villagers, in fear for their lives and not knowing who he was, fled (cf. Kamakau 1964:15; N. Emerson 1903:20–21).

40. Kamakau 1961:126; Fornander 1880:319; Kuykendall 1957:34. Two sources place the war of Hāpu'u in 1784 (*Ke Au Okoa* 1865: May 22; Lyman 1857). N. Emerson (1903:22) said Kamehameha's forces actually were encamped at Hilo Bay for several months, when Keawema'uhili and his forces were in Ka'ū with his ally Keōua.

41. Fornander (1880:228–229, 320) placed this series of events ca. 1785–1786; Kuykendall (1957:34) suggested 1786. Seventeen eighty-six is also reinforced by Dixon's 1786 observation that no high chiefs were about Kealakekua Bay; he was told that all the absent chiefs were engaged in a war with a neighboring island (Dixon 1789:51).

42. Kamakau 1961:143–144; Fornander 1880:229.

43. Meares 1790:4–9, 336–441; Kamakau 1961:153; Fornander 1880:222, note 1 on p. 231. The dates for Ka'iana's return are established in the historical records (Meares 1790:336–341). Kamakau (1961) had this return after the *Fair American* event and after the invasion of Maui and the battle of 'Īao, which is clearly incorrect, since accounts by Western traders arriving soon after the battle placed the taking of the *Fair American* in March of 1790 (cf. Ingraham 1971:79–81), as did Young and Davis, the survivors (Vancouver 1798, 2:136–139). Considerable jealousy among Kamehameha's original chiefs seems to have been directed against Ka'iana, who was both more knowledgeable in Western ways and weapons and was also a more successful general than Ke'eaumoku. This seems particularly to have been the case after 1792. [Note: In Lyman's 1857 list of dates, Ka'iana is said to have gone to Kahiki in 1787—"Holo o Kaiana i Kahiki" (Lyman 1857).]

44. Meares 1790:354.

45. Meares 1790:354, 356.

46. Fornander 1880:235; Quimper, told by Kahekili's son in April 1791 (Minson 1952:76); Vancouver (1798, 3:66), told by Young and Davis; Bingham (1847:39); Kuykendall (1957:24).

47. Kamakau 1961:147; Fornander 1880:235. Dibble, 1909 [1843]:48, said Keawema'uhili also sent along Kalanimanokaho'owaha, a renowned warrior of Kalani'ōpu'u's time, who many said had slain Cook.

48. Kamakau 1961:148; Fornander 1880:236.

49. Fornander 1880:236.

50. Fornander 1880:237.

51. Fornander 1880:237; Kamakau 1961:148–149.

52. Kamakau 1961:149; Fornander 1880:212; *Ke Au Okoa* 1865:May 22; Lyman 1857.

53. Kamakau 1961:149; Fornander 1880:238–239.

54. Kamakau 1961:149.

55. Kamakau 1961:150. Fornander, 1880:239, gave a very similar version.

56. Kamakau 1961:150; Fornander 1880:240.

57. Kamakau 1961:151; Fornander 1880:240; *Ke Au Okoa* 1856:May 22; Lyman 1857.

58. Kalola's daughters and granddaughter were taken back to Hawai'i, and Keōpūolani was raised as Wahine-pio at Keauhou until she was grown. She was not an official wife of Kamehameha's until 1795 (Kamakau 1961:260).

59. Kamakau 1961:151–152; Fornander 1880:323–324.

60. Quote from Dibble, *History of the Sandwich Islands*, given in Fornander 1880:324–326. Fornander believed that Dibble's account was the "most graphic and correct," noting that it corresponded with a firsthand observation (from Mona) that Kamakau (1961:152) recorded. Ellis' (1963:174) account referred to people being struck by stones and covered by ashes and lava, which was not correct, but he did give the gist of the tragedy. Also, he "had heard the account several times before, with some little variation as to the numbers killed, and the appearance of Pele to Keōua, in the column of smoke as it rose from crater" (Ellis 1963:175).

61. Geologists now believe the warriors died from "asphyxiation from hot, ash-laden gasses...in a lateral blast" similar to that of Mt. St. Helens (Wright, Takahashi & Griggs 1992:fig. 19, p. 19).

62. Kamakau 1961:152.

63. Fornander 1880:326.

64. Ellis 1963:174—"Some of the natives say, the warriors of two districts [ahupua'a], about eighty men, perished on this occasion."

65. Kamakau 1961:153.

66. Fornander 1880:326.

67. Fornander 1880:326.

68. Kamakau 1961:153; Fornander 1880:326–327.

69. Kamakau 1961:154; Fornander 1880:327. Ellis' guide in 1823—apparently a Ka'ū native—pointed out the hill Makanau as a place where Keōua, defeated by Ka'iana, surrendered to warriors of Ka'iana and went to Kawaihae (Ellis 1963:143). This account, however, was clearly incorrect in many details: in saying that Keōua did not control western Ka'ū, Keōua was marching to attack Kona when Pele struck down his division, he met Ka'iana's force right after the eruption, Ka'iana routed Keōua at Pu'ukoki, and Keōua surrendered to Ka'iana to be taken to Kawaihae (1963:143–144). The oral account that was given Ellis seems to be a melding of fact and fiction, combining several discontinuous events—perhaps by an individual who was not present or even alive then. Bingham, whose chief informant was usually his protégée Ka'ahumanu, had Keōua in Hilo when Ka'iana arrived off Ka'ū, then hurrying to Ka'ū and losing his men to Kīlauea, and finally induced to surrender (1847:40–41). This sequence of events was very similar to Ellis'.

70. Kamakau 1961:154.

71. Fornander 1880:328, note 1.

72. Kamakau 1961:155; Fornander 1880:327–328.

73. Soehren 1964; Bonk 1968; Barrera 1974; M. S. Allen 1987; Hammatt, Shideler, Borthwick, Stride, McDermott & Nakamura 1991.

74. Barrere 1983:27.

75. Kuykendall 1957:37. The basis for Kuykendall's conclusion was that in October of 1791, Ingraham returned to the islands, having been there in May. Some time between May and October, Keōua had been killed (Ingraham 1971:162).

76. Ellis 1963:55–56. Bingham (1847:84) visited the heiau in 1820 in the company of Kalanimoku, and recorded its area as 240 feet x 120 feet.

77. Ellis 1963:55–56.

78. Ellis 1963:56.

79. Ellis 1963:57.

80. Ellis 1963:56.

81. Ellis 1963:56.

82. Ellis 1963:57.

83. Freycinet 1978:18.

84. Freycinet 1978:74.

85. Ladd 1986:3–5.

86. C. J. Lyons 1853; Alexander 1869; Stokes 1919; Fowke 1922:183–184; Soehren 1964; Kikuchi & Cluff 1969; Ladd 1986b.

87. HEN 1:266 in Valeri 1985:385, note 4.

88. Kikuchi & Cluff 1969.

89. Ladd 1986b:3. See also Kinney (1913:43) referenced in Kelly (1974:6). At least one oral historical account said Pu'ukoholā heiau was present during the reign of Lonoikamakahiki (1640–1660) (Fornander 1917, 4(2):324–327; Thrum 1924:15).

90. Valeri 1985:163.

91. Fornander 1880:329; Kamakau 1961:155.

92. Ladd 1986b.

93. Kamakau (1961:159–162) and Fornander (1880:241–244) provided accounts for this invasion. Fornander argued that the invasion took place before the completion of the heiau and Keōua's death. Kuykendall (1957:37, note 18) reiterated this point, referencing the journals of Ingraham and Quimper. Indeed, the journals of Western visitors showed all the high chiefs and Kamehameha at Kawaihae from the end of March 1791 to May 1791 (Quimper in Minton 1952; Colnett n.d.:220; Ingraham 1971:69). In April, Quimper spoke with Kahekili's son, Manono, at Waikīkī and learned that a battle had been fought shortly before with Kā'eo speared by Ka'iana and that Kā'eo and Kahekili were still on Maui (Quimper in Minton 1952:76–77). [A 1865 *Ke Au Okoa* article (1865:May 22) placed the invasion in 1791 and Keōua's death in 1792. Lyman's 1857 list had both in 1791, with Keōua's death after the invasion.]

94. Fornander 1880:73–74, 243.

95. In a 1907 account, two Maui chiefs (Manono and Kahekilinuiahumanu) were said to be slain either in Kahekili's raids or in the battle off Waimanu. They supposedly were placed on the altar of Mo'okini heiau (J. Ena, 1907, in McKenzie 1986:120—story from L. M. Kekupuohika-pulikoliko and S. L. K. Pelioholani).

96. Ingraham 1971:69.

97. Kamakau 1961:155. Fornander (1880:331–335) agreed with Kamakau's account, as Dibble and Jarvis gave few details, and Malo no information on this sequence of events.

98. Kamakau 1961:155.

99. Kamakau 1961:155.

100. Cf. Fornander 1880:333.

101. Ellis 1963:144.

102. Kamakau 1961:156. Valeri (1985:163) gave other references supporting the view that Keōua knew he would die.

103. In 1823 Hawaiians did tell Ellis: "Pele, they said, was propitious to Tamehameha, and availed herself of the opportunity afforded by the contiguous encampment of Keōua to diminish his forces and aid the cause of his rival" (Ellis 1963:174).

104. Kamakau 1961:156.

105. Kamakau 1961:156.

106. Kamakau 1961:156.

107. Kamakau 1961:157. Valeri

(1985:163) suggested that Keōua landed to the traditional mock spear attack (kali'i ritual), which proved through deceit to be a real attack.

108. Kamakau 1961:157; Fornander 1880:334. Keali'imaika'i, Kamehameha's brother, apparently demanded that Ka'ōleiokū—Keōua's half-brother and according to some Kamehameha's son—also be slain, but Kamehameha refused. This difference among brothers may mark an existing or developing schism between Kamehameha and his younger brother,
for Keali'imaika'i received little land in the redistribution (Puget, 1793, in Sahlins 1981:62). Kala'imamahū and Kamehameha's son, Kīna'u, also fell from favor several years later, when opposing Kamehameha's way ('I'i 1959:49–50).

109. Kamakau 1961:158; Bingham 1847:42. Young stated that 13 humans were offered that day (Apple 1969:17, from a source withheld by request). Keōua's body remained on a lele for several days, and was then taken down and cooked in an oven to remove the flesh and prepare his bones (HEN 1:266; Valeri 1985:338, note 266; 385, note 4).

110. Kamakau 1961:158.

111. Kamakau 1961:123.

112. Fornander 1880:301, 309, note 1.

113. As this book was being prepared for press, I came across an article which said Keawema'uhili married Kekikipa'a (a daughter of Kame'eiamoku) after the battle of Moku'ōhai (Morris 1925:41–42), and another reference that he also was married to Kalola of Moloka'i and had a son Pi'imaiwa'a with her (Desha in press).

114. Fornander 1880:235; Kamakau 1961:147.

115. Fornander (1880:335) for Hi'iaka; Desha (in press:1921, Aug. 11) for Kaiolani.

116. Kamehameha was in Kealakekua in December of 1788 (Douglas in Meares 1967:337), in September of 1789 (Mortimer 1791:51–52), and in March of 1790 during the *Fair American* incident.

117. Kamehameha was living in Kawaihae in March of 1789 (Douglas in Meares 1967:354) and from the end of March into May of 1791 (Ingraham 1971:69, 74; Quimper in Minson 1952:31–42).

118. Quimper was told in 1791 by Keali'imaika'i that Kamehameha also resided in Kailua (Minson 1952:47). Three years later (Feb. 26, 1794), Vancouver described "the royal residence at this place; which consisted of three of the neatest constructed houses we had yet seen; but not having been constantly inhabited for some time past, they were not in good repair. This habitation of the king, like that at Karakakooa, was in the neighbourhood of a grand morai [luakini heiau], close to the sea side" (1798, III:61). 'I'i (1959:110, 116–117) placed this residence's location at the same spot where Hulihe'e Palace is today, just south of Pa o 'Umi—the residence of 'Umi.

119. Waipi'o (Fornander 1880:324). In Kohala, Kamehameha resided in the Hālawa to Hala'ula area, with the surf spot Kauhola being in Hala'ula (Fornander 1880:319–320).

120. Older Hawaiians who grew up in Kawaihae say the streams once flowed more constantly at the shore.

121. Upland soils begin at the 1,200–1,400-foot elevation (Barrera 1974:14).

122. There are numerous accounts of pigs and vegetables obtained in trade by ships at Kawaihae, and it is assumed they came from Waimea (cf. J. Clark 1983a:42, table 3.1). In 1793, Menzies traveled up to Waimea and commented on "the number of people that I met loaded with the produce of their plantations...bringing it down to the water side to market" (1920:55–56). Recent archaeological reconnaissance work in upland Kawaihae uka has identified extensive agricultural fields, often watered by irrigation canals, and associated permanent houses and religious sites (Hammatt & Shideler 1991)—suggesting that many food items may also have come down to the shore from this upland area.

123. Freycinet 1978:17–19.

124. The Pelekane sites are labeled site 2297 in the State of Hawaii's inventory of historic places. Barrera (1974:6) and Kelly (1974:23) minimally discuss the ruins.

125. See Kelly (1974:3) and Kamakau (1961:58) for Lonoikamakahiki's presence. See Kamakau (1961:77) for Alapa'inui's presence.

126. Cf. Kelly 1974:67–71.

127. Vancouver 1798,II:116–117.

128. Ellis 1963:288.

129. Meares 1788:342.

130. M. S. Allen 1987; Hammatt, Shideler, Borthwick, Stride, McDermott & Nakamura 1991.

131. Rosendahl & Carter 1988.

132. Carlson & Rosendahl 1990a.

133. Kamakau 1961:155; Fornander 1880:331.

134. Cf. Cordy (1987b) which summarized these Māhele period patterns.

135. Barrera & Hommon 1972; Crozier & Barrera 1974.

136. Kelly 1980:fig. 28.

137. Barrera & Hommon 1972; Crozier & Barrera 1974.

138. Stokes 1919; Kelly 1980. This heiau is also labeled Kāne'ele'ele by some. Thrum had so labeled it, but Stokes (1991:132–133) when asking Ka'ū people in 1906 could find no people in the Punalu'u area who knew it by that name.

139. Kamakau 1961:152.

140. Stokes 1919; Crozier 1972.

141. Native Register n.d., 8:144, 656.

142. Kelly, Nakamura & Barrere 1981:20; McEldowney 1979:18–24; Byron 1826:96, 168, 176; Bloxam 1925:51; Macrae 1922:7, 46.

143. 1794, Whidby, in Menzies 1920:140–141.

144. Stewart 1970 [1830]:360–361.

145. C. J. Lyons 1875:111; Kelly, Nakamura & Barrere 1981:16.

146. Ellis 1963:241.

147. Kamakau 1961:75.

148. Desha in press:1921, June 23.

149. Ellis 1963:231.

150. Kelly, Nakamura & Barrere 1981:4.

151. C. Lyman 1846; Kelly, Nakamura & Barrere 1981:14; Stewart 1970 [1830]:363.

152. After 1791, when the court was in Hilo, Kamehameha resided in Waiākea and John Young in Kūkūau (Ellis 1963:230–231).

153. Kamakau 1961:15–17.

154. Stokes 1991:154.

155. Kamakau 1961:174.

156. Stokes 1991:155.

157. Ching 1971:100.

158. Bonk 1969:79.

159. Haun & Walker 1988:35, 37, 128–129; Spriggs 1983. A second Kapua refuge cave is site 3705—a huge 730-meter-long and 30-meter-wide cave with three main openings, at different sinkholes up to 0.9 miles inland. All openings were fortified with stone walls, well faced on the inside (cf. Haun & Walker 1988:34, 37, D-20).

## NOTES FOR CHAPTER 11

1. "A Prophecy of the Overthrow of the Kingdom by Kamehameha" in Fornander 1920, 6(3):363–389.

2. I should add that these are not the only sources for studying the past. Historical linguistics, paleobotany, and physical anthropology also have contributed, and will continue to contribute, to our understanding of Hawai'i Island's history. And quite likely there are other sources that I am forgetting.

# References

Allen, Jane .1981. Archaeological Excavations at Kawainui Marsh, Island of O'ahu. Bishop Museum manuscript. On file, State Historic Preservation Division Library, Kapolei [O-156].

———.-. 1987. *Five Upland 'Ili: Archaeological and Historical Investigations in the Kane'ohe Interchange, Interstate Highway H-3, Island of O'ahu.* Hawaii Historic Preservation Report 87-1. Bishop Museum, Honolulu.

———.-. 1989. Preliminary Report: Archaeological Investigations at Sites 50-Oa-G6-17 and G6-69 through G6-71, Royal Hawaiian Country Club, Inc., Makai Golf Course Project Area, Maunawili, Kailua, Ko'olaupoko, O'ahu. Bishop Museum manuscript. On file, State Historic Preservation Division Library, Kapolei [O-840].

Allen, Melinda S. 1984. Archaeological Reconnaissance Survey, Waiono Meadows Development Project Area. PHRI ms. On file, State Historic Preservation Division Library, Kapolei (H-394).

———.. 1987. Archaeological Inventory Survey of DHHL Lands, Kawaihae, South Kohala, Hawai'i. Bishop Museum manuscript. On file, State Historic Preservation Division Library, Honolulu [H-589].

Alexander, W. D. 1869. "Puu Kohola Heiau"—Map. In W. Kikuchi and D. Cluff, "An Archaeological Survey of Puu Kohola Heiau, South Kohala, Kawaihae, Hawaii Island," p. 44. In D. Cluff, W. Kikuchi, R. Apple, and Y. H. Sinoto, *The Archaeological Surface Survey of Puu Kohola Heiau and Mailekini Heiau, South Kohala, Kawaihae, Hawaii Island*, pp. 35–66. Hawaii State Journal, 69-3. State Parks, State of Hawaii, Honolulu.

———.. 1887. "History of Umi in His Birth and his Youth." *Hawaiian Almanac & Annual for 1888*, pp. 78–85.

———.. 1899. *A Brief History of the Hawaiian People.* American Book Company, New York.

———.. 1951 [1903]. "Introduction." D. Malo, *Hawaiian Antiquities*, pp. xvii–xviii. Bishop Museum, Honolulu. [First printed 1903.]

Anderson, Lisa. 1998. Archaeological Inventory Survey of the Helani Church Lot (TMK 7-8-14-45), KahaLu'u AhuPua'a, Hawai'i Island. Anderson Archaeological Research Consultants ms. On file, State Historic Preservation Division Library, Kapolei.

Alvarez, Patricia. 1989. Land Use at Ka'awaloa, Kealakekua Bay State Historical Park, South Kona, Island of Hawaii: 1848–Present. State Parks manuscript. On file, State Historic Preservation Division Library, Kapolei.

Apple, Russ. 1969. "A History of Historic Structures, Kawaihae, South Kohala, Hawaii Island." In D. Cluff, W. Kikuchi, R. Apple, and Y. H. Sinoto, *The Archaeological Surface Survey of Puu Kohola Heiau and Mailekini Heiau, South Kohala, Kawaihae, Hawaii Island*, pp. 10–34. Hawaii State Journal, 69-3. State Parks, State of Hawaii, Honolulu.

Athens, J. Stephen. 1983. Archaeological Excavations at a Beach Midden Deposit, Kailua, O'ahu: The H.A.R.C. Site (50-Oa-G6-40). On file, State Historic Preservation Division, Library, Kapolei [O-245].

Athens, J. Stephen, and Jerome Ward. 1991. Paleoenvironmental and Archaeological Investigations, Kawainui Marsh Flood Control Project, O'ahu Island, Hawai'i. International Archaeological Institute, Inc. manuscript. On file, State Historic Preservation Division Library, Kapolei [O-719].

Athens, J. Stephen, and Michael Kaschko. 1988. Prehisoric Upland Bird Hunters: Archaeological Inventory Survey and Testing for the MPRC Project Area and the Bobcat Trail Road, Pohakuloa Training Area, Island of Hawaii. International Archaeological Institute, Inc. manuscript. On file, State Historic Preservation Division Library, Kapolei [H-841].

Atkinson, I. A. G. 1970. "Successional Trends in the Coastal and Lowland Forest of Mauna Loa and Kilauea Volcanoes, Hawai'i." *Pacific Science*, 24:387–400.

Awards Books. n.d. *Awards Books* (with maps of each LCA parcel). Handwritten copy, on file, Lands Division, Department of Land and Natural Resources, State of Hawaii, Honolulu.

Baker, Albert. 1916. "Ahua a Umi" *Hawaiian Almanac & Annual for 1917*, pp. 62–67.

Barratt, Glynn. 1987. *The Russian Discovery of Hawai'i.* Editions Limited, Honolulu.

Barrera, William. 1971. *Anaehoomalu: A Hawaiian Oasis.* Pacific Anthropological Records, 15. Bishop Museum, Honolulu.

———. 1974. "Archaeological Survey." In W. Barrera & M. Kelly, *Archaeological and Historical Surveys of the Waimea to Kawaihae Road Corridor, Island of Hawaii.* Hawaiian Historic Preservation Report, 74-1. Department of Transportation, State of Hawaii, Honolulu.

———. 1977. Waipio Valley Archaeological Survey. Chiniago Inc. ms. On file, State Historic Preservation Division Library, Kapolei [H-16].

———. 1988. Kohanaiki, North Kona, Hawaii: Archaeological Excavations Interim Report. Chiniago Inc. ms. On file, State Historic Preservation Division Library, Kapolei (H-722).

———. 1990a. Kaawaloa, South Kona, Hawaii Island: Archaeological Inventory Survey. Chiniago ms. On file, State Historic Preservation Division Library, Kapolei [H-1274].

———. 1990b. Kahauloa, South Kona, Hawaii Island: Archaeological Inventory Survey and Data Recovery. Chiniago ms. On file, State Historic Preservation Division Library, Kapolei [H-964] .

———. 1990c. Kaumalumalu and Pahoehoe, North Kona, Hawaii Island: Archaeological Inventory Survey. Chiniago ms. On file, State Historic Preservation Division Library, Kapolei [H-983].

———. 1990d. Draft: Kohanaiki, North Kona, Hawaii Island: Archaeological Inventory Survey and Data Recovery. Chiniago ms. On file, State Historic Preservation.

———. 1994. Ouli and Lanikepu, South Kohala, Hawaii: Archaeological Inventory Survey of TMK 6-2-01:9. Comstock Cultural Resource Management, Inc. ms. On file, State Historic Preservation Division Library, Kapolei [H-1346].

Barrera, William, and Robert Hommon. 1972. *Salvage Archaeology at Wailau, Ka'ū, Island of Hawaii.* Department of Anthropology Reports, 72-1. Bishop Museum, Honolulu.

Barrere, Dorothy. 1959. "Political History of Puna." In K. Emory et al., Natural and Cultural History Report on the Kalapana Extension of the Hawaii National Park. Bishop Museum ms. On file, State Historic Preservation Division Library, Kapolei [H-377].

———. 1961. Cosmogonic Genealogies of Hawaii. *Journal of the Polynesian Society*, 70(4):419–428.

———. 1964. "Foreword." In S. Kamakau, *Ka Po'e Kahiko: The People of Old*. Bishop Museum, Honolulu.

———. 1967. "Revisions and Alterations in Polynesian Creation Myths." In G. Highland et al. (eds.), *Polynesian Culture History: Essays in Honor of Kenneth P. Emory*. Bishop Museum Special Publication, 56. Honolulu.

———. 1969. *The Kumuhonua Legends: A Study of Late Nineteenth Century Hawaiian Stories of Creation and Origins*. Pacific Anthropological Records, 3. Bishop Museum, Department of Anthropology, Honolulu.

———. 1970. "An Historical Sketch of Makaha Valley." In Roger Green (ed.), *Makaha Valley Historical Project: Interim Report No. 2*, pp. 3–14. Pacific Anthropological Records, 10. Department of Anthropology, Bishop Museum, Honolulu.

———. 1971a. "Glimpses of History." In K. Emory, P. McCoy & D. Barrere, *Archaeological Survey: Kahaluu and Keauhou, North Kona, Hawaii*, pp. 1–9. Department of Anthropology Report, 71-4. Bishop Museum, Honolulu.

———. 1971b. "Historical Survey: Pualaa, Puna, Hawaii." In S. N. Crozier & D. Barrere, *Archaeological and Historical Survey of the Ahupuaa of Pualaa, Puna District, Island of Hawaii*, pp. 7–21. Department of Anthropology Report, 71-1. Bishop Museum, Honolulu.

———. 1975. *Kamehameha in Kona: Two Documentary Studies*. Pacific Anthropological Records, 23. Bishop Museum, Honolulu.

———. 1976. "Preface." In S. Kamakau, *The Works of the People of Old: Na Hana a ka Po'e Kahiko*, pp. v–vi. Bishop Museum Special Publication 61. Honolulu.

———. 1980. "Kona: Kai Malino a 'Ehu." In Jane Allen-Wheeler, Archaeological Investigations in Kailua-Kona, Hawaii. Bishop Museum ms. On file, State Historic Preservation Division Library, Kapolei.

———. 1983. "Report 2. Notes on the Lands of Waimea and Kawaihae." In J. Clark & P. Kirch, eds. *Archaeological Investigation of the Mudlane-Waimea-Kawaihae Road Corridor, Island of Hawaii: an Interdisciplinary Study of an Environmental Transect*, pp. 25–38. Department of Anthropology, Bishop Museum, Honolulu.

———. 1986. "A Reconstruction of the History and Function of the Pu'uhonua and the Hale o Keawe at Honaunau." In Emory et. al., *The Natural and Cultural History of Honaunau, Kona, Hawai'i*, pp. 117–136. [1957 manuscript]. Bishop Museum Departmental Report Series, 86-2. Honolulu.

———. 1989. "A Tahitian in the History of Hawai'i: The Journal of Kahikona." *The Hawaiian Journal of History* 23:75–107.

Barrere, Dorothy, and Marshall Sahlins. 1979. "Tahitians in the Early History of Hawaiian Christianity: The Journal of Toketa." *The Hawaiian Journal of History* 3:19–35.

Bastian, Adolf. 1881. *Die Heilige Sage der Polynesier: Cosmogonie und Theogonie*. Leipzig.

Bath, Joyce, Margaret Rosendahl, and Paul Rosendahl. 1984. Subsurface Archaeological Reconnaissance Survey: Kuilima Resort Expansion Project. PHRI manuscript. On file, State Historic Preservation Division Library, Kapolei [O-316].

Beaglehole, J. C. ed. 1967. *The Journals of Captain James Cook on His Voyages of Discovery. Vol. 3. The Voyage of the Resolution and Discovery 1776–1780.* The Hakluyt Society, Cambridge.

Beckwith, Martha, ed. 1932. *Kepelino's Traditions of Hawaii.* Bishop Museum Bulletin, 95. Honolulu.

———. 1940. *Hawaiian Mythology.* Yale University Press, New Haven. (Reprinted in 1970).

———. 1972. *The Kumulipo: A Hawaiian Creation Chant.* University of Hawai'i Press, Honolulu. [First published 1951]

Beggerly, Patricia. 1987. Archaeological Investigations at Morse Field and Pacific Missile Range Facility, Kama'oa-Pu'u'eo, Ka'ū, Island of Hawai'i. International Archaeological Research Institute, Inc. ms. On file, State Historic Preservation Division Library, Kapolei [H-586].

———. 1990. Kahana Valley, Hawai'i, A Geomorphic Artifact: A Study of the Interrelationships Among Geomorphic Structures, Natural Processes, and Ancient Hawaiian Technology, Land Use and Settlement Patterns. Unpublished Ph.D. thesis, Dept. of Anthropology, University of Hawai'i at Manoa.

Bell, Edward. 1929—1930. "Log of the Chatham." *Honolulu Mercury* I(4):7–26, I(5):55–69, I(6):76–96, II(1):80–91, II(2):119–129.

Belt, Collins and Associates. 1981. Environmental Impact Statement for the Proposed Manukona Resort. Honolulu.

———. 1985. Draft Environmental Impact Statement Revised Master Plan for Mauna Lani Resort. South Kohala, Hawaii. Honolulu.

Bennett, Wendell 1931. *Archaeology of Kauai.* Bishop Museum Bulletin, 80. Honolulu.

Bennett, Wendell. and Junius Bird 1964. *Andean Culture History.* The Natural History Press, Garden City. [First published in 1949. The American Museum of Natural History, New York.]

Best, Simon, P. Sheppard, Roger Green, and R. Parker. 1992. "Necromancing the Stone: Archaeologists and Adzes in American Samoa." *Journal of the Polynesian Society* 101:45–85.

Bevacqua, Robert, and Tom Dye. 1972. *Archaeological Reconnaissance of Proposed Kapoho-Kalapana Highway, District of Puna, Island of Hawaii.* Department of Anthropology Report, 72-3. Bishop Museum, Honolulu.

Biggs, Bruce, D. S. Walsh, and Jocelyn Waga. 1970. Proto-Polynesian Reconstructions with English to Proto-Polynesian Finder List. Working Papers in Linguistics, Department of Anthropology, University of Auckland, Auckland.

Bingham, Hiram. 1847. *A Residence of Twenty-one Years in the Sandwich Islands.* New York.

Birdsell, J. 1957. "Some Population Problems involving Pleistocene Man." *Cold Springs Harbor Symposium on Quantitative Biology* 22:47–69.

Bishop, Charles. 1897. February 22, 1897, Letter to Bishop Estate Trustee Henry Holmes. On file, State Historic Preservation Division, Kapolei.

Bishop, Charles. 1967. In *The Journals and Letters of Captain Charles Bishop on the North-west Coast of America, in the Pacific and in New South Wales,* 1739–1799, Michael Roe, ed. Cambridge University Press for the Hakluyt Society, Cambridge.

Bloxam, Andrew. 1925. *Diary of Andrew Bloxam, Naturalist of the "Blonde" on Her Trip from England to the Hawaiian Islands,* 1824–25. Bishop Museum Special Publication, 10. Honolulu.

Bloxam, Rowland. 1924. "Visit of the H.M.S. *Blonde* to Hawaii in 1825." *Hawaiian Annual* for 1924, pp. 66–82. Honolulu.

Board of Genealogy of Hawaiian Chiefs. n.d. Letter to Charles T. Gulick, Minister of the Interior. Kalanianaole Collection, Bishop Museum Library, Honolulu.

Bond, Elias. 1885. "Puuepa Heiau." *Saturday Press,* editorial response, April 25, 1885. Honolulu.

Bonk, William. 1968. An Archaeological Survey of a Coastal Tract in North and South Kohala, Hawaii. Manuscript. On file, State Historic Preservation Division Library, Kapolei [H-705].

———. 1969. "Lua Nunu o Kamakalepo: A Cave of Refuge in Ka'ū, Hawaii." In R. Pearson, ed, *Archaeology on the Island of Hawaii,* pp. 75-92. Asian & Pacific Archaeology Series, 3. Social Science Research Institute, University of Hawai'i at Manoa, Honolulu.

(BCB) Boundary Commission Books. n.d. Boundary Commission Books. 5 volumes, microfilm. Archives of the State of Hawaii, Honolulu (records from the 1870s–1880s).

Brigham, William. 1899. *Hawaiian Feather Work.* Memoirs of the Bernice Pauahi Bishop Museum, 1(1):1–86. Honolulu.

———. 1902. *Ancient Hawaiian Stone Implements.* Bishop Museum Memoirs, 1(4). Honolulu.

———. 1903. *Additional Notes on Hawaiian Featherwork.* Bishop Museum Memoirs, 1(5). Honolulu.

Broughton, William. 1804. *A Voyage of Discovery to the North Pacific Ocean.* London, for T. Cadell and W. Davies.

Brown, Barton. 1983. Floor Area and Population Size: A Worldwide Cross-Cultural Study. Paper presented at 48th Society for American Archaeology Meetings, Pittsburgh.

———. 1985. Floor Area and Population Size: A Worldwide Cross-Cultural Study (revised). Manuscript, personal copy.

Buck, Peter (Te Rangi Hiroa). 1938. *Vikings of the Sunrise*. F. A. Stockes Co., New York.

———. 1957. *Arts and Crafts of Hawaii*. Bishop Museum Special Publications, 45. Honolulu.

Burgett, Berdena, and Paul Rosendahl. 1993. Summary of Archaeological Inventory Surveys: Kapaanui Agricultural Subdivision and Mahukona Property. PHRI manuscript. On file, State Historic Preservation Division Library, Kapolei [H-1368].

———. 1994. Archaeological Inventory Survey, Kealakekua Bay Club Parcel 39. Land of Kealakekua...PHRI ms. On file, State Historic Preservation Division Library, Kapolei [H-1275].

Burney, James. 1776–1780. Journal. ms. Additional ms. 895. British Museum, London.

Burrows, E. G. 1938. *Western Polynesia: A Study of Cultural Differentiation*. Ethnologiska Studier, 7. Gothenburg.

Burtchard, Greg. 1996. Population and Land Use on the Keauhou Coast, The Mauka Land Inventory Survey, Keauhou, North Kona, Hawai'i Island. International Archaeological Institute, Inc. ms. On file, State Historic Preservation Division Library, Kapolei [H-1310].

Byron, George A. 1826. Voyage of *H.M.S. Blonde to the Sandwich Islands in the years 1824–1825*. Murray, London.

Cachola-Abad, Kehau. 1993. "Evaluating the Orthodox Dual Settlement Model for the Hawaiian Islands: An Analysis of Artifact Distribution and Hawaiian Oral Traditions." In M. Graves and Roger Green, eds, *The Evolution and Organization of Prehistoric Society in Polynesia*, pp. 13–32.

Campbell, Archibald. 1967 [1822]. *A Voyage Round the World (1806–1812)*. University of Hawai'i Press, Honolulu [First published in 1822.]

Carlson, Arne, and Paul Rosendahl. 1990a. Archaeological Inventory Survey, Queen's Lands at Mauna Kea. Land of Kawaihae 2nd, South Kohala...PHRI manuscript. On file, State Historic Preservation Division Library, Kapolei [H-988].

———. 1990b. Archaeological Inventory Survey Palani Development—Phase II. Lands of Puapuaa 1st and 2nd, North Kona...PHRI manuscript. On file, State Historic Preservation Division Library, Kapolei [H-799].

Carter Case. 1915. A. W. Carter, Trustee, Parker Ranch vs. Territory of Hawaii. Transcript of Testimony. Attorney General Case File 2311, Archives of the State of Hawaii, Honolulu.

Cartwright, Bruce. 1930. "Note on Hawaiian Genealogies." *Thirty-Eighth Annual Report of the Hawaiian Historical Society for the Year 1929*. Honolulu.

———. 1933. "Some Aliis of the Migratory Period." *Bishop Museum Occasional Papers*, 10(7). Honolulu.

Chamberlain, Levi. n.d. Copy of Chamberlain's Memorandum [naming those in the Hale o Keawe mausoleum]. Hawaiian Mission Children's Society Library, Honolulu.

Char, W. 1986. Botanical Survey, Proposed Kohana-iki Resort Community, North Kona, Island of Hawai'i. In Hastert, Helbert, Van Horn & Kimura, *Kohanaiki Draft EIS*, Appendix. Hastert, Helbert, Van Horn & Kimura Planners, Honolulu.

Char, W., and M. Kjargaard. 1986. Biological Survey, Proposed O'oma II Project, North Kona, Island of Hawai'i. In *O'oma II Draft EIS*, Appendix.

Charvet-Pond, Ann, and Bertell Davis, 1991. Draft, Volume I: West Beach Data Recovery Program. Phase 4—Archaeological and Paleontological Excavations. Ko Olina Resort, Land of Honouliuli, Ewa, Island of Oahu. PHRI ms. On file, State Historic Preservation Division Library, Kapolei [O-869].

Cheever, Henry. 1851. *Life in the Sandwich Islands.* Banet & Co., New York.

Ching, Francis. 1971. *The Archaeology of South Kohala & North Kona: From the AhuPua'a of Lalamilo to the AhuPua'a of Hamanamana.* [*Surface Survey Kailua-Kawaihae Road Corridor (Section III).*] Hawaii State Archaeological Journal, 71-1. Division of State Parks, Honolulu.

Christensen, Carl. 1983. Report 17. "Analysis of Land Snails." In J. Clark and P. Kirch, eds, *Archaeological Investigation of the Mudlane-Waimea-Kawaihae Road Corridor, Island of Hawaii: an Interdisciplinary Study of an Environmental Transect*, pp. 449–471. Department of Anthropology, Bishop Museum, Honolulu.

Chun, Malcom, ed and trans. 1988. I *Ka Wa of Kamehameha: In the Time of Kamehameha. Selected Essays by Samuel M. Kamakau.* Kapiolani Community College, The Folk Press, Honolulu.

Clark, Jeffrey. 1980. Phase I Archaeological Survey of Castle Estate Lands Around the Kawainui Marsh, Kailua, O'ahu. Bishop Museum ms. On file, State Historic Preservation Division Library, Kapolei [O-96].

———. 1981. Archaeological Survey of the Proposed Lalamilo Agricultural Park, South Kohala, Island of Hawaii. Bishop Museum ms. On file, State Historic Preservation Division Library, Kapolei.

———. 1983a. "Report 3. The Waimea-Kawaihae Region: Historical Background." In J. Clark and P. Kirch, eds. *Archaeological Investigation of the Mudlane-Waimea-Kawaihae Road Corridor, Island of Hawaii: an Interdisciplinary Study of an Environmental Transect*, pp. 39–57. Department of Anthropology, Bishop Museum, Honolulu.

———. 1983b. "Report 8. Archaeological Investigations of Agricultural Sites in the Waimea Area." In J. Clark and P. Kirch, eds, *Archaeological Investigation of the Mudlane-Waimea-Kawaihae Road Corridor, Island of Hawaii: an Interdisciplinary Study of an Environmental Transect*, pp. 293–314. Department of Anthropology, Bishop Museum, Honolulu.

———. 1987. Waimea-Kawaihae: A Leeward Hawaii Settlement System. Unpublished Ph.D. Thesis, Department of Anthropology, University of Illinois at Urbana-Champaign.

Clark, Jeffrey and Patrick Kirch, eds. 1983. *Archaeological Investigation of the Mudlane-Waimea-Kawaihae Road Corridor, Island of Hawaii: an Interdisciplinary Study of an Environmental Transect.* Department of Anthropology, Bishop Museum, Honolulu.

Clark, Ross. 1975. "Comment on Polynesian Sibling Terms." *American Anthropologist* 77:85–88.

———. 1979. "Language." In J. Jennings (ed), *The Prehistory of Polynesia*, pp. 249–270. Harvard University Press, Cambridge.

Clark, Stephan. 1986. "V. Stratigraphy." In T. Han, S. Collins, S. Clark and A. Garland, *Moe Kau o Ho'oilo: Hawaiian Mortuary Practices at Keopu, Kona, Hawai'i*, pp. 23-53. Hawaii Historic Preservation Report, 86-1. Department of Anthropology, Bishop Museum, Honolulu.

Clark, Stephan, E. Dow Davidson, and Paul Cleghorn. 1990. Archaeological Testing and Data Recovery for the Waimea School Improvements Lot A (TMK: 6-7-2: por. 17), Waikoloa, South Kohala...Bishop Museum ms. On file, State Historic Preservation Division Library, Kapolei [H-1361].

Cleghorn, Paul. 1984. An Archaeological Reconnaissance Survey and Auger Testing at Kaulana Bay, Ka'ū, Hawai'i Island. Bishop Museum ms. On file, State Historic Preservation Division Library, Kapolei [H-369].

———. 1986. "Organizational Structure at the Mauna Kea Adze Quarry Complex, Hawaii."" *Journal of Archaeological Science* 13:375–387.

Cleghorn, Paul, and Elaine Rogers-Jourdane. 1983. Archaeological and Historical Research in Waipi'o Valley, Hamakua District, Hawai'i Island. Bishop Museum ms. On file, State Historic Preservation Division Library, Kapolei [H-503].

Clerke, Charles. 1967. Journal. In J. C. Beaglehole, ed, *The Journals of Captain James Cook on His Voyages of Discovery*. Vol. 3. *The Voyage of the Resolution and Discovery 1776–1780.* The Hakluyt Society, Cambridge.

Colnett, James. n.d. The Journal of Captain James Colnett Aboard the Prince of Wales & Princess Royal from 16 Oct. 1786 to 7 Nov. 1788. Copied by Donald Angus from Public Record Office, London, Admiralty, 55 Series II 146. Hawaiian and Pacific Collection, Hamilton Library, University of Hawai'i at Manoa, Honolulu.

Connolly, Robert. 1974. An Archaeological Phase I Survey of Puuhonua Road Section, South Kona...Bishop Museum ms. On file, State Historic Preservation Division Library, Kapolei [H-172].

Cook, James. 1944. *Captain Cook's Voyages of Discovery.* J. M. Dent and Sons, London. [edited by John Barrow]

Cook, James, and James King. 1784. *A Voyage to the Pacific Ocean in the Years 1776, 1777, 1778, 1779 and 1780*...3 volumes. Nicol and Cadell, London.

Cordy, Ross. 1974a. "Cultural Adaptation and Evolution in Hawaii: A Suggested New Sequence." *Journal of the Polynesian Society* 83(2):180–191.

———. 1974b. "Complex-rank Cultural Systems in the Hawaiian Islands: Suggested Explanations for Their Origin." *Archaeology and Physical Anthropology in Oceania* 9(2):89–109.

———. 1974c. "The Tahitian Migration to Hawaii ca. 1100–1300 A.D.: An Argument Against Its Occurrence." *New Zealand Archaeological Association Newsletter* 17(2):65–76.

———. 1974d. Traditional History of Oahu Political Units: Its Use for Explaining the Origin of Complex-Rank Systems in the Hawaiian Islands. Manuscript. On file, Department of Anthropology Library, University of Hawai'i at Manoa.

———. 1975. Archaeology at Anaeho'omalu (Hawai'i Island): A Reanalysis of Social Organization. Manuscript. On file, State Historic Preservation Division Library, Kapolei [H-558].

———. 1978. A Study of Prehistoric Social Change: The Development of Complex Societies in the Hawaiian Islands. Ph.D. thesis, Department of Anthropology, University of Hawai'i, Manoa.

———. 1981. *A Study of Prehistoric Social Change: The Development of Complex Societies in the Hawaiian Islands.* Academic Press, New York.

———. 1984. "Sampling Problems in Regional Interpretation in Hawaiian Archaeology." *Archaeology in Oceania* 19(1):21–28.

———. 1985a. Archaeological Data Recovery at C22-27 in Kalamakapala AhuPua'a in the Kealakekua Bay Region. Manuscript. On file, State Historic Preservation Division Library, Kapolei [H-486].

———. 1985b. "Settlement Patterns of Complex Societies in the Pacific." *New Zealand Journal of Archaeology* 7:159–182.

———. 1986a. South Point: Early Historic Land Use Patterns in the AhuPua'a of Kamā'oa, Pu'u'eo, Mohowae, Waiopua and Kea'a. Manuscript. On file, State Historic Preservation Division Library, Kapolei.

———. 1986b. Observations on Pinao Bay Archaeological Sites, Kamā'oa AhuPua'a, Ka'ū, Hawai'i. Manuscript. On file, State Historic Preservation Division Library, Kapolei [H-669].

———. 1986c. Archaeological Fieldcheck of HapaiAli'i Heiau. KahaLu'u, Kona, Hawai'i Island. Manuscript. On file, State Historic Preservation Division Library, Kapolei [H-607].

———. 1986d. Archaeological Fieldcheck and Historical Overview of Kapuanoni Heiau, KahaLu'u, Kona, Hawai'i Island. Manuscript. On file, State Historic Preservation Division Library, Kapolei [H-1519].

———. 1987a. Hamakua & Waipi'o: The Homeland of Hawai'i Island's Political System. Manuscript, in press, Festschrift for K. Emory, edited by M. Spriggs & P. B. Griffin. On file, State Historic Preservation Division Library, Kapolei [H-580].

———. 1987b. An Overview of Ka'ū District & Some Thoughts on Island-Wide Settlement Patterns. Paper presented at the 1st Annual Society for Hawaiian Archaeology Conference, Hawaii Volcanoes National Park. Manuscript, State Historic Preservation Division, Honolulu.

———. 1987c. Archaeological Survey. Keauohana AhuPua'a, Puna, Hawai'i Island. Manuscript. On file, State Historic Preservation Division Library, Kapolei [H-606].

———. 1987d. 'Anaeho'omalu's Ahupua'a Altar, Ke Ahu a Lono (HA-E1-63): An Archaeological and Archival Overview, South Kohala, Hawai'i. Manuscript. On file, State Historic Preservation Division Library, Kapolei [H-603].

———. 1988a. Archaeological Reconnaissance Survey of a Portion of Waipi'o's Upper Valley. Manuscript. On file, State Historic Preservation Division Library, Kapolei.

———. 1988b. Kahuwai Village. Kahuwai AhuPua'a, Puna. Recommendations for Preservation. Manuscript. On file, State Historic Preservation Division Library, Kapolei.

———. 1989a. 1989 Survey Work at Kahuwai Village. Kahuwai, Puna, Hawai'i. Manuscript. On file, State Historic Preservation Division, Kapolei.

———. 1989b. Additional Archival and Archaeological Information on a Portion of the Waimea Field System, Waimea Area, South Kohala, Hawai'i Island. Manuscript. On file, State Historic Preservation Division Library.

———. 1989c. Initial Information on Trails in Keauhou 1 AhuPua'a, North Kona, Hawai'i Island. Manuscript. On file, State Historic Preservation Division Library, Kapolei [H-675].

———. 1991. 1848–1851 Māhele Records on Land Use in Waimanu AhuPua'a, Hamakua District, Hawai'i Island. Manuscript. On file, State Historic Preservation Division Library, Kapolei [H-956].

———. 1994. *A Regional Synthesis of Hāmākua District, Island of Hawai'i.* State Historic Preservation Division, Honolulu.

———. 1995. Central Kona Archaeological Settlement Patterns. Manuscript. On file, State Historic Preservation Division Library, Kapolei [H-1441].

———. 1996. "The Rise and Fall of the O'ahu Kingdom: A Brief Overview of O'ahu's History." In J. Davidson, G. Irwin, B. F. Leach, A. Pawley and D. Brown, eds, *Oceanic Culture History: Essays in Honour of Roger Green*, pp 591–613. New Zealand Journal of Archaeological Special Publication. New Zealand.

Cordy, Ross, and Michael Kaschko. 1980. "Prehistoric Archaeology in the Hawaiian Islands: Land Units Associated with Social Groups." *Journal Field Archaeology* 7:403–416.

Cordy, Ross, Joseph Tainter, Robert Renger, and Robert Hitchcock. 1991. *An AhuPua'a Study: The 1971 Archaeological Work at Kaloko AhuPua'a North Kona, Hawai'i.* Western Archaeological and Conservation Center Publications in Anthropology, 58. National Park Service, Honolulu.

Cordy, Ross, and H. David Tuggle. 1976. "Bellows, Oahu, Hawaiian Islands: New Work and New Interpretations." *Archaeology & Physical Anthropology in Oceania* 11:207–235.

Crozier, S. Neal. 1971. *Archaeological Excavations at Kamehameha III Road, North Kona, Island of Hawaii, Phase II.* Department of Anthropology Reports, 71-11. Bishop Museum, Honolulu.

———. 1972. *Archaeological Survey and Excavations at PunaLu'u, Island of Hawaii.* Department of Anthropology Reports, 72-6. Bishop Museum, Honolulu.

Crozier, S. Neal, and William Barrera. 1974. Archaeological Survey and Excavations at PunaLu'u, Island of Hawaii. Bishop Museum ms. On file, State Historic Preservation Division Library, Kapolei [H-67].

DaSilva, Armando, and Rubellite K. Johnson. 1982. "Ahu a 'Umi Heiau." *Annals New York Academy of Sciences* pp. 313–331.

Davis, Eleanor. 1979. *Abraham Fornander: A Biography.* University Press of Hawaii, Honolulu.

Davis, Bertell, Alan Haun, and Paul Rosendahl. 1986. Phase 3 Data Recovery Plan for Archaeological and Paleontological Excavations: West Beach Data Recovery Program. PHRI ms. On file, State Historic Preservation Division Library, Kapolei [O587].

Daws, Gavin. 1968. *Shoals of Time: A History of the Hawaiian Islands.* University Press of Hawaii, Honolulu.

Denham, Timothy, Peter Brennan, and Jerome Ward, Serge Avery, 1993. Draft: Paleoenvironmental Reconstruction Adjacent to the Mouth of Halawa Stream: Monitoring Report of the Waiau-Makalapa No. 2 138 kV Overhead Lines (Phase II), Halawa AhuPua'a, 'Ewa District, Island of O'ahu. Archaeological Consultants of Hawaii ms. On file, State Historic Preservation Division Library, Kapolei [O-808].

Desha, Stephen. In press. *A Tale of Kekūhaupi'o, The Famous Warrior of the Era of Kamehameha the Great.* Translated by Frances Frazier. Kamehameha Schools Press, Honolulu. [Original in Hawaiian in *Ka Hoku o Hawaii*, Sept. 7, 1922–Sept. 11, 1924].

Dibble, Sheldon, ed. 1838. *Ka Moolelo Hawaii.* Lahainaluna.

———. 1909 [1843]. *A History of the Sandwich Islands.* Honolulu, T. G. Thrum. [First published 1843].

Dicks, Merrill, Alan Haun, and Paul Rosendahl. 1987. Archaeological Reconnaissance Survey for Environmental Impact Statement, West Loch Estates—Golf Course and Parks. PHRI ms. On file, State Historic Preservation Division Library, Kapolei [O-437].

Dixon, George. 1789. *A Voyage Round the World: But More Particularly to the North-West Coast of America.* George Goulding, London.

DLNR Department of Land & Natural Resources. 1971. Site Inventory File, State of Hawaii Inventory of Historic Properties. Archived at State Historic Preservation Division, Dept. of Land & Natural Resources, State of Hawaii, Kapolei.

Dollar, S. 1986. Baseline Assessment of the Marine Environment in the Vicinity of the O'oma II Resort Development. In *O'oma II Draft EIS*, Appendix.

Donham, Theresa. 1987. Archaeological Reconnaissance Survey, Resort Expansion Area and Selected Undeveloped Parcels, Waikoloa Beach Resort. PHRI ms. On file, State Historic Preservation Division Library, Kapolei [H-595].

———. 1990a. Archaeological Inventory Survey, Honokohau Industrial Park (Parcel VII). PHRI ms. On file, State Historic Preservation Division Library, Kapolei [H-876].

———. 1990b. Archaeological Inventory Survey, Kealakehe Planned Community Project Area. Lands of Kealakehe and Keahuolu, North Kona...PHRI ms. On file, State Historic Preservation Division Library, Kapolei [H-1063]

———. 1990c. Archaeological Inventory Survey, Queen Liliuokalani Trust Property. Land of Keahuolu, North Kona...PHRI ms. On file, State Historic Preservation Division Library, Kapolei.

DOT (Department of Transportation, State of Hawaii). 1975. *EIS Administrative Action for Development of Honokohau Boat Harbor, Hawaii.* Department of Transportation, State of Hawaii, Honolulu.

DOT (Department of Transportation, State of Hawaii) and FHWA (Federal Highways Administration, United States) 1980. *Final Environmental Impact Statement, Hawaii Belt Road.*

Dunn, Amy, Leta Franklin, and Susan Goodfellow. 1995. Archaeological Inventory Survey, A & O Golf Course Project. Lands of Ahalanui, Oneloa, and Laepao'o, Puna District...PHRI ms. On file, State Historic Preservation Division Library, Kapolei [H-1429].

Dunn, Amy, Alan Haun, and Susan Goodfellow. 1991. Intensive Archaeological Survey and Test Excavations, Ewa Marina Community Project—Phase I. PHRI ms. On file, State Historic Preservation Division Library, Kapolei [O-675].

Dunn, Amy, and Paul Rosendahl. 1989. Archaeological Inventory Survey, Kapaanui Agricultural Subdivision. Lands of Kapaanui and Kou, North Kohala...PHRI ms. On file, State Historic Preservation Division Library, Kapolei [H-846].

Dye, Thomas. 1989. "A Tale of Two Cultures: Traditional Historical and Archaeological Interpretations of Hawaiian Prehistory." *Bishop Museum Occasional Papers*, 29:3–22. Honolulu.

———. 1992. "The South Point Radiocarbon Dates Thirty Years Later." *New Zealand Journal of Archaeology*, 14:89–97.

———. 1994. "Population Trends in Hawaii Before 1778." *The Hawaiian Journal of History* 28:1–20.

———. 1995. "Comparing 14C Histograms: An Approach Based on Approximate Randomization Techniques." Radiocarbon, 39(3):851–859

———. 1991. "A Reputation Unmade: J. F. G. Stokes's Career in Hawaiian Archaeology." In J. Stokes, *Heiau of the Island of Hawai'i: A Historic Survey of Native Hawaiian Temple Sites*, pp. 3–20. (edited and introduced by Thomas Dye). Bishop Museum Bulletin in Anthropology, 2. Bishop Museum, Honolulu.

Dye, Thomas, and Eric Komori. 1992a. "A Pre-censal Population History of Hawai'i." *New Zealand Journal of Archaeology* 14:113–128.

———. 1992b. "Computer Programs for Creating Probability Curves and Annual Frequency Distribution Diagrams with Radiocarbon Dates." *New Zealand Journal of Archaeology* 14:35–43.

Dye, Thomas, and D. Steadman. 1990. "Polynesian Ancestors and Their Animal World." *American Scientist* 78:207–215.

Earle, Timothy. 1978. *Economic and Social Organization of a Complex Chiefdom: The Halele'a District, Kaua'i, Hawaii.* Anthropological Paper 63. University of Michigan, Ann Arbor.

Ehle, John. 1988. *Trail of Tears: The Rise and Fall of the Cherokee Nation.* Anchor Books, New York.

Elbert, Samuel. 1951. "Hawaiian Literary Style and Culture." *American Anthropologist* 53(3):345–354.

———. 1953. "Internal Relationships of Polynesian Languages and Dialects." *Southwestern Journal of Anthropology* 9:147–173.

———. 1982. "Lexical Diffusion in Polynesia and the Marquesan-Hawaiian Relationship." *Journal of the Polynesian Society* 91(4):499–518.

Ellis, William (Rev.) 1963. *Narrative of a Tour of Hawaii, or Owhyhee.* Advertiser Publishing, Honolulu. [Reprint of 1827 London publication]

Ellis, William (Surgeon). 1784. *An Authentic Narrative of a Voyage Performed by Captain Cook and Captain Clerke.* G. Robinson, J. Sewell & J. Debrett, London.

Emerson, J. S. 1880. Fieldbook—Waipio, Hamakua. Hawaii Survey of Kuleanas. No. 1. On file, Surveys Division, Dept. of Accounting & General Services, Honolulu.

———. 1892. "The Lesser Hawaiian Gods." *Papers of the Hawaiian Historical Society* 2.

Emerson, Nathaniel. 1893. "The Long Voyages of the Ancient Hawaiians." *Papers of the Hawaiian Historical Society,* 5. Honolulu.

———. 1951 [1903]. "Biographical Sketch of David Malo." In D. Malo, *Hawaiian Antiquities,* pp. vii–xv. Bishop Museum, Honolulu. [First printed in 1903]

———. 1903. "Mamala-Hoa." *Tenth Annual Report of the Hawaiian Historical Society,* pp. 15–29.

Emory, Kenneth. 1928. *Archaeology of Nihoa and Necker Islands.* Bishop Museum Bulletin, 53. Honolulu.

———. 1933. *Stone Remains in the Society Islands.* Bishop Museum Bulletin, 116. Honolulu.

———. 1943. "Polynesian Stone Remains." In C.S . Coon and J. M. Andrews, eds, *Studies in the Anthropology of Oceania and Asia,* pp. 9–21. Papers Peabody Museum Archaeology & Ethnology, 22. Harvard University, Cambridge.

———. 1959. "Origin of the Hawaiians." *Journal of the Polynesian Society,* 68(1):29–35.

———. 1968. "East Polynesian Relationships as Revealed Through Adzes." In I. Yawata and Y. Sinoto, eds, *Prehistoric Culture in Oceania,* pp. 151–169. Bishop Museum Press, Honolulu.

———. 1970. "A Re-examination of East Polynesian Marae: Many Marae Later." In R. Green and M. Kelly, eds, *Studies in Oceanic Culture History,* vol. 1, pp. 73–92. Pacific Anthropological Records, 11. Department of Anthropology, Bishop Museum, Honolulu.

———. 1971. "Preface to the 1971 Reprinting." In D. Malo, *Hawaiian Antiquities,* pp. xix. Bishop Museum Special Publication, 2 (1971 re-printing.) Honolulu.

———. 1977. "Comparison of Polynesian Genealogies in the Bishop Museum." *Pacific Studies* 1(1):1–14. Brigham Young University Hawaii, Laie.

———. 1979. "The Societies." In J. Jennings, ed. *The Prehistory of Polynesia,* pp. 200–221. Harvard University Press, Cambridge.

———. 1986. "Honaunau Village and Vicinity." In Emory et al., *The Natural and Cultural History of Honaunau, Kona, Hawai'i,* pp. 89–110 [1957 manuscript]. Bishop Museum Departmental Report Series, 86-2. Honolulu.

Emory, Kenneth, William Bonk, and Yosihiko Sinoto. 1959. *Hawaiian Archaeology: Fishhooks.* Bishop Museum Special Publication, 47. Honolulu.

———. 1969. *Hawaiian Archaeology: Fishhooks.* 2nd ed. Bishop Museum Special Publication, 47. Honolulu.

———. 1969. *Waiahukini Shelter, site H8, Ka'u, Hawaii.* Pacific Anthropological Records, 7. Bishop Museum, Honolulu.

Emory, Kenneth, and Yosihiko Sinoto. 1961. *Hawaiian Archaeology: Oahu Excavations.* Bishop Museum Special Publication, 49. Honolulu.

———. 1964. "Eastern Polynesian Burials at Maupiti." *Journal of the Polynesian Society* 73(2):143–160.

———. 1965. Preliminary Report on the Archaeological Investigations in Polynesia: Fieldwork in the Society and Tuamotu Islands, French Polynesia, and American Samoa in 1962, 1963, 1964. Bishop Museum ms. Bishop Museum Library, Honolulu.

———. 1969. *Age of the Sites in the South Point Area,* Ka'ū, Hawaii. Pacific Anthropological Records, 8. Department of Anthropology, Bishop Museum, Honolulu.

Emory, Kenneth, John F. G. Stokes, Dorothy Barrere, and Marion Kelly. 1986. *Part II, The Cultural History of Honaunau. The Natural and Cultural History of Honaunau, Kona, Hawai'i.* [Bishop Museum 1957 manuscript. Published in 1986 with annotations.] Bishop Museum Departmental Report Series, 86-2. Honolulu.

Erkelens, Conrad. 1993. The Archaeological Investigation of the Kukanono Slope, Kawainui Marsh, Kailua, Ko'olaupoko, O'ahu. Unpublished M.A. thesis, Dept. of Anthropology, Univeristy of Hawaii at Manoa (O-1182).

———. 1996. Draft: The Kuleana Lots at Pukalani, Waimea Town Center Project Area. Waimea, Hawai'i Island. International Archaeological Research Institute, Inc. ms. On file, State Historic Preservation Division Library, Kapolei [H-1380].

Fager, Mikele, and Donna Graves. 1993. Archaeological Inventory Survey, Holualoa 3rd Development Parcel. PHRI ms. On file, State Historic Preservation Division Library, Kapolei [H-1155].

Finney, Ben. 1967. "New Perspectives on Polynesian Voyaging." In G. Highland et al., eds, *Polynesian Culture History: Essays in Honor of Kenneth P. Emory,* pp. 141–166. Bishop Museum Special Publication, 56. Honolulu.

———. 1977. "Voyaging Canoes and the Settlement of Polynesia." *Science,* 196:1277-1285.

———. 1979. "Voyaging." In J. Jennings, ed, *The Prehistory of Polynesia,* pp. 323–351. Harvard University Press, Cambridge.

———. 1991. "Myth, Experiment and the Re-invention of Polynesian Voyaging." *American Anthropologist* 92:383–404.

Firor, James, and Paul Rosendahl. 1990. Hyatt Regency Kauai Golf Course Archaeological Preservation Program Phase II. Land of Paa, Koloa District, Island of Kauai. PHRI ms. On file, State Historic Preservation Division Library, Kapolei [K-474].

Fitzpatrick, Gary. 1986. *The Early Mapping of Hawai'i.* Editions Limited, Honolulu.

Fornander, Abraham. 1878. *An Account of the Polynesian Race, its Origins and Migrations, and the Ancient History of the Polynesian People to the Times of Kamehameha I,* vol 1. Trubner, London.

———. 1880. *An Account of the Polynesian Race, its Origins and Migrations, and the Ancient History of the Polynesian People to the Times of Kamehameha I,* vol. II. Trubner, London.

———. 1916–1920. *Fornander Collection of Hawaiian Antiquities and Folk-lore.* Memoirs of the Bernice Pauahi Bishop Museum, vols. 4–6. Bishop Museum, Honolulu. (1916–1917 = vol. 4, 1918–1919 = vol. 5, 1919–1920 = vol. 6).

Fowke, Gerard. 1922. "Archaeological Work in Hawaii." *Bureau of American Ethnology Bulletin*, 76:174–195. [Washington, D.C.]

Franklin, Leta, Kepa Maly, and Paul Rosendahl. 1994. Archaeological Inventory Survey, Hawaii Preparatory Academy Campus Expansion. Land of Waiaka 2nd, South Kohala...PHRI ms. On file, State Historic Preservation Division Library, Kapolei [H-1381].

Frazier, Frances. In press. "Foreward." In S. Desha, *A Tale of Kekūhaupi'o.* Kamehameha Schools Press, Honolulu.

Freycinet, Louis. 1978. *Hawaii in 1819: A Narrative Account by Louis Claude de Saulses de Freycinet*, trans. Ella Wiswell. Pacific Anthropological Records, 26. Bishop Museum, Honolulu.

Fuller, J. 1853. Letter to A. Thurston, May 30, 1853. Interior Miscellaneous file, Archives of the State of Hawaii, Honolulu.

Gagne, W. C. and L. W. Cuddihy. 1990. "Vegetation." In W. Wagner, D. Herbst, S. Sohmer, eds, Ma*nual of the Flowering Plants of Hawaii, Volume 1*, pp. 45–114. Bishop Museum Special Publication 83. Honolulu.

Garanger, Jose. 1967. "Archaeology and the Society Islands." In G. Highland et al., eds., *Polynesian Culture History: Essays in Honor of Kenneth P. Emory*, pp. 377–396. Bishop Museum Special Publication, 56. Honolulu.

Genealogy Books. n.d. Genealogy Books. On file, Bishop Museum Library & Archives, Honolulu.

Gilbert, George. 1982. *Captain Cook's Final Voyage: The Journal of Midshipman George Gilbert.* University Press of Hawaii, Honolulu.

Gladwin, Thomas. 1970. *East is a Big Bird.* Harvard University Press, Cambridge.

Goldman, Irving. 1970. *Ancient Polynesian Society.* University of Chicago Press, Chicago.

Golson, Jack, ed. 1962. *Polynesian Navigation: A Symposium.* Polynesian Society Memoir, 34. Auckland.

Goto, Akira. 1986. Prehistoric Ecology and Economy of Fishing in Hawaii: An Ethnoarchaeological Approach. Ph.D. Thesis, Department of Anthropology, University of Hawai'i at Manoa.

Graves, Donna, and Susan Goodfellow. 1993. The Gardens of Kona Revisited: Pualani Residential Community Phase II—Archaeological Data Recovery. Lands of Puapuaa 1st and 2nd, North Kona...PHRI ms. On file, State Historic Preservation Division Library, Kapolei [H-1353]. (Appendix D. "Historical Documentary Research" by Kepa Maly.)

Graves, Donna, and Leta Franklin. 1998. Archaeological Inventory Survey, Kahua Makai/Kahua Shores Coastal Parcels. PHRI manuscript. On file, State Historic Preservation Division Library, Kapolei [H-1315].

Green, Roger. 1966. "Linguistic Subgroupings within Polynesia: The Implications for Prehistoric Settlement." *Journal of the Polynesian Society* 75:6–38.

———. 1968. "West Polynesian Prehistory." In I. Yawata & Y. Sinoto, eds. *Prehistoric Culture in Oceania*, pp. 99–110. Bishop Museum Press, Honolulu.

———. 1971. "The Chronology and Age of Sites at South Point, Hawaii." *Archaeology & Physical Anthropology in Oceania* 6(2):170–176.

———. 1974. "Tahiti-Hawaii, A.D. 1100–1300: Further Comments." *New Zealand Archaeological Association Newsletter* 17:206–210.

———. 1995. Hawaiian Origins: A Multi-Disciplinary Approach. Keynote speech, 8th Annual Society for Hawaiian Archaeology Conference, Kapiolani Community College, Honolulu.

Group 70. 1979. *Environmental Impact Statement for Hale Pohaku. Mid-Elevation Facilities Master Plan. Hamakua, Mauna Kea, Hawaii* (appendix A = Vegetation survey by Grant Gerrish; Appendix on avifauna by Maile Stemmerman).

———. 1985. *Amended Environmental Assessment for Waiono Meadows Ranch. North Kona, Hawaii.*

Hammatt, Hallett. 1992. Draft: Archaeological Survey, Testing and Excavation of a 174-Acre Parcel, Holualoa, North Kona, Hawaii. Cultural Surveys Hawaii ms. On file, State Historic Preservation Division Library, Kapolei [H-1329].

———. 1994. Archaeological Reconnaissance Survey of 16 Acres, Holualoa, North Kona, Hawaii (7-7-4:11). Cultural Surveys Hawaii ms. On file, State Historic Preservation Division Library, Kapolei [H-1250].

Hammatt, Hallett, and Douglas Borthwick. 1986. Archaeological Survey and Excavations at Kohala Ranch. Cultural Surveys Hawaii ms. On file, State Historic Preservation Division Library, Kapolei [H-665].

Hammatt, Hallett, Douglas Borthwick, Rodney Chiogioji, Jennifer Robins, Joy Collins, and Ted Novak. 1995. An Archaeological Data Recovery of a 4.27 Acre Parcel in the AhuPua'a of Holualoa 4, District of North Kona, Island of Hawai'i. Cultural Surveys Hawaii ms. On file, State Historic Preservation Division Library, Kapolei.

Hammatt, Hallett, Douglas Borthwick, Brian Colin, Ian Masterson, and Jennifer Robins. 1994 Draft: Archaeological Inventory Survey and Limited Subsurface Testing of a 1540-Acre Parcel in the AhuPua'a of Honuaino 3-4, Hokukano, Kanaueue, Haleki'i, Ke'eke'e, 'Ilikahi, Kanakau, Kalukalu, and Onouli 1. Vol. 1. Cultural Surveys Hawaii ms. On file, State Historic Preservation Division Library, Kapolei [H-1210].

Hammatt, Hallett, Douglas Borthwick, and David Shideler. 1986. Archaeological Survey and Excavations on a 20-Acre Parcel, Holualoa, Kona, Hawaii Island. Cultural Surveys Hawaii ms. On file, State Historic Preservation Division Library, Kapolei [H-591].

———. 1988. Intensive Archaeological Survey of 12.4 Acres for Proposed Lalamilo House Lots, Unit 2. Lalamilo, Kohala, Hawaii. Cultural Surveys Hawaii ms. On file, State Historic Preservation Division Library, Kapolei [H-698].

Hammatt, Hallett, and Stephen Clark. 1980. Archaeological Testing and Salvage Excavations of a 155-Acre (Ginter) Parcel in Na AhuPua'a Pahoehoe, La'aloa and Kapala'alaea, Kona, Hawai'i Island. Archaeological Research Center Hawaii, Inc. ms. On file, State Historic Preservation Division Library, Kapolei [H-296].

Hammatt, Hallett, and William Folk .1980. Archaeological Surveys (Phase A): Portions of Keauhou-Kona Resort, Keauhou and Kahalau'u, Kona, Hawai'i Island. Archaeological Research Center Hawaii, Inc. ms. On file, State Historic Preservation Division Library, Kapolei [H-214].

Hammatt, Hallett, William Folk,, and David Shideler. 1992. Archaeological Survey, Testing and Excavation of a 174-Acre Parcel, Holualoa, North Kona, Hawaii. Cultural Surveys Hawaii ms. On file, State Historic Preservation Division Library, Kapolei [H-1329].

Hammatt, Hallett, and David Shideler. 1989. Archaeological Investigations at Ka La Loa Subdivision. Lalamilo, South Kohala, Hawai'i. Cultural Surveys Hawaii ms. On file, State Historic Preservation Division Library, Kapolei [H-766].

Hammatt, Hallett, David Shideler, and Douglas Borthwick. 1987. Archaeological Survey and Test Excavation of a 15-Acre Parcel, Kealakehe, Kona, Hawaii. Cultural Surveys Hawaii ms. On file, State Historic Preservation Division Library, Kapolei [H-581].

Hammatt, Hallett, David Shideler, Douglas Borthwick, Mark Stride, Matt McDermott, and Kirstie Nakamura. 1991. Archaeological Survey and Testing, Kawaihae 1 (Komohana), South Kohala, Hawaii. Cultural Surveys Hawaii ms. On file, State Historic Preservation Division Library, Kapolei [H-852].

Hammatt, Hallett, David Shideler, Rodney Chiogioji, and Douglas Borthwick. 1993. Archaeological Excavations at Lanihau 2 and Moeauoa 2, North Kona, Hawaii. Cultural Surveys Hawaii ms. On file, State Historic Preservation Division Library, Kapolei [H-1149].

Han, Toni, Sara Collins, Stephan Clark, and Anne Garland. 1986. *Moe Kau o Ho'oilo: Hawaiian Mortuary Practices at Keopu, Kona, Hawai'i.* Hawaii Historic Preservation Report, 86-1. Department of Anthropology, Bishop Museum, Honolulu.

Handy, E. S. C. 1923. *The Native Culture of the Marquesas.* Bishop Museum Bulletin, 9. Honolulu.

———. 1930. *History and Culture of the Society Islands.* Bishop Museum Bulletin, 79. Honolulu.

———. 1940. *The Hawaiian Planter.* Bishop Museum Bulletin, 161. Honolulu.

Handy, E. S. C. and E. Handy. 1972. *Native Planters in Old Hawaii.* Bishop Museum Bulletin, 233. Honolulu.

Handy, Elizabeth. 1972. "Ka-'u, Hawai'i, in Ecological and Historical Perspective." In E. S. C. Handy & M. K. Pukui, *The Polynesian Family System in Ka-"u, Hawaii*, pp. 207–252. Charles Tuttle, Tokyo.

Harner, Michael. 1970. "Population Pressure and the Social Evolution of Agriculturalists." *Southwestern Journal of Anthropology*, 26(1):67–86.

Hather, J. G., and Patrick Kirch. 1991. "Prehistoric Sweet Potato (*Ipomoea batatas*) from Mangaia Island, Central Polynesia." *Antiquity* 65:887–893.

Haun, Alan. 1986. Archaeological Survey and Testing at the Bobcat Trail Habitation Cave Site (50-10-30-5004). Pohakuloa Training Area, Island of Hawaii. PHRI ms. On file, State Historic Preservation Division Library, Kapolei [H-532].

Haun, Alan, and Alan Walker. 1987. Final Report: Archaeological Reconnaissance Survey, Hawaiian Riviera Resort Project Area. Land of Kahuku, Kau District...PHRI ms. On file, State Historic Preservation Division Library, Kapolei [H-609].

———. 1988. Archaeological Reconnaissance Survey, Farms of Kapua Mauka Lands Project Area. Land of Kapua, South Kona District...PHRI manuscript. On file, State Historic Preservation Division Library, Kapolei [H-649].

Head, James, Wanda Pua-Kaipo, and Susan Goodfellow. 1994. Supplemental Archaeological Inventory Survey, Ali'i Drive Sewer Project, Roman Catholic School Parcel. Land of Pahoehoe 1st, North Kona District...PHRI ms. On file, State Historic Preservation Division Library, Kapolei [H-1443].

Helber, Hastert, Van Horn and Kimura Planners. 1986. *Kohaniki Draft EIS.* Helber, Hastert, Van Horn and Kimura Planners, Honolulu.

Helekunihi, S. C. n.d. Moolelo Hawaii. Ms. in Hawaiian, on file, Bishop Museum Library (ms. S. C. Helekunihi).

———. 1893. Letter to Rev. Oliver Emerson from Elia Helekunihi. February 25, 1893. Translated by E. Sterling. Bishop Museum Library, Honolulu.

HEN (Hawaiian Ethnographic Notes). n.d. Volume I. Typescript. Honolulu, Bishop Museum Library.

Henry, Jack, and Paul Rosendahl. 1993. Archaeological Inventory Survey, Hienaloli 3-4 Mauka Parcel. PHRI ms. On file, State Historic Preservation Division Library, Kapolei.

Henry, Teuira. 1896. "Tahiti." *4th Annual Report of the Hawaiian Historical Society* 9–13. Honolulu.

———. 1897. "Tahitian Folklore Compared with the Samoan and Hawaiian." *5th Annual Report of the Hawaiian Historical Society*, pp. 16–21.

———. 1928. *Ancient Tahiti, Based on Material Recorded by J. M. Orsmond.* Bishop Museum Bulletin, 48. Honolulu.

Hezel, Francis X. 1983. *The First Taint of Civilization: A History of the Caroline and Marshall Islands in Pre-Colonial Days*, 1521–1885. Pacific Islands Monograph Series, 1. University of Hawai'i Press, Honolulu.

Hommon, Robert. 1969. An Intensive Survey of the Northern Portion of Kaawaloa, Kona, Hawaii. Bishop Museum ms. On file, State Historic Preservation Division Library, Kapolei [H-94].

———. 1970. An Intensive Survey of the Southern Portion of Kaawaloa, Kona, Hawaii. Bishop Museum ms. On file, State Historic Preservation Division Library, Kapolei [H-236].

———. 1975. Use and Control of Hawaiian Inter-Island Channels. Polynesian

Hawaii: A.D. 1400–1794. Manuscript. On file, State Historic Preservation Division Library, Kapolei.

———. 1976. The Formation of Primitive States in Pre-contact Hawaii. Unpublished Ph.D. thesis, Department of Anthropology, University of Arizona.

———. 1980. Historic Resources of Kaho'olawe. National Register of Historic Places Inventory Nomination. Manuscript. On file, State Historic Preservation Division Library, Kapolei.

———. 1986. "Social Evolution in Ancient Hawai'i." In P. Kirch, ed. *Island Societies: Archaeological Approaches to Evolution and Transformation*, pp. 55–68. Cambridge University Press, Cambridge.

———. 1989. "The Kahiki Connection: Extra-Archipelagic Contact and the Development of Complex Polities in Ancient Hawaii." Paper prepared for Circum-Pacific Prehistory Conference. Personal copy.

Hommon, Robert, and Hamilton Ahlo. 1983. A Research Design for Archaeological Studies at the Pohakuloa Training Area, Island of Hawaii. Science Management Inc. ms. On file, State Historic Preservation Division Library, Kapolei [H-290B].

Houghton, Phillip. 1980. *The First New Zealanders*. Hodder & Stoughton, Auckland.

Howard, Alan. 1968. "Polynesian Origins and Migrations." In G. Highland et al., eds., *Polynesian Culture History: Essays in Honor of Kenneth P. Emory*, p. 45–101. Bishop Museum Special Publication, 56. Honolulu.

Hudson, Alfred. 1932. Archaeology of East Hawaii. Bishop Museum ms. On file, State Historic Preservation Division Library, Kapolei.

Hunt, Terry. 1976. Hydration-rind Dates from Archaeological Sites in the South Point Area: A Contribution to Hawaiian Prehistory. Paper Presented at the 1976 First Conference in Natural Sciences in Hawaii.

Hunt, Terry, and Robert Holsen. 1991. "An Early Radiocarbon Chronology for the Hawaiian Islands: A Preliminary Analysis." *Asian Perspectives* 30:147–161.

'I'i, John Papa. 1869. "Na Hunahuna o ka Moolelo o Hawaii." *Ka Nupepa Kuokoa*, Februrary 6, 27, April 10, 17, 24, May 8, June 5. Honolulu.

———. 1889. "Ancient Idolatrous Customs and Kapus of the Hawaiian People." *Hawaiian Almanac and Annual for 1890*, pp. 59–62. Honolulu. [1841 Thanksgiving address at Kawaihao Church.]

———. 1959. *Fragments of Hawaiian History*. Bishop Museum Special Publication, 70. Honolulu.

Ingraham, Joseph. 1918. The Log of the Brig "Hope," called the "Hope's trek Among the Sandwich Islands." *Hawaiian Historical Society Reprints*, 3. Honolulu.

———. 1971. *Joseph Ingraham's Journal of the Brigantine Hope on a Voyage to the North West Coast of North American 1790–1792* (edited by M. Kaplanoff). Imprint Society, Barre (Mass.).

Irwin, Geoffrey. 1992. *The Prehistoric Exploration and Colonisation of the Pacific*. Cambridge University Press, Cambridge.

Jensen, Peter. 1988. Archaeological Data Recovery and Intensive Survey, Resort Expansion Area and Selected Undeveloped Resort Parcels, Waikoloa Beach Resort. PHRI ms. On file, Historic Preservation Division Library, Kapolci [II-645].

———. 1989a. Archaeological Inventory Survey. Undeveloped Portions of Lots 8 of File Plan 1562, Waikoloa Beach Resort. Land of Anaehoomalu...PHRI ms. On file, State Historic Preservation Division Library, Kapolei [H-767].

———. 1989b. Archaeological Inventory Survey, Waikoloa Beach Resort Parcels 20, 21, 22, and 23 and Strip Located Between Parcel 23 and Kiholo Puako Trail. Land of Waikoloa...PHRI ms. On file, State Historic Preservation Division Library, Kapolei [H-763].

———. 1990a. Archaeological Data Recovery and Site Preservation. Undeveloped Portions of Lots 22 and 23 of File Plan 1562 and the Strip Between Lot 23 and Kiholo Puako Trail, Waikoloa Beach Resort. Land of Anaehoomalu...PHRI ms. On file, State Historic Preservation Division Library, Kapolei [H-858].

———. 1990b. Archaeological Data Recovery Program. Lots 1, 2, 6, 7, 17, 24, Waikoloa Beach Resort. Land of Anaehoomalu, South Kohala District...PHRI ms.On file, State Historic Preservation Division Library, Kapolei [H-854].

———. 1991a. Archaeological Data Recovery, Surface Collection, and Excavation. Mauna Lani Cove Project Area. PHRI ms. On file, State Historic Preservation Division Library, Kapolei.

———. 1991b. Archaeological Mitigation Program. Site 5694—TMU A, Waikoloa Beach Resort. Land of Waikoloa, South Kohala District...PHRI ms. On file, State Historic Preservation Division Library, Kapolei [H-940].

Jensen, Peter, and Theresa Donham. 1991. Archaeological Mitigation Program. Honokohau Industrial Park (Parcel VII). PHRI ms. On file, State Historic Preservation Division Library, Kapolei [H-645].

Jensen, Peter, and Susan Goodfellow. 1993. Archaeological Mitigation Program, Honokohau Industrial Park (Parcel VII). Phase II: Data Recovery. PHRI ms. On file, State Historic Preservation Division Library, Kapolei [H-1340].

Joesting, Edward. 1984. *Kauai: The Separate Kingdom.* University of Hawai'i Press, Honolulu.

Johnson, Rubellite. 1979. "From the Gills of the Fish: Hawaii's Genealogical Ties with the Rulers of Tahiti." *Pacific Studies* 3(1):51–67. Brigham Young University Hawaii, Laie.

Joppien, Rudiger, and Bernard Smith. 1988. *The Last of Captain Cook's Voyages.* Vol. 3. *The Voyage of the "Resolution" and "Discovery"" 1776–1780.* Yale University Press, New Haven.

Kaelemakule, J. L. 1867. Map: "Waikoloa, Waimea, Hawaii." Hawaiian Government Survey. Registered Map 574. On file, Department of Accounting & General Services, Survey Office, Honolulu.

Kaeppler, Adrienne. 1975. *The Fabrics of Hawaii: Bark Cloth.* World's Heritage of Woven Fabrics, 14. F. Lewis, Leigh-on-Sea.

———. 1985. "Hawaiian Art and Society, Traditions and Transformations: Featherwork." In *Transformations of Polynesian Culture*, pp. 105–131. Memoir 45.

Kahaulelio, A. D. 1902. "Fishing Lore." *Ka Nupepa Kuakoa*, February 28, March 7, 14, 21, 28, April 4, May 2, 16, 23, 20, June 20, 27, July 4. Translation by M. K. Pukui, Bishop Museum Library, Honolulu.

Kalākaua, David. 1990 [1888]. *The Legends and Myths of Hawaii*. Mutual Publishing, Honolulu. [First published in 1888.]

Kamakau, Samuel. 1961. *Ruling Chiefs of Hawaii*. Kamehameha Schools Press, Honolulu.

———. 1964. *Ka Po'e Kahiko: The People of Old*. Bishop Museum Special Publication, 51. Honolulu.

———. 1976. *The Works of the People of Old: Na Hana a ka Po'e Kahiko*. Bishop Museum Special Publication, 61. Honolulu.

———. 1991. *Tales and Traditions of the People of Old: Na Mo'olelo a ka Po'e Kahiko*. Bishop Museum Press, Honolulu.

Kaneinei. n.d. Manuscript in Hawaii (untranslated). Bishop Museum Library, Honolulu.

Kaschko, Michael, and Melinda S. Allen. n.d. The Impact of the Sweet Potato on Prehistoric Hawaiian Cultural Development. Manuscript. On file, State Historic Preservation Division Library, Kapolei [G-289].

Kaschko, Michael, and Paul Rosendahl. 1987. Full Archaeological Reconnaissance Survey, Kealakekua Ranch Makai Land Subdivision. PHRI ms. On file, State Historic Preservation Division Library, Kapolei. [H-571].

Ka'ū Station Reports. 1846, 1852. Kau Station Reports 1842–1863. Mss 2-A, H31, Kau. Hawaiian Mission Children's Society Library, Honolulu.

Kawachi, Carol. 1989. Pua'a 2: An Upland Habitation and Agricultural Complex in North Kona, Hawaii Island. M.A. thesis, Department of Anthropology, University of Hawai'i at Manoa.

Kawaharada, Dennis. 1992. "Introduction." In M. Nakuina, *The Wind Gourd of La'amaomao*, pp. vii–x. Kalamaku Press, Honolulu.

Ke Au Okoa. 1865. "Ka Moookuauhau, a he Papa Hoomanao hoi, o na mea Kaulana maloko o na mooolelo Hawaii." *Ke Au Okoa*, May 22, 1865. Honolulu.

Kekahuna, Henry. 1950. Map of Pakiha Enclosure and Residence of Queen Kekealani. Blueprint map. On file, State Historic Preservation Division Library, Kapolei.

———. 1952. "Map Showing Kaha-Lu'u Beach." On file, State Historic Preservation Division Library, Kapolei.

Kelly, Marion. 1969. *Historical Background of the South Point Area, Ka'ū, Hawaii*. Pacific Anthropological Records, 6. Bishop Museum, Honolulu.

———. 1974. "Historical Survey of the Waimea to Kawaihae Road Corridor, Island of Hawaii." In W. Barrera, Jr. and M. Kelly, *Archaeological and Historical Surveys of the Waimea to Kawaihae Road Corridor, Island of Hawaii*. Hawaiian Historic Preservation Report, 74-1. Department of Transportation, State of Hawaii, Honolulu.

———. 1980. *Majestic Ka'ū: Mo'olelo of Nine Ahupua'a*. Department of Anthropology Reports, 80-2. Bishop Museum, Honolulu.

———. 1983. *Na Mala o Kona: Gardens of Kona*. Historic Preservation Report, 83-2. Department of Transportation, State of Hawaii, Honolulu.

———. 1986. "Annotated List of Puuhonua in the Hawaiian Islands." In Emory et al., *The Cultural History of Honaunau. The Natural and Cultural History of Honaunau*, Kona, Hawai'i. [1957 manuscript.] Bishop Museum Departmental Report Series, 86-2. Honolulu.

Kelly, Marion, Barry Nakamura. and Dorothy Barrere 1981. *Hilo Bay: A Chronological Study*. Bishop Museum, Honolulu.

Kelsey, Theodore. 1949–1950. Field Notes. On file, Kekahuna Private Collection, Archives of the State of Hawaii, Honolulu.

Kennedy, Joseph, Mary Anne Maigret, and James Moore. 1993. An Archaeological Inventory Survey with Subsurface Testing, Report for the Proposed Keopu Loa Subdivision...Archaeological Consultants of Hawaii ms. On file, State Historic Preservation Division Library, Kapolei [H-1224].

Kent, Harold. 1961. "Acknowledgement." In S. Kamakau, *Ruling Chiefs of Hawaii*,p. x. Kamehameha Schools Press, Honolulu.

Kepelino, Keauokalani. 1868. Moolelo Hawaii. Manuscript. Bishop Museum Library, Honolulu.

———. 1932. *Traditions of Hawaii* (edited by M. Beckwith). Bishop Museum Bulletin, 95. Honolulu.

Kikuchi, William, and Deborah Cluff. 1969. "An Archaeological Survey of Puu Kohola Heiau, South Kohala, Kawaihae, Hawaii Island." In D. Cluff, W. Kikuchi, R. Apple, and Y. H. Sinoto, *The Archaeological Surface Survey of Puu Kohola Heiau and Mailekini Heiau, South Kohala, Kawaihae, Hawaii Island*, pp. 35–66. Hawaii State Journal, 69-3. State Parks, State of Hawaii, Honolulu.

King, James. 1967. Journal. In J. C. Beaglehole, ed. *The Journals of Captain James Cook on His Voyages of Discovery*. Vol. 3. *The Voyage of the "Resolution" and "Discovery" 1776–1780*, The Hakluyt Society, Cambridge.

Kinney, Henry. 1913. The Island *of Hawaii*. Hilo Board of Trade, Hilo.

Kirch, Patrick. 1973. Early Settlement and Initial Adaptation Models in the Hawaiian Islands. Paper read at the 38th Society for American Archaeology Conference, San Francisco. Manuscript.

———. 1974. "The Chronology of Early Hawaiian Settlement." *Archaeology & Physical Anthropology in Oceania* 9(2):110–119.

———. 1979. *Marine Exploitation in Prehistoric Hawaii: Archaeological Excavations at KalahuiPua'a, Hawaii Island*. Pacific Anthropological Records, 29. Department of Anthropology, Bishop Museum, Honolulu.

———. 1984. *The Evolution of the Polynesian Chiefdoms*. Cambridge University Press, Cambridge.

———. 1985. *Feathered Gods and Fishhooks*. University of Hawai'i Press, Honolulu.

———. 1986. "Rethinking East Polynesian Prehistory." *Journal of the Polynesian Society* 95(1):9–40.

———. 1989. "Prehistory." In A. Howard and R. Borofsky, eds, *Developments in Polynesian Ethnology*, pp. 13–46. University of Hawai'i Press, Honolulu.

Kirch, Patrick, and Thomas Dye. 1979. "Ethnoarchaeology and the Development of Polynesian Fishing Strategies." *Journal of the Polynesian Society*, 88:53–76.

Kirch, Patrick, and Marion Kelly, eds. 1975. *Prehistory and Ecology in a Windward Hawaiian Valley: Halawa Valley, Molokai.* Pacific Anthropological Records, 24. Bishop Museum, Honolulu.

Kohala Station Reports. 1845, 1848, 1849. Kohala Station Reports 1838–1863. On file, Hawaiian Mission Children's Society Library, Honolulu.

Kolb, Michael. 1991. Social Power, Chiefly Authority, and Ceremonial Architecture in an Island Polity, Maui, Hawaii. Unpublished Ph.D. thesis, Department of Anthropology, UCLA.

Komori, Eric. 1993. "An Analysis of Matched Volcanic Glass and Radiocarbon Samples from Lana'i and Kaho'olawe." Paper presented at 6th Annual Society for Archaeology Conference, Kaluakoi, Moloka'i.

———. 1984. Intensive Archaeological Survey of Land at Kalamakapala, South Kona, Island of Hawaii. Bishop Museum ms. On file, State Historic Preservation Division Library, Kapolei [H-368].

Kotzebue, Otto von. 1821. *A Voyage of Discovery into the South Sea...in the Years 1815–1818.* 3 volumes. London, Longman.

———. 1831. *A New Voyage Round the World During the Years 1823–1826.* London.

Kuykendall, Ralph. 1957 [1938]. *The Hawaiian Kingdom.* Volume 1, *1778–1854 Foundation and Transformation.* University of Hawai'i Press, Honolulu. [First published in 1938].

Laanui, Gideon. 1838. "Reminiscences of G. Laanui." *Kumu Hawaii.* March, p. 144 (translation by Mary K. Pukui). On File, Bishop Museum Library, Honolulu.

Ladd, Edmund. 1969a. "Alealea Temple Site, Honaunau: Salvage Report." In R. Pearson, ed, *Archaeology on the Island of Hawaii*, pp. 95–132. Social Science Research Institute, Asian & Pacific Archaeology Series No. 3. University of Hawai'i, Honolulu.

———. 1969b. "The Great Wall Stabilization: Salvage Report." In R. Pearson, ed., *Archaeology on the Island of Hawaii*, pp. 133–162. Social Science Research Institute, Asian & Pacific Archaeology Series No. 3. University of Hawai'i, Honolulu.

———. 1969c. "Hale-o-Keawe Temple Site, Honaunau: Pre-Salvage Report." In R. Pearson, ed., *Archaeology on the Island of Hawaii*, pp. 163–190. Social Science Research Institute, Asian & Pacific Archaeology Series No. 3. University of Hawai'i, Honolulu.

———. 1985. *Hale-o-Keawe Archeological Report. Archeology at Pu'uhonua o Honaunau National Historic Park.* Western Archeological and Conservation Center Publications in Anthropology, 33. National Park Service.

———.- 1986a. *Test Excavations at Sites B-105, B-107, and B-108. Archaeology at Pu'uhonua o Honaunau National Historic Park.* Western Archeological and Conservation Center Publications in Anthropology, 34. National Park Service.

———. 1986b. Ruins Stabilization and Restoration Record. Pu'ukohola Heiau National Historic Site, Kawaihae, Hawaii. National Park Service ms. On file, State Historic Preservation Division, Kapolei.

———. 1987. *Excavations at Site A-27. Archaeology at Pu'uhonua o Honaunau National Historic Park.* Western Archeological and Conservation Center Publications in Anthropology, 43. National Park Service.

Ladefoged, Thegn, Gary Somers, and M. Melia Lane-Hamasaki. 1987. *A Settlement Pattern Analysis of a Portion of Hawaii Volcanoes National Park.* Western Archeological and Conservation Center Publications in Anthropology, 44.

Landrum, J., A. Haun, P. Rosendahl, and K. Delimont. 1990. Archaeological Inventory Survey and Test Excavations, Kahakai Development Project Area. Lands of Puapuaa 1st and 2nd, North Kona, Island of Hawaii. PHRI ms. On file, State Historic Preservation Division Library, Kapolei [H-1243].

La Paz. 1871. "A Ride Through Puna and Discovery of the Ancient Ruins of Kukii." *Pacific Commercial Advertiser*, June 10, 1871.

Law, John. 1779. Journal of J. Law, Surgeon 1779. Additional mss. 37327, British Museum. Photostat copy, Captain Cook Collection #94 in Archives of the State of Hawaii, Honolulu.

Leach, B. Foss, and Horwood, Ian Smith. 1988. Analysis of Archaeological Fauna from Kaloko. Manuscript. On file, State Historic Preservation Division Library, Kapolei.

Ledyard, J. 1963 [1783]. John Ledyard's *Journal of Captain Cook's Last Voyage* (edited by J. Munford). Oregon State University Press, Corvallis. [Originally published 1783, Nathaniel Patten, Hartford]

Levison, Michael, R. Gerard Ward, and John W. Webb. 1973. *The Settlement of Polynesia: A Computer Simulation.* University of Minnesota Press, Minneapolis.

Lewis, David. 1972. *We, the Navigators.* University of Hawai'i Press, Honolulu.

Libby, W. F. 1951. "Radiocarbon Dates, II." *Science* 114:295.

Lieb, Amos. 1949. *Hawaiian Legends in English: An Annotated Bibliography.* University of Hawai'i Press, Honolulu.

Lili'uokalani, Queen., trans. 1897. An *Account of the Creation of the World According to Hawaiian Tradition.* Boston.

Lisiansky, Urey. 1814. *Voyage Round the World,* 1803–1806, in the Ship "Neva." Longmans, London.

Liston, Jolie, and Greg Burtchard. 1993. Historic Preservation Mitigation Plan, Development Parcel 35. Keauhou, North Kona, Island of Hawai'i. International Archaeological Research Institute, Inc. ms. On file, State Historic Preservation Division Library, Kapolei.

———. 1994. Archaeological Data Recovery, Development Parcel 34, Keauhou, North Kona, Hawai'i Island. International Archaeological Research Institute, Inc. ms. On file, State Historic Preservation Division Library, Kapolei [H-1268].

Loo, Virginia, and William Bonk. 1970. A Historical Site Study and Evaluation of North Hawaii Island. Manuscript. On file, State Historic Preservation Division Library, Kapolei [H-272].

Lyman, Chester. 1846 [1924]. *Around the Horn to the Sandwich Islands and California 1845–1850.* Yale University Press, New Haven.

Lyman, Frederick. 1857. List of Dates. Case Files of the Fourth Circuit Court. Case File 82, Folder 3, Archives of the State of Hawaii, Honolulu.

———. 1868. "Extracts from a Letter...Dated Hilo, April 10th, 1868...." In

J. D. Dana, ed., "Recent Eruptions of Mauna Loa and Kilauea, Hawaii," pp. 109–112. *American Journal Science Arts* Series 2, 46(13):105–123.

Lyons, C. J. 1853. Map of Puu Kohola Heiau, Kawaihae, Hawaii. Copy in W. Kikuchi & D. Cluff, "An Archaeological Survey of Puu Kohola Heiau, South Kohala, Kawaihae, Hawaii Island," p. 43. In D. Cluff, W. Kikuchi, R. Apple, and Y. H. Sinoto, *The Archaeological Surface Survey of Puu Kohola Heiau and Mailekini Heiau, South Kohala, Kawaihae, Hawaii Island*, pp. 35–66. Hawaii State Journal, 69-3. State Parks, State of Hawaii, Honolulu.

———. 1875. "Land Matters in Hawaii. Volume I." *The Islander:* 103–104, 111, 118–119, 126–127, 135, 143, 150–151, 159, 168–169, 174–175, 182–183, 190–191, 206–207, 214–215, 222–223.

Lyons, Lorenzo. 1842. Statisticks Book. On file, Hawaiian Mission Children's Society Library, Honolulu.

———. 1847. Waimea Church Records (1832–1847). Manuscript. On file, Hawaiian Mission Children's Society Library, Honolulu.

MacDaniels, Laurence. 1947. A Study of the Fe'i Banana and Its Distribution with Reference to Polynesian Migrations. Bishop Museum Bulletin, 190. Honolulu.

Macdonald, Gordon, and Agatin Abott. 1970. *Volcanoes in the Sea: The Geology of Hawaii.* University of Hawai'i'Press, Honolulu.

Macrae, James. 1922. With Lord Byron at the Sandwich Islands in 1825. New Freedom Press, Honolulu.

Malo, David. 1840. Moolelo Hawaii. Manuscript. Microfilm, Bishop Museum, Honolulu.

———. n.d. He Buke no ka 'Oihana Kula. Manuscript. Copy on file, State Historic Preservation Division, Kapolei.

———. 1951 [1903]. *Hawaiian Antiquities.* Bishop Museum Special Publication, 2. Honolulu. [Originally published in 1903.]

Manby, Thomas. 1959. "With Vancouver at Kealakekua Bay." In Day, A.G. and Carl Stroven, eds., 1959. *A Hawaiian Reader.* Mutual Publishing Paperback Series, Honolulu.

Martin, Jean. 1971. State of Hawaii Site 10-07-2115 Inventory File. On file, Historic Preservation Division, Department of Land & Natural Resources, State of Hawaii, Kapolei.

McAllister, J. Gilbert. 1933. *Archaeology of Oahu.* Bishop Museum Bulletin, 104. Honolulu.

McArthur, Norma, J. W. Saunders, and R. L. Tweedie. 1976. "Small Population Isolates: A Micro-simulation Study." *Journal of the Polynesian Society,* 85(3):307–326.

McCoy, Patrick. 1977. "The Mauna Kea Adze Quarry Project: A Summary of the 1975 Field Investigations." *Journal of the Polynesian Society* 86:223–243.

———. 1986. Archaeological Investigations in the Hopukani and Liloe Springs Area of Mauna Kea, Hawaii. Bishop Museum ms. On file, State Historic Preservation Division Library, Kapolei [H-525].

McCoy, Patrick, Kenneth Emory, and Dorothy Barrere. 1971. *Archaeological Survey: Kahaluu and Keauhou, North Kona, Hawaii.* Department of Anthropology Report, 71-4. Bishop Museum, Honolulu.

McEldowney, Holly. 1979. Archaeological and Historical Literature Search and Research Design. Lava Flow Control Study, Hilo, Hawai'i. Bishop Museum manuscript. On file, State Historic Preservation Division Library, Kapolei [H-127].

———. 1983. "A Description of Major Vegetation Patterns in the Waimea-Kawaihae Region During the Early Historic Period." In J. Clark & P. Kirch, eds., *Archaeological Investigation of the Mudlane-Waimea-Kawaihae Road Corridor, Island of Hawaii: an Interdisciplinary Study of an Environmental Transect,* pp. 407–448. Department of Anthropology, Bishop Museum, Honolulu.

———. 1986. A Narrative Summarizing and Analyzing Historical and Archaeological Documents Gathered on the Kamoa Point State Park. Manuscript. On file, State Historic Preservation Division Library, Kapolei [H-1197].

McKenzie, Edith. 1983. *Hawaiian Genealogies Extracted from Hawaiian Language Newspapers,* vol. 1. The Institute for Polynesian Studies, Brigham Young University Hawaii, Laie.

———. 1986. *Hawaiian Genealogies Extracted from Hawaiian Language Newspapers,* vol. 2. The Institute for Polynesian Studies, Brigham Young University Hawaii, Laie.

Meares, John. 1790. *Voyages Made in the Years 1788 and 1789 from China to the North-West Coast of America.* Logographic Press, London.

Menzies, Archibald. 1920. *Hawaii Nei 128 Years Ago: Journal of Archibald Menzies, Kept During His Three Visits to the Sandwich Islands when Acting as Surgeon and Naturalist on Board HMS Discovery.* The New Freedom Press, Honolulu.

Michener, James. 1959. *Hawaii.* Fawcett Publications, Greenwich.

Minson, William. 1952. The Hawaiian Journal of Manuel Quimper. M.A. thesis, University of Hawai'i at Manoa.

Mission Committee Report. 1830. Map of Waimea. Hawaiian Mission Children's Society Library, Honolulu.

Morris, Penrose. 1925. "Kapiolani." *The Hawaiian Annual for 1926,* pp. 40–53. Honolulu.

Mortimer, George. 1791. *Observations and Remarks Made During a Voyage to the Islands of Teneriffe, Amsterdam, Maria's Islands near Van Diemens Land &*

*Otaheite, Sandwich Islands: Owhynee...in the Brig Mercury, commanded by Captain John Cox.* T. Cadell, London.

Nakuina, Moses. 1992. *The Wind Gourd of La'amaomao* (translation by Esther Mookini and Sarah Nakoa). Kalamaku Press, Honolulu.

Napoka, Nathan. n.d. Mo'okini Heiau, Summary of Archival Data. Manuscript, in Mookini Heiau Site File. State Historic Preservation Division, Kapolei.

Naroll, Rauol. 1962. "Floor Area and Settlement Population." *American Antiquity* 27:587–589.

Native Register. n.d. (ca. 1848–1849). Native Register of Kuleana Claims Recorded by the Board of Commissioners to Quiet Land Titles in the Hawaiian Islands. Ms. (translation) on file, Archives of the State of Hawaii, Honolulu.

Native Testimony. n.d. (ca. 1849). Native Testimony Recorded by the Board of Commissioners to Quiet Land Titles in the Hawaiian Islands. Ms. (translation) on file, Archives of the State of Hawaii, Honolulu.

Newman, T. Stell. 1968. "Cultural Adaptations to the Island of Hawaii Ecosystem: The Theory Behind the 1968 Lapakahi Project." In R. Pearson, *Archaeology on the Island of Hawaii*, pp. 3–14. Asian & Pacific Archaeology Series, 3. Social Science Research Institute, University of Hawai'i at Manoa, Honolulu.

———. 1970. *Hawaiian Fishing and Farming on the Island of Hawaii in A.D. 1778.* Division of State Parks, Honolulu.

———. 1974a. Ahua a Umi Heiau State of Hawaii Inventory Form. On file, State Historic Preservation Division (site 10-29-3810), Kapolei.

———. 1974b. Kona Field System. Hawaii Register of Historic Places Nomination Form. Site 10-37-6601. On file, State Historic Preservation Division, Kapolei.

O1 Consultants, Inc. 1986. Impact Analysis of Resort Development at Kohanaiki on the Near-Shore Marine Environment and Anchialine Pond Resources. In Helber, Hastert, Van Horn and Kimura, *Kohanaiki Draft EIS*, Appendix. Helber, Hastert, Van Horn and Kimura Planners, Honolulu.

O'Hare, Constance, and Susan Goodfellow. 1992. Koana-Iki Resort. Phased Archaeological Mitigation Program. Phase 4—Data Recovery. Land of Kohana-Iki, North Kona, Island of Hawaii. PHRI ms. On file, State Historic Preservation Division Library, Kapolei [H-1339].

O'Hare, Constance, and Paul Rosendahl. 1993. Archaeological Inventory Survey, Makai Portion of 'Ohi'a Cave. PHRI ms. On file, State Historic Preservation Division Library, Kapolei [H-1241].

Oliver, Douglas. 1974. *Ancient Tahitian Society.* 3 volumes. University Press of Hawaii, Honolulu.

Pawley, Andrew. 1966. "Polynesian Languages: A Subgrouping Based on Shared Innovations in Morphology." *Journal of the Polynesian Society* 75:39–64.

Pawley, Andrew. and Kaye Green. 1971. "Lexical Evidence for the Proto-Polynesian Homeland." *Te Reo*, 14:1–36.

Pawley, Andrew. and Roger Green. 1984. "The Proto-Oceanic Language Community." *Journal of Pacific History*, 19:123–146.

Pearsall, D., and Deborah Trimble. 1983. "Report 18. Phytolith Analysis of Soil Samples." In J. Clark and P. Kirch, eds., *Archaeological Investigation of the Mudlane-Waimea-Kawaihae Road Corridor, Island of Hawaii: an Interdisciplinary Study of an Environmental Transect*, pp. 472–497. Department of Anthropology, Bishop Museum, Honolulu.

Pearson, Richard, Patrick Kirch, and Michael Pietrusewsky. 1971. "An Early Prehistoric Site at Bellows Beach, Waimanalo, Oahu, Hawaiian Islands." *Archaeology & Physical Anthropology in Oceania* 6:204–234.

Pfeiffer, Michael. 1995. "Distribution and Design of Pacific Octopus Lures: The Hawaiian Octopus Lure in Regional Context." *Hawaiian Archaeology* 4:47–56.

Pietrusewsky, Michael. 1970. "An Osteological View of the Indigenous Populations in Oceania." In R. Green and M. Kelly, eds., *Studies in Oceanic Culture History*, vol. I, pp. 1–12. Pacific Anthropological Records, 11. Bishop Museum, Honolulu.

———. 1971. "Application of Distance Statistics to Anthroscopic Data and a Comparison of Results with Those Obtained by Using Discrete Traits of the Skull." *Archaeology & Physical Anthropology in Oceania* 6:21–33.

Pirie, Peter. 1972. "The Effects of Treponematosis and Gonorrhoea on the Populations of the Pacific Islands." *Human Biology in Oceania* 1(3):187–206.

Pogue, John. 1858. *Ka Moolelo Hawaii*. Honolulu.

———. 1978. *Moolelo of Ancient Hawaii*. Charles Kenn (translation). Honolulu. [Original published in 1858 in Hawaiian.]

Pukui, Mary Kawena. 1983. *'Olelo No'eau: Hawaiian Proverbs & Poetical Sayings*. Bishop Museum Special Publication, 71. Bishop Museum, Honolulu.

Pukui, Mary Kawena, and Samuel Elbert. 1971. *Hawaiian Dictionary*. University of Hawai'i Press, Honolulu.

Pukui, Mary Kawena, Samuel Elbert, and Esther Mookini. 1974. *Place Names of Hawaii*. University of Hawai'i Press, Honolulu.

Puna Geothermal. 1985. Draft Supplemental Impact Statement to the Revised Environmental Impact Statement for the Kahauolea Geothermal Project. True/ Mid-pacific Geothermal, Inc.

Reeve, Roland. 1983. "Report 6. Archaeological Investigations in Section 3." In J. Clark & P. Kirch, eds., *Archaeological Investigation of the Mudlane-Waimea-Kawaihae Road Corridor, Island of Hawaii: an Interdisciplinary Study of an Environmental Transect*, pp. 181–236. Department of Anthropology, Bishop Museum, Honolulu.

———. 1994. Na Wahi Pana o Kaho'olawe. Kaho'olawe Island Conveyance Commission Consultant Report, 17. Manuscript. On file, State Historic Preservation Division Library, Kapolei.

Reinecke, John. 1929–1930. Hawaiian Remains on the Shoreward Flat of Kaawaloa and Keopuka, District of South Kona. Bishop Museum ms. On file, State Historic Preservation Division Library, Kapolei [H-376].

———. 1930a. Survey of Sites on West Hawaii. Bishop Museum ms. On file, State Historic Preservation Division Library, Kapolei [H-674].

———. 1930b. Part 7. Survey of Coast from Honaunau to Kaawaloa. Bishop Museum ms. On file, State Historic Preservation Division Library, Kapolei.

Reinman, Fred, and Alan Schilz. 1992. Archaeological Data Recovery at the MPRC, Pohakuloa Training Area, Island of Hawaii. Odgen ms. On file, State Historic Preservation Division Library, Kapolei.

Remy, Jules. 1979. *Contributions of a Venerable Native to the Ancient History of the Hawaiian Islands.* Outbooks, Reno. [Originally published in 1859. Translated by W. T. Brigham, with translation originally published in 1874.]

Renger, Robert. 1970. *Archaeological Reconnaissance of Coastal Kaloko and Kukio 1, North Kona, Hawaii.* Department of Anthropology Reports, 70-10. Bishop Museum, Honolulu.

———. 1973. Human Adaptation to Marginal Coastal Environments: The Archaeology of Kaloko, North Kona, Hawaii. Ph.D. thesis, Department of Anthropology, University of California at Santa Barbara.

Richards, William. 1824–1825. August 13, 1824 Letter to Evarts. William Richards file, 1824–1825 Lahaina. Hawaiian Mission Children's Society Library, Honolulu.

Rickman, John. 1781. *Journal of Captain Cook's Last Voyage to the Pacific Ocean on Discovery, Performed in the Years 1776–1779.* London.

Riley, Thomas. 1975. "Survey and Excavations of the Aboriginal Agricultural Systems." In P. Kirch & M. Kelly, eds., *Prehistory and Ecology in a Windward Hawaiian Valley: Halawa Valley, Molokai*, pp. 79–115. Pacific Anthropological Records, 24. Bishop Museum, Honolulu.

Riou, Edward. 1778–1779. A Logg of the Proceedings of his Majesty's Sloop Discovery, 1778–1779. Ms. Adm. 51/4529. Pacific Records Office, London.

Roe, Michael, ed. 1967. *The Journals and Letters of Captain Charles Bishop on the North-west Coast of America, in the Pacific and in New South Wales*, 1739–1799. Cambridge University Press for the Hakluyt Society, Cambridge.

Rose, Roger. 1978. *Symbols of Sovereignty: Feather Girdles of Tahiti and Hawai'i.* Pacific Anthropological Records, 28. Bishop Museum, Honolulu.

———. 1992. *Reconciling the Past: Two Basketry Kē'ai and the Legendary Liloa and Lonoikamakahiki.* Bishop Museum Bulletin in Anthropology, 5. Bishop Museum, Honolulu.

Rosendahl, Paul. 1972. Aboriginal Agriculture and Residence Patterns in Upland Lapakahi, Island of Hawaii. Unpublished Ph.D. thesis, Department of Anthropology, University of Hawai'i at Manoa.

———. 1973. *Archaeological Salvage of the Hapuna-Anaehoomalu Section of the Kailua-Kawaihae Road (Queen Kaahumanu Highway), Island of Hawaii.* Hawaii Historic Preservation Report, 72-1. Department of Transportation, State of Hawaii, Honolulu.

———. 1984a. Archaeological Field Investigation: Private Subdivision Development, Waipunaula and Kalamakumu, South Kona...PHRI ms. On file, State Historic Preservation Division Library, Kapolei [H-355].

———. 1984b. Archaeological Field Investigation: Private Subdivision Development, Waipunaula, South Kona. PHRI ms. On file, State Historic Preservation Division Library, Kapolei [H-378].

Rosendahl, Paul, and Laura Carter. 1988. *Excavations at John Young's Homestead, Kawaihae, Hawai'i.* Western Archeological and Conservation Center Publications in Anthropology, 47. National Park Service.

Rosendahl, Paul, Alan Haun, Joseph Halbig, Mikk Kaschko, and Melinda S. Allen. 1988. Kaho'olawe Excavations, 1982-3 Data Recovery Project. Island of Kaohoolawe, Hawaii. PHRI ms. On file, State Historic Preservation Division Library, Kapolei [Ko-27].

Sahlins, Marshall. 1958. *Social Stratification in Polynesia.* American Ethnological Society, Seattle.

———. 1971. An Interdisciplinary Investigation of Hawaiian Social Morphology and Economy in the Late Prehistoric and Early Historic Periods. Proposal to the National Science Foundation. On file, State Historic Preservation Division Library, Kapolei.

———. 1973. Historical Anthropology of the Hawaiian Kingdom. Proposal to the National Science Foundation. On file, State Historic Preservation Division Library, Kapolei.

———. 1981. *Historical Metaphors and Mythical Realities: Structure in the Early History of the Sandwich Islands Kingdom.* Ann Arbor: University of Michigan Press.

———. 1985. *Islands of History.* Chicago, University of Chicago Press.

———. 1992. *Anahulu: The Anthropology of History in the Kingdom of Hawaii: Volume One: Historical Ethnography.* The University of Chicago Press, Chicago.

Sahlins, Marshall, and Dorothy Barrere, eds. 1973. "William Richards on Hawaiian Culture and Political Conditions of the Hawaiian Islands in 1841." *The Hawaiian Journal of History,* 7:18–40.

Samwell, David. 1786. *A Narrative of the Death of Captain James Cook*...For G. and J. Robinson, London.

Sanders, William, and Barbara Price. 1968. *Mesoamerica: The Evolution of a Civilization.* Random House, New York.

Sarfert, Ernst. 1920. *Kusae,* vol. 2: *Geistige Kultur.* L. Friederichsen & Co., Hamburg.

Sato, H., W. Ikeda, R. Paeth, R. Smythe, and M. Tekehiro, Jr. 1973. *Soil Survey of the Island of Hawaii, State of Hawaii.* U.S. Government Printing Office, Washington, D.C.

Schele, Linda, and David Freidel. 1990. *A Forest of Kings: The Untold Story of the Ancient Maya.* William Morrow, New York.

Schilt, A. Rose. 1980. Archaeological Investigations in Specified Areas of the Hanalei Wildlife Refuge, Hanalei Valley, Kaua'i. Bishop Museum ms. On file,

State Historic Preservation Division Library, Kapolei.

———. 1984. *Subsistence and Conflict in Kona, Hawai'i: An Archaeological Study of the Kuakini Highway Realignment Corridor.* Department of Anthropology Reports 84-1. Bishop Museum, Honolulu.

Schilz, Alan, Kanalei Shun, Scott Williams, and Richard Nees. 1994. Archaeological Survey and Evaluation, Lands of Kau, North Kona, Hawai'i Island. Ogden ms. On file, State Historic Preservation Division Library, Kapolei [H-1118].

Schmitt, Robert. 1971. "New Estimates of the Pre-Censal Population of Hawaii." *Journal of the Polynesian Society* 80:237–243.

———. 1973. *The Missionary Censuses of Hawaii.* Pacific Anthropological Records, 20. Bishop Museum, Honolulu.

———. 1977. *Historical Statistics of Hawaii.* University of Hawai'i Press, Honolulu.

Schmitt, Robert, and Lynn Zane. 1977. How Many People Have Ever Lived in Hawaii? Manuscript. On file, Department of Anthropology, Bishop Museum, Honolulu.

Sharp, Andrew. 1956. *Ancient Voyagers of the Pacific.* Polynesian Society Memoir, 32. Wellington.

———. 1963. *Ancient Voyagers in Polynesia.* Pauls Book Arcade, Auckland.

Shun, Kanalei, and Alan Schilz. 1991. Archaeological Investigations in Waimanu Valley, Hamakua District, Hawaii Island, Hawaii. Ogden ms. On file, State Historic Preservation Division Library, Kapolei.

Simmons, D. R. 1976. *The Great New Zealand Myth: A Study of the Discovery and Origin Traditions of the Maori.* A. H. & A. W. Reed, Wellington.

Sinoto, Yosihiko. 1962. "Chronology of Hawaiian Fishhooks." *Journal of the Polynesian Society* 71(2):162–166.

———. 1966. "A Tentative Prehistoric Cultural Sequence in the Northern Marquesas Islands." *Journal of the Polynesian Society* 75(3):287–303.

———. 1967. "Artifacts from Excavated Sites in the Hawaiian, Marquesas, and Society Islands: A Comparative Study." In G. Highland et al, eds., *Polynesian Culture History: Essays in Honor of K. P. Emory*, pp. 341–361. Bishop Museum Special Publication, 56. Honolulu.

———. 1970. "An Archaeologically Based Assessment of the Marquesas Islands as a Dispersal Center in East Polynesia." In R. Green & M. Kelly, eds., *Studies in Oceanic Culture History:* volume 1, pp. 105–130. *Pacific Anthropological Records*, 11. Bishop Museum, Honolulu.

———. 1979. "The Marquesas." In J. Jennings, ed., *The Prehistory of Polynesia*, pp. 110–134. Harvard University Press, Cambridge.

Sinoto, Yosihiko, and Marion Kelly. 1975. *Archaeological and Historical Survey of Pakini-nui and Pakini-iki Coastal Sites: Waiahukini, Kailikii, and Hawea. Ka'ū, Hawaii.* Department of Anthropology Reports, 75-1. Bishop Museum, Honolulu.

Sinoto, Yosihiko, and Patrick McCoy. 1975. "Report on the Preliminary Excavation of an Early Habitation Site on Huahine, Society Islands." *Journal de la Societe des Oceanistes* 47:143–186.

Smith, Clifford, William Hoe, and Peter O'Connor. 1982. Botanical Survey of the Mauna Kea Summit Above 13,000 Feet. Bishop Museum ms.

Smith, S. Percy. 1897. "Synopsis of a Lecture on the Origins and Migrations of the Polynesians Considered from the South Polynesian Point of View." *5th Annual Report of the Hawaiian Historical Society*, pp. 10–16.

———. 1898. "Hawaiki: The Whence of the Maori." *Journal of the Polynesian Society* 7:137–177.

———. 1910. Hawaiki: The Original Home of the Maori. [3rd ed] Whitcombe & Tombs Ltd., Christchurch.

———. 1920. "Kava Drinking Ceremonies Among the Samoans." *Journal of the Polynesian Society* 29(114):Supplement 1–21.

Soehren, Lloyd. 1962. Archaeological Excavations at City of Refuge National Historic Park, Honaunau, Kona, Hawaii. Bishop Museum ms. On file, State Historic Preservation Division Library, Kapolei. [Published as Soehren & Tuohy 1987.]

———. 1964. An Archaeological Survey of the Shores of Ouli and Kawaihae, South Kohala, Hawaii. Bishop Museum ms. On file, State Historic Preservation Division Library, Kapolei.

———. 1968. An Evaluation of the Archaeological Features Between Honaunau and Kaawaloa, South Kona, Hawaii. Bishop Museum ms. On file, State Historic Preservation Division Library, Kapolei.

———. 1977. Letter Report: Archaeological Reconnaissance of Portions of TMK 8-2-08:22 and 55, Kehauloa 1st, South Kona, Hawaii. Manuscript. On file, State Historic Preservation Division Library, Kapolei [H-91].

———. 1980. Letter Report: Archaeological Reconnaissance Survey of TMK: 8-2-05: 18. Manuscript. On file, State Historic Preservation Division Library, Kapolei [H-142].

Soehren, Lloyd, and T. Stell Newman. 1968. Archaeology of Kealakekua Bay. Manuscript. On file, State Historic Preservation Division Library, Kapolei [H-95].

Soehren, Lloyd, and Donald Tuohy. 1987. *Archaeological Excavations at Pu'uhonua o Honaunau National Historical Park, Honaunau, Kona, Hawai'i.* Bishop Museum, Honolulu.

Somers, Gary. 1986. *Mapping and Stabilization of Alahaka and Oma'o Heiau. Archeology at Pu'uhonua o Honaunau National Historical Park.* National Park Service, Pacific Area Office, Honolulu.

———. 1991. "The Effects of Rapid Geological Change on Archaeology in Hawai'i." *Asian Perspectives* 30(1):133–145.

Spoehr, Alexander. 1961. "Introduction, Kamakau: The Man and the Manuscript." In S. *Kamakau, Ruling Chiefs of Hawaii*, pp. vii–viii. Kamehameha Schools Press, Honolulu.

Spriggs, Matthew. 1983. A Field Trip to the "Farms of Kapua" Property, Kapua, Kona, Hawai'i Island. Manuscript. On file, State Historic Preservation Division Library, Kapolei [H-502].

Spriggs, Matthew, and Atholl Anderson. 1993. "Late Colonization of East Polynesia." *Antiquity* 67:200–207.

Stannard, David. 1989. *Before the Horror: The Population of Hawai'i on the Eve of Western Contact*. Social Science Research Institute, University of Hawai'i at Manoa, Honolulu.

Stearns, Harold, and Gordon Macdonald. 1946. *Geology and Groundwater Resources of the Island of Hawaii*. Territory of Hawaii, Division of Hydrography Bulletin 9.

Sterling, Elspeth. 1960. Important Sites between Ku'emanu Heiau and Paniau Point in Kahaluu, North Kona, Hawaii. Bishop Museum ms. On file, State Historic Preservation Division Library, Kapolei [H-73].

Stevenson, Christopher, Wal Ambrose, Peter Sheppard, and Doug Sutton. In press. "Advances in Hydration Dating of New Zealand Obsidian." *Journal of Archaeological Science*.

Stewart, Charles. 1970 [1825]. *Journal of a Residence in the Sandwich Islands, During the Years 1823, 1824, and 1825*. University of Hawai'i Press, Honolulu. [First published in 1830.]

Stokes, John. 1919. Heiaus of Hawaii. Bishop Museum manuscript. On file, State Historic Preservation Division Library, Honolulu [G-22].

———. 1921. "Notes on Polynesian Featherwork." Bishop Museum Special Publication, 7(1):75–85.

———. 1925. "Notes on Polynesian Featherwork." *Journal of the Polynesian Society* 34:24–35.

———. 1928. "Whence Pa'ao?" *Hawaiian Historical Society Papers* 15:40–45. Honolulu.

———. 1930a. "Burial of King Keawe." *Papers of the Hawaiian Historical Society* 17:63–73. Honolulu.

———. 1930b. "An Evaluation of Early Genealogies Used for Polynesian History." *Journal of the Polynesian Society* 39(153):1–42.

———. 1932. "The Hawaiian King." *Hawaiian Historical Society Papers* 19:1–28.

———. 1933. "New Bases for Hawaiian Chronology." *Forty-first Annual Report of the Hawaiian Historical Society for the Year 1932*, pp. 23–65.

———. 1986. Archaeological Features of the Pu'uhonua Area. In Emory et. al., *The Natural and Cultural History of Honaunau, Kona, Hawai'i*, pp. 163–210. (Written in 1957)

———. 1991. *Heiau of the Island of Hawai'i: A Historic Survey of Native Hawaiian Temple Sites*. (Edited and introduced by Thomas Dye.) Bishop Museum Bulletin in Anthropology, 2. Bishop Museum, Honolulu.

Streck, Charles. 1986. Trip Report, Aerial Archeology Reconnaissance Survey for the Revised Proposed Site for the Multi-purpose Range Complex, Pohakuloa Training Area, Hamakua, Island of Hawai'i; 31 Mr - Apr 1986. U.S. Corps of Engineers ms. On file, State Historic Preservation Division Library, Kapolei [H-561].

Streck, Charles, and Farley Watanabe. 1988. Archaeological Reconnaissance of Areas Proposed for Emergency Flood Control Repair and Replacement of Structures, Bellow Air Force Station (BAFS), Waimanalo District, Oahu Island. U.S. Corps of Engineers ms. On file, State Historic Preservation Division Library, Kapolei.

Suggs, Robert. 1961. *Archaeology of Nuku Hiva, Marquesas Islands, French Polynesia.* Anthropological Papers of the American Museum of Natural History, 49(11).

Sutton, Doug, and Peter Sheppard. n.d. Dating New Zealand Prehistory Using Obsidian Hydration. Manuscript. Personal copy.

Tainter, Joseph, and Ross Cordy. 1977. "An Archaeological Analysis of Social Ranking and Residence Groups in Prehistoric Hawaii." *World Archaeology* 9(1):95–112.

The Traverse Group. 1985. *Draft Environmental Impact Statement High Tech D C Development Plan for the HOST Park and Expansion of the NELH, Keahole, North Kona, Hawaii.*

Thompson, Linda, and Paul Rosendahl. 1992. Archaeological Inventory Survey, Potential Sites for North Hawaii Community Hospital. PHRI ms. On file, State Historic Preservation Division Library, Kapolei [H-989].

Thrum, Thomas. 1907. "Heiaus and Heiau Sites Throughout the Hawaiian Islands. Island of Hawaii." *Hawaiian Almanac & Annual for 1908*, pp. 38–47.

———. 1908. "Heiaus and Heiau Sites Throughout the Hawaiian Islands. Island of Hawaii." *Hawaiian Almanac & Annual for 1909*, pp. 38–78.

———. 1918. "Brief Sketch of the Life and Labors of S. M. Kamakau, Hawaiian Historian." *Hawaiian Historical Society Twenty-sixth Annual Report*, pp. 40–61.

———. 1924. "Heiau (Temples of Hawaii Nei)." *32nd Annual Report of the Hawaiian Historical Society for the Year 1925*, pp. 14–36. Honolulu.

Tomonari-Tuggle, Myra. 1985. Cultural Resource Management Plan, Cultural Resource Management at the Keauhou Resort. PHRI ms. On file, State Historic Preservation Division Library, Kapolei [H-467].

———. 1988. North Kohala: Perception of a Changing Community. A Cultural Resources Study. State Parks ms. On file, State Historic Preservation Division Library, Kapolei [H-687].

Trevenen, James. 1959. *A Memoir of James Trevenen*, Christopher Lloyd and R. C. Anderson, ed. Navy Records Society.

Tuggle, H. David. 1976. A Windward Kohala-Hamakua Archaeological Zone, Island of Hawaii. Manuscript. On file, State Historic Preservation Division Library, Kapolei [H-36].

———. 1979. "Hawaii." In J. Jennings, ed., The *Prehistory of Polynesia*, pp. 167–199. Harvard University Press, Cambridge.

———. 1990. Azabu Kona Resort: Historic Preservation Mitigation. Phase I Archaeological Investigations. International Archaeological Research Institute Inc. ms. On file, State Historic Preservation Division Library, Kapolei [H-1426].

———. 1997. Archaeological Research of Areas Proposed for Development of Military Family Housing...Task 1: Literature Review of the Cultural Resources of the Bellows Area. International Archaeological Research Institute Inc. ms. On file, State Historic Preservation Division Library, Kapolei [O-1382].

Tuggle, H. David, Ross Cordy, and Marcus Child. 1977. "Volcanic Glass Hydration-rind Age Determinations for Bellows Dune, Hawaii." *New Zealand Archaeological Association Newsletter* 21:58–77.

Tuggle, H. David, and P. Bion Griffin, eds. 1973. *Lapakahi, Hawaii: Archaeological Studies.* Asian and Pacific Archaeological Series, 5. Social Science Research Institute, University of Hawai'i at Manoa, Honolulu.

Tuggle, H. David, and Myra Tomonari-Tuggle. 1980. "Prehistoric Agriculture in Kohala, Hawaii." *Journal of Field Archaeology* 7:297–312.

———. 1997. Synthesis of Cultural Resource Studies of the 'Ewa Plain. International Archaeological Research Institute Inc. ms. On file, State Historic Preservation Division Library, Kapolei [O-1480].

Tuohy, Donald. 1965. Salvage Excavations at City of Refuge National Historic Park, Honaunau, Kona, Hawaii. Manuscript. On file, State Historic Preservation Division Library, Kapolei. [Published in 1987 as Soehren & Tuohy.]

Underwood, Jane Hainline. 1969. *Human Skeletal Remains from Sand Dune Site (HI), South Point (Ka Lae), Hawaii.* Pacific Anthropological Records, 9. Bishop Museum, Honolulu.

United States Army Corps of Engineers. 1971. Pub*lic Announcement Summary Brochure Concerning Application for Department of Army Permit for Dredging and Alteration of Kaloko Pond, Island of Hawaii.* Pacific Ocean Division, United States Army Corps of Engineers, Fort Shafter.

———. 1979. *Draft Interim Report and Environmental Impact Statement, Hilo Lava Flow Control. South Hilo.*

———. 1980. Reconnaissance Report for Flood Damage Reduction, Alanaio Stream, Island of Hawaii.

———. 1985. *Final Environmental Impact Statement. U.S. Department of Agriculture Permit Application, Waikoloa Beach Resort. Waikoloa, South Kohala District, Island of Hawaii.*

United States Department of Commerce. 1976. *Final Environmental Impact Statement, Proposed Estuarine Sanctuary Grant Award for Waimanu Valley, Hawaii County, Hawaii.* Office of Coastal Zone Management.

Valeri, Valerio. 1985. *Kingship and Sacrifice: Ritual and Society in Ancient Hawaii.* University of Chicago Press, Chicago.

———. 1985b. "The Conqueror Becomes King: A Political Analysis of the Hawaiian Legend of 'Umi." In A. Hooper and J. Huntsman, eds., *Transformations of Polynesian Society*, pp. 79–103. The Polynesian Society, Wellington.

Vancouver, George. 1798. *A Voyage of Discovery to the North Pacific Ocean and Round the World.* 3 volumes. For G. G. and J. Robinson and J. Edwards, London.

Vansina, Jan. 1965. *Oral Tradition: A Study in Historical Methodology.* Aldine, Chicago.

Varigny, Charles de. 1981 [1855]. *Fourteen Years in the Sandwich Islands 1855–1868.* University of Hawai'i Press, Honolulu. [First published in 1855.]

Vayda, Andrew, and Roy Rappaport. 1963. "Island Cultures." In R. Fosberg, ed., *Man's Place in the Island Ecosystem*, pp. 131–142. Bishop Museum, Honolulu.

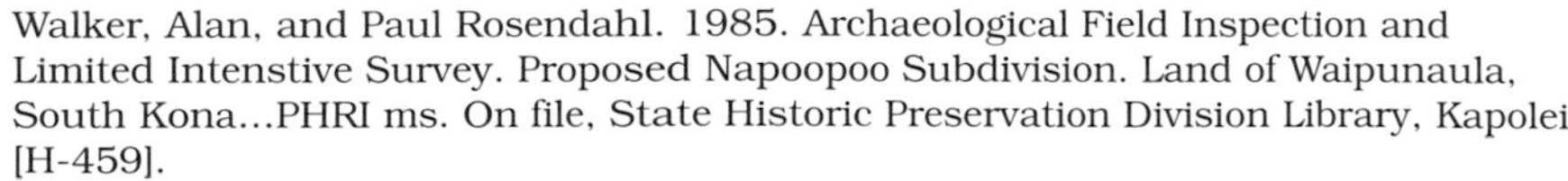



Walker, Alan, and Paul Rosendahl. 1985. Archaeological Field Inspection and Limited Intenstive Survey. Proposed Napoopoo Subdivision. Land of Waipunaula, South Kona...PHRI ms. On file, State Historic Preservation Division Library, Kapolei [H-459].

———. 1986. Intensive Survey and Test Excavations, Waikoloa Beach Resort Off-Site Electrical Work Project Area. Lands of Anahoomalu and Waikoloa, South Kona...PHRI ms. On file, State Historic Preservation Division Library, Kapolei [H-548].

———. 1988. Archaeological Reconnaissance Survey Pualani Subdivision. Lands of Puapua'a 1st and 2nd. PHRI ms. On file, State Historic Preservation Division Library, Kapolei [H-650].

———. 1989. Archaeological Reconnaissance Survey for Environmental Impact Statement (EIS). Azabu Keauhou Resort Project. Land of Kahalulu, North Kona...PHRI ms. On file, State Historic Preservation Division Library, Kapolei [H-769].

———. 1994. Archaeological Inventory Survey Azabu Keauhou Resort, Mauka Project Area. Land of Kahalulu, North Kona...PHRI ms. On file, State Historic Preservation Division Library, Kapolei [H-1352].

Walker, Alan, Alan Haun, and Paul Rosendahl. 1988. Intensive Survey and Test Excavations, Site 50-OA-2911, Kahuku Point Archaeological Area, Kuilima Resort Expansion Project. PHRI ms. On file, State Historic Preservation Division Library, Kapolei [O-580].

Walker, Alan, Lehua Kalima, and Susan Goodfellow. 1991. Archaeological Inventory Survey, Kealakekua Ranch Development—Kaawaloa Parcel. Land of Kaawaloa, South Kona...PHRI ms. On file, State Historic Preservation Division Library, Kapolei [H-1280].

Walker, Winslow. 1931. Archaeology of Maui. Bishop Museum ms. On file, State Historic Preservation Division Library, Kapolei [M-55].

Walsh, D. S., and Bruce Biggs. 1966. *Proto-Polynesian Word List I.* Te Reo Monographs. Linguistic Society of New Zealand, Auckland.

Watanabe, Farley. 1986. Final Report for Archaeological Aerial and Limited Ground Reconnaissance of Various Parcels Situated at Hawaii Island Selected as Potential Military Training Areas. U.S. Corps of Engineers ms. On file, State Historic Preservation Division Library, Kapolei [H-539].

Welch, David. 1983. "Report 5. Archaeological Investigations in Section 2." In J. Clark and P. Kirch, eds., *Archaeological Investigation of the Mudlane-Waimea-Kawaihae Road Corridor, Island of Hawaii: an Interdisciplinary Study of an Environmental Transect,* pp. 138–180. Department of Anthropology, Bishop Museum, Honolulu.

———. 1988. Archaeological Investigations at Pauoa Bay (Ritz Carlton Mauna Lani Resort), South Kona, Hawai'i. International Archaeological Research Institute, Inc. ms. On file, State Historic Preservation Division Library, Kapolei [H-694].

Westervelt, William. 1913. "The Legend of Paao and Pili from Samoa." In *Around the Poi Bowl and Legend of Paao,* pp. 5–60. Paradise of the Pacific, Honolulu.

———. 1916. *Hawaiian Legends of Volcanoes.* Boston and London.

Wickler, Stephen, J. Stephen Athens, and Jerome Ward. 1991. Vegetation and Landscape Change in a Leeward Coastal Environment, Paleoenvironmental and Archaeological Investigations, Fort Shafter Flats Sewerline Project, Honolulu, Hawai'i. International Archaeological Research Institute, Inc. ms. On file, State Historic Preservation Division Library, Kapolei [O-793].

Wilkes, Charles. 1845. *Narrative of the United States Exploring Expedition during the Years 1838–1842*, vol. 4. Lea & Blanchard, Philadelphia.

Williams, Scott. 1992. "Early Inland Settlement Expansion and the Effect of Geomorphological Change on the Archaeological Record in Kane'ohe, O'ahu." *New Zealand Journal of Archaeology* 14:67–78.

Williamson, Robert. 1939. *Essays in Polynesian Ethnology*, edited by R. Piddington. Cambridge University Press, Cambridge.

Wilson, Okamoto and Associates. 1981. *EIS Kaloko Light Industrial Subdivision*. Wilson, Okamoto and Associates, Inc., Honolulu.

Withrow, Barbara. 1989. Prehistoric Distribution of Stone Adzes on the Island of Hawaii: Implications for the Development of Hawaiian Chiefdoms. Paper Presented at 54th Annual Meeting of the Society for American Archaeology, Atlanta.

Wolforth, Thomas. 1998. Data Recovery for the New Konawaena School: Kona Field System Development in 'Apa'a. PHRI ms. On file, State Historic Preservation Division Library, Kapolei.

———. 1999. Data Recovery (Phase II) for the North Hawai'i Community Hospital: Investigations at an 'Auwai in the Lalamilo Field System. PHRI ms. On file, State Historic Preservation Division Library, Kapolei.

Wolforth, Thomas, Warren Wulzen, and Susan Goodfellow. 1997. Archaeological Data Recovery at West Loch Estates: Residential Increment I, and Golf Course and Shoreline Park. PHRI ms. On file, State Historic Preservation Division Library, Kapolei.

Wright, Thomas, Taeko Takahasi, and J. D. Griggs. 1992. *Hawai'i Volcano Watch: A Pictorial History, 1779–1991*. University of Hawai'i Press, Honolulu.

Yen, Douglas. 1971. "Construction of the Hypothesis for Distribution of the Sweet Potato." In C. L. Riley et al., eds., *Man Across the Sea*, pp. 328–342. University of Texas Press, Austin.

———. 1973. "The Origins of Oceanic Agriculture." *Archaeology & Physical Anthropology in Oceania* 8:68–85.

———. 1974. *The Sweet Potato and Oceania: An Essay in Ethnobotany*. Bishop Museum Bulletin, 236. Honolulu.

———. 1978. The Amy Greenwell Bequest: 3rd Report, A Preliminary Report on the Archaeological Survey of March, 1978, and its Bearing on Ethnobotanical Garden Planning. Bishop Museum ms. On file, State Historic Preservation Division Library, Kapolei [H-557].

———. 1987. "The Hawaiian Ti Plant (*Cordyline fruticosa* L.): Some Ethnobotanical Notes." *Notes from Waimea Arboretum & Botanical Gardens* 14(1):8–11.

Yent, Martha. 1984. Memorandum: Archaeological Reconnaissance Survey of Proposed Residential Parcels in Kealakekua, South Kona, Island of Hawaii. State Parks ms. On file, State Historic Preservation Division Library, Kapolei [H-379].

———. 1985. Archaeological Survey & Mapping of the Hikiau Complex (Site 1963) and Napoopoo Section of the Proposed Kealakekua Bay State Historical Park, South Kona, Island of Hawaii. State Parks ms. On file, State Historic Preservation Division Library, Kapolei [H-388].

Yent, Martha, and Jason Ota. 1981. Archaeological Reconnaissance Survey of the Napoopoo and Kaawaloa Portions of Kealakekua Bay, South Kona, Island of Hawaii. State Parks ms. On file, State Historic Preservation Division Library, Kapolei [H-388].

Yzendoorn, Reginald. 1927. *A History of the Catholic Mission in the Hawaiian Islands.* Honolulu Star-Bulletin, Honolulu.

Zimmerman, Heinrich. 1781. *Reise um die Welt, mit Captain Cook.* C. F. Schwann, Mannheim.

## A



## B



## C



## D



## E

# F



# G



# H

## I



## K

## N



## O



## P

## About the Author

Dr. Ross Cordy is the Branch Chief for Archaeology in the State of Hawai'i's Historic Preservation Division, having headed that office and program for 15 years. He currently teaches archaeology, history, and Hawaiian studies at the University of Hawaii at West O'ahu and helps teach archaeology to students in Wai'anae High School's and Nanakuli High School's Hawaiian Studies Programs. Dr. Cordy has conducted research on Hawaiian archaeological and historical topics since 1968. He has done fieldwork throughout the Hawaiian Islands, on all the major Micronesian Islands, and in the Society Islands, and taught at universities in New Zealand. Dr. Cordy's writings include over 50 published articles books and monographs and numerous manuscript papers on a wide variety of Pacific subjects.